MAJOR
SOCIAL ISSUES

Other Joint Publications of The Free Press
and
The American Sociological Association

Peter M. Blau, *Approaches to the Study of Social Structure*

This is the most concise and definitive statement of sociological conceptions of social structure. Some of the world's foremost sociologists present different, sometimes opposite, theories of social structure. This book illuminates the diverse ranges of vision, and dramatically illustrates the parallel as well as contrasting features of various theoretical conceptions of structural analysis. Contributors include: Robert K. Merton, George C. Homans, William J. Goode, James S. Coleman, Talcott Parsons, Walter L. Wallace, Gerhard E. Lenski, Robert S. Bierstedt, Tom Bottomore, Seymour Martin Lipset, Lewis A. Coser, and Peter M. Blau.

The 1974 meeting in Montreal

Lewis A. Coser and Otto N. Larsen, *The Uses of Controversy in Sociology*

This is a critical assessment of some of the major controversies in sociology today. Twenty-three distinguished sociologists examine several areas of concern:

- . trends in American society
- .. cleavages in the social structure
- . individual and societal modernity
- . conflict and revolution
- . the resurgence of ethnicity
- . labeling theory
- . the links between knowledge and policy
- . theoretical and methodological problems

The contributors express divergent views of each of these issues. For example, Walter Gove questions the effectiveness of labeling theory, while both Patrick Conover and Edwin Lemert find it a viable guide to research and practice.

The selections in *The Uses of Controversy* represent a wide range of issues but each is a probing of the tools or the results of the sociological enterprise.

The 1975 meeting in San Francisco

MAJOR
SOCIAL ISSUES

A Multidisciplinary View

edited by

J. Milton Yinger
and
Stephen J. Cutler

A Publication of
The American
Sociological Association

THE FREE PRESS
A Division of Macmillan Publishing Co., Inc.
NEW YORK

Collier Macmillan Publishers
LONDON

The Free Press
A Division of Macmillan Publishing Co., Inc.
866 Third Avenue, New York, N. Y. 10022

Collier Macmillan Canada, Ltd.

Library of Congress Catalog Card Number: 78-50846

Printed in the United States of America

printing number

1 2 3 4 5 6 7 8 9 10

Library of Congress Cataloging in Publication Data

Main entry under title:

Major social issues.

  "A publication of the American Sociological Associa-
tion."
  Bibliography: p.
  Includes indexes.
  1. Social problems--Addresses, essays, lectures.
2. Social history--1945-   --Addresses, essays, lec-
tures. I. Yinger, John Milton. II. Cutler, Stephen J.
III. American Sociological Association.
HN17.5.M337   309   78-50846
ISBN 0-02-935840-X

Contents

VI. On the Multidisciplinary Analysis of Fertility

VII. The Social Sciences and Public Policy

VIII. The Attitude-Behavior Complex

About the Contributors

WALTER ADAMS, Distinguished University Professor and Professor of Economics at Michigan State University, received his B.A. from Brooklyn College and his M.A. and Ph.D. from Yale University. Former President of Michigan State University, he has served frequently as an expert witness on economic policy before Congressional committees. Among his books are *The Structure of American Industry* and *The Test*.

WENDELL BELL, Professor of Sociology and Director of Undergraduate Studies at Yale University, received his B.A. from California State University, Fresno, and his M.A. and Ph.D. from the University of California, Los Angeles. His writings include *Jamaican Leaders: Political Attitudes in a New Nation* and the coediting of *The Sociology of the Future* and *Ethnicity and Nation-Building*.

ROY S. BRYCE-LAPORTE is Director of the Research Institute on Immigration and Ethnic Studies at the Smithsonian Institution. He studied in the Canal Zone, the Republic of Panama, Nebraska, and Puerto Rico, and took his Ph.D. at the University of California, Los Angeles. He was formerly Director of the Afro-American Studies Program and Associate Professor of Sociology at Yale University. Some of his recent publications are *Contemporary Perspectives on Alienation* and *Exploratory Fieldwork on Latino Migrants and Indochinese Refugees* (coeditor).

WILLIAM R. CATTON, JR., Professor of Sociology at Washington State University, is a graduate of Oberlin College (B.A.) and the University of Washington (Ph.D.). He has served as Vice-President of the Pacific Sociological Association and of the New Zealand Branch of the Sociological Association of Australia and New Zealand and has chaired the American Sociological Association's section on Environmental Sociology. He is the author of *From Animistic to Naturalistic Sociology* and *Overshoot: The Ecological Basis of Evolutionary Change*.

ALBERT K. COHEN, University Professor of Sociology at the University of Connecticut, received his M.A. from Indiana University and his Ph.D. from Harvard University. He has served as President of the Society for the Study of Social Problems. His published works include *Delinquent Boys* and *Deviance and Control*.

STEPHEN J. CUTLER, Associate Professor of Sociology and Anthropology at Oberlin College, received his B.A. from Dartmouth College and his M.A. and Ph.D. in sociology from the University of Michigan. He is the author of numerous articles on aging and coauthor of *Middle Start: An Experiment in the Educational Enrichment of Young Adolescents*.

GEORGE A. DeVos, Professor of Anthropology at the University of California, Berkeley, received his B.A. in sociology, his M.A. in anthropology, and his Ph.D. in psychology from the University of Chicago. His books include *Japan's Invisible Race* (coauthor), *Socialization for Achievement,* and the recently edited volumes of *Ethnic Identity* and *Responses to Change*.

RICHARD A. EASTERLIN, Professor of Economics at the University of Pennsylvania, studied at the Stevens Institute of Technology (M.E.) and the University of Pennsylvania (Ph.D.). He is President of the Population Association of America and was Vice-President of the Economic History Association. Among his publications are *Population Redistribution and Economic Growth, United States: 1870–1950; Population, Labor Force, and Long Swings in Economic Growth: The American Experience;* and *America's Economic Growth: An Economist's History of the United States* (coeditor).

ISAAC EHRLICH is Professor of Economics at the State University of New York, Buffalo, and the University of Chicago and Senior Research Associate at the National Bureau of Economic Research. He received his B.A. from the Hebrew University of Jerusalem and his Ph.D. from Columbia University. His most recent research has appeared in the *Journal of Political Economy* and *The American Economic Review*.

DORIS R. ENTWISLE is Professor of Social Relations and Engineering Science at The Johns Hopkins University, from which she received her Ph.D. She is the current editor of *Sociology of Education,* and the author of *Word Associations of Young Children,* and coauthor of *Introductory Systems and Design* and *Too Great Expectations*.

MARTIN FISHBEIN (Ph.D., University of California, Los Angeles) holds the positions of Professor of Psychology and Research Professor, Institute of Communications Research at the University of Illinois, Urbana–Champaign. His major publications include *Readings in Attitude Theory and Measurement* and *Belief, Attitude, Intention, and Behavior: An Introduction to Theory and Research* (coauthor).

JAMES A. GESCHWENDER, Professor of Sociology at the State University of New York, Binghamton, received his B.A. from SUNY, Buffalo, and his M.A. and Ph.D. from Michigan State University. Among his published works are *Stratification in America* and *Class, Race, and Worker Insurgency: The League of Revolutionary Black Workers*.

TAMARA K. HAREVEN is Professor of History and Director of the History of the Family Program at Clark University and a Research Associate at Harvard's Center for Population Studies. She is also the editor of the *Journal of Family History*. Several works in press include *Family Transition and the Life Course in Nineteenth Century Populations* and *Family and Work in an Industrial Town*.

REUBEN HILL, Regents' Professor of Family Sociology at the University of Minnesota, obtained his Ph.D. from the University of Wisconsin. He has been a Fellow at the Center for Advanced Study in the Behavioral Sciences and served as President of the International Sociological Association. His books include *The Family and Population Control* and *Family Development in Three Generations*.

JOAN HUBER, Associate Professor of Sociology at the University of Illinois, Urbana–Champaign, received her B.A. from Pennsylvania State University, her M.A. from Western Michigan University, and her Ph.D. from Michigan State University. She has served on the Council of the American Sociological Association and the Board of Directors of the Society for the Study of Social Problems. Among the works she has coauthored or edited are *Income and Ideology; The Sociology of American Poverty;* and *Changing Women in a Changing Society*.

ALEX INKELES, Margaret Jacks Professor of Education and Professor of Sociology at Stanford University, will join the Hoover Institute as a senior fellow in the autumn of 1978. He received his Ph.D. from Columbia University. He taught previously at Harvard where he directed the Harvard Project on Social and Cultural Aspects of Development and Studies in Social Relations at the Russian Research Center. He is the editor of the *Annual Review of Sociology*, and his latest book (with David Smith), *Becoming Modern*, received the first Hadley Cantril Award.

SUZANNE KELLER holds a joint appointment in the Department of Sociology and the School of Architecture at Princeton University. Her Ph.D. is from Columbia University. She has served as Vice-President of the American Sociological Association and of the Eastern Sociological Society. Her books include *Beyond the Ruling Class* and *The Urban Neighborhood*.

HERBERT C. KELMAN, Richard Clarke Cabot Professor of Social Ethics at Harvard University, was trained at Brooklyn College (B.A.) and Harvard University (Ph.D.) Previously he was Professor of Psychology and Chairman of the Doctoral Program in Social Psychology at the University of Michigan. He served as President of the Society for the Psychological Study of Social Issues, the Division of Personality and Social Psychology of the American Psychological Association, and the International Studies Association, among other professional offices. His publications include *International Behavior: A Social Psychological Analysis* (coeditor); *A Time to Speak: On Human Values and Social Research;* and *Cross-National Encounters* (coauthor).

ELEANOR E. MACCOBY, Professor of Psychology at Stanford University, received her undergraduate training at the University of Washington and her M.A. and Ph.D. at the University of Michigan. Among her publications are *Patterns of Child Rearing; Experiments in Primary Education;* and *The Psychology of Sex Differences* (coauthor).

GEORGE L. MADDOX, Professor of Sociology and of Medical Sociology (Psychiatry) and Director of the Center for the Study of Aging and Human Development at Duke University, obtained his Ph.D. from Michigan State University. He is currently President of the Gerontological Society and Vice-President of the Southern Sociological Society. He is an advisory editor of *The Handbook of Aging and the Social Sciences* and the author of *Drinking Among Teenagers*

RANDALL MARK did his undergraduate work at Knox College and graduate study at the University of Chicago. He has worked with Isaac Ehrlich in research on the economics of crime, punishment, and deterrence. They recently published "Fear of Deterrence: A Critical Evaluation of the Report of the Panel on Research on Deterrent and Incapacitative Effects" in the *Journal of Legal Studies* (June 1977).

E. SCOTT MAYNES is Professor and Chairman of the Department of Consumer Economics and Housing, New York State College of Human Ecology, at Cornell University. His Ph.D. is from the University of Michigan. He has served on the Editorial Boards of the *Journal of Consumer Research* and the *Journal of Consumer Affairs.* Included among his publications is *Decision-Making for Consumers.*

N. KRISHNAN NAMBOODIRI is Chairman and Professor of Sociology at the University of North Carolina at Chapel Hill. He obtained a B.S. in mathematics and an M.S. in statistics from the University of Kerala, India, and an M.A. and Ph.D. in sociology from the University of Michigan. He is the author of numerous articles, coauthor of *Applied Multivariate Analysis and Experimental Designs,* and has served as the editor of *Demography.*

GWYNN NETTLER, Professor of Sociology at the University of Alberta,

Canada, received his Ph.D. from Stanford University in sociology and psychology. He previously held the position of Senior Clinical Psychologist in the Nevada State Department of Health. His books include *Explanations; Social Concerns;* and *Explaining Crime.*

DONALD C. PELZ holds appointments as Professor of Psychology and Director of the Center for Research on the Utilization of Scientific Knowledge at the Institute for Social Research at the University of Michigan, from which he received his Ph.D. in social psychology. Among his publications is the book *Scientists in Organizations.*

THOMAS FRASER PETTIGREW is Professor of Social Psychology and Sociology at Harvard University. His B.A. is from the University of Virginia, and his M.A. and Ph.D. are from Harvard. He was President of the Society for the Psychological Study of Social Issues and now serves on the advisory board of *Social Psychology.* His publications include *A Profile of the Negro American; Racially Separate or Together?* and *Racial Discrimination in the United States* (editor).

ROY A. RAPPAPORT, Chairman and Professor of Anthropology at the University of Michigan, was awarded his Ph.D. from Columbia University. His recent books include *Pigs for Ancestors: Adaptation and Maladaptation in Social Systems* and *The Sacred in Human Evolution.*

RICHARD SCHACHT, Associate Professor of Philosophy at the University of Illinois, Urbana–Champaign, received his B.A. from Harvard, studied at Tübingen, and took his M.A. and Ph.D. from Princeton. His writings include *Alienation* and *Hegel and After.*

HOWARD SCHUMAN, Professor of Sociology and Program Director in the Institute for Social Research at the University of Michigan, received his Ph.D. from Harvard's Social Relations Department. He is the current editor of *Social Psychology.* In addition to numerous articles on attitude change, he is the coauthor of *Black Racial Attitudes* and *Social Change in a Metropolitan Community.*

JEROME H. SKOLNICK is Director of the Center for the Study of Law and Society and Professor of Law (Jurisprudence and Social Policy) at the University of California, Berkeley. He did his undergraduate work in economics and philosophy at City College of New York and received his M.A. and Ph.D. in sociology from Yale. His publications include *Justice Without Trial; The Politics of Protest;* and *Family in Transition* (with Arlene Skolnick).

LAWRENCE B. SLOBODKIN is Professor of Biology in the Department of Ecology and Evolution at the State University of New York, Stony Brook. He received his B.A. from Bethany College and his Ph.D. from

Yale University. Former Senior Visiting Scientist at the Smithsonian Institution, and Guggenheim Fellow, he has served as President of the General Systems Research Society and as Vice-President of the American Society of Naturalists. His writings include *Growth and Regulation of Animal Populations.*

HAROLD W. WATTS, Professor of Economics and Director of the Center for the Social Sciences at Columbia University, received his B.A. from the University of Oregon and his M.A. and Ph.D. from Yale University. Among his publications he has coedited *Income Maintenance and Labor Supply: Econometric Studies* and *The New Jersey Income Maintenance Experiment*, Vols. II and III.

BEATRICE B. WHITING is Professor of Education and Anthropology at the Laboratory of Human Development, Graduate School of Education, Harvard University. Her B.A. is from Bryn Mawr College and her M.A. and Ph.D. in anthropology from Yale University. Her writings include *Six Cultures: Studies of Child Rearing* (editor) and *Children of Six Cultures: A Psycho-Cultural Analysis.*

HAROLD L. WILENSKY, Professor of Sociology and Research Sociologist in the Institutes of Industrial Relations and International Studies at the University of California, Berkeley, holds a Ph.D. from the University of Chicago. He has served on the Councils of the American Sociological Association and the Industrial Relations Research Association and was a Fellow at the Center for Advanced Study in the Behavioral Sciences. His several books include *Intellectuals in Labor Unions; Industrial Relations;* and *Organizational Intelligence: Knowledge and Policy in Government and Industry.*

ROBIN M. WILLIAMS, JR., Henry Scarborough Professor of Social Science at Cornell University, received his Ph.D. from Harvard. He has been President and Secretary of the American Sociological Association, President of the Eastern Sociological Society, and is the current editor of the Arnold and Caroline Rose Monograph Series. He is a member of the American Academy of Arts and Sciences. Among his several books are *American Society: A Sociological Interpretation; Strangers Next Door;* and *Mutual Accommodation: Ethnic Conflict and Cooperation.*

J. MILTON YINGER, Professor of Sociology and Anthropology at Oberlin College, was trained at DePauw University (B.A.), Louisiana State University (M.A.), and the University of Wisconsin (Ph.D.). He has served as Secretary and President of the American Sociological Association and has held fellowships from the Guggenheim Foundation, the National Endowment for the Humanities, the East-West Center, and Clare Hall, Cambridge University. His writings include *Toward a Field Theory of Behavior; The Scientific Study of Religion;* and *Racial and Cultural Minorities* (with George E. Simpson).

Foreword

It has become increasingly apparent in recent years that the several disciplines interested in the study of human behavior converge on similar sets of issues. The sociologist who examines the literature of anthropology, political science, economics, psychology, and to an increasing degree history, biology, and philosophy, often has the sense of déjà vu, of parallel programs of research and theory corresponding to those in sociology. The sharing of interests, however, is not always accompanied by a sharing of vocabularies, assumptions, methods, or data. As a result, the gains that come from the diversity of perspectives are reduced by poor communication, inconsistencies, and gaps that leave us with unresolved differences in the formulation of topics of mutual concern, and with many contradictory findings.

Believing that this situation creates serious difficulties for the social sciences, the 1977 Program Committee of the American Sociological Association (Leo P. Chall, Stephen J. Cutler, William H. Form, Suzanne Keller, Otto N. Larsen, S. M. Miller, Charles U. Smith, and J. Milton Yinger) selected as the theme for the Annual Meeting the topic: Sociology and Related Disciplines: Shared and Divergent Perspectives. The aim was not simply to carry out an exercise in the sociology of knowledge by showing how professional location can influence scholarly work—although that proved to be one of the consequences. The deeper aim was to advance our understanding of major social scientific problems by examining them from divergent and to some degree competing points of view.

In the development of a discipline, we see a dialectic between specialization (major attention to small, closed systems that can be dealt with by sharper and sharper analytic methods) and synthesis (major attention to the interactions between and among systems, to the interfaces, to the permeability of the boundaries that have been closed for analytic purposes). With apologies to Kant: Synthesis without analysis is blind; analysis without synthesis is empty. Most professional pressures (e.g., advancement in one's career) favor analysis. We need from time to time to counter those pressures with those based on the nature of the problems with which we deal, their holistic qualities, lest we mistake our analytic statements about the world for reality. This statement is in no way intended to disparage analytic research. Only by closing off some part of nature for study can we begin to get into some of its secrets. But we need to come back often to larger systems of interaction. This will, in fact, improve analysis by placing technically sociological, or anthropological, or economic, or psychological, or other specialized work into the framework from which it has been abstracted.

Having decided to emphasize a multidisciplinary approach to issues of major sociological importance, the Program Committee had no difficulty in identifying appropriate topics—that is, topics being actively studied by scholars from several disciplines. In fact, there were soon about forty topics on the potential list—a larger number than we could schedule. The list was pared to twenty-one only with some difficulty. Each of these topics was the subject of a plenary session or a thematic panel at the 1977 meeting in Chicago.

The present volume is composed of papers presented at that meeting. Most of them have been revised, many extensively, and they have been clustered into sections built around common themes. Despite the diversity of topics, the sections share two important characteristics: Each examines a problem or a set of problems that is currently the subject of active research in two or more disciplines. (Of the thirty papers included here, not counting the brief introductions or commentaries, fourteen have been written by sociologists and sixteen by scholars from other disciplines.) For lack of space a number of excellent papers on additional themes of multidisciplinary interest could not be included.

The second characteristic that binds the sections together is the shared emphasis on topics of vital concern today not only to scholars but also to the public at large. The several chapters deal with major social issues as well as major social scientific issues (overlapping but not identical categories). It is our hope that these multidisciplinary studies can enlarge our understanding and lend some clarity to problems that are the stuff of headlines as well as of the professional journals.

In the selection of participants, we have not sought consensus. There is substantial agreement, but also some sharp disagreements. It is our hope, however, and indeed our expectation, that these papers will contribute significantly to our understanding of some of the most critical issues of our time.

J. Milton Yinger
Stephen J. Cutler

I

Competing Models of Multiethnic and Multiracial Societies

I

Introduction

Wendell Bell

IN THE PAPERS of part I, a psychologist-anthropologist, a social psychologist, and two sociologists explore the questions selected for a panel created to discuss multiethnic and multiracial societies: "How do societies, viewed comparatively, deal with ethnic and racial complexity? What options are open? What are the major trends?" In response, one panelist, Robin M. Williams, Jr., mused, "And after I have disposed of these questions, will it be all right to answer a few others, such as whether the universe is open or closed?"

They are big questions. In lesser circles they would be conversation stoppers. But if they can be answered, then these four authors are among the best equipped to do so. Each has spent the bulk of his professional career trying to understand ethnicity and race. Each, however, has taken a somewhat different tack, not so much competing or divergent and only partly shared, but certainly complementary. If we put aside our sociological imperialism and defensiveness for a moment, we can see the need not only for structural answers, such as what society does to groups and what groups do to society, but also for psychological and cultural answers, such as what internal mechanisms occur as the person copes with the challenges of ethnicity and what values different cultures inculcate that facilitate or impede a person's adjustment to the larger society.

Here is where psychologist-anthropologist George A. DeVos' psychocultural answers are important. His own personal mix of "sociology and related disciples" includes a B.A. in sociology, an M.A. in anthropology, and a Ph.D. in psychology. He developed his psychocultural approach during his investigations with different ethnic groups in a variety of different sociocultural settings, including Japanese Americans,

3

Koreans in Japan, rural and urban Algerians, a variety of ethnic groups in Europe, and rural and urban Japanese.

His paper on role degradation is an effort to build a bridge, a theoretical connection between psychological theory related to specific mental mechanisms on the one hand and role theory as we in sociology relate it to socialization on the other. Thus he explores problems of social identity using the concepts of differential role expectations, reference group pressures, and automatic ego functions. He stresses an active, consequential self that through the process of "selective permeability" excludes certain external stimuli while allowing others to enter.

One theme of DeVos' work is achievement, although his particular emphasis, I think, is rendered better by "success." If people are trapped in a maze, then what explains why some people make it to the reward at the end and others get caught in a blind alley? At least part of the answer is to be found, according to DeVos, in the nature of the different cultures in which people have been reared. If achievement leads to individual "success," that is, adaptation to the constraints of a particular maze created by the larger society, it may cool out rebellion and revolution. But here is a bridge to the eminently structural analysis given by Williams, where the aggregate of such individual successes is seen as one of the conditions affecting the chances for collective action. Furthermore, and here I think Bryce-Laporte misreads DeVos, the costs of such success, great as they often are, may be less than the costs of failure, and in the long run they may be less, too, than the costs of rebellion and revolution, despite—in Williams' terms—the personally satisfying dramatic, often ritualistic, opportunities for expressiveness that the latter immediately provide.

Thomas Fraser Pettigrew is concerned less with the movements of particular individuals within a society than he is with changes in the positions of entire groups. That is, if people are trapped in a maze, he asks about their perceptions that may lead them as members of groups to be willing to mobilize their efforts to reach the "reward" either by "running the maze" together as a collectivity or by tearing down a few of the walls and creating some new passageways. His discussion of the ethnic group structure of perceived deprivation is particularly important in this regard in that he stresses not the individual comparisons that people make but the politically and socially more crucial comparisons with other groups made by people *as members of a group.* "Fraternal" rather than "ego" deprivation is at the root of collective action.

Pettigrew is a major figure in the social psychology of race relations. Dealing mainly with race in the United States, he has written on the related subjects of the dynamics of desegregation, sociocultural factors in intergroup attitudes, racial stereotypes, racial prejudice, psychological gains and losses in black American protest, racial differences in intelligence and personality, urban growth and race, and school integration. And he has descended from the ivory tower many times in an effort to communicate to wider audiences through popular magazines and newspapers.

Robin M. Williams, Jr., began his sociological life studying farm tenancy and rural youth in North Carolina in the 1930s. Since 1947, however, when the Social Science Research Council published his well-known propositional survey of ethnic studies, *The Reduction of Intergroup Tensions,* Williams has been recognized for his contributions to race and ethnic studies. He has done many other things, including writing an enduring book on American society, upon which many of us cut our sociological teeth, and shaping sociological thinking about values. Yet he has returned to the subject of race and ethnicity repeatedly throughout his career. With his contribution to this volume he brings us up-to-date with his mature reflections.

At the risk of overburdening a simple analogy, I think Williams adds to our consideration of people trapped in a maze by introducing some conditions of the maze itself and of the location of people in it that minimize or maximize the likelihood of organized protest, pressure for change, and conflict. Williams incorporates some of the considerations of Pettigrew, such as the importance of fraternal relative deprivation, and even of DeVos, such as individualized adjustments and striving, which he sees as one type of behavior outcome in response to deprivation. Yet he concentrates on variables that define aspects of the structure, often of the larger containing society, the maze within which people are trapped. Thus he discusses the effects of inequality, social change, geographical mobility, exposure to mass media, the rates of vertical mobility, and the importance of kinship as a basis of social organization. Although he is interested in the sources and consequences of discontent, he focuses on the structural conditions whereby such discontent may be translated into collective dissent, protest, or structural opposition. What conditions of the maze itself facilitate or impede people's willingness to tear it down and redesign it? Thus he looks to structural variables, including patterns of communication, leadership, and authority.

And, as we have learned, we can count on Williams to make his thinking systematic, organized, and testable. Thus he concludes with a list of propositions that will challenge us for some time to come.

Roy S. Bryce-Laporte, Panamanian-born of West Indian ancestry, has studied or done research in the Panama Canal Zone, among Jamaican immigrants to Costa Rica, in Puerto Rico, in the black community in Los Angeles, among black leaders in Chicago, among Mexican Americans, and among other groups in other places. He has written on the slave plantation and the slave family, alienation and race, migration and ethnicity, Caribbean migration, the new immigration, inequality and the black experience, black culture and the ghetto, the black experience in Central America, and urban relocation and family adaptation in Puerto Rico. Fluent in Spanish as well as English, he has become a major link between Afro-United States studies and Afro-Latin American and Afro-Caribbean studies. As a former colleague, I should add that he played an important role in establishing Afro-American Studies at Yale.

Bryce-Laporte's critical discussion is essential to round out our consideration of the questions posed to the panel. It is a prod to our easy satisfaction with our concepts and models. As a black and Third World sociologist, he adds still another perspective. For him, if people are trapped in a maze, it is a complex one, perhaps with more than a single end and more than one kind of reward; there are mazes within mazes, interconnected in complex and consequential ways.

No matter how much "progress" people make by individually running the maze, collectively making their way through it together, or tearing it down and creating new paths, the maze may keep changing so that the ends and the rewards remain elusive. We should not be deceived, he reminds us, into believing that all changes—even those that greatly alter some aspects of the structure of society—really have altered the fundamental differentials of power, prestige, and control over property among different ethnic and racial groups. If the maze can be changed, there is no guarantee that "success" won't move, too, forever out of reach for members of some groups.

Not only can the structure of society be redesigned, but the value of the ends can be questioned. Thus "success" should be made problematic, the value of the "rewards" questioned.

Finally, although Williams mentions it, Bryce-Laporte insists on it: Ethnicity not only has its macrosociological aspects, but also has international dimensions. In consciousness and identity, in networks of communication, in shared past and fate, and in common struggle, race and ethnicity are being internationalized. Our social science net must be enlarged to incorporate this phenomenon.

2

Selective Permeability and Reference Group Sanctioning: Psychocultural Continuities in Role Degradation

George A. DeVos

MARX IS OFTEN QUOTED as having said that "religion is the opiate of the masses." To make such a statement is not to give explanation of why some seek opiates and others do not. Why is it that some individuals cling to forms of religious belief or to forms of social submission to exploitive authorities? Why do not more individuals, once recognizing their plight, seek direct political or economic redress? It is not simply that people are ignorant and maintain religious or social beliefs that go counter to their self-interests. Individuals are sometimes painfully aware that their behavior is counterproductive. They seem to be swayed by needs that cause them to become self-defeating or even apparently self-destructive.

Such reactions are sometimes deeply entwined with an ambivalently held ethnic identity. There are many features of collective cultural traditions that make them inhibitory of change even when change is positively desired. I shall not, for purposes of brevity, enter into the many problems of collective interaction in pluralistic societies. Rather, I shall focus on some of the problems specific to social self-identity inherited by individuals as part of a given cultural background. How does the internal psychological structuring of an ethnic identity, to be specific, facilitate or impede change? In this particular presentation I will extract one of several themes that contributors brought together in my recently edited volume, *Responses to Change* (DeVos, 1976). Here I shall focus on the particular issues of role degradation. How and to what degree is a

7

degraded role part of the self? As I use the term, "role degradation" is somewhat different from, but related to, problems of role subordination and self-concepts as experienced by women in traditionally defined male-dominant cultures. The issues that I shall bring forward are now receiving systematic attention in women's studies. I shall only allude to such concerns incidentally, but the similarity if not identity of problems should be apparent.

Wagatsuma and I used certain key psychocultural concepts in our previous volume, *Japan's Invisible Race* (DeVos and Wagatsuma, 1966), devoted to consideration of the Japanese former outcastes or Burakumin. We found it conceptually convenient to concern ourselves with "differential role expectations," "reference group pressures," and what I term "selective permeability," as these concepts interrelate with problems of social self-identity.

Ethnic Identity as an Aspect of Social Identity

Central to any examination of childhood socialization in any culture is the issue of how a social self-identity becomes internalized. Increasingly, both anthropology and sociology are according recognition to the fact that in complex societies an essential aspect of the development of a "self" is some concern with what is conceived to be one's ethnic origin. In situations of social or cultural pluralism one now notes how alternative theories are developing to explain a variety of social problems, including how an ethnic identity is influenced by discrimination. Why is a particular minority group successful or unsuccessful in status adjustments within a given society? Explanations are often attempted in purely economic or political forms of analysis. I myself find such analysis rather insufficient because there are, in all cases, some intermediary psychocultural considerations that are crucial. These considerations have to do with how and why there is generational continuity in the internalization of social expectations. Particular groups have experienced historical circumstances that have influenced primary socialization within the home. Generational continuity in adaptive patterns is mediated within primary family units as well as reinforced within the immediate face-to-face communities defined by kinship and ethnicity, or by class or caste segregation. Should these agents of mediation become in conflict in particular ways with the expectations of a host society or a dominant culture, radically different forms of conflict or accommodation may occur, depending upon historical circumstances.

The point of view that I am attempting to present is that social science must attempt to understand directly the psychological mechanisms involved in specific situations of historical change. Change takes place not simply in social structures of systems but in the internal perceptions of individuals. How change occurs within the perceptual structure of the individual, influenced by the history of his group and the historical circumstances he experiences in growing up, is an important consideration in understanding how social structures are modified by contemporary economic and political forces.

If we look at our multiethnic American society, we can observe a varied spectrum of responses among as well as within given minorities, from situations of relative facility in what has been termed "assimilation," to situations in which individuals or groups enclave themselves and resist incorporation. These responses are not simply complementary to the relative degrees of receptivity on the part of the host society.

There is no doubt, of course, that the degree of social receptivity in the majority culture is a major determinant in minority attitudes toward assimilation. There has been extensive documentation in social science studies of how certain ethnic groups are selectively appreciated or depreciated in accord with cultural and racial assessments that persist over generations. Individuals originating from northwest Europe are accorded a rapid receptivity far different from that experienced by those originating in eastern or southern Europe. In turn, individuals of Asian or African origin or Caucasoids from outside the European sphere have been treated with relative degrees of continuing rejection based on what are generally termed "racist" attitudes.

However, one must quickly note that such acceptability or rejection is also crosscut with forms of traditional social behavior that are judged relatively acceptable or unacceptable, and that to some degree again are not completely congruent with racial prejudices. There are further complications related to the internally maintained cohesiveness and exclusiveness of given groups that derive from given cultural traditions. In sum, there are a number of overlapping and intertwining determinants in the nature and type and persistence of specific ethnic identity found characteristic for any given group. Within any given situation there are to be found psychological patterns—some general to given sociological determinants, others specific to given cultural-historical continuities.

Let me illustrate by examining Japanese psychocultural behavior, both in circumstances where three generations of Japanese origin comprise a minority group within American society and where they operate in their own country as the dominant majority with a Korean minority. The behavioral responses of Japanese Americans have, in some instances, gone directly counter to many sociological hypotheses concerning the negative effects of discrimination in American society. By and large, they have succeeded relatively well educationally and occupationally, despite the history of strong prejudice against them (Caudill and

DeVos, 1956). They have now, in three generations, for the most part shown a singular social invulnerability to discrimination relative to other groups. This is witnessed in social statistics in a relative lack of delinquency in youth and a relative lack of socially observable mental illness. Statistics on the amount of schooling achieved and on relative income received, where they are available, attest to a relatively positive social adaptation as it would be defined by the society in which they live.

I would like to single out for examination one psychocultural variable that I believe plays a considerable part in the Japanese American response to their minority problem. I would like to suggest that role-playing behavior, within the primary group as well as in face-to-face community relationships, creates a socialization situation in which the Japanese child, whether in the United States or elsewhere, becomes relatively invulnerable against the later "societal diseases" of deviancy and alienation so often contracted by individuals of minority status. (DeVos, 1973:13). In what I say I hope not in any way to discount the numerous experiences of personal discomfort or stress suffered by Japanese living in a white-oriented American society.

The type of role playing that one witnesses within the Japanese family protects the individual from the severely deleterious effects of his minority status as an adult. Contrary to some other groups we will presently mention illustratively, the Japanese adult male in the United States, for example, tends not to use alcohol excessively, nor does he become involved negatively in crime or other forms of legal difficulty with relative frequency. Rather, he achieves some form of middle-class economic and professional status.

Americans consider the ideal personal relationship to include considerable capacity for individuals to relate directly to one another in intimate nonhierarchical contact. This contact is defined as occurring between "selves" rather than individuals playing roles defined by status considerations. The Japanese tradition, in contrast, subordinates concern with the self to role expectation. To illustrate, the traditional Japanese concept of "sincerity" sees the sincere individual acting in accordance with his role expectations, *not* in accordance with his own personal subjective feelings. In a contrary sense, for an American to be "sincere" is to behave in accord with his feelings rather than acting only from the standpoint of what might be expected of him in the exercise of a given role. Indeed, the person who acts in accordance with role expectations at the expense of feelings would be seen as insincere and dissimulating. This concept, as it works out in the Japanese primary family, creates considerable psychological security for the growing child. Of course, this is at a price. There is the frequent complaint reported by Japanese Americans that they have experienced personal distance vis-à-vis the father. Keeping distance emotionally is aided and abetted by the mother's insistence in her manifest behavior that the father's role as head of the family is irreproachably legitimate, demanding unquestioned respect from the child.

I have witnessed examples of this even in the lower-status Japanese families with which we worked in urban Tokyo. As part of our delinquency study, started in the early 1960s, Wagatsuma and I, with our Japanese colleagues, conducted intensive observations, interviews, and psychological tests with fifty Japanese families (DeVos and Wagatsuma, n.d.). Thirty of these were families with a delinquent child and twenty families were a control group matched from the same schools and neighborhoods. Briefly, one of our most notable findings was the fact that in the families of delinquents the mothers tended *not* to role play. They expressed attitudes in front of children that conveyed their sense of dissatisfaction with the father. The father's manifest social and personal inadequacy was not hidden from the children; rather, it was emphasized. Conversely, in the families of the nondelinquent controls, whatever the personal and economic failures of the father, he was nevertheless accorded deference and supported by his wife, who, in playing the role of mother, saw to it that her children observed a proper attitude toward the head of the family in their day-by-day behavior.

To illustrate by a diagram (see figure 1), Japanese males inhabit a well-defined role, whether it be in their family or in their occupation. A father is not nakedly observed. His role serves as a protective covering that hides his inadequacies. It is a breach of social distance to penetrate within and make obvious, in any social context, the manifest limitations of the other person. A male child and a female child both grow up to expect similar conduct accorded to mother and father. A little girl observes mother's constrained behavior and thereby learns her expected role in her relationship with men. The mother demonstrates as central to her expected behavior self-control rather than confrontation by complaint or castigation.

This is not to say that such role playing takes place without considerable internal psychological cost for many Japanese. Nor do I want to give the impression that such behavior is invariant within Japanese culture. The very fact that we are able to observe differences in families related to the appearance of delinquency attests to a possible range of variability. However, if one takes into consideration statistics of any form of problem behavior, it is notable how members of a Japanese family in Japan as well as in the United States are surviving other sociological forces so manifest in situations of modernization and change. As witnessed by international statistics on delinquency, the urban Japanese uniquely in both Japan and the United States are maintaining a very low overall rate in direct contrast with what we find in other countries, certainly in very great contrast to the overall statistics for Americans.

Figure 1. Effects on Son's Occupational Achievement of Father's Roles and Mother's Attitudes Toward Husband in Various Social Status Situations

Many majority Japanese families

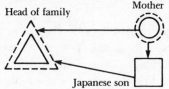

Father protected within role, treated as if he inhabits role.

Boy motivated to succeed into the safe role of family head.

Many Irish families (acc. to James Joyce)

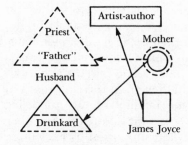

Relationship to priest idealized, husband not protected by "father" role but looked down on as inadequate.

Child observes degradation and escapes into the marginal ideal role of artist.

Many lower-class British miner families (acc. to D. H. Lawrence)

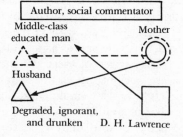

Child refuses and seeks escape into marginal observer's role.

Many minority Jewish families

Minority role outside of family not as important for male status. Father protected by inhabiting religious role. Mother must accord him status in this role.

Child motivated by "learning" as guarantee of family status.

Lower-class caste minority black families

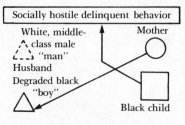

Some black women ambivalent about black males. Communicate ambivalence to children, esp. in anger. Boy witnesses degradation of black man, but cannot become white.

Let me quickly add that sociological problems of social degradation related to minority status operate similarly in Japan and the United States. Among the former pariahs of Japan, the present-day Burakumin, there is, indeed, a high delinquency rate, four times that of majority youth (DeVos and Wagatsuma, 1966). Among Koreans in Japan, whom we are currently studying, in the city of Kobe, where we have done some systematic appraisal, the rate is approximately up to seven times as high as that of majority Japanese. These rates are comparable to the official rates recorded in California for Mexican Americans and blacks (five times the delinquency rate compared with those classified as majority "white"). But if the delinquency rate was simply a matter of the societal pressures related to minority status, why is it that the Japanese in the state of California have a rate that has been calculated at one-eightieth of that of the majority?

The clue to understanding, I believe, is the cultural-historical circumstances that have come to prevail over several generations in given cultures or given minority segments of a complex culture. The occupational role degradation experienced *outside* by men who are forced to compete occupationally in situations of relative discrimination can become somehow echoed *inside* the family by mutual husband-wife attitudes both self-directed and incurred from one's spouse. Even in those instances where the internal relationships of the family do not reflect some vulnerability to outside social degradation, men and women in some cultures are less "trained" toward forms of parental role playing that shield the child from the negative implications of social degradation experienced by those experiencing outside contact. Perhaps uniquely, in the case of the Jews of Europe, where the high-status role of the father was supported internally within ghettoed communities by religious considerations, and in the case of the Japanese, where the role of head of family has had a quasi-religious meaning, do we find family structures that are comparatively resistive to the deleterious effect of minority status outside the ethnic community.

Traditions of parental status in some segments of a culture may not obviate forms of overt tension and conflict with families. Where there are long traditions of occupational exploitation, as among the peons and the ex-peons of Mexico, the ex-slaves of the American South, and the serfs of eastern Europe, men in degraded class or caste status are not accorded the formal respect afforded higher-status males within the same society. Their women may submit to their authority only by force; an attitude of conflict and submission is transmitted to their offspring.

Despite the fact that the Koreans and Japanese share a common heritage of Confucian ideology about the high status of the father in the family, we are finding a great deal of actual role degradation of father, both within the family as well as outside, in the Korean minority in Japan (Lee and DeVos, n.d.).

This experience is explicable in a cultural-historical context. From 1919 on, an increasing number of abjectly impoverished Koreans migrated to Japan from what had become an economically exploited Japanese colony to seek some form of unskilled labor in an industrializing Japan. Later, as a by-product of Japanese militarist adventure in Asia from the 1930s on, over three and a half million Koreans were brought to Japan involuntarily to replace Japanese who had been drawn into the armed forces. Today there are 750,000 second- and third-generation Koreans who are not accorded citizenship due to a rather complicated situation that we cannot discuss here. These Japanese "Koreans" for the most part know no Korean language. They speak and think as do the majority Japanese. They are nevertheless still accorded a semipariah state as the offspring of illiterate Korean peasants, already despised and degraded from their moment of entry into Japan. (It must be stressed that even before migration the poor Korean peasant within his own culture did not receive the status support traditionally accorded the Japanese farmer who, despite widespread poverty, was still ranked socially above more wealthy artisans and merchants in premodern Japan.)

In our field experiences as well as in newspaper reports, we are finding many instances of drunkenness and general despair among minority Koreans and many problems of mutual physical as well as verbal abuse occurring in the home between parents. The growing child is often exposed to the mother's overtly expressed negative attitudes toward a socially degraded father. In many instances he or she witnesses, but does not understand until later, a type of helpless violent rage that can only be vented in the home by men who feel a deep sense of personal inadequacy. Such behavior corresponds closely to that witnessed in the U.S. in some families derived from a degraded heritage of eastern European serfdom, where in similar fashion the peasant father at home was accorded very little formal social respect by the mother.

Polish miners in the United States have in some instances perpetuated a family interaction pattern in which the man's insistence on male dominance elicits him no respect or even fond acquiescence by his wife. The anticipated parental interaction from one generation to the next may be a negative one. Periodic drunken behvaior of the husband includes beating.

In rural Ireland the cultural-historical pattern condemned many men to a lifelong role as "boy" if they possessed no land through inheritance. Social disparagement of men is still relatively prevalent in rural Ireland, as is recourse to drink and a high rate of hospitalization. James Joyce, in his sensitive novel, *A Portrait of the Artist as a Young Man*, depicts the alternate images of the male roles he saw himself destined to inhabit. On the one hand there was the desexualized priest, who is respected as a "father," and on the other hand the actual technical heads of families and biological fathers of children who are disparaged by women, and perceived generally as being drunken, inadequate males. Joyce sought to escape this perceived dilemma of Irish destiny by becoming a marginal man in his role as artist (see figure 1).

Similarly, perhaps emphasizing less the ethnic variable and more the class problems of lower status, D. H. Lawrence depicts, in his autobiographically influenced novels such as *Sons and Lovers,* a situation in which the lower-class British coal miner father seeks in his inarticulate way some kind of respect from his wife, but can only, as so many others, bolster himself with alcohol and in effect demand brutally what is not given freely from a wife who has no respect for his role in society. Lawrence depicts the way his mother's image of male respectability and status is derived from middle-class models. She instills in her son a need for social mobility. The son witnesses the degradation of his father. He cannot sympathize with him, for he cannot completely escape identifying with his mother's perceptions. He nevertheless revolts against the status definitions of his society because he cannot identify with the destiny of so many from his own class background. Note well how the author depicts how the mother teaches the individual child the destiny of deep shame related to status degradation.

Turning to the recent social revolution taking place in American society, there has been an increasing awareness of how some black mothers have debilitated their own male children (cf. *The Autobiography of Malcolm X,* with Alex Haley). Long before the child is exposed to the outer world and its cruel discrimination, he has often heard his own mother place an angry curse on his own destiny, such as "You black bastard. You will never amount to anything." Too many black women have accepted, perhaps not consciously in most instances, the attitude that the only legitimate role for a "man" is performed by white middle-class males. Their own children grow up in the shadow of ambivalence about themselves cast upon them by their own mothers. They have in many instances personally witnessed the social degradation of an older generation of males who have already succumbed to their destiny. Wishing to fight against these forces, some find themselves curiously unable to overcome a sense of inner debilitation that prevents an optimal exercise of potential (Kardiner and Ovesey, 1962).

There are Mexican American children whose mothers, in effect, tell them that the only reason she stays with a "macho" father is the fact that without some form of economic provision they would be helplessly destitute. The Mexican child witnesses the defensive assertion of a precariously believed masculine image. As an adolescent he may seek refuge outside the home with peers. At a later date he, too, may succumb finally to adulthood and, in so doing, to a culturally shared "macho" image. Women are not to be trusted; one can only demand their respect by the use of force (cf. M. Clark, 1959).

What we often find in these various minority communities is that, while there are some families and elements within given communities who form social attitudes that help their members survive in a generally degraded social atmosphere, a notable proportion of individuals find it difficult to surmount the difficulties of degradation extending back generationally. Nevertheless, no matter how degraded a group, there are individuals who can respond to the challenge of dignity and set up examples within their families that are resistive to the later corrosive experiences of the outer world.

Sometimes there are relatively successful movements within minority groups to reestablish bases for dignity. I discussed elsewhere (DeVos, n.d.:chap. 3) how revivalist religious movements are attempts to restore a lost sense of personal worth and social dignity to a given group (cf. Theodore Schwartz, "The Cargo Cult," in DeVos, ed., 1976). The astounding reaction to the television series "Roots" must be attributed to the implicit knowledge of both blacks and whites that if one can trace one's origin to some past period of dignity, the subsequent degradation of intervening generations can be overcome.

Peer Group Functions and Ethnic Identity—Reference Group Theory Reconsidered in Relation to Selective Permeability

Whereas Sherif and Sherif and others (1964, 1967) have made of reference group theory a powerful instrument for understanding social processes in communities, the emphasis too often in the use of these concepts has been on the conscious face-to-face affiliation of individuals. Relatively less attention is paid to the dynamic, sometimes conflictful, interrelationship between the internalized conscience more or less acquired in the family, and the immediate reference group influence. Apparent in those individuals who have strongly internalized a family identity with less conflict is the maturation of a social identity somehow more tuned to past family directives and relatively less susceptible to immediate group influences coming either from outside the peer community or from within. Such inner-directed individuals, to use Riesman's term (Riesman, Glazer, and Denney, 1958), in some sense have more autonomy and are less subject to the vagaries of immediate social experience. In ethnic groups where family interaction is generally less homogeneous, or in individuals within a particular family where conflicts are greater, there is dependence on the reference group as a secondary medium of socialization. This priority of peer group over family is quite apparent in many acculturative situations. The parents become viewed as "foreigners" or as out of date. Children are alienated from the past adult community and seek identification of a mutual sort among their young peers. This has been a notable process in the "Americanization" of previous generations of ethnic minorities coming from Europe. But for European immigrants, the reference group itself was defined as "American" by the growing youth. More recently, however, for youthful Mexican Americans, blacks, Puerto Ricans, and Chinese in San Francisco, the peer reference group itself serves to maintain a separateness in orientation that prevents ready identification with the majority white population.

This peer group alienation has traditionally operated in a similar fashion among Native Americans. The peer group has been historically overrun by an expanding European population. It has resisted any incorporative definitions by the white culture. Note well, however, how this type of separateness in peer group orientation is somehow directly related to a sense of status degradation in perceived parental roles. It is in such situations of relative adult status degradation that the family moral authority has itself been replaced by peer group orientation. (This topic needs much more explication than can be pursued here.)

In our recent study of minority Koreans in Japan we note, for example, that an extreme complexity of peer group involvement in identity can occur. The conflictual identity of being a despised Korean in a culture in which the individual's parents do not speak Korean but Japanese; where their legal status remains that of foreigners; where the father is often unemployed or works ambiguously at a dubious occupation; where the mother is very often constrained to work as a bar hostess; where the children are not supervised with the constancy that they need, especially in early childhood; where the Korean child is often ridiculed as dirty and uncouth, or feared as tough and belligerent by his Japanese mates—in all these circumstances, even with the help of peer group socialization, the Korean youth finds it most difficult to resolve with any finality his chronic problem of belonging.

Individual instances reveal how complex this problem can become. In some of the individual cases we have studied, a Japanese peer reference group at times is accepting to the individual Korean child without any negative reference to his background. At other times, however, the individual must make selective identification with either a Korean group against Japanese or a Japanese group in which there is animosity expressed toward Koreans. In other instances, some individuals who are accepted by a Japanese group will, in peer group conflicts in school, be forced to make a loyalty choice that at times can pit them against other Korean youth. The situation can become very complex for the individual.

Looking at the problem longitudinally, in childhood and adolescence, in given instances the same individual may at one time make an identification with Japanese peers and at other times make affiliation with other Koreans of his own age. In this movement back and forth the individual is often struggling with self-conflicts of a self-deprecatory nature. He may experience a sense of worthlessness should he too readily identify with his degraded Korean community. Yet at any given rebuff or setback in relation to Japanese, whether based on prejudice or not, what comes into focus very often is his own basic lack of self-confidence derivative of the inescapable knowledge that he is of Korean origin. In some cases, however, one also notes how a secure family identity leads to a persistence and a sense of dedication in overcoming barriers to accomplishment.

The point of all this is to recognize that in some situations individuals can maintain their identity and still take on acculturative traits from other groups without in any way feeling inferior or giving up their sense of ethnic origin. We will discuss this further when we examine "selective permeability" as a function of the ego related to individual identification and identity.

From the standpoint of modernization, the point to be made here is that, in any particular situation of culture contact, one must explore acculturative change—what new experiences mean subjectively to the individual. What are the dangers to self when one takes on a reference group composed of other backgrounds or other traditions? Can a new sense of larger belonging be attained without injury to the values and sense of ethnic self-dignity the individual wishes to preserve?

In adaptive acculturation a person can utilize a reference group of actual available peers with whom one comes in direct contact. He or she, however, may take on as a reference group one that is only contacted indirectly through available mass media. This process can progress through more than one generation. For example, a young lower-class girl, in her fantasies, may wish for a middle-class husband. Her destiny, however, brings her into contact only with lower-class men. When she marries, she may never accept emotionally the economic and behavioral limitations of her husband. He is measured against the standards put together out of far-off glimpses of another world. For some women in a class-stratified society, or for some living themselves in a minority status, the dominant group provides an orienting life style that is not actualized for them, but is used as a measure of one's own incapacities or the degraded conditions of one's family background or the insufficiencies of one's spouse. These models are used also to measure the potential inadequacy of one's children. For many women, marriage is the only perceived vehicle for realization of status—hence, a "good" marriage is the life goal for many.

Discontent with one's fate is passed on to the children by parents, as we have already discussed. The aspirations of the mother in this sense are in turn internalized as an orienting reference with which the growing child must contend, as is, unfortunately, the sense of the father's failure. For some children it may mean an impetus toward social mobility. This implies a rejection both of immediate peers and of parents, and a seeking out of opportunities or avenues of actual contact with members of a distant yet desired group. This dynamic of mobility is apparent in some members of every minority group.

The peer group, youthful or adult, however, tends in self-preservative reactions continually to sanction against individuals trying to leave a group. The mechanisms employed can be subtle or directly coercive. An account told me by another anthropologist is a paradigm of such peer group pressure. A Native American Apache high school graduate, upon being awarded a college scholarship, came home shortly afterward only to receive a severe beating and to find his dog killed by his peers. Change of reference orientation in a member of the group can be experienced as a threat to the collectivity. This threat is not simply to the cohesion of the group, but to the implicit defensive posture of the group against the intrusion of alien expectations of accomplishment that would entail an examination of personal inadequacies. In contrast, more often youthful peer groups are used to ward off the expectations of adulthood. In a plural society, minority peer groups not only resist the demands of the dominant society, they sometimes prepare the individual for a sense of group failure for which responsibility is placed on the majority. To attempt to succeed and then to fail is to acknowledge the possibility that failure is in the self or the inferiority of the group to which one belongs, hence a negative circle exists in which one cannot try to succeed without becoming alienated from one's group. The negative stance of the group ironically perpetuates the very need to defend against implications of inferiority by denying the competitive goals thrust upon the group by a disparaging host society that already judges a group incapable of picking up the challenge.

To illustrate cross-culturally, in some instances the reference group may facilitate adaptation, while in others it is resistive to adaptive change in situations of modernization. Edward Bruner is an anthropologist who has worked both with Native Americans and with the Toba Batak of Sumatra (Bruner, 1976). Influenced by Herbert Blumer, he uses an interactionist interpretation to illustrate the differences in adaptation to change in these two instances.

He has witnessed the dilemmas of integrity experienced by Native Americans. Relatively few succeed in modern "white" terms, or succeed to enclave and isolate themselves in traditional customs, so that they do not become anomic or self-destructive. In contrast, the Toba Batak adapt well to modernization in urban settings. This challenges the idea that "tradition" need be static. For the Batak, at least, their tradition is created and constructed anew in contemporary situations as the situations change. The socially constructed conception of what has been the group tradition also changes imperceptibly. The past is subtly reconstructed to accommodate present self-definitions. Bruner states:

> A Toba Batak in Sumatra or an American Indian in Arizona is not completely free to choose his cultural symbols or his slot in the structure; there are limitations inherent in the situation. In this sense there is no opposition between structuralism, which defines what is possible within the social arena, and symbolic interactionism, which focuses on the interactions and images that emerge within it (Bruner, 1976, p. 235).

In brief, the basic difference in identity formation for most Native Americans in contrast to Toba Batak, in Bruner's observation, is that until very recently an Indian identity had to be renounced in order to modernize, but the model of orientation for a Batak is a "modern" Batak. The Batak have been able to bend tradition to modern purposes. Their adat or "customary law" in their view has not changed. For the Batak no choice of group is necessary, no sense of betrayal is aroused, nor do they isolate themselves from their past by attempting to succeed in modern occupational terms.

Sometimes success in a new occupational role necessitates disguise as a member of the majority. Among the Japanese Burakumin, or former pariahs, Wagatsuma and I have been given examples of several youths who have initially "passed" by leaving for Tokyo. They return to their ghetto life, preferring it to living without personal contact. The individual may be encouraged to become "successful" in a Japanese society, but cannot be satisfied by "passing." A need for affiliation or nurturance cannot be transferred from one's own group to occupational success among majority Japanese. All segments of Japanese culture, including that of the Burakumin, socialize the individual to emphasize group belonging over individual self-sufficiency. One example will suffice.

One young man Wagatsuma interviewed had succeeded in "passing." He was seen as having a promising career in Tokyo. After two years he returned to become a refuse collector in Kyoto. He could not bear the dissimulation necessary in Tokyo. He could not identify with majority Japanese despite his interest in his work. He needed to return to a despised group he had sought to abandon (cf. DeVos and Wagatsuma, 1966, chap. 12).

The major part of his dilemma was a continuous internal conflict over his identity. For many, it is not simply a matter of adapting to an alien reference group that better exemplifies what the individual holds to be his values and his life goals. One cannot abandon a deep sense of identity. This is true even if the individual cannot find any rapport with his group of origin, due to education and personal accomplishment that remove him conceptually from his former peers. One must choose which form of alienation is less intolerable.

SELECTIVE PERMEABILITY: A FORM OF AUTOMATIC REPRESSION

Finally, related to continuity of social class or caste there are psychological coping mechanisms or, if you will, defensive mechanisms related to ego functioning, that induce the selective perception and execution of behavior related to particularized learning experiences. Let me consider very briefly problems of relative "nonlearning" evidenced in particular ethnic minorities as well as in men or women of majority culture. To do so, one cannot escape some psychological examination of how the self is selectively defined, progressively. By the time individuals are collectively exposed to formal education, they are not perceiving the same stimuli in the school situation.

Recently there has been what I believe to be a serious misapplication of theories around the effects of linguistic differences as an important determinant of differential learning in school situations. The reasoning of those talking about language disadvantage, even "cultural" disadvantage, is, I believe, somewhat overly simplistic.

For example, one often hears expressed the idea that a basic reason why Mexican American or black children do not learn well in American schools is that they use a separate language at home. Why is it that this disadvantage is overcome by some children with equally different cultural background? Why is it that Nisei children of Japanese immigrants, for example, from the 1930s on, did so well in school despite the poor linguistic competence in English of their parents and their evident difficulty themselves with English on achievement tests administered them? I believe that the disadvantages of speaking a foreign language at home are secondary to the social and personal meaning attached to learning an alien tongue. The fact of the matter is that in some circumstances the peer group as well as the family facilitates the *permeability* of learning experiences in the school situation. This was so in the case of the Japanese. In other instances, the peer group especially can buttress a pattern of learning resistance on the part of the child. I hasten to add that such lack of learning is not necessarily consciously controlled. Individuals "freeze up" when asked to learn something that might threaten an "incompetence" that is a protective part of one's identity, be it sexually or socially defined. For example, many boys and men "cannot cook," just as many women or scholars "cannot learn" to replace a rubber gasket in a leaking faucet.

Of course, the attitude of the teachers, whether in a formal school or in an informal learning situation, is also crucial. Without knowing it, teachers deliver attitudinal messages to individuals being taught as to whether or not they are capable of learning something, or whether or not a particular type of learning is appropriate for them (Warner et al., 1944; Davis and Havighurst, 1947).

From the vantage point of how a social self-identity or ethnic identity is formed, the question becomes not a direct one of values, but of how particular learning experiences may be perceived, automatically and unconsciously, as harmful or helpful to the integrity of the individual. The very process of formal learning itself may arouse a sense of impending conflict over one's future identity. Adults as well as children maintain as best as possible a consistent concept of self. This process operates through the automatic functioning of their perceptual apparatus. There is the automatic selecting out of those aspects of the environment that are stimulating to growth within a more or less well-defined sense of present and future role.

In situations of cultural pluralism or class differentiation, strongly defined separate sex roles, certain forms of behavior, certain ways of expressing oneself, certain forms of comportment are in a sense not to be entertained or practiced without emotional as well as cognitive dissonance. In another context (DeVos, 1975), I have argued against the *cognitive* dissonance theory of Leon Festinger in favor of a concept of *affective* dissonance. It is the arousal of dissonant emotions that necessitates some form of consequent cognitive resolution. When an individual is not affectively aroused he can readily tolerate without discomfort confusing concepts or conceptual inconsistencies. But human beings cannot tolerate contradicting emotional states without calling into use psychological defense mechanisms such as denial, repression, projection, or displacement.

Some modes of social adaptation, however instrumentally advantageous, may not be accessible because they go counter to an affectively aroused sense of consistency and stability in self-awareness. There is selective permeability to experience. The incorporation of inconsistencies demands the expenditure of considerable psychic energy. The individual may wish to forgo instrumental social advantage to avoid the inevitable internal conflict that accompanies some aspects of acculturation or upward social mobility.

Individuals experiencing some forms of change in themselves may sense the possible vertigo of alienation. Rather than face such an internal stress, during youth they may turn to an available peer group that offers psychological security. Most operative in the pre- and postpubescent period of formative social development, the peer group mutually reinforces for its members the maintenance of types of social self-identity that are in the process of being established.

Where there is no general resistance to social acceptance, the individual may find that he can manage within a reference group that espouses transition toward a socially acceptable adult identity toward which he aims. In such a circumstance the peer group facilitates conformity, yet permits the individual psychologically to leave the family.

In some circumstances the peer group can be used to reinforce a previous identity. It reinforces positive attitudes in the family toward having a child better his status through the educational process. In the Japanese American Nisei studied by Caudill and myself in the late 1940s, such a process manifestly was at work (Caudill and DeVos, 1956).

In understanding acculturation or identity maintenance, therefore, it is crucial to understand the critical functioning of peer groups in the acculturative process. Unfortunately, today too little direct attention is paid to the crucial role of peer groups within the formal education system. Too much emphasis is put instead on the nature of the curriculum, or the functioning of the teacher, neglecting how the peer group may be the most crucial feature of the educative process in some minorities. Whether an individual functions within a peer group or not, whether the peer group is facilitative or inhibitive will to a great extent determine whether or not education occurs.

As one can document from working intimately with an ethnic minority, whether it be the Koreans in Japan or the Bretons in France, no child survives a situation of cultural pluralism without taking in some experiences that cannot be consciously accommodated as consistent with one's self-image. Such experiences are repressed, again indicating the selective permeability of experience. Over and over we find there is conflict between one's consciously embraced identity and what has been experienced but denied or repressed. Some of these repressed experiences remain alive and potentially disruptive, though buried deep in the individual's unconscious. It takes energy to repress—energy that could be used for more constructive forms of self-development.

Few individuals can avoid some degree of enervating conflict or stress in suppressing parts of an ethnic past, or conversely, a defensiveness that disavows what one has experienced of a majority culture. In one case the individual is frequently besieged by shame over what is disavowed. He refuses to acknowledge what is a true part of him. In another case the individual cannot free himself from some expectations that are inherent in the majority society. He has internalized them and develops a sense of failure if they are not realized.

Strong family definitions are crucial for many individuals in developing a social self-identity, as they are crucial for the establishment of a firm social sex role. There is less internal conflict in situations of cultural pluralism where individuals are able to gain some genuine security by internalizing a firm ethnic image of self through positively perceived parental models. One can face subsequent social disparagement with less vulnerability when one is already secure within oneself, by identifying with parents who are loved regardless of their acceptance by the outside world.

Unhappily, this early security is lacking in groups where family integration has suffered. In working with either the Burakumin or the Koreans in Japan, one finds repeated evidence of internalized negative self-images that have actually been transmitted within the primary family itself and have interfered with family cohesion. However they are subsequently denied, these negative images come back to haunt the individual from within. Negative images of oneself can haunt with the most destructive force in those cases where parental interaction has been conflictful and mutually damaging to the witnessing child as well as to the parents themselves.

Three Issues in Ethnicity: Boundaries, Deprivations, and Perceptions

Thomas Fraser Pettigrew

The Concept of Ethnicity

ETHNICITY AS A CONCEPT reminds one of St. Augustine's anguish over the concept of time: "For so it is, oh Lord my God, I measure it, but what it is that I measure I do not know."[1] Indeed, we are in an even more unenviable position than Augustine, for we are not certain even how to measure ethnicity, nor can we rescue it fully from heated ideological usage. Yet, like time, we are agreed upon its importance.

Ethnicity is widely accorded importance because it appears to be virtually a universal phenomenon. Human beings around the globe live and participate in groups presumed to be of common origin, groups larger than kinship units yet smaller than societies. They identify with such groups, and they are identified by others as members of such groups. And, like time again, human beings typically can "tell" you their ethnicity without being able to delve into its deeper significance.

The near-universality of ethnicity complicates its definition, for it appears in radically different forms across the world. A further complication involves the lack of fit between objective and subjective definitions. Objective definitions include such criteria as the sharing of a

☐ I wish to express my appreciation for invaluable suggestions for this paper made by Shelley Taylor of Harvard University, Morton Weinfeld of McGill University, and Wendell Bell of Yale University

[1] From Book XI of St. Augustine's *Confessions*.

common culture and fundamental values, biological self-perpetuation, enhanced communication, and *Gemeinschaft* relations (F. Barth, 1969; Isajiw, 1974). Fredrik Barth attacks such exclusively objective definitions as begging "all the critical questions... in the genesis, structure, and function" of ethnic groups (Barth, 1969: 11). Thus the existence of a common culture is best seen as a result rather than a criterion of an ethnic group; to make it a definitional requisite is to ignore cultural change over time and the shaping of diverse cultural forms by diverse ecologies within the same ethnic group.

Such critics prefer subjective definitions that stress ingroup identification and outgroup recognition. Scots comprise an ethnic group when a collectivity identifies itself as of common Scottish origin, and when it is seen as Scottish by such significant others as the English and Welsh. Though not without its own problems, such a subjective definition lends itself better to quantifiable variables, to the study of change and social organization, and to social psychological considerations. It leaves open to empirical investigation questions of biology, culture, and intragroup interaction and communication as well as questions about the overlap between ethnicity and such related concepts as race, class, and nationality. Finally, it raises the three issues I wish to address at the social psychological level: *the complexity of ethnic group boundaries, the ethnic group structure of perceived deprivation, and attributional distortions and ethnicity.*

The Complexity of Ethnic Group Boundaries

Subjective definitions of ethnicity necessarily place critical emphasis upon "the ethnic *boundary* that defines the group, not the cultural stuff that it encloses" (Barth, 1969:15; italics added). If the boundary between members and nonmembers is maintained, the ethnic group continues through time even if the distinctive physical and cultural traits that objectively define the group change sharply. This systems view of the importance of boundaries is a critical consideration for the study of ethnicity that has emerged within cultural anthropology from ethnographic materials of recent decades. But this view is still often overlooked in sociology and social psychology, especially in the study of ethnic groups in North America.

THE NON-CONVERGENCE OF ETHNIC BOUNDARIES

LeVine and Campbell (1972:chap. 7), in their valuable volume, *Ethnocentrism,* outline the evidence that "indicates that the ideal-typical ethnic community, in which boundaries, loyalties, and labels coincide in a single order of predecence, is not the general case for nonindustrial peoples..." (LeVine and Campbell, 1972:99). First, territorial inter-penetration of ethnic communities is more often the rule than the excep-tion. It is usually impossible to draw a single continuous territorial boun-dary. An ethnic ideology, a sense of kind and peoplehood, separates them rather than territory, though there are usually one or more con-spicuous differences between ethnicities in language, mode of subsis-tence, material culture, religion, life style, and social organization.

Second, there is continuous variation in linguistic and cultural characteristics rather than sharp discontinuities. Moreover, there is often noncongruent variation among these characteristics, so that dif-ferent ethnic maps will be produced for each characteristic. Third, there is also confusion among subjective criteria of ethnicity. It is not unusual for peoples within the same region to disagree about ethnic labels and community boundaries. LeVine and Campbell (1972) believe that such inconsistency is more commonly found in areas with continuous cultural variation that lack political centralization. Finally, ethnic communities typically engage in stable and significant interaction across boundaries.

For these reasons, Barth (1969) maintains that the study of bound-aries is strategic to understanding the persistence of ethnic groups. If the old assumptions of territorial isolation and discontinuous cultural varia-tion are largely invalid, how is it that ethnic groups seem generally to be tenaciously persistent? This question will be addressed in a variety of ways throughout this paper.

The psychological complexity generated by ethnic boundaries is re-vealed by Brewer and Campbell (1976) in their analysis of ethnic stereotyping from samples of fifty respondents in each of thirty East African tribes. In analyzing trait ratings between groups, these inves-tigators soon found that a simple one-dimensional space of acceptance and rejection does not reflect the results. Three dimensions are re-quired: (1) trust–conflict; (2) attraction–repulsion, and (3) admiration–disrespect. Thus there is little relationship between evaluative ratings (admiration–disrespect) and affective ratings (attraction–repulsion) of outgroups. Admiration reflects the power and status of tribes. Attraction ratings toward low-status, disrespected outgroups are uniformly low, while they are highly variable toward high-status, admired groups. Envy is two-edged. Powerful groups are both respected and constitute targets for resentment. Attraction ratings also covary with such intergroup con-tact factors as cultural-linguistic similarity and geographic proximity. Most respondents "feel psychologically closer to a 'familiar enemy' than to a little-known stranger" (Brewer and Campbell, 1976:142).

A principal psychological consequence of the widespread noncon-vergence of ethnic boundaries may be an "institutionalized sustained ambivalence in intergroup relations." Such an ambivalence permits flexibility in meeting divergent demands, and is dramatically illustrated by East African groups that combine frequent military confrontations with high rates of intermarriage.

From this perspective, Sumner's (1906) complete form of ethnocentrism represents a limiting case of near-total convergence of boundary-defining mechanisms rather than the typical intergroup state of affairs. Either threats to group survival or institutionalized barriers to equal-status contact between groups appear necessary to induce such a situation (as in the American South of Sumner's time and modern South Africa). "Convergent ethnocentrism," conclude Brewer and Campbell (1976:145), "is not a necessary or universal pattern of intergroup relations in a pluralistic society."

But can nonconvergent boundaries between two ethnic groups achieve stability? Or, as balance theory maintains, is there a "strain toward symmetry," boundary convergence, and hence Sumner's full-blown pattern of ethnocentrism? These investigators believe that their new East African data argue against such a trend being inevitable or even typical. This judgment can be supported as well on theoretical grounds. Balance theory, like most social psychological theories, is limited to situations of *mechanical* solidarity. Stable, nonconvergent ethnic boundaries, however, invoke principles of *organic* solidarity. Barth (1969) and his colleagues provide numerous illustrations of intricate boundary equilibria reached by interdependent ethnic groups, such as market exchanges. Organic solidarity raises divergent intergroup demands; "institutionalized ambivalence" and boundary nonconvergence serve such demands better. Yet Sumner (1906) was not all wrong. Extreme ethnocentric patterns do occur throughout the world. The point is that such patterns, with their relative convergence of boundaries, are not the rule; they deserve to be studied as problematic exceptions.

This analysis has been developed primarily around preindustrial peoples in Africa and Asia. How much of it can be applied to ethnic groups in modern states? Clearly, nation-states apply strong pressures for boundary convergence of their total populations. But I wish to argue that much of this anthropological boundary analysis *is* valid for ethnic groups within modern polyethnic states.

Consider again the four lines of evidence for tribal nonconvergence of boundaries: territorial interpenetration, continuous variation in linguistic and cultural characteristics, ethnic labeling inconsistencies, and stable and extensive cross-boundary interaction. Inconsistent labeling is less evinced when a centralized polity contributes to common definitions throughout the society. However, the remaining three phenomena would seem to hold largely true for most polyethnic situations in industrial nations. To be sure, these phenomena assume shadings that contrast with preindustrial forms. But if there are systematic differences, I suspect that two of these nonconvergent phenomena, territorial interpenetration and cross-boundary interaction, hold with even greater force in the modern setting.

The controlling words here, however, are "argue" and "suspect." Little attention has been given to the boundary issue in the study of ethnic groups in industrial societies, especially in North America.[2] Thus one recent survey study of American ethnicity (Greeley, 1974) asked only, what is your nationality or background? Or, where do most of your ancestors come from? If more than one nationality was provided, only the father's nationality was employed as the respondent's ethnicity. Such a procedure obviously obscures the issue of boundaries. Mixed-ethnic marriages and their offspring are vital elements in understanding ethnicity and its persistence. This is particularly true in a country where Yinger (1976) estimates that 35 to 40 percent of all religious intermarriages that could have occurred in 1957 did occur. Denying the intermarriage issue through dubious empirical procedures will not aid our understanding of the complexities of ethnic boundaries in industrial countries.

Greater concern for boundaries would also clarify the relationship between ethnicity and race in the United States. Ideological debate has unproductively dominated this discussion to date. A boundary perspective, however, points to a solution. We have defined ethnicity so broadly—in terms of ingroup identification and outgroup recognition—that black Americans are included. Race makes its unique contribution in the extreme degree of boundary convergence (Pettigrew, 1964, 1975). Intermarriage is minimized. Housing segregation is intense and qualitatively a different problem than that facing white ethnic groups. Racial role prescriptions are narrow and enforced. Even the terms of past American race relations describe this convergence—segregation, color line, knowing your place. In short, black Americans are an ethnic group limited by unusually extreme boundary convergence that is only now beginning to recede.

The degree of boundary convergence not only distinguishes racial from white ethnic phenomena, but distinguishes among North America's white ethnic group situations as well. If we simultaneously considered residential separation, intraethnic marriage, intraethnic organizational participation, and other boundary indicators, such late arrivals to North America as the Eastern Europeans would probably have stronger relationships between the indicators and greater boundary convergence than such earlier arrivals as the Irish.

---

[2]Thus the excellent paper by Donald Horowitz (1975) on ethnic boundaries and identity necessarily has to draw virtually all of its examples from nonindustrial societies.

AFFECTIVE ETHNICITY

A prime place to look for this phenomenon is Toronto, North America's most ethnically heterogeneous city of recent arrivals.[3] Richmond (1974) provides such a look with a 1970 ethnic survey utilizing a probability adult sample of metropolitan Toronto.

In a secondary analysis of these data, Weinfeld (1977) devised a broad composite ethnic index consisting of seven indicators: ethnic preferences as reflected in choice of a residence, spouse, friends, language, and community participation, together with self-identification and support for cultural pluralism. For his three major groups—Jews, Slavs, and Italians—generation and social class yield the highest independent predictions of the ethnic index. As the assimilationist model predicts, ethnicity is strongest for the first-generation Canadians and the least educated, with sharp declines with each generation and with increased education. The effects of age on ethnicity, interestingly, are largely mediated through education. Consistent with our earlier discussion, perceived discrimination against one's own group relates positively to the ethnic index for only the nonwhite respondents.

Weinfeld (1977) also analyzes each of the seven ethnicity indicators as separate dependent variables. Here he discovered meaningful differences between his five structural and preference variables and his two psychological and identification variables. More than American cities, Toronto still reflects high levels of intraethnic living. Nevertheless, each of Weinfeld's five structural indicators fit the assimilationist model; they decline with each generation and with greater educational attainment. But the assimilationist model does *not* fit the two psychological variables—self-identification and support for cultural pluralism. Weinfeld labels this psychological component "affective ethnicity"; it is this element that is the persistent core of North American ethnicity that effectively resists assimilationist pressures.

Weinfeld's findings contribute to Milton Gordon's (1964) classic analysis. Gordon distinguished between *acculturation,* in reference to behavioral and cultural assimilation, and *assimilation,* in reference to "large scale entrance into . . . institutions of the host society" with dissolution of group differences even at the most intimate primary levels of friendship and family. The United States, Gordon argued, witnesses mass acculturation alongside only moderate social assimilation. A sense of "peoplehood" necessarily lessens, Gordon felt, when significant structural entry is made. Weinfeld's Toronto results question this prediction about less-

---

[3]Richmond's (1974) 1970 survey reveals that half of metropolitan Toronto's household heads were born outside of Canada, and only 29 percent were native born of native parentage.

ened "peoplehood," and add a third domain of psychological assimilation that is not as closely linked to forms of cultural and social assimilation as previously envisaged.

Relatively strong affective ethnicity side-by-side with marked acculturation and growing social assimilation appears to characterize much of the ethnic scene in North America (sans Quebec). Such a description fits with the recent ethnic revival, with much of Greeley's (1974) survey data, and with Alba's (1976) demonstration that by 1963 mixed ethnic marriage and friendship among American Catholics was widespread. The current ethnic revival in America may represent largely affective ethnicity. But such ethnic identification is just as "real" a social phenomenon in American society as are the patterns of extensive acculturation and increasing social assimilation. We go wrong in both our social analyses and ideological debates when we assume close boundary convergences among these affective, cultural, and social components of ethnicity. Moreover, the most lasting core of ethnicity may be its affective basis.

Such contentions do not imply that these three realms of ethnicity are independent. But they do imply that these affective, cultural, and social components interact in complex ways, and that the apparent exceptions to convergent boundaries are numerous and meaningful. One can be, like the author, a second-generation Scots-American with scant cultural and virtually no social traces of ethnicity remaining, yet identify strongly with Scotland, visit it often, and sympathize with its aspirations for nationhood. Such mixed cases, as Yinger (1976) points out, are probably typical in North America. As the popularity of Alex Haley's (1976) *Roots* suggests and Weinfeld's results bear out, there appear to be continuing psychological needs to identify ethnically even when ancestry is mixed and the cultural and social supports of such identification have withered. Erikson (1966) and others have explored this realm. Further progress might be made by social psychologists in extending the work on the human need and search for meaning—in this case, the central meaning of ethnicity to the self and its social situs.[4]

[4]The human need and search for meaning, understanding, and predictability are widely accepted in social psychology. But, as Berkowitz (1969: 87–88) points out, this motive has suffered from vague terminology and analytic imprecision. The postulated drive for meaning derives from the Gestaltists, and Cantril (1941) made it a central explanation for how such social movements as Nazism arise in threatening, ambiguous situations. Clearly, meaning has instrumental value, for without it we are lost in "an unorganized chaotic universe." And meaning has reinforcing properties like the satisfaction of biological drives (Munsinger, 1964). This promising line of theorizing has not, however, been brought to bear on an analysis of the personal functions served by ethnic identity, functions that could perpetuate affective ethnicity even after the cultural and social supports for ethnicity have eroded. Yet the meaning of the self and of the social coordinates supplied by ethnicity appear crucial. Such personal meaning could be supplied by other, nonethnic collective identifications, but the near-universality of the ethnic phenomenon suggests that it is uniquely qualified to play this role.

The Ethnic Group Structure of Perceived Deprivation

The central importance of affective ethnicity leads to our second issue. A sense of ancestral roots, peoplehood, and common fate structures an ethnicity's perceptions of itself and of its group deprivations. A group's past triumphs and even more its defeats and humiliations shape its present views and select the relevant comparison groups upon which deprivation will be assessed. Consequently, the thesis advanced here is that *past analyses of relative deprivation have too often stressed individual comparisons and perceived deprivation at the expense of the societally and politically more crucial group comparisons and perceived deprivations.*

Relative deprivation has been utilized to explain both individual and societal phenomena ranging from stress symptoms and self-improvement to revolution. Two excellent reviews of relative deprivation by Crosby (1976) and R. M. Williams (1975b) demonstrate this sweeping range in the use of the concept across different subjects, situations, societies, and dependent variables. Yet this breadth of the concept has been achieved in part at the expense of a lack of consistency and depth in its use. Relative deprivation as an explanatory concept has often been invoked in *post hoc* fashion, its causal relationships left ambiguous, its measurement varied and questionable, and its application confused by the failure to specify precisely its operation at both the individual and social levels of analysis (Pettigrew, 1967). Nonetheless, relative deprivation ideas can be formalized and their predictions made testable (J. A. Davis, 1959). And careful empirical use of the ideas have repeatedly borne fruit (e.g., Spector, 1956; Vanneman and Pettigrew, 1972).

Basically, relative deprivation or gratification occurs when an individual or class of individuals feels deprived or gratified in comparison to relevant reference individuals and groups. Thus comparison with a nondeprived referent leads to high expectations that, if unfulfilled, lead in turn to severe feelings of deprivation and unfairness. Blau (1964) and Homans (1961) contributed the notion of *investment* to the formulation. If a reference individual or group is perceived as making a larger investment, then proportionately greater rewards to the referent are not likely to be seen as unfair. Perceived injustice occurs when the rewards to the referent are proportionately greater than its investment relative to you or your group. More recent statements of so-called "equity theory" advance a similar equation of investment to reward ratios (Walster, Berscheid, and Walster, 1973).

Runciman (1966:33–34) added a critical refinement. He distinguishes between *egoistic* and *fraternal* deprivation. Egoistic deprivation describes *individual* deprivation sensed through comparisons made between one's self and others within one's own ingroup. By contrast, fraternal deprivation describes *group* deprivation sensed through comparisons made between one's ingroup and other groups. Runciman found in England and Wales, as had been found earlier in France (Stern and Keller, 1953) and the United States (Hyman, 1942), that his survey respondents typically restrict their comparisons to friends and relatives within their own ethnicity and social class. Cross-group comparisons are minimal, and this limits the degree of fraternal deprivation. Yet Runciman maintains that it is perceived *group,* not individual, deprivation that is most conducive for the perception of injustice. And my research on white voters and black mayoralty candidates over the past decade bears out his contentions.

FRATERNAL DEPRIVATION AND RACIAL VOTING

Using survey techniques during mayoralty campaigns in Gary, Cleveland, Newark, and Los Angeles, we have found fraternal deprivation an important correlate of white opposition to serious black candidates (Vanneman and Pettigrew, 1972). Table 1 shows how we operationalized Runciman's two concepts. It is formed with two pieces of information: how respondents view their own economic gains over the past five years in relation to (1) their ingroup (whites) and (2) the relevant outgroup (blacks). Type A respondents are *doubly gratified,* for they feel they have been doing as well as or better than both their ingroup and outgroup. Type B, the *fraternally deprived,* believe that they have kept up with or surpassed the gains of their own group but that they have slipped behind those of the outgroup. Consequently, their deprivation is fraternal in that it is their group as a whole that is seen as losing ground in comparison with the outgroup. By contrast, the *egoistically deprived,* type C, consists of individuals who sense their gains to have been less than those of

T A B L E 1 .   Four Types of Relative Deprivation and Gratification

PERSONAL ECONOMIC GAINS COMPARED TO INGROUP (WHITES)	PERSONAL ECONOMIC GAINS COMPARED TO OUTGROUP (BLACKS)	
	Equal or *Greater than*	*Less than*
Equal or greater than	A. Doubly gratified	B. Fraternally deprived
Less than	C. Egoistically deprived	D. Doubly deprived

From Vanneman and Pettigrew, 1972.

T A B L E 2 . Racial Deprivation and the Reactions of Whites to
Black Mayoralty Candidates

REACTIONS TO BLACK CANDIDATES	RACIAL DEPRIVATION TYPE			
	A. Doubly Gratified %	B. Fraternally Deprived %	C. Egoistically Deprived %	D. Doubly Deprived %
Mayoralty voting				
For *Stokes* v. Perk, Cleveland 1969*	31	12	49	29
For *Bradley* v. Yorty, L.A. primary vote, 1969	26	17	34	30
Run-off preference, 1969	51	30	46	46
Run-off vote, 1969	35	21	52	42
For *Gibson* v. Addonizio, Newark, 1970	19	14	29	20
For *Hatcher* v. Williams, etc., Gary primary, 1971	17	7	30	15
Candidate image (% favorable)†				
Stokes, 1969	57	33	64	50
Bradley, 1969	65	44	71	49
Gibson, 1970	25	18	27	36
Hatcher, 1970	35	17	36	29

From Vanneman and Pettigrew, 1972.

*For Democrats only, since this was a partisan final election.

†The respondents were each presented a printed card with twelve adjectives from which three were chosen as the most descriptive of the black candidate. Half of the adjectives were favorable in tone (e.g., intelligent, honest) and half were unfavorable (e.g., out-for-himself, prejudiced). The favorable percentages provided here represent those whites who chose three favorable adjectives in the cases of Stokes and Gibson, and two or three favorable adjectives in the cases of Bradley and Hatcher.

their ingroup but at least equal to those of the outgroup. Finally, type D respondents are *doubly deprived,* for they feel they have lost economic ground to both their ingroup and outgroup. These individuals are typically older and often retired; their fixed incomes in a time of inflation have in fact been surpassed by younger groups generally.

The greatest reluctance to vote for Hatcher, Stokes, Gibson, and Bradley and the most negative images of these black politicians were consistently found among the fraternally deprived. Table 2 shows this phenomenon replicated in all of the four cities on both of the dependent variables. Note, too, that the egoistically deprived tend to be the *most favorable* to the black candidates. Controls for age, education, and other status variables do not substantially alter these results. A detailed item analysis reveals that the fraternally deprived score especially high on a factor of "competitive racism," comprised of statements that attacked poverty programs, welfare recipients, and "Negroes pushing themselves in where they are not wanted." The other, more common orthogonal factor of "contact racism" uncovered its highest scores among the doubly deprived respondents.

Fraternal racial deprivation provides a partial explanation for the widespread phenomenon in industrial countries that the lower middle class (the skilled, "affluent workers") of the majority group report the most hostile views of minority groups (Vanneman and Pettigrew, 1972; 466–69). Unlike the poorer workers below them, they have both the fraternal solidarity of achieving better than most white workers and the increased aspirations and hopes resulting from this success. But, unlike the truly affluent, they are not doing so well as to be free from the threat of unemployment and deprivation. This should reflect itself in a curvilinear relationship between our fraternal deprivation measure and socioeconomic status. In general, the results confirm this expectation. Only 12 percent of the white respondents who were not high school graduates and made less than $5,000 annually in the late 1960s felt fraternally deprived relative to blacks. But this percentage increases to a high of 26 percent among high school graduate whites making $7,500 to $10,000 anually and declines to 16 percent of college graduate whites making over $15,000 annually.

THE ETHNIC GROUP IMPLICATIONS OF RELATIVE DEPRIVATION

Structural change by definition involves changes in the positions of groups within society and not the movements of particular individuals within that structure. Obviously, then, attitudes about structural change would involve group-to-group, fraternal comparisons and not individual-to-group, egoistic comparisons. Yet this point has been ignored or obscured by most of the researchers who have sought to link relative deprivation to movements for and against social change. There has been, then, a consistent and erroneous individualistic bias throughout this research literature.

The most frequent definition of relative deprivation in these studies refers to the gap between individual aspirations and satisfactions (e.g., Gurr, 1969, 1970). But defined in this way, relative deprivation is cut adrift from its original reference group moorings. The hypothesized comparison is entirely within the individual: "How are the blacks doing relative to me?" instead of "How are the blacks doing relative to whites?"

The point is not that such individualistic comparisons are never relevant to social action. Rather, the problem with this past work is that it fails to distinguish between self-evaluations and structural evaluations and, thus, between the different comparisons that underlie these evaluations. The failure of individual whites to keep up with the perceived gains of blacks has important consequences for one's self and, perhaps, for how one interacts with blacks. But not until this deprivation is generalized to one's entire membership group are there implications for desired changes in the fundamental structure of society. Our research indicates that evaluations of structural changes in race relations are related to fraternal comparisons, while attitudes toward contact with blacks are more closely associated with individualistic cross-group comparisons.

Moreover, the success of predicting civil violence by those who employ egoistic definitions of relative deprivation does not disconfirm this reasoning. On closer examination, the operational definitions of relative deprivation in this research are typically structural, with their relationships to individuals only tenuously inferred. Consider Gurr's (1969, 1970) work. He accounts for about two-fifths of the variance of his combined measure of civil violence across 119 nations using twenty-nine predictor variables (Gurr, 1969:45). His direct measures of relative deprivation among these predictors include the proportion of the population excluded from valued positions and the increase in migrants to the cities. His indirect measures include such variables as school attendance and economic growth rates. But these variables measure neither relative deprivation nor any other individual-level phenomenon. Even if one were willing to join Gurr in making the enormous inferential leap between these gross aggregate indicators and the level of individual relative deprivation in a society, fraternal deprivation is indicated more than egoistic deprivation.

In understanding the role of ethnicity in perceived deprivation, a fraternal deprivation focus has two advantages. First, the weak link in reference group and relative deprivation ideas is the failure to explain adequately how the relevant comparisons are selected in the first place (Pettigrew, 1967). But this weakness holds with less force for fraternal deprivation. When groups are the referent, as opposed to individuals, the number of possibilities are sharply reduced. And reference groups tend to be reciprocally paired much in the manner of social roles: white–black; native–immigrant; blue-collar–white-collar. Even in polyethnic states, groups often form two political factions. Thus, in Kenya from 1960 to 1964, the many tribes formed into the Kenya African National Party and the Kenya African Democratic Union (Duran, 1974).

Consequently, once an individual has identified with his ingroup, the relevant group referent with which to compare the societal status of the ingroup is largely determined. This does not imply that an ethnicity's principal comparison groups do not change over time. Indeed, such shifts have major consequences for a society precisely because of the critical role played by fraternal deprivation. The civil rights movement in the United States, for example, helped to trigger shifts in group comparisons not just for blacks but ultimately for many other groups as well.

Second, fraternal deprivation presents a unique solution for the tension created between mobility aspirations and the Gemeinschaft bonds of the ingroup. As one rises in the social structure, there necessarily are created pressures for breaking old ingroup ties. This tension is implicit in Durkheim's distinction between organic and mechanical solidarity. DeVos, in Chapter 2 of this volume, provides telling examples of minority group members failing to achieve in order to avoid this conflict. But fraternal aspirations skirt the problem by opting for group, instead of individual, mobility. If structural change succeeds in raising the status of one's group, then one achieves a type of personal mobility while maintaining—indeed strengthening—ingroup bonds.

Fraternal aspirations and deprivations are, then, quite different from the more often studied egoistic aspirations and deprivations. And they often involve cohesive ethnic groups. Our discussion suggests the following hypothesis: *Fraternal aspirations and deprivation will be most prevalent in societies where rapid mobility is perceived and cohesive groups (often ethnic) exist. Put differently, fraternal deprivation is created when perceptions of rapid mobility raise aspirations while ingroup solidarity channels the aspirations into group terms.* This hypothesis is consistent with proposition 2 of Robin Williams' fascinating chapter in this volume. It is also consistent with the "interest group" analysis of ethnic groups in New York City advanced by Glazer and Moynihan (1970).

The operation of fraternal relative deprivation does not require accurate perceptions of comparative groups. Actually, these cross-group perceptions are often highly distorted, and it is to this issue we now turn.

Attributional Distortions and Ethnicity

Psychological social psychology is unusually prone to fads in theory and research. The present fad is attribution "theory"—how ordinary people ("naive psychologists") order their perceptual worlds by determining the causes and implications of their actions and the actions of others (Jones, 1976; Jones et al., 1971; H. H. Kelley, 1967, 1973; Ross, 1977). But this latest enthusiasm, unlike some past passions, strikes at such central issues that advances are likely to have far-reaching applications. We wish to advance one such application to ethnicity in order to suggest the possibilities.

Attributional theory and research have so far emphasized logical schemata of how causal attributions might be made by humans (H. H. Kelley, 1967, 1973), as well as the many types of illogical "distortions" that characterize human attributional processes. The dominant result of the work on distortions is what Ross (1977) calls the *fundamental attribution error*. This error consists of observers consistently underestimating the force of situational and societal pressures and overestimating the force of an actor's personal dispositions on his behavior. It occurs over a wide range of situations and has extensive social implications.

The fundamental attribution error can be easily demonstrated in the laboratory. One study (Jones and Harris, 1967) showed that listeners inferred a "correspondence" between communicators' private opinions and their anti-Castro remarks, even though the listeners were well aware that the remarks were made only to obey the explicit instructions of the experimenter. In another study (Ross, Amabile, and Steinmetz, 1977), subjects played a quiz game with the assigned roles of "questioner" and "contestant." Though the game allowed the "questioners" the enormous advantage of generating all of the questions from their own personal store of knowledge, later ratings of general knowledge were higher for the questioner. This dispositional attribution was made not only by the questioners and uninvolved observers but especially by the disadvantaged contestants themselves.

Note the three common elements of this fundamental error illustrated in these two experiments: (1) powerful situational forces (the experimenter's instructions and the quiz game's format) are minimized; (2) internal, dispositional characteristics of the salient person (the communicator and the questioner) are causally magnified; and (3) role requirements (of being an experimental subject or quiz contestant) are not fully adjusted for in the final attribution.

There are systematic exceptions to the phenomenon. Actors often attribute their own behavior to situational causes when there are salient extrinsic rewards (Lepper and Greene, 1975), few choices open, and few similarities with past behavior (Monson and Snyder, 1977). The typical attribution study maximizes these conditions likely to elicit situational attributions from actors about their behavior. But the "real world" is far more likely to elicit dispositional attributions, correctly or in error, from actors when they perform familiar acts in situations under their control.

There are other qualifications. Dispositional and situational causal attributions do not form a neat, single dimension; that is, a dispositional attribution is not necessarily the opposite of a situational attribution. Moreover, there appears to be a positivity bias, particularly for intimate others, such that you grant them the benefit of the doubt by attributing positive actions to dispositional causes and negative actions to situational causes (S. E. Taylor and Koivumaki, 1976).

THE ULTIMATE ATTRIBUTION ERROR

Granting members of another ethnic group the benefit of the doubt, however, may not be so common. Indeed, the hypothesis can be advanced that the fundamental attribution error will be stronger and the positivity bias weaker for across-ethnic perceptions. This *ultimate attribution error* is neatly illustrated by an experiment conducted by B. L. Duncan (1976). One hundred undergraduates were shown a videotape depicting one person (either white or black) ambiguously shoving another (either white or black). Duncan's white subjects tended to attribute the shove to personal, dispositional causes when the harm-doer was black, but to situational causes when the harm-doer was white. In addition, the shove was labeled as more violent when it had been administered by a black.[5] More formally, we propose that *across-group perceptions are more likely than within-group perceptions to include the following:*

1. *For acts perceived as antisocial or undesirable, behavior will be attributed to personal, dispositional causes. Often these internal causes will be seen as innate characteristics, and role requirements will be overlooked.* ("He shoved the white guy, because blacks are born violent like that.")
2. *For acts perceived as prosocial or desirable,[6] behavior will be attributed either: (a) to the situation—with role requirements receiving more attention* ("Under the circumstances, what could the cheap Scot do but pay the whole check?"); *or (b) to motivational, as opposed to innate, dispositional qualities* ("Jewish students make better grades, because they try so much harder."); *or (c) to the exceptional, even exaggerated, "special case" individual who is contrasted with her/his group*—what Allport (1954) called "fence-mending" ("She is certainly bright and hardworking—not at all like other Chicanos.").

In short, negative acts of the outgroup are more often seen as caused by the distinctive biological origins of the outgroup, while positive acts

---

[5]Three decades ago, Allport and Postman (1947) noted this violent stereotype in their study of rumor transmission. One of their pictures employed to initiate a rumor chain showed a white man holding a razor while arguing with a black man. In over half of the all-white experimental groups, the final report indicated that the black in the picture (instead of the white) held the razor. The black was sometimes described at the end of the rumor transmission as "brandishing it wildly" and "threatening" the white.

[6]This precondition bypasses the most primitive response: namely, denial of either the act or its prosocial character.

are more likely to be explained away either situationally, and motivationally, or exceptionally. These predictions connect with the two previous issues. *The more bounded the groups, the greater the ultimate attribution error is likely to be. Similarly, if racial, national, and socioeconomic differences overlap with the ethnic differences, then these systematic attributional tendencies will be proportionately greater.* Thus the sharpest empirical demonstrations to date of the ultimate attribution error have involved black–white relations in the United States (e.g., B. L. Duncan, 1976). Finally, *outgroups which as comparisons evoke strong feelings of fraternal deprivation would also be expected to evoke more sharply the ultimate attribution error.*

Full, direct tests of these predictions have not as yet been conducted. However, the B. L. Duncan (1976) study supports the first prediction concerning the perception of undesirable acts. Other laboratory studies support in part each of the three alternatives that comprise the second prediction concerning desirable acts. Thus two classic experiments by Thibaut and Riecken (1955) demonstrate the differential use of situational explanations for prosocial behavior as a function of social status. In two investigations conducted on different campuses, college sophomores and juniors were asked to make requests of two experimental confederates. One of these target persons was presented as of higher status (law student or new instructor) than the subject, the other as lower status (freshman) than the subject. Ultimately, the confederates complied with the requests for positive actions (loan a dictionary or donate blood to the Red Cross). Subjects were then asked to explain the compliance. As predicted, the lower-status confederate was more often perceived to be complying because of the subject's pressure, while the upper-status confederate's compliance was more often attributed dispositionally.

Prediction 2b concerning motivational, rather than innate, attributions for across-group positive behavior receives support from another recent racial study. Banks, McQuarter, and Pryor (1977) employed an attributional approach to achievement with black and white high school students. Forty white subjects evaluated identical performances of black and white targets in ability and effort terms. Consistent with 2b, the white students placed greater emphasis upon the role of effort in evaluating blacks than in evaluating whites. However, equal emphasis was given to the importance of ability for both races. Forty black students repeated the experiment, but did not reveal the effect. The experimenters explain the difference in results in terms of differential racial association. The community and school in which they worked had less than 10 percent black participation. Hence, the black subjects were more familiar with their white peers than the white subjects were with them; this differential familiarity could have caused the differential findings. If true, such an effect would support our speculation that convergent boundaries enhance the *ultimate attribution error*.

Both predictions 2a and 2b receive partial confirmation in a series of interesting investigations concerning the evaluation of female performance. On a male-oriented task, women are regarded by undergraduates as succeeding relative to men less because of ability than of luck—an external evaluation of desirable behavior (Deaux and Emswiller, 1974). And when men and women perform equally well in an emergency situation identified as masculine, women are more often viewed as trying harder—a motivational attribution (Taynor and Deaux, 1973). But complications are raised by the fact that both female and male undergraduates tend to make these attributions. The ultimate attribution error can occur for ingroup as well as outgroup perceptions when: (1) the behavior being evaluated arouses cognitively available group stereotypes held by both groups; and (2) the outgroup typically possesses more power, prestige, and status. The interesting difference between the results of these female studies and the Banks et al. (1977) failure to find the effect with desegregated black high school students may reflect the differential development of the black and feminist movements.

Prediction 2c, positing the exaggerated, special case means of interpreting prosocial acts of outgroup members, has not received a direct test. But incidental findings from research aimed at other issues have in part uncovered it. Consider the fascinating work underway on "solo status." Taylor and her associates (S. E. Taylor et al., 1976; S. E. Taylor, in press) have conducted experiments in which the perceptions of a solo black, man, or woman in groups of six are contrasted with perceptions of blacks, men, and women in racially or sexually balanced groups. They found that solos are viewed as more prominent, active, and influential than are the same individuals in balanced groups. The solos are more likely to be cast into special, frequently stereotyped roles. And, relevant to our predictions, the solos are more likely to be evaluated in an extreme manner, either positively or negatively. The researchers explain these effects in terms of greater attention being directed at the salient solo person, with the solo's behavior being disproportionately available to the perceiver for evaluation.

Taylor's laboratory findings are replicated in a field study by Kanter (1977) of solo women in the sales offices of a large industrial corporation. Kanter noted three perceptual phenomena associated with solo status: (1) visibility (solos received disproportionate attention); (2) assimilation (views of solos were melded into preexisting stereotypes); and (3) polarization (the exaggeration of sex differences with extreme evaluations). She also noted that solos are often cast in the role of spokespersons for their entire group. Though the Taylor and Kanter findings are not differentiated by whether positive or negative acts are being evaluated, they appear consistent with both predictions 1 and 2c.

While these studies supply largely indirect evidence for the hypothesized ultimate attribution error, they do provide clues for further specification. In judging desirable acts by outgroup members, under what conditions will each of the alternatives listed under prediction 2—situational, motivational, or exceptional explanations—be most likely to be utilized? The Thibaut and Riecken (1955) research suggests that *situational attributions are more likely to be evoked when there is an unequal power distribution between the two groups such that the outgroup can be perceived as having committed the positive act because of its weaker position.*

The Banks, McQuarter, and Pryor (1977) research suggests that *motivational attributions are more likely to be evoked when the evaluated behavior is regarded as internally determined.* And the Taylor (S. E. Taylor et al., 1976; S. E. Taylor, in press) and Kanter (1977) work suggests that *the exceptional explanation is more likely to be evoked when there is high visibility of the outgroup and/or there has been extended contact between the group perceiver and the outgroup person.* These specifications are obviously speculative and require refinement and testing.

What is there about social groups that would activate this systematic attribution error? The cognitive literature proposes a variety of interlocking processes that do not require motivational and affective involvement. First, the group's distinctiveness is critically important. The more two ethnic groups contrast with each other, the more distinctive, salient, and dissimilar they will appear to each other and the greater the likelihood for the ultimate attribution error to be evoked.

Salience and distinctiveness shape causal attributions. This can occur from prominent roles, as in the dispositional attributions made in evaluating the knowledge of the questioner in the quiz game study (Ross, Amabile, and Steinmetz, 1977). It has also been demonstrated with point-of view paradigms using videotape replays (Storms, 1973) or special seating arrangements (S. E. Taylor and Fisk, 1975). Visual field engulfment generally leads to dispositional attributions, and the distinctiveness of most outgroup members generally assures them such a position of prominence.

Extremity also plays a role, for extreme cases are more salient, distinctive, and available to memory. Rothbart and his colleagues (Rothbart et al., in press) have shown that the proportion of individuals in a group who are extreme either in terms of height or criminal acts is retrospectively overestimated. Furthermore, since we know our ingroup better than the outgroup, extreme instances observed among the outgroup are more likely to be accepted as representative. And much of our information about outgroups derives from the mass media, which disproportionately report extreme instances.

Degrees of familiarity and dissimilarity, critical elements in cross-ethnic perception, also relate to causal attribution. Banks' (Banks, McQuarter, and Pryor, 1977) subjects reported particular difficulty in "knowing and predicting the behavior" of target persons whom they were led to perceive as dissimilar to themselves. Nisbett et al. (1973) asked their college subjects to explain the reasons for their own and their best friend's choices of girl friends and academic majors. Dispositional attributions were approximately the same for self and best friend explanations, but more situational attributions were made for the self.

Finally, the positivity effect of dispositional attributions for desirable acts and situational attributions for undesirable ones was found by S. E. Taylor and Koivumaki (1976) to operate strongest for familiar persons (spouse and friends) and weakest for the less familiar (acquaintances and strangers). While similarity and familiarity do not operate in any simple, linear fashion, an obvious extension of these findings involves members of dissimilar and unfamiliar ethnic groups being perceived for negative acts in the least situational terms of all (prediction 1).

Familiarity and similarity also play a role in judging behavioral acts in a somewhat different way. Social psychologists have proposed, under such terms as "egocentric attribution" (Heider, 1958) and "false consensus" (L. D. Ross, 1977), that people tend to see their own responses as appropriate and common, and alternative acts as inappropriate, even deviant. This tendency leads to attributions of stable dispositions to explain behavior that is not similar to our own. Ross, Greene, and House (cited in L. D. Ross, 1977) have shown this "false consensus" phenomenon operating for a wide variety of characteristics, results that support prediction 1.

Taylor and Fiske (1977) have drawn together these diverse threads by focusing upon attention processes. Their convincing argument holds that:

1. Distinctive, extreme, and unfamiliar stimuli lead to these features being salient and attended to disproportionately.
2. "[W]hen the salient stimulus is a person, differential attention affects learning and recall; evaluations of prominence, leadership, and causality; attitudinal and behavioral consistency; affective judgments; perceived representativeness; and (possibly) ratings of the role of dispositional and situational stimuli as perceived causal factors for that person's behavior."
3. These effects are mediated by the fact "that information about salient stimuli is both more plentiful and more available. . . ."
4. Finally, "these processes may occur primarily in situations which are redundant, unsurprising, uninvolving, and unarousing."

In short, these salience and attention phenomena may well be largely a function of "automatic processing" as opposed to more intentional, conscious "controlled processing" (Schneider and Shiffrin, 1977; Shiffrin and Schneider, 1977). The broader cognitive phenomenon of stereotyping also appears to be largely a function of automatic processing, so we shall assess the significance of this new social cognition literature for a better grounded conceptualization of social stereotyping.

THE COGNITIVE BASIS OF ETHNIC STEREOTYPES

The concept of group stereotypes has been constrained by its uniform measurement in the traditional form of adjective checklists. However, recent investigators, utilizing new methods and theories, have questioned three basic tenets of traditional thinking about stereotypes. Are they developed to serve motivational needs, to rationalize prejudice and discrimination? Are stereotypes a product of a "faulty reasoning process"? And do they always reflect at least a "kernel-of-truth?" difference between the two groups involved (Brigham, 1971; D. L. Hamilton, 1976)? Current thinking answers each of these queries in the negative. Defining stereotyping broadly as "the attribution of general psychological characteristics to large human groups" (Tajfel, 1969:81–82), the process is thought to arise naturally from standard cognitive biases. Neither motivational force nor any special faulty reasoning process nor even a "kernel-of-truth" is necessary to trigger stereotyping (Banks, McQuarter, and Pryor, 1977; D. L. Hamilton, 1976; Rothbart et al., in press; Tajfel, 1969).

This argument can be organized around Tversky and Kahneman's (1974) three basic heuristic principles that human beings employ to reduce complex tasks to simpler cognitive dimensions. All three can lead to characteristic errors, and all three seem intimately interwoven with the stereotyping process. *Availability* occurs in situations when individuals estimate the frequency of a class or the probability of an event by the ease with which concrete instances can be recalled. Systematic biases result from the use of this heuristic when such factors as salience, recency, and faulty search strategies influence the retrievability of instances.

Representativeness involves the estimation of probabilities by the degree to which an object resembles a whole class or category. When object A resembles class B, it is thought to be representative of class B and hence likely to have originated from B. Systematic errors result from such widespread tendencies as being insensitive to the base-rate or probability of outcomes, to sample size, and to the reliability of the evidence, as well as misconceptions about chance and regression.

The third heuristic, *adjustment and anchoring,* refers to the modification of an initial anchor or starting point to make an estimation. Again, standard errors emerge. Different starting points lead to different estimates, since typically insufficient adjustments yield estimates biased toward the initial values. Similarly, there are systematic biases toward overestimating the probability of conjunctive events and underestimating disjunctive events.

Tversky and Kahneman (1974) show that these recurring judgmental errors, traceable to the three heuristics, are not motivationally created. Experienced researchers as well as laymen are prone to them "when they think intuitively." And automatic processing as well as informational overload (Rothbart et al., in press) enhance these biases.

Availability

Stereotypes are highly available images of social groups. Even the mere mention of group membership can trigger stereotypical attributions (Gurwitz and Dodge, 1977). We have noted how availability is enhanced by the solo role, with solo persons often being assigned stereotyped roles and viewed in stereotypical terms.

Distinctiveness, salience, and extremity all contribute to availability, and all three often underlie the development of stereotypes. Indeed, these stimulus characteristics can establish a negative stereotype even without the slightest "kernel-of-truth." D. L. Hamilton (1976; Hamilton and Gifford, 1976) has shown how this can occur through "illusory correlation." The cooccurrence of two distinctive, low-probability events can lead to a sharp overestimation of the frequency with which the two events occur together. Hamilton and Gifford (1976) paired thirty-nine descriptions of behavior with thirty-nine statements describing individuals of either group A or group B ("John, a member of group A, is rarely late to work.") Twelve of the behavior descriptions were negative, twenty-seven positive. One-third of the individuals were of group B, two-thirds of group A, and negative and positive behaviors were distributed equally between the two groups. But subjects still grossly overattributed the rarer, undesirable behaviors to the rarer, minority group B. The subjects also rated group A's members as less likely to possess undesirable traits and more likely to possess desirable traits. The distinctiveness of both group B members and negative acts made them both more available, and hence created an illusory correlation between them.[7]

---

[7]This finding could also reflect mere exposure or a generalized bias against groups in the minority, so Hamilton and Gifford (1976) also demonstrated the effect for a positive bias toward the smaller group B by making positive instances of behavior rare.

Representativeness

Outgroup members who appear to possess the accepted stereotypes are seen as particularly representative of the group. The informational value of nonoccurrences is typically overlooked (L. D. Ross, 1977). Consequently, the numerous instances of outgroup members who do not possess the stereotype tend to be less salient, and therefore less likely to be seen as "representative."

The availability and representativeness heuristics are often bound together, so that most of the salience and distinctiveness research we have reviewed speaks to both principles. Recall Kanter's (1977) observation that solo women were often asked to be spokespersons for all women. Moreover, individuals rely more heavily on the representativeness of the specific, concrete case than on abstract, base-rate data. This effect should be even more powerful in the "real world," for rarely are we privileged to know accurate base-rate data.

Biased operation of the representativeness heuristic is heightened in interethnic perception through differential association. We know our ingroup better and have more contact with its members. Thus extreme instances among the outgroup are more salient, more available to memory, retrospectively overestimated, and more likely to be utilized as representative (Rothbart et al., in press). Group members on the boundaries who have far more contact with the outgroup should, therefore, reveal some meaningful differences in their stereotype of the outgroup. One investigation that compared white stereotypes of blacks as a function of residential distance from Chicago's black areas did find systematic differences (Kramer, 1950, cited in Allport, 1954). These differences may well reflect at the cognitive level what we noted at the social level—intricate boundary equilibria (Barth, 1969) and an "institutionalized sustained ambivalence in intergroup relations" (Brewer and Campbell, 1976).

The results of Banks, McQuarter, and Pryor (1977) from an interracial high school provide further evidence for this possibility. Remember that only the white students, who comprised over 90 percent of the school, evinced the ultimate attribution error. The black students, who as a small minority had far more cross-racial contact, did not reveal the error. Similarly, Aboud and Taylor (1971) found that ethnic stereotypes were used less by their English and French Canadian subjects who had experienced the most interethnic contact. Presumably, such contact leads to a larger sampling of outgroup behaviors, which acts to counter stereotypes. Yet, as we learned from the East African research of Brewer and Campbell (1976), intergroup contact can have differential effects upon stereotypes. It depends on the conditions of the contact (Pettigrew, 1971), as well as the particular dimensions of stereotypes in question.

Adjustment and Anchoring

People know that not all Scots are thrifty. But such general stereotypes act as anchors, as initial starting points. And adjustments from these anchors are typically insufficient. It becomes difficult, then, to demonstrate the opposite of a stereotypical attribute; only a vivid, "exceptional" performance that contrasts with the stereotype can keep from being assimilated to the stereotypical anchor.[8]

This process probably affects negative stereotypes more than it does positive. Greater weight is given to negative than to positive characteristics in evaluations generally (Kanouse and Hanson, 1971). And if Parducci (1968) is correct in his contention that the most prevalent life outcomes are moderately favorable, then highly favorable outcomes are viewed as less extreme than highly unfavorable outcomes. This could help to explain the preponderance of extremely negative over extremely positive stereotypes. The negativity bias is also rooted in social structural factors that make undesirable outcomes more costly and more worthy of vigilance. Likewise, the disproportionate frequency of negative stereotypes can also be traced to intergroup conflict and the lessened level of trust across group boundaries.

The selection of particular stereotypes held about a social group also reflects the anchoring and adjustment process. Since "the greatest contrasts provide the strongest stimuli," D. T. Campbell (1967) predicts: "The greater the real differences between the groups on any particular custom, detail of physical appearance, or item of material culture, the more likely it is that that feature will appear in the stereotype imagery each group has of the other." Notice that Campbell does not deny the possibility that stereotypes can emerge without even a "kernel-of-truth," as experimentally shown by D. L. Hamilton (1976). But anchoring considerations make it doubtful that such a possibility will be likely in everyday life.

An Assessment of the "New Look" at Social Stereotypes

The general observation that stereotyping is grounded in normal, useful, even necessary cognitive processes is not new. Allport, in his classic volume *The Nature of Prejudice* (1954), made this point forcefully a generation ago. He emphasized that the fundamental process of categorization underlies stereotyping by accentuating differences between categories and minimizing them within categories.

[8]One laboratory study, utilizing 120 college women as subjects, found that prize-winning paintings were rated equally highly when ascribed to female and male painters. But paintings thought to be just contest entries were judged more highly when ascribed to men (Pheterson, Kiesler, and Goldberg, 1971).

What modern cognitive social psychologists have contributed is a significant extension of this insight. They have detailed an array of basic cognitive processes that often contribute to stereotyping, misattributions, and other biases in intergroup perception. And they have convincingly demonstrated that group stereotyping can occur from cognitive processes alone, apart from motivational and affective factors. In short, the "new look" has mapped out the essential cognitive structure that undergirds social stereotyping; it has demonstrated the depth of the stereotyping process in cognitive structure.

But no one level of analysis can do justice to the phenomenon. Stereotypes are patterned and shared, and this highlights their *social* significance. Analyses at levels other than cognition are required to complete the picture. Even at the individual level, to show that cognitive processes are sufficient in themselves to develop and trigger stereotyping is not to prove that it does in fact often happen in this manner beyond the confines of the laboratory. Once stereotyping involves real ethnic groups with long histories of interaction and conflict, instead of mythical groups A and B, motivational and affective influences become significantly involved.

At the interpersonal interaction level, stereotypes persist in part because role requirements are not fully adjusted for and role behavior is consequently attributed to dispositional characteristics (Jones and Harris, 1967; Ross, Amabile, and Steinmetz, 1977). Snyder and Swann (1978) show another reason why stereotypes are so tenacious. They find that a perceiver's actions based upon initially erroneous beliefs about a target individual shape the social interaction between them in ways that cause the target to confirm the perceiver's initial beliefs. But studies involving interpersonal interaction are rare, for cognitive social psychologists typically study their subjects under static conditions with minimal personal involvement (S. E. Taylor and Fiske, 1977).

At the societal level, little or no integration of this material has been made with the larger social processes of ethnic group interaction. We conclude that the process of stereotyping is now being well grounded in cognitive structure, but awaits similar progress in being grounded in social structure. Applications of the "new look" in the "real world" will gain power as attribution ideas are melded with what Stryker (1977:156) calls the "fundamental insight" of sociological social psychology: namely, "that social structure and social person mutually constrain one another. . . ."

A Final Word

There are a multitude of issues concerning ethnicity that require theoretical and research attention. This paper has explored only three of them from a social psychological perspective: boundaries, deprivations, and perceptions. Greater attention to group boundaries, affective ethnicity, fraternal relative deprivation, and interethnic misattributions, it has been argued, would further our understanding of this near-universal phenomenon. So would a range of perspectives, close coordination with work in related fields, and less ideological influence. The critical importance of ethnicity deserves no less.

4

Competing Models of Multiethnic and Multiracial Societies: An Appraisal of Possibilities

Robin M. Williams, Jr.

Terms of Discourse

THE FIRST PROPER ORDER of business in dealing with a large and complex topic is to decide what meaning we shall attach to the central terms of discourse: in this case, "ethnic" or "ethnicity," "models," "competing," and "societies."

First, let us look at a few examples of recent efforts to define or describe ethnicity and ethnic groupings.

A report on a conference concerning ethnicity organized by the Social Science Research Council notes:

> It was proposed that ethnicity (1) involves a past-oriented identification emphasizing origins; (2) includes some conception of cultural and social distinctiveness; and (3) relates to a component unit in a broader system of social relations (Bell, 1974:61).

But because this characterization does not allow us clearly to distinguish ethnic formations from units based on kinship, locality, religion, or social class, Bell observes, three other criteria may be involved:

> (4) ethnic groups are larger than kin or locality groups and transcend face-to-face interaction; (5) ethnic categories have different meanings both in different social settings and for different individuals; and (6) ethnic categories are *emblematic*, having names with meaning both for members and for analysts (Bell, 1974:61).

An ethnic group has been characterized by Yinger (1976:200) as

> a segment of a larger society whose members are thought, by themselves and/or others, to have a common origin and to share important segments of a common culture and who, in addition, participate in shared activities in which the common origin and culture are significant ingredients.

A closely related definition is:

> An ethnic group is defined here as a collectivity within a larger society having real or putative common ancestry, memories of a shared historical past, and a cultural focus on one or more symbolic elements defined as the epitome of their peoplehood (Schermerhorn, 1970:12).

LeVine and Campbell (1972) readily accept the terms "ingroup" and "outgroup," but treat the concept of ethnic group as problematic—variously referring to "segments," "groups," "ethnic communities," and "ethnic entities." The variations reflect skepticism about the definiteness, impermeability, and duration of ethnic boundaries. The authors choose the term "ethnic community" to designate "the ideal type of named, bounded, culture-sharing entity conventionally referred to as 'society' or 'a culture' (LeVine and Campbell, 1972:85).

Without unnecessarily multiplying examples, we can easily see that definitions of ethnicity and ethnic group (see Francis, 1976) are enumerative or range definitions: They list a range of characteristics, and the *degree* of the property of "being ethnic" varies roughly but directly with the number of characteristics present in a particular case. But the characteristics do not form a unidimensional scale; ethnicity not only varies from "very little" to "a great deal" but also varies "qualitatively," i.e., the various combinations of characteristics produce different *types* of ethnicity. For example, Yinger (1976) has proposed eight major types of ethnic identity; Schermerhorn shows four generic types of subordinate-superordinate ethnic relation (1970:82–84)—which are crosscut by eight cultural-historical types of contemporary society (1970:165–87).

With the recognition of types we already have moved close to the problems of model building. Thus three "models" of ethnic relations have been proposed on the dual basis of whether ethnic boundaries are fluid or rigid and whether interethnic relations are fluid or rigid (Despres, 1975). A broad contrast exists between societies in which the economic system is more nearly autonomous, or in which economic interest groupings strongly affect state actions. "Competitive" ethnic relations are most marked in the second case. The crucial difference among the "fluid competitive" societies (van den Berghe, 1967:9) is whether individuals or collectivities are the units. In a competitive system, emphasis upon ethnic membership quickly politicizes the process and puts a premium upon organization and collective action. Individualized competition in which there are many winners from subordinate ethnic categories minimizes ethnic solidarity. Another form of the same generalization is Parkin's hypothesis (1971:165): "Favorable chances for individual advancement tend always to undermine collectionist resentments over inequality."

We cannot here review the various meanings that accrue to the term "societies." For the present it will suffice to note that "state," "nation," and "society" are not synonymous, but that the modern period has been marked by the practical disappearance of stateless societies, by a vast growth in state activity all over the world, and by strong pressures to transform states into nations and nations into states. Self-sufficiency is no longer a decisive criterion of a society, but maintenance of distinctive boundaries remains crucial.

Divergent Models

We have been mandated by the title of this section to deal with "competing models" of multiethnic and multiracial societies.

By "models," I take it here, we mean conceptual constructions that in important ways are supposed selectively but validly to represent or depict the processes or structures of actual societies. Main types of societies can be defined by answers to questions such as the following:

1. Are ethnic or racial formations to be regarded as important or *constitutive* collectivities, or should they be seen as secondary or *derivative* phenomena?
2. Are nation-states (or "national societies") the essential units within which ethnic relationships occur and are determined?
3. Are racial and ethnic categories and collectivities long enduring?
4. Is it inevitable that multiethnic and multiracial societies will be, or tend to be, societies of dominance and subordination?
5. Is it the case that multiethnic and multiracial societies, as political entities, can only be held together by force?
6. Do multiethnic societies tend to have high levels of collective conflict?
7. Is cultural assimilation necessarily accompanied by structural/social assimilation?
8. Do high levels of either enforced segregation or voluntary social separatism inevitably develop as a feature of multiethnic or multiracial societies?

Evidently one could go at great length with additional questions about the possibly important aspects in which multiethnic societies can differ. We hope that the eight just listed are important enough to warrant close examination. They certainly are enough to generate more models than we would care to work with, i.e., even if the eight characteristics formed a Guttman scale, we would have nine models, and if the characteristics combine in all possible ways we would have 3,025 "models." In addition, we almost certainly will want to include two major preconditions or correlates that are empirically salient: (9) the number of socially recognized ethnic/racial groups within a defined "society"; and (10) the absolute and relative size of each.

Clearly some simplification would be welcome. How may it be achieved?

One of the great virtues of polemics is that they enormously simplify reality. Sociological controversies in the comparative study of ethnic relations often polarize around two sharply contrasting generalized images, or conceptual models of societies. One conception assumes that a society (or a set of subgroupings) is a stable set of relationships that tends, in the absence of interfering influences, to become self-regulating through exchange, socialization, persuasion, and consensus-based social control. The whole set of relationships is thought to become over time an integrated system, with many feedback sequences that reduce deviance and reinforce conformity to the constitutive norms of the total system. In this conceptual scheme, to the extent that collective conflict appears at all it is regarded as primarily a by-product of "strain" or of an inevitable residue of resistance to social control. In contrast, the opposing model assumes that societies and other collectivities are continually falling apart or breaking up—that, in the absence of interfering influence, social systems are highly entropic. Their "natural state" is either chaos or a precarious condition of continuous conflict. Opposition of interests, contradictions between beliefs, and incompatibilities among values—these are inevitable and universal characteristics. *All* social relationships tend toward instability. Conflict is normal, peace is an interlude between wars, consensus is rare and fleeting.

Analyses that begin with the assumption of tendencies toward reciprocally rewarding consensual relationships will be recurrently confronted with the anomalies of frequent and severe conflicts. Analyses that start with the model of opposition, conflict, and instability continually will be faced with the fact that much stability and peace actually can be found.

Rarely are we told why an exclusive choice has to be made between only two perspectives, each of which is highly unrealistic. Why must we be surprised when "naturally integrated" societies suddenly show massive conflicts or major disintegration? Why, on the other hand, should we have to regard it as remarkable when collectivities endure or integrated relationships develop and are maintained? An enormous accumulation of current, historical, and comparative data and analyses show that both models always apply in varying degrees and varying modes to all societies. Each of the opposing perspectives is simplistic. Generalized debate about their empirical accuracy is speculative and unproductive. An end to the reiteration of extreme claims is overdue. What is needed is a continuous effort to explain the varying mixes of conflict, accommodation, and cooperation in specified societal contexts (R. M. Williams, 1975b, 1972).

Several ground-clearing generalizations are suggested by this exercise in mechanical extremism.

First, ethnic collectivities and relationships rarely disappear through assimilation or convergence from multiethnic societies except over very long periods (Greeley, 1974).

Second, many careful reviews of historical experiences agree in showing that territorial partition of states does not succeed in abolishing ethnic minorities: "It is practically impossible to secure a territory of significant size which is ethnically homogeneous" (Hunt and Walker, 1974:440; see also 424–25). The implication is that multiethnic national societies will be the mode for the foreseeable future.

Third, ethnicity is only one among the many different social formations and the many different ideologies and symbols through which the assembling and mobilization of collective interests in political struggles may be carried out. Ethnicity may compete or converge or combine with class, region, nation, religion.

Fourth, it is impressive to see how regularly "models" are conceived as polar opposites and how regularly the opposites both turn out to be partly correct and partly wrong.

Fifth, the usefulness of a model can be assessed in two ways. The first is by examining its ability to represent accurately, i.e., to describe, a given state of affairs ("Yes, South Africa fits; no, Switzerland does not"). The second test resides in its capacity to predict, e.g., "This multiethnic society seems politically stable now, but it surely will disintegrate through ethnic oppositions and conflicts in the near future."

Illustrative Problems and Hypotheses

Let us briefly review a few examples of how several of the ten characteristics listed above have been used in efforts to describe and analyze concrete cases.

There is a great actual variation in the degree of continuity (persistence) of distinctive ethnic culture, ethnic self-identification, and ethnic social separation (enclosure). It is an empty exercise to argue the generalized question, is ethnicity highly persistent? The answer is, sometimes yes, sometimes no. On the other hand, an interesting, nonempty question is, under what conditions does ethnicity remain strong? Answers to the question have been classified by Yinger (1976) as structural, cultural, and characterological. The structural argument is that ethnic membership is retained when it is advantageous in struggles for prestige, power, authority, wealth, income. The cultural hypothesis treats ethnicity as deeply rooted in family, religious group, locality grouping—in both primordial sentiments and basic particularistic social ties. The characterological thesis is that (especially under conditions of rapid change, low consensus, and weak group memberships) individuals hang on to ethnicity as a source of identity and security (cf. Stein and Hill, 1973:82).

Both *size* and functional *connectedness* affect the strength of collective boundaries. To paraphrase what several investigators have noted, under otherwise comparable conditions: The larger the relative size of politically subordinate minority ethnic population, the greater the disparities between the majority and the minority in income and, usually, in occupational status (Blalock, 1956; Frisbie and Neidert, 1977; Glenn, 1964, 1966; R. H. Turner, 1951).

Representative of propositions about functional connectedness is the hypothesis that maximum likelihood of severe collective conflict occurs when two or more interdependent ethnic collectivities differ greatly in economic position and political power. The same generalization holds for ascriptive religious collectivities. Thus, although "wars of religion" have ceased in Western societies, communities of faith still represent strong loyalties and moral commitments. Hence religious allegiance easily can become a focus to express other conflicts—political, social, and economic (class)—as in the case of Protestants and Catholics in Ulster. Regional segregation and the cumulation of distinct economic and political differences congruent with the lines of religious differences encourage the expression of conflict through the social organization and symbolism of a religious "community."

If we want to predict for any society which social statuses, relationships, or collectivities will be the most important loci of opposition and conflict, it is reasonable to look first for social units that incorporate the most important interests. We then ask whether there are *accessible* and *interacting* units that represent *incompatible claims to or expressions of these interests*. As between any two social units, we will expect the extent of opposition to be the greater, the larger the number and the higher the ranking of the incompatibilities.

In these terms, a fully polarized society would be one in which all

individuals belonged to two mutually exclusive collectivities each claiming to control economic resources, coercive means, and social honor.
Thus the number of significantly different collectivities is a factor. The
greater the number of overlapping memberships of individuals in
statuses and collectivities each of which represents only a specialized and
narrow interest, the less the basis for massive cleavages. The expected
outcome is that of many small oppositions rather than polarized struggle. Two implications seem plausible (R. M. Williams, 1970:608, 609):

> *The larger the number of conflicts in any particular context, the less likely that any
> one will become all-inclusive with respect to persons, groups, energies, and re-
> sources.*

> *Conflicts between collectivities within a national society are least likely to develop
> or to become intense when the members of each potentially conflicting unit are
> subject to cross-pressures of interests and reference-groups with regard to the
> diverse issues.*

Plainly the same basic conditions of size and heterogeneity can lead to
diametrically opposed effects upon the likelihood of relatively uncontrolled conflicts. How is this possible? Obviously, only if there are important mediating variables that are not being taken into account. Here the
influence of interdependence is a central variable of this kind. If, and
only if, a division of labor increases rewarding interdependence will it
increase solidarity and reduce conflict. And these effects will be reduced,
or even reversed, if the specialized interests created by the division of
labor coincide, rather than cut across, the ethnic segments implicit in the
cultural heterogeneity. Another major mediating factor is social
separation—which includes both ecological separation (and segregation)
and separation in both formalized and informal association and groupings (Pettigrew, 1971).

This review thus suggests that maximum likelihood of relatively un-
limited conflicts will occur when there is a *large population* organized *into
a highly specialized division of labor* in which the main lines of *differentiated
and incompatible interests* coincide with *social segmentation* of *culturally distinct and divergent groupings*.

We noted above that LeVine and Campbell (1972:85) use the term
"ethnic community" to refer to "the ideal type of named, bounded,
cultural-sharing entity conventionally referred to as 'a society' or 'a culture.'" They then go on to point to five sets of observations that cast
doubt on the empirical definiteness of such ideal-type units: (1) territorial interpenetration; (2) continuous and gradual rather than sharp and
discontinuous variations in cultural characteristics; (3) disagreements,
among both "members" and "nonmembers" and groups; (4) frequent
interaction across ethnic boundaries; (5) shifts in lifestyles and self-
chosen changes in ethnic identities (LeVine and Campbell, 1972:85–99).

Further, the evidence is convincing that sharply bounded and enduring ethnic collectivities are not simply "primordial" but rather are heavily derivative from the exactions, pressures, inducements, and opportunities generated by complex state societies.

This generalized assertion can be specified in a variety of contexts. For instance, if a politically and economically dominant segment of a society segregates most members of a subordinate segment and keeps them in only a few conspicuous occupations, rigid stereotyping will be accentuated. Attitudes and behavior toward members of a distinctive ethnic category always will be strongly affected by the character of major occupations carried out and by the consequent relationships of trade and exchange, employer and employee, ruler and ruled, creditor and debtor, landlord and tenant, and so on. In general, the more diverse the occupations (and other major statuses) of the members, the less distinctive an ethnic grouping will be and the less will occupational stereotypes and evaluations be generalized as attributes of the ethnic category.

The more varied the social statuses and activities of members of an identifiable ethnic category, the less homogeneous and rigid will be the stereotypes imposed on it. Maximum inaccuracy of group stereotypes is to be expected when ethnic groupings are spatially segregated, rarely interact directly, interact exclusively in dominant-subordinate relationships, and impinge upon one another in only one status or a few statuses or other social contexts.

Not cultural similarity but complementarity of interests often is the crucial factor encouraging mutual accommodation between ethnic collectivities (Lockwood, 1975). Just as consensus has its limits as a basis for practical *modus vivendi*, so the market has limits as an integrative mechanism. Nevertheless, there is no doubt at all that rewarding economic interdependence is a silent factor of pervasive importance in muting and regulating competition and conflict (R. M. Williams, 1970:chap. 14).

A crucial mediating factor that helps to decide whether assimilative integration or cultural retention and separatist tendencies will prevail is the degree of social respect and honor accorded the "outsider" ethnics by the insider ethnics. Among major propositions developing this hypothesis is the following:

> Ethnic groupings that have retained distinctiveness, especially in language, in multiethnic states and that are treated as outsiders and inferior by the politically dominant grouping(s) will retain ethnic solidarity (Hechter, 1975; cf. C. H. Williams, 1976; Guindon, 1964; Le Magazine Maclean, 1963:23–26, 80–82).

So far we have treated the boundaries of the situations discussed as nonproblematic. But they are problematical (Barth, 1969). During the last two decades, the ideas of "center" (or "core") and "periphery" have proved useful in this connection by suggesting the possibility that ethnic minorities often will be peripheral, territorially or culturally, to dominant central groupings within nation-states.

These concepts further indicate that national societies must be seen as open subsystems of relationships among societies—affecting and affected by the "world-system" (Wallerstein, 1974), to the extent that they are connected with it. Indeed, it has become evident that nation-states are so far open systems that one cannot safely treat their internal ethnic relations in isolation from internation relationships and transactions. Glazer (1975b) proposes that ethnicity is becoming less and less coincident with the boundaries of nation-states at the same time that ethnicity often—although not always—shows itself to be a stronger focus than social class for terminal loyalties (Ragin, 1977). To the extent that these tendencies exist, an obvious implication is an intensification of subnational ethnic movements (cf. Pinkney, 1976), increased *inter*national influence on *intra*national ethnic relations, and increased influence of domestic ethnic relations upon international relations. Even in a period of extraordinary strength of the state as a worldwide institution, ethnicity seems heightened by the growth of supranational organizations and by international communication and economic organization, leading to the political mobilization of ethnic segments of state-societies (Enloe, 1973; cf. Esman, 1973).

The "larger society" or "broader system of social relations" within which ethnic groupings exist is today almost universally, first, the nation-state and, second, a set of relationships among nation-states. Ethnic categories and groupings extend across national boundaries; these groupings are used by nation-states in power struggles, and ethnic lines of communication across nations affect interethnic relations within nation-states (Bell and Freeman, 1974:12–13). Furthermore, new ethnic "peoples" often appear as public entities as a fairly direct result of political events—as in the recent instances of the Moldavians and the Macedonians (King, 1973). Finally, intranational ethnic relations are strongly shaped by massive events of conflict or cooperation between "parent" collectivities of ethnic groupings.

Examples of what Hunt and Walker (1974:429–30) call "classic cultural pluralism" include the Ottoman *millet* system, Swiss federalism, Soviet doctrines of central direction but cultural diversity, and Yugoslavia's decentralized regional system. Each of their four examples shows the severe strains of reconciling a centralized polity with "ethnic autonomy." And today new states attempting to govern multiethnic/multiracial societies almost always encounter serious problems of disunity and intergroup conflict (see, e.g., Enloe, 1973; Rabushka and Shepsle, 1972; Ryan, 1972).

It is no news to point out that the interests of various elites and would-be elites clearly are of great importance in determining whether or not a particular ethnic grouping will develop collective self-consciousness and capacity for collective action. For example, in case after case new nationalistic movements claiming to represent a distinctive ethnic identity have been stimulated and led primarily by urban classes, not by the rural people, and particularly by the aspiring intelligentsia—teachers, writers, professors, journalists, professionals (Hroch, 1968). With great regularity, resurgent or ethnogenic movements are begun and led by a subelite, usually urban and relatively well educated, whose members feel themselves deprived of political, economic, and cultural-prestige opportunities. Such elites "attempt to portray inequalities of social and political deprivation as community grievances rather than as individual or class-based inequalities" (C. H. Williams, 1976:19).

Ethnic Relations, Conflict, and Social Change in Multiethnic Societies

The specific character of intergroup relations is not constant across different societies or in the same society over historical time. The basic structures of well-described societies show enormous variations, although they also exhibit consistent types of social change over fairly long periods (Buck and Jacobson, 1968). And different types of conflict characterize both different historical periods and types of society (Paige, 1975; Tilly, Tilly, and Tilly, 1975; Jacobson, 1973; Gurr, 1970, 1972; Nesvold, 1969). For example, the so-called developing countries have had high frequencies of large-scale violent political conflict ("internal war"), whereas the industrialized countries have a high incidence of "turmoil" (protests, demonstrations, strikes, riots) but a low frequency of the more violent conflicts. The effects of political policies appear to differ systematically in the two groups of national societies.

Three of the more important structural changes that occur in the transformation from a traditional society to a modern nation are: (1) the differentiation of the political system from other societal subsystems and the establishment of authority over a territory; (2) the differentiation of the occupational structure from the kinship system; (3) the inclusion of the major subcollectivities into the political system. Each of these changes is likely to generate considerable conflict (Hobsbawn, 1965; Eidelberg,

1974), but the most important for present purposes are political differentiation and inclusion. Because of the uneven development of these processes, ethnic conflicts within developing countries may be more significant structurally than those experienced in the recent past in Western societies. Not only do the cleavages represent cumulative overlapping of group alignments, but the parties are open to few crosspressures and see their interests in communal rather than individualistic terms.

Ethnic distinctiveness is maximized by highly visible cultural differences, by territorial separation or residential segregation, by close association with certain occupations, by separate participation in community organizations (schools, churches, voluntary associations), by marked interethnic differences in wealth, income, power, and authority. The central facts, therefore, are *separateness* in social participation, *inequality*, and *cultural differences*. These components are mutually reinforcing. Indeed, long-continued inequality and separate community life always will produce cultural distinctiveness.

It is well known that language diversity is negatively correlated with "national development" as indicated by gross national product, industrialization, urbanization, literacy, communication, and consumption of energy. Longitudinal analyses, however, show that the correlations primarily reflect the fact that new nations tend to be "underdeveloped" and also linguistically diverse; if age of nation is controlled, there is little association between language diversity and development (Lieberson and Hansen, 1974).

In rural, isolated, and segmentary local systems, cultural distinctiveness can become stable and traditionalized. In urban situations of change and diversity, ethnic mobilization is more likely to occur. For example, in American cities widespread political participation is most frequently found in centers of economic and ethnic diversity rather than homogeneity (T. N. Clark, 1968). One reason for the association of diversity and participation is *subcollectivity mobilization:* When competition and rivalry exist among ethnic and economic-interest groupings, the effect is to accentuate intragroup cohesion and partisan political contests. Ethnic and class solidarity in turn enhance political mobilization (Gamson, 1968).

Thus collective conflict depends upon a complex set of interactions between "partisans" (claimants and protestors) and "authorities" (those who control resources and make collectively binding decisions). It follows that neither discontent alone, nor "social control" or "repression," can ever be sufficient to explain ethnic conflict (Hibbs, 1973). Evidently other, thus far unexamined, factors are crucial. To some of the others we now turn. They include relative deprivation, inequalities, external intervention, and variations in the organization of collectivities.

This is not the place for any extended discourse on the generic features of social change (cf. R. M. Williams, 1969). Only a few central issues need attention.

The origins of change in intergroup relations very frequently have nothing to do with intergroup relations. This is a shorthand way of saying that racial and ethnic relations often are primarily shaped by values and interests that are "nonethnic"—changes in technology (the cotton gin; mass production techniques), in economic opportunities, in feasibility of suburban living, in international politics, and so on indefinitely.

Within the narrower class represented by changes originating in the facts of intergroup relations themselves, a primary locus of change lies in those sociocultural conditions that produce organized reactions to collective *relative deprivation* (R. M. Williams, 1975b). In particular, organized efforts to change social allocations are favored when a large collectivity sees itself as arbitrarily blocked from achieving advantages enjoyed by other comparable collectivities. In this connection, "protoelites" who feel themselves excluded from power and influence are "crucial catalysts" in mass mobilization of ethnic groupings within multiethnic states (Fishman, 1972:15).

Open-class societies of increasing affluence tend to experience initially a weakening of segmentary social structures and of insulating barriers to emulation and invidious comparisons (Duesenberry, 1967; Eisenstadt, 1971:79).

PROPOSITION 1. *Responses of relative deprivation are minimized by: slow social change, low geographic mobility, low education, little exposure to mass media, sharp boundaries between strata and among ethnic groups and local communities, low rates of upward and downward social mobility, and primary importance of kinship as a basis of social organization. Individualized relative deprivation will be high under the opposite set of conditions.*

But discontent alone is not sufficient to produce collective action. Unorganized and dispersed masses of discontented people are not in a position to generate effective political pressure. Only through communication and the subsequent emergence of leadership, authority, and division of functions—i.e., organization—can discontent be mobilized and focused into collective dissent, protest, and structured opposition. Revolutions, for example, require not only increased expectations and widespread frustration or threat, but also that relative deprivation must be extended over a period long enough to activate organized protest, and must strongly affect all or most of the main social formations supporting the political regime (Brinton, 1965; Davies, 1962; Janowitz, 1970; R. M.

Williams, 1976). Furthermore, the main repressive forces of the regime (primarily the armed forces and the police) must not be overwhelmingly committed to quelling protest—otherwise one will have "abortive" rebellion that will be decisively crushed (Russell, 1974).

It follows from the preceding hypotheses that a particular constellation of conditions will maximize the likelihood of organized protest and pressure for change.

PROPOSITION 2. *Maximum incentives for collective action will exist under the following conditions: (a) there is widespread and severe relative deprivation, especially in (b) prestige or social respect and in political power, which (c) occurs suddenly and results in an increased absolute gap between deprived and advantaged collectivities, when (d) the deprived collectivity is large, commands substantial economic and political resources, has recently increased in relative power, is internally cohesive, and is linked together by rapid and extensive communication, and when (e) the established regime and other control elements of the society have given signals of weakness, indecision, disunity, or actual encouragement of militant dissent.*

Not all conflicts are based upon one collectivity's dissatisfaction with its position relative to another. Important as relative deprivation undoubtedly is, it is possible for intercollectivity conflict to arise simply because one party encroaches upon another. Conflict arises from efforts to attain goals or to realize values, efforts that happen to deprive or threaten another party. Thus an expanding group may continue to expand just because its past growth has been highly rewarding and its members anticipate future rewards. Then, in the "natural" course of using resources, claiming markets, spreading ideas, and so on, it usually will enter into confrontations with other collectivities—regardless of whether or not "position relative to another group" had been involved in its major incentives to assert itself.

Evidently an enormous part is played in intergroup relations by *power*—in allocating rewards and penalties, in establishing collectivity boundaries, in determining the outcome of conflicts, and in establishing and maintaining systems of authority. To account for the ubiquity of power and of conflict we do not need to postulate specific predispositional instincts of aggression or territorial imperatives. Our only biosocial assumption need be that individuals and collectivities tend to explore and use their environments. This tendency may be called "assertiveness."

Assertiveness is a directly observable characteristic of persons in society, just as scarcity represents a similarly inherent relationship to the environment of symbol-using humans who are able to aspire beyond their current condition. Given assertiveness and scarcity, it is reasonable to posit encroachment as a statistical tendency and to predict that processes of opposition always will appear in any relationships of interdependence.

The incidence and prevalence of oppositions accordingly are increased by social *inequalities*. Inequalities can even be generated by random processes operating in relation to any selective mechanism that makes attainment cumulative. For reasons that can be specified but must be passed over here, valued attainments in social life tend to create cumulative advantages. Further, the acquisition of power creates additional inequalities and tends to perpetuate and increase them (Meade, 1973).

We have said that both the size of a social aggregate and the degree of its organization, i.e., the extent to which it actually is a collectivity, are aspects of its potential power and bargaining power. The more that modern societies make available resources for rapid transportation and communication to all segments of the population, the more likely it is that political mobilization of discontented strata or collectivities will occur. The more that potential partisans are assembled in large clusterings (either residentially or in educational, military, or work organizations), the more likely it is that grievances will be shared, collective solidarity developed, concerted action attempted. To the extent that grievances involve claims against vested interests of other collectivities, the likelihood of collective conflict is increased (Gamson, 1975).

Most large-scale political societies are composed of thousands of collectivities, among which there are many divergent and mutually opposing interests and claims. Because of the great heterogeneity and the multiplicity of overlapping and crosscutting complementaries and oppositions, it seems at first difficult to conceive how bipolar conflict—a single basic cleavage—could develop. Yet we know that such polarization often occurs in rebellions, revolutions, and civil wars (as well as in class and ethnic political cleavages short of collective violence). It follows that there must be processes that combine mutually antagonistic elements in a common movement against a similarly unified adversary. How is this possible?

Either one of two main sets of conditions seems necessary. In the first, the incumbent authorities represent a single set of interests that are simultaneously blocking or depriving major interests of other politically mobilized segments of the society, e.g., an ineffective government that cannot defend the nation against foreign attacks even while it imposes ruinous taxation on all strata. In the second case, most of the subcollectivities are apathetic or otherwise preoccupied while two highly mobilized groupings fight one another. The first situation is likely to produce a genuine revolution; the second, a coup d'état, local rebellion, and the like.

Conclusion

To be a part of basic sociology, the analysis of intergroup relations must deal with enduring, not merely topical, social realities, i.e., with recurring processes and structures. It has to recognize that intergroup relations are *constrained*. They are rooted, on the one hand, in the constraints of human biological characteristics and of the biophysical environments within which concrete social groups either do or do not survive. On the other side, they are constrained by exigencies of necessary social interactions. Nominalistic and atomistic models that depict societies as indefinitely fluid, variable, and plastic are literally fantasies. Not every social arrangement that anyone can imagine or that someone may prefer is workable as a long-term basis for actual societies. In short, societies are structures, and all enduring social systems inevitably develop self-generated directions and limits.

In many multiethnic societies marked inequalities of income or wealth and of political power coincide with conspicuous cultural differences as well as with sharp discontinuities in communal social interaction (intermarriage, interdining, informal social interaction; common participation in religious and educational activities). These societies inevitably face difficult problems of political integration. The only solutions that thus far have proved to be compatible with a parliamentary democray have been either: (a) a high degree of assimilation; or (b) *political* pluralism and federalism (R. M. Williams, 1975a:146). If assimilation is not feasible, the various pluralistic arrangements seem to survive well under quite specific conditions, e.g., demographic stability, decentralized allocations of public goods (Switzerland), absence of provocative intervention from other nations. Given such benign conditions, it is possible for astute elites to recognize the perils of extreme claims and of drastic means of struggle. Recognizing the self-defeating results of intransigence, such authorities may strive intensively and persistently to find ways of accommodating the differences between their constituencies. Under these (rare) circumstances, *"overarching cooperation at the elite level can be a substitute for crosscutting affiliations at the mass level"* (Lijphart, 1975:200; italics in original).

There are important differences between the *cultural pluralism* of distinct ethnic groupings and the much more complex interethnic relations represented by *structural pluralism* (Gordon, 1964). In the latter case there is widespread acculturation to a common language and to the primary political and economic institutions. Realistic interdependence is great. There is also substantial "behavioral assimilation" to a central life style (clothing, dress, education, recreational patterns, and so on). At the same time, there can be considerable voluntary separation in residential areas, churches, voluntary associations, informal social relations, and marriage. The United States is a society of structural pluralism, not of rigid ethnic segments that severally have separate economic institutions and quasi-autonomous agencies of communication, education, welfare, and local governance. *To the extent that* flexible mediating structures can be maintained, even in the face of increasing efforts to accentuate politicized ethnicity, the most severe types of conflict can be minimized through mutual accommodation (R. M. Williams, 1977). Of course, the minimization of severe conflict is not always a desired goal in collective processes.

On Models of Multiethnic Societies: A Commentary

Roy S. Bryce-Laporte

THE TASK OF BEING A DISCUSSANT is generally not easy, but I find this particular assignment rather awesome, given the relatively open nature of the panel's task, and the length, complexity, and range of presentations. The expectations of being congenial, critical, and controversial are generally difficult to reconcile. They become even more so when the subject at hand involves intimate aspects of one's life, status, selfhood, and scholarship, as does the issue of ethnicity or race, and when the presenters are respected friends and formidable scholars, as is the case with this panel.

Turning to the papers, we find that they are all conceptually rich, insightful, and provocative. In certain ways they are both complementary and contradictory in relation to each other, since they represent different levels of analysis. I shall attempt to assess the merits and limits of each such level and to offer some of my own thoughts on the subject from the perspective of a black, minority, and third world sociologist.

□ Acknowledgment is due to Stephen Couch, Betty Dyson, Cheryl Gilkes, David Harris, Georgia Moen, and Mark Schneider, for their kind assistance in the preparation of this paper. However, the comments do not represent or reflect policies of the Smithsonian Institution, and the author holds himself solely responsible for any mistakes or shortcomings therein.

I

Early in his paper DeVos asks the question: How does the internal psychological structuring of an ethnic identity facilitate or impede change? DeVos seemingly believes that the ethnic experience in multiracial societies necessarily involves changes on the part of the ethnics themselves due to the expectations (demands) of the host society. These changes are expected on various levels and often require or include changes on the level of role, self, and internal perceptions of individuals. It is these latter aspects toward which DeVos directs his concern, and he opts to concentrate on conflict; specifically, role degradation versus self- or ethnic identity as a *negative* aspect of the ethnic experience. Thus he asks: "How and to what degree is a degraded role part of the self?"

In the process of developing an answer to the latter question, DeVos expresses disdain for purely political and economic analyses of status adjustments of ethnic groups. At best he views them as insufficient and goes on to prove this latter point rather well but not without showing the liabilities of an equally one-sided reductionism. Such structural analyses, he argues, tend to bypass very important issues regarding self-structure, mediating or socializing agents such as the family and peer groups, and their roles in the formation of self-concept, role adaptation, or adjustment techniques of individuals to the larger society.

In his own analyses he purposefully plays down the importance of social receptivity and corresponding structural changes that the society (or its dominant host groups) would have to undergo in order to meet even the more structural needs and demands of its ethnic minorities in order for the latter to enjoy widespread success. Rather he equates change with role accommodation or role conformity by the minorities, and is convinced that certain minorities are less than successful because they (must) reject such change, even discourage reception and assimilation against what he considers their best interests. Such resistance DeVos attributes to: (1) conflicts over roles and their evaluation stemming from differences in permeability among cultures; and (2) particular kinds of socialization for ethnic, self, and identity formation and role flexibility learned within families and peer groups.

DeVos himself finds the Japanese American and Jewish American families in the U.S. and higher classes of Japanese in Japan as the heroes in his schema. He sees them as successful in terms defined by their host societies, but then proceeds to view the steps they take in order to achieve such success as necessary and in their "best" self-interest. Additionally, he claims them to portray low rates of the "societal diseases" that he contends usually characterize such ethnic groups in the U.S. as the Native Americans, black Americans, Chicanos, Italian Americans, and Irish Americans, and the Koreans in Japan. DeVos seemingly attributes much of these so-called diseases—i.e., unemployment, delinquency, crime, alcoholism, and so on—not to the larger society or the differing stages of experience and formation among ethnic groups in the U.S., but rather to the culture of these groups (or certain strata within them). For him, the absence of conflicts, failures, and frustrations correlates with the propensity of a given ethnic or class culture to provide: (a) strong selves; (b) strong families; and (c) supportive peer groups. The maximum personification of DeVos' model is found in a culturally determined self that has a high propensity toward: (1) role detachment and analytical thinking; (2) continued sense of belonging and commitment; and (3) concentration on social role, while excluding what would be disruptive personal influence.

Obviously, this work has much to say on an important level of analysis that is not, unfortunately, usually pursued by most structurally bounded sociologists. There is much that it does not say, however, and much that it says that deserves to be challenged and criticized insofar as it obviously espouses a nonstructural, overly simplified, and by inference a static model of society. DeVos concentrates on lower-class and low-status ethnic minorities. It remains an item of conjecture what would have been his line of argument had DeVos chosen to probe more deeply into the middle classes or dominant host groups as the focus of his study. Already we see him treating them largely as models of success and ideal adjustment behavior. He hints at difficulties within these segments but does not elaborate. It would have been preferable for him to have reported as well on the social and psychological price of their success and to have analyzed the fuller nature of that success before inviting its exaltation as ideal or goal.

The publicized excursions into violent, counterculture political acts by disillusioned children of successful Jewish, WASP, and lately Japanese families should be seen alongside the critical and resistive behavior of peer groups in the other ethnic minorities. These latter also merit serious consideration within the concepts of: (1) counterculture and contracultural values by which Roszak and Yinger respectively acknowledge societal conflict; and, (2) "hidden injuries of class," which Sennett and Cobb consider as alienation of working, stable classes of white ethnic families of Boston. Increasingly, Japanese and other Asian American scholars have begun to feel the need to reanalyze and revitalize their acclaimed "success" in American society. Census data and new conceptual tools suggest that their "success" is exaggerated, situationally specific, and may have been costly and against their best interests as a middleman minority group relative to the major groups. Such revelations will likely bring into question the usual cultural deterministic explanations for Japanese American stability and success such as is being offered here by DeVos (see Hune, 1977).

DeVos stresses accommodation/adjustment on the part of the individual and conformity or adaptation on the part of mediating groups—on both scores toward "changes" that do not disturb the status quo of the overarching structural system. As a consequence he eschews questions on the properties and propensity of the society. His arguments provide no clues as to what changes will be required of society itself in order to accommodate extensive cases of instrumental role aggrandizement rather than degradation, reduce the price of success, or the incidence and cost of failures. Rather he overplays the potential of family strength, self-formation, and socialization as if they were root causes of high incidences of success or failure in a society in which they are all ultimately shaped by more powerful institutional forces. These latter forces determine the objective opportunity structures and the range and selection of roles (even though less so for particular persons or families). They also determine the spatial-temporal context in which minorities may play them, as well as the value such roles hold in the larger society.

DeVos also adds to the negative stereotyping of certain ethnic minorities by his failure to accommodate for variation, stage, and situation, and by a methodology that leans too heavily on anecdotes and examples to make broad generalizations. He thus anchors them to failures that, if so widespread, may well be failures of the larger society. He attributes to culture what in some cases are perspectives and practices that may be seen in particular sections of almost all ethnic groups—to be sure, with variation in frequency and distribution. For example, immigrant/migrant and other groups in crises or mobility generally may display such behavior largely because of: (1) temporality and purpose of their stay; (2) predispositions associated with motives and conditions even prior to actual arrival; (3) unawareness of social stigma or its importance due to socialization and marginality (see Bryce-Laporte, 1972, 1973; Bryce-Laporte and Mortimer, 1976). Other minority groups may pursue such a course because their references and their community structure have remained sufficiently intact and viable to withstand assaults from (or are sanctioned or reinforced by) the larger society. And yet others may be so atomized or devastated that they have no practical alternative or rivaling disposition. Additionally, DeVos overlooks the historical facts that most of the groups he compares with Japanese Americans are larger and older American groups whose socialization, reference, and measurement of self-worth are understandably more American than the Japanese. Numerically, though perhaps not proportionally, some of these groups do have more representation in the higher echelons of American society.

The dichotomy between American and Japanese cultures as the extension of self into role versus the separation of self from role, and the seeming superiority that DeVos assigns to the latter, seem overdramatized. In the first case, not only are there conventional images via folk and public media but a substantial scientific, historical, and literary tradition (involving rather important foreign observers as well) that views the American culture in just the opposite terms—"artificial," "mechanical," "inhuman," "calculating," "pecuniary," "insensitive," and "detached." Some prominent American sociologists have sought to analyze this quality of role playing/role taking that not only involves a distancing of role from self but the pursuit of sanctioned ends by spurious means.

DeVos also overlooks the character, pervasiveness, and persistence of the so-called "societal diseases," some of which are not simply ritualistic, rebellious, or pathologic behavior in themselves, but are more extreme uses of devious or "deviant" means for acquiring highly sanctioned ends (or symbols of such ends). He does not imply that the drive for mobility and sense of responsibility for effecting such mobility to the subsequent generation extends beyond Japanese and Jewish Americans to the other groups he mentioned. An investigation of these latter groups beyond motif of behavior and without blindness due to normative or personal evaluations (some of which I may even share with him) would show that some proportions of them share these ambitions of success for themselves and/or for their children. And necessarily they, and/or their spouses and children, have had to reconcile disparities involved in order to survive and later to become successful. Like the old robber-barons-turned-philanthropists, many ethnic Mafia gangsters and black numbers runners engage in calculated detachment of self from role. Some obtain sympathy or respect, even though at times in retrospect, from their progeny who become successful, respectable socialites. On the other side of the coin is the hardworking garbage collector or custodian who educates his children through college and whose spouse often beseeches their children to respect their father, despite his lowly work, for "he is a good, decent, hardworking man."

DeVos leaves us confused or uninformed as to his model of multiracial society. He criticizes cultural pluralism-as-is but provides no alternatives or correctives. Indeed, if the experiences of the Japanese and Jewish American middle-class minorities are as universally benign as he presents them, then it is as important to know about the compatibility and reinforcement they obtain from the larger society (including its culture and its attitudes toward other less successful minorities) as it is to learn of the appropriateness of the internal dynamics and sociocultural traditions of these two groups and their propensities for retaining such stability and success over time. Additionally, while it is not clear what DeVos conceives of as society per se, he treats culture as superorganic—not only as behavior but also the cause of behavior and the explanation of social fate. He leaves us with the strong impression that he shares (perhaps unconsciously) many of the underlying assumptions of the theorists of *cultural* deprivation, *culture* of poverty, and black family as a "tangle" of pathology, and of social pathology ("blame the victim" version). By so doing he undercuts the extremely important thrust of his paper as a call to macrosociologists, many of whom tend to overlook the importance of dynamics involving self-structure, primary groups, and other psychological and cultural matters in their analysis of the workings of complex, multiracial societies. Consequently, many public policies intended to have an impact on urban minorities have indeed failed because of the absence of an appreciation of how they are responded to on the lower levels, or because of the erroneous assumption of the monolithic or monocultural character of minority populations in the United States. Having suggested and demonstrated these intricacies without showing their connections to structure and the need for corresponding structural changes, DeVos leaves us with an esoterically rich but futile situation for certain minority groups-as-groups.

II

The discussion by Pettigrew represents an escalation of complexity and level of focus. Pettigrew's concerns are largely on the (small) group level, and he hastens not only to distinguish objective from subjective and group from individual attributes in the definition of ethnicity, but also to champion the predicting or explaining powers of the subjective group perspective. Pettigrew explores from a sociopsychological orientation three issues concerning ethnicity that he thinks merit sociological attention—boundaries, deprivation, and perceptions. Generally, ideal and simplified models of society are characterized by their claim of ethnic homogeneity and the convergence of boundaries. Pettigrew contends, however, that in modern reality such simplistic solidarities are likely nonexistent. For various reasons, modern societies tend to be heterogeneous in ethnic composition and culture.

Even in the United States ethnic groups range from disparate to crystallized formations. Blacks in the U.S., according to Pettigrew, are unique insofar as they suffer extremely narrow boundary convergence—a function of race. He believes that the combination of subjective identity, common experience of fate, and especially the degree of boundary convergence not only help to distinguish racial from ethnic phenomena, but to distinguish among the white ethnics along lines of historical periods of original entry of each group and the presumed correspondence in change and mobility experienced by each group. Sounding somewhat like DeVos, Pettigrew subscribes to the notion that the persistent case of ethnicity in the U.S. is affective in nature (i.e., shared identity or sentimentality). Despite high acculturation and growing social assimilation, there are suggestions of deep psychological needs by people of given ethnic groups to identify and share meanings that, when combined with their sense of common fate, overshadow other cultural and social factors used to indicate ethnic presence.

More important to us as sociologists is Pettigrew's discussion of the concept of relative deprivation. His thesis is that too much stress has been on individual rather than on group levels of perceived relative deprivation. He contends that it is *fraternal*, not egoistic, deprivation that results in movement for and against structural change, and it is also the former that provides greater predictive and explanatory powers.

By his own studies he ably demonstrates the advantages of looking at both levels of perceived deprivation. These studies suggest that it was the fraternally deprived groups that tended to display competitive racism most highly and were reluctant to support black political candidates. The egoistically deprived were most favorably disposed to support black candidates, and the doubly so deprived (also the older segments of his sample) demonstrated high incidence of contact racism. All of these presumably are reflective of *perceived* deprivation. Partially by inference, Pettigrew contends that perceived fraternal deprivation is the key factor operating in the hostile behavior of white ethnic workers toward blacks, and really represents a sense of competition and therefore of threat in their perception of assertiveness and advances on the part of blacks.

In an interesting display of the relative advantages of an approach that begins to address conflict in positive terms and takes account of the potential for collective movement over psychocultural entrapment, Pettigrew proposes a breakthrough in the Freudian-like dilemma constructed by DeVos. Rather than the individual route that involves the risk of alienation, whether one changes or does not change, the fraternal route avoids the dilemma by pursing change in status *as a group process* while retaining group support and reference for the individual members.

Pettigrew concludes this section of his paper with an interesting hypothesis: "Fraternal aspirations and deprivation will be most prevalent in societies where rapid mobility is perceived and cohesive groups (often ethnic) exist. . . . Fraternal deprivation is created when perceptions of rapid mobility raise aspirations while ingroup solidarity channels the aspirations into group terms." However, his application of the principle to Third World countries is simplistic, ahistorical, and thus distorted. Contrary to his observations, deprived groups and classes in many Third World societies demonstrate fraternal deprivation in the early stages of their countries' development. In fact, many such manifestations began to be evident in prenationalist periods, e.g., Haitian slave revolution, Rastafarians of Jamaica, untouchables of India. Many of the early manifestations of fraternal deprivation in these countries take political or racial, not ethnic, forms, for the confrontation usually is between Europeans and nonwhite natives. Variations take place where alien middlemen populations or tribal–ethnic contests are encouraged by the colonial regimen. The widespread expulsion of orientals and antiwhite assaults in settlement colonies in East and South Africa and the bitter civil or tribal wars in exploitation colonies of West and Central Africa, even though on one level drawing their leadership from competing elites, really express tensions between one ethnic group and another due to institutional inequality inherited from the colonial period; they represent feelings of fraternal deprivation or disdain among these competing groups.

Pettigrew's final section on stereotyping simply reinforces the fact that this phenomenon is still an important aspect of interethnic relations; that it involves specific cognitive processes; and by inference is of high importance even in the work of social scientists themselves. In acquainting us with the concept of fundamental attribution error—the overestimation of personal/dispositional factors, and underestimation of situational factors and inadequate adjustment—he hypothesizes that such error and its various combinations are likely to heighten in correlation with the nature of contrast between two interacting groups. Curiously enough and despite obvious admiration for DeVos' work, Pettigrew's treatment of the subject can be directed with devastating criticism to DeVos who, in my own opinion, one-sidedly emphasized motivational and dispositional attributes in his treatment of what he considered negative or counterproductive adjustment behavior by members of low-status/low-class ethnic groups.

From a more standard sociological viewpoint, I do have some curiosity and criticism to voice about Pettigrew's presentation as well. To begin, I would have liked to see a more comparative and close-up analysis of whites, especially the so-called WASPs, as an ethnic versus racial group. While Pettigrew characterized blacks as a race, since they experience high convergence of boundaries, he spent little time establishing: (1) that those boundaries and their convergences have largely been imposed by whites (or if by blacks themselves, then mostly in response to historically exclusive and exploitative actions against them by whites); and (2) that the more endogenously derived boundaries among blacks are generally vulnerable and unstable in the face of threat due to institutionalized and technological power differences between them and whites as groups. In fact, vis-à-vis blacks and some other visible minorities, whites as a group also represent a highly bounded entity, only more aggressively racist and more successfully defensive. Speaking in terms of both will and resource

differentials, the boundedness of blacks, though not without its internal
collective aspects of social identity, is largely, then, a matter of the power
of white racism rather than the characteristics of race per se (K. Clark,
1965).

I would have liked to see Pettigrew not stop his analysis on the study
of *perceived* relative deprivation, but investigate as well the *objective* conditions of deprivation both relative and absolute. As one with some training in interpretive sociology and symbolic interaction, I can appreciate
the importance of shared perception. Yet it is the objective situation in
the long run that composes the structural bases and contextual limitations of given social arrangements. To what extent did Pettigrew's sample represent the objective situation of blacks versus whites in terms of
mobility, income distribution, and the like? And to what extent do these
objective vis-à-vis subjective situations of his subjects really provide the
answers to the dynamics of black-white relations?

It is curious that the whites who perceived themselves as the doubly
deprived were older and retired, for in objective situations they occupy
perhaps one of the two points in the age spectrum (the other is at birth)
when there is the closest similarity in objective economic conditions between the races, in real and absolute terms. Also, at the older end of the
age spectrum, it is the last opportunity for economically moderate or
lower-income whites to avoid, by way of uncommitted income and
mobility, close interracial residential proximity, and the final likelihood
for moderate and middle-income blacks, due to accumulation of income
and stability, to share the same. Thus it represents a precarious point of
contact and, therefore, has heightened potentiality for contact racism.
Moreover, the phenomenon of the increasing objective relative deprivation between whites and blacks as groups, as well as within each group,
demands serious policy attention if: (1) the morale and equality of the
society is to be improved; and (2) the propensity for negative use of
fraternal aspirations by white ethnics and even collective competition
among nonwhite minorities are to be ended.

Such concerns immediately indicate the limitations of group-level
analysis, especially on the subjective level, for it is known that one of the
consequences of stereotyping is not merely stigmatization and self-
definition, but its tendency toward structural self-fulfillment on the
societal level, which in turn reinforces the former. Even though Pettigrew's concerns are more clearly social than cultural, like DeVos, he still
leaves us without an example of his model of multiracial societies in
objective terms, its impact on ethnic and race relations, and how these
correspond to the subjective concerns he has presented. I find it curious
that he did not proceed with his argument as to the applicability of his
notion of fraternal aspiration to concerns not only with retaining individual identity while carrying out change in the status of the group, but

also in the use of this group phenomenon for changing aspects in the nature of the society. Here our concern includes both macrosociological and international problems, such as: (1) the quest for crucial changes toward equality rather than simply adjustments and mobility within the existing system(s); (2) the location of major responsibility for such changes on the dominant segments, powerful institutions, and higher levels of interaction than one-to-one intergroup relations; (3) the escalation of fraternity to levels beyond race or ethnicity to include class, nations, and regions, which would then function to unify oppressed groups beyond sometimes deceiving and divisive racial/ethnic issues; and (4) the enhancing of mobilization on more universalistic and international levels to combat exploitation, oppresssion, and inequality.

III

The work of Robin M. Williams, Jr., clearly operates on the macrolevel and indeed raises questions of the structural order I am proposing. Unlike DeVos and to some extent even Pettigrew, who do not treat their material as resources for generating ethnic movements, Williams concludes that not individualized needs for psychological reassurance generated by anomie or alienation but "realistic" demands for economic security and for protection are the main sources of ethnic movements. Unlike Pettigrew, Williams appreciates the early emergence and expression of ethnic conflicts in developing countries, characterized by less overlapping and strong communal rather than individualistic needs, but he does agree with Pettigrew that collective or fraternal relative deprivation is highest under circumstances of rapid social changes, mobility, inequality, and so on.

Having discussed conditions most likely to create a sense of deprivation and need for change, Williams proceeds to discuss conditions that maximize the likelihood of parts of society organizing for change. It is not clear, however, what is the level of change that most highly preoccupies Williams, but here again we find that he is concerned with averting what he calls the most severe kinds of conflict. Either he is concerned with modes of rectifying the conditions or needs that in the first place would lead particular groups to seek drastic change and engage in severe conflict, or he is more satisfied to have presented not only the conditions for probable severe conflict but also the structural mode that would prevent that outburst. It seems safer to assume that his concerns are more the latter than the former. Williams ends with a more explicit model of society than his counterparts; he calls not for cultural but rather structural pluralism—not a society made up of subsocieties or smaller substates with replicas of separate but similar institutional systems, but one in which common language and primary political and economic institutions are shared, at the same time that social separation exists on levels of residence, informed networks, associations, and so on. Yet, Williams ends: "To the extent that flexible mediating structures can be maintained, even in the face of increasing efforts to accentuate politicized ethnicity, the most severe types of conflict can be minimized. . . ."

I must conclude that despite my greater comfort with the level of analysis of Williams, his conclusion is insufficient as an end or an explanation. What, after all, does "politicized ethnicity" mean? Why does he anticipate its persistence in ethnic struggle, especially after denouncing the primordial characterization subscribed to by DeVos and Pettigrew?

Williams, earlier, has recognized the issue at stake as economic, political, and technical inequality. This—not the absence, level, or type of pluralism—is the primary disruptive issue that in the final analysis characterizes many multiracial societies. As long as such institutional inequality in power, resources, prestige, and so on, continues to exist and is cherished as the property and interest of particular groups; as long as there is a high convergence of attributes within powerful and bounded economic/ethnic groups at the expense and denial of others, then no matter what kind of plural society may be proposed—cultural or structural—discrimination and discontent will persist. The challenge is then much more serious; it is neither sufficient to have the existence of many cultures, nor to have ethnics represented in various dominant institutions where structural inequality and a deceptive ideology of rationalization nevertheless prevail. Yet I submit this latter to be the prevailing pattern of racial affairs in the United States, and I daresay even in the ASA, today (see Committee on the Status of Racial and Ethnic Minorities in Sociology, 1977; Blackwell, 1974). Hence, while minorities cannot deny that they have gained representation, too often such representation is merely symbolic, token, visible but not viable; having moral influence at best but generally no power really to defend, negotiate, match, or impose will in the behalf of those communities or in the interest of the objectives they represent.

Institutionalized racial inequality persists today but its manifestations are less blatant and crude. Up through the recent past the inequality suffered by blacks was marked, among other things, by their obvious absence and restriction from participation because of the then highly convergent boundaries of white-dominated institutions and styles of life. At present, through struggle and also by way of concession, blacks and other low-status groups have gained minority representation in many formerly all-white organizations or communities. The practice of maintaining the minority representation indeed minor in number and power is often accompanied by formulas that put the representative of one specific ethnic or minority group against the others, or that collapse the responsibilities of a given ethnic or minority representative, thereby forcing him to defend interests of more than one competing minority constituency. These formulas have provided the white majority with a deceptive claim of compliance and goodwill. They also provide them with time to create new strategies of delay and dominance and to experiment with more subtle forms of exploitation and cooptation. Hence even when they may be useful as rallying points of pride and concerted actions by blacks or minorities themselves, on examination many of these newly sponsored symbols of ethnic presence in the United States—e.g., black capitalism, minority aesthetic and cultural goods, and ethnic programs—have been used also as devices of delusion, diffusion, and divisiveness by the dominant groups.

Speaking, similarly, not only from the cross-cultural and "plural" perspectives of the main panelists but also from the vantage point of the victimized minorities themselves, it would do Williams and our colleagues of the panel well to take heed of the persistent articulation of black spokesmen. There is a current West Indian Reggae song now played on American radio stations that goes, "Some people want peace but we want equal rights and justice" (Tosh, 1977). Similarly, the imagery posed by Martin Luther King of white and black youth holding hands was not simply a plea for racial peace and nonviolence in the abstract but a model of the depths of justice and equality that black people sought. These are both necessary if there is to be peace, that is, the effective and universal reduction of conflict, tension, and anxiety in the society/world.

Conclusion

The challenge, then, is clear: A model for multiethnic society must be a model for crucial societal and moral changes and a new society where equality and justice will be made to prevail. In terms of the concerns raised by the authors of the previous articles, it must be a society where: (1) success is neither defined nor structured to require the negative alienation of self (or identity) from role or behavior from values; (2) the obsession with exploitation, dominance, and ethnocentrism does not lead its members to be preoccupied with the creation of symbols and stereotypes to justify acts of injustice and inequality; and (3) a commitment on the societal level and consistency on the institutional and leadership levels will not simply be geared to resolve conflict but to maximize the experience of equality and justice for all (see Bryce-Laporte in Bryce-Laporte and Thomas, 1976:358–81; Kelman, 1977).

6

Comments on the Discussion of Roy S. Bryce-Laporte

George A. DeVos and Thomas Fraser Pettigrew

Comments of George A. DeVos

I FIND DR. BRYCE-LAPORTE'S comments somewhat unfortunate in their concentration on what was *not said* in the paper, rather than the simple points I chose to emphasize. He accuses me of falling into the opposite reductionism of those whom I find antagonistic to a psychocultural approach. Granted, I spent no time in my discussion reiterating the effects of political and economic forces on minority groups within a plural society. I assume that one is aware of these arguments without having to state their cogency. On the contrary, I was trying to supplement and point out the alternative considerations that help explain statistical differences in social indices. My approach is an interactional one; I am not a psychological determinist, but I certainly would not leave out motivational considerations in explaining social statistics.

Dr. Bryce-Laporte chides me for not considering the costs paid by middle-class oriented individuals within American society. This is a worthy topic, but was not the point at issue. I did not concern myself with the amount of psychoneurosis (harder to index by statistical means) or the personal costs in intimacy and personal satisfaction paid by the socially mobile individual. Indeed, I have discussed these issues elsewhere.

The point I was seeking to make was that one cannot neglect the cultural background of individuals, either statistically or individually, in ascertaining adaptation to American society. And I demonstrated that one aspect of family interaction, that is, the upholding of the authority of the father within the family, is adaptive to social and economic success within American culture. There are other problems and other issues that one could explore. Certainly in a few pages one can do little more than illustrate. I did not seek to examine in my paper how change comes about through the inclusion of ethnic minorities within a total society. This is a very real problem that demands considerable exploration, for indeed, as a group becomes accommodated, there is a total change in the society, depending upon the numbers and positions of influence assumed by any minority group. This is a legitimate study, to see how cultural positions are a source of further cohesion or disruption within a total society.

Unfortunately, the negative aspects of a culture are the ones that often receive greater attention. The social science literature does not concentrate on Italian contributions to food or music; instead, one is usually made aware of Sicilian contributions to organized crime in the United States. Ethnic Americans are sometimes justifiably incensed that social scientists pay heed to their negative traditions rather than the totality of their traditional culture. I, too, am guilty, in that my paper was a clinical examination of role degradation rather than a positive statement concerning the totality of impact of any particular ethnic group on American society. Since in the past few years I have been concerned with understanding delinquency and crime cross-culturally, I have perhaps given a one-sided impression of undue attention to social indices related to disorganization, rather than to the positive inputs related to cultural pluralism.

Dr. Bryce-Laporte accuses me of assuming "superiority" for the Japanese and Jews; in this respect I beg not to be accused of using judgmental terms in describing what I believe to be statistical indices of particular forms of behavior. I do agree, however, with Dr. Bryce-Laporte that it is incumbent upon social scientists to find ways of assessing the costs of social success as well as the manifestations of social failure. Social mobility as an ideal in American society places great frustration on its members, and is a source in itself of the concept of failure in American culture. I am sufficiently "Buddhist" in my thought to find it impossible for a society to adhere to a concept of success without creating an equal possibility for failure. To use a statistical analogy, one cannot have an upper part of a normal curve without having a counterpart for the lower 50 percent of a population on any measurement. The emphasis on mobility in American society is itself a source of concern with the potential failure and degradation of many of its members.

Finally, I did not attempt in my paper to offer any solutions; this was not my purpose. Before one can concern oneself with solutions one has to attain some objectivity about all determinants of human behavior, not only those one chooses as congenial to one's point of view or ideology.

Amelioration of society is ultimately best served by consideration of all factors, including psychological ones, rather than slighting some because they create discomfort and are not flattering to the individuals involved. As social scientists we must gain a degree of dispassionate analysis that separates advocacy from statements about the forces operative within a society, and within individuals who are members of society.

I do not think that amelioration is something to be easily obtained. However, this does not imply that one does not use all means possible. Let us not be too disappointed when change is not effected automatically by our goodwill.

Comments of Thomas Fraser Pettigrew

Roy Bryce-Laporte raises several interesting issues concerning my paper to which I would like to respond.

As the lone social psychologist on the panel, I stated at the onset that my contribution was confined to the subjective and social psychological levels of analysis. Though he notes this limitation, Bryce-Laporte launches a critique that is at once too broad and too narrow. On the one hand, he would have preferred an analysis that involved objective as well as subjective factors, structural as well as social psychological considerations. On the other hand, he would also have preferred an analysis that limited itself to black-white conflict rather than attempting the larger task assigned the panel of addressing ethnicity in its widest sense. Actually, I share Bryce-Laporte's biases for structural analyses aimed specifically at black-white issues; most of my past work as well as applications in this paper reveal these biases. They were not central, however, to the task at hand.

But there is a more fundamental theme that ties together most of Bryce-Laporte's varied criticisms: namely, the paper is too "white" in its orientation. Why were problems "couched as minority problems"? Why did it seek "to alleviate societal tension" or "to communicate esoterica among peers" instead of seeking "crucial change" and directing the responsibility for racism on whites? After all, he points out, the boundedness of black Americans is largely an imposed pattern.

Before responding in more generic terms, I wish to answer these serious charges specifically. In my view there is nothing about my treatments of ethnic boundaries, deprivations, or perceptions that is "couched" largely as minority problems, nor are these treatments necessarily aimed at alleviating societal tension. The paper views these problems as societal in scope and conflict as often beneficial. And (as Bryce-Laporte admits) the analyses of fraternal deprivation and stereotypical attributions can be applied easily to majority groups. Indeed, the one empirical demonstration of the paper deals with white Americans who are unwilling to vote for black mayoralty candidates. As for communicating "esoterica among peers," one can only say that one person's esoterica is another's practical and crucial conceptualization.

I agree with Bryce-Laporte that social scientists in this area have a duty to seek structural change and justice, a task that necessarily directs responsibility to groups in power. Virtually all of my work in race relations over the past generation has been so directed (e.g., Pettigrew, 1971, 1973, 1975). I further agree that the boundedness of black Americans is largely imposed; the paper makes that clear, supported by referring to a recently edited volume that provides a structural analysis of *Racial Discrimination in the United States* (Pettigrew, 1975). But these themes were not pursued here because we were asked to tackle the infinitely more difficult task of providing conceptualizations that might prove of value for *both* majority and minority groups across various types of interethnic societies.

Finally, there is an insider-outsider distinction being raised by Bryce-Laporte. One cannot improve on Merton's (1972) handling of this issue. But I think the distinction is not fully appropriate here. In the all-embracing realm of interethnic interaction, there are many "sides" but everyone is both "an insider" and "an outsider."

II

On the Effectiveness of Public Programs: Poverty and Civil Rights

7

Introduction

The Editors

THE FOUR CHAPTERS that follow are important both because they examine major issues confronted by almost every society in the world today and also because they ask whether these issues can be dealt with in an effective way by governmental action. Although the two topics under review here are studied separately, they are highly interdependent, and they are closely related to the topic of the first section. Multiethnic and multiracial societies find, almost without exception, that poverty hits some ethnic and racial groups more strongly than others. Civil rights movements have as one of their chief goals the elimination of the economic disadvantages faced by those groups.

Despite a widespread belief that democracies are inherently liberalizing (is it not natural for the majority to so govern that their lot is improved?), the evidence is decisive that efforts to reduce income inequality and the disadvantages faced by racial and ethnic minorities and by women face serious obstacles. The unintended effects of actions not designed to affect income distribution or civil rights often have proved to be more powerful than direct efforts to reduce poverty or discrimination. In his careful review of the evidence, Professor Wilensky finds that the structure of earnings is relatively impervious to direct attack. Tax policies and government expenditures are more effective in reducing income inequality. They also can run into serious obstacles, however. Professor Huber's comparative study of public assistance programs reveals how sensitive they are to political currents. During the last several years, both the United States and many of the countries of Western Europe have experienced a strong backlash against welfare programs designed to aid one-parent families and minority workers.

Professor Watts wonders, "Does anyone really want to reduce income inequality?", and notes that in the United States, at least, equality of opportunity has far more appeal than equality of result. The level of opportunity, he observes, is to an important degree the effect of current income, hence is not likely itself to be the cause of significant changes in the distribution of income.

As is true of many of the topics dealt with in his book, there are difficult problems of definition and measurement in studies of inequality. These are carefully reviewed in the chapters that follow, particularly by Professor Watts, in a way that can clarify our thinking about public policy and poverty programs.

Professor Skolnick focuses more directly on the legal process, particularly as it relates to efforts to reduce inequalities borne by members of racial and ethnic minorities. Critical to his discussion are two questions: What do the lawmakers define as civil rights? And do existing institutional arrangements make the exercise of those rights possible? As is the case with efforts to reduce income inequality, activities to increase civil rights involve not only political and legal processes, but the whole range of institutional structures and the basic values of a society.

These four papers contribute significantly to our understanding of the social programs designed to reduce the burdens of poverty and discrimination.

8

The Political Economy of Income Distribution: Issues in the Analysis of Government Approaches to the Reduction of Inequality[1]

Harold L. Wilensky

ECONOMIC INEQUALITY IS one of those problems in social science that inspires the unhappy combination of maximum passion and minimum systematic study. Drawing on the contributions of economists and sociologists, this paper attempts to set a context for the analysis of government approaches to inequality in the chapters that follow. It outlines some questions, distinctions, and propositions we must consider if we

[1]Throughout this paper the following definitions should be kept in mind: *Income:* the increase in command over goods and services received by a person or other social unit (e.g., a corporation) during a particular time period. This includes earnings from work, property income, and transfers in cash or kind. *Earnings or pay:* income derived from work. This includes overtime, incentive pay, and fringe benefits. *Wages or salaries:* the basic rate of pay received per unit of time—hour, week, month. *Property:* a system of rights and duties, socially recognized and sanctioned, of persons and other social units (e.g., a corporation, the state) with respect to valued objects (tangible like a house, or intangible like an idea). *Wealth:* a stock of natural resources and previously produced goods in existence at one moment, such as land, structures, machinery, consumer goods, and business inventories, as well as any financial claims of individuals such as cash, stocks, government or corporate bonds, and retirement claims. *Economic inequality* refers to all differentials in income, earnings or pay, wages or salaries, property or wealth. It should be distinguished from *poverty*, which refers only to limited economic resources in the hands of persons or other social units below some absolute or relative minimum.

□ This chapter is part of a forthcoming book on the politics of taxing and spending based on research made possible by the support of the National Science Foundation (Grant SOC77-13265), the Institute of International Studies, and the Institute of Industrial Relations of the University of California, Berkeley. I am grateful to Claire Vickery, Barbara L. Heyns, Philip S. Selznick, and Lloyd Ulman for critical readings and to Theodore M. Crone, Anne T. Lawrence, and Timothy L. McDaniel for research assistance.

want to understand the nature and sources of economic inequality in modern societies and thereby grasp the possibilities for its reduction.

I shall present four arguments. First, the theoretical and ideological disputes between economists and sociologists who deal with inequality have shown that economists are often weak on the analysis of the structure of opportunity as it is shaped by the power and status of groups, while sociologists are often oblivious to the workings of labor markets. Second, both sociologists and economists have arrived at several distinctions that are crucial for any progress in understanding economic inequality. These distinctions are obvious but they are often forgotten in general discussions of inequality: concentration of wealth vs. inequality of income distribution; trends in absolute levels of poverty vs. trends in relative poverty; primary income vs. post-tax, post-cash transfer income. There is also the nontrivial distinction between the distribution of cash and the distribution of services. These distinctions often lead us to opposite conclusions about the main drift in economic equality.

Third, in achieving equality, income maintenance programs are more effective than attempts to change the structure of earnings, which is one reason authors in this section of the book focus on taxes and public expenditures. My central theme is that pay structures—relative wages and salaries—are remarkably stable across time and place. Pay differentials do not yield readily to government or union action, whether through collective bargaining or legal enactment such as increased minimum wages or attempts to compress salaries (limit by law the salaries of the "fat cats" in administration, management, and the professions). To reduce income inequality or to overcome poverty we must instead look elsewhere—to tax structures and government expenditures. Finally, when we seek to understand how taxes and spending affect income distribution in cross-national perspective, we encounter formidable difficulties in concepts, measures, and data. Nevertheless, we can defend a few propositions about gross differences and similarities in the income distribution of rich countries and link these to policies.

Economists and Sociologists Approach Economic Inequality

As economists and sociologists eye each other across the barriers of specialization and ideology they often vulgarize one another's views. Yet in explaining variations in income, earnings, or rates of pay, the work of the two disciplines is largely complementary; they deal with different aspects of the same problem. Economists focus on: (1) the size and shape of the income distribution as determined by sources of income or by fiscal and monetary policy; and (2) the market determinants of the level and structure of wages and earnings, as well as impediments to the free workings of labor markets. Sociologists concentrate more on: (1) the determinants of which individuals, groups, and strata gain access to various positions in the stratification system, including occupations and related economic rewards; and (2) the social structures within which social mobility takes place.

Their stereotypes function to insulate each discipline from the most fruitful work going on in the other. If sociologists interested in economic equality read the relevant economics, they would find substantial evidence that within the market for adult workers the forces of supply and demand—expressed in competition for training and job opportunities—explain a large percentage of the variance in income and pay. They might also learn that their ideas of what economists do are a caricature of the actual work. Economists are said to make oversimplified assumptions regarding self-interest, rationality, and near-perfect knowledge. Worse, they are accused of ignoring government, bureaucrats, political parties, unions, the mass media, and, more generally, the power of elites or ruling classes, as well as the ignorance and drift of masses and elites alike.

In fact, most sophisticated economists coping with substantive problems have so modified their assumptions and theories that the parody is a poor guide to economic literature, especially research bearing on the issue of equality. Like sociologists, economists do not let the irrelevant or weakest parts of their theories stop good work and, of course, the best of them transcend their introductory texts.[2] Economists who work with free market models almost always modify their explanations of economic inequality by noting many forms of restriction of both the number of jobs and the number of entrants to the market. For instance, here is a typical list of "market imperfections" that keep the labor supply down, the price of labor up, and therefore, demand below the "equilibrium

---

[2]For an idea of what economists are doing see Walter Heller (1975). Not only is Heller able to show impressive diversity of traditional economic theory but he notes general consensus in economists' diagnosis and policy prescriptions. Although the consensus is obscured by media coverage of failures in short-run forecasting and of confrontations between monetarists (e.g., Friedman) and their enemies (e.g., Galbraith), it is nonetheless substantial. For instance, a vast majority of academic and government economists, Heller suggests, favor "tougher antitrust policy, freer trade, deregulation of transportation, pollution taxes in place of most prohibitions, and tax reform to remove tax shelters." They agree that "budget deficits need not spell inflation, nor national debt a burden on our grandchildren; that thriftiness can be a mixed virtue; that while exploding oil prices *in*flate costs, they *de*flate demand; that in an overheated economy, greater taxes can be the lesser evil; and so on" (p. 5). He tells us further that students of public finance have now "measured the growing burden of income, payroll, and consumption taxes on the lower income groups and developed techniques for removing them—most recently, in the context of the impact of inflation on the same groups" (p. 12)—no mean achievement, if one is interested in the reduction of inequality.

price": differential amenities of jobs; regional immobility (as in mining); lack of knowledge (poor information and disorientation); training costs; limits of personal qualities (physical, mental, temperamental) (Phelps-Brown, 1977:14–15).

Although when economists confront anomalous findings they sometimes seek refuge in the vague residual categories of "custom" and "convention," and although they often invoke market imperfections ritualistically without studying their effects, students of inequality typically abandon simple versions of the marginal productivity theory of earnings distribution and instead concentrate on the imperfections themselves. (Work of this sort includes Thurow, 1975, and Pen, 1971. For research on the economics of discrimination, see Marshall, 1974; Kahne, 1975; Masters, 1975.)

For their part, if economists took the trouble to read the relevant sociology, they would find a much richer picture of the "customs and conventions" and "market imperfections" they themselves have been forced to discuss. Students of social organization, social stratification, and economic life have developed a useful language for describing the social structures within which people act out their strivings. More precisely, sociologists have uncovered those patterns of preadult socialization in family, school, and community that shape occupational fate. They have studied the social groups that structure opportunity, channel information, and shape motivations and abilities, thereby allocating persons variously situated to jobs and occupations and associated income or to an economic position outside the labor force. They have also described norms of industrial justice, analyzing variations by group and society in popular consensus regarding the criteria by which rewards should be allocated. Without such data no explanation of economic inequality is complete.[3]

[3]On opportunity structures see Blau and Duncan (1967); Coleman (1966); Boudon (1973); Sewell and Hauser (1974). On the effect of family and schooling on later training and occupational fate see Hollingshead (1949); Cicourel and Kitsuse (1963); Jencks et al. (1972); Levine and Bane (1975). For the effect of schooling on knowledge see Hyman, Wright, and Reed (1975). On racial, ethnic, and religious variations in education and jobs see Warner and Srole (1945); Hutchinson (1956); Coleman (1966); Mosteller and Moynihan (1972); Glazer and Moynihan (1970); Light (1972); Beattie (1974); Rainwater (1966); Levitan, Johnston, and Taggart (1975). On variations in motivation by class and minority group see J. A. Davis (1964); Sewell and Hauser (1974); Strodbeck (1958:135–94); Liebow (1967); Howell (1973); Padfield and Williams (1973). Sociologists have given little attention to the diffusion of job information. For an exception see Sheppard and Belitsky (1966; cf. Wilensky, 1967). On abilities see Jencks et al. (1972); Eells, Davis, et al. (1951); Goslin (1963); O. D. Duncan, Featherman, and Duncan (1972:69–105); Halsey (1977). On the norms of industrial justice that help explain workplace pay differentials see Selznick (1969). Cf. Tannenbaum et al. (1974) for analysis of national variations in such norms. On popular consensus in the U.S. regarding income differentials see Rainwater (1974). For a general review of the interplay of opportunity, motivation, information, and abilities in the development of a modern labor force see Moore (1951); Wilensky and Lebeaux (1965:Introduction; pt. I; chap. 9); Inkeles and Smith (1974); Halsey, Floud, and Anderson (1961); cf. O. D. Duncan, Featherman, and Duncan (1972).

In sum, compared to sociologists, economists have presented a more coherent, more powerful analysis of the political and economic forces affecting the interplay of supply and demand as a source of inequalities in income and pay. Sociologists have doubtless presented a richer picture of the structural and cultural determinants of variations in the abilities, skills, motivations, orientations, and information of the workers who enter the economist's market. In other words, there is a standoff in theoretical emphasis, with the economist accenting market determinants of income and pay and the sociologist accenting the social determinants of status, the relation of status to income (using the idea of relative deprivation), and the cultural and political determinants of the definition of who is eligible to join which parts of the labor supply.[4]

Perhaps more important than these differences in perspective, which are complementary, is the failure of both sociologists and economists, especially in the U.S., to adopt a systematically comparative approach. We read, for instance, of the slowdown in the drift toward income equalization. After marked downward redistribution during the Depression of the 1930s and during World War II, "income distribution in the United States has remained virtually unchanged for one-quarter of a century" (Miller, 1975:40). Such findings are cited by Marxists as indicating "increasing inequality" rooted in the "dynamics of capitalism." None of these studies checks one country in which a cause is alleged to be linked to an effect against another country where the effect appears without the cause or the cause without the effect. We shall see that such propositions do not stand up to comparative tests.

Fortunately there is a new breed of social scientist emerging who can give a critical and yet sympathetic reading to research in adjacent disciplines. All are interdisciplinary, most are participating in the recent revival of political economy. And by their effort to understand their own countries or by their interest in more general theory, many of these scholars have been increasingly forced to attempt cross-national comparisons. From their work we can derive some important distinctions, a few propositions about economic inequality that are probably true, and also locate some unsettled questions.

Useful Distinctions, Propositions, and Open Questions

There are many ways of describing a country's income distribution. Much futile controversy arises when politically important assertions and counterassertions are made about "the" distribution of income when

[4]Sociologists and anthropologists have not entirely ignored market phenomena. See Blau (1964, 1968); Homans (1958); H. K. Schneider (1974).

differences in research procedures explain most of the differences in dispute. Studies use different recipient units, definitions and sources of income, periods over which income is accumulated, levels of aggregation, positions within the distribution to be compared, and dates chosen for comparison (Wilensky, 1975:87–89). Because Harold Watts in this volume discusses ways of conceiving and measuring income distribution, I can omit such crucial matters here.

Instead I shall sketch a few distinctions I find especially useful as guides through the thicket of income distribution theories and data, using a few illustrative propositions to indicate that these are distinctions that make a difference.

WEALTH OR PROPERTY vs INCOME OR PAY[5]

Many sociologists who are aware of long-term reductions in income inequality say "So what?" The main source of social, political, *and* economic inequality, they say, is the concentration of wealth and the accumulation of property in private hands. It is the hidden income from wealth, often excluded in studies of income distribution, and the power rooted in private property that count. This argument echoes the hopes of nineteenth-century socialists who thought that once the capitalists were removed through such measures as the nationalization of industry, remaining income and earnings differentials would take care of themselves.

The distinction between wealth and income is crucial. Income is a flow of goods and services produced or received during a particular time period; wealth is a stock of natural resources and previously produced goods in existence at one moment (Lampman, 1968:59). The two are obviously connected, but what evidence we have on the place of wealth and the effects of the public ownership of wealth casts doubt on the claim that wealth and private property should be our main focus of attention. It suggests that for students of economic inequality the strategy of analyzing income distribution is of central and even increasing importance. Several findings support this view.

With Economic Growth, Income from Property as a Share of National Income Falls Relative to the Share of Income from Work

In a study concentrating on Canada, France, Germany, Switzerland, and the U.S., Kuznets (1966:218) observes that, excluding the equity of individual entrepreneurs,

[5]Although the abstract definitions of property and wealth are distinct (rights and duties with respect to valued objects vs. the valued objects themselves), studies of their distribution use overlapping or even interchangeable measures.

the proportion of property income in national income . . . which ranged between 20 and 40 percent in the mid-19th century has, after a long period of stability or slight rise, declined—in some countries beginning with World War II—and is now at or below 20 percent. Even more clearly discernible is the decline in the share of income from capital, including that on equity of individual entrepreneurs, from almost a half to about 20 percent. . . .

(Cf. the similar conclusions of Lampman, 1968:62.) The reasons are not obvious. First, technological change, far from increasing the capital investment for a given output, may actually reduce it. Other things being equal, more technologically advanced processes absorb less capital (Temin, 1966). Many artisans, each working with his own equipment, can use more capital per unit of output than the more mechanized processes that displace them. Second, the labor force has been upgraded: Healthier, more educated, and better-trained workers and managers are more productive (Wilensky and Lebeaux, 1965:56–67, 90–100); there has therefore been some substitution of human capital for physical capital (cf. Schultz, 1961; Phelps-Brown, 1977:4ff).

Wherever We Have Evidence, Wealth Has Followed the Recent Trend of Family Income Toward Equalization (pp. 95 –96 below), Although it Remains Far More Concentrated Than Income

The ownership of property in the U.K. has diffused away from a narrow band of large landowners, industrialists, and financiers and toward far more numerous owners of houses, household equipment, cars, life insurance, savings accounts. (Royal Commission, 1975:97–109.) Against the possible objection that the U.K. is more egalitarian than other countries, we can cite the similar conclusions of the most careful historical study of wealth distribution in the U.S. (Soltow, 1975). Using Gini coefficients, the author observes that "perhaps wealth in 1963 was 5 percent less concentrated than in 1870" (p. 115). The shift is recent. "The inequality of wealth remained the same from 1800 to 1940 and then decreased a little, particularly among middle wealth groups" (p. 123). Using a measure of an absolute poverty level which is based on wealth and standardizing for the age distribution of the population, Soltow also calculates that the percentage of the U.S. population in "poverty of wealth" has decreased over this entire period by approximately one-third (p. 53). At the other end of the scale, the top 1 percent of the population held about 29 percent of the total wealth in 1860, 32 percent in 1922, and 25 percent in 1953 (p. 123). Even if the change is hardly dramatic, inequality of wealth in the United States has decreased.

This is not to deny that wealth differentials are much more skewed than the distribution of earnings or that large fortunes, while they are made almost overnight, are passed on through the generations (about half of the great American fortunes are inherited fortunes). Wealth yields power—one reason that wealth concentration is far greater than income concentration. Nor am I arguing that the mechanisms that produce great wealth are the same as those that produce large incomes (Thurow, 1975:xi–xii, 14–15, 129–54). What meager data we have merely suggest that in rich countries in the past fifty to one hundred years, if the distribution of property and physical wealth has changed at all, it has drifted toward equalization. And whatever the trend, inequalities of earnings have become dominant in the picture of economic inequality.[6]

There Is No Evidence That Collective Ownership of the Means of Production Reduces Inequalities in the Distribution of Income or Pay

Comparisons of earnings spreads in the "socialist" countries (USSR and Eastern Europe) show them to be similar to those in the Western democracies (Phelps-Brown, 1977:38ff., 285ff.; cf. Lane, 1976:177–211; Wiles, 1974). True, the relative position of particular occupations varies across nations (the relative pay of civil servants is high in France, the U.K., and India; doctors make out very well in the U.S., and badly in the USSR and the U.K.; the relative pay of managers in France is higher than that of managers in Germany; managers in Yugoslavia have the edge over managers in the USSR). But these are minor variations on the main theme. The most wide-ranging, thorough study of pay differentials concludes:

> With the partial exception of the lower white-collar occupations, and the notable exception of the Kibbutzim, in every society and period we have surveyed we have found that the grades of work requiring more education, experience, and skill, and carrying more responsibility, have been the more highly paid. This has been found to be so even in Mao's China and Castro's Cuba. It shows that the inequality of pay arises from factors common to societies of very various economic, political, and social complexions (Phelps-Brown, 1977:65).

Thus sociologists who have discovered one of the great structural uniformities of modern and modernizing societies—the rank order of prestige of occupations across decades and nations (Hodge, Siegel, and Rossi, 1966; Hodge, Treiman, and Rossi, 1966)—can now look at the economists' evidence for a parallel uniformity in the structure of pay. Many questions remain for further research. What is the precise relationship between the occupational rank order of pay and that of status,

---

[6]This is illustrated by the case of Holland, where we find an estimate that in the 1950s one-quarter of the variance in incomes was attributable to inequalities of property holding, and three-quarters to inequalities of earnings (Pen, 1971:65).

and why? How can we explain national differences in the spread of base wage rates or earnings by nation (why, for instance, was Mao's China less egalitarian than Castro's Cuba)? How can we explain deviations from the general pattern mentioned above?

As for collective ownership and income distribution, the most recent and most wide-ranging study of post-tax household income shares based on standardized household size, covering ten rich non-Communist countries, shows that the most inegalitarian by any measure is France (OECD, 1976). It happens to be the Western country with the largest fraction of its commerce and industry nationalized (Pryor, 1973:14–15). Conversely, Holland and Norway rank high in egalitarianism but low in nationalization (31 percent). What about East-West comparisons? If we measure inequality by the ratio of the average per capita income after taxes of the top 5 percent of income recipients to the average of the bottom 5 percent, we find more cross-national variation in income spreads in the West (from egalitarian Sweden to less egalitarian U.S.) than in the Soviet bloc (from egalitarian Bulgaria to less egalitarian USSR). Nevertheless, Sweden, with low nationalization, is the world-beater in economic equality, while the U.K. edges out the USSR (Wiles, 1974:xiv, 48).[7] Without countervailing evidence, no one can assert that public ownership reduces income inequality.

European socialists have not been oblivious to these facts, and in democratic countries without a strong Communist party social democrats long ago shifted their attention away from nationalization of industry toward measures to reduce income inequality. Recent conflicts between "Eurocommunists" and "socialists" in France over nationalization and related issues indicate the same shift even where socialists must compete with Communist party ideologues. Socialists are saying, "egalitarianism, yes; socialism, no."

TRENDS IN ABSOLUTE LEVELS OF POVERTY vs. TRENDS IN RELATIVE LEVELS OF POVERTY

How can we assess the idea that inequalities of income since World War II are rooted in the "crisis of capitalism" and are getting worse (Weisskopf, 1972; Ackerman et al., 1972)? Only by cross-national comparison of diverse measures of income distribution. As we shall see, the

---

[7]Wiles (1974) notes in passing that these difficult comparisons do not take account of fringe benefits and unofficial income. These "extras" may be correlated with occupational status and authority in *both* East and West. But it is likely that many more well-placed Soviet citizens have much greater opportunity for corruption (bribes and favors in housing, education, medical care, etc.) than their Western counterparts. Thus, the income spreads in the Soviet bloc are probably wider than Wiles estimates.

statement, generally based on American data, is quite dubious. But suppose it were true of the U.S.? Is it a capitalist phenomenon, a product of American exceptionalism, or what?

If we concentrate on an absolute level of minimum needs, below which people are seen as poor for purposes of government attention and which does not change over time, then the trend is clear. Since World War II absolute poverty has declined fairly rapidly in all rich countries for which data are available, mainly because of economic growth.

If we are concerned about the misery of people with low incomes, absolute poverty is the appropriate concept, and the results give grounds for optimism (cf. Schiller, 1973). If we are concerned not about misery but about the unequal distribution of income, then relative poverty is the appropriate concept; the results vary by country and are mixed. The best study of recent trends drew the poverty line at 40 percent of median family income and assumed that family size and composition of the population did not change much between the early 1960s and early 1970s. The study shows that relative poverty declined in France, Germany, and the United States, but rose in Canada and possibly in Britain (cf. Wiles, 1974:47).[8] We cannot say anything with much certainty about longer-run trends in relative poverty (OECD, 1976:68; see also Gillespie, 1976). The major work on trends over several decades (covering various segments of the period from the late nineteenth century to the 1950s), however, suggests a long-run leveling tendency: For seven countries the rise in the before-tax share of lower brackets was less conspicuous than the decline in the shares of upper brackets; for three countries for which after-tax income could be compared, the rise in the relative income of the poor was more marked (Kuznets, 1966:206-7).[9]

In any case, this cross-national exercise forces us to look beyond "capitalism" as the driving force behind poverty, whether we define it as absolute or relative poverty.

Occupational Differentials in Pay Have Declined but the Trend in Educational Differentials Is Uncertain

An important aspect of relative income distribution is the relative pay of various occupational groups and strata. Is the skilled upper crust of

---

[8]Forty percent of the median is somewhat below the threshold of relative deprivation found in Gallup polls for the U.S. since World War II. On seventeen different occasions Americans were asked, "What is the smallest amount of money a family of four needs to get along in this community?" Their answers indicate a fairly consistent fraction of the average income of the year in which the question was asked—a little over half (Rainwater, 1974:52-58; cf. Runciman, 1966).

[9]The seven countries are the U.K., Germany, Sweden, U.S., Holland, Denmark, Norway. The three countries are the U.K., Sweden, U.S. The income-equalization argument of Kuznets is strengthened if we consider changes in purchasing habits or "budget struc-

the working class sinking into the unskilled class, or is it becoming bourgeois, merging with the lower middle class? Are lower white-collar workers sinking into the proletariat because the income and educational basis for their status is eroding (Mills, 1951)? Comparisons across time and place permit no firm answer to these questions.

A hint of the difficulties can be seen in both cross-sectional and trend studies of the relative economic position of occupational strata and groups and of educational strata, controlling for various background characteristics. Students of the effects of education and occupation on rates of pay, earnings, and income have often been surprised at the weak relationships they have found. When Jencks et al. (1972) found that only 22 percent of the variance in white nonfarm workers' annual incomes could be explained by family background, educational attainment, intelligence test scores, and occupational status (p. 245), they fell back on the importance of luck plus specific skills and personality attributes not captured in their analysis of determinants of personal income (pp. 8–9, 131, 226–78). Economist Thurow (1975:75) introduces a more sociological explanation—which he calls a "job competition model"—as a supplement to the old "wage competition" versions of marginal productivity: "Instead of competing against one another based on the wages they are willing to accept, individuals compete against one another for job opportunities based on their relative costs of being trained to fill whatever job is being considered." In fact, too much wage competition would undermine not only the wage standards that excite unions but also economic efficiency. The reason is that most learning occurs on the job or in work-related contexts and depends on the collaboration of job incumbents. Direct wage competition—or any clear job threat—gives oldtimers an incentive to restrict the flow of information and knowledge to job applicants and newcomers (pp. 81–84). In this view the main function of the labor market is "to allocate individuals to on-the-job training ladders." The "background characteristics" invoked by sociologists or psychologists are here seen as clues to variations in training costs and hence job opportunities. Nevertheless, when he observes that education is a limited cue to training costs, Thurow, like Jencks et al., falls back on a grab bag residual explanation: "Physical dexterity, personality, or a host of other characteristics," he says, "may eventually prove to be more important personal background variables than those we typically consider" (p. 128).

A brief look at the categories of occupation and education typically used may help explain these results.

---

ture"; middle and upper-middle incomes now go more to services, which in the last one hundred years or so have not benefited much from technological change (Fourastié, 1960:30, 52ff., 88ff.).

Occupation and Relative Income or Earnings.   Broad occupational strata
explain only a small percentage of variance in income or earnings,
whether the strata are defined in Marxian terms (common structural
positions within the social organization of production) or status terms
(people sharing a common position within a status hierarchy).

For instance, if we substitute such categories as "employers, managers, workers, and petty bourgeoisie" for a standard occupational status
index (continuously graded scores of the prestige of job titles), we find
that either "class" or "status" explains about 14 percent of the variance in
income. A multiple regression analysis of sources of total annual personal income before taxes among white, male, nonfarm, full-time workers in the U.S., 1973, shows that education, age, decile occupational
status, and "employer class" and "worker class" (dummy variables for
two of the four class categories) together explain about 27 percent of the
variance in income. Status (net of education and age) yields a .041 increment in R^2; the two "class" variables together (net of education and
age) yield an increment of .094 (Wright and Perrone, 1977:44, 50).

There are two main reasons that broad occupational strata explain so
little of the variance in income, one obvious, the other less obvious.
First, income includes a component of money not derived from earnings
at work, so we cannot expect a tight link between income and occupation.
Second, and more important, there is a vast heterogeneity within each
stratum in entry requirements, authority, responsibility, and status (often
labeled "skill"), in freedom (discretion in choice of tools, techniques,
pacing and timing of work), and in work setting (private vs. public,
large vs. small, entrepreneurial vs. other, stable and growing vs. other)—
not to mention hours of work and job security, hence lifetime earnings
(Wilensky, 1962, 1964b:141-142). The finer we slice the occupational
structure, the more our classification will capture variations in earnings
and, to a lesser extent, in income and associated life styles. Phelps-
Brown (1977) is persuasive in his cross-national analysis of pay differentials by occupational group partly because he uses a level of disaggrega-
tion appropriate to his problem; he locates contrasts and similarities
in earnings by the demands of work roles that are obscured by broad
strata.

When one is necessarily confined to broad occupational strata, the
failure to disaggregate and classify appropriately can result in erroneous
conclusions about social stratification. Thus some sociological research
reports behavior and attitudes of "skilled workers" similar to those of
the less skilled, and concludes that the skilled are not becoming "middle
class." These findings often result from weak classifications. For instance,
a detailed study based on two nationwide surveys comparing "clerical,
sales"; "craftsmen, foremen"; and "operatives" shows that the latter two
are similar in level of organizational affiliation, types of affiliation, union

membership, religious involvement, media behavior, politics, home owner-ship, and attitudes toward education and foreign affairs (Hamilton, 1964: 42–57). Such studies not only fail to control for education (which is often the only distinction that matters when the "classes" are compared), they also lump stably employed, high-income operatives with unstably em-ployed, low-income workers to form the lowest stratum, thereby obscur-ing crucial differences between the two segments of the working class (Wilensky in Wilensky and Lebeaux, 1965:xxix).

What about trends in the internal differentiation of the working class? We have seen that the main story about earnings differentials is their remarkable stability over time and place. Yet there are obviously short-run changes; there may even be a long-run leveling tendency. What changes we find in relative earnings by occupation within a generation or so can be explained in large part by changes in supply and demand. And they seem to be similar for "capitalist" and "socialist" countries. Phelps-Brown (1977:98) notes that "the rise in the differential for skill in the British industrial revolution and its subsequent contraction was mirrored in Russian economic development from the First Five Year Plan to 1956." Skilled labor shortages followed by increased supply is the main reason. Similarly, poor countries evidence wider differentials for skill than those in rich countries. At low levels of development poor countries lack the educational and training apparatus to produce skilled workers. As they modernize, their supply of literate trained workers increases and the differential for skill contracts.

The strongest case against the idea of this tendency to earnings equality within the working class is stated by William Form (1976b:57–61). He notes some variations among nations at similar economic levels but concedes the general trend.

It is likely, as Phelps-Brown suggests, that for the long pull and for the entire occupational structure few differentials have widened, many have contracted, although a crucial advantage to "skill" (i.e., train-ing, responsibility, and so on) remains. The usual explanation is that: (1) the spread of public education and rising living standards mean reduced differences among individuals for all kinds of capabilities; and (2) sophisticated equipment and better forms of organization—themselves related to the spread of education—reduce dependence on the skill of the worker and increase the productivity of the less skilled. What do empirical studies show?

Education and Relative Income or Earnings. In explaining income dis-tribution, if we focus on the effects of changes in the supply of workers defined as qualified, using formal education as the criterion, the results are ambiguous.

Economists who see education as an investment in human capital have generally adopted the following argument. The spread of mass higher education increases the supply of people who can quickly (and cheaply) learn new jobs and adapt to changing job requirements. This has recently led to an "oversupply" of college graduates—another force for reducing inequalities in primary income, at least in the short run. If public financing reduces the cost of education for the individual, the supply of educated labor increases and the dispersion of incomes is reduced, although long-run adjustments in supply may tend to reestablish the differentials (Freeman, 1971:107-11)—perhaps at a slightly more equal level.

The effect of short-run fluctuations in the supply of educated labor is illustrated in two U.S. studies, one by Thurow covering 1949-1969, the other by Freeman extending into the 1970s. Thurow's job competition model (1975) leads him to argue that making grade-school workers into high-school workers can worsen the relative wage of the remaining grade-school workers: "The extra high-school workers take what had been the best jobs available for grade-school workers" (pp. 189-90). Using money income for white males twenty-five years and older in the U.S. from 1949 to 1969, he shows that high-school earnings fell relative to college earnings: "The increasing college work force spread down the earnings distribution and forced high-school workers to take lower-paying jobs. The effect was compounded for grade-school workers since they faced competition from more college workers and more high-school workers" (p. 125). Thus high-school earnings fell relative to college earnings and rose relative to grade-school earnings (p. 127).

Freeman's more recent study (1976), however, shows that the salary advantage of college graduates over high-school graduates, as well as the economic return on the costs of a college degree, have declined since the late 1960s. The picture is one of short-term fluctuations in relative pay rooted in supply and demand—the standard case of increased demand in attractive occupations requiring college education followed by oversupply. The fortunes of currently advantaged lawyers, engineers, and business managers (M.B.A.'s) should similarly decline as the recent flood of recruits saturates the labor market.

If we turn to long-run effects, we encounter data limitations that make the best judgment speculative. Covering half a century in two countries, Tinbergen (1975) had to rely on the earnings of one educational stratum compared to the earnings of everyone rather than the more appropriate comparisons of adjacent educational strata. He shows (pp. 102-4) that the ratio of earnings of university graduates to the average income recipient in the U.S. and the Netherlands since 1900 declined with the growth in the supply of college graduates. The same trend appears for the ratio of family income (university-trained head) to average family income.

Thus, in the development of mass education, the always tentative resolution of tension between meritocracy and equality may slightly favor economic equality. What these three studies together suggest is a slow, long-run tendency toward earnings compression among educational strata, with short-term ups and downs, and a losing struggle of college graduates to restore large differentials.

The question of the effect of mass education on income distribution is far from settled, either in theory or in research findings. Just as broad occupational strata obscure earnings-related differences in work roles, so broad educational strata obscure earnings-related qualitative differences among graduates of different types of educational institution. High-quality schools and colleges may graduate people whose abilities, motivations, and information give them a competitive advantage in the job scramble over people with identical formal levels of education. Further research must take account of the riotous diversity of modern mass educational systems. (For a demonstration of the utility of measures of quality of education, see Wilensky, 1964a:187–189).

Why Minimum Wages and Other Government Attempts to Compress the Pay Structure Have Little Impact on Economic Inequality

What are the prospects for reducing relative income inequalities by government action aimed at the structure of pay? (This is a major recommendation of Jencks et al., 1972:230.) If experience with minimum wage laws and with attempts to use legislative or executive authority to reduce earnings spreads is any guide, the prospects look dim.

Economists present a strong case in their consensus that whatever minimum wage laws do to redistribute income from one group to another, and even if they slightly increase the share to "labor," they are weak tools for helping the poor. Such laws do not typically shock employers into a recognition that they were undervaluing the cheaper labor they had previously hired. Instead, raises in the minimum wage inspire a great range of responses with one underlying theme: return to the status quo ante. Where the relationship between wages and productivity as employers (managers) measure it is disturbed, they try to restore it. Where differentials thought to be justified by training, experience, or seniority are violated, workers press for their restoration. What employers in fact do is to deny jobs to teenagers; they also hire illegals below the minimum, or they fire some low-paid workers while they take steps to increase the productivity of the remaining workers via the technical and social reorganization of work (cf. Phelps-Brown, 1977:177).

Minimum wage legislation, especially if it applies a uniform standard, clearly reduces employment opportunities for the group most marginal to the labor force, teenagers. During normal periods they get fewer jobs; on downswings their jobs become less secure. In a period when the U.S.

finds youth unemployment an urgent if short-run structural problem, a flexible minimum wage may be sensible. Lower youth minimums are commonly set by collective bargaining in West Germany, Holland, and the U.K.; the same result is achieved by law in France and Canada (U.S. Bureau of Labor Statistics, 1970).

Of course, a lower minimum wage for youth could inspire displacement of older, more expensive workers, including many heads of households, which explains the strong opposition of the AFL-CIO to such a policy. However, on the assumption that the experience of adult workers increases their productivity, modest differentials in the minimum wage would likely involve only a slight displacement effect. This, in turn, could be counteracted by active labor market policies, including job creation and training programs, moving allowances, and the spread of job information—measures that in any case are more effective than minimum wage increases in combating poverty among the working population.

If generous minimum wage laws threaten employment opportunities for marginal workers in the labor force, they do nothing for the majority of the poor who are not in the labor force. Earned income is a smaller share of income for the lowest stratum than for all others. Even economists who worry about the displacement effects of a youth differential concede that a high minimum wage does little to reduce poverty (cf. Kaufman and Foran, 1971).

Now, what about the fat cats? Can we not reduce income inequalities by lowering the salaries of those at the top of the heap? There are theoretical grounds for believing that we would encounter trouble. Underlying cross-national similarities in both pay differentials and standard-of-living minima are several functional necessities and their apparently contradictory ideological correlates (Wilensky, 1975:32–49). Although the demands of modern technology impose no rigid mold on a culture, all modern societies face similar problems, and their solutions to these problems are similar. For instance, every industrial system requires some competition for occupational position on the basis of criteria relevant to the learning and performance of the role, as well as some system of special reward for the development of scarce talents and skills. The same system requirements should foster related ideas of distributive justice. All modern countries evidence considerable popular consensus about: (1) equal pay for equal work; and (2) the content of jobs as related to job rewards (unequal pay for unequal skills and job demands) (Wilensky in Wilensky and Lebeaux, 1965:33–48; 1975:89; cf. Rainwater, 1974; Huber and Form, 1973). Far from being an ephemeral expression of the wild economic individualism of late nineteenth-century capitalism (Selznick, 1969), this free-mobility ideology is an enduring feature of modern society, varying only in degree.

As I have shown elsewhere, a similar elite demand for incentives underlies pro-welfare state doctrines—the idea that by political right everyone is entitled to government-protected minimum standards of income, nutrition, health, housing, and education. Such entitlements as pensions and job injury insurance are not incentives to make people train for and perform in demanding careers, but incentives to keep the least successful working, even in unattractive jobs. This elite necessity for stable economic incentives is matched by universal mass demands that the shock of mobility failures be cushioned and the risks of modern life be tempered. Thus, although the necessary cross-national data are severely limited, in every rich country where data can be found the mass of citizens simultaneously embrace a free-mobility ideology that favors earnings differentials based on education, training, and responsibility, and a welfare-state ideology that favors family security through a just minimum as well as wage differentials for seniority and family needs, e.g., marital status and family earnings (cf. Wilensky, 1975; Coughlin, 1977; Jasso and Rossi, 1977:639ff.).[10]

If my argument about conflicting system requirements and the corresponding ideological ambiguities is correct, we should find similar earnings differentials among countries with different political ideologies and political economies. Strategic empirical data come from studies of pay structures in Soviet-type economies, where an ideology of equality, with varying intensity, has been articulated for some time; in democratic countries where labor governments are strong and have articulated an ideology of wage solidarity; and finally in the Israeli Kibbutz, with its communal ideology. Many indications in existing data suggest that a thorough investigation would support the theory. Significant pay differentials appear in sharply contrasting political and ideological settings. "In the Soviet-type economies," Phelps-Brown concludes, "the planners seek . . . to arrive at differentials that will be 'correct.'" The differentials are correct, the planners tell us, if "they encourage entrants to acquire needed qualifications, bring about the desired allocation of labour between different occupations, industries, and regions, and stimulate performance in posts of responsibility" (Phelps-Brown, 1977:325). As in more decentralized economies, relative pay is adjusted to a labor market in which workers are more-or-less free to change jobs. Middle and top echelons in Soviet-type economies are, of course, subject to what Wiles (1962) calls "planners' tension," the pressure of the planners' impossible demands—an excess of administratively ordered output over capacity output. Among other adjustments, managers violate wage regulations to

[10]In American data both Rainwater (1974:163ff.) and Jasso and Rossi (1977) find that popular support for ideal earnings differentials is accompanied by more tolerance for equality than present earnings spreads reflect.

obtain scarce help, thereby coming closer to earnings differentials that would prevail without the regulations (Wiles, 1962:132–37; cf. Berliner, 1957; Wiles, 1974).

The major deviation from convergence in the pay structures of "capitalist" and "Soviet-type" economies is the Soviet success in lowering the pay and status of already marginal white-collar workers further than they have been lowered in the West (relative to the most skilled manual workers). By criteria relevant to role performance, one can argue that Soviet-type economies are adopting the stiffer meritocratic line. Considering the training costs, job responsibilities, and task complexities of clerks, checkout cashiers, keypunch operators, and so on, compared to the most skilled manual workers, Soviet planners seem to have arrived at the "right" differentials. The Soviets may be the best structural-functionalists around.

It is even possible, as Phelps-Brown suggests (1977:86–87), that if demand for clerical and administrative services had not kept pace with supply in the West, we would by now have found lower white-collar occupations far below the working-class elite.

The exception that clarifies the rule is the Israeli Kibbutz: If the fraction of the economy covered is small (Kibbutzim comprise less than 5 percent of the labor force), if the division of labor is relatively simple, if the members share a high cultural and educational level, and if their relations are personal and intimate—in contrast to all other cases mentioned above, where contractual relations prevail—then the radical separation of qualifications and pay can be sustained, more or less. (For some variations even among the Kibbutzim and some signs that the structure of rewards creates trouble in recruiting managers, see Spiro, 1970:210–11, 268; Weller, 1974:249–55, 260–73; and Tannenbaum, 1974:33ff., 210ff.).

Finally, if we turn to the West and locate the most heroic efforts to reduce income inequalities by reducing wage differentials, we once again see the nearly impermeable character of wage structures, whatever the short-run fluctuations. In Sweden since the early 1940s, the LO (Swedish Confederation of Trade Unions) and the Social Democratic party have collaborated with the Confederation of Swedish Employers to pursue a general national policy of "wage solidarity"—bringing low-wage workers closer to the skilled levels and, later, manual workers closer to upper white-collar workers. This, of course, provoked strong informal pressure from skilled workers to restore their usual differentials. It was also a factor in the 1971 strike of SACO, a federation of white-collar college graduates (Heidenheimer, 1976). Since the adoption of wage solidarity the wage structure has compressed and opened like an accordian until now a formally negotiated sum must be put aside at each round of wage increases to accommodate "wage drift" (Ulman and

Flanagan, 1971)—the informal restoration of wage differentials in the workplace where official wage compression violates local consensus regarding distributive justice. Similar experience is noted in the U.K. and Holland.[11]

In short, if pay structures are virtually immutable, if rich countries, whatever their political economies and official doctrines, display a convergent array of differentials roughly matching the prestige rankings of occupations, then hardly anything the government does to change relative wages will be effective as a long-run redistribution policy. Egalitarians must look instead to the more powerful tools of government taxes and expenditures.

PRIMARY INCOME vs. POST-TAX/POST-TRANSFER INCOME AND THE SPECIAL PROBLEM OF WHO BENEFITS FROM SERVICES

This final distinction is crucial for judging trends in economic inequality. To examine the primary income distribution in isolation from the effect of taxes, social security, and other benefits in cash and kind is misleading (Wilensky, 1975:93ff.). Similarly, we cannot make accurate trend statements without taking account of substantial changes in the nature of recipient units. For discussion of these problems see Harold Watts' chapter below. I shall here merely illustrate these two difficulties and give my impression of what we might find if we could fully surmount them with an ideal data base.

The complexities are illustrated in an article that begins, "Income distribution in the United States has remained virtually unchanged for one-quarter of a century... the poorest 20 percent of all families received 5 percent of the cash income in 1947 and they receive the same share today" (Miller, 1975:40; cf. U.S. Bureau of the Census, 1966:2). This is the typical summary statement repeated in many popular books and even academic articles. Its accuracy depends first on the income unit as well as the quintile share remaining stable. Yet no adjustment is made for changing family size. The families represented in the bottom fifth contain fewer individuals to be supported by that 5 percent and more old and young people, who are at less than peak earnings.

The author, a leading expert on income distribution at the U.S. Bureau of the Census, goes on to make educated guesses regarding "missing income" for 1968—unreported income as well as capital gains,

---

[11]The long-run equalization of income is consistent with a much slower contraction of relative earnings, if we take account of the changing occupational composition of the labor force. For instance, when workers in higher-paying occupations increase as a fraction of all workers, incomes will tend toward less concentration in the upper brackets even though earnings differentials among occupations do not change.

undistributed profits, and imputed income—and concludes that the rich must be getting richer. But then he also estimates the value of transfer payments and distributes the estimated value of government services to various strata on various assumptions. Here he finds much more equality—a net outcome of less to the rich, more to the poor than he reports for the quarter century.

Based on existing clues, if we had good cross-national data on recent trends in income distribution, taxes, and cash transfers, I think we might find the following for any recent year:

1. Income taxes in action (counting evasion and avoidance) are not highly progressive, although national variations—from Sweden (more progressive) to France (less progressive)—are considerable.
2. Although the regressivity of indirect taxes and property taxes has been exaggerated (Aaron, 1975), they often substantially offset the progressivity of income taxes. Thus the tax structures of rich countries as a whole are seldom more than mildly progressive and at their worst they are quite regressive (France). The U.S. is perhaps somewhere in the middle of that range. (Cf. Pechman and Okner, 1974; OECD, 1976. Neither of these studies deals with a sticky technical problem: how to impute the incidence of indirect taxes to households of different size and income level on the basis of their observed patterns of spending on products taxed at different rates.)
3. But if we take account of cash transfers such as social security, rent supplements, family allowances, and public assistance, the pattern changes and the typical net effect is downward redistribution, especially to the bottom fifth.

What would happen to this picture of economic inequality if we could place a monetary value on each of hundreds of government services—from health and education to transportation and family services (which vary greatly from country to country)—and allocate them to each income unit? Would we discover the net benefit to the poor that appears in Miller's study for the U.S. or in other studies for the U.K. (Wilensky, 1975:92–94)? The problem of defense spending indicates the mind-boggling complexity and yet underscores the need for still more difficult cross-national comparison. Miller (1975:48–49) says that the net benefit to the poor might change if we assume that the rich have more to lose from death than the poor and that defense is an insurance policy for property rather than a protection for freedom or for lives. Thus defense spending in the U.S., he shows, could make the net outcome less egalitarian. In the higher theology of the law it is true that the rich have more to lose: You can sue for damages for wrongful death on the basis of the present value of expected lifetime earnings of the deceased. If, however, we reject these legal fictions and make other, perhaps more realistic assumptions, we find an egalitarian effect by allocating defense among more classes.

Again, however, a comparative perspective helps. At the peak of the cold war only a few rich countries had a defense burden heavy enough to make a big difference in their income distribution picture—U.S., USSR, Israel, France, Canada, and U.K. Because defense expenditures at very high levels subvert public civilian spending (Wilensky, 1975:74–80), and because nonmilitary cash transfers and services probably have a net downward distributional effect, the indirect effects of defense spending in the 1950s and 1960s were perhaps regressive. Others might argue that the training in literacy and work and the health programs of the armed forces represent a redistribution to the working class and minorities who are overrepresented in their ranks—an indirect effect in the opposite direction.

A final difficulty, which may be most intractable, is the difference between long-run and short-run effects on economic inequality of many government services. Consider the outcome of the national health service of the U.K. There is some evidence that it is used most intensively by the least well-off—the old, the young, the poor, the single. If we consider long-run possibilities, however, the effects of public health expenditures might be highly regressive. The poor die young—before they can contract the chronic diseases that dearly cost national health schemes. The more affluent citizens live to a riper age, chronically collecting health services paid for by the lifelong taxes of the deceased poor. A program that is highly progressive at a cross-sectional moment may be highly regressive in the lifetime of particular generations (Wilensky, 1975:96).

It is hardly astonishing that most social scientists interested in equality shy away from comparative studies of its economic aspects.

Summary

While rich countries are not identical in their pay structures and the spread from top to bottom varies from place to place and time to time, the similarities are more striking than the differences. The successive widening and compression of occupational differentials—reflecting cycles of over- and undersupply—may constitute short-term fluctuations around a long-run equalization trend. If we turn to income distribution, including income not derived from work, we find substantial national differences, especially in the number and relative deprivation of the poor. Again, however, and even more than the drift in earnings differentials, what meager evidence we have indicates a long-run leveling tendency in the total flow of income, mainly because of the changing composition of the labor force, the spread of mass education and literacy, and the increased importance of government transfers.

The persistence of pay differentials through thick and thin, their resistance to minimum wage laws and salary compression alike; the declining importance of private property and wealth in the picture of income distribution (and the probable irrelevance of public ownership of industry)—all this suggests a reorientation of research toward comparative analysis of the redistributional effects of taxes and public expenditures. Until we have that research, neither egalitarians who are repelled by the income gap between top dogs and underdogs nor conservatives who think that the gap is closing at the cost of efficiency and freedom will know whether the policies they so fervently advocate serve their own values or the values of their enemies.

9

The Politics of Public Assistance: Western Europe and the United States

Joan Huber

SOCIAL WELFARE PROGRAMS in the U.S. and Western Europe are in trouble. Designed for relatively stable families in homogeneous polities, programs grew as a patchwork response to changes in the economy. Two trends since World War II have politicized welfare problems by producing two strata with high risk of poverty. First, rising divorce rates are increasing the number of families headed by a single parent. Second, labor demand in "advanced" economies and/or labor surplus in less developed areas stimulates the migration of low-skilled workers who are racially or ethnically different from their "hosts." This paper is concerned with political backlash against these two strata. To clarify the politics of public assistance, I shall: (1) examine the historical origin of welfare troubles; (2) compare social security programs in the U.S. and Western Europe; (3) review research relating social security expenditures to welfare backlash; and (4) show why the new strata of poor require new program perspectives.

The Origin of Welfare Troubles

Modern poverty—the inability to obtain adequate subsistence in a wage system—appeared in England in the fourteenth century after the

□ I am indebted to Marilyn Flynn for intellectual stimulation and for generously making her library available to me. This paper has benefited from the criticism of William Form and Harold Wilensky.

Black Death. Labor was in short supply but estates were improverished, hence migrant workers left their parishes in search of wage work. The Statute of Laborers in 1349 tried to control vagrancy: It forbade migration, set maximum wages, and penalized almsgiving. But vagrancy increased. In the fifteenth century it was dangerous for citizens to move on public roads because of packs of roving paupers. By the end of the century England had a real welfare mess (Flynn, 1973).

Four hundred years later, after masses of peasants had shifted from status to contract labor, a labor movement emerged, the men's movement of its time—for white men. Whether prompted by fear of revolution, by compassion, or by the desire to remain in power—the franchise had been broadly extended—European governments cushioned workers against the uncertainties of industrial life with welfare programs that substituted for the declining distributive importance of the extended family. By the beginning of the twentieth century, a social security patchwork blanketed Western Europe (Rimlinger, 1971). Workers' compensation was usually the first identified risk; health and employment insurance were last to be funded (Flynn, 1975). By the end of the Great Depression even the U.S. had insurance and assistance programs that covered a substantial portion of the work force.[1]

After World War II, rising affluence in Western Europe and the U.S. the womb-to-tomb security plan in Britain, and the strength of socialist parties on the Continent helped to stimulate the belief that poverty had been alleviated. U.S. editors of influential mass media and economists in both major parties believed that income equality was increasing (Miller, 1964:37; Levitan, 1969:12), as did British scholars (Titmuss, 1962). Sociologists celebrated America as a middle-class society (Pease, Form, and Rytina, 1970). Meanwhile, a line of worms was queueing up to file into the apple: Sociodemographic change was laying a base for future political conflict.

The most immediate cause of current welfare troubles is that unemployment rates recently have been higher than during the 1950s and 1960s, hence an identifiable although fragmented understratum is more obvious. Because the consolidation of oligopolies, the partial unionization of the labor force, and discrimination against women and ethnic/racial groups has internally stratified the working class (Form, 1976), the nineteenth-century rhetoric of class war poorly describes the political arena. Industrial societies are increasingly stratified into relatively stably employed workers who share productivity gains and workers left behind in unstable or low-wage jobs (Bibb, 1977). High-wage workers are typi-

[1]Social insurance links contributions paid by the insured person and benefits granted; the amount of the benefit and qualifying conditions are fixed by law. Social (or public) assistance provides from general taxation cash payments or services on the basis of a means-test (Rys, 1966:250).

cally covered by social insurance while many low-wage workers join the nonworking poor on public assistance.

The problem of labor market segmentation has been thrown into relief in the U.S. because of higher unemployment rates than in Europe and because blacks are much more likely than whites to be unemployed. But recently Europe has been thrown into a tangle of functionally linked questions concerning the breakdown of the international monetary system: oil, recession, unemployment, and inflation (Delpérée, 1975; Fabius, 1976). Although U.S. unemployment rates remain markedly higher (Moy and Sorrentino, 1975), postwar highs have been reached in Europe (European Coal and Steel Community et al., 1975). Like their U.S. counterparts, European leaders now worry about full employment strategies (International Social Security Review, 1976:196).

Although the politics of income distribution has become more important, social scientists are hampered in their approach to it by disciplinary segregation. Analysis should begin with a theory of personal income distribution but no one has put the relevant factors together. Economists have failed to link data on vertical mobility and income distribution because they had a certain contempt for sociology;[2] sociologists know too little of the problems of theoretical economics (Pen, 1971:264). We need a theory specifying the relationship between wage levels, the social characteristics (ethnicity, sex, race, education) of the people who experience upward or downward mobility, and the institutional forces responsible for the sifting process, such as family sponsorship, the seniority system, and the impact of law. All of these factors affect the politics of welfare. I shall refer again to this gap later in the paper. Let us now turn to a comparison of Western European and U.S. social security programs.

Comparative Social Security Programs

Most industrialized countries have instituted the same program ingredients in similar sequence: social insurance for the aged, disabled, or widowed; help in paying medical bills; unemployment benefits; and, often, family allowances. Once begun, these programs expanded coverage to include larger portions of the population, typically from a limited (often poorer) segment to a broader (often better-off) segment (Heidenheimer, Heclo, and Adams, 1975:188). Public assistance components are minor because the insurance programs were thought to be adequate. To grasp the differences, let us first examine income-maintenance programs in the U.S. then in Western Europe.

[2] Rossi and Lyall (1977) report that the economists responsible for the income-maintenance experiments had low regard for sociologists' interests and skills.

The fastest growing component of U.S. income-maintenance programs is Old-Age, Survivors, Disability, and Health Insurance (OAS-DHI); it increased from 9 percent of social security expenditures in 1949–1950 (when it was OASI) to 49 percent in 1970–1971. In contrast, public assistance decreased from 27 percent in 1949–1950 to a low of 12 percent in 1964–1965, then increased to 14 percent in 1970–1971 (Turnbull, Williams, and Cheit, 1973:678).[3] The major part of the public assistance increase was due to higher medical-care costs; its largest single program is Aid to Dependent Children (ADC or AFDC), which has grown vigorously since 1958. ADC is the chief target of public controversy over "the welfare mess."

The typical European social security network, more extensive, consumes a higher proportion of the GNP than in the U.S. (Flynn, 1977:4).[4] The cash transfer programs are older, structurally more diversified, and reflect a wider philosophical range than in the U.S. Three distinct patterns emerged in Europe.

The first, the Bismarck tradition, characterizes most Continental nations except Scandinavia and the Netherlands (Flynn, 1977:5). At least until recently, it moved toward more comprehensive schemes covering everyone. Schemes are tied to occupational status; individual entitlement is based on previous earnings, length of service, and type of work. Except for family allowances, benefit structures aim to replace preretirement differences in living standards. Supplementary means-tested aid is locally financed and its administration is discretionary. Since social insurance schemes presumably relieved poverty, data on low incomes have not routinely been collected. This benign premise is now being reassessed because public assistance expenditures have recently risen in unprecedented manner.

The second, the Beveridge pattern, evolved in Britain, Ireland, the Netherlands, and the Scandinavian countries (Flynn, 1977:7). Rather than a basic earnings-rated benefit, the "Beveridge countries" rely on flat-rate payments derived from general revenue; entitlement derives from citizenship. Since the benefit is insufficient, a second tier of payments in Scandinavia is based on an employer payroll tax. In Britain the flat rate has remained very low, hence a means-tested scheme retains an

---

[3]U.S. public assistance includes all means-tested cash and in-kind benefits: Aid to Families with Dependent Children (ADC or AFDC); Supplemental Security Income for the aged, blind, and disabled poor (SSI); Work Incentive Training and allowances (WIN); employment and training programs under Titles I and III of the Comprehensive Employment and Training Act (CETA); vendor medical payments under Medicaid; social services to low-income families through Title XX of the Social Security Act; public service employment and other work relief; emergency assistance payments; surplus food and school lunch programs; food stamps; and repatriate and refugee assistance.

[4]I follow the excellent account in Flynn (1977).

importance unknown on the Continent. These patterns, however, are gradually moving toward a mixed system in which earnings-related principles are joined to flat-rate minima.

The third pattern, unprecedented, is neither insurance as conventionally defined nor assistance as traditionally administered. Benefits consist of categorical demogrants based neither upon prior earnings nor economic need. The program identifies a specific category of risk, such as disability, establishes a single nonincome test to determine eligibility, then provides universal payments for all persons meeting the test. Denmark has abandoned the concept of long-range financing and has decentralized the program, along with health care and public assistance, placing it in the hands of county administrators. A similar program obtains in the Netherlands.

Since World War II most planners expected public assistance schemes to wither away as the insurance system matured (Flynn, 1977:9). Instead, an unanticipated demand for assistance resulted in unexpectedly high program costs. Almost one-third of all aged insurance beneficiaries may also qualify for means-tested assistance, whose benefit levels trail behind accepted minima. Almost all European insurance programs that had not already done so are adopting cash benefit principles to incorporate a concept of minimum social benefits.

Western European benefits to the able-bodied poor and to dependent children show the greatest diversity, but four common themes occur: All countries provide family allowances, although some countries have increased the benefits at less than the rate of inflation. Family benefits are small relative to those of old-age pensions and health-care benefits. All benefits are paid on a flat-rate basis. Family allowances have received attention in the last few years as a means of reducing poverty (Flynn, 1977:12). Family allowances have been popular because they presumably stimulated population growth, although no evidence demonstrates such an effect.

The biggest difference between U.S. and European patterns concerns family benefits. Since population decline never threatned U.S. survival, family benefits and family policy have received only erratic attention. The U.S. resembles West Germany in its stress on benefits for the aged. U.S. benefits are relatively lower as a percent of past earnings, although between 1968 and 1972 real benefits increased by about 60 percent, with coverage extended to about 90 percent of the population. In contrast, handling family benefits under ADC places in public assistance programs persons whose needs in Europe are met by social insurance.

The U.S. would probably be classed with France and West Germany in that its pension and unemployment programs relate benefits to previous earnings, but it appears closer to British practice in its provision of means-tested public assistance (OECD, 1976:13). Features of the Bismarck and Beveridge patterns coexist within individual countries and some movement toward convergence has appeared in both patterns.

A major question for all these programs is the degree to which disadvantaged strata can form groups to press demands, and the degree to which their pressure invites backlash from higher-income strata. Let us now turn to the literature that focuses on the backlash problem.

Program Expenditures and Backlash

Causal explanations of comparative social security expenditures in countries with differing cultures and levels of economic development highlight the importance of economic factors in determining expenditure levels (Cutright, 1965:Aaron, 1967). Studies focusing on a narrower range of nations tended to find that the role of economic factors was unclear; institutional factors—age of population and age of system— were more important (Taira and Kilby, 1969; Pryor, 1968). Reconciling these findings, Wilensky (1975a:47) concludes that, although the root cause of the welfare state is economic development, its effects are felt chiefly through demographic change and the momentum of the programs themselves. Because of fertility decline, economic development produces large proportions of older people who then become a political force in societies with enough surplus to make old-age benefits possible.

Wilensky's (1975a, 1976) research is the first to link welfare and political backlash. Omitting education and housing,[5] Wilensky (1975a) asked what structural attributes in 22 "rich" countries explained welfare-spending variations. He found that the welfare state is most developed where a centralized government can mobilize a well-organized working class, where the middle mass neither perceives its tax burden as grossly unfair relative to that of the rich nor feels great social distance from the poor, and where the tax system relies least on direct taxes.

A second study focuses on centralization of government and employer/labor federations, social cleavages, party stability, and backlash as expressed in antitaxing, antispending, and antibureaucratic sentiments/actions opposing state welfare programs (Wilensky,

---

[5] Good housing data are scarce. Higher education tends to transfer money from the parents of less affluent children to the children of more affluent parents (Wilensky, 1975a:4–9).

1976:56–68). Two roads that lead to the containment of mass discontent center on taxes, social spending, and bureaucracy. A strong corporatist democracy that relies on invisible taxes dampens welfare backlash whether it has an old dominant party (Belgium, the Netherlands) or not (France, Italy, Israel, Austria). A young party system that provides several channels for party opposition and that relies on invisible taxes also dampens backlash whether it has strong corporatist-technocratic linkages (France, Italy, Israel) or not (West Germany, Japan, Ireland, and New Zealand). Denmark, the U.S., the United Kingdom, Switzerland, Canada, and Norway attained top backlash scores.

While Wilensky's pioneering research is exciting political sociology, it has two problems. First, focusing on backlash, Wilensky lumps together as "social security expenditures" both the social insurance and public assistance components, as if both components were equally likely to annoy taxpayers. This seems unlikely. Common sense tells us that backlash focuses on welfare bums, chiselers, and loose women rather than on respectable senior citizens—despite the fact that pensions comprise by far the largest and most rapidly growing portion of welfare expenditures. The broad masses in the U.S. and Britain have accepted contributory social insurance in contrast to their unease about public assistance (Titmuss, 1969:152); the U.S. middle mass accepts heavy payroll taxes while rebelling against similar, even smaller, payroll deductions for federal income tax (Wilensky, 1975a:60).

A second problem in the comparative study of social security involves using expenditure data for international ranking. Rys (1966:259) notes that the International Labour Office reports (1972, 1976)—which Wilensky used—comprise the best available data on national social security receipts and expenditures, but the ILO itself (1964:6) claims that these data are not adequate to evaluate national efforts because the cost elements differ. Costs of protection against a given contingency vary with the incidence of the contingency; hence if cost analysis is used for international comparisons, one would have to decide what constituted a higher achievement: high-level benefit schemes in nations with low-frequency risks or low-level schemes in countries with high risks. The only solution would be to group nations according to the level of social needs and make comparisons only within such groups (Rys, 1966:260).

Current data do not permit expenditures to be related to social needs. We do not know what social needs really are. After the Swedes discovered poverty in the 1970s, they found about one-third of the working population living at or below a relative poverty standard (Heclo, 1974:323). Since Sweden has the best social statistics in the world, their "discovery" helps to explain why it is nearly impossible to find comparative data on the smaller components of total programs. Other data gaps abound: Data on discouraged workers are available only in the U.S. and

Sweden (Moy and Sorrentino, 1975:9). Little is known about the extent to which pension systems meet their objectives (J. Schulz et al., 1974:32), or about the size and composition of the hard-to-employ in Northwest Europe (Reubens, 1970:13), or about income distributions during the life cycle, especially in socialist countries (Chlumsky, 1974). Even comparisons among the six founding members of the European Community are difficult (James and Laurent, 1974).

The effect of social security expenditures is hard to assess, in addition, because the programs are so complex. Since this complexity reflects the real world, it cannot be avoided by statistical manipulation (OECD, 1976:11). The diversity of arrangements is bewildering (Veldkamp, 1973). The French system seems to be a juxtaposition of systems (Laroque, 1969). The German system is hardly a system at all (Young, 1975), nor is the U.S. really a system (Barth, Carcagno, and Palmer, 1974:14). The degree of overlapping coverage and gaps in coverage cannot be ascertained in the U.S.; neither program data nor census data suffice to estimate how many people satisfy the complex eligibility requirements (Lurie, 1975:10). Nor is there a systematic relationship among the various means tests, either in Western European or U.S. programs (International Social Security Association, 1975:60). The net impact of cash grants and social services in France, Sweden, and Great Britain on income distribution is increasingly hard to untangle because of the difficulty in assigning either costs or net benefits for different income, occupational, or family-size groupings (Marmor, Rein, and Van Til, n.d.:283).

Does the problem of obtaining good comparative data mean that social scientists should confine themselves to global armchair theories and avoid testing empirical hypotheses? No. Although we should remain nervously aware that national comparisons may be more suggestive than definitive, the Wilensky studies show that, until a pioneer publishes findings for others to mull, data problems remain obscure and important social problems remain unaddressed. Wilensky's variable mix sensitizes us to important new relationships, for example, the impact of tax visibility on welfare backlash. To U.S. "liberals" who view invisible taxes as somehow immoral, the idea that visible taxes invite welfare backlash is a shock. The Soviets also vigorously disapprove of indirect taxes—yet the outstanding feature of Soviet tax structure is heavy reliance on them (Holzman, 1955:5). Social scientists clearly need to analyze the function of the tax structure in the modern state.

Because tax backlash strikes at certain groups, I shall now discuss why some groups tend to be overrepresented among public assistance clientele and then examine why these groups attract so much welfare backlash.

The Clients of Public Assistance

In industrial societies people with low skills often experience unstable employment and low wages. Migrants from less developed areas typically have low skills; an additional burden for most migrants is the racial/ethnic prejudice in the U.S. and Western Europe. Migrants often encounter discrimination, which may ease in several generations if the "wrong" characteristics were linguistic or cultural. If the "wrong" characteristics are ascriptive, discrimination may persist. I shall start with a discussion of the situation of U.S. blacks, a world prototype for the problem of racism.

U.S. BLACKS

Although blacks had long experienced coercion, a wide-scale civil rights movement appeared only in the 1960s, as a response to sociodemographic events that followed World War II. After 1950, the machine harvesting of cotton and corn drastically cut the need for unskilled labor in the South. Blacks increasingly migrated to metropolitan areas where they encountered massive discrimination in housing and jobs; this increased the disadvantage of their low-skill levels because the demand for unskilled labor was declining (Fusfeld, 1974).

By the 1960s the middle mass—upper-working and lower-white-collar classes (Wilensky, 1975a:116)—worried about crime and the rising ADC caseload. The Democratic party worried about how to carry the urban vote in cities increasingly populated by blacks. The War on Poverty—which consisted mostly of warmed-over programs from the 1930s (Levitan, 1969:215)—was in great part a response to these factors. Its impact on blacks was modest. In the early 1970s college enrollment increased more rapidly for blacks than for white but other indicators led some observers to conclude that deep pessimism within the black community was justified (Brimmer, 1976:14). During the 1970s male unemployment increased more rapidly for nonwhites than for whites. The jobless rate for blacks in late 1977 was over 14 percent while that for whites was 6.1 percent.

Two strata are emerging within the black population: Young, two-earner black families are economically abreast of their white counterparts because young black married women are more likely to work full time than their white counterparts. The earnings of individual blacks, however, especially older ones, lag behind those of their white counterparts.

U.S. SPANISH-ORIGIN

Increasing in size and political importance, Spanish-origin Americans include Mexican Americans, Puerto Ricans, South Americans, and Cubans. They comprise about 5 percent of U.S. population, yet 8 percent of U.S. children under eighteen live in Spanish-origin families (Grossman, 1977). Mexican Americans, the largest single group (60 percent), and Puerto Ricans (14 percent) are the least educated. In 1975 about a third of both groups had incomes below $5,000 (U.S. Bureau of the Census, 1976:9).

Mexican Americans continue to enter the U.S. at high rates, spurred by high fertility coupled with Mexico's lower rate of industrial development (Grebler, Moore, and Guzman, 1970). Most Mexican Americans are urban-dwellers, a shadow labor force (Briggs, 1975).

U.S. MIGRANT WORKERS

In the U.S. in the 1950s about 400,000 persons a year worked as migrants, a decrease from about one million in the 1940s (Ornati, 1974). After World War I the migrant labor population declined, but at a decreasing rate. Migrants became a larger proportion of all agricultural workers and foreign workers became an increasing proportion of all migrant workers, most of whom are now black or Mexican American (Ornati, 1974).

FOREIGN WORKERS ON THE CONTINENT

Because of high labor demand after World War II, some Northwest European countries admitted workers from less developed countries. By 1970, for example, West Germany had 1.8 million foreign workers, the largest number from Yugoslavia, followed by Italy, Turkey, Greece, Spain, and Portugal (Schewe, Nordhorn, and Schenke, 1972:42). Switzerland has 600,000, creating upward mobility for Swiss workers who rely on foreigners for low-skill jobs (Siegenthaler, 1975:276). In France about 7 percent of the population is foreign. Increasing rapidly in the 1960s (Ancelin and Dumas, 1974:7), their presence has improved the income and status of French workers. Foreign workers are weakly organized but their discontent is growing (Reynaud, 1975:216).

By 1975, however, unemployment was a problem. Unemployment rates for foreign workers are higher than those for native workers, although both rates are low by U.S. standards. Despite the increase in unemployment, not as many foreign workers as expected returned to their countries. A number of countries in the European Community have banned immigration of foreign workers and some have set up commissions to combat illegal employment (European Coal and Steel Community et al., 1975). The problems of illegal entry leaves one with the feeling that the real number of foreign workers may be higher than published data indicate.

The problem with foreign workers is that, unless the demand for labor remains very high, they are unabsorbable in the short run. Sending foreign workers home during recessions may improve matters for host countries but it ruins the economies of nations who had exported their surplus labor. If all European nations returned foreign workers as energetically as have the Germans and the Swiss, the Turkish and Yugoslav economies would be badly damaged.

MIGRANTS IN BRITAIN

After World War II, persons from less developed Commonwealth countries migrated to Britain, after the pattern of Puerto Rican and southern migration in the U.S. The Labour party's record on immigration, race, and unemployment did little to improve things for migrants. By 1968 a Commonwealth Immigration bill restricted migration to the United Kingdom. Despite the fact that race is an important problem, little statistical information is available (Stein, 1976:31).

WOMEN IN THE U.S. AND WESTERN EUROPE

Women of all ages comprise a potentially large group of public assistance recipients in the U.S. and Western Europe but—despite their problems[6]—I shall exclude older women from this analysis because they attract little welfare backlash. The problems of younger women stem from interlocking factors that increase the probability that they will head families with children. I shall first state these factors and then spell them out in detail.

Women's labor force participation continues to rise, hence employment becomes increasingly normative for them. But their wages are little more than half those of their male counterparts. Women care for home and children but the marital dissolution rate also continues to rise. Since

---

[6]Social security systems tend to ignore the problem of compensating women for lower earnings and/or child rearing, or of insuring them against the risks of widowhood, separation, or divorce. Still missing from ILO standards is a forthright declaration outlawing sex discrimination in social security systems (Gelber, 1975:432).

divorced/separated women receive skimpy financial support from their husbands, women who head households that include children are likely to need public assistance, especially if they are also black, Spanish-origin, or recent migrants to the Continent or to Britain. And women receiving public assistance invite taxpayer backlash.

The key factor in women's position is the increase in their labor force participation since the end of World War II (Krebs, 1975). Adjusted to U.S. concepts of participation, about 55 percent of Swedish women, 47 percent of U.S. women, 46 percent of British, 44 percent of French, 38 percent of German, and 26 percent of Italian women were employed in 1976 (U.S. Department of Labor, forthcoming).[7] An important factor is the increase in the employment of women with children (Ancelin and Dumas, 1974; Grossman, 1977:41; Flamm, 1974:2).

Yet all over the industrialized world women workers receive from one-half to two-thirds the wages of men (Lydall, 1968:55), basically because of their occupational/industrial distribution (Form and Huber, 1976). The wage gap has recently widened in Britain (Commission of European Communities, 1974) and the U.S. (Sexton, 1977:3). The situation is worse for women not in the dominant race or ethnic group. In France, for example, foreign women workers earn 62 percent of the wages of French women and 61 percent of the wages of male foreign workers (Granier and Marciano, 1975).

Divorce rates are increasing markedly in twenty-six industrialized countries but the trend is sharpest in the United Kingdom, Denmark, and the U.S. (Cockburn and Hoskins, 1976). Schoen and Urton (1977) estimate that at current rates one in every two U.S. marriages will end in divorce.

Hence the number of female-headed families grows; by the mid-seventies, one of every seven U.S. children will live in a father-absent family (Ross and Sawhill, 1975:1). A five-country study (Denmark, Norway, Sweden, West Germany, the Netherlands) found one in ten families with a dependent child headed by a single parent, most of them women, and a tendency for these families to increase (International Social Security Association, 1975).

Female-headed families have three economic problems. First, alimony and child-support payments are low. Eckhardt (1968) reports that 67 percent of Wisconsin fathers were in total noncompliance five years after child-support payments were ordered by the court. Ross and Sawhill (1975:175) report that only 22 percent of court-ordered payments to AFDC mothers were being met in full. In Europe absent

---

[7]Rupert Evans brought these data to my attention. U.S. concepts of labor force participation distort data for countries with high proportions of workers in agriculture; differences in defining "economically active" make comparisons of women's labor force participation, using ILO data, very difficult (Ferber and Lowry, 1977).

fathers often fail to meet their obligations (Conference of European Ministers, 1971:35).

Second, working women with young children need child-care services. The shortage of child care, a major obstacle to equality in employment, is the most difficult problem of the female-headed family (International Social Security Association, 1975:50). In the U.S. little is known about the current demand for or supply of child-care services (Grossman, 1977:43). In Europe the supply lags far behind the demand (European Coal and Steel Community et al., 1974).[8]

Third, even if women work, their low wages imply high poverty risk for female family heads (Osmond and Grigg, 1975; Liljeström, Hellström, and Svensson, 1975). The situation is worse for minority women. Over half of black and two-thirds of Mexican American and Puerto Rican female-headed families are poor (U.S. Commission on Civil Rights, 1974:2). European women's wages are similarly low but I cannot estimate the extent to which female-headed families are poor because comparable poverty definitions are not available.

Hence the trend in Western Europe and the U.S. is for female-headed families to increase proportionately and to face greater income insecurities (Heidenheimer, Heclo, and Adams, 1975:206), marked in Britain and the U.S. by the steady rise in the number of such families who receive public assistance (Stein, 1976:28). AFDC families comprise about one-tenth of families with children (Oberheu, 1976); in Western Europe the comparable proportion is slightly smaller.

In the U.S. most AFDC families are eligible for such benefits as Medicaid, food stamps, and child-care subsidies. The direct cash benefits vary among the fifty states, ranging from $14.39 in Mississippi to $77.41 in New York, an average of $56.95 per person per month—56 percent of the poverty line for a family of four (Levitan and Taggart, 1976:57).[9]

The situations of U.S. and European assistance recipients differ because European countries typically use a mix of non-means-tested programs to aid single-parent families; public assistance is only a last resort (Heidenheimer, Heclo, and Adams, 1975:106ff). These programs include:

1. Family allowances. The amounts are modest. The value of tax allowances and cash transfers for two children in 1972 as a percent of gross earnings of the "average production worker" was

[8]Considering the importance of socializing the next generation, one would expect much research on the effects on children of different kinds of child care. Yet Sexton (1977:3) reports that there is little U.S. research; my impression is the same for Europe.

[9]The quasi-official U.S. poverty line is adjusted for inflation but not for wage increases, hence the declining proportion of persons reported to be poor each year is misleading. By 1972, for example, the poverty line had fallen from its 1959 level of 55 percent of median family income for a family of four to only 38 percent (OECD, 1976:63).

almost 14 percent in France and Belgium, 6 to 9 percent in Denmark, Sweden, the Netherlands, and Austria, and about 5 percent in the United Kingdom (OECD, 1976:27).

2. Maintenance grants, legal mechanisms for fixing the obligations of an absent parent.
3. Maternity benefits, an important transitional income support.
4. Housing allowances.
5. Tax deductions and credits, which vary considerably. In West Germany single parents (except widows) pay taxes on substantially lower incomes than do the married, but in Sweden single parents are better off than the married in this respect (International Social Security Association, 1975:57).
6. Job-training grants, the last program, are also available in the U.S. A variety of vocational training programs is available in Western Europe (Conference of European Ministers, 1971:55). The income support and potential for long-term security can be substantial; training grants and expense allowances have been relatively generous to encourage participation (Heidenheimer, Heclo, and Adams, 1975:209). Yet some observers feel that traditional occupational stereotyping pervades vocational guidance and training for women in Western Europe (Commission of European Communities, 1974:15). Even in Eastern Europe women's job training includes a much narrower range of skills than does men's (H. Scott, 1974:8).

In contrast to the European programs discussed above, U.S. job training for single parents is part of the public assistance program rather than general labor market policy. The federal Work Incentive Program (WIN), directed to lone parents on welfare, is designed to encourage welfare recipients to train for jobs. But there is little evidence of successful training and considerable indication that quick job placement has been emphasized at the expense of long-term earning capacity (Heidenheimer, Heclo, and Adams, 1975:209). In any one month, only 10 to 20 percent of welfare mothers work (Wilensky, 1975b:8).

A basic problem with job-training programs—in addition to the fact that they are not very effective in the absence of a brisk labor market and a strong employment service (Wilensky, 1975b:7)—is that women's needs for skill training have been given short shrift. Fewer than 44 of the 252 studies of U.S. job-training programs provided any data on minorities or women (Perry, 1975). The *Dictionary of Occupational Titles* rates women's jobs at such low skill levels that it is hard for training programs to qualify for federal funds (Sexton, 1977:39); for example, kindergarten teaching is rated as having almost no skills in dealing with ideas, people, or things (Babcock et al., 1975:204). An early review of the impact of the Comprehensive Employment and Training Act of 1973 said almost nothing about women in CETA programs, although 42 percent of the participants were women (Sexton, 1977:55).

WHY BACKLASH?

Why do public assistance clients make taxpayers so nervous? First, the general public in both the U.S. and Western Europe dislikes supporting able-bodied persons. Second, many public assistance recipients are already targets of race or ethnic bias. Third, the men who run things— such men have never tended children full time—apparently do not define child care as "work." Fourth, taxpayers dislike subsidizing "immoral" women and their "boyfriends"; even the ILO in a number of its conventions specifically allows for the suspension of social insurance and cash benefits to a widow living in immoral circumstances (Gelber, 1975:433).

Middle-mass taxpayers have political clout because they are involved in organizational networks. Public assistance strata have little cohesive force vis-à-vis trade unions and occupational associations (Lisein-Norman, 1974:531), yet their presence in a society implicitly threatens possible governmental disruption. Governments which would avoid both middle-mass backlash or disruption by the unemployed must devise means to improve matters without arousing mass resistance. Can this be done?

A New Perspective on Public Assistance

Recently both the U.S. and Western Europe have encountered a mix of problems—unemployment, inflation, foreign trade imbalance—that have the unpleasant feature of politically acceptable remedies for one making the others worse. These conditions create political instability because their solutions are not apparent.

The size of the public assistance population depends on unemployment levels that, in turn, are linked to price stability. An ideal public assistance program would provide universal benefits at reasonable levels, would preserve work incentives, and would be sufficiently inexpensive that the public would tolerate it. The reason that the U.S. Congress has not found such a plan is that, given current institutional patterns, no such plan can be devised. These objectives are mutually inconsistent (Aaron, 1975a:187). Programs that combine full employment and price stability cannot avoid measures to redistribute income. For example,

Lekachman's (1975) program includes guaranteed employment, income maintenance for the nonemployed, wage and price controls, redistribution of the tax burden, and a long-range shift in social investment if private investment should be depressed by altered profit expectations. Whether such a program is feasible in the U.S. or in many Western European countries is another question.

Social science research on the "welfare mess" has been limited because each discipline has chosen problems suited for its methods rather than problems that require a multidisciplinary approach. An almost unresearched area, bounded by economics, sociology, and political science, is the politics of social welfare. Since economists typically omit institutional factors, they have trouble applying their theories to problems in the public sector (Musgrave, 1959:4). Sociologists have been slow to develop policy suggestions that make legislative sense. For example, the tax structure, a central factor in welfare backlash, marvelously mirrors the distribution of socioeconomic power, yet social scientists rarely try to relate it to political problems—to say nothing of ignoring its political impact in their introductory tests. The general public understands the tax structure very poorly (Pechman, 1971), increasing the probability that tax issues can be used for demogogic purposes.

Perhaps the worldwide scope of current troubles will induce us to go beyond our own disciplines in our research. There are grounds for optimism. Some sociologists now work on models that use aggregate data for large-scale problems (Land, 1975), while economists are becoming more aware of politics—the first public finance text to consider politics appeared a few years ago (Buchanan, 1970). The research of Watts and Wilensky shows that social scientists can simultaneously address theoretically and substantively important problems.

What can social scientists do? My suggestions raise more questions than answers. We need to incorporate three interrelated ideas in our research. First, the basic public assistance problem is a worldwide system of economic inequality that makes the position of workers migrating from less to more industrialized areas a continuing political irritant. The migration of foreign workers in Europe is akin to the migration of southern blacks, Mexican Americans, and Puerto Ricans within the U.S. They cannot be stopped. These migrations occur just when advanced industrial nations are undergoing an energy crisis that exacerbates the difficulties of controlling inflation, maintaining full employment, and balancing foreign payments. National social security programs should recognize migration as a permanent feature of economic life and should develop systems that grant benefits on an international basis.

Second, economic dependency for women is outdated. Women are in the labor market to stay. The divorce rate continues to rise. Yet the assumption that only men should be defined as primary earners still undergirds most public assistance and job-training programs in the U.S. and Western Europe. This leads to blaming family "pathology" for the increase in public assistance, rather than women's low wages and inadequate job training. For example, Levitan and Taggart (1976:57) assert that the "accelerated deterioration" of U.S. family structure is of deep concern because the expansion of welfare rolls is caused by people with marital problems. Some federal officials also hold this view. On 14 March 1977 Arnold Packer, assistant secretary of labor for policy evaluation and research, included these statements in a memo to Secretary of Labor Ray Marshall:

> One can think of the traditional American family structure with two parents and children in which the family head goes to work and makes enough of a living to keep the family together. The major thrust of the program ought to be to support this as the predominant situation.[10] ... The incentives should be arranged so that individuals prefer the two-parent arrangement (Tenenbaum, 1977:1-2).

Such thinking fails to confront the central issue for ADC women: how to get decent work and care for their children (Wellisch, 1977:7).

Third, it is risky to tolerate persistently high unemployment rates because they inevitably imply higher public assistance rates. The more unemployment, the larger the proportion of able-bodied adults who must live on transfer incomes derived from general taxation. In turn, this increases the probability that "hard-working taxpayers" will become restive at supporting "welfare bums." Middle-mass confrontation with an underclass threatens governmental stability. The problem is how to increase the employment of the old, of women, of foreign workers, migrant workers, and the urban "underclass" while maintaining international price stability. The solution will require the collective effort of those social scientists whose research transcends the boundaries of their own discipline.

---

[10]Packer's definition of the predominant family type is wrong. Families with employed father, nonemployed mother, and two children constitute 7 percent of U.S. husband-wife families; such families with any number of children comprise about 20 percent of U.S. families (computed from Johnson and Hayge, 1977).

10

Why, and How Well, Do We Analyze Inequality?

Harold W. Watts

As an economist who has a long-standing interest in income inequality and redistributional policies, I welcome this chance to discuss some of the problems that I have encountered in my own approach to these issues. I begin, however, with a digression that challenges the notion that policies and programs are deliberately chosen to have a specific effect on inequality. If they are not, our analyses take on the character of studying unintended consequences. But whether or not inequality is a primary objective of policy, I share the idea that it is important for the general health and welfare of a society and that policies *do* affect it.

The problems that I want to discuss have mainly to do with the lack of both concepts and measurements equal to the task of analyzing inequality and the impact of a wide range of policies on that inequality. Until we have consistent measurement of the phenomena, it is impossible to go very far with our efforts to understand how policies are chosen or how well they work.

Does Anyone Really Want to Reduce Income Inequality?

It is of some interest and significance that redistribution, or direct reduction of income inequality, is nowhere a salient issue in the area of social welfare policy. Taking from the "rich" and giving to the "poor," despite the continuing popularity of the Robin Hood legend, has never developed a widespread and sustained political appeal. Programs and policies that accomplish redistribution have flourished in the modern welfare state, but they do the job almost by stealth and indirection and do not acknowledge specific distributional goals. There are episodes, to be sure, when a "soak-the-rich" campaign may gain some general support, but the narrow definition of the group defined as "rich" yields small revenues. Even these gains erode rapidly as "confiscatory" rates are evaded through loopholes of various kinds, often before the passion has gone out of the effort.

The United States and some other countries have recently witnessed a spasm of concern for the poor, during which some limited gains were made. But, at least in the U.S., the main motive force came from policies and events that were not overtly redistributive. Moreover, the problem of poverty was defined in such a way, by reference to *absolute* requirements for nutritional adequacy (on a temporary basis), that it could eventually be eliminated without any change in inequality. Judged by relative standards, the official poverty thresholds have steadily drifted downward in relation to median income. Judged by surveys of what people feel is necessary to "just get along," the official thresholds have moved from skimpy about half the distance to ridiculous in the thirteen years since they were set as standards.

But in between episodes that strike, ineffectively, at the two extremes of the distribution, no broad-based concern about income inequality is evident. Income security or, even better, "social" security receives dependable, perennial attention. The ordinary hazards of old age, death, sickness, disability, and unemployment are all very important causes of low or interrupted income. Interest in securing against losses of purchasing power due to such events is widespread at all levels of earning, and political support for maintaining or expanding such coverage has been correspondingly strong. There is no question that these programs redistribute income, at least when conventionally analyzed on an ex post basis, and they make inequality less extreme by usual measures. But it is possible to explain their vitality in a society that is, finally, quite indifferent to income inequality per se.

As Senator Moynihan used to point out, the U.S. stands almost alone among developed western countries in not having a child or family allowance system. Such systems redistribute income from childless to childed households, and also from the more wealthy to the poor. They have also enjoyed dependable political support, perhaps because they were aimed at fertility objectives at least as much as at familial hardship. It is noteworthy that these allowance systems do not usually have income-tested benefits and are tax exempt. These and other child-oriented programs including public education can also be related to the goal of equal opportunity, which is at the very least complexly related to income inequality. Again, there is no need to impute a general interest in greater income equality in order to understand a major redistributive policy.

Income taxation is another major policy related to redistribution, and is perhaps the only one where income inequality gets anywhere close to the surface as an element in the debate. It is possible for progressive taxation to reduce the dispersion of aftertax income relative to pretax income. But the record in terms of accomplishment is not very impressive, at least in the U.S. A major study showed remarkably constant *effective* tax rates as distinct from the *nominal* rates displayed in the tax regulations (Pechman and Okner, 1974). While inequality may be mentioned as the rate schedules are being negotiated, it appears that the resulting progressivity is more symbolic than real.

Equality of opportunity enjoys a level of support that far exceeds "equality of result," which is what we are talking about here. It is no accident that the honor guard of the war on poverty was called the Office of Economic Opportunity, and that most of the initiatives were directed toward opportunities, not toward outcomes in the income dimension. Since we don't have equal opportunities, it speculative and gratuitous to suppose that the consequent distribution of incomes would be satisfactory on ethical, aesthetic, or political grounds. But it is worth remembering that causation also proceeds from current income "results" to the opportunities for future earnings of the generations now growing up. Universal and compensatory education; nondiscriminatory labor, housing, and credit markets; and affirmative action are unlikely, in the end, to be able to offset all the consequences of impoverished home environments. Thus there may be degrees of income inequality that are incompatible with reasonable achievement of equality of opportunity.

In short, there is little evidence that reduction of income inequality is a distinct and important goal of social policy. Certainly there is no well-defined notion of how much inequality is too much, and the infrequent surges of envy or guilt are the only signs that such limits exist. While I regard inequality a very critical social phenomenon and a policy issue much to my own taste, it often seems that most people aren't listening.

What Do We Mean by Income Inequality?

There are a number of very important issues involved in arriving at a specific definition of "income inequality." While there are some conventional answers, heavily influenced by the availability of statistics, they are not, on balance, very satisfactory. The issues or questions have to do with what is counted as income, what aggregation of persons into units is appropriate, and over what period of time income should be measured. What we have in the United States is usually limited to "census money income," which includes earnings before tax and other cash receipts such as income from property or benefits from public transfer programs. This income is measured for a single year, and is usually tabulated separately for individuals and for families of more than one person. Now consider how alternative specifications might change the indications about inequality, and whether the measures we have are likely to be misleading. This is particularly relevant for making cross-national comparisons, whether in terms of absolute levels of inequality or in terms of changes in inequality.

The money income concept has at least two major drawbacks. First of all, the effect of taxes is not shown, and consequently any effect of progressive taxation in reducing dispersion at the top end fails to be shown. If one is interested in the command over market goods and services as an indicator of welfare, then a disposable income concept would be much more appropriate. Second, the money income concept leaves out in-kind benefits which are, to greater or lesser extent, close substitutes for unconstrained money income. Food stamps, or more properly the "bonus value" of them, are not counted as money income, yet for most families that use them the main effect is to release dollars for other purposes. An appreciable amount of public subsidy is also embodied in housing programs (and in tax law provisions), and the money income concept does not reflect this means of augmenting family income. Some in-kind benefits are received by the relatively well-to-do in the form of expense-account living and other consumptionlike perquisites. These are not direct public programs, but the tax laws have a great deal to do with their prevalence.

If there were a stable and consistent pattern of either taxes or in-kind benefit structures, it might be reasonable to use a money income measure of inequality for comparisons over time or across countries. But these policies are frequently changed and vary widely, at least in detail, from country to country. Whenever there are large differences or changes in the amount of the ordinary expenses of daily life for which families are expected to pay out of their disposable income, inequality of money income may be very misleading. Depending on whether or how much the in-kind benefits are conditioned by income, the distortion can go in either direction.

There is also an issue concerning whether in-kind benefits, such as medical services or education, should be included at cost (or some fair market price) as an addition to income. Here the question is how much the free or subsidized services replace expenditures that would otherwise be made voluntarily. It is a matter of how much the consumer's "sovereignty" is being violated either by the quantity or quality of the in-kind benefits. Clearly free medical care for families that previously purchased none does not reduce *income* inequality because it does not release previously committed funds. This is not to say that such policies do not affect a more broadly defined sort of inequality. In this connection, it should not be assumed that only the public medical care programs involve coercion, since most of the "private" health insurance plans are partly paid by the employer and cannot be converted fully to cash by employees who do not want to participate.

Certainly a substantial amount of equalization is shown if one adds major in-kind transfers (food stamps, housing assistance, child nutrition, Medicare, and Medicaid) to the money income figures. The Congressional Budget Office has recently produced estimates showing that these programs, combined with taxes in the form of state and federal income taxes and Social Security contributions, change the quintile shares quite substantially. The share of the bottom 20 percent of households is increased from 4.5 percent to 7.2 percent, while the share at the top falls from 45.6 percent to 41.3 percent (Congressional Budget Office, 1977). The effect on the Gini measure is comparable to, though smaller than, the effect of the cash transfer programs. Noncash transfers have grown rapidly over the last ten years, but the conventional statistics do not reflect their impact.

Additional puzzles are provided by the choice of unit for counting and the normalization used for ranking the units by income. There would be no problem if everyone were in a family and each family were of the same size and composition. Alternative treatments are mainly attempts to approximate that situation from data on the real, and much more disorderly, world. The most common tabulations segregate individuals from families containing two or more persons. This is helpful, at least, because many of the individuals are elderly or very young. The families that remain are somewhat more homogeneous, although they still vary widely in size, age composition, and stage in the life cycle.

It is simple, but rarely done, to rank families by per capita income, and to form quintiles based on fraction of the relevant population, rather than on fractions of the total number of families. Here, again, there is the objection that economies of scale are ignored (while in the usual tables they are assumed to be so complete that ten can live as cheaply as two!). Compromises are possible that utilize adult-equivalent scales for children or other dependents. Sometimes the scales built into the poverty thresholds are used to "normalize" income for diverse family types, and this device could be used for ranking families in an analysis of inequality.

The best procedure depends, of course, on what you are trying to find out. For market research of some kinds, the family distributions produced by the Census Bureau might be appropriate. For any assessment of inequality that presumes a relation to individual well-being, some sort of normalization is required. The per capita measure is too crude, but almost any improvement on that would be better than the one we customarily use.

Household units have been getting smaller, probably because privacy or "separateness" is an income-elastic phenomenon. Lower fertility rates play a role here, too, and public tax and transfer policies tend to reinforce the "small nest" pattern. Unless the measure of inequality is somehow adjusted to take this factor into account, it is easy for spurious indications of increased inequality to show up as families "unpack" themselves into separate units. Private transfers, both in cash and in kind, are important in some cases of "unpacked" households, and these are not well reflected in the inequality measures.

Finally, there is a question of the time interval for measuring income. Income for a one-year period is the standard measure; again, this may be as much a matter of availability as of deliberate choice. It is frequently suggested that a longer period would be more appropriate, and there are now some limited sources of longitudinal data that make it feasible to examine, say, five-year averages. A difficulty arises, however, if the composition of the family unit is not constant—one simply doesn't find a large number of families that remain the same over a five-year period. Some sort of normalization has to be used to adjust for changes in size, and additional rules are required to determine when a family simply ceases to exist.

An extreme form of long-period measure would be a lifetime income. This would have to be specified as a distribution of persons rather than families. Some rule of allocation would be required to define the income of children in families, not to mention other earning and nonearning members of the family. This sort of income measure would only be useful for evaluating inequality within birth cohorts, or perhaps for cohorts that entered the labor market at the same time.

For purposes of evaluating the performance of a society in achieving social justice, I find a variant of the lifetime income more appealing. My choice, unconstrained by measurement feasibility, would be for a distribution of permanent income, as defined by Friedman, for specific age groups (Friedman, 1957). I would be particularly interested in the distribution for "new" adults of around twenty to twenty-five. The permanent income concept provides a smoothed income flow that is equivalent in present value to the more irregular flow expected by a person. Depending on the rate of discount applied to the future income stream, the measure may be more or less sensitive to income components in the distant future. For present purposes I would opt for a relatively low discount rate, so that incomes well into the future would receive substantial weight. I would also specify a uniform number of hours worked per year (or some other indicator of effort), in order to abstract from inequalities that derive from voluntary choices along the ant-grasshopper scale of industriousness as well as from involuntary unemployment. This approach emphasizes inequalities of human wealth, although it includes existing holdings of nonhuman wealth as well as expected future bequests of or receipts of public transfers. Using this income measure, it might be reasonable to set goals specifying the largest acceptable dispersion, with the further proviso that none of the dispersion should be the result of mean differences between racial, sex, or ethnic groups.

Longitudinal data, of the sort gathered by the Income Dynamics study or the National Longitudinal survey, provide a basis for examining more long-term measures of income and inequality. Some work has been carried out, and it has confirmed that short-run variations add substantially to the inequality measures based on annual income. So far relatively little has been done toward estimating the effect of public policies on equality measured for longer periods.

Altogether there are plenty of reasons for suspecting that we are not perfectly clear on what we mean by "inequality," and even more for doubts about the information that comes from typical statistical tabulations. There is room for a great deal of conceptual work to sharpen the distributional questions we ask and for exploratory empirical work to find ways of getting better answers to these questions.

Life Cycle Influences on Inequality and Public Policy

The inequality of *primary income*, meaning by that term money income received by household units prior to any modification by public policy, is trivially "explained" by a few elementary considerations. Many persons have no primary income, i.e., they are dependents. These are concentrated at the beginning and end of the life cycle, but some adults are disabled or incapacitated as well and hence fall into the dependent category. Able-bodied adults, on the other hand, have unequal primary income both because of unequal endowments of human or nonhuman wealth and because of different outcomes in the use of that wealth—more specifically, how much they choose or manage to engage that wealth in money-earning activities. Some, including the traditional housewife, employ their efforts in nonmarket activities, and of course there are variations in the amount of effort devoted to productive activities of any kind.

In the absence of any sort of public action to redistribute income, dependent persons must necessarily rely on private transfers, usually by being part of an income-pooling household or spending unit. This process remains important even when public policies do redistribute income. It is clear that many of those policies are directed toward supplementing the private transfers to dependents. What is not so clear is the extent to which they have substituted for private transfers instead of augmenting them. But we do find that policies that make income transfers to the aged and disabled and to children deprived of a "breadwinner" are among the first to be considered and adopted in developed countries. It is impossible to say whether these policies were motivated more by a desire to relieve the hardship and deprivation of those who "lost out" in the private transfer process, or more by the inequality of burden placed on the active and productive adults. In any case these sorts of policy are very prevalent, seem to be politically durable, and accomplish substantial reduction of inequality.

Child or family allowances are also common in developed countries. Where cash benefits are not provided there are, as in the United States, tax provisions that work in the direction of equalizing the burdens on households with numerous children. The redistribution involved is primarily from childless household units to those with children and, depending on the country, may be designed to yield greater transfers to those who have higher incomes. Various explicit and implicit motives can be cited for such payments, but reduction of inequality or poverty is not usually one of them. Regardless of the reason for implementing child allowances, they do have the effect of reducing inequality of per capita or per adult-equivalent money income. Policies of this kind have also maintained a high degree of public support, but there may be significance in the fact that the benefits have not generally kept pace with inflation in the last decade.

The public attention to the aged and to children can be seen as a partial collectivization of the basic societal task of supporting dependent members. To the extent that all persons figure to pass through dependent stages in their life cycle, they can regard the taxation that is entailed as a repayment of costs of childhood and as prepayment of support during old age. Viewed in this manner, one wishes for lifetime income data and an assessment of the equalization produced by public policies on lifetime income. Without such data it is not obvious whether or how much equalization is produced.

Turning to inequality in the primary income received by nondependents, consider first the unequal endowments of nonhuman wealth. There are policies that aim at reducing large intergenerational bequests in most countries. While there is not, to my knowledge, very much evidence or analysis related to the effect of such policies, it seems likely that they make some contribution to the reduction of income inequality based on inherited wealth in the form of real or financial assets. The equalization is, of course, accomplished by reducing a few very large endowments and encouraging a larger number of smaller ones. There is no corresponding policy for distributing wealth, per se, to those who have none.

The endowment of human wealth is another, and perhaps the most important, source of inequality. At the same time it is probably the least well understood. The various attributes and capacities that can command income in modern societies are not at all well sorted out, nor are the ways that persons acquire them. The nature-nurture controversy illustrates many deficiencies in the way we ask questions about human endowments as well as the scarcity of evidence available for answering them. But it seems clear that policies have been based on a presumption that a great deal of human wealth is formed in childhood. Public universal education, however it works out in practice, has been urged on the basis of a notion that schooling can provide a "floor" on human wealth for all who are exposed to it. It is also possible to view cash transfers to families with children as a means of influencing the formation of human wealth and, depending on how they are structured, could yield some equalization of endowments within the eventual generation of adults. But these possible consequences are long-run at best and largely unevaluated as major influences in income inequality (this does not deny that strong beliefs can be found about their efficacy).

More direct policies that offset inequalities in human wealth are relatively scarce. In part this is due to the difficulty of distinguishing low income due to low wealth from that due to low effort, and there is a disinclination to "reward" the latter. Unemployment insurance was a relatively late entrant in the social insurance area, and is usually wage related in an attempt to reduce the "moral hazard." While unemployment benefits show substantial reduction of income inequality when measured over short periods, it seems likely that any impact on long-period measures is an unintended or unavoidable minimum.

It should be noted that the level of unemployment, inflation, and other dimensions of performance of the general economy have important impacts on income inequality. Low rates of unemployment are much more effective in reducing inequality than are the social insurance benefits aimed at diluting the worst effects of slack labor demand. The effects of inflation are more complicated, and depend upon the composition of the price changes as well as on the institutional framework. In general the holders of fixed-money claims lose to those who owe fixed-money obligations, and there is a consequent tendency for the wealthy/old to lose purchasing power to younger groups who have access to credit. This can be offset by "indexing" various contracts or benefits, and as a consequence it is hard to say what happens to overall inequality.

Unqualified guarantees of income or universal demogrants provide mechanisms that could offset inequalities in endowments, but these have, so far, not achieved much popularity, and concerns about incentive effects are the most prominent reason for this. Usually some form of work requirement is used as a qualification for benefits and there are attempts to assure that there is a substantial gain from working. But

TABLE 1. **Differences in Social Benefits, by Country**

Country	Old-age Benefits	Child Benefits	Total Social Expenditure Benefits
West Germany	100	19	51
France	80	30	39
United Kingdom	65	10	27
Denmark	92	33	48

From Eurostat, 1974.

there are inevitable conflicts among the goals of providing an adequate income floor, financial incentives to earn, and concentrating the benefits to the very poorest. This conflict has usually been resolved by keeping the floor well below a reasonable "living level" and by using nonfinancial coercion to discourage "slackers."

There is little evidence that shirking is a quantitatively important component of present expenditures, or that it is likely to become so under reasonable programs that preserve substantial possibilities for self-help. Nevertheless, there is a general view that policies should not reinforce *any* laziness, and this has justified costly measures to detect and prevent such abuse.

There are substantial differences among countries in the relative emphasis placed on policies to help equalize the support of dependents. A tabulation for 1972 for European Community countries found the differences noted in Table 1 in social benefits (not all of which are in cash) among four countries. The index used here takes the West German old-age benefits (per person over sixty) as the base. Clearly the benefits for the aged are substantially higher per person than the child-related social benefits (per person under fifteen), but the ratio varies from less than 3:1 to more than 6:1. The last column shows the same index calculated for total social expenditures (which do not include education) on a per capita basis. It appears that there is less variation in the benefits for the aged than there is for either total social expenditures or benefits for children.

There is no directly comparable calculation for the United States, but as a guess, we should stand close to the top on old-age benefits and well below the bottom on benefits for children.

STRUCTURAL DIFFERENCES IN PROGRAMS AFFECTING INCOME INEQUALITY

If one looks at aggregated social expenditure accounts one can find differences among countries in other elements of structure. An important characteristic is the division of benefits among cash payments, reimbursement of claimed expenditures, and direct provision of goods and services. Denmark pays about 45 percent of its benefits in kind, only 2 percent as reimbursed costs, and the rest in cash. France pays 72 percent in cash and uses reimbursement for most of the rest. Germany and England pay cash benefits for 76 and 70 percent, respectively, and make in-kind transfers for most of the rest. The United States pays about two-thirds of its social welfare benefits in cash, and the share has been shrinking since the introduction of Medicare, Medicaid, and food stamps (Eurostat, 1974).

Because any equalization effects of in-kind benefits are not reflected in distribution of money income, the share represented by in-kind benefits may lead to differences in income equality that are more apparent than real. There is not any easy generalization about trends favoring increased or decreased use of in-kind benefits among the countries examined. The administration's welfare reform proposes to "cash out" food stamps, which are not exactly in-kind benefits anyway, but was unwilling to do the same for the in-kind housing benefits.

The source of funds for social benefits also varies strongly among countries. France and West Germany rely heavily on employer taxes, and finance less than a fourth of the costs out of general tax revenues. Denmark, on the other hand, charges 81 percent to general revenue, and the United Kingdom is intermediate with 40 percent (Eurostat, 1974). Both employee and employer taxes on earnings are likely to be flat-rate taxes with ceilings that are somewhat regressive in impact. (I assume that employer taxes are shifted to the employee.) General revenue, on the other hand, is usually levied by a progressive tax, even allowing for the loopholes that dilute the nominally progressive structures.

If only the distribution of social benefits is considered, as the use of money income implies, the differential impact of the financing system is obscured. Hence the Danish system might have a relatively small measured effect on inequality if only the cash benefits are considered, but a more substantial effect when the progressive effects of general revenue finance are considered. France, which gets more than 80 percent of the cost of its social benefits from flat earnings taxes, has to achieve most of its equalization via the benefit structure.

BETTER WAYS OF MEASURING IMPACT ON INEQUALITY

A major problem in comparing policies that reduce inequality lies in the wide variety of program combinations that one finds, and the absence of descriptive measures that are sufficiently general to abstract from what may be unimportant differences. The argument developed here suggests that inequality is sufficiently complex to justify recognition of several aspects of redistribution policies.

To begin with, the treatment of dependent members of society should be considered separately, and probably subdivided into three categories: children, aged/retired, and other adult dependents. For these groups it would be very useful to have comprehensive measures of the net differential in disposable income for a household that contains such a person relative to one that does not. The differential could be made up of direct cash transfers, tax reliefs of various kinds, or subsidies that directly substitute for money income, such as the food stamp bonus. The average differentials of this kind would be a helpful overall index of the treatment of the different categories of dependents. More detail on the relation of those differentials to household size, composition, and primary income level would provide a compact means of comparing the overall impact of public programs or policies on the inequality deriving from the presence of dependent persons who, by definition, have no primary income.

Nations may differ, as we have seen, in the relative generosity toward children and the aged. Their policies may be more or less progressive according to how the income of the household is related to the size of comprehensive dependent benefit levels. The degree to which economies of scale are reflected in benefits is another important parameter that bears on choices of household formation and subdivision. Clearly it is possible for benefit structures to facilitate separate quarters for some dependents and, as pointed out earlier, this may produce an apparent increase in inequality even though all parties regard the change as desirable.

For the nondependent adults a separate description is needed to focus more directly on the relation between primary income, which is simply earnings for most people, and final or disposable income available for spending by the household. Here it is the tax system that plays a paramount role, both because most countries avoid major transfers to able-bodied adults, and because revenues for the benefits to dependents have to be extracted from the currently active and productive part of the population. Unemployment benefits and, in most countries, health and medical benefits account for most of the social expenditure directed at this group.

Again it is possible to combine the impacts of benefits and taxes into a comprehensive measure of disposable income, from which all household benefits occasioned by dependent members should be deducted. Necessary costs of earning income, most prominently child-care expenses, should also be deducted, and the resulting net amount could be related to primary income of the household. This would produce a schedule

Figure 1. Policy Effects on Disposable Income

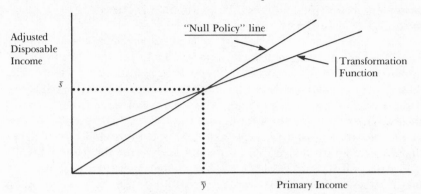

that indicates how the particular set of policies yields a transformation between primary income and final income. The diagram indicates such a transformation function set against a "null policy" reference that would tax all primary income received by adults at a flat rate sufficient to yield the same aggregate of adjusted disposable income. By definition this line passes through the point with coordinates equal to the means of primary and disposable income. A transformation function that is flatter than the reference line indicates some progressive redistribution. The slope of the transformation curve indicates the marginal gain in disposable income from an added unit of primary income; the complement of the slope might be called a comprehensive marginal tax or impact rate.

It is also possible, and worthwhile, to consider how such transformations operate for different kinds of household. Provisionally, it would be interesting to consider single-person households, childless couples, couples with children, and one-parent households as separate cases. Where the income tax is based on individual incomes, and there is an increasing tendency to do this, it will often make a substantial difference whether the income of a couple has been earned by both or by only one of them.

Unfortunately, the data required for such a thorough analysis are not readily available for most countries. Approximations to transformation curves for the United States and the United Kingdom have been estimated, and the OECD has estimated some useful parts of the schedule, namely, the impact in the vicinity of the average industrial production worker's earnings. At average earnings a production worker with a wife and two children gets disposable income ranging from 67 percent of gross nominal earnings in Denmark to 101 percent in France. In the United States the ratio is 83 percent, in the United Kingdom 79 percent, and in West Germany 76 percent. These differences are exaggerated, however, by not allowing for the payroll taxes paid by employers. Making a rough allowance for these reduces the figure to 75 percent in France and places the United States at the extreme with 78 percent (OECD, 1975).

The average tax rates on gross earnings (including employer taxes) appear to range from 33 percent in Denmark to 22 percent in the United States for average production workers with four-person families. The marginal rates are generally higher than the average rates, and range from around 55–60 percent in Denmark to around 30 percent in the United States; the other three countries discussed cluster around 36 percent, again after adjustment for employer payroll taxes. It is interesting that in both Denmark and the United Kingdom the marginal tax rate is lower if the added income is earned by the wife. In France and Germany the rate is higher, and in the United States there is almost no difference (OECD, 1974, 1977).

A transformation function for a couple and two children in the United Kingdom (1975) shows an interesting pattern. Disposable income reaches a local peak of £25/week of earnings that is not surpassed until earnings exceed £39/week. These earning rates are low—around half of the average industrial earnings—but they do illustrate how benefits and taxes can combine to produce an actual penalty for additional earnings. The transformation does not become convex, as would be the case for increasing marginal rates until well beyond median earning rates (Central Statistical Office, 1975).

Estimates of the effects of public programs on disposable income in the United States can be derived from figures prepared by the Congressional Budget Office. This work combines the effect of the social insurance programs, welfare programs, in-kind benefits (except education), and the taxes levied on income. The patterns showed a marked nonconvexity, indicating declining marginal tax rates for higher-income groups. Comparisons between units with and without children confirmed a general pattern of neglect of children in United States policies and a relatively generous treatment of the aged, particularly at high levels of income.

In terms of a static analysis, which simply looks at distribution of income with and without the modifications introduced by public policy, there is a clear and strong equalizing effect. Groups that are heavily dependent on public income subsidies, supplements, and so on, appear, by definition, much worse off, if one simply subtracts those benefits. But such statistical or mental exercises do not tell you what the world would look like in the absence of the programs. There certainly is some replacement of private transfers. Programs alter the incentive structures within which households are formed and reformed. Work and saving incentives are changed as well, sometimes providing absolute penalties for increased earnings. These are the difficult questions about policies to reduce inequality, and they cannot be answered without an understanding of the behaviors involved.

But static descriptions of the combined impact of such programs on dependents and on productive adults can be structured in such a way that the consequences of incremental changes in structure can be readily discerned, and questions about the relevant behaviors can be more sharply focused. The measures of impact outlined above are at least a beginning framework within which cross-national and intertemporal analysis of inequality can be carried out.

Concluding Remarks

Despite the fact that inequality seems to have limited and sporadic appeal as a political issue, and without general agreement on exactly what "inequality" means, there is a persistent belief that inequality is a critical determinant of the quality of life in a society. Moreover, there are, with various rationales, a wide range of public policies that modify the distribution of income and may have long-run effects on income inequality. But to analyze and compare those policies it seems essential to secure more sensitive and standardized measures of what the existing programs are doing and how they do it.

11

Changing Civil Rights Through Law: Can It Be Done?

Jerome H. Skolnick

IN HIS RECENT BOOK ON SLAVERY, Eugene Genovese opens his chapter on "The Hegemonic Function of the Law" with a nod to both Mao Tse-Tung and Max Weber (Genovese, 1972:25–49). Both of them, he points out, recognized two facts about the relation between law and power. First, the conquest of state power is the object of all serious political struggle. Second, that once achieved, state power employs law to discipline and legitimize "the command of the gun." Law is thus a civilizing and a coercive instrument. It coerces by ultimately threatening violence, and civilizes both by minimizing the necessity for violence and by disguising that state power does in fact rest on force.

Nowhere is the relation between civilization and coercion more evident than in the area of so-called "civil rights." The real question has always been not whether civil rights can be achieved through law, but: (1) whether those who control state power will define through law a given political, economic, or social activity as a civil right, so that the power of the state can be employed to enforce the right; and (2) whether, if law defines an activity or thing of value as a civil right, prevailing institutional arrangements will permit that right to be exercised.

Thus the law does not necessarily either advance or retard civil rights. Whether it does or not depends upon the prevailing realities of dominance in the history of class relations, in this country importantly defined by race. Those out of power, seeking change toward equality, may be hindered by those holding it. But even when those who genuinely seek change gain formal governmental power, established institutional patterns may still impede the law's capacity to influence social equality. This paper in effect adapts a labeling-theory perspective to the area of law and civil rights and argues that, like deviance, whether a line of conduct will be regarded as a "civil right" depends on factors other than the quality of the conduct. Nowhere is this more evident than in the question of racial intermarriage, which during a span of less than twenty years was redefined from an impermissibly deviant act to a civil right.

Defining Civil Rights: "Miscegenation"

In what seems like ancient history, but was as recent as 1948, the state of California declared void all marriages of white persons with Negroes, Mongolians, members of the Malay race, or Mulattoes, a classification scheme that would today seem quaint, were it not so individious.

The county clerk of Los Angeles defended the California law on grounds that Negroes were physically and intellectually inferior to whites, and justified the prohibition of miscegenation on grounds similar to those set forth in the frequently cited 1869 Georgia case, *Scott* v. *State.* "The amalgamation of the races," the Georgian court intoned, "is not only unnatural, but is always productive of deplorable results. Our daily observation shows us, that the offspring of these unnatural connections are generally sickly and effeminate, and that they are inferior in physical development and strength, to the full blood of either race" (*Scott* v. *State,* 1869:324).

Writing for the majority in 1948, Justice Traynor of the California Supreme Court contrasted the opinions of modern experts with the older view. The progeny of such marriages, it was now believed, are not inferior to both parents. Furthermore, he pointed out that lots of people—especially Californians—belong to more than one race, and that the California law was therefore vague and uncertain. Accordingly, he concluded, it violated the equal protection clause of the U.S. Constitution "by impairing the right to marry on the basis of race alone and by arbitrarily and unreasonably discriminating against certain racial groups" (*Perez* v. *Sharp,* 1948:711).

Although freedom to marry a partner of one's own choosing regardless of race might seem today to be a fundamental civil right, there is no question that an overwhelming majority of the United States legislatures historically did not see it that way at all. A total of thirty-nine states passed statutes barring marriages between individuals of different racial groups. Thirteen states with miscegenation statutes were located in the North. In fifteen southern and border states, as late as the 1960s, a miscegenous marriage constituted a felony (Harper and Skolnick, 1962:98).

Lest anyone think courts routinely protect civil rights, until 1948, in the California case, courts throughout the country played an important role in perpetuating these bigoted marriage acts, finding them to be consistent with the equal protection and privileges and immunity clauses of the Fourteenth Amendment, as well as with the impairment of contracts clause of Article I, paragraph 10 of the U.S. Constitution.

Thus courts for years consistently concluded that the marriage contract is to be free from federal interference, and that the civil rights act of 1866 did not bind the states in the standards they set for marriage. The typical rationale was expressed by the North Carolina court in 1869 as follows: "But neither the Civil Rights Bill, nor our State Constitution was intended to enforce social equality but only civil and political rights" (*State* v. *Hairston,* 1869:451).

It took nearly one hundred years and considerable social protest, sometimes violent, sometimes not, to effect a basic change in race relations, a change reflected in the legal attitude toward civil rights. Thus not until 1967 did the chief justice of the U.S. Supreme Court write: "Marriage is one of the basic civil rights of man, fundamental to our very existance and survival . . ." (*Loving* v. *Virginia,* 1967:1). Of course, for more than one hundred years courts of law had not understood what was now so clear.

The Impact of Redefinition

By the time this decision came about, it was already a sociological anachronism in a number of respects, stemming in large part from the limitations of legal rules in effecting social goals. The U.S. Supreme Court could outlaw racial segregation in the schools, but it could not enforce residential integration. It could define racial intermarriage as a civil right, but it could not make it socially acceptable. The Congress was scarcely more effective. The civil rights act of 1964 was a sweeping legislative landmark. It addressed the right: to vote (Title I); to use places of public accommodation (Title II); to use public facilities (Title III); to a desegregated public education (Title IV). It also dealt with the powers of the Civil Rights Commission (Title V), nondiscrimination in federal employment (Title VI), and, most significantly, employment opportunity (Title VII).

Nevertheless, racism did not disappear upon passage of the civil rights act. The capacity of the law to affect civil rights, that is, to represent the actuality of a recognition of changing class relations, is also limited by history and associated institutional lag. When institutions have for many years developed a vested interest in patterns of racism, they are not—in the interests of stability—going to bend easily to the decisions of courts. If I may quote from my report to the National Commission on the Causes and Prevention of Violence, discussing the effects of the passage of federal civil rights legislation:

> The deepest or most entrenched meaning of racism began to emerge, and it made considerable sociological as well as historic sense: A society that has been built around racism will lack the capacity, the flexibility, the institutions to combat it when the will to change belatedly appears. The major American institutions had developed standards, procedures, and rigidities which served to inhibit the Negro's drive for equality. It was as if a cruel joke had been played; the most liberally enshrined features of democracy served to block the aspirations to equality—local rule, trade unionism, referendums, the jury system, the neighborhood school. And to complete the irony, perhaps, the most elitist aspect of the constitutional system—the Supreme Court—was for a time the cutting edge of the established quest for equality, for which it came under considerable populist fire (Skolnick, 1969:133–134).

The U.S. Supreme Court recently ruled that racially discriminating seniority plans started before the civil rights act could stand (*International Brotherhood of Teamsters* v. *United States,* 1977:4506). These seniority plans represented a truly vested interest in racism. And as we shall see, the real and contemporary problem in civil rights and the law emerges when legitimate and apparently conflicting claims of civil rights clash, e.g., the black worker's right to equal opportunity and the white worker's right to vested seniority interests. This clash between normative expectations is most evident in what has come to be known as "affirmative action." Whites characteristically claim a right to be judged on ostensibly meritocratic criteria. Minorities argue that criteria that result in substantially less than statistical parity are not really meritocratic and therefore are racially discriminatory.

Affirmative Action

As the inadequacy of civil rights legislation to affect the life chances of minorities became increasingly apparent, the remedy of affirmative action became increasingly popular and widespread, partly under the pressure of executive orders of the federal government, partly under pressure from minority activists, and partly because, as a result of the protests of the 1960s, the reality of racism in America became an acknowledged fact, both in law and in the wider society.

Nathan Glazer, who otherwise views affirmative action as affirmative discrimination, nevertheless nicely describes how subterfuges to avoid legal observance led to statistical rules of parity as the basis for proving discrimination:

> The South was endlessly ingenious in devising regulations for registration that were on their face fair but that were used in many jurisdictions to deny the blacks the right to vote.... Similarly, in 1968, the Supreme Court, tired of endless delay in desegregating dual school systems, accepted a statistical rule for desegregation of schools, under which "freedom of choice" was outlawed....
>
> It was relatively easy for a statistical rule to develop in the discrimination cases brought under the Civil Rights Act of 1964, for here, too, endless subterfuge was possible. Indeed, it was owing to the resistance of craft unions to the entry of blacks that the first affirmative action programs requiring fixed statistical quotas for employment were instituted by the Federal government through its power as a Federal contractor, in the Philadelphia Plan in 1969, and many similar plans which followed (Glazer, 1975a:50).

The concept of affirmative action implies that objectivity is possible only when a prior history of racism and associated institutional impairments has not prevailed. Thus the idea of affirmative action in university admissions grew out of a combination of experience and impatience. Experience showed that a rough statistical parity of racial minorities would not, because of institutionalized consequences of racism, become doctors, lawyers, and bankers. Nor were minorities or civil-rights activists willing any longer to be patient. A generation of both black and white civil-rights activists had learned that "deliberate speed" too often meant procrastination.

The Bakke Case

As I write, we are approaching what is probably the most important, controversial, and potentially divisive U.S. Supreme Court case involving race in this country since *Brown* v. *Board*. That case is *Allan Bakke* v. *The Regents of the University of California*.

The Bakke case involves access of minorities to professional education and careers. Bakke—who is white—applied to the U.C. Davis Medical School and was rejected. He argues that if there were not a special program for minorities, taking some of the spaces, he would have been admitted. The Bakke case thus raises what seems to be the contemporary American dilemma: how to reconcile the moral claim of individual merit with the moral claims of minority-group membership.

Actually, however, the issue raised in the Bakke case is not a strictly meritocratic one, if by meritocracy we mean selection on the basis of test scores and grades. The California Supreme Court did not, in upholding Bakke's claim, assert that the University's Davis Medical School cannot or should not take factors other than scores and grades into account. Medical schools have traditionally employed factors other than grades in admissions. Scores alone can perhaps predict which graduates will prove the most successful medical researchers, but not the most artful practitioners.

Only the use of a racial classification per se was found to be impermissible by the California court. In fact, the court urged the university to develop a category, such as "disadvantaged," that would substantially raise the number of black and other minority admittees to professional schools (*Bakke* v. *The Regents of the University of California*, 1977:55). The California Supreme Court seemed to be urging the university to accomplish by indirection what it was already doing straightforwardly. Indeed, Justice Tobriner's dissenting opinion described this proposal as a "cruel hoax" (*Bakke* v. *The Regents of the University of California*, 1977:90).

The university's brief responded pointedly to the necessity for employing racial categories: It states:

> Today, only a race-conscious plan for minority admissions will permit qualified applicants from disadvantaged minorities to attend medical schools, law schools and other institutions of higher learning in sufficient numbers to enhance the quality of the education of all students; to broaden the professions and increase their services to the entire community; to destroy pernicious stereotypes; and to demonstrate to the young that educational opportunities and rewarding careers are truly open regardless of ethnic origin. (Brief for Petitioner, 1977:13-14).

The hard, compelling, and unpleasant facts are that when the Medical School at U.C. Davis opened in 1968, racial and ethnic minorities comprised more than 23 percent of California's population. The 1968 entering class contained no blacks, no Chicanos, three Asians, and no American Indians (Brief for Petitioner, 1977:2). Yet the Carnegie Commission on Higher Education commented in 1970 that "The greatest single handicap of the ethnic minorities is their underrepresentation in the professions of the nation" (Carnegie Commission, 1970:13).

It is also important to distinguish, when assessing the fairness of race-conscious plans, between the use of racial classifications motivated by prejudice or contempt, and those motivated by aspirations of social justice. "In the past," writes Ronald Dworkin in a closely reasoned article, "it made sense to say that an excluded black or Jewish student was being sacrificed because of his race or religion; that meant that his or her exclusion was treated as desirable in itself, not because it contributed to any goal in which he as well as the rest of society might take pride." If race is a permissible consideration, rather than the more indirect "disadvantaged," there really is no justification for a meritocratic argument, unless test scores are to stand as the only criterion of merit. Dworkin continues:

> Allan Bakke is being "sacrificed" because of his race only in a very artificial sense of the word. He is being "sacrificed" in the same artificial sense because of his level of intelligence, since he would have been accepted if he were more clever than he is. In both cases he is being excluded not by prejudice but because of a rational calculation about the socially most beneficial use of limited resources for medical education (Dworkin, 1977:15).

Conclusion

The Bakke case will have an impact for decades. It will decide whether blacks, Chicanos, and other minorities will have meaningful access to American professions, or are to continue indefinitely in the occupations assigned by previous centuries of discrimination. The Bakke case presents several "ironies of history." It has divided the liberal civil rights community, and in particular has strained relations between organized Jewish and black groups. Even the students at the University of California, Berkeley, have split over the case, with the Editorial Board of the normally liberal to radical *Daily Californian* voting four to three to support Bakke and oppose preferential admissions based on race. At the same time, the normally liberal to conservative chancellor supports preferential admissions, as does the dean of the Law School plus a substantial majority of law school faculty who have not in the past been noted for radical leanings.

Finally, the outcome of the case could rest less on social concerns than on the conservative philosophy followed by the U.S. Supreme Court in recent years, giving considerable weight to local government and administrations.

During the days of slavery and Jim Crow, the U.S. Supreme Court was prone to leave the state and local governments to their own devices. Not until the 1950s and 1960s, especially during Earl Warren's tenure as chief justice, were national standards imposed on the states. Generally, liberals applauded the Warren Court's federal stance, while conservatives deplored it.

In this instance, probably the most powerful legal argument of the university centers around the conservative affirmation of local control. Local officials are here accused of unfairly favoring minorities, and the university's lawyers defend the right of local officials—the faculty—to solve problems on the basis of local judgment. The university does not argue that professional schools must have special-admissions programs, or that when they do, the programs must look like the Davis program. Rather, the university takes the position that when a professional school voluntarily chooses to adopt such a program, the equal protection clause does not prohibit them from doing so. In effect, the brief argues that distant judges and courts have no business in making decisions properly the province of local educators. Obviously, this assertion invokes a conservative and elitist principle in the interests of what is normally considered a liberal cause.

To uphold Bakke and the California Supreme Court, where he won, the brief concludes, "would not only sacrifice this essential discretion to an arid formula, it would also stand as one of those rare but tragic instances in which the judiciary has contributed to the continued subordination of racial minorities" (Brief for Petitioner, 1977:86–87).

A backward look at the history of courts and racism in this country would suggest, however, that during the entire span of American history the law has often contributed to the subordination of racial minorities. The law has also advanced such interests. Whether we are discussing racial intermarriage or affirmative action, we can be confident only that the definition of a "civil right" will rest less on neutral principles of law than on the Court's perception of the political and social requirements of the nation. Given a case like Bakke's, with its implications for the future of American society and American justice, it will be interesting to see whether a judicial pronouncement in this case will in fact provide a forum for the "civilization" of this dispute, or will merely add to a conflict that will ultimately be resolved primarily by coercion.

III

The Explanation and Control of Crime

12

Introduction: The Study of Crime, Items for an Agenda

Albert K. Cohen

IN THE STUDY OF CRIME there are five areas of inquiry where concentrated effort is likely to be particularly rewarding.

1. The first has to do with the definition of crime and the scope of the field of criminology. Are we concerned with explaining infractions of legal rules or with the labeling of persons as criminals? The question has seemingly been debated ad nauseam but it is by no means resolved, and it still lurks disturbingly in the background of all criminological discourse.

From one point of view, it is a matter of definition, an argument over words, not substance. Suppose that members of society, or at least the actors in the criminal justice sector, are in pretty fair agreement on the meaning of legal rules, that these meanings can be known to the scientific investigator, and that the investigator can therefore compare what people have done with what the rules say they should have done, and in this way determine whether crimes have been committed without waiting for the verdict of the criminal court. Suppose further that the labeling of acts as crimes and of persons as criminals varies, in some degree, independently of infraction itself. And suppose, finally, that infraction cannot be fully understood without considering the consequences of labeling, and that labeling, in turn, is to some degree influenced by infraction. If we accept these suppositions, then infraction and labeling are both real, they are both legitimate objects of study, they are complementary and in no way contradictory. Whether we define crime as the one or the other is arbitrary and of no theoretical consequence.

Suppose, on the other hand, that the meaning, objectivity, and reliability of rules are, as the phenomenologists are fond of saying, radically problematical, that the language in which rules are couched may be fixed but their meanings are constantly being renegotiated, and that, in any case, rules are not so much standards for judging behavior as they are rhetorics for legitimizing official outcomes and "constructing accounts." If these suppositions are correct, then the only possible meaning of the statement that a given act is an infraction of such-and-such a rule is that the participants in the criminal justice process have cranked out a verdict to that effect. It would then follow that the study of crime can only be the study of the methods and procedures by which people arrive at judgments that are phrased in the language of the criminal law. Furthermore, since crime is a product of the criminal justice system rather than an independent reality to which the criminal justice system responds, the social control of crime is identical to the process whereby crime is produced. That is to say, both expressions point to the same set of activities. To dispute this conception of crime is not to argue over terms; it is an argument over the nature of the social reality. Many of us are uncomfortable with this position. It seems to trivialize what we have been doing and implies that many of the great theoretical issues of traditional criminology are like disputes about the characteristics of unicorns. Still, we cannot reject it out of hand in favor of rule breaking. Its conclusions may be distasteful but its reasoning is persuasive and must be met on its own ground. Many sociologists shuttle back and forth between the phenomenological and the traditional views. Crime, they say, is part of a "socially constructed reality"; it is whatever gets to be labeled crime. Then they proceed to talk about infractions of the criminal law as though they had an existence independent of the judgments pronounced by the criminal justice system. We are going to have to do better than that. I suspect that a solution that is intellectually defensible and that does justice to both views will provide us with a way of looking at the phenomena of crime that is rather different from either one of them or some uneasy combination of them.

2. American criminology has been disproportionately concerned with the social psychology and microsociology of crime. It has been too little concerned with the macrosociological question: How are the properties of the larger, more encompassing social system and changes in those properties related to the kinds, the scale, and the social distribution of crime within the system? The two levels of analysis are not independent. Social psychological and macrosociological theories deal with the properties of the situations in which persons find themselves (legitimate and illegitimate opportunities, moral and material support from others, the role of the victim, and so on), and the interactions among the elements of these "local fields." To the extent that such a theory is valid, the

distribution of crime in the social system must correspond to the distribution of the kinds of local field that that theory asserts to be necessary for the production of criminal acts, but the theory itself does not address the question of what kind of organization of society is capable of producing that kind of distribution of local fields. One way of approaching the macrosociological question is to ask how variations in the polity, the economy, social class and other modes of social differentiation, and the bases, organization, and distribution of power are related to and generate the composition and distribution of the kinds of local field that are relevant (according to the theory) for the production of crime. Or one may take as his starting point a theory of society and develop its implications for the distribution of crime as one of the properties of that system, although in doing so he will surely make assumptions about the psychological and microsociological "black boxes" that provide the motivation for criminal behavior. In any case, there is a macrosociological question that calls for a macrosociological answer. This level of analysis has not been completely neglected but, by comparison with the microsociological level, it is grossly underdeveloped. For example, Merton's paper on social structure and anomie (1938) had the potential of providing a framework for a comparative macrosociology of crime, but there have been only a few modest beginnings in the direction of exploring that potential.

The chief exceptions to my characterization of American criminology have been the Marxists who, since they are committed to the exposure of the iniquities of capitalism, take satisfaction in revealing the complicity of our most sacred institutions in the generation of crime. We should welcome the Marxists as a serious and constructive force in American criminology, but I do not think that they should be left with a near-monopoly of the macrosociological sector. I am not calling for an army of bourgeois criminologists to refute the heresies of Marxism, but it will not do to leave the task of macrosociological analysis to the partisans of any single system of theory, especially one with a powerful ideological animus. Much of the Marxist work is able and provocative, but much of it is impaired by dogmatism, omission, distortion, and sheer sloppiness. However, I am not contrasting the propagandistic bent of Marxism with a presumably value-free approach by more conventional criminologists. I am suggesting, rather, that objectivity and *Wertfreiheit* in science are not so much a *property* of individual practitioners or of schools of thought as a *product* of dialogue, of confrontation, of challenge and response. Indeed, the quality of Marxist scholarship itself can only gain if Marxist scholars speak not only to one another but to a larger community of scholars dealing with the same issues but from a variety of theoretical perspectives, and if this larger community listens and responds.

3. The study of the social control of crime is vigorous but frag-

mented. In the last twenty-five years criminology has discovered the criminal justice system, and research on its anatomy and physiology has become a thriving industry. The emphasis, however, has been on the internal operations of its subsystems: why the police conduct and misconduct themselves as they do, the symbiotic relationships among the personnel of the criminal court, how prisons are organized and what effect they have on their involuntary clients, and so on. I am not aware of a comparable interest in this country, despite the heritage of Marx, Weber, Durkheim, and other European antecedents, in explaining why societies have the systems of criminal justice that they do and why those systems vary as they do in space and time.

We also have a theoretical literature on the informal controls inherent in the normal functioning of the everyday world outside the criminal justice system. We have a modest literature, mostly descriptive, on the vast, market-oriented private security industry, including private police services, the manufacture and servicing of hardware, and environmental design. We have a meager literature on the measures that individuals take to reduce their vulnerability to crime—measures that sometimes amount to radical reorganizations of their lives. All of these are facets of the societal reaction to crime. They are intimately interrelated in ways that we have hardly begun to explore. It is now time to approach, in a serious and systematic way, the interfaces and interactions of all these sectors with one another and with the politically organized criminal justice sector and the study of their joint effects.

4. Traditionally, criminological theory has been concerned with the crimes of natural persons, men and women like you and me. However, the criminal law extends also to "artificial persons," such as corporations and other collectivities, and the collectivities have been as busy and productive turning out crime as natural persons. The collectivities I am speaking of are not just business firms; they include also governments, their agencies and departments, labor unions, patriotic societies, ball teams, and so on. There is a modest literature on collectivity crime, but most of it is descriptive. There has been hardly any work on the explanation of collectivity crime and not much on its control. I think that this is a sort of a scandal and a continuing embarrassment to criminology. The most important questions have hardly been touched. What sort of an actor is a collective actor anyway? What kind of theory is appropriate to the criminal behavior of collective actors? What relation does it bear to established criminological theory, which is designed to explain why natural persons commit crimes? Do we need a special kind of theory, *sui generis,* to deal with collectivity crime? Are explanations of collectivity crime somehow reducible to explanations of criminal behavior of concrete human beings or natural persons? These questions have hardly been raised, much less seriously addressed. Whether our interests are

purely theoretical or concerned with policy, we should be wrestling with these questions.

5. The application of economic analysis to the study of crime has jolted criminology, and especially sociological criminology, out of its strange reluctance to take account of rational decision making, market forces, and the calculation of costs and benefits in its theories of crime. Economists, newly come to the study of crime, but drawing upon long experience with economic analysis, have been able rather quickly to identify a host of variables, distinctions, and relationships that are part of the actual complexity of rational decision making, market processes, and the like, in the world of crime. Sociologists, having become somewhat reconciled to the idea that it is not necessarily reactionary, mean, or dehumanizing to recognize that these processes operate in the world of crime as they do everywhere else, would probably eventually have arrived where the economists have, but would have taken much longer to get there. (Opportunity structure theorists, had they rigorously analyzed the concept of opportunity, would have discovered that their theories very largely resolve themselves into a number of elements that are commonplaces of economic theory, but they have not done so.) There is much more to be done along this line, but there is another kind of task ahead of us: the integration of economic theory as it bears upon crime and the societal response to crime with the variables, distinctions, and relationships to which sociological theory is especially sensitive, such as organizational relationships, the role of power, belief systems, value elements, problems and forms of legitimacy, subcultural processes, and so on. The integration will have to take place on all the levels on which criminological issues arise: on the levels of models of man, of interaction processes, and of social systems. It will not be accomplished by sociologists becoming amateur economists or by economists becoming amateur sociologists so that each can perform now in this role, now in that. Nor will it consist of an eclectic aggregation or congeries of sociological and economic ideas. Criminology has the potential of becoming the meeting point between economics and sociology where the power of the two disciplines may become fused in a single, coherent, logically articulated, and empirically relevant body of theory. If this should happen, the chief beneficiary may turn out to be not criminology but the larger discipline, parent to both: the science of human action.

13

Description, Prescription, and Science: On Differences Between Knowing Something and Knowing Enough, Promising and Predicting

Gwynn Nettler

WE HAVE BEEN ASKED to look at competing "perspectives" of crime. A perspective is, of course, a way of thinking about our lives. In criminology, a perspective is an intellectual site from which to view the rights and wrongs of our conduct.

Criminologists, however, do not have a scalpel with which to cut cleanly between right and wrong, crime and not crime. There is no essence of "crime" or "criminality." There is no one dimension among all the injuries we inflict on ourselves and others that is universally and timelessly called "criminal" and accorded the same social value. The quality of assigned injury flickers as it ranges across the gamut of wrongs nominated for attention by the state—from the "wrong" of damaging one's own body, to that of producing "too many" children, to the "wrongs" of lying, cheating, stealing, killing one another, and failing to fasten one's seat belt.

In short, "crime" is a morally burdened word. It is part of a family of ideas whose siblings include conceptions of "right," "wrong," "sin," "vice," "justice," and "harm." This family of concepts has troubled philosophers for centuries and quarrel in this house has united some of us while estranging others—at least since Cain killed Abel. Given such a history, I see no reason to prophesy harmony among criminologists.

□ My appreciation is due colleagues Timothy Hartnagel and Robert A. Silverman, and Professor William Avison of the University of Western Ontario, who have counseled me on some of these issues. They are not responsible, of course, for the present construction.

A STRANGE JOB

However, we are workers who have chosen the job of being professionally thoughtful. We have defined our work and justified it—to consumers of our product and to ourselves—by appealing to canons of truth, objectivity, science. Some unknown proportion of criminologists even consider themselves to be "social scientists." In addition, some unknown proportion of criminologists consider themselves to be useful, but useful in a special sense—in the sense of being moral and helpful.

Many of us are descendants, then, of the *philosophes*. We try to develop knowledge on the premise that knowing something may relieve misery and resolve moral conflict. The attempted conjunction between knowledge and correct action has worked frequently enough in the handling of physical objects to suggest its application to social subjects. But when the connection between knowing and right action is elevated to an article of faith, it is bound to be schizophrenogenic. This faith leads to lunacy, particularly as knowing a little is confused with knowing enough and having information is mistaken for having knowledge.

Insofar as criminologists conform to this job description—one that mixes seeking the truth with doing good and confuses being informed with being knowledgeable—our work standards are likely to conflict. How frequently sociological work standards conflict, and how much, for which individuals, constitute a set of unknowns. But without giving numbers to these unknowns, one can find in this strange vocation a source of our continuing invention of "perspectives" and several holes in our scientific robes.

The conflict in work standards is apparent in the competing criteria offered to justify rival orientations in the study of crime. If, on the one hand, we regard perspectives as built on a scientific foundation, five interacting criteria are applicable to their evaluation:

- the clarity of the concepts employed
- the reliability and validity of measures of those concepts
- the reliability of the taxonomies of acts, actors, and situations used in explanation—implicitly or explicitly
- the fit of empirical propositions with facts
- the predictive utility of those propositions ("predictive utility" may be translated as having a causal theory that works)

On the other hand, if we regard perspectives as political statements, then obscurity may be preferable to clarity. Concepts will be emotionally resonant and "sensitizing" rather than referential. This means, in turn, that measurement will be degraded. Facts will be used selectively, inconvenient facts will be denied, and promise will be more important than prediction. By the ethicopolitical work standard, an orientation is to be judged principally by "the side it takes" and the policy it proposes.

This difference in job standards is a matter of degree, of course. No absolute demarcation need be drawn between thinking scientifically and thinking politically. We recognize an interplay between facts and values so that we often say, "Every scientific statement has political implication," and, the other way around, "Every ethicopolitical position selects different facts in its defense."

Nevertheless, matters of degree are important, and our evaluations of competing interpretations of moral issues employ some unstable mixture of scientific and political standards. However, since most criminologists have donned the gown of doctor of philosophy rather than that of doctor of divinity, we are prone to cover our ethic with a façade of science. In the battle of perspectives, we propose that facts, like God, are on our side. Our morals and our politics, it is claimed, are based on truth while our opponents are mired in error.

This faith is sometimes shaken by full immersion in the contending explanations of crime. After such baptism, one is more willing to believe, with me, that competing perspectives originate with our preferences and are only secondarily, and meagerly, nourished by facts. As in some courts of law, so it seems with us: decisions first, facts afterward.

This impression is reinforced as one looks for factual ground and proven predictive utility among the more popular professional attitudes toward crime. Over the past ten years the two most visible interpretations of crime in the West have been the ideas of radical criminologists and those of "labeling" theorists. Neither of these conceptions is supported by citizens in general and neither is defended by a distinctive set of well-verified propositions. The evidence for my statement is abundant and it can be read at your leisure.[1]

Now that the shouting is almost over, some advocates of these exciting perspectives can admit that their arguments were far from a scientific theory, but rather, in Howard Becker's words (1974:6); "a way of looking at a general area of human activity; a perspective whose value will appear, if at all, in increased understanding of things formerly obscure."

Ah, what a relief to be able to put down the heavy burden of science with its effort to develop knowledge and, instead, to look for "increased understanding." Our relief is only temporary, of course, because the skeptic then asks us what we mean by "understanding," and how we will know when we have it, and what we can do with it that we could not have done before. The skeptic's questions return us to the nagging debate about which criteria to use in judging the quality of our work.

[1]Arguments and references can be found in Nettler (1978), particularly chaps. 11 and 15.

Obstacles to Competence

If we are not to behave as propagandists first and truth-seekers second, we shall have to be clear about the nature of our competence and its limits. Clarification of our competence requires recognition that there are differences between being able to describe and being able to explain, between having information and having knowledge, and between promising and predicting.

Confusion of these intertwined abilities is generated by hope and desire, and hope and desire are fueled under high pressure by moral concern. Our expertise as would-be scientists is limited by our choice of moral subject matter.

Studying issues that are inflamed with moral concern and employing moral ideas in attempting to do a science are obstacles to knowledge. Obstacles are not absolute deterrents, of course; they are more like hurdles that we may leap, but only if we are in training.

I should like to describe some of the dimensions of these hurdles without measuring them. And I should like to discuss, but briefly, a training regimen that may improve our track record and clarify the nature of our competence.

A study of moral issues that aspires to be objective faces three high hurdles, sometimes approached singly and sometimes approached one piled on top of the others. These obstacles may be termed those of selection, conception, and explanation.

SELECTION

Competing perspectives in criminology derive from differences in preference. Professional students of "crime" want different things, or the same things in varying order. We bring to our studies different visions of social relations—actual, possible, and preferable. We therefore nominate a varied assortment of conceivable wrongs to be called "crime," and to be punished, if not prevented, by an organization with a monopoly of power, the state.

Some students look at robbery and rape, others at perfidy in high places. Some criminologists attend to price fixing, fraudulent advertising, and fraudulent bookkeeping—when accomplished by private persons, of course, but seldom when perpetrated by favored governments. Still others are concerned with the "violent crime" (their words) of "[designing and manufacturing] automobiles that kill and maim occupants in low-speed crashes" (Galliher and McCartney, 1977:x). Additional scholars call our attention to the crimes of "racism, sexism, poverty, and imperialist war" (Schwendinger and Schwendinger, 1975), while there are others who wish us to attend to the crimes of tyranny (Solzhenitsyn, 1975).

The very prescriptions of one band of scholars become the crime-generators of other inquirers. Thus, although it is popular to call for decriminalization of a host of present offenses, it is equally in vogue to call for government regulation and punishment of a multiplicity of new offenses. The supply of "crime"—its quality and its level—may be expected to move with these new demands. As it does, we who are criminologists out of the humane studies will be reminded of older voices—those of Fyodor Dostoyevsky (1950:291) and Arthur Koestler (1945), for example, and Karl Popper (1967:270) and Max Weber (1946). These voices warned us that to engage in politics—that is, to employ power—to right wrongs is itself to run the risk of generating misery, cruelty, and crime.

Determining the Hierarchy of Injury

We debate, then, which wrongs are wrong enough to be deemed criminal, and we are unable to resolve the debate by reference to an agreed-upon test of damage. There is no social accountancy—no cost accounting of injuries—that can assign objective values to the range of wrongs nominated to be crimes. Lacking such a standard of deciding the proper hierarchy of damage, we can adopt a democratic measure—the weight of injury assigned by people who suffer these nominated wrongs and who are subject to the sanctions of a particular state.

But some criminologists—the "newer" ones in particular—disdain such a democratic test on Lenin's ground that "The people themselves do not know what is good or bad for them." This reason is camouflaged today by claiming that "the people" are uninformed and that *our* information will elevate their debased "consciousness."

I think, however, that if we deny a democratic measure of the social injuries to be criminalized, we are pushed back to the childhood argumentation that so often typifies moral quarrels: " 'Tis. 'Tain't." Moral sentiment is characteristically immune to fact.[2]

The conflict of perspectives begins here. It begins in preference, not in knowledge. It is illustrated by the repeated performance of criminologists who condemn researchers for addressing one set of questions rather than the critic's preferred set (Nettler, 1972).

---

[2]Those who doubt the impotence of facts when confronted by beliefs will not be moved, although they may be disturbed, by the illustration Simone de Beauvoir (1962:30) provides of the outcome of the endless quarrels between the prominent intellectuals Raymond Aron and Jean-Paul Sartre. "I cannot recall," she writes, "one occasion on which he [Sartre] convinced Aron—or on which Aron succeeded in shaking Sartre's own beliefs."

Avoiding the Hurdle

A way to handle this obstacle is to run around it. Given the premises of academic freedom and our resistance to intellectual despotism, the questions asked from one perspective are as justified as those proposed from other orientations. Scratching an intellectual itch is a persistent habit among *Homo sapiens* and you and I shall not be put off from scratching where we itch rather than where others do.

People who are curious about other things than we are may offend us at times, or bore us, but, in the Western world thus far, there is no Commissar of Inquiry with a mandate to specify which questions shall interest us or whose interests our answers must satisfy.

There are markets for questions and answers, of course, and we may find ourselves in a situation in which no one wishes to pay us to search for answers to our questions. But those of us who work for publics, as do most of us, are constrained to address ourselves, occupationally at least, and some of the time, to some of the questions our supporters raise.

CONCEPTION

A second obstacle to the study of moral issues is conceptual. We approach the study of "crime" with a vocabulary that is morally loaded. Now, moral terms are both a comfort and a necessity in communicating evaluations of our social worlds, but such comfort and necessity do not make morally saturated concepts useful for a science. Since moral terms have to do with approval and disapproval, they have an uncertain nucleus of denotation and a broad and shifting range of connotation. Concepts of such ambiguous reference are useful for "appreciating" our situations and each other, but they are not reliable instruments for knowing what we are talking about. Morally burdened words do not make firm structures for a taxonomy of actors and events, and taxonomy, we are reminded, is the foundation of any science.

The vocabulary of sociology is a common one. It is therefore highly evaluative (Osgood et al., 1957). It is therefore unsatisfactory for a study that requires clear referents of its terms. We have recently been instructed in the slippery quality of morally useful and scientifically useless ideas by the performance of an ambassador to the so-called United Nations who has shown us how to apply the concept, "racist." Ambassador Young's lesson would be applauded by Humpty Dumpty, who agreed that words mean whatever the user says they do.

With variations, this instruction applies to many of the concepts adopted by social studies that would be sciences. Many of the terms with which we try to conduct rigorous studies have been borrowed uncritically from philosophy, journalism, and the street. No student of social relations who wishes to be clear, as opposed to being popular and persuasive, can use morally contaminated ideas without stripping them down to some thin meaning that omits so much connotation as to make the concept unrecognizable. The trouble with these terms is that they are multidimensional. They are many-faceted, splendid alarms with which to ring Pavlovian bells in our heads. This means that scholars are at high risk of speaking at cross-purposes and testing different qualities of action when they employ such ambiguous words as "discrimination," "prejudice," "stereotype," or "alienation," "exploitation," "oppression."

This is but a sample, of course, of the vague vocabulary with which we try to be objective. Charles Lachenmeyer's book, *The Language of Sociology* (1971), extends this sample and shows us how comfortable and obscure are the words with which we do our work. Indeed, our philosopher-friend Ortega y Gasset (1946:24) assures us that "the very name, 'society,' as denoting groups of men who live together, is equivocal and utopian."

A Weak Solution

We have tried to leap this linguistic hurdle with a technique known in sociological argot as "operationalizing" our terms. This is some help, but it is help with a price. One price is that of connotative poverty: Every precisely indicated meaning of a moral idea omits something considered important for some consumers of that concept. In addition, we pay a price in diminished or uncertain validity. Measures applied to attempted clear definitions of morally tinctured terms normally yield so many dimensions of a seemingly singular idea that we have to ask which meaning of "unemployment," or "intelligence," or "justice" is being tapped by a particular indicator. Given the diversity of reference in our common vocabulary, it is little wonder that so few measures of sociological constructs have undergone trial by replication (Bonjean et al., 1967).

Resolution

The training prescribed thus far for those who would be professionally truthful in reply to morally burdened questions requires:

1. That we know what issue we are addressing.
2. That we use clean concepts in searching for answers.
3. That we recognize that no measure of a clean concept will tap all possible meanings of the tangled ideas that concern us. This is a recognition that the political connotations of morally infused terms are always broader than the referent we have measured.

This is the best we have been able to do thus far in clearing the occupational hurdles of selection and conceptualization in the study of moral issues. But these obstacles are only prelude to the highest hurdle: that of useful explanation. In fact, our difficulties in selecting "crimes" from among the vast repertoire of wrongs, and of thinking about crimes and their alleged causes and remedies with words made slippery by morality—these difficulties intrude upon our poor attempts at taxonomy and explanation.

EXPLANATION AND CAUSATION

I have argued that explanation is encumbered by preference. Explanation is encumbered because every description that passes for explanation is causal—however well or ill the causal model is explicated. Locating causes, in turn, directs policy; the process says "yea" or "nay" to recommendation in response to crime.

We are made dizzy, then, by the constant turning of our attention between what is described and what seems to follow by way of prescribed societal response. We often attend to the consequence before we look at the evidence.

Professional students of social affairs are vulnerable to the common tendency to locate the causes of action by an operation that balances sympathy for the actor with approval of the act to be explained (Evans, 1968; Regan et al., 1974; Schiffman and Wynne, 1963). When *our* good people do good deeds, we locate the causes of their conduct "internally"—in their characters, dispositions, purposes. And we respond similarly when people we dislike do their characteristically wicked deeds. However, when people with whom we sympathize behave badly, or when people of whom we disapprove behave well, there is a tendency to move the locus of causation from within actors to forces outside them, and causation is attributed to situation, accident, or luck.

It is preference, not observation, that defines some wrongdoers as victims of circumstance and others as rational actors. It is ideology, not knowledge, that makes schizoid determinists of sociologists who regard some sympathetic bad actors as pawns, "caused" to do evil, while unsympathetic bad actors are regarded as agents, who "should have known better." Think, for a moment, where *you* locate the causes of Richard Nixon's "dirty tricks" as opposed to John Kennedy's.

Two Urgencies

Exculpation and accountability move with the moral scenery. However, what morality allows, logic forbids. And logic does not allow us to get on and off the causal train at convenient moral stations.

We are hoist between two urgencies: the moral need to assign responsibility and the practical need to assess causal power.[3] We are torn between the scientific assumption that behavior is caused and the moral assumption that some behavior, at least, is chosen. We are trapped by the hushed doubt whether we can live together if we assume that people are nothing but pawns and never agents. We are confused by the possibility that an assumption required of a science may be corrosive of social life.

Sparse and Dense Causal Webs

Our explanatory schizophrenia does not end with the unresolved tension between determinism and indeterminism. We are further divided by our inability to decide whether the causes of human action are loosely or tightly packed.

As we become more politically active, it becomes more convenient to think of human action as produced in causal webs that are sparse: a few powerful, noninteracting causes accounting for conduct. Practical politics requires such thinking because promises depend on simple remedies: If we do this, we shall get that.

It is conceivable, however, that the social world works differently. It may be more like a dense causal web in which myriad causes interact, and interact with little perceptible uniformity and with powers that change as interactions move. When we think with such a dense model, we become aware of possible threshold effects of an innumerable variety so that we cannot be sure, as one geologist poetically put it, that "the flutter of a moth's wing may not precipitate a hurricane."

Furthermore, to assume a dense causal web is to acknowledge that we can know what the causes *can be* without knowing what they *will be*. It is slippage between these abilities that accounts for the poor prognostic record of economists and other gamblers in the social arena. It is recognition of this slippage that distinguishes historians from social reformers.

A picture of the human situation as densely packed calls caution to zeal and pushes reasonable people toward prudence. The prudential advice is exemplified in a physician's pragmatic approach to the "right act" in medicine (Dagi, 1976:364–66):

1. If it works, don't stop;
2. If it doesn't work, stop;
3. If you don't know what to do, don't do anything;
4. Never call a surgeon.

[3]The conflict between moral and scientific ends in the assignment of causation is another source of the perennial warfare between truth and utility. It is another reason why collective action so frequently produces the opposite of that which is intended. This conflict also accounts for suicidal moralities.

In the hospital for social ills, the surgeon is, of course, the revolutionary.

Being prudent does not always require that one "do nothing." We are all aware that the decision to "do nothing" is itself a "doing." But calling caution makes us aware of differences between promise and prediction, and between *doing* something and *knowing* what we are doing. The lesson was taught us long ago by the physiologist Claude Bernard. "True science," he said, "teaches us to doubt and, in ignorance, to refrain."

Conclusions

Given the conflicting demands made of a vocation that would be expertly humane and truthful, what inferences can we draw from competing views of crime?

Professional perspectives of crime all describe some truths. This follows from their blind groping of different parts of the elephant. But the partial truths told by some perspectives have achieved resonance beyond their evidence. Some ideas have been persuasive on ethicopolitical grounds where they have been inadequate on scientific grounds. Theories of crime production, crime prevention, and criminal correction are poor ones. They do not improve much upon common sense and they do not hold up well when translated into policy.

With this acknowledgment, I should like to draw a picture of where we are intellectually and to make some suggestions—most of which do not depend on a strongly held particular "theory" of crime. My suggestions are written against a moral backdrop, of course. This means, again, that disagreement is to be expected. Space limitation requires that one comment bluntly, without the proof and qualification fuller discourse would allow. Lacking such protection, may I suggest the following:

First, the structure of social relations and its moral justification, however these are conceived and measured, change the definition of crime, the quality and quantity of crime, and the mode of societal response. There is no end to crime.

Second, there is no *science* of crime prevention and correction. We have not developed a knowledge of human action—either individual or aggregate—that improves much upon truisms to be found in the Great Books.

During its ninetieth congress, the American Correctional Association (1960) issued a high-sounding *Declaration of Principles,* the first of which reads:

> The prevention and control of crime and delinquency are urgent challenges to the social sciences. The growing body of scientific knowledge, coupled with the practical wisdom and the skill of those professionally

engaged in society's struggle with the problem of criminality, provide the soundest basis for effective action.

This statement is misleading. It is saddening. It promises more than it can deliver.

Tools thus far developed in the social studies assist us somewhat in forecasting behavior, but little in predicting it. A forecast, you recall, is a prognosis publicly replicable from empirical data where the prognosticator has no control over the outcome he or she foretells. A prediction, by contrast, is a prognosis from empirical data that accurately foretells the outcome of purposive *intervention*. Intelligent control of causes is required.

Our professional inability to predict does not justify our assuming the role of doctors to the body politic, although we may function as cautious counselors. To change the metaphor, we are not societal engineers equipped with a technology of social melioration based on a science of conduct.

It is presumptuous, then, for so-called "new" criminologists (I. Taylor et al., 1973:282) to propose to "create" (their verb) "a society in which the facts of human diversity . . . are not subject to the power to criminalize." This proposal covers ignorance and impotence with promise. The promise of that perspective is a vision. One may hold it or reject it, but having such a vision is not a sign of professional competence. Enthusiasm requires no knowledge.

Third, it is time to divest ourselves of the sloganized notion that some students and journalists think they have learned from "social science": the notion that "punishment does not work" or that "the threat of punishment does not deter."

When the distinguished psychiatrist Karl Menninger (1968) tells us that punishment is a crime, he is expressing his moral opinion. When he assures us that "being against punishment is not a sentimental conviction. It is a logical conclusion drawn from scientific experience" (p. 204), he is taking the titles of logic and science in vain.

Our trouble, again, is with the morally infected word, "punishment." This word does not refer to one kind of intentionally produced pain with one kind of consequence. Punishment refers to an assortment of painful events whose consequences are contingent.

We object to punishment because it is costly although, as usual, we have no accountancy that can calculate an optimal balance among styles of punishment, reward, and neglect. We also object to punishment on moral grounds. It is unpleasant and we prefer to reward good conduct rather than to penalize bad action. But none of these objections permits the categorical denial of deterrent effects, specific and general.

However, when we object to "punishment" with the allegation that it is ineffective, clarity demands that we specify the quality and probability of the punishment we are talking about. Every "criminologist" on the street knows that punishment loses efficacy if it is tardy and improbable, as is the case in many Western jurisdictions. Every recent econometric model, except one, demonstrates that the probability of punishment is associated with reduced attacks on person and property (Nettler, 1978, chap. 10).

We have for too long assumed an ill-defined continuum of action called expressive-instrumental or impulsive-rational. This assumption has carried with it the belief that we could make a *predictively efficient cut* on this vague continuum such that we could identify points above and below which punishment does and does not deter. Moreover, we have built into these tangled assumptions the additional premise that *degrees of deterrence*—for example, the number of potential homicides inhibited each year for each murderer executed or otherwise punished—could be assigned with ascertainable probabilities to discernible segments along the impulsive-rational continuum. May I remind you that we have not been able to live up to this series of assumptions. Nevertheless, these notions have been married in a popular but defective syllogism:

If murder is impassioned, it is not affected by consequences.
Much murder is passionate.
Therefore, punishment will not deter much murder.

The argument, of course, draws a circle. It arrives at its conclusion by definition, not by predication. By definition, passionate homicide is that which presumably could not have been deterred. The question is begged.

PUNITIVE CONTINGENCIES

Honesty requires that we come out of the moral closet misleadingly labeled "social science" and admit the distasteful evidence that "punishment works." Pain and its threat change us, but they do so conditionally.

Our difficulty is that we cannot predict whose acts will be changed how much in which direction for how long by which penalty inflicted with what timing and severity by whom (Nettler, 1978:199–204, 316–17). Our difficulty is that we have ignored threshold effects, and we have ignored such turning points because we have been unable to specify them outside the laboratory. These difficulties reflect some of the contingencies reported, but imperfectly tallied, by a behavioral science whose little, good name has been sorely abused for moral causes.

Fourth, the professional competence of a sociologist is actuarial. The training of a sociologist develops some forecasting skill, but little predictive ability. It provides no moral credentials.

An actuary can count, crudely, how things are. This means that a sociologist can test for *effects* of public policy—quite a different talent, incidentally, from predicting what will happen if. . . .

What we have counted thus far among the consequences of different responses to crime has produced some consensus about policy. For example, most of us agree that it is stupid (that is, inefficient) to collect large numbers of bad actors behind walls where they have years in which to get to "know" one another, exchange criminal skills, and infect each other with their varieties of distemper. Such moral consensus as there may be among us also calls this foolish procedure inhumane.

We know better than to believe that imprisonment *in this form* will "teach them a lesson"—in the sense of the "right" lesson. We know better than to believe that this is the way to provide "opportunity" for vocational training. We are slowly approaching a similar agreement about the folly of therapy: the idea that criminals need some vague response called "treatment," that we know what that is, and that our therapies (mostly of the talking variety) provide cures. We are moving beyond the comforting and incorrect assumption that one who breaks the criminal law is necessarily "sick" and seldom rational.

This is as much as we may agree upon as a result of what we have counted. Consumers of our product ask for more than this, however. They ask for recommendation and remedy. At this point our vocational competence thins and moral philosophy enters. Morality enters because prescription depends upon definition of ends and an assessment of how much others—the consumers of our advice—are willing to pay for recommended responses to crime that carry no guarantee of their consequences.

Given such uncertainties, criminologists of varied orientation recommend experimentation. For example, we agree that many youthful hoodlums need homes, not jails, and that all young people need to be apprenticed to lawful work. However, we do not know how to implement these prescriptions at acceptable cost with the tools available in a free society. Our states, as opposed to communist governments, lack the power and justifying ideology with which to conscript youth for social work.

Other experiments have been suggested but, since our goals are in conflict, every means advocated is challenged. We are interested in restitutive contracts in lieu of imprisonment, but we shall have to use jails as a backup against breach of contract. We have agreed, I trust, that prisons as presently constructed are unsatisfactory, but we disagree about whether the very idea of incarceration is obsolete.

Other experiments have been suggested that would "prevent" crime by changing laws. Thanks in part to the labeling hypothesis and to overloading of criminal justice systems, we propose that many current crimes be reduced to offenses, and that many offenses be annulled. However, we have no sooner given this general prescription than some among us see new wrongs to be righted by the state. It would make an interesting doctoral dissertation, incidentally, to compute a balance sheet for criminologists of differing persuasion that tallies the number of present crimes they wish waived against present wrongs they wish the state to sanction.

None of these experiments foresees realization of an ideal that some of us share: the end of imprisonment and of governmental coercion. And none of these suggestions fully faces a perennial demand made of criminal justice systems—that they do justice.

DOING JUSTICE

Justice is, of course, another coruscating term, resplendent in its many meanings. It is an emotional term; a "fighting word," Holmes called it.

The concept of justice is moral. This means that justice is an end in itself. A criminal justice system expresses this morality. It symbolizes what we are for and against. Satisfaction of this sentiment may be at least as important a function of criminal justice as is any other consequence.

However, we know little about the quality of a citizenry's demand for justice. Criminologists have not studied the public's sense of justice, other than to ask survey questions about approval-disapproval of capital punishment and other penalties. But no one has adequately investigated the quality of justice expected in response to crime or the salience of a people's demand for justice.

In anticipation of research on this matter, it may be expected that the sense of justice may be peculiar to a people. The quality of demand for justice may be expected to vary with region and ethnicity, and with vulnerability to different quantities and qualities of crime, but, I repeat, we have not studied demand for justice and we know little of its nature. Such study may reveal both universals and local peculiarities in the definition of crime and in the sense of justice. And such study may have different effects upon audiences of differing moral persuasion.

If, as I expect, we were to find some parochial standards of justice in response to some categories of crime, such a finding should reinforce the moral relativism of those who are confirmed cultural relativists. On the other hand, for those who are moral absolutists (whether or not they know it), such a finding may unmask an ideology and reveal the morality that so often hides behind an appeal to rationality.

For example, consider the attitude of East Texans to domestic murders among them. Following sociological logic, grand juries there assess the impulsivity of the crime, the justice of the attack (usually "victim-precipitated," which translates as "he had it comin' to 'im"), and the utility of imprisoning the accused. Houstonians do not prosecute most such murders. Lundsgaarde (1977:42) reports that "the majority of homicide cases are dismissed."

Some criminologists find this abhorrent and want prosecution and punishment to follow murder. Punishment is to follow murder not so much because it may be deterrent—an idea with low credence among sociologists—but rather because *one* sense of justice requires official condemnation of domestic killing. Criminologists, like other citizens, demand justice, and justice remains a moral term, not a utilitarian concept.[4]

Where We Are

A review of perspectives of crime is disappointing to those who may have thought that social scientists were "really scientists" whose objectivity was little affected by morality and whose inventory of information constituted knowledge. Such a review is doubly disappointing to those parts of the populace—usually the "better-educated" parts—that have been misled into believing that unsatisfactory social relations are "problems" that have "solutions" if only we think hard enough with good intentions.

A less American perspective regards the notion of "social problems" as an optimistic and arrogant parochialism imposed upon recurring human difficulties. In accord with this "foreign" perspective, my thesis has been that our competence is limited and that what little we know is not enough to guide us toward "getting it all together"—love, liberty,

---

[4]If justice is a moral term, it is therefore an idea applied relative to a time and a people. Moralities seem to be everywhere the same *only if* moral principles are kept general as, for example, in "the condemnation of aggression, injustice, and deceit" (Nowell-Smith, 1967:153). Moralities are temporal and local, however, in application of these broad maxims. Thus what is prohibited within our tribe may be required in meeting foreigners. The particularity of the moral principle is reflected in the lexical distinctions made—as instanced in the different names given to homicide.

This gap between the general and the particular in the conception of the moral has disturbed philosophers for centuries. The disturbance has stimulated search for a universal principle based on reason that would justify an absolute code of conduct and allow the weighing of parochial norms against a reasoned, rational, and ecumenical standard. Thus far this search has failed and what is just remains a matter of municipal interpretation. Thus Carl Friedrich (1963:31) insists that "The most just act is the one compatible with the greatest number—and the greatest intensity—of values and beliefs." To which Perelman (1967:67) adds, "It goes without saying that the values and the beliefs in question are those of the community in whose name political power is being exercised."

peace, and prosperity, and the end of lying, cheating, stealing, and killing.

We in the Western world are in a criminogenic condition, halfway between community and anarchy and torn between the quest for community and the preference for freedom. The moral condition of Western countries does not permit an end to crime or a single best response to it. The condition is one in which the load of responsibility for conduct is being shifted—with some help from sociology—from the individual and his/her family to the new deity, Society. This shift is occurring along with an affluence that permits the proliferation of useless youth and the elevation of appetite. It is occurring in an atmosphere saturated with violence, an atmosphere that now seeps electronically into every household. Thieving and killing have always been with us, but never has so grand a variety of these activities been so repetitively well-modeled and justified.

In this moral climate, republics that attempt to govern many nations face a dilemma between defending liberty and maintaining the order that freedom requires. Dilemmas are not solved like puzzles; they are worked through, more and less happily, but always in conflict.

14

Deterrence and Economics: A Perspective on Theory and Evidence

Isaac Ehrlich and Randall Mark

UNDERLYING THE CLASSICAL deterrence hypothesis is the fundamental notion, shared by leaders of economic thought since Adam Smith, that human behavior is to a considerable degree a matter of choice prompted by opportunities. Translated in the context of illegitimate behavior, the idea is that man is endowed with a capacity for both good and evil and that his decisions to pursue one or the other, or a combination of the two, will be influenced by the opportunities associated with each type of behavior. Recent explorations in applied economics amount to a revival of this classical or liberal approach to criminality, most notably identified with Beccaria and Bentham. But whether derived through Bentham's felicific calculus of pain and pleasure or from the expected utility formulations of contemporary theorists, the deterrence hypothesis finds natural expression in economics, for its presumption of man's responsiveness to incentives mirrors the most basic laws of the economic theory of choice: price deters demand and profit motivates supply.

A central issue that we wish to explore in the following section is the extent to which economists of past generations actually have demonstrated acceptance of the deterrence hypothesis. Our research permits two principal observations. First, the evidence examined indicates that classical economists strongly adhered to the idea that offenders are responsive to incentives in general and to criminal sanctions in particular. While classical economists occasionally differed in their advocacy of particular sanctions and even in their conception of the normative princi-

□ We are indebted to Aaron Director and George Stigler for useful suggestions.

ples underlying punishment as it relates to specific acts, they did share the fundamental belief that punishment serves as an instrument for altering behavior. Indeed, we are unaware of any systematic work by an economist in either the classical or the neoclassical tradition that has directly challenged the deterrence theory. The second observation, however, is that economists devoted markedly less attention to the economics of crime and to "nonmarket" types of behavior generally following the period of classical economics until the recent past. The first section of this paper explores the reasons why economists' interest in crime receded over that period. The second section surveys the empirical evidence accumulated on deterrence prior to the present resurgence of interest in deterrence among economists and other social scientists. The third section then addresses the importance of a systematic formulation of the deterrence hypothesis as a guide to devising empirical tests of this hypothesis and for interpreting the evidence so obtained.

Economists on Deterrence

The period of preeminence of the classical approach to criminality is largely coincident with what is known as the classical period in economics, roughly from Adam Smith through John Stuart Mill. The coincidence is accentuated by what is regarded as the founding of modern criminology shortly afterward. Our reading of the literature reveals that with the notable exception of Karl Marx, economists of the classical period accepted with apparent unanimity the view that punishment deters crime.[1] While the classical school of thought on crime is quite properly associated with the detailed and systematic writings of Beccaria and Bentham,[2] other major figures in classical political economy—Adam Smith, William Paley, Thomas Malthus, Edwin Chadwick, James Mill, and John Stuart Mill—shared in the belief in the basic tenets of the deterrence hypothesis. Although the emphasis and scope of the analysis of crime and punishment by these scholars vary widely, each demonstrates a fundamental acceptance of the proposition that potential offenders

[1]We should emphasize that our primary interest here was to establish whether these economists accepted the essential, positive, i.e., behavioral, principles associated with the deterrence hypothesis. We did not attempt to assess comprehensively their individual contributions to the evaluation of the economic approach to crime, or to analyze systematically the differences among them, though both pursuits could provide fruitful future research.

[2]Beccaria's "Dei Delitti E Delle Pene," initially published in 1764, is his singular work in this area. We used the Farrer (1880) translation. The major works by Bentham that we have reviewed are his "Introduction to the Principles of Morals and Legislation," "Principles of Penal Law," and "The Rationale of Reward," all contained in Bowring (1843).

respond to incentives and the corollary proposition that an optimal social policy in connection with certainty and severity of punishment must be predicated on the deterrence theory, with due recognition of the costs and gains involved. Space limitations unfortunately preclude further elaboration on some of the penetrating treatises.[3] We would merely point out that none of the writers cited above would dispute Adam Smith's view that

> nature has implanted in the human breast that consciousness of ill-desert, those terrors of merited punishment . . . as the great safe-guards of the association of mankind, to protect the weak, to curb the violent, and to chastise the guilty (Smith, 1777:133-34).

Karl Marx is the only prominent economist of the period whom we find denying the deterrence proposition. His argument, however, is an empirical one directed toward both capital punishment and punishment in general:

> It would be very difficult, if not impossible to establish any principle upon which the justice or expediency of capital punishment could be founded. . . . Punishment in general had been defended as a means either of ameliorating or of intimidating. Now what right have you to punish me for the amelioration or intimidation of others? And besides, there is history—there is such a thing as statistics which prove with the most complete evidence that since Cain the world has been neither intimidated nor ameliorated by punishment. Quite the contrary (Marx, 1956).

Marx's casual empiricism with respect to the intimidating effects of punishment is unfortunate in that he mistakenly attributes to the deterrence theory the expectation that crime in the aggregate will be nil if some, even severe, punishment is enforced. Preceding the significant theoretical developments associated with the marginal revolution in economics some years later, Marx does not recognize the potential influence of punishment as a check against further crime on the margin for both actual offenders and those contemplating a criminal endeavor. Marx also fails to consider the role of certainty of punishment in determining and modifying the deterrent effect of punishment's severity. Indeed, his reasoning is equivalent to the contention that the aggregate quantity demanded of a good will be zero if its price is positive.

[3]A longer version of this paper prepared for the September 1977 ASA meetings presented illustrations from works by Beccaria, Bentham, Smith, Paley, Malthus, James Mill, and J. S. Mill to document their belief in deterrence. The sources relied upon, in addition to those cited at n.2 supra, included Smith (1777, 1896, 1937), Paley (1882), Malthus (1798), James Mill (n.d.), J. S. Mill (1907), and comments by J. S. Mill in Hansard's Parliamentary Debates (1868). Chadwick's work is discussed by Hebert (1977:539-50) and Radzinowicz (1957:448-74).

Now, despite their prior evident interest in crime and punishment, economists' attention to illegitimate behavior and the deterrence hypothesis apparently receded for about a century following the latter part of the nineteenth century. While traces of deterrence theory possibly can be detected in the literature on business regulation—in connection, say, with antitrust activity[4] or prohibition—the clear impression from our search of the economic literature is that the domain of economic analysis following the classical period largely excluded consideration of felonious behavior and so-called nonmarket activity in general. Though we can offer no definitive explanation of why economists' interest declined, some possible reasons, which we shall briefly explore, suggest themselves.

Our basic explanation concerns the perceived "marginal product" of research efforts—in terms of innovation and discovery—to be realized by focusing on a narrower range of topics than that cultivated by classical economists. Ricardo's attempt at formalizing a theory of market equilibrium in connection with value and distribution was a first step toward the professionalization of economics as a science that already involved a narrowing of the scope of issues of political economy analyzed by Smith and the utilitarians. The later emergence of marginal economics in utility and production theory occupied the attention of the finest economists of the last half of the nineteenth century and the early twentieth century as well. Jevons, Menger, Walras, Marshall, J. B. Clark, Edgeworth, Pareto, and Irving Fisher all devoted their talents to the systematic development of marginal utility and marginal productivity theories and the resulting laws of equilibrium in production, investment, and distribution.[5] Efforts to resolve and systematize these theoretical matters partly through use of mathematics and geometry not only preoccupied the thoughts of economists of the time, but firmly oriented economics toward analysis of traditional market-related activity.

Second, developments elsewhere in the social sciences also help account for the waning of economists' interest in issues of crime and punishment. The classical approach was supplanted in academic thought, if not in law, by a variety of alternatives known collectively as the positivist approach which, in its various forms, was strongly deterministic in methodology.[6] The positivist theoretical approaches were articulated along two general lines: one emphasizing the innate constitu-

[4]See Thoreilli (1955, esp. chaps. VI.3 and III.5) for a discussion of economists' views on antitrust policy and related issues at the time of passage of the Sherman Act.
[5]The substance of these developments and their historical importance are elaborated upon in Howey (1960), Black et al. (1972), and Stigler (1965, chap. 5; 1968).
[6]See Radzinowicz (1966, esp. chap. 2) for a review of the development of the positivist approach. De Quiros (1911, chaps. 1-3) provides a more detailed review by a contemporary of the major figures in criminology in its early decades.

tional factors characterizing "criminal man"; the second emphasizing the environmental factors that shape him. Possibly reflecting then-contemporary advances in biology and medicine, including Darwin's writings and Pasteur's discoveries, the constitutionalists related crime to considerations of inheritance, disease, and race. The environmentalists sought the factors determining a social behavior in various, primarily social, phenomena reflecting, in part, the Marxist reliance on economic and social structure.[7] Of course, there are formal similarities between the positivists and classicists, for some of the environmental factors, e.g., wages or legal income, raised by the positivists can be interpreted as objective opportunities. But the two approaches differ over the fundamental issue of individuals' capacity to choose among alternative opportunities and to respond to changes in those opportunities. As Bonger puts it in 1936, "He who . . . still adheres to the doctrine of free will cannot be admitted to the criminologist fraternity. An indeterminist criminologist is a living *contradicto in adjecto*" (Bonger, 1936:21). In the late nineteenth century the various strands of positivist thought provided the foundation for the establishment of criminology as a new academic discipline with its own schools of thought and specialists. Thus the progress of the division of labor in the social sciences generally, as well as within economics itself, further removed economists' interest from criminal activity.

At least with respect to Great Britain, where prominent classical economists accepted the deterrence principle, another reason can be offered for the diminished interest of subsequent economists in crime: The importance of crime as a social problem decreased dramatically at least during the last half of the nineteenth century and quite probably earlier. From 1857 to 1900 alone the rate of offenses known to police in England and Wales dropped about 42 percent.[8] Given this trend, and

---

[7]Bonger (1916) contains a notable exposition of an early Marxist analysis of crime.

[8]The data used for the calculation are from Great Britain—Parliament (1907:79 of pt. I). The offense rates are annual averages over five-year intervals of the aggregate, indictable Class I–VI crimes known to the police per 100,000 population. The year 1857 apparently is the first year of this system of maintaining criminal statistics; the first interval for which an annual average is taken is 1857–1860.

We note in passing that this sharp decline in crime rates, possibly starting a few decades earlier, is not inconsistent with an explanation based on the economic model. In the first place, the level of crime might have been expected to decline over the most part of the nineteenth century because of the progress of growth enhanced by the Industrial Revolution, and the accompanying ultimate increase in legitimate opportunities for those in the lower earnings brackets. Second, the decline in crime followed a significant structural shift from a system of private to public enforcement in the early nineteenth century. The likelihood of offenders being apprehended and tried may have increased significantly in the second quarter of the nineteenth century due to the increased role granted to police with the establishment of the metropolitan London police in 1829. Police activity spread gradually until it became compulsory throughout England in 1856 (see Stephen, 1883, vol. 1:197–200).

the economic expansion accompanying England's nineteenth-century industrialization, it is clear that relative to, say, gross national product the social costs of the criminal sector were reduced by an even more considerable proportion than the absolute fall in crime rate. The hypothesis that economists' interest in crime may fluctuate, in part, due to the seriousness of crime as a social problem is at least consistent with the revival of economists' interest in the United States and elsewhere in the 1960s. Aggregate offense rates in the U.S., rising generally since World War II, increased most precipitously starting in the late 1950s.[9] As rational men, scholars apparently respond to opportunities to further knowledge in those areas where social payoffs, and as a consequence the "value" of the product of research efforts, may be high.

Economists and criminologists alike cannot evaluate the deterrence hypothesis strictly on logical grounds. As compelling as the a priori logic of deterrence was to, say, Malthus, Ferri was fully persuaded to the contrary.[10] Whether punishment deters, and criminal behavior generally is responsive to incentives, ultimately must be established on empirical grounds in the same way that the responsiveness of other types of human behavior has been tested. The accumulation of evidence by criminologists and other scholars, allegedly rejecting the deterrence hypothesis and confirming the hypotheses of alternative approaches, may have further "deterred" economists from pursuing the study of criminality. Indeed, there is some indication that two notable economists—Pareto (1935:1282–83) and Irving Fisher (1909:51–54, 124–25)—may have been influenced by evidence of the second sort that was gathered by positivists of the Italian school in support of their theories. Because of its independent importance, we undertake an evaluation of empirical evidence, bearing directly on deterrence, in the following section.

Evidence and Inference: Studies by Sellin, Schuessler, and Some Predecessors

The focus of much of the empirical work on deterrence in both the nineteenth and the twentieth centuries has been the deterrent efficacy of the death penalty. Researchers' interest in the topic, while partly at-

[9]For example, the aggregate estimated offense rate in the U.S. (for FBI index crimes) increased about 33 percent from 1946 to 1959, and about 150 percent from 1959 to 1969.

[10]"No man ... can doubt for a moment," writes Malthus, "that if every murder in Italy had been invariably punished, the use of the stiletto in transports of passion would have been comparatively but little known" (Malthus, 1798:259). By contrast, Ferri writes, "punishments, in which until now ... the best remedies against crime have possibly been seen, have none of the efficacy attributed to them" (Ferri, 1917:214).

tributable to the historical and political significance of the debate on the general merits of the death penalty as a social instrument, seems to have been prompted to a large extent by the unique opportunity to test the deterrence hypothesis in connection with what most of them considered to be the most extreme of sanctions. As Schuessler interprets the deterrence hypothesis, "Since people fear death more than anything else, the death penalty is the most effective deterrent, so runs the argument" (Schuessler, 1952:54).

The overall impression one obtains from surveying the twentieth-century literature on the deterrent effect of capital punishment in connection with the crime of murder is that the penalty has had no effect whatever on the incidence of murder in the population. More than fifty years of intermittent empirical analysis of varying scope yielded remarkable, indeed enviable, agreement among researchers who uniformly concluded that the death penalty is inconsequential, and who differed only in the definitiveness with which this general conclusion was expressed. The consistent failure of the researchers to observe any deterrent or preventive effects thus was interpreted as a categorical rejection of the deterrence hypothesis in general. In fact, so great was the impact of this research that the issue of deterrence was considered by criminologists and other social scientists throughout most of this century as closed.[11] This section reconsiders some of the evidence that has served as a basis for the strong inferences on deterrence, in particular works by Thorsten Sellin.[12]

It may come as a surprise to some readers that in the nineteenth century investigations were conducted on the deterrent efficacy of sanctions, and capital punishment in particular, that relied on a methodology apparently similar to that used by twentieth-century researchers, but that provided evidence not so unambiguous as the subsequent twentieth-century research. A few examples will illustrate. Reviewing European studies on the deterrent effect of the death penalty, Tarde (1912:chap. 9) refers to evidence of his own and others from Rhode Island, Michigan, Switzerland, Finland, Belgium, and Austria, where the frequency of murder and other capital offenses increased following the abolition of the death penalty. He finds the balance of the evidence "generally favorable to deterrence" (Tarde, 1912:562). Garofalo

---

[11]Cf. Tittle and Logan (1973:371–72). It is interesting to introduce in this connection Bedau's congressional testimony: "History is yet to record a single empirical study undertaken by those who defend the death penalty on deterrent grounds" (U.S. House of Representatives, 1972:215).

[12]Evidence compiled by Sellin, allegedly rejecting the deterrent efficacy of the death penalty, has figured prominently in the legislative deliberations in England, Canada, and the United States; see, for instance, Royal Commission on Capital Punishment (1953:23); Canada—Parliament (1956:12–13); and U.S. House of Representatives (1972:162–64).

(1914:202), after examining available data on crime levels in Europe, attributes the increases in crime in France, Italy, Germany, and the Austrian Empire in the nineteenth century, in part, to diminished punishment severity in those countries, while similarly attributing England's falling crime rates to the maintenance of relatively severe punishments, including the death penalty. Garofalo's recognition of an appreciable deterrent efficacy of the death penalty[13] is remarkable in that he was one of the noted positivists of his time. But perhaps most interesting, an anonymous 1832 article in the prestigious *Quarterly Review,* later attributed to Charles Edward Dodd, a barrister,[14] presents English evidence in which the incidence of murder, rape, forgery, arson, stabbings and wounding, housebreaking, and sheep stealing are shown to vary inversely with the probability of execution for those crimes. This is the first instance we are aware of in which an empirical analysis of crime fluctuations uses a probability of punishment measure to indicate the actual threat of punishment and to correlate it with variation in crime.

However, not only does evidence from the nineteenth century defy the frequent assertion[15] that the death penalty has never been shown to have any discernible effect on the incidence of murder, but one of the pioneering modern studies in this area (Schuessler, 1952) also presented evidence not inconsistent with the deterrence hypothesis.[16] The 1952 study by Karl Schuessler is noteworthy because it proposed some of the statistical methodology that was also adopted in other studies discussed in this section. However, Schuessler's work goes beyond later work in attempting to arrive at a more direct parametric test of the deterrence hypothesis. After examining the deterrence hypothesis and stating his disbelief in its scientific value, Schuessler proposed to test it directly through an investigation of the impact of the certainty of imposition of

---

[13]Tarde (1912:544) comments in this context: "Garofalo believes himself authorized with the figures at his disposal to prove that everywhere the scaffold has been overthrown . . . the evidence of the deplorable results by its overthrow had compelled the government to restore it."

[14]See Houghton (1966) in reference to "Punishment of Death—Wakefield on Newgate," *Quarterly Review* 47 (March and July 1832):170–216. We are grateful to Aaron Director for providing this most illuminating reference. Aside from the direct issue of deterrence, Dodd considers in this article the association between the probabilities of execution and conviction for different crimes.

[15]Cf. Sellin (1959:80–84) and Bedau's congressional testimony cited at n. 11 supra.

[16]In fact, an earlier twentieth-century study by MacDonald (1910) considered data from countries throughout Europe and elsewhere bearing on the association between the death penalty and crime. He reached the conclusion that "in certain localities at certain times the death penalty has been shown with great probabilities to lessen certain forms of crime" (p. 115). While MacDonald does not present a systematic analysis of his data that would support a strong inference, his research and conclusions have been widely ignored in the popular literature.

capital punishment on the rate of murder in places where the death penalty is actually imposed. He implemented this test by defining the risk of execution as the ratio of executions to 1,000 homicides for the period 1937–1949 in forty-one executing states, and correlating it with the homicide rate in these states. The correlation coefficient was found to be $-.26$, indicating a tendency for the homicide rate to diminish as the unconditional probability of execution rose. Nevertheless, Schuessler dismissed his finding by arguing that this tendency was not uniform across all states and that it was barely significant. A reanalysis of Schuessler's findings indicates, however, that the correlation he estimated is significant statistically at the 5 percent level for a one-tail test.[17]

In evaluating Schuessler's results one may notice, first, that he used homicide rather than murder statistics in calculating the dependent and independent variables. This may lead, in part, to a spurious negative association between the two resulting from identical errors in the numerator and denominator of the dependent and independent variables, respectively.[18] In contrast, since the correlation analysis was performed for values of the variables averaged over a period of thirteen years, the true correlation between contemporaneous values of the relevant variables may not have been measured appropriately, and in fact may have been understated because of offsetting correlations between current and lagged values of the relevant dependent and independent variables. Schuessler's simple correlation coefficient may also be biased downward because of a reversed causal relationship. An unusually high murder rate may create an incentive to retain and enforce the death penalty. And, of course, Schuessler does not control for the effect of other relevant factors, a point returned to later in this section. His "low" correlation coefficient is thus not entirely unexpected. Indeed, by using murder statistics and estimates of the conditional probability of execution given conviction for the years 1940 and 1950, and by implementing an efficient multiple regression procedure, Schuessler might have obtained a much higher correlation between murder and the risk of execution— one that is also free of a spurious negative association—as a recent study indicates (Ehrlich, 1977).

Despite its intriguing approach and findings, Schuessler's work received relatively little attention in the literature on capital punishment.[19]

[17]Schuessler does not explain his method of constructing the relevant indices and performing the correlation analysis with sufficient detail to permit a rigorous evaluation of his test statistic. On the assumption that his simple correlation $r = -.26$ is based on just 39 degrees of freedom, the implied t statistic associated with his measure of execution risk would be about 1.684, which is significant at the 5 percent level for a one-tail test. The formula connecting r and t is $t = \sqrt{d.f. r^2/1 - r^2}$, where $d.f.$ denotes the number of degrees of freedom (see R. A. Fisher, 1954:193).

[18]For a specific illustration see I. Ehrlich (1974:App. 1 to sec. IV).

[19]For example, Schuessler's paper is not included in the popular collections of papers on the deterrent value of the death penalty assembled by Sellin (1967) and Bedau (1967).

Far more frequently cited are the studies by Thorsten Sellin (see Sellin, 1959, 1961, 1967). While we shall henceforth focus on Sellin's research, the general comments also apply to other studies using a similar methodology.[20]

Sellin proposed to test the hypothetical deterrent effect of capital punishment mainly through testing three related hypotheses. First, he argued, the incidence of murder should be less frequent in states having the death penalty than in those that have abolished it, all other factors being equal. Second, murders should increase when the death penalty is abolished and decline when it is restored. Third, law-enforcement agents should be safer from murderous attacks in states that have the death penalty than in those without it.

To perform the first test, Sellin compared homicide death rates in six groups of contiguous retentionist and abolitionist states in the United States over the period between 1920 and 1963. Each group included an abolitionist state and two bordering retentionist states. Visual inspection of the data revealed no evidence distinguishing the abolitionist state from the others, asserted Sellin. "The conclusion is inevitable that the presence of the death penalty—either in law or in practice—does not influence homicide death rates" (Sellin, 1967:138; 1959:34).

In the second test, Sellin attempted to examine the effect of a temporary removal of the death penalty from the statutes of eleven states for periods varying in duration on the average annual rate of murder and nonnegligent manslaughter committed during the abolition period, as compared with the same datum in the five-year period immediately preceding and following the abolition period. By Sellin's own evaluation, the quality of the pertinent data from these states is poor in many instances. Only a fraction of them had the complete relevant data for the purpose of the desired comparison. For some states Sellin reports statistics on the total *number* of murders (which is likely to rise over time simply because of an increase in population size) and for some he reports statistics on murder rates. Even so, the few complete comparisons yielded mixed results, some consistent with the deterrence hypothesis, some inconsistent. Nevertheless, Sellin's inference from these data has been that "there is no evidence that the abolition of the death penalty

---

[20]For example, the earlier twentieth-century studies of Bye (1919) and Sutherland in 1925, and some later studies cited below, utilized methodologies similar to that of Sellin. Bye looks at homicide rate data across (reporting) states, grouped regionally, from 1904 to 1915. He infers that no relationship exists between the legal status of the death penalty and the homicide rate either across neighboring states or over time in states where the legal status has changed. Sutherland (1973) engages in the two same types of comparison over the period of 1913 to 1922, limited, as was Bye, to registered states in the vital statistics mortality tabulations. He concludes similarly: "There is no evidence of a significant relation between the murder rate and the probability or practice of using the death penalty as a punishment for murder" (p. 182).

generally causes an increase in criminal homicides, or its reintroduction
is followed by a decline" (Sellin, 1967:124).

To test the third hypothesis, Sellin examined information from a
sample of 128 cities in seventeen states—six abolitionists and eleven bordering the abolitionist states—on the number of policemen killed by
lethal weapons during the period between 1919 and 1954. The rates of
policemen murdered in the population of different city size classes were
then computed using the respective city population figures from 1950 as
a deflator. These rates were compared across abolitionist and retentionist states and found to be roughly equal. From examination of this
evidence Sellin inferred "it is impossible to conclude that the states which
have abolished the death penalty have thereby made the policeman's lot
more hazardous" (Sellin, 1967:147).

While Sellin's hypotheses are, in principle, relevant for the purpose
of an empirical test of an overall deterrence or incapacitating effect of
capital punishment, his actual test procedure suffers from three fundamental shortcomings. The first concerns the nature of the tests as they
were conducted. Unlike Schuessler, Sellin does not provide any
parametric or nonparametric statistical inference tests that could justify
his rather strong conclusions. Also, no sensitivity analysis is reported in
reference to the particular groupings of states compared in testing the
first and third hypotheses, even though the choice of two retentionist
states bordering on an abolitionist state is in many cases arbitrary. Moreover, the comparison made in connection with the third hypothesis is not
the desired one. What Sellin should have compared is not the number of
policemen killed relative to the state population but rather the number
killed relative to either the relevant size of the police force or the number
of violent crimes committed in the state.[21] It is the latter ratios that
indicate the probability of a policeman's death from a felonious attack.
Unfortunately, the raw data and information concerning the size of
police forces in the cities included in Sellin's work are not available in
published sources, and so no attempt was made here to calculate the
proper ratios.

A more serious shortcoming of all three tests is that comparisons of
homicide rates are made between states in which the death penalty has
been declared illegal and states in which it has remained legal, with no
account taken of the extent of the actual enforcement of the death
penalty in practice. But the relevant variable, by Sellin's own analysis, is
the risk of execution, not its legal status, for "where [the death penalty] is

[21]The comparisons between "abolition" and "death penalty" states are also troublesome
because of the very unequal representation of these states in Sellin's sample of cities and
because the sample did not contain data from some key cities; in a few comparisons,
states were represented by a single city only (see Sellin, 1959).

present in the law alone it would be completely robbed of its threat" (Sellin, 1959:20). The point is far from being subtle, because in a number of the groups examined by Sellin in testing his first and third hypotheses, the risk of execution in the so-called retentionist states has been negligible throughout the period considered. For example, in Vermont, New Hampshire, South Dakota, and Nebraska, the death penalty was hardly ever applied between 1930 and 1963 (or afterward), and in Massachusetts it was not enforced after 1947; in fact, the risk of execution has become negligible in most "retentionist" states since the late 1950s. Indeed, the differences between the homicide death rates of "retentionist" and "abolitionist" states in the various groups examined by Sellin are generally greater in the early years relative to the later years included in the sample. This is not inconsistent with the hypothesis that the risk of execution does have a systematic effect on the incidence of murder.

A similar criticism applies to the test performed in reference to the second hypothesis. For example, in both Delaware and South Dakota, the objective risk of execution in the five-year periods preceding and following their experiments in the legal abolition of capital punishment is nil.[22]

The most important shortcoming common to all three tests is the lack of any systematic standardization of the data to insure that the effect of

---

[22]This criticism applies even more strongly in connection with tests performed by Bowers (1974: chap. 6) to determine the effect of the moratorium on executions in the United States since 1967 on murder trends across abolition and death penalty states. Following Sellin's methodology, Bowers compares the levels of murder rates in nine groups of arbitrarily chosen mixes of neighboring "abolition" and "death penalty" states in the four years preceding the judicial moratorium and in the four years subsequent to it and finds similar patterns in most groups. However, the plain fact is that *none* of the states classified in eight of the nine groups has had a single execution throughout the period investigated by Bowers. Moreover, in the ninth group Bowers creates a distinction between New York, which he classifies as an abolitionist state, and New Jersey and Pennsylvania, which he classifies as retentionists, although New York ceased all executions in 1963—the same year as New Jersey and one year after Pennsylvania. Wolfgang, in U.S. House of Representatives (1972:181, 184–89), reports upon the very same type of exercise for the period 1963–1970. Bowers also reports the results of another extension of Sellin's analysis where neighboring death penalty states are distinguished by whether they are either "discretionary" or "mandatory" death penalty states by law, and their crime rates compared. Again, a brief examination of actual execution policies since 1930 shows that "mandatory" and "discretionary" provisions on the books bear little relation to the extent of execution in practice. For example, South Carolina actually executed more convicts than North Carolina after it became a "discretionary" capital punishment state. Massachusetts and Vermont stopped executions in 1947 and 1954 respectively, or about three to four years before the changes in their status took place. In New York, where the change to discretionary status in 1963 was also coupled with cessation of executions, the murder rate did in fact go up sharply in subsequent years, and the same increase occurred in neighboring Pennsylvania, which also stopped executions in 1962, although its status as a discretionary state remained unchanged both before and after it ceased all executions.

other factors that might influence the frequency of murder in the population, and that are expected to be systematically related to the risk of execution, be in some way controlled so that the partial effect of the death penalty may be properly isolated.[23] Clearly aware of this problem, Sellin (1959:21) has emphasized the need to compare states that are "as alike as possible in all other respects." However, Sellin's assumption, like that of Schuessler (1952:57), that neighboring states satisfy such a prerequisite, is unacceptable. Pairs of states such as New York and Rhode Island, Massachusetts and Maine, or Illinois and Wisconsin, which are included in comparisons made by Schuessler, Sellin, and others, differ in their economic and demographic characteristics, in their overall crime rates, in their law enforcement activities, and in the efficiency of medical services provided victims of aggravated assault (see I. Ehrlich, 1977:sec. II). In addition, variations in the legal status of the death penalty may occasionally be caused by, rather than be the cause for, significant changes in the rate of murder, and thus may give rise to an apparent positive association between the two variables. The true effect of the death penalty on the murder rate might not then be readily observed through simple comparisons. This difficulty has been ignored in practically all the studies surveyed; when recognized in theory (as in Sellin, 1961:6; Sutherland, 1973:180), it was not dealt with in the empirical investigation and did not lead to any modifications in the inferences drawn. Clearly, the task of controlling for all possible variations in relevant factors or circumstances affecting cross-sectional and time series comparisons is impossible to achieve in practice, as Schuessler notes. However, the extent to which the criterion "all other things being equal" is satisfied in principle can be judged only if the major determinants of murder and law enforcement activity are identified in light of some theoretical considerations. Since the null hypothesis concerns the deter-

[23]Bailey (1975) uses Sellin's methodology to compare estimates of *conviction* rates per 100,000 population relating to persons convicted of murders of various degrees across states labeled as "death penalty" and "abolition" states in 1967 and 1968. The choice of these two years for the purpose of cross-state comparisons seems unfortunate, given that no executions took place in 1968 and a total of only two occurred in two states in 1967. In addition, the annual number of executions in individual retentionist states approached negligible dimensions throughout the 1960s. Inferences drawn from cross-state comparisons over that period would be highly imprecise. Moreover, Bailey does not control systematically for differences in the level of deterrence (and other) variables across the two subsets of states. Controlling for conviction risks is particularly important in his analysis, however, since the variables he compares are estimates of conviction, rather than offense, rates. It is interesting to note, however, that when Bailey calculates the correlation between estimates of the unconditional probability of execution, based on the ratios of executions to criminal homicides in the five years preceding 1967 and 1968, and the murder indices in the latter two years he, not unlike Schuessler before him, finds the correlation coefficient to be negative. Moreover, he finds the correlation coefficient between execution risk and the murder index to be higher in absolute value than the corresponding correlation coefficient between execution risk and homicide rate defined to include both murders and nonnegligent manslaughters.

rent effect of capital punishment predicted by the utilitarian approach, it seems appropriate to expect a systematic test of this hypothesis to implement the general implications of that approach. No such systematic implementation was attempted in the studies noted or in other studies following a similar methodology.

It is evident from a survey of the main studies on the deterrent effect of capital punishment that these studies do not provide a direct test of the deterrence hypothesis. What, then, is the basis for the strong inferences denying the existence of any effect of the death penalty? At the basis of most such inferences lies the following reasoning: The analysis shows, most authors asserted, that other factors besides capital punishment, and certainly not the death penalty alone, are responsible for variations and trends in the homicide or murder rates across "abolition" and "death penalty" states. Even if the comparisons made are relevant and the results obtained are valid, such findings cannot be considered as evidence against the deterrence hypothesis unless that hypothesis is entirely misconstrued to imply that the death penalty *alone* determines movements in the murder rate. Specifically, if differences in the true risk of execution are effectively accounted for in comparisons of trends in the murder rate in different states over time, then these trends may be expected to exhibit great similarities because of common factors operating at the national level, such as fluctuations in business cycles, changes in federal government and Supreme Court policies in the area of law enforcement and criminal justice procedure, and improvements in the technology of saving lives, which may have caused considerable reduction in the proportion of all murderous assaults resulting in "murder" (i.e., the death of the victim). Clearly, similarity in trends of murder in different states over time cannot be interpreted by any conventional logic as implying that demographic, economic, and political factors *alone* determine changes in the crime rate, as some researchers seem to imply (see, e.g., Sellin, 1961:6).

The Role of Theory in Guiding Empirical Research

Just as the ultimate measure of success of a positive theory is its ability to explain observed phenomena of interest, an effective and valid test of the theory's explanatory power must systematically and rigorously implement its relevant set of empirical implications. Without such systematic implementation an empirical investigation runs the risk of being just a futile experiment in tautology, reflecting the artificial environment of the experiment conducted rather than the reality of the phenomena to be explained.

Does punishment exert a deterrent effect, and, if so, how may its existence be verified? By what statistical tests can one, in principle, accept or reject the proposition that punishment in general, or capital punishment in particular, deters the commission of crime by actual or potential offenders? And what are the relevant null hypotheses? Should it be posited, for example, that capital punishment has *no* effect on the incidence of murder, or can executions be expected to exert some preventive or incapacitative effects that are independent of any deterrent influence? The last question is particularly intriguing because a theory that states that offenders do not respond to incentives surely must recognize that executions nonetheless may reduce crime by eliminating categorically the possibility of recidivism on the part of those punished. A similar argument applies also in connection with punishment by imprisonment or detention. The analytical challenge, then, is to distinguish such preventive effects from the hypothesized "pure" deterrent effects. Furthermore, a key question to be addressed in testing the deterrent effect of capital punishment specifically is not whether any such effect exists, but whether the death penalty has a differential deterrent effect over and above that of the most common alternative. This issue would be particularly important in those instances where the alternative is actual imprisonment for life rather than the present-day typical "life imprisonment" term of ten years or less. More important, in testing for the deterrent effect of the criminal sanctions from empirical observations concerning crime rates and severity and certainty measures of punishment, would the actual correlations exhibit responsiveness of offense rates to variations in punishments or reactions of law enforcement agencies to variations in crime levels? To the extent that the deterrence hypothesis is valid and punishment is an efficient instrument for the prevention of crime, wouldn't society react to increases in the risk of criminal victimization by setting more severe penalties and expanding resources to enforce those penalties so as to achieve a proper balance between the marginal social gains from crime prevention and the marginal social costs of law enforcement? To test for the validity of the deterrence hypothesis, it thus becomes necessary for researchers to recognize that by the very same hypothesis observed associations between indicators of crime and punishment might exhibit apparently perverse results due to society's response to the threat of crime, although the underlying true causal relationships may be perfectly consistent with the deterrence hypothesis.[24]

The brief overview of some of the past evidence on deterrence in

---

[24]For a more detailed exposition of those aspects of the economic formulation of the deterrence theory see Becker (1974), I. Ehrlich (1974, 1975, 1977), and Ehrlich and Gibbons (1977).

the preceding section has attempted to provide some notion of the methodology upon which previous inferences have been based. More generally, the argument we have attempted to develop is this: To devise an adequate procedure for testing for the classical deterrence hypothesis, one must test the full set of implications emanating from the deterrence theory rather than view separately and in isolation particular associations between specific variables of interest. While the existence of deterrent effects ultimately is an empirical matter, it cannot be studied effectively without thorough considerations of related theoretical issues. An adequate analytical framework should recognize, for example, that if capital punishment deters potential murderers, then surely other punishments imposed on convicted offenders should also impart deterrent effects, and their influence on the rate of murder must be properly accounted for in the context of the statistical analysis. The converse follows *a fortiori:* If investigations indicate that apprehension and temporary imprisonment of convicted murderers do impart statistically significant deterrent effects, then failure of research to demonstrate specifically the deterrent efficacy of capital punishment may be taken more as evidence of shortcomings in research design and methodology or imperfections of measures of the theoretically relevant variables than as a reflection on the validity of the deterrence theory. And, whether considering capital punishment or punishment by imprisonment, one cannot expect sanctions imposed only rarely and with much delay to affect offenders' behavior as they would if imposed with greater frequency and swiftness. Actual enforcement must always be taken into account. The theory of deterrence indicates not only the direction of the effects of specific deterrence instruments such as the risk of apprehension, the conditional risk of conviction given apprehension, and the conditional risk of specific punishments given conviction, but also the relative magnitudes of these effects (I. Ehrlich, 1977). A systematic test therefore must address ranking as well as signs of the relevant parameters. An adequate analytical framework should also recognize the role played by "positive" as well as "negative" incentives. Inasmuch as empirical evidence indicates that crime is enhanced by reductions in legitimate earning opportunities, such evidence can provide support for the deterrence hypothesis derived from economic theory in much the same way as would evidence on the deterrence efficacy of criminal sanctions. An empirical implementation of a comprehensive theory of deterrence should thus seek to control for the effects of all *relevant* incentives. More important, in view of the expected simultaneous relations between offense and defense against crime, causal relationships must be identified so that deterrent effects might be approximately estimated. Finally, an effective link must be established between the theoretical framework, which identifies the relevant theoretical constructs and predicts their respective roles, and the empirical implementation, which includes choice of efficient empirical counterparts of the relevant theoretical variables as well as selection of statistical data that exhibit genuine and sufficiently large variations in crime and sanction levels so as to insure statistically meaningful tests of the hypothesis of no deterrence.[25] All these considerations must be taken into account before any systematic inferences can be drawn about the validity of the deterrence hypothesis.

[25]These considerations apparently have been overlooked not only in some of the statistical studies reviewed in the last section but also in some of the more recent research that purports to implement an economic methodology. For example, the analyses by Passel (1975) and Forst (1977), based on cross-sectional data relating to homicides and executions in 1960 and 1970, depend entirely on the presumed distribution of the execution risk measures in these years. However, no *meaningful* distributions of execution risk are available in these years since there were no executions in 1970, and in 1960 in twelve out of twenty "executing" states for which complete data are available only a single execution occurred, with the trend in all such states clearly leading toward a practical abolition of the death penalty. At such small levels of execution in each state and with an attenuated distribution of execution risk measures, the effects of errors in the estimates are likely to dominate the comparisons across states both in a given year and for changes over time. For a meaningful test of the hypothesis of *no deterrence* (which is what the statistical tests are about), one must be careful to analyze those situations in which such a hypothesis can conceivably be rejected. To do otherwise would amount to searching for the lost coin under the streetlight.

IV

The Impact of Contemporary Trends in the Family on Socialization

15

Introduction

Reuben Hill

THE FOLLOWING THREE PAPERS are concerned with the impacts of contemporary trends in the family on socialization viewed from the perspectives of sociology, psychology, and anthropology. Although these three disciplines have been deeply concerned among the social sciences with the issues of socialization and the family, we should note that in recent years economists, political scientists, social gerontologists, demographers, and historians have all brought distinctive perspectives to these issues. Each discipline is inclined to ascribe the impacts of recent demographic family trends on the dimensions of socialization of higher interest to the specialty: consumer choices and the rise of consumerism for consumption economists; patterns of political participation and party affiliations for the behaviorally oriented political scientists; styles of life and career management in the middle and later years for social gerontologists; patterns of family formation and family size control for social demographers; and the search for the historical origins of contemporary family forms and socialization patterns by family historians.

The three authors have interpreted contemporary trends in the family to refer to post–World War II changes to give us a common time frame, and have focused on the North American region of the world for the statement of trends. However, Dr. Whiting has utilized the scope that anthropoligical and comparative researches require to place North American developments in a broader perspective. We will also assume that socialization occurs over the entire life span rather than solely in the period of early childhood. This allows discussion of the acquisition and activation of roles in middle and later adulthood, for which shaping is provided by one's juniors and peers as much as by one's seniors, thus

making intergenerational socialization a two-way process over the life
span of the participants. To achieve something of a common focus, the
authors have been selective in their choice of trends. Ideally one would
spell out *which trends* in the family have *what impacts* on *what aspects of
socialization.* This may involve a degree of precision that the research
data don't justify. Panel members will alert us when that is the case.

In completing this introductory statement may I present a series of
trends drawn largely from U.S. census sources, preceded by caveats
about their durability. Complicating the assertions of trends since World
War II is the curvilinear nature of a number of the trends. Marriage and
divorce rates peaked immediately after demobilization (1945–1947) and
then declined into the early 1960s. The rate of first marriages has continued to decline in the 1970s, whereas second marriages increased with
the divorce rate, after about fifteen years of decline, suggesting that
remarriage is a function of divorce. The recent dramatic increases in the
divorce rate hardly warrant extrapolation into the future until we can
explain the downswing of fifteen years earlier. The declining birth rate
of the 1970s must also be seen as a downturn in 1965 after more than
twenty years of sustained and largely voluntary high rates of family
building. The fertility rate in 1970 (87.9) was still higher than the prewar
1940 rate of 79.9 births per 1,000 women. Interpretation of trends is
always precarious when the phenomenon is cyclic and subject to fads and
fashions as well as to the vagaries of the business cycle.

Without further reservations, let me list some recent trends in family
structure and functioning that have implications for fulfilling the crucial
socialization function:

1. Decrease in average completed family size and with that a decrease in numbers of brothers and sisters to participate in peer
   socialization.
   a) Compared to the 1950s, children of the late 1970s live in a
      world of fewer children, fewer siblings, and more adults.
2. Decrease in average family size is not the result of increased
   childlessness nor of increase in families of only children, but is
   due to a decline in families of five or more children.
   a) Childlessness remains at 8–10 percent of marriages and only-
      children families at 10 percent over the past twenty years.
   b) Expectations of childlessness in surveys is up from 2 percent in
      1970 to 5 percent in 1975, a negligible trend that has been
      exaggerated by the mass media.
3. Decline in marriage rates for late adolescents and those in their
   early twenties accompanied by an increase in unwed motherhood
   among teenagers.

4. Increase in divorce rates and of rates of remarriage after fifteen
   years of decline.
   a) Increase of divorces involving children but a continued de-
      crease of widowhood involving children.
   b) More parents divorcing than remarrying.
   c) Mary Jo Bane (1976:15-20) notes that compared with the
      nineteenth century there is a net decline in children being
      placed out with relatives or in foster homes when the marriage
      is fractured—most children are reared by both parents who
      survive to see them launched, and where death or divorce has
      occurred the children continue living with at least one parent.
5. An increase in neolocal independent households of one or two
   generations; namely, single young adults, aged adults, unrelated
   adults, newly married adults, and single-parent households.
   a) Most of the increase in single-parent households is due to in-
      creases in marital disruption (23 percent) and to increases in
      marital disruption involving children (20 percent), but the in-
      crease in the unmarried with children setting up separate
      households is not negligible (21 percent for blacks, 9 percent
      for whites).
   b) The distaste for three-generation households in America is of
      long duration. They have been uncommon except under situa-
      tions of severe economic crisis. Boundary setting to insure pri-
      vacy is a high value for newly marrieds, single parents, and
      aged couples who might, however, have mutual gains from
      doubling up.
6. The last of the trends to be cited, and possibly the most powerful
   of all is the improvement in the status of women in and out of the
   family setting, associated with increased educational and career
   opportunities, choice of residence, and control of property.
   a) Increased gainful employment of women since World War II
      is most marked among mothers who had remained out of the
      labor force earlier. Employment of mothers of children under
      six years tripled from 1948 to 1975, and doubled for mothers
      of children six–seventeen years old.
   b) But the highest maternal employment rates are among women
      heading single-parent households.

A committee of the National Academy of Science (1976) charged to
recommend a national policy for children and families worked from the
same factual data I have cited, but interpreted the trends as damaging to
families and to the socializing of children. They saw employment patterns and residential mobility as increasing the isolation of children from

adults. With both parents working or with the sole parent in a single-parent household away all day, they saw inadequate supervision. Observing virtually no three-generation households, they saw a decreased utilization of the extended family. In effect, "they saw nobody about to mind the store"! There was diversity of perspectives in this committee made up of economists, psychologists, pediatricians, lawyers, and social workers, which may explain their "trendy-type" conclusions. I for one would disagree vigorously with most of them, as would most family sociologists.

16

Current Changes in the Family and Their Impact Upon the Socialization of Children

Eleanor E. Maccoby

THE CHANGES THAT ARE taking place in the family are profound, widespread, and well documented. The divorce rate continues to rise. Both the number and proportion of children born out of wedlock also continue to rise. There is a growing proportion of unwed mothers who are very young—not merely in their teens, but in their fairly early teens. Both the rising divorce rate and the increase in births to unwed mothers mean that there is a dramatic increase in the number of children being raised by a single parent. In Western industrialized societies, the birthrate has also undergone a remarkable decline.

Linked to all these changes is the increasing representation of women in the labor force, and the increasing tendency of women to work while their children are young. The nature of the linkages among these various trends is indeed difficult to understand. Are women working more because they are bearing and rearing fewer children, and need something to do with their time? Or are they bearing fewer children because they must work for economic reasons? Is the divorce rate going up because, once women work, they are economically able to free themselves from bad marriages? Or is it the case that divorce is occurring for other reasons and that women work as a consequence, not as a cause, of divorce? No doubt the lines of influence run in both directions and we are dealing with a closely interwoven matrix of circular processes. Economic factors are certainly involved in such a cycle. As one example: The rising interest rates—part of a tight-money policy intended to combat inflation—increased housing prices and slowed down the rate of construction of new housing at a time when the postwar baby boom population bulge was reaching marriageable age. Housing was scarce and prices rose. The fact that some women were working meant that their families had the purchasing power to pay more for scarce houses. But this contributed to further increases in housing prices, to the point where families with only one wage earner were virtually priced out of the market, and many mothers who might have preferred to remain home with their children were forced into the job market so that they and their husbands could earn enough to buy a house. Thus the factors that led *some* women to work have fed back into increased pressure for other women to work.

Please understand that I do not mean to deplore the entry of women into the job market nor to attribute the inflation of house prices entirely, or even mainly, to their incomes. I only mean to illustrate the complexity of forces underlying the current changes in the family. My own intuition is that the widespread availability of cheap and effective contraception is the single most powerful factor underlying the present changes. If I am right, it means that the changes are not transitory and perhaps not self-limiting. It means that there is little chance that we will go back to our former birthrates, divorce rates, single-parent rates, or female employment rates. It therefore does behoove us to examine closely the consequences of the current trends.

As I see it, there are several bodies of research that are relevant to our understanding of the probable impact of current changes in the family on the socialization of children. One is the work on family size and ordinal position: their effects on the way parents rear children, and ultimately on the children themselves. The second is the research on working mothers, and the effects of maternal employment on the intellectual and emotional development of children. Linked to this work is the large body of current work on day care: the comparison of center care vs. home care, studies of the adult-to-child ratio, studies of the kind of training day-care workers ought to receive. All of this is relevant to the issue of how best to care for the children of the increasing number of mothers who are entering the labor force. And finally, the work on father absence and its effects is clearly relevant to the fate of children growing up in single-parent households, since the vast majority of these are headed by mothers.

It would be foolhardy to attempt to review the current state of our knowledge in each of these areas—the task would be formidable indeed, and we do not have time. Furthermore, many are already familiar with the relevant work, since these are topics in which both sociologists and psychologists have worked intensively. I would simply like to comment briefly on some aspects of each of these issues. Let us begin with family size. From the standpoint of the earth's resources, zero population growth is of course good news wherever in the world it can be achieved. From the standpoint of our concern about the quality of the socialization of children, it may not be altogether good news. The first question, I suppose, is how childbearing is being redistributed among the people of childbearing age. We could have a low birthrate in two ways: One would be a kind of specialization in which some couples devoted themselves to child rearing and had large families, while other couples elected to remain childless. The other path involves a large proportion of couples continuing to have children, but having very small families. This latter appears to be the path we are taking, and it is the choice in other countries (China, and Western Europe) that have succeeded in bringing their birthrates under control. What will be the effect of vast numbers of children growing up as members of one-child or two-child families? Many people are complacent, or even pleased, about this prospect. I imagine that my colleague Robert Zajonc must be one of these, since he has been so active in calling our attention to the relationship between family size and scores on intelligence tests (Zajonc and Markus, 1975). We used to think that the tendency of children from smaller families to have higher intelligence scores was an artifact of the fact that larger families were more often found at lower socioeconomic levels. Zajonc presents evidence from very large sample studies in Holland and elsewhere in which education and economic level have been factored out. It remains true that the child who has fewer siblings is the brightest. His thesis is, simply, that a child's intelligence is a function of the collective mental ages of the people with whom he spends the most time, and he presents clear data to support the contention that this factor is operative. It may not be a *strong* factor in the complex web of forces affecting a child's measured intelligence, but Zajonc has certainly made a case for its being present.

All of this might be a source of considerable comfort as we look at the demographic trend toward smaller family size. The Zajonc work suggests that the reduction in average family size does not imply that the "quality" of child rearing is being reduced; indeed, it suggests the opposite. And the Zajonc findings are consistent with other things we know about families: Parents who have few children have more time to spend with each child. This not only means more intellectual stimulation for the child, but presumably also closer affective ties and possibly a more relaxed atmosphere. Parents should be in a better position to enjoy their children if they do not have the burden of caring for a large brood.

What, then, could possibly be wrong with a society composed largely of people who have grown up in one- or two-child families? In the first place, the emotional intensity of the affective ties in those families may not be altogether good for children. This possibility was highlighted in the early work of Schachter. In his small classic book *The Psychology of Affilia-*

tion, Schachter (1959) was able to show that firstborn and only children were motivated to seek the company of others when placed under stressful conditions, while later-borns did not show this effect of stress. According to Schachter's hypothesis, we ought to find that with decreasing family size there would be more and more people in the population who become depressed when alone and find it difficult to adjust to jobs in which they must function independently under stress. Many are aware of the vicissitudes of the work on ordinal position and personality conducted since Schachter's book was published. As the review by Schooler (1972) shows, if birth-order effects exist they are not robust—they are not easily replicated, and there are complex interactions with sibling spacing and sibling sex. Perhaps the main point we should take away from Schachter's work is this: If children growing up in different positions within families do turn out to have different characteristics, this diversity is something to be valued. The roles to be filled in an industrialized society are diverse. We are probably better off, therefore, to have a good mixture of large *and* small families so that, continuing Schachter's example, we produce some people who are well adapted to working alone, others who work better in teams, and so on. In all honesty, through, we would have to say that the existing evidence indicates that we would get almost as much diversity if most people grew up in two-child families as we do from the greater range of family sizes represented in our present population.

I feel a certain nagging reluctance to conclude that family size makes no difference at all. The intensity of the parent-child relationships in small families deserves further comment. Parents report that they are considerably more nervous, more unsure of themselves, in dealing with their first child. And indeed, the studies that have involved observations of parents dealing with the eldest vs. later children (with age of child at the time of observation held constant) do show that parents seem more anxious, more intrusive, less relaxed, and in some respects less skillful, with their eldest child. In studies of mother-child interaction the tension is particularly evident between mothers and their eldest *daughters.* I suspect, but do not know, that a parallel tension might be found between a father and an eldest son. What I am suggesting is that the familial conditions that Zajonc found to be associated with higher IQ's may not be an unmixed blessing—that there is an associated cost.

A possible cost that we need to be concerned about is the absence of opportunity, in small families, for children to learn mutual responsibility and cooperation. Bossard's classic work on large families (Bossard and Boll, 1956) underlined this. As an example selected from recent work: In a cross-cultural study, Ember analyzed the aggressive behavior of children during free play with age mates. She found that boys who had been assigned responsibility for taking care of younger siblings were less aggressive with their peers during times of the day when they were not baby-sitting. In other words, their experience in being responsible for younger siblings affected their social behavior in other spheres.

It should be noted too, that Zajonc found that there is an especially great intelligence deficit associated with being a *last* child, regardless of total family size. He attributed this drop to the lack of opportunity for the last child to serve as teacher of younger children. Even the intelligence data, then, are sensitive to the boost to a child's maturity that comes from having younger siblings.

Finally, when children are grown, their brothers and sisters frequently are an important part of their personal support system. Siblings help one another in emergencies. The sense of personal isolation, of vulnerability, will surely be greater among people who grow up in small families.

I do not think, then, that we can regard the trend toward small families as an unmixed blessing. The values of zero population growth are so enormous that they surely overshadow any losses that we might encounter from the absence of large families. We might consider, however, whether there is some way that we can replace the positive experiences that children used to have in large families through other institutional arrangements.

Let us turn now to the trend toward increasing numbers of working mothers. Here again, substantial review papers exist, and I shall not try to review their findings in any systematic way. As you might expect, the effect of a mother's working depends on many factors: her income level, whether she is a single parent, her reason for working, her satisfaction with her domestic situation, the quality of the substitute care available for her children while she works, and so on. My own reading of the literature leads me to conclude that there is nothing about a mother's working per se that is damaging to a child. Children can form normal attachments to their mothers even though care taking is shared with others while she works. And their intellectual development seems to move along at a normal pace. There is one curious contradiction that is now emerging from studies of working mothers: Although the children have not been shown to suffer, certain groups of mothers themselves do show signs of extra stress. The women who have low incomes and very young children report that their lives are more stressful when they work than when they do not (see McAdoo, 1977). It is curious that these maternal stresses have not yet been found to reflect themsevles in the progress of their children. Perhaps we have not measured the relevant aspects of the children's development. Or perhaps mothers are simply absorbing the stress themselves and not passing it on to their children.

But there is another side to the picture. In certain circumstances there are aspects of going to work that are extraordinarily beneficial to the *mothers,* and hence indirectly to the children. An example comes from observations by Ira Gordon in the mid-sixties, in connection with a Headstart program in Florida. His program involved selecting a group of women from underprivileged neighborhoods and training them to be home visitors. Their duties were to train mothers in how to stimulate their young children and be responsive to them in ways that would foster their intellectual development. Gordon reported that regardless of whether his interventions succeeded in improving the quality of mother-infant interaction, or in raising the intellectual competence level of the children, there was one benefit of his program that he was absolutely sure of: the effect upon the women who had been selected and trained as home visitors. Most had never worked before. Many had been isolated and depressed. Having a meaningful job had revolutionized their lives. Their lives had become purposeful and meaningful; they acquired a respected status in their own communities; they got up earlier in the morning and began to organize their activities so that they became energetic, efficient people—a sharp contrast to the impression they gave when they first entered training.

This experience illustrates the fact that for certain women, the benefits of working are very great, and they extend beyond the value of the money they earn. It is difficult to believe that such improvements in morale would be anything but beneficial to the children of the women involved. Of course, there are many women who continue to find fulfillment, and a sense of purpose and value in their lives, through devoting themselves exclusively to the roles of wife and mother. It is my impression that these satisfactions are declining. Social pressures have reversed themselves in the last decade, at least among middle-class people, and the college woman who says openly these days that her main objective in life is to marry and raise a family is treated with a certain scorn by most of the women she meets, and by many of the men as well. I do not know, frankly, how we can maintain the sense of self-worth of people engaged primarily in child rearing in the face of declining family size and greater involvement of women outside the home. What seems clear is that work will inevitably occupy an increasing place in the lives of women. If children are not to be the victims of our shift in values, if they are not to be neglected, it seems necessary that we continue to press for the creation and maintainance of adequate child-care facilities that will function as a backup system for traditional family care. If a good-quality backup system exists, I think our evidence to date is that children will not suffer, and may gain, from maternal employment.

Quite a different picture emerges when we consider the trend toward more single-parent families. Social scientists have concerned themselves for many decades with "broken homes." For a long time the primary concern was whether there was a connection between broken homes and delinquency. Among psychologists, at least, the focus shifted to father absense and its impact upon the development of the child's sex identity and sex-role adoption. This concern stemmed largely from psychoanalytic theory, which holds that each parent is the model for the sex-role development of the same-sex children in the family. From this view, the absence of a father during the child's formative years ought to be especially damaging to a son, who could be expected to show disturbances in sex-role development. He could become overtly feminine, or he could become manifestly hypermasculine in an effort to compensate for covert feminine tendencies. This theory has stimulated enormous amounts of research and writing about father absence and its effects, and about the role of the two parents in the development of sex typing. There is still considerable difference of opinion about what it all adds up to. Portions of the relevant work has been summarized in several places (Biller, 1971; Lynn, 1974; Herzog and Sudia, 1973; Maccoby and Jacklin, 1974). My own reading of the findings is that a firm connection between the absence of a parent and specific sex-role disturbances in the same-sex child has not been adequately demonstrated. Certainly boys who grow up without a father are usually within the normal range for masculinity. Children of both sexes seem to construct their sex-role concepts from many sources, outside the family, as well as within it. When a father is absent, this may indeed have an effect upon the ability of a child to interact smoothly with members of the opposite sex in adolescence. But this does not imply that the fatherless adolescent boy is *feminine;* he may show a good deal of "masculine" aggression, be good in sports, and so on, but may simply not know how to deal with girls, not having had sufficient opportunity to observe normal male-female interaction at home.

In fact, and contrary to simple identification theory, the greatest impact of father absence upon sex-role performance seems to be with *daughters*. In Hetherington's excellent work (1977) on father-absent adolescent girls, we see the daughters of widows being shy, prim, and excessively conventional in their interactions with men, while the daughters of divorcees are flirtatious, tend to be promiscuous, but are also fairly hostile in many of their attitudes toward men. Clearly, there is a reflection here of their mothers' experiences and of the daughters' concepts of their absent fathers, but the results are hardly to be understood in terms of the simple absence or presence of a sex-role model at home. In our preoccupation with sex-role development, I believe that psychologists have tended to lose sight of the larger issues that are involved in the rearing of children by a single parent. It is to these issues that I now wish to turn, and I will draw upon some recent studies in which interaction has been observed in intact families, as well as studies of broken families. In this enterprise I have found a recent paper by Ross Parke (1977), called "Perspectives on Father-Infant Interaction," very useful indeed. I would like to discuss first the part that fathers play in normal intact families. This should give us a better perspective than have the earlier orientations toward father absence on what it means for him to be absent. Then I will turn to direct observational work on child rearing by single-parent mothers.

As Parke notes, there are a number of ways in which fathers can affect the child-rearing process. The first, of course, is through their direct interactions with the child; they can stimulate, soothe, teach, arouse anxiety by harshness, and so on. And of course, whatever effects the father's behavior has on the infant may reverberate by creating a different sort of infant for the mother to react to. If he makes the baby tense, she has a more difficult task in attempting to soothe it, and this may have an impact upon her morale and her attitudes toward the child. Other modes of father influence are more indirect: The mother observes how her husband interacts with the infant and how he seems to feel toward it. Her own attitudes may be affected. She could either be influenced to feel the same way her husband does, or feel that she needed to compensate, in her own child rearing, for something the father does or fails to do. And finally, the husband's attitudes toward the wife—toward her in relation to himself, toward her pregnancy, and toward her performance as a mother—can have profound effects on her ability to function effectively in interaction with children. We can see this interweaving of family dynamics in the results of a number of recent observational studies. Let me give you a few sample findings to transmit the flavor of what I am talking about:

> Each parent shows more positive affect toward an infant when the other parent is present (Parke and O'Leary, 1976).
>
> Mothers engage in less interaction with their children when the father is present than when they are alone with the child (Clark-Stewart, 1977).
>
> Mothers are more intimately involved with their children if they perceive that their child rearing has the approval and support of their husbands (or of some other significant person) (Feiring and Taylor, 1977).
>
> The presence of a supporting husband during the period immediately following the birth of a child lessens postpartum depression (Parke and O'Leary, 1976).
>
> The amount of positive affect shown by a mother toward her infant when the two are alone together is correlated with the amount of positive affect shown by the father when he is alone with the infant (Pedersen, Anderson, and Cain, 1977).

From this sampling of findings we can see the value of studying the family as a multiperson system. Each person has direct effects on other members of the family, plus indirect effects on the interactions of other family members in which he/she is not directly involved. Here are some further generalizations that seem to emerge from present and earlier research on the father's part in socialization:

1. Fathers, when they do engage in caretaking with infants, are as skillful as mothers and as sensitive to the infant's needs and reactions.
2. There is a difference here between performance and competence: Although fathers are entirely competent in caretaking, in fact they do much less of it than mothers in almost all families. However, the father's participation increases if he is allowed close contact with the newborn (Lynn, 1974).
3. As children grow out of infancy, a differentiation of function usually occurs between their parents. The nature of the division varies greatly from one family to another, but one difference appears to be fairly general: Mothers spend a larger proportion of their interaction time in caretaking, soothing, and control, fathers in fun and games. (It should be noted that the difference does not fit the Parsonian hypothesis that mothers adopt an expressive role, fathers an instrumental one.) This hypothesis has not stood the test of time and replication. The children react to this by going to their mothers when distressed, and being somewhat more likely to turn to their fathers when they want to play. However, when only the father is present, he is usually just as effective as the mother in providing the child with security and comfort in the face of anxiety-producing situations, and the child shows as much reliance on his presence and as much distress if he leaves.
4. Mothers use fathers for respite from child care: When fathers are home, mothers tend to withdraw from interaction with the children and turn to other tasks.
5. Children obey their fathers more readily than their mothers. This is quite a consistent finding, and rather mysterious. We do not know whether mothers are less consistent in following through on their demands, whether fathers are more imposing because of their size and louder voices, whether children see their fathers as dominant over their mothers and therefore assume they are the final authority of the household, or what.
6. Fathers differ more in their treatment of sons and daughters than mothers do.

What are the implications of these facts for single-parent child rearing? It is true that there is an increasing number of fathers who have custody of the children following separation of the parents, but the fact remains that in the vast majority of cases it is the mother who rears the children, especially if the children are young at the time of separation. Therefore, in discussing single-parent families I will focus on those families where a divorced or widowed woman, or an unwed mother, is rearing children without the close and continuous involvement of a man. If we think in terms of the relationships of fathers to their families that have just been reviewed, it is immediately apparent what stresses mothers must be under when the father is absent. Many of these points are so obvious that they do not need the weight of social science evidence to validate them, but let me list a few all the same:

1. The mother has no one who accepts a major responsibility for relieving her—for taking over child care when she is tired or ill or temporarily unable to cope for any reason. True, she can hire baby-sitters if she can afford it, but this is temporary and the baby-sitter does not have the commitment to the children or the sense of personal responsibility for their continuing welfare that fathers do.

2. The mother has no one to give her emotional support—to tell her she is doing a good job, sympathize with her difficulties, laugh with her over something unexpected or charming that the children do, help lift her out of a bad mood.

3. The household lacks variety in the adult approach to the children. The playful element that fathers so often contribute can lighten the household atmosphere at crucial moments; the skills the father has are likely to be different from, and complementary to, the ones the mother possesses, so the activity resources, the possibilities for involving the children in useful and interesting enterprises, are much reduced when no father is present.

4. When disciplinary issues arise, the authority of one parent—the ability of that parent to follow through and maintain a firm set of guidelines for the child's behavior—is greatly reduced by comparison with the situation that prevails when two parents are working together with a reasonable degree of agreement about their child-rearing goals and methods. The fact that children obey their fathers more readily than their mothers means that their presence is particularly missed on those occasions where the need for obedience is real.

5. The mother has an increased burden of household management, beyond the child-rearing functions themselves. Her child rearing, then, occurs in a setting of less free time, more worry about money, greater general responsibilities.

The most powerful work that I know of that demonstrates these deficits in child rearing in the single-parent home has been done by Mavis Hetherington (1977), in her longitudinal study of families following divorce. She has studied the parents and their children at two months, one year, and two years following the legal divorce action. Of course, most of the couples have been separated for a period of time prior to the official divorce. The research includes extensive interviews with the two parents, and observations of the children with their mothers both in the naturalistic home setting and in structured observation situations. All the families included in the study had a child in nursery school at the time of the divorce, and in all cases the children were living with the mother, although most were seeing their fathers fairly regularly as well. A comparison study was done with a group of intact families having children in the same nursery schools as those where the children of divorced families were enrolled.

From the standpoing of child rearing, the point of greatest disorganization in family functioning seemed to occur one year after the divorce. Here are some of the characteristics of families at this point in their lives:

Meals, baths, and bedtimes were irregular.

Mothers were making relatively few maturity demands on the children.

The quality of communication between mothers and children was poor.

Shows of affection were rare, and angry outbursts frequent.

Discipline was inconsistent, and there was poor control of the children's activities: Mother's directives tended to be ignored by the children.

The tension seemed to be particularly great between mothers and sons, who were more likely than daughters to show defiance and resistance toward the mother.

Fathers were highly permissive and indulgent during the year following divorce, following which their frequency of contact with the children diminished, while they also began to return to making some maturity demands.

In all the ways described, the interactions of divorced parents and their children differed significantly from those seen in intact families. Furthermore, the comparisons across time showed closer to normal family interactions at two months following divorce, quite abnormal patterns one year following divorce, and some recovery of normal functioning by the end of the second year. Many disturbances remained at that time, however.

The repercussions in the children's behavior outside the home could be seen in some of the time-lag analyses. For example, children who were defiant and poorly controlled at two months following the divorce showed poor focusing of attention in nursery school at the end of the first year. And the children who showed deficits in attention focusing at one year showed losses in quantitative ability when they entered first grade a year after that. And so the effects of ineffective parenting continue to spread out into new situations and new behavioral manifestations.

This is not a pleasant story. Clearly, divorce is very hard on parents and children. The socialization process that normally occurs within the family is seriously disrupted. We should note, too, that the deficits in family functioning that Hetherington has described are often found in the interactions of unwed mothers with their children, particularly when the mothers are very young. What are the implications for social policy of these findings? Should we attempt to reverse the clock, outlaw divorce, and encourage couples to stay together "for the sake of the children" even when very serious disharmony exists? Obviously, there are many still-married families in which one or the other parent is not carrying out his or her share of the parenting, in which the partners do not give each other emotional support, but on the contrary add to one another's stress. There is no simple answer to whether divorce is the best alternative under these conditions. The root problem, of course, is the poor interpersonal functioning that leads to divorce and single-parenthood in the first place, and eventually we must try to understand why marital tension is so high in our society. I won't attempt to enter this thorny thicket. The main point I want to close with is this:

Of all the current trends in the family—decreasing birthrates and family size, increases in mothers working, increases in divorce and unwed motherhood, I think the increase in single-parent families is the one that poses the most serious dangers for the socialization of children. This is the trend that calls for the most careful thought on all our parts, and the greatest efforts at solution. As a nation, we are currently struggling with matters of public policy in which the fate of single parents and their children is intimately involved. The architects of our new welfare policies are struggling with the question of whether single mothers of preschool-aged children should be encouraged to work and place their children in day care, or whether we should set up our income-support systems so that there will be incentives for single parents to remain home with their children. The welfare reform proposals that have just been announced tip the balance in favor of creating incentives for single parents to remain home while their children are of preschool age. Perhaps a more accurate way to put it would be to say that they create *dis*incentives for these parents to work. I think we need to think very carefully about this aspect of the proposed policies. Child rearing, I believe, is something that many people cannot do adequately as single adults functioning in isolation. Single parents need time off from parenting, they need the company of other adults, they need to have other voices joined with theirs in transmitting values and maturity demands to their children. Because of these needs, I believe that many single parents are better served by having opportunities to work and to share child rearing with the staff of a day-care center than by being required to remain home as full-time parents. Of course, for many single parents there may be little choice: There may be no jobs available and some may prefer full-time parenting. I only wish to argue that we keep as many options open as possible while we are experimenting with possible ways of helping and supporting single parents and their children.

17

Socialization and the Young Family

Doris R. Entwisle

PROFESSOR HILL HAS CALLED our attention to some striking recent changes in family structure—there are now more one-parent families; couples tend to have fewer children; and so on. A principal reason for these changes he did not emphasize—the high degree of conception control now possible, including abortion backup. And the structural and demographic changes are paired with family changes of another sort— the *quality* of family life itself is becoming different. Attitudes and behaviors of young couples starting families today reflect this. For example, fewer children per family probably means that a family attaches a social premium to producing and nurturing each child. Scarce commodities are always valued more highly and certainly this is no less true because the commodities are children, as the social status of children through history testifies.

Parents now embarking on parenthood want to savor the experience. Young people starting families—that is, going through a pregnancy and a first birth—realize that this pregnancy may be a one-and-only experience for them. At least partly for this reason, then, I think both men and women today view their parental roles differently than parents did a decade ago.

Let me be specific. In a study Susan Doering and I recently conducted, we interviewed 120 couples[1] having their first child. Many couples wanted to experience *every* part of parenthood together, starting

---

[1] The sample consisted entirely of Caucasian couples residing in the greater Baltimore-Washington area reached through informal friendship networks (Doering and Entwisle, 1977).

from pregnancy exercises, continuing with both parents taking an active part in the birth event, and then with both parents going on to share in nurturing of the neonate. Change in family attitudes and behaviors seems particularly noticeable in the case of fathers, as I will point up in detail later on.

Actually, then, my perspective in speaking on socialization and the family will interchange the two terms—I will talk not about how small family size affects socialization of children, or about how single parents manage child rearing, but will talk instead about how the current socialization of young men and young women affects the way they start families of their own. In other words, I will talk about how current socialization patterns impinging on young adults seem to be affecting the way they start family life. One consequence of declines in marriage rates for adults in their early twenties, for example, is that many of those who do marry and decide to bear a child take on their childbearing task with considerable enthusiasm and forethought.

More women are working. Just about all young women work from before marriage up to the time their first child is born. Women's activities in the labor market have led young men and women to broaden their conceptions of one another's sex roles. With wives working, for example, there is a companion change in that young men more commonly share in household tasks, at least if our data can be trusted. Perhaps more interesting, it turns out that what were formerly exclusively female tasks—childbearing and the care of very young infants—are tasks many husbands now wish to share and actually do share. The large majority of young fathers we interviewed, for instance, wished to be present at the birth of their children. Their wives were in full sympathy with such desires. The young men, furthermore, gave their wives much support through both pregnancy and childbirth. They were eager also to begin "fathering" as soon as their babies were born. The men we interviewed by and large saw little incongruity between a masculine role and the kinds of nurturant behavior a new baby requires. Actually, since today's young women are so little prepared for a mother's tasks, both parents are about equally inexperienced in child care, perhaps an advantage in the encouragement of early fathering.

It is startling to reflect on how times have changed. How different this state of affairs is from what was true even a decade ago. In 1965 men almost never entertained the thought of witnessing the birth of their own children. The few who did were actively barred from the delivery suite even when they themselves were physicians! Social scientists ignored fathers. As Nash (1976) points out, there was complete lack of interest in fathers. There are no data on what prospective and new fathers thought about themselves prior to about 1965. Socialization for the father role was certainly different then from what it is today, but, unfortunately, we do not know anything much about how it used to be.

One manifestation of the desire of today's young couples to share in the birth of their children is the current popularity of childbirth preparation classes. Difficult as attendance at such classes is to estimate on a nationwide basis, the appeal of the classes is nonetheless apparent.[2] In a survey of 269 mothers we conducted during the late 1960s (Doering and Entwisle, 1975) we had trouble finding couples who *were* enrolled in childbirth education classes. In a study recently concluded (1973–1976), our trouble was just the opposite. It was hard to find pregnant couples who were *not* enrolled in some sort of childbirth preparation class (even though half the couples studied were blue collar). We naturally wanted to interview a set of parents not attending classes as a sort of control group, but we had great difficulty in finding such persons.

Childbirth preparation classes encourage couples to approach birth as a joint experience. Fathers are expected to help their wives in labor and to assist, when possible, in delivery. These classes may be one explanation for what seems to be a national resurgence in breast-feeding, but the deeper cause for increased rates of breast-feeding is probably the same as the reason for class attendance—young couples want to experience parenthood to the fullest. Many of the women who did not attend classes planned to breast-feed. With fewer children expected and fewer actually being born, young parents seem disposed to treasure the experience of parenthood and to plan for it carefully. Couples planned to have fewer children (2.4) than they would have preferred (3.4), and among the couples we interviewed, over 20 percent postponed childbearing from four to six years after marriage, testimony to the importance of life planning and conception control.

The desire to experience all facets of parenting was as characteristic of the young men as it was of the young women. Today's expanded sex-role attitudes allow new fathers to share comfortably in the care of young infants, and the extent of this caretaking, if our small study is any barometer, is truly astounding. For example, 65 percent of the husbands in our study had diapered their new baby before it was a week old, and when their new baby was two to three weeks old, fathers on the average were holding their babies one and one-half hours a day, even though a substantial majority of the babies were being breast-fed.

Let me back up for a moment, and reflect very briefly on how and why socialization prior to a child's birth may be important for family formation and family life patterns.

A couple's first pregnancy, followed by the birth of a child, and the ensuing early months of an infant's life actually constitute a critical period in the evolution of a family. Even now, despite the mushrooming of childbirth preparation classes, there is little formal socialization of either parent for their new family roles. Yet if a couple manages to cope well with the arrival of their first child, one would expect the threesome (mother, father, infant) to be off to a successful beginning as a family. This successful beginning may be reflected in the role integration of both parents. That is, the man must integrate the father role with roles he has previously held, his husband role, his work role, and others. The woman must also integrate the mother role into a role set she possesses, including that of wife, daughter, and possibly employee. A successful beginning of parenthood may also be reflected in an increase in both parents' sense of well-being, an improvement in the couple's marital relationship, and, most important, in the enhancement of developing relationships between parents and child.

If, on the other hand, a couple copes poorly with pregnancy, childbirth, and the early weeks of parenting, problems may ensue, and problems at one stage may create problems at the next stage. During pregnancy, for example, if *the couple* does not take steps to prepare realistically for the birth, the birth event may be traumatic for both spouses and actually drive them apart. As always, there are more ways to err than to be successful.

Surprisingly, despite sociologists' extensive research on the family as a social unit and particularly despite their extensive research on aspects of family life that may be associated with psychiatric disorders, they have paid little attention to the normal family at the time when its first child arrives—the exact moment when the couple metamorphoses into a "family." And what little attention has been paid has targted the mother. Fathers have been almost entirely neglected.

Many sociologists, of course, have commented upon birth as a life-cycle event, noting that parenting is a role for which our society offers little preparation, and also that there is no period of apprenticeship analogous to the courtship preceding a marriage. Put another way, there is no period for "trial parenting." But casual observations have not led to much actual research. The lack of research on emergent families is all the more curious when one considers that society as a whole tacitly recognizes the challenge posed by pregnancy and childbirth. Just the fact that there are specialized personnel and specialized institutions concerned with pregnancy and birth is proof that society at large recognizes the need for support at the time of birth.

In the research by Susan Doering and myself, we followed 120 couples experiencing their first birth from the sixth month of pregnancy, through birth, and then through the early postpartum period. So far we have data up to a phone check when the infant is six months old. Both mother *and* father were interviewed pre- and postpartum. One purpose was to investigate how the stress of pregnancy and birth affected the male. Another purpose was to see whether (and to what extent) successful coping with the birth event enriched the husband-wife relationship and family life in general. For example, the husband's interest in his wife's pregnancy was studied in relation to his later parenting behavior. The research focused particularly on the couple's specific preparation during pregnancy and their prior life experience in caring for infants as "socialization" for family life. In other words, the research aimed to see how young men's and women's prior socialization, whether intentional or unintentional, affected a family's beginning.

I will limit my remarks to the husband's role both because time is short and also because so little research in the past has concerned the father's role. (The first report on fathers is apparently that of Pedersen and Robson, 1969.) Research on the socialization of men for their family roles, as already mentioned, is scarce. But, as I also mention, changing ideas about sex roles and core gender identity are strongly pushing young men toward becoming involved in even the tasks of labor and delivery. For example, 78 percent of the wives in our study wanted their husbands to be present during delivery, and 72 percent of the husbands expected to be there. (Sixty-three percent actually were present.) Wives' ideas on the desirability of the husband's being present in delivery did not change postpartum. Ninety-six percent of women whose husbands were in delivery were positive about their husbands' having been there. This is a complete about-face compared to what went on in the 1960s and earlier. As far as we can tell, fathers then waited in hospital waiting rooms and sometimes fainted when told of the birth.

The average couple in our study exhibited much sharing of household tasks in the sixth month of pregnancy, much more than previous reports would have led us to suspect. Further, husbands increased the amount of household help they gave their wives as pregnancy progressed. They also helped when the new mother returned from the hospital—about a fourth of the husbands took vacation and stayed home full time.

There turned out to be a highly significant relation between division of household labor in the sixth month of pregnancy and several variables involving husband's later care of his new baby, including how often he diapered it and how much he held it. Socialization of young men leading them to share in household chores, then, is associated with a more active father role, at least when the child is a young infant.

Both the young men and young women in our study expected before birth that the men would take an active part in the care of the neonate. Gone are the days, at least for most of these families, when the baby is viewed as the "mother's property." These young men no doubt were reacting to their wives' expectations. Ninety-six percent of the women believed the most important quality in a father is the warmth and interest he shows his children, and 87 percent believed (postpartum) that new fathers would resent not being able to hold their newborn child. But the young men themselves also expressed opinions consistent with an active father role—over 75 percent of the young fathers said men are just as interested in their children when they are babies as when they are older.

Our study is small and deliberately unrepresentative—only 120 couples, half middle class and half blue collar, and all Caucasian—so it may or may not reflect general trends, yet compared with young families of a decade ago even the most traditional of our couples gives evidence of remarkable shifts in both attitudes and behaviors. Probably the paramount example of a shift is that only four babies in this sample were completely unplanned, and even these babies could have been avoided because of the easy availability of abortions in Maryland. (Twelve percent of the women in the same had actually had abortions before.) This amount of conception control contrasts sharply with that possible a decade ago—a recent preliminary report by the foundation for Child Development (1977:19) based on a national probability sample of children born between 1964 and 1969 states that "less than half of the youngsters in the survey were the result of a planned pregnancy, in the sense that the mother wanted to become pregnant at that time." No one would doubt that early parenting behavior is likely to be affected by whether or not the pregnancy is wanted. We found, for example, that a man's interest in his wife's pregnancy is related to how much he holds the baby in the first six weeks of its life and also to whether he picks up the baby when it is crying in the first few weeks. Also, husbands' attitude toward pregnancy as rated by the husband prepartum predicted wife's enjoyment of motherhood.

What is the significance of the father's active involvement in pregnancy and childbirth? Answers are many, but two stand out:

1. Such involvement can enrich life for the man himself.
2. The involvement seems to affect early parenting both directly and indirectly.

I will not dwell on the first point. Everyone can imagine the excitement and wonder many men experience on seeing their first child born, and how profound their emotions can be at this time. One direct quote from a father who witnessed the birth of his child is worth citing: "I was elated. I was filled up. There was no—to me there was no room for words. I was crying. Just looking and crying. . . ."

The second point, how active involvement prior to and during birth affects fathering, is another matter, and to detect such relationships requires a longitudinal or panel design plus some fairly complex causal models. Such designs and models require considerable computer capability. The level of technology available may be one reason why longitudinal studies of emergent families were not undertaken earlier, of course.

Let me cite just a few of the findings relating prepartum variables to later parenting.

We found some fascinating relationships linking wives' attitudes toward their husbands as fathers with how actively husbands participated in pregnancy and delivery. Using a semantic differential instrument, we found that women's views of their husbands as fathers were unchanged or improved if their husbands were present during delivery or if husbands *wished* to be present. If husbands stayed away by choice, however, their wives' views of them as fathers (*not* as husbands) changed in a negative direction. We found also that wives' views of themselves deteriorated if their husbands chose not to be present in delivery.

If a wife stated at the sixth month of pregnancy that she wished her husband to be present in delivery, the husband was more likely postpartum to report the baby as being a source of happiness in marriage ($r = .44$). In other words, it seems that if husbands are made a part of the pregnancy and birth experience from the beginning and wish to take part, they enhance their own potential and their wives' potential as parents and have more positive views of the child later on.

Using a set of structural equations presented in detail elsewhere (see Doering, Entwisle, and Quinlan, 1977), we found that a husband's presence in delivery enhanced the quality of his wife's birth experience significantly *and* directly. That is, his presence did not lead his wife to feel less pain or to remain more fully conscious (indirect effects), but when husbands were present wives reported birth experiences of higher quality. As might be expected, the quality of women's birth experience predicted both the likelihood and duration of breast-feeding. Father's participation, then, contributed to making breast-feeding more successful.

There was a significant correlation between husband's previous experience with newborns and a wife's confidence in her own ability to care for a baby. A husband's previous experience with baby care was correlated with his enjoyment of fatherhood, and also, but less strongly, with his wife's enjoyment of motherhood.

All these findings point in the same direction: Young men, whether as a consequence of current sex-role ideology or of demographic trends in family structure, are taking an active role in family life, especially early on. Because we have no baseline data from a decade ago, we cannot compare things now with how things were then, but we suspect the quality of family life is undergoing marked changes.

Marriage, births, and parenting in this decade seem like nothing before. Couples want fewer children, they have control over childbearing, they are very interested in the *quality* of their childbirth experience and in sharing it with their mate, and, especially for men, the parent role has been expanded. The most dramatic change in American marriage during the twentieth century, as Bane (1976) points out, is not the proportion marrying or the proportion divorcing but the *pattern* of marital life—in what husbands and wives do and in the number of years they spend with and without children. Our data are entirely consistent with Bane's conclusion.

All of these changes do not necessarily lead childbirth to be less stressful, however. Young fathers are expected to measure up to standards they have had no role models for. The kinds of stress couples face are not the same as those they faced a decade ago, but sources of stress are probably just as numerous. Almost all babies in this study were planned, for example, yet many couples found the actuality of pregnancy unpleasant. An active desire to take part in childbirth laid the groundwork for disappointment when husbands were barred or chose to stay away from delivery. The number of mothers undergoing major surgery seems to have tripled in the past decade (Klassen, 1975), and over one-sixth of the women in this sample were delivered by Caesarean section. Despite professed egalitarianism between the sexes, most fathers still wanted a male child—a joy only half of them could experience. The high cost of living and inflation make it hard for families to get by on one paycheck, and all the women were forced to cease or interrupt their outside work. Financial stress may be severe. Fully a third of the women expected to return to work by the time their infant was six months old, but only 8 percent had been able to return to work full time by then.

So in returning to Professor Hill's main question—which trends have what impacts on what aspects of socialization—I see current trends in socialization of young men and young women having considerable impact on the quality and style of early family life. And the end is not in sight.

Socialization in the direction of broader sex roles for both men and women encourages women to work outside the home, both before and after the birth of their children. Such socialization also seems to be encouraging men to take active part in household work and early child care. The desire for small families, together with the wish that it were possible to have more children, makes childbearing a voluntary act and one calling for the exercise of restraints. It places birth in a new perspective. If the family will produce few children, those it does produce are more highly valued. One apparent consequence of these trends, in our data at least, is that young fathers are very active in early parenting.

There are a number of unresolved issues that are bound to arise as time goes on, however. Many inequities between husband and wife surface at birth. The couples in our sample believed in women's sexual fulfillment and in equal-pay-for-equal-jobs, but they also leaned in the direction of "women's place is in the home with preschool children."

They believed that women are more likely to be attached, or more easily attached, to infants emotionally. Their stated egalitarian beliefs aside, the couples in our study, whether they consciously realized it or not, had acted in ways to decrease the pressure of egalitarian beliefs on *themselves*. For example, women's work roles were devalued by both husbands and wives, even though many wives continued to work or planned to return. Prior to resigning their jobs, women in this sample held jobs of lower prestige than their husbands'. Devaluing their own "women's work" makes it easier for these couples to sidestep conflicts after birth between a woman's work role and her parent role. We also saw that child-spacing plans were not related prepartum to women's work plans, but there was a shift after birth in women's child-spacing desires, suggesting that women (the majority in this sample) who planned to return to work after children were old enough to go to school had already decided to remain out of the labor force longer than they earlier anticipated.

In fact, an egalitarian ideology involves profound difficulties when applied to child rearing. Lorber (1977) wonders how children will be produced and then socialized if the reforms currently called for by women's liberationists are actually realized: "When women's liberation succeeds . . . [we will need] alternatives to the system currently being breached." We note, along with Rosaldo and Lamphere (1974), that current legislation guarantees job equality and nondiscrimination because of parental status, but *that status must still be dealt with*. How a woman can combine a demanding career with early parenting is not easily solved, short of changes societywide. The stresses generated may be great except in rather unusual circumstances like those Bailyn (1970) points to—families in which "work-integrated" women are matched with family-oriented men, with housework and children shared *and* income high.

18

The Dependency Hang-up and Experiments in Alternative Life Styles

Beatrice B. Whiting

THE YOUNG OF EVERY GENERATION, in the process of becoming adult, identify the weaknesses of their parents and of the current social institutions and seek to change them. This phenomenon has been sometimes characterized as an adolescent revolt. In this paper, however, I am not concerned with protest but with the innovative attempts of young adults to set up viable alternatives to the institutions they dislike. In our society in recent times the emphasis has been on economic institutions and the military–industrial complex, institutions that prove difficult to change in a well-established capitalistic society. More recently, attention has been focused on the family and its structure. The isolated nuclear family consisting of husband, wife, and children has been under fire. Divorce rates are up, increasing the number of single-parent households. The more dissonant and adventurous of the new generation are experimenting in alternative life styles involving both new household arrangements

□ The research in Kenya reported in this paper was financed by the Carnegie Corporation and was conducted by the Child Development Research Unit of the Faculty of Education of the University of Nairobi under the direction of John and Beatrice Whiting between the years 1968-1973. Standardized observations were collected by university students. Data analysis was supplemented by a grant from NIMH (01096). The Six Culture Project was directed by Irvin Child, William Lambert, and John Whiting, and financed by the Ford Foundation and an NIMH grant (01096). The behavior observations were made by John and Ann Fischer, Barbara Lloyd and Robert LeVine, Thomas and Hatsumi Maretzki, Leigh Minturn, William and Corinne Nydegger, A. Kimball, and Romaine Romney. With the exception of the Fischers, who studied Orchard Town, all the field teams were assisted by educated members of the ethnic group studied.

and new community organizations. Will they be more successful working on this micro level than their predecessors were in trying to change the economic institutions? How easy is it to change these well-established family patterns? What are the weaknesses that these young people have identified and what do the new social institutions offer by way of improvement? Why is the nuclear family under attack?

The study of family structure and socialization practices in other parts of the world is useful in understanding the weaknesses of this isolated unit. As I see it, this type of family as a socializing institution, along with the associated school system, leads to what we have called the "dependency hang-up." We teach the value of independence and self-reliance and at the same time reward a type of dominant-dependence.[1]

There are two aspects of socialization in the United States that are peculiar from a cross-cultural perspective and responsible for this conflict over dependence: one is the early detachment of the baby from the mother, followed by an unusual amount of interaction between mother and child in the home, a characteristic of the small isolated nuclear family; the other is the long hours of schooling, with their emphasis on individual achievement and the enforced confinement of children with same-aged peers. Intensive interaction with the mother encourages seeking or "dependent" behavior, while interaction with same-aged peers involves a competitive and mildly aggressive type of sociability, often not conductive to protracted intimacy. Interactions with older and younger children, missing from the experience of many, are dyadic relationships that encourage helpful and responsible behavior (see Whiting and Whiting, 1975; Lodish, 1976).

In sharp contrast is the life cycle of an individual in societies where the nuclear family is imbedded in a larger group—usually kin based—where there is prolonged physical attachment and there is no schooling. Since I have been studying Kenyan families, in particular Kikuyu families, I will use them as a base for comparison and as a way of highlighting certain problems engendered by our life style.

In Kenya the newborn baby lives in close physical contact with his mother or surrogate mother. He is carried in close body contact in the day and sleeps with his mother at night. Thin clothes separate his skin from that of his mother and communication is primarily kinesthetic. One rarely hears Kenyan village babies crying. There were no cribs, cradles, or cradleboards in traditional Kenyan groups. Baby carriages are not suited to rough terrain. Infants up until the time they can walk are carried for most of the day.

---

[1]"Dominant-dependent" is defined to include behavior judged to be seeking help and attention or demanding that some other act in such a way as to meet ego's stated desires (see Whiting and Whiting, 1975:54–82).

Contrast the infant of our colder clime. He must be dressed in the fall, winter, and spring in thick clothes. He sleeps in a crib, is propped in various sitting devices, or wheeled in a carriage. If he is born in a conventional hospital, from the moment of birth he is clearly detached from his mother's body. He must summon a caretaker vocally, and since this caretaker is often not in sight, is never sure his needs will be satisfied promptly (J. Whiting, 1964, 1971).

The fact that most U.S. middle-income households have only one adult woman who cares for infants is responsible in part for this early detachment. My Kenyan mothers have helpers, unlike U.S. mothers, and for that matter unlike almost all of our worldwide sample of families. Few societies expect a woman to be the sole caretaker of an infant. Large polygynous homesteads abound in children of various ages, one of whom is appointed as a child nurse. Cowives and grandparents, young aunts and uncles who live in the extended homestead are available to furnish assistance when the mother or child nurse is busy, sick, or temporarily away from the homestead.

Thus there are two important differences between the life of an infant in the U.S. and in Kenyan society. The U.S. baby is physically detached from his mother for most of the time from birth onward, while the Kenyan baby is not detached from physical contact until he can walk. Even then, at night, he continues to sleep with a sibling or other relative. The U.S. baby must learn to summon the mother vocally for help and await her caretaking. The Kenyan baby does not need to elicit help vocally. He can signal his needs kinesthetically. The Kikuyu mother does not have to anticipate the needs of her baby, since the communication system is continuous and immediate. The U.S. mother attempts to learn the rhythm of her infant's needs and to anticipate them. In the second place, when it is time for the Kenyan child to be weaned from the back, he is already attached to other persons who have been his surrogate caretakers. In the isolated nuclear family with few children, there is rarely a sibling old enough to serve as a caretaker. Furthermore, even when there is a sibling, we do not consider him/her capable of responsibility for an infant or toddler until he/she is teenaged. In most of the cultures of the world, eight- to ten-year-olds are the primary surrogate caretakers of infants and toddlers. Although men in U.S. families may be willing helpers, they are rarely home and conventionally have seen their role to be that of occasional helpers.

The early detachment in U.S. families is followed by the pressure on toddlers toward what has been called "independence." The child is encouraged to feed himself early, put on his clothes, wash himself, and entertain himself with various objects or TV programs. This is essential if the young mother is to manage two closely spaced children without help.

For the traditional Kenyan child there was no great fuss made about "independence," but in fact the toddler had more opportunity to be autonomous. Weaned from the back, his mother turned him over to the child pack, and he trailed after his numerous siblings and courtyard half-siblings and cousins. Until the introduction of schools, this was a multiaged group. They were responsible for the toddler's safety. They were also his stimulation, and his adjacent sibling was a constant companion and teacher by the demonstration of his newly acquired skills. His older siblings were available for help when needed. Dependency was not focused on one individual, as in the nuclear family setup.

The pattern of anticipating the needs of children continues after infancy in the U.S. middle-income families. It is our hypothesis that it leads to a form of dominant-dependence. In observations made by Ann and John Fischer in Orchard Town, New England, and in more recent observations of other middle-income families in the New England area, mothers are frequently offering resources they think their child wants before he expresses the desire. These guesses are often incorrect and are followed by dominant-dependent demands.

A mother alone at home with her two-year-old who appears to be restless suggests, "Shall we wash the dishes together?" The two-year-old responds, "No, read me a book." The mother complies. Later, "Would you like a glass of orange juice?" Child, "I want to go for a ride." A five-year-old alone with his mother after school constantly demands her attention. He works for a few minutes with a crayon and then approaches his mother. "See my picture." The mother responds, "That is very good. The house is very pretty."

In our comparison of children's behavior in six different societies, the Orchard Town children ranked first in dominant-dependent demands to parents (Whiting and Whiting, 1975:158). The Kenyan sample, the Nyansongo, were proportionately low in all forms of dependent behavior to parents. They ranked lowest in seeking help and physical contact and third in dominant-dependent behavior. U.S. children ranked first in dominant-dependent behavior and third in seeking help and physical contact. Or, stated another way, the preferred form of dependency among the Kenyan sample was simple requests for help; among the Orchard Town sample the preferred form was demands for attention or demands that the mother act in such a way as to meet the stated desires of the child, not identified by observers as instrumental help.

The U.S. lone mother seems to enjoy the social interchange with her children; a mutual seeking and offering pattern of interaction is established. The children are "seekers," initiating interaction with adults, seeking primarily attention, information, and sociability. The lone non-working mother is responsive to such behavior. She both gives and seeks

TABLE 1. Percent of Interaction with Adults in Six Societies

	TAIRA (OKINAWA)	TARONG (PHILIPPINES)	KHALPUR (INDIA)	JUTLUHUACA (MEXICO)	ORCHARD TOWN (U.S.)	NYANSONGO (KENYA)
Young boys	7%	26%	42%	19%	55%	12%
Young girls	10%	25%	62%	38%	65%	14%
Both	8.5%	25.5%	52%	28.5%	60%	13%

Based on behavior observations collected by field workers in the Six Culture Study (Whiting and Whiting, 1975).

in the interchange. In comparing the six cultures, the children of Orchard Town ranked first in the percent three- to six-year-olds interacted with adults—60 percent of their coded interaction was with adults; in contrast, in the Kenyan sample, only 13 percent was with adults (see Table 1). In comparing the percent figures of the six groups, it is clear that they reflect the workload of the mothers (see Whiting and Whiting, 1975:83ff.). On the other hand, it should be noted, however, that Kikuyu mothers are with their children during the afternoon. The five to seven-year-olds were actually observed to be around adult females more than U.S. children in one of the comparisons the Munroes made using spot observations.[2] The rate of interaction with adults, however, is lower if we can judge by our other studies. In a comparison of Kikuyu two-year-olds with Burton White and Jean Carew's (1973) sample of Brookline, Massachusetts, two-year-olds, there was a significant difference in the amount of interaction with the mother (Bronson and Whiting, 1972). Thus it appears that, although Kikuyu young children are in the presence of the mother, the interaction between them is far less than in U.S. middle-income groups.

At the next stage in life after early childhood, there is another sharp contrast between traditional Kenyan and U.S. families: universal education, compulsory school. Compulsory education and the long school day make the latency period in traditional Kenyan society and the U.S. dramatically different. Spending six hours or more, five days a week, in the company of same-aged peers is associated with patterns of interaction that are proportionately high in competitiveness and mildly aggressive sociability.

The "seeking" behavior already established in U.S. middle-income homes is rewarded in the schoolroom setting as well as in the home. Teachers are taught to offer praise to those who seek information and seek to get the attention of the teacher by good performance. The use of praise seems essential in teaching symbolic and abstract material. Praise was rarely used in traditional Kenyan society. The skills Kenyan parents transmitted were better suited to demonstration, and effective performance—intrinsic reinforcement—seemed adequate reward. It is interesting to note that with the introduction of emphasis on schooling and reading and writing, praise by Kikuyu mothers becomes more frequent, and with it the children's dominant-dependent behavior becomes focused on adults. The children of the Kikuyu families who are educated and wish their children to succeed in school are significantly higher in

[2]Children five–seven were in the presence of adult females in 27 percent of observations made after school using randomized spot observations of sample children. A sample of U.S. children in California were with adult females in 19 percent of the observations made using the same methodology (see B. Whiting and Edwards, n.d.).

the proportion of dominant-dependent behavior than the children of traditional mothers.

Seeking attention for performance and being rewarded by praise have been identified as correlated with achievement motivations. A mother who incites her child to competitive striving and autonomous problem solving using praise as a reward produces a child who is more apt to be successful in our schools (McClelland, 1961; Rosen and D'Andrade, 1959; Winterbottom, 1958). Since achievement motivation is essential for success in a competitive industrial society, parents who reward these characteristics are apt to have successful children. However, parents at the same time are producing what we have labeled dominant-dependent children by rewarding demands for attention.

In traditional Kenyan society individual achievement is not a highly valued trait. It is recognized, however, by modern Kikuyu mothers that the traditionally valued traits are not adapted to school success (Whiting, Whiting, and Herzog, n.d.). Mothers who are convinced that success in school is essential for economic success are consciously changing their behavior.

The characteristics our sample of Kikuyu mothers considered essential for success in school included cleverness as evidenced by a quick mind, confidence, obedience as defined by attentiveness to the teacher, and boldness as defined by the ability to speak up to the teacher in class, to ask and answer questions. This latter trait requires that a new skill be learned, and modern Kikuyu parents are encouraging this behavior by allowing children to ask more questions. They are exchanging information with children more frequently, taking an interest in their schoolwork and using praise to reward their newly acquired symbolic skills (Whiting, Whiting, and Herzog, n.d.). A similar change in parental behavior based on mother and father interviews has been reported by Lloyd (1966, 1970) and LeVine, Klein, and Owen (1967) in their study of modern Yoruba parents in Nigeria.

That initiating interaction to adults is rare in traditional societies has also been documented in the studies by Gallimore, Howard, and Jordan (1969) and Howard (1974) in Hawaii. It is interesting to note that teachers consider the children who do not speak up in class "passive" and "dependent." Their concept of dependence is obviously the obverse of the definition we are using here.

There is an obvious confusion in the U.S. concept of independence. We are training children to be "seekers," to have strong habits of dominant-dependent behavior, and yet we value independence and self-reliance. How do we interpret this inconsistency?

It seems clear that valued characteristics, rather than being isomorphic to behavior, are often indicators of problem areas. Traditional

Kikuyu mothers stated that the traits they most valued in their children were generosity, goodheartedness, obedience, and respect for elders. Their children, as we have observed them, are no more obedient or respectful than U.S. children. But these traits are essential for the peaceful existence of the extended living group. The U.S. mother values independence, a trait that makes it possible for her to have a breather in the intensive parent-child interaction, a trait essential for success in a competitive world, but her children are no more independent than other children, and in some ways perhaps less so.

The type of dependence encouraged by U.S. and traditional Kikuyu socializers differs. The Kikuyu child seeks instrumental help, food and material goods, and permission. The U.S. child demands attention and praise. The former is more compatible with a nurturant-responsible interchange between the old and the young; the latter demonstrates a striving for individual achievement and self-reliance.

The U.S. middle-income individual may be taught to value independence and aspire to self-reliance, but the dependency bonds remain. The affective bonds in the isolated nuclear family are within the small group—all needs are focused on the members of the family. Since siblings in small families tend to be close in age, what have been called "dependency" needs are focused on the two adults and most frequently on the responsive mother. The siblings compete for her attention. In the Kenyan family structure, from infancy onward there are a variety of people to choose from and all wants need not be satisfied by one person. Seeking behavior is frequently focused on older children. Women are bonded to other women, men to men. The dyadic marital relationship is not the only emotional bond, and in the young years of marriage is frequently exclusively sexual. In contrast, the ultimate healthy adjustment in the Eriksonian scheme is the capacity for exclusive intimacy between husband and wife (Erikson, 1950), the implication being that in the perfect relationship all dependent and sexual needs are satisfied by one person.

Early on, the Kenyan child is considered an adult and is capable of marrying and raising a family. The Kenyan man may still remain within the family compound. It is his choice if he wishes to leave. The conflict continues in the U.S. home. Encouraged to be independent, adolescent boys and girls remain bound to the family. The work world has no room for the young and our specialized economy requires prolonged education. In those families who can afford to finance this, the young adult remains dependent into his late twenties. Both parent and now adult child are caught up in a dependency conflict—one must be independent but one has been trained from early childhood to be a seeker from adults, and economic factors allow this behavior to continue. Parents have established strong dyadic bonds with their children, habituated to intense social interaction. They continue to attempt to anticipate their children's needs but often resent the continuing dependency demands. Both members of the dyad are caught in the conflict that we have labeled the "dependency hang-up."

The young adults who are attempting to set up new styles of family life are aware of part of this syndrome. They see the lack of early physical contact between caretaker and child. They are encouraged by the new breed of pediatricians and psychologists to develop a sensitivity to the rhythm of each individual infant's needs (Brazelton, 1976). These young parents carry infants more frequently, advocate the lying-in of the infant with the mother in the hospital, are not so anxious as in the 1920s about sleeping with their infants. They see the isolation and loneliness of the mother. They understand her desire for a career outside the home, for contact with other adults. There are now many women who are working and who feel comfortable in delegating some of child care to surrogate mothers. They see the danger of the close dyadic relationships engendered by the isolated nuclear family, where all emotional needs are focused on one or two individuals. They see the danger of even closer bonds with smaller-sized families. They seek to increase the number of potential reciprocal partners by developing support groups for both men and women. In some cases they seek to break the exclusive dyadic intimacy of the marital bond by encouraging the exchange of sexual partners. They all wish to embed the nuclear family in a larger household unit larger than the nuclear family or to organize some type of microcommunity. But living in a viable microcommunity requires some of the traits valued by traditional Kikuyu—an ability to share, to cooperate with people beyond the confines of the nuclear household, to feel responsible for others, to value interdependence rather than independence. New patterns of interaction are called for.

How successful have these experiments in alternative life styles been? Is it easy to break the bonds of the small intimate family group, to embed it in a larger unit? Living in a larger unit requires new social habits as well as new values. Intellectually one can change one's values, but it is more difficult to change one's styles of social interaction.

It is our hypothesis that styles of interaction are developed in those settings where children spend the majority of their waking hours. Our research suggests that our children need less training in settings that encourage seeking interaction with adults, less time with same-aged peers, which encourages competition and sociable aggression, more time with younger children and infants. It is caring for and associating with these younger children that encourages responsibility and responsive nuturance. Orchard Town ranks fifth in our sample of six societies in this type of behavior (Whiting and Whiting, 1975:71). To equip our children to participate now and in the future in microcommunities, we need to teach new habits of dyadic interaction. To take a lesson from tribal societies, we need to encourage the young to feel responsible for siblings and younger community members, to feel responsible for the welfare of the social group, to interact in nonschool settings in work that is focused on the welfare of the group. We need more cross-age grouping of children, less same-age peer interaction, more young caretakers of infants. We need more emotionally receptive, noncompetitive individuals over whom to spread our intimacies. We need practice in sociable, non-task-oriented behavior that requires that adults be able to interact with other adults in the community without the constant interruption of young who are seekers, demanding attention from the older generation rather than enjoying noncompetitive sociability with older and younger children. Until we train such a generation, the young idealistic adults who are experimenting with styles of cooperative living arrangements will find it difficult to maintain viable mutual support groups and we will find it difficult to set up much-needed microcommunities.

V

On the Quality of Life: Population, Resources, and Community Design

19

Introduction

The Editors

IF PERCEIVED QUALITY of life may be taken as one standard by which to assess the effects of change in postindustrial society, the results are not entirely favorable. In a recent Harris Survey, for example, 43 percent of the respondents reported that the quality of life in the United States has grown worse over the past decade, compared with 34 percent who felt that it has improved (*Cleveland Plain Dealer,* November 21, 1977). The papers that follow explore the ways in which this elusive notion of quality of life can be conceptualized. They add significantly to our understanding of the wide range of factors influencing it and demonstrate the usefulness of applying a multidisciplinary perspective in analyzing quality of life.

Professor Catton draws heavily on the findings of biology and anthropology in discussing how quality of life might change as the number of energy consumers, with resource appetites enlarged by prosthetic technologies, increases. As one scenario, he suggests that we may be entering the overshoot phase of the bloom-crash cycle characteristic of some species. That our expanding search for energy might be viewed as "industrial hunting and gathering" also leads him to explore possible future patterns of interaction and organization based on patterns characteristic of primitive hunters and gatherers.

A central theme of Professor Slobodkin's chapter is that continued population growth will make resource management an increasingly complex, political issue. He expresses a concern that recent developments in sociobiology, resting on weak biological foundations, may be interpreted by policy makers as limiting the range of possible responses to ecological problems. Since decisions concerning the management of ecological resources are likely to have a profound effect on the quality of life, he argues that sociologists should school themselves in biology in order to be in a better position to contribute to this area of policy formulation.

While acknowledging the role of demographic factors in ecological destruction and deteriorating quality of life, Professor Rappaport's paper directs our attention to a number of other explanations: differentiation and specialization making systemic stability more problematic, the dominance of industrial subsystems, and changing belief systems about our relationship to nature. Among the many factors influencing quality of life, his analysis highlights the critical role of thought and social organization.

Finally, Professor Keller's paper considers still another component of the quality of life: the built environment. She reviews the ways in which perceptions of the environment relate to planning and design, and she draws upon the results of a long-term study of one planned community to demonstrate that design considerations are of consistent relevance to the residents' evaluation of and satisfaction with the community.

There can be little doubt about the continuation of the types of change identified in these chapters. This should ensure that quality of life will become increasingly prominent as a topic of social scientific investigation. In their thoughtful efforts to clarify the concept of quality of life, to specify its determinants, and to provide multidisciplinary models for analysis, these papers represent an important contribution.

20

Carrying Capacity, Overshoot, and the Quality of Life

William R. Catton, Jr.

QUALITY OF LIFE DEPENDS strongly on the relation between population and the carrying capacity of the habitat occupied and exploited by that population. Carrying capacity greatly in excess of population affords opportunities for a very different quality of life than is possible when population has expanded to fill carrying capacity or has even overshot it.

An Essential Concept

Carrying capacity is the maximum population of a given species that a particular environment can support indefinitely. In the human case, it is the maximum population that can be indefinitely supported by a particular environment under exploitation by specified technology and organization.

Because carrying capacity is seldom mentioned in sociological literature, sociologists who now recognize its importance must draw upon biological literature in which the concept has been systematically developed (e.g., Edwards and Fowle, 1955; P. Ehrlich, Ehrlich, and Holdren, 1973; Heady, 1975; Whittaker, 1975) and anthropological literature in which a good start has been made toward applying the concept to human populations (e.g., Bayliss-Smith, 1974; Brush, 1975; Hardesty, 1977; Rappaport, 1967; Zubrow, 1971, 1975).

Properly understood, carrying capacity enables us to avoid some of the difficulties that beset discussions of the sociologically more familiar "optimum population."[1] Optimum population has meant the number that cannot be exceeded without beginning to lower *the population's* per capita wealth. The major flaw in such a concept was that it did not make explicit both the environmental dependence and the environmental impact of the population. Carrying capacity does do this, for it means the number that cannot be exceeded without reducing *the environment's* capability of providing sustenance for the given species.

Population that exceeds carrying capacity entails habitat damage. The effect of habitat damage upon the population is adverse but may be delayed. Population can thus sometimes exceed carrying capacity and suffer no *immediate* adverse consequences; it may therefore not *seem* to be greater than optimum. One result of such biocultural lag has been that the optimum has seemed less measurable than a useful quantitative concept ought to be. As long as indices of departure from optimum were sought in the condition of the population rather than in the condition of the habitat, the difficulty could not be overcome. Until population-habitat interactions became the focus of analysis, the indices would not be sought in the right place, and the analyses had to remain essentially sterile—and it was tempting to explain away the sterility by insisting that "optimum" population was, after all, a matter of value judgment. Adoption of the carrying capacity concept can redirect sociological attention toward habitat condition and habitat modification.

Quality Quantified and Qualified

Quality of life is also a difficult concept. Attempts to measure it have gone through three stages that implied three rather different definitions (Dillman and Tremblay, 1977). At first, quality of life was more or less equated with economic standard of living (e.g., Fairchild, 1939). It was assumed that increased economic abundance would increase the quality of life. But in the decades after World War II it turned out that certain higher-level needs (see Maslow, 1954) were often left unsatisfied, or thwarted, by even the dramatically successful pursuit of material abundance. Moreover, industrial progress turned out to yield such by-products as increasingly visible degradation of environment (Wagar,

---

[1]The latter has been a troublesome concept; Thompson devoted a whole chapter to it in the second edition of his population textbook (1935:422–35), deleted the chapter and replaced it with a perfunctory paragraph in his third edition (1942:40), expanded upon this in his fourth edition (1953:44–45, 446–52, 455–56), and reverted to perfunctory mention without index citation in his fifth edition (1965:47). But recognition that the problem had been ill conceived did not make it vanish. It has demanded renewed attention (Singer, 1971).

1970), and "painful increases in crime, drug addiction, civil disorder and violence, and a steady deterioration of confidence in public authority" (A. Campbell, Converse, and Rodgers, 1976:2).

In its second stage of development, therefore, the phrase "quality of life" came to refer to statistical indicators of environmental quality (Train, 1972; Sears, 1975) as well as measures of educational achievement, health, health-care provisions, leisure time, leisure activities, crime rates, and political participation (Bauer, 1966). Some of these second-stage indicators began to suggest that quality of life might be enhanced by *less* (rather than more) of some things.

In a third (very recent) stage, measurement of quality of life has focused on *perceptions* of well-being (Andrews and Withey, 1977), and on *subjective* assessments of happiness or satisfaction (A. Campbell, Converse, and Rodgers, 1976).

All three measurement approaches had one thing in common: They all took "quality" of life to mean the degree of *goodness* of life. A brief look at a dictionary, however, will show that the word "quality" can refer just as well to the "basic nature of" something, or the "characteristic attributes of" something, rather than to something's goodness or excellence. For example, the quality of senior citizens' life is more sedentary and reminiscent compared to adolescents, who have typically lived more active and anticipatory lives.

The decline of anticipation and the rise of something like nostalgia among youth is thus an indicator of serious change in the quality of their society's life (Gutmann, 1972). A society whose people live with pervasive despair certainly has a different quality of life than a society characterized by opportunity. A society in which one's fellow humans are rivals for insufficient resources, in which life is fundamentally and implacably competitive, has a manifestly different quality of life than one in which a carrying capacity surplus makes feasible a more fraternal style of relationship between persons. I propose, therefore, to take the attribute of competitiveness as a key element in conceptualizing quality of life, and to consider in ecological terms why exuberant confidence in the future has waned.

Exuberant Life vs. Postexuberant Life

Any population (human or nonhuman) that has the opportunity to undergo logistic growth (as depicted in the middle part of figure 1) must experience a transition from minimal intraspecific competition to increasingly intense intraspecific competition. In the period prior to the growth curve's inflection point, when growth is accelerating, the basic

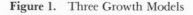

Figure 1. Three Growth Models

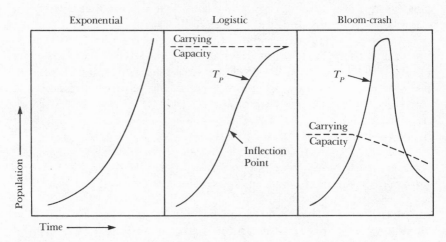

fact of life is that a large carrying capacity surplus minimizes competition between conspecifics, permitting life to be lived expansively. In the period after the inflection point has passed, the basic fact of life is the increasingly depressive effect of the conspicuous shrinkage of this carrying capacity surplus. As the surplus approaches zero, competition between members of the growing population approaches maximum intensity and has to become a major parameter of the quality of life.

Population data from the first seventeen decennial censuses of the United States fit a logistic curve remarkably well. It is not surprising that the fit was so close for so long, for the American population was an almost classic case of population of invaders expanding into a land that was (for the European mode of agricultural-industrial exploitation) still an almost virgin habitat. The cultures of its native peoples held them to much less intense exploitation; for them its carrying capacity was much less than for the invaders, with their more advanced technology.

The upper asymptote of a best-fitting logistic would have been about 197 million. According to the implications of this model, loss of much of the traditional American optimism was to be expected once the inflection point had been passed. On the toe of the curve a society can have a youthfully anticipatory quality of life; high on the shoulder of the curve, however, it begins to face the plight of the elderly, with a shrinking future.

The 1960 and 1970 censuses turned up numbers appreciably higher than the logistic trend would have predicted, and we are now quite conspicuously above its asymptote. Odum (1971:183) took the upper asymptote of the logistic curve as a measure of the implied carrying capacity of a population's habitat. In terms of a logistic growth model, then, it can be said that U.S. population now exceeds the implied carrying capacity of U.S. territory. But, of course, a population that rises above the asymptote either indicates that the logistic model is inapplicable or that something has happened to launch a new growth surge transcending previous limits. Even if the logistic is not finally the appropriate model, however, it has at least made us aware of the distinction between an exuberant phase in our history and a postexuberant phase. The quality of life in the postexuberant phase (after the point of inflection) is necessarily different from the quality of life in an age of exuberance (prior to the inflection point).

Humanness in Ecological Perspective

Before going on to consider other growth models and their implications for what is happening to the quality of life, it will help to clarify issues if we first consider the special ecological nature of the human species and infuse special meaning into the word "population." We need to see that a population as a number of energy-consumption units may be many times larger and more impactful than a population as merely a given number of persons.

THE MISLEADING POSTULATE

Conventional sociological throughtways have usefully taught us that human beings are organisms with two kinds of inheritance, one genetic, the other cultural. But quite misleadingly, it has come to be assumed by most sociologists that the cultural heritage that our species has so remarkably elaborated now overshadows so enormously the biological properties humanity shares with all other species that we sociologists can almost forget biology. Ever since Sumner (1906) told us that "the mores can make anything right" we have tended to suppose that the arbitrariness of human life styles can approach 100 percent. It cannot. Human social life does not occur in a vacuum. It occurs in adaptation to environmental opportunities and constraints.

If reproductive success is the definition of Darwinian fitness, then in the special case of *human* evolution what matters is not only a gene's future prevalence in a gene pool but also the future prevalence of a given norm or a given tool in the "norm and tool pool" we call culture. But by this standard, when we think with carrying capacity in mind we can begin to see that many of today's most powerful norms and titanic apparatus are going to prove "unfit" because they are leading to creation of conditions in which their continued implementation and replication will be impossible. Cultural elements are adaptive or progressive only *in relation to* environmental circumstances. Environmental circumstances differ both from place to place and from one historic period to another. Some of the changes that enhanced human life as recently as the nineteenth century will be disastrous under the changed circumstances of the twenty-first century.

NEW ASSUMPTIONS NEEDED

To understand present and future social reality, it is time for sociologists to revise three assumptions. First, we must abandon our traditional postulate of human exceptionalism. At the very least we must now recognize that human beings, as truly as other species of organisms, "have no way of leaving the ecological scene" and are therefore as truly engaged in what mathematical biologists can describe as the game of "existential Gambler's Ruin," wherein the optimal strategy in our encounters with environmental selection pressures is to minimize the stakes (Slobodkin and Rapoport, 1974). Sociology must acknowledge that the various life styles and social organizations developed by assorted segments of our species are subject to ineluctable constraints arising from physical, chemical, and biological dimensions of the world upon which human living depends.

Second, it is time to rethink the significance of a methodological rule we inherited from Durkheim. In the interest of disciplinary purity (which was important when we still had to establish ourselves institutionally), sociologists have made a fetish of the notion that social facts cannot be explained in terms of relations to other facts that are not distinctly social. But now we live in a time when some very important social facts can *only* be explained in terms of their relations to facts we have long supposed were irrelevant to sociology.

Third, it is also time to reconsider our habitual notions of the part technology plays in human life. Ogburn (1956) steered our thinking in what I now believe was not the most incisive direction when he distinguished three categories of "environment." All organisms, he said, have to adapt to a natural environment—temperature, moisture, soil, atmosphere, sunlight, and so on. All social organisms have to adapt to a social environment as well—associations of conspecifics. Mankind has to adapt to both a natural and a social environment *and* to what Ogburn called a "technological environment," all the objects of material culture. It was in conceiving technology as part of our environment rather than as part of us that I think Ogburn led us astray.

His ultimate aim was to call attention to derivative, indirect adaptations that follow among societal institutions in the wake of technological change. Today, of course, the very convening of an interdisciplinary panel to consider relationships among population, resources, and the quality of life is a derivative adaptation by the American Sociological Association in response to a new anxiety about technology increasingly felt in various sectors of modern society (see, for example, Fernandez, 1977). Resource depletion has begun to confront us with the specter of a technological civilization running out of the fuels and materials that sustain it. But we are also confronted with valiant efforts at "whistling in the dark," the significance of which is that they assume a practical substitute can always be found for any natural resource we exhaust, because new technology will give us new abilities to use substances not now usable and not now defined as resources.

This faith in technology as a solver of problems (when dissident voices have begun worrying about it as a *generator* of problems—e.g., Douglas, 1971; Teich, 1977) has been clearly expressed by Hawley (1975:10) as follows:

> Historically, the accumulation of technical knowledge has followed an exponential curve. A simple extrapolation extends that curve ever more steeply into the future. The expectation of further developments need not rest solely on a mathematical exercise. It has a sound basis in the enormous fund of information that has been gathered into our libraries, data repositories, and the minds of technical specialists. The unexploited potentialities that lie in that vast accumulation are immeasurable; they may be infinite.

A MORE INCISIVE VIEW OF TECHNOLOGY

In the face of such sublime optimism I take the view that more realistic insights into the ecological prospects for human life will arise if we begin to view technology not as part of the environment *to* which we adapt but as a vast extension of the (originally organic) apparatus *by* which we adapt. In short, I believe we must learn to view all artifacts as essentially prosthetic devices.

In medicine, a prosthetic device is an artificial replacement for a missing part of the body. The most obvious example is a wooden limb. A prosthesis enables its user to perform again at least some of the functions for which he used to use the now-missing part of his body. With a wooden leg, an amputee can walk again. By wearing a hearing aid, a person with hearing loss hears again.

In some cases it may not be feasible to replace amputated or incapacitated legs, so we use a wheelchair to restore partial mobility. Form is different, but function is what matters. And if it is reasonable to regard as prosthetic any device that *restores* a function, it seems heuristically useful to view as no less prosthetic whatever devices *extend* our abilities beyond what was possible with our genetic endowment. Those of us who may not need hearing aids to listen to persons speaking to us from across the room do need radios if we want to listen to persons speaking to us from across the continent. A bicycle adds to the mobility of the unin-jured as truly as a wheelchair adds to the mobility of the paraplegic. Natural selection had not equipped our bodies with wheels in either case, so we do it with culture.

The selection pressures operating upon our ancestors did not endow us with wings. Today we fly with prosthetic wings, so huge that several hundred of us can use a single pair at once. Today, too, we have other kinds of seven-league boots, with four wheels and V-8 engines. What we must now recognize is that all these devices make us more space consum-ing. They have also given us tremendous per capita appetites for petro-leum products. Thus the latest generation of supertankers that we now require to bring petroleum to us from overseas sources (with the con-stant risk of oil spills disastrous to marine life) are among the "derivative adjustments" entailed by our most modern prostheses.

Technology was prosthetic from the start. The hafting of weapons and the invention of spear throwers provided detachable extensions for our hunting and gathering ancestors' arms. But we must remember that one result was "pleistocene overkill"—when many species of game ani-mals were hunted to extinction (Boughey, 1975:137–42). This should remind us, then, that technological extensions of our bodily apparatus may do more than just make available to us resources that would oth-erwise not serve our needs; prosthetic technology enlarges our environ-mental impact. It can increase our resource appetites.

FROM HOMO SAPIENS TO HOMO COLOSSUS

Technology, in short, has the power to turn us into "enlarged" crea-tures for which a given environment may have *less* carrying capacity than it had for our prosthetically "smaller" forebears. With this in mind, perhaps we can see that the logistic model of growth was invalidated for contemporary human experience not merely by the increase of the number of Americans beyond the asymptotic 197 million. What re-quired us to begin thinking of "population" growth in a different way was the enlargement of each American's resource appetite and en-vironmental impact. At the same time as we were becoming more nu-merous at a greater-than-logistic rate we were also becoming effectively larger and more voracious through major technological changes—the cultural analogue of mutation.

The "population" whose growth matters environmentally today consists not merely of two-legged mammals that consume up to 3,000 kilocalories of energy by daily food intake. It consists in America of about 220 million elaborately equipped persons who consume a per capita average of over 200,000 kilocalories of energy daily, mostly derived from fossil fuels.

We have become, in effect, a species of giants, and it would be useful to begin calling ourselves Homo colossus instead of merely Homo sapiens. The more colossal we become by virtue of our prosthetic extensions, the fewer of us it takes to fill up a given habitat or exceed a given carrying capacity. It would even be useful to append numerical subscripts to our species name, reflecting the ratio of our per capita energy consumption (as wielders of vast technology) to the energy we would consume as mere naked apes. Thus today, globally, mankind can be regarded as Homo colossus$_{10}$, and the American subspecies would perhaps be designated Homo colossus$_{80}$. Until very recently we have assumed that whatever enlarged the subscript always improved the quality of life. In relation to the carrying capacity concept, however, it becomes apparent that this is not always the way it works. It takes fewer Homo colossus$_{80}$ to subject each other to a postexuberant quality of life with intensified competition (for finite space and depleted resources) than would be the case for, say, Homo colossus$_{40}$. With this in mind, let us consider alternatives to the logistic growth model.

Alternative Growth Models

The exponential curve in figure 1—representing the growth pattern one gets when each successive time period brings a *constant percentage* increase over the previously accumulated total—is the model implicit in the traditional American faith in perpetual progress. The image of a "land of opportunity," and the tacit expectation of universal opportunities for upward social mobility, were consistent with the exuberant growth represented by this model (or by the preinflection portion of the logistic model).

People whose expectations have been nurtured by traditions that developed in the exuberant phase of our history cannot help feeling that "something has gone wrong" in the postinflection period.

In figure 1, on the shoulder of the logistic curve there is a point T_p representing "Time, present." Postexuberant Americans, reluctantly adjusting to the changed shape of our ecological future, may feel they have been courageously realistic to abandon the exponential model and accept the diminishing-increments view of the future embodied in the logistic model. But by supposing we are merely undergoing the kind of change that can be represented by a logistic curve, we let ourselves expect that the misfortunes in store for us consist merely of "the end of progress."

Suppose, however, that we are really undergoing a process of change that is most accurately portrayed by the bloom-crash curve in the third section of figure 1. Suppose the point T_p on *that* curve best represents

Figure 2. Birth and Death Patterns

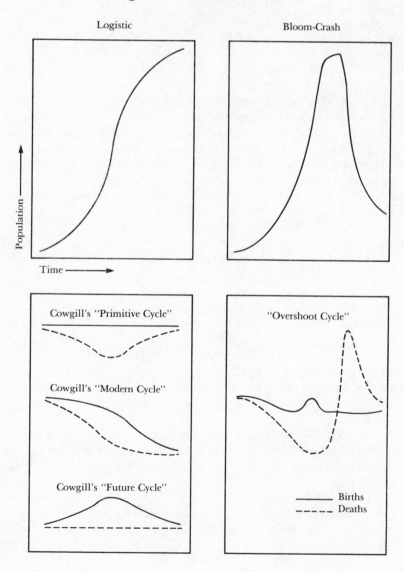

our present situation. In that case, our future is even more drastically "out of shape" than we had let ourselves imagine. It has in store for us a plummeting *decline* in numbers, or standard of living, or both. The quality of life ahead of us is very different if this model is valid than if the logistic model is the applicable one.[2] (For anthropological indications of what happens to quality of life during the high-mortality crash phase, see Mulloy, 1974; C. Turnbull, 1972).

In figure 2 we look at mechanisms behind growth curves. On the left-hand side, below the logistic curve, three alternative patterns of change in birth and death rates that could produce it are shown, as analyzed by Cowgill (1949). The middle one, Cowgill's "modern cycle"—a birthrate decline lagging behind a death rate decline—is the pattern sociological demographers have formed the habit of calling "the demographic transition" (K. Davis, 1945; Taeuber, 1960; Kirk, 1971). It has been misleading to speak of "the" demographic transition, as if the pattern were universal, and necessarily a transition to a steady state. It has also been unwise to study demographic change as if it were uniquely human, failing to use vast funds of knowledge about its processes obtained from studies of other species. From other species a good deal is known about the bloom-crash model, and in the lower right-hand portion of figure 2 an "overshoot cycle" is schematically represented, showing changes in births and deaths that would produce the bloom-crash curve. Looked at closely, it can be seen to combine Cowgill's "modern cycle" and his "future cycle," but it also takes into account the idea that population increase can, in certain circumstances, overshoot permanent carrying capacity, so it follows these cycles with a phase in which deaths exceed births. Such a dieback phase would obviously be, like a tragic war, a time of unsatisfactory quality of life.

Understanding Bloom and Crash

To gain insight into problems of overshoot and crash, social scientists have much to learn by turning to studies of other species. Figure 3 is adapted from a study of the population dynamics of an Australian species of psyllid, or plant louse, that lives on the foliage of a particular species of Eucalyptus tree (L. Clark, 1962, 1964). Phase 1 represents a long period in which the psyllid population remains at a low level, con-

[2]If, for reasons given later in this paper, the bloom-crash model *is* applicable to Homo colossus, then the ostensible realist who has belatedly recognized the obsolescence of the exponential model and has embraced the logistic model is only superficially realistic. He is quite egregiously superficial, moreover, if he continues to imagine not only that we are following a merely logistic trajectory but also that we are not yet far into its postinflection

Figure 3.   Population Dynamics of *Cardiaspina Albitextura*

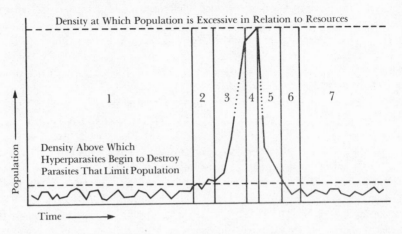

Adapted from L. Clark (1964).

trolled by prevailing weather, density-reactive predation, and parasites. Phase 2 happens when a change of weather reduces percentage parasitism, allowing the psyllid population to rise to a level at which it becomes possible for a species of hyperparasites to mulitply and destroy the primary parasites that helped control the psyllid numbers. Then, in phase 3, the psyllid population explodes.

At this point, to understand clearly the *applicability* of psyllid experience to the human case, let us recall Durkheim's venerable study of the division of labor in human society; it explicitly recognized the ecological equivalence of an occupation to a species, and the functional parallel between interoccupational and interspecific relationships (Durkheim, 1933:266-67).[3] With this in mind, let us note that there is an occupational category, medical practitioners, who depend for their living on attacking the microbes that attack human bodies. Thus the advances in medicine, public health practices, and so on, that have so greatly increased human life expectancy in the last century are clear instances of the opportunistic destruction of parasites, which, among the psyllids, is

---

portion. Herman Kahn (Kahn, Brown, and Martel, 1976), whom one does not *lightly* dismiss as superficial, *quite arbitrarily* assumed point T_p to be located much lower on the logistic curve than it appears in figure 1. He took the American bicentennial year as the inflection point. This put the upper asymptote as far above our present status as our present is above the 1776 level of living, letting Kahn suppose the next 200 years would bring magnificent further improvements in the quality of life. His reasoning seems typical of the technological optimists who persistently discount concerned investigation of ecological limits (e.g., studies by the Club of Rome and the M.I.T. group).

[3]The importance of these equivalences has been reiterated by a recent sociological advocate of a multispecies model of human communities (Stephan, 1970).

done by hyperparasites. If phase 3 is the natural sequel to phase 2 among these plant lice, the irruption of human population in recent generations is a manifestation of the same pattern. This is why it is instructive to go on and examine phases 4, 5, 6, and 7 in the psyllid case. They tell us about our own situation.

Phase 3 depletes the resources upon which the population depends for its life style. In phase 4 habitat damage becomes so severe it imposes strong environmental opposition to population growth. The aftermath of this habitat damage is the population crash of phase 5—involving both increased mortality and a reduced reproductive rate. In phase 6, when crash has brought the population back down to a level where the percentage effectiveness of predation and parasitism becomes more significant, these agencies further reduce the population, bringing it below the threshold level at which it was originally controlled in a steady state (phase 1). Phase 7, then, is another phase 1—and the whole cycle may be repeated *if* the exploited resource is one that can recover and provide renewed opportunities for another outbreak. It is important to note, however, that in the case of Homo colossus, crash following overshoot would probably not give us a second chance, for the resource depletion we are inflicting upon our habitat involves not just defoliation of host trees but draw-down of natural reservoirs of abiotic substances and fossil fuels whose rate of replacement by geological processes is enormously slow in relation to a human generation.

Figure 4 depicts the comparatively well-known case of the deer population on the Kaibab Plateau, which irrupted following the slaughter of predators (by human hyperpredators). It is included here to suggest two things. First, inasmuch as very nearly the same pattern can be observed among species as different as deer and plant lice, we ought to question the notion (traditional among sociologists) that inferences from the experience of other species have no implications for the human species because man is so different. The burden of proof should be reversed; except when we have explicit contrary indications, we should assume that patterns of population dynamics observed among a varied assortment of other species probably *are* applicable to mankind (because they are probably due to ecological principles from which we, as living beings, are not exempt).[4] Second, in figure 4, note that the observation of fawn starvation was subsequent to the observation of habitat damage. Fawn starvation would certainly be an indication that the deer population had exceeded its optimum. But habitat damage indicative of overshoot (and consequent carrying capacity reduction) occurred and was observed *before* the population began to suffer in that way. This sequence should

---

[4]To gain knowledge of such principles, sociologists would be well advised to read Nicholson (1954).

Figure 4. Kaibab Plateau Deer Irruption

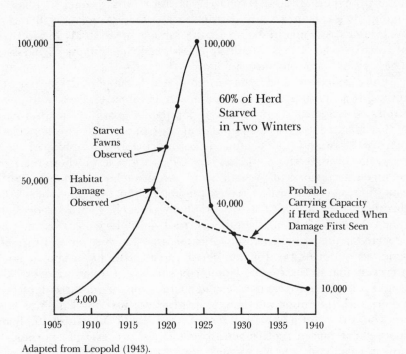

Adapted from Leopold (1943).

suffice to show why we ought to get away from discussing "optimum population" and think instead in terms of carrying capacities.

Carrying Capacity Enlargement: Fateful Change of Method

A population can sometimes enlarge the carrying capacity of its habitat, but it can also reduce the carrying capacity by what it does to its habitat. For different species (or different cultures) the carrying capacity of a given environment differs.

Homo sapiens, on the way to becoming Homo colossus, several times raised the earth's human carrying capacity by taking over (through cultural innovations) portions of the ecosphere that had been supporting other forms of life. Because these takeovers were accomplished by major cultural transformations, sociologists are as apt as any other group to suppose this can be done again if necessary.

Use of fire extended the range of our hunter-gatherer ancestors into areas where winter would have been unendurable had man not learned to release, through wintertime combustion, supplies of solar energy stored in wood by summertime photosynthesis. The arm-extending breakthroughs that resulted in Pleistocene overkill increased the earth's human population from something like three million persons to perhaps eight million. Discovery of techniques of plant cultivation enabled Homo sapiens to take over for the growth of human food areas of land that would otherwise have been occupied by humanly inedible plants and the animals dependent on them; as a result, our species became about twenty-five times as numerous in the course of some five thousand years. Then invention of the plow (and irrigation systems) further added to the human power to manage ecosystems; increasingly numerous agricultural man kept more and more extensive tracts of land in the early seral stage we call a farm. By this power to turn back tides of natural succession, human numbers were boosted (at the expense of other species) to almost a billion before industrialization began.

Industrialization, however, was a breakthrough of such a different kind that we may find it necessary to begin regarding its addition of another three billion people to the planet's population as a clear case of overshoot. That is, the billion the earth supported by preindustrial agriculture may be an approximate measure of the carrying capacity ultimately achievable by the *method of displacement* of competitors. Industrialization added illusory (i.e., temporary) carrying capacity by the *method of depletion* of geological savings deposits, as we began ambitiously withdrawing underground stores of prehistoric solar energy. An oil well I saw recently pumping fuel from beneath a Kansas cornfield nicely symbolizes our dependence today on simultaneously harvesting both contemporary crops of vegetation and vast accumulations of the remains of "crops" that grew in the Carboniferous period before humans existed. The demand of industrial societies for such organic remains is so great in proportion to our demand for contemporary organic substances that we can almost call Homo colossus a detritovore. And among detritus-consuming organisms, the bloom-crash pattern is common.

Accordingly, the larger we make the energy-ratio subscript that our technology enables us to attach to our new species name, the more our behavior is ecologically equivalent to that of the irrupting psyllids—committed by their numbers and their appetites to drawing down the reserves of redgum foliage upon which their way of life depends. The very technology that seems to validate the notion that humans are so superior to other species that they are exempt from principles applying to lower forms actually puts us squarely into the predicament depicted in phases 3 and 4 of figure 3.

Moreover, as we have all become increasingly aware during congressional and national debate over energy policy, an industrial society depends on massive programs of "exploration and development." What has been too seldom recognized is that these high-sounding words are euphemisms for *hunting* and *gathering*. A high-energy industrial way of life is as dependent as our pre-Neolithic ancestors were on *finding* usable materials generated by processes man does not and cannot control or accelerate.

Insights Into Our Future

As industrial hunters and gatherers, we have irrupted from one billion to four billion. Because of our colossal character, the four billion of us are deeply dependent on depleting resources that nature cannot renew as fast as we use them.[5]

The *prospect* of crash (taking the form either of an actual dieback in human numbers, or a reduction of our colossal level of living, or both) will be a fundamental attribute of the quality of life in the years ahead. Population redundancy will erode democratic values and will impede processes of self-actualization.

Because we have become colossal hunters and gatherers but have not heretofore seen ourselves as such, considerable light may be shed on our future and the quality of life we may anticipate if we enumerate some basic characteristics of life in primitive societies we do recognize as hunters and gatherers; examine features of modern industrial life that may or may not constitute parallels; and consider the reasons for both the similarities and the differences.

Hunting and gathering societies have generally been characterized by the following traits (Lenski and Lenski, 1974:135–54):

1. Nomadism.
2. Limited development of political institutions.
3. Minimal inequality of power and privilege.
4. Kinship as the central organizing principle.
5. Religion comprising (a) animistic beliefs, (b) minimal religious differentiation and conflict, and (c) the role of shaman.

These characteristics doubtless reflect not merely the dependence of hunting and gathering peoples upon unmanaged nature, but also the combined influences of their crude technology together with the small scale of their societies and the resulting face-to-face nature of interac-

---

[5]Certain technological innovations *may* permit resource substitutions that may somewhat postpone crash, but other technological progress may continue in the meantime to make us even more colossal in our resource demands. Technology cannot be depended upon to mitigate permanently or fundamentally the precariousness of life for a population that has overshot carrying capacity.

tions within them. So we would hardly expect all five traits to be replicated among modern peoples whose commitment to industrialism has renewed (on a colossal scale) their dependence on natural processes they cannot expect to manage and accelerate.

The second and third characteristics in particular—undeveloped political systems and minimal social stratification—are presumably attributable almost entirely to modesty of scale and hardly at all to dependence on nature. On the other hand, the traits of nomadism, kinship-based organization, and animistic religion may have more direct counterparts among industrial peoples because they may have resulted more directly and fully from hunter-gatherer dependence on unmanaged and intractable nature.

Primitive hunting and gathering groups were nomadic because their method of harvesting resources tended to exhaust local carrying capacity and compelled them to move elsewhere and exploit other plant and animal populations until those in a previously exploited area had recovered. That the United States now imports some 40 percent of the petroleum it uses is a manifestation of part of this same process. We escalated use of this resource by becoming more colossal, and drew down the reserves that existed within our national boundaries, so we have increasingly turned elsewhere for replacement supplies. The fundamental difference is that this turning elsewhere does not mean our own drawn-down fields will recover.[6] In fact, it is probably the wave of the future for industrial societies to find themselves beset with internal resource depletion and to seek vast quantities of essential substances from wherever they can be found, with increasing disregard for territorial claims of other peoples. Intersocietal conflict may become chronic as a consequence, and will hardly be curbed by mere denunciation of imperialism.

Among primitive hunter-gatherer groups, a common mechanism for providing resource-access insurance consisted of exogamy rules. Out-marriage helped ensure peaceful movements between the territories claimed by related groups and could ease temporary local variations in food resources (Service, 1962:49). Modern societies have long since transcended kinship as the major organizing principle (Parsons, 1977), but our dependence on dwindling and uncertain resources has pressured us to evolve functionally equivalent mechanisms of resource-access insurance (L. Brown, 1974:29).

Seeing industrial nations as colossal hunting and gathering societies should enable us to see international cartels and multinational corpora-

---

[6]General failure to see what we are really up against is perhaps epitomized by universal public acceptance of the utterly unecological meaning assigned to the word "recovery" in oil-industry jargon. In the ecology of psyllid populations, "recovery" means the *regrowth* of drawn-down Eucalyptus foliage after the psyllid dieoff. In the human case, we blindly use "recovery" to mean the process of draw-down (of oil reserves, and so on).

tions as agencies engaged in a struggle between a natural tendency of peoples in a competitive era to assert *exclusive* territorial rights to resources and the opposite tendency to assert principles of *inclusiveness* to ensure wider access to resources in the manner of exogamous primitive communities. Sociologists have not always found it easy to penetrate emotional rhetoric and understand the forces underlying events like the Fourth Conference of Heads of State or Government of Non-Aligned Countries in 1973, or to perceive the ecological significance of documents such as the "Economic Declaration" that conference issued. We need to learn to read much of today's political jargon (e.g., specimens appearing in P. Rogers, 1976:112, 119) as symptomatic of a struggle between exclusive versus inclusive tendencies. Resource depletion will very probably intensify that struggle.

Finally, in the religious sector, if religion is basically an institutionalized way of dealing with life's precariousness, the new hazards spawned by our becoming so colossal may well have stimulated new religious interests. Industrial societies remain too complex, however, for us to expect religious differentiation and conflict to be minimized here as in primitive hunting-gathering groups. The pressures of population redundancy may even foster religious conflict; more or less genocidal responses toward religious outgroups may be tempting ways of trying to ensure that the burdens of crash afflict "superfluous" others rather than one's own ingroup. At the same time, however, we may have generated a new market for shaman-like roles, as occupants of more sophisticated roles are discovered to be incapable of providing desired protection from the consequences of overshoot. By industrializing, mankind has reverted to a massive dependence on natural forces that not even the achievements of modern science can put under human control; we are thus increasingly pressed toward animistic thoughtways that will sustain comforting *illusions* of control through magic, ritual, and so on.

Conclusion

Quality of life has to be very different under conditions of a carrying capacity deficit than under conditions of a carrying capacity surplus. Exuberant American expectations for perpetual progress were formed when there was a conspicuous surplus of human carrying capacity (at least in the then-New World). Sociological thoughtways were powerfully shaped by that heritage. Sociologists have therefore shared the difficulty of the general public in comprehending the repercussions of a fundamental shift from expansion of carrying capacity by the method of displacement to prodigal living by the method of depletion. If we are to avoid hopeless bewilderment by the aftermath of overshoot, we need to avail ourselves of everything anthropology can tell us about human cultures that have adapted to constraints they could not bend or circumvent. And we will need every insight we can obtain from the biological sciences about the experiences of other species that have undergone the kind of postirruptive transition now confronting humanity.

21

Sociology and Ecology: The Need for Mutual Concern

Lawrence·B. Slobodkin

Ecological Problems of an Obvious Kind

LET US FIRST BRIEFLY consider the obvious. We will then look at the less obvious.

It is obvious that above some critical size of human population all increments in either population size itself, or in the material quality of life of the members of the population, will make some problems easier and some problems more difficult to solve.

The things that become easier are those that depend on the fact that people differ and that the differences are occasionally very valuable. As human population increases, we can expect a breaking of athletic records since somewhere in those teeming masses there is someone who can run a mile a fraction of a second faster than anybody else has done—someone can swim a bit faster or jump a bit higher.

We do not anticipate any major genetic alterations in mankind; i.e., we wouldn't expect a three-minute mile, since anyone who had the muscles, bone structure, and cardiac physiology to permit him to run a three-minute mile would be a major aberrancy. He would be a mutant of a rather serious kind, and we would expect that he would have other problems—like getting through first grade. This is an important point

□ This is contribution no. 244 from The Ecology and Evolution Program, State University of New York at Stony Brook. It is in part a result of support from the Guggenheim Foundation and the National Science Foundation (General Ecology Program).

for several reasons. We would expect to see in actuality specimens of the full range of existing theoretical genetic potential—which will show itself in minute alterations in excellence.

It should be emphasized, of course, that quite aside from the opportunity that a very large population gives to sample the full range of the genetic pool, a large enough population with a sufficient diversity also presents a sufficient array of environmental and child-rearing circumstances to give us an occasional extraordinary chess master or pole vaulter who does not necessarily represent a genetic extreme of any kind. Papa Mozart training Wolfgang is to be expected to be repeated over and over again—and maybe Papa Mozart could have done it a trifle better, or if we had a sample of a hundred Papa Mozarts we may have gotten an extra-good Wolfgang out of it.

As population becomes more dense we would expect to find more specialized activities in any given location—brain surgeons in the back woods of Oklahoma, orthodox rabbis in Grosse Point, master chefs in the Maine woods, and so forth—not because any of these areas must be expected to alter drastically its sociological complexion, but because as populations get more dense we might expect each population to contain a sampling of concerns and interests of the sort that are now found only in larger cities.

All those things that involve physical properties and manipulations of the world will become considerably harder.

A wild population of elephants leaves its droppings behind. It can be anticipated that before they return to that same place these droppings would have been recycled by an army of beetles and flies and worms into mineral material, and in turn this would have entered plants or the soil or water. In any case it would no longer be there as droppings so long as the elephant population is small enough. Staying with the elephants, as an arbitrarily chosen example, there is reason to believe that under natural conditions (that is, prior to the occurrence of railways) the elephant's annual migration pattern in Africa was of several hundred miles. During the course of this migration the elephants were feeding on plants that were becoming ripe or were coming into an appropriate edible stage, leaving behind half-digested material but not returning to the same feeding grounds more than once a year. This gave approximately ten months for the regeneration process to occur behind them before they returned. It also seems to be the case that many of the kinds of plant eaten on this migration differed somewhat in nutritive quality and that eating a balanced diet involved a time scale at the order of a year and a distance of many miles. By contrast, as the space available per elephant contracts, there is no possibility of maintaining them in any state of physical (or psychological) health without imposing manipulations on the world (Laws, Parks, and Johnstone, 1975; Hamilton, 1972).

A clever manager of elephants can maintain elephants in good condition in a small enclosure. This means that he must provide food of appropriately balanced sort, clean up the remains, and in general do for the elephants the job that the natural world did for them in the wild. In return, he is imposing some kind of a load on his environment that will have to be accounted for somehow.

In zoos and game parks it is necessary to replace the major reserves and buffering systems of natural ecological cycles with intellect, labor, and energy-intensive management.

While the elephant example may seem in a sense ludicrous, it is a completely general phenomenon. It is possible to formalize the notion that the only ecological system that is known to be largely self-regenerating is the whole earth (Botkin et al., 1978). The process of putting partitions of any kind around ecological subsystems cuts them off from storage, buffering, and slow regeneration processes. As the confines of an ecological system become smaller and smaller, the greater is the amount of intelligence and management labor that is involved in doing the job that these buffering systems would normally do. The ratio of rates of cycling to buffer capacity goes up. If one put a plastic dome over a forest, we anticipate the death of the forest due to the absence of free air flow and free exchange of carbon dioxide and oxygen.

Conversely, as the populations increase—particularly if that increase is due to only one or a small number of species, as would be in the case of human population increase—the local buffering and recycling systems may very well become taxed. The effect would be the same as cutting off a section of an ecosystem, and requires the management and intellect that would not have been required were the human population and its associated animal and plant populations smaller. These problems then will become more difficult since—in general—intelligence and managerial talent are always relatively rare commodities.

What occurs at the limit? The spaceship Earth image has become part of our general consciousness over the last twenty years. What actually might be expected to occur in a spaceship? It is clear that in an actual spaceship of any reasonable dimensions it would be quite impossible to maintain anything but an ecologically sophisticated *agricultural* system. That is, there is no real possibility of maintaining anything having the semblance of natural ecology.

Biological systems are very good at manufacturing complex molecules. Sugars, proteins, carbohydrates, vitamins, and fiber molecules are very difficult to prepare without the aid of sugar cane, soybean plants, and sheep. However, the process of maintaining the sugar cane and the sheep in functional condition cannot be left to the natural cycling processes in a spaceship since there would not be the large capacity for buffering that characterizes the extant earth. An artificial energy-intensive breakdown of wastes and leftovers to the form of mineral fertilizer, without waiting for the normal activities of soil and of soil-living microorganisms, would be required. That is, we expect in the spaceship to find a soilless agriculture, with a high use of energy and of engineering skills to turn the waste products of that agriculture back into usable form for agricultural purposes (Botkin et al., 1978). We anticipate that as the world approaches the spaceship the same considerations would apply.

In that sense there is a general class of problems that are guaranteed to become more difficult as either populations increase or resources dwindle.

I have assumed the essential constancy of quality of life. Quality of life is the most ambiguous of terms. It is important to realize that the definition of what quality of life *should be* is neither politically nor morally the decision to be made by the scientist or engineer whose expertise lies in how the world can be manipulated to produce some desired goal. That is, in some sense the answers to ecological management questions hinge on the acceptance of some defined life quality and on some population level. Both of these are themselves resultants of a complex of forces that are certainly much less obvious than what to do with elephant droppings.

The technical distinction between a crowded world and an uncrowded world relates to such factors as how much water can be used by each household or by each individual if industrial and other demands are to be met, how much food can be rationed out, and so forth. The form of these problems is relatively clear even if the solutions are not self-evident. We can say with fair certainty that to the degree that the world becomes more heavily peopled, the amount of managerial skill and nonphotosynthetic energy required to maintain an ecological system will increase.

A formal property of managing this type of system is that there are at least two things to optimize simultaneously, so that one cannot do as well as one would like for one without correspondingly diminishing the second. Assume that assertions made by the central managing agency of a fishery have associated with them sufficient sanctions so that poaching or illegal fishing is minimal. It would be good to be able to maximize the following:

1. Income per hour to the fisherman.
2. Return on investment in equipment.
3. Total yield in edible food from the fishery.
4. Economy to the consumer.
5. Continuity of the fish population as a resource.

It is obvious that the income to the fisherman and yield on investment cannot be maximized if price to the consumer is to be minimized. It is just slightly less obvious that maximal yield from the fishery can only be maximized if the income per fishing hour of the fisherman is held relatively low. Conversely, if the fishermen are to get proper return for their investment, the total yield must be held down, and so on (Parrish, 1973; Gulland, 1974).

Also, from the purely ecological standpoint, maximizing the durability and persistence of the fish population is quite often incompatible with appropriate amortization of the capital investment in fishing equipment. This is one of the great problems in the control of the whale industry, in which enormous investments have been made in whale-catching ships that are expected to earn their amortization costs, almost regardless of the ecological consequences (C. W. Clark, 1975).

The set of things to be optimized can be summarized under the two headings of local and global properties. The local properties include such things as the catch per unit effort of the fisherman and the ease of finding fish. The global properties involve such things as the size of the fish population, the total yield from the fishery, and the total fishery earnings. The first of these can be referred to as intensive variables—variables that are defined at each point in the system and are of particular interest to the more intimate participants in the system: e.g., the fish and the fisherman themselves. Such things as net size are paramount-intensive variables. The second category is defined as extensive variables—integrals over the entire system that are of interest on the level of the managerial or governmental agencies and are of secondary importance to the actual participants in the system. The total yield from a fishery matters less to the individual fisherman than does his particular income. The total yield from a fishery is less interesting to the individual fish than is his probability of being captured by a net. It is generally the case that a deterioration of intensive variables is associated with a maximization of extensive variables and the converse (Slobodkin, 1972). The greater the total number of fishing boats permitted, the poorer the livelihood of each fisherman. The smaller the individual net size, the less likely the fish population is to survive, but the greater the immediate yield from the fishery, and so on.

These are real and fundamental difficulties. They are with us at the moment and will change in intensity but not in kind as we pass into the future. Note that an altruistic fisherman will be willing to take a lower income and to compete with a greater number of fisherman for the sake of the large food supply of the world, while a selfish fisherman will want to keep a minimal number of fishermen working on the grounds of maximizing his own yield per unit effort and his own income per pound of fish. As a rule, however, decisions about management process are made not altruistically but by a governmental supervisory agency having some legal rights to decision making.

These problems will not be turned on at some future moment in history. They are already here.

Social Problems of a Nonobvious Kind

There is an extensive homiletic literature on the difficulties of the future being written in the present in the name of ecology. These tracts can act as political and moral switch mechanisms of several sorts.

The simplest is the *slant-headline-switch*. For example, the idea that intensive and extensive variables cannot be simultaneously maximized as summarized by Garrett Hardin (1968) in his well-known essay, "The Tragedy of the Commons." There he points out that people owning private herds of cattle must of necessity degrade any land that is held in common between them, since there is incompatibility between the global management process and their own profit. The word "tragedy" in the essay title is a slanted headline of the sort current in yellow journalism of the 1930s and 1940s. It is equivalent in its emotional effect on the reader to a headline saying "Black Suspect in Rape."

As Murdoch and Oaten (1975) indicate, we could have been talking instead about the tragedy of private ownership. That is, if the herds were, in fact, all owned in common, if profits from all the herds were divided among the herdsmen, the incompability between the private and the public, between the global and the intensive would have disappeared. Hardin draws the conclusion that the commons must be regulated for the sake of private ownership. An equally tenable solution would be that the elimination of private ownership would also eliminate the conflict situation.

Let us consider another example. One of the most significant books in the popularization of ecology is Paul Ehrlich's (1968) *The Population Bomb*. The word "bomb" is gratuitous. We have discussed the family of problems associated with population increase. But, by asserting that population constitutes a "bomb" we are saying that there is a drastic emergency situation that justifies abrogation of normal political and social procedures in response.

There are a variety of rather mundane social and political reforms that seem to carry as their consequences a reduction in birthrate, or at least permit a feasibility of reduction in birthrate, but these seem of great inadequacy when faced with the word "bomb." It trivializes, in a sense, such approaches as enhancement of social security benefits, so that the desire for children to support one in one's old age may be less, equalization of women's role in the professions, so that the role of mother becomes just one of the choices available to an intelligent woman, and so forth.

A collection of such loaded titles can be found in an anthology prepared by Dr. Hardin (1969) called *Population, Evolution and Birth Control: A Collage of Controversial Ideas*. Some of the titles are original, some were introduced by Dr. Hardin, but words like "Cassandra," the "wail" of

Kashmir, the "bomb" of population, and the "utterly dismal theorem" set a tone for an apocalyptic sense of the ecological future and lead to the purely emotional conclusion that normal political processes must be abandoned in favor of some other procedure.

There are two types of apocalyptic procedure made available by this class of ecological popularizers. One is the managerial fix that short-circuits normal political and ethical standards, and the other is a reliance on (or return to) some supposed natural law that is presumed to have been violated by normal political and ethical standards. In either case, the *fear* of the ecological future becomes a political and social force in the present—additional to the ecological problems of the present or the future. As we have already seen in our section on the obvious, the problems do exist and hard decisions about our living standards, political machinery, and so forth, are, in fact, necessary. In what sense does ecology or biology in general provide a guide to these hard decisions? While there are management procedures that are available from the ecologists, can ecological and, more generally, biological thinking provide the goal of management as well?

Can the ethical criteria be derived from the biological? Ten years ago it would have been clear to the vast majority of people that the answer was "no." There was a semicrank literature of Ardrey, Lorenz, Morris, and others that defined a biological natural state of man that was terrifyingly similar to the heroic figures in German propaganda movies from the 1940s, and this period was still close enough in memory to produce an immediate revulsion from curious definitions of the desirable style and quality of life for humanity (Bateson, 1978).

The arguments of Ardrey, Lorenz, Morris, and before them of Grant (1916), were of curiously poetic derivation, making use of dubious anthropology and more dubious history and acting as if it were of no interest to write music, develop theology, or be concerned with art and poetry. It was in a sense based on an esthetic of the human couched in the language of an oddly masculine Darwinian struggle, but gave no illusion of being natural law in the sense that physics would be thought of as natural law.

More recently, there has been a curious development of the notion that social science is a simple consequence of rigorous biological law. This has been most firmly attached to the name of E. O. Wilson (1975) in his rather large book *Sociobiology*. The only portions of the sociobiological controversies that are immediately relevant to us are those that purport to provide a biological paradigm for the setting of quality of life standards, as if there were evolutionary laws that restricted the choice of such standards. That is, he is countering the notions of cultural relativism with a doctrine (claimed to be based on biology) that limits the diversity of cultural standards.

While a full critique of the biological basis of sociobiology would be excessively long for this presentation, it is probably necessary to give some idea of the problem. I will abbreviate Wilson's views in this process and I can understand if the reader is dubious about my abbreviation. I would strongly suggest that the concerned reader refer to the references cited. It must be emphasized also that the study of social interactions in biological systems (i.e., sociobiology) is a much broader and richer field than would be indicated by simply following the publications of the Wilsonian school. My criticisms are addressed only to the specifically Wilsonian sector of sociobiology.

Just as physics can be divided into the theoretical and experimental, there exists an independent discipline, mathematical population genetics, that is concerned with exploring the properties of a system consisting of particulate hereditary material subject to various constraints and assumptions (Lewontin, 1974). The type of problem that can be analyzed is, for example, "What will be the future frequency in a freely interbreeding population of a gene subject to some particular selective regimen?" While selection and fitness can be used as mathematical constructs in the formal theory of population genetics, it is quite often very difficult indeed to assess their actual value in a field or natural situations involving actual organisms. This is not a condemnation of population genetics. Noting the experimental difficulties associated with many of the predictions of theoretical physics is not to condemn the internal logic, ingenuity, or scientific validity of theoretical physics itself. The notion of fitness in particular is a difficult one since, in the meaning developed for population genetics by the pioneers in the field, it is considered to be a quantitative measure of the success of an organism at being an ultimate ancestor. That is, it is not adequate simply to measure the number of young born to an organism; one must consider the descendants present at some future moment, taking into account the full range of environmental alterations that might occur during the intervening period. It is for this reason that it is much simpler to speak about fitness in the context of a mathematical theory than in that of an actual biological situation.

W. D. Hamilton (1964) expanded on a concept implicit in R. A. Fisher (1930) and developed the notion of "inclusive fitness." In brutal brevity, this concept takes cognizance of the fact that genes as such may be thought of as being subject to selective forces, the organism simply being their carrier. If a particular organism performs some act that, in the extreme case, terminates its own life but at the same time sufficiently enhances the survival and reproductive potential of other organisms who share genes identical with itself, the genes would be considered as having a high selective value, if these shared genes were to be found in a segment of the population and were not to be found in another segment.

If it were the case that all of the individuals in a population were genetically identical, then no selective change would arise, since by definition
selection involves a relative alteration in the frequency of a particular
gene as compared with its existing alelles.

The implication of this analysis is that in some situations in nature
one might expect to be able to show that apparently altrusitic activity,
with altruism rather narrowly defined, may be of selective advantage to
the genes shared by the beneficiary of the altruistic act and its performer. It must be emphasized that this demonstration is contingent in
any actual case on proof of the presence of genetic differences between
the set consisting of *the performer of the altruistic act and its beneficiaries* on
the one hand and *nonperformers of the altruistic act* on the other. In fact,
however, no single case has shown that one subclass of a population
performs altruistic acts that benefit its immediate relative and is also
genetically different from some other subclass of the same population
that does not perform these altruistic acts. That is, for many organisms,
and for many properties, it is possible to show that: (1) there are in fact
genetic differences between individuals in the population; and (2) there
is a selective value under specific environmental circumstances that ac-
crues to one genotype rather than another.

To my knowledge no such demonstration has been made for any
organism with reference to genes that would activate or in some sense
cause this type of altruistic behavior, i.e., empirically confirm the theory
of inclusive fitness.

Despite this lack of direct evidence, many examples make it seem
plausible that if such a gene had existed it *would have been* selected. This
selection would have occurred in essentially the way indicated by Hamilton.

For example, E. O. Wilson (1971) has discussed the evolution of the
social insects in which many of the genetic females fail to reproduce but
act to feed and care for the progeny of their mother, with whom they
share a large component of their genotype. The plausible argument
based on the theory of inclusive fitness in this case is that there once was
a population in which there were animals suitably genetically different
and that it maximized inclusive fitness if some individuals abandoned
their own reproductive activity so as to enhance the reproductive activity
of their mother, and that this mechanism of caring for the young was
selected over the alternative in which adults cared for their own young.
But even for the social insects equally plausible alternatives exist. For
example, E. O. Wilson (1971) has asserted that the origin of the sterile
castes may be due to nutritional deficiencies in ontogeny that make
development of reproductive organs impossible. Another possible explanation of the evolution of insect sociality has been suggested based on
the larvae-digesting proteins and exuding amino acid solutions (Grogan

and Hunt, 1977). This would permit interpreting the care of the young as a method of processing food for the adults and would not require the idea of inclusive fitness.

The use of young as a way of processing food for adults is also illustrated by some fishes. As young these fish feed on plankton, but cannot feed on plankton as adults. The adults feed extensively on their own young, i.e., use their own young as a food-gathering device (Nikolsky, 1963).

It is generally felt that the strongest case for the role of inclusive fitness in the development of apparently altruistic activity can be made in the social insects. But notice even here that the rigorous requirements for application of the theory have not ever been met. Studies claiming to confirm the role of kin selection and inclusive-fitness theory in social insects by indirect tests, such as measuring the amount of effort animals put into aiding others as a function of degree of relatedness (Trivers and Hare, 1976), seem to be subject to serious criticism (Alexander and Sherman, 1977).

The plausibility chain has been extended to assert that *wherever* one finds apparently altruistic behavior, the notion of inclusive fitness is to be invoked in developing a hypothetical ancestral reconstruction, even in the absence of direct genetic evidence of any sort. At this point in the argument we have a single plausible theory assumed to act over a broad range of species. By the same kind of plausibility extension, many of the apparently unique altruistic properties of humans are now seen in a new evolutionary light.

As E. O. Wilson says:

> For example, certain general traits [of humans] are shared with most other Old World primates, including size of intimate social groups on the order of 10–100; males larger than females, probably in relation to polygyny; a long period of socialization in the young, shifting in focus from the mother to age- and sex-peer groups; and social play strongly developed, with emphasis on role practice, mock aggression, and exploration. It is virtually inconceivable that primates, including human beings, could be socialized into the radically different repertories of insects, fish, birds, or antelopes; or that the reverse could be accomplished. Human beings, by conscious design, might well imitate such arrangements; but it would be a fiction played out on a stage, running counter to deep emotional responses and with no chance of persistence through as much as a single generation.
>
> *Homo sapiens* is distinct from other primate species in ways that can be explained only as the result of a unique human genotype. Universal or near-universal traits include the facial expressions that denote basic emotions, and some other forms of paralinguistic communication; elaborate kinship rules that include incest avoidance; a semantic, symbolical language that develops in the young through a relatively strict timetable;

close sexual and parent-offspring bonding; and others. Again, to socialize a human being out of such species-specific traits would be very difficult if not impossible, and almost certainly destructive to mental development. People might imitate the distinctive social arrangements of a white-handed gibbon or hamadryas baboon, but it seems extremely unlikely that human social systems could be stably reconstructed by such an effort.

It is significant that not only do human beings develop a species-characteristic set of social behaviors, but that these behaviors are generally mammalian, and most specifically Old-World primate in character. Furthermore, even the species-specific traits are logically derivable in some cases from the inferred ancestral modes still displayed by a few related species. For example, the facial expressions and some nonlinguistic vocalizations can be plausibly derived in phylogenetic reconstructions. This is precisely the pattern to be expected if the human species was derived from Old-World primate ancestors (a fact) and still retains genetic constraints in the development of social behavior (a hypothesis) (E. O. Wilson, 1977:132).

He is saying that there are in fact genetic constraints on the development of social behavior. Deviations from these plausibly generated genetic constraints are probably unhealthy and "biology is the key to human nature and social scientists cannot afford to ignore its emerging principles." Further, he asserts that "the last remnants of social Darwinism died with the advent of sociobiology, which delineated the roles of cooperation and altruism in societies and rendered them consistent with population genetics."

Notice this is all built without any genetic evidence whatsoever. The generalizations about primate behavior are generally subject to question and a family of considerations related to the special biology of man is ignored. As I pointed out elsewhere (Slobodkin, 1977):

1. In general, evolutionary units make minimal responses to environmental perturbations.
2. Humans, chimpanzees, and orangutans share the biological capacity to develop a normative introspective self-image which permits them to deviate from the general paradigm of minimal response. So far, no other organisms have been unequivocally shown to have this capacity.
3. The capacity for normative introspective self-image development, combined with learning capacity, interacts with environmental differences between individual humans so as to produce extraordinarily weak canalization in the development of human decision-making behavior.
4. By normal biological standards it would, therefore, be expected that it would be extremely difficult to demonstrate genetically

significant heritability for particular decision-making behavior in humans, chimpanzees, or orangutans. In fact, no such heritability has been demonstrated in these organisms.

5. If it could be demonstrated for some particular species that kinds of social behavior have high canalization, high heritability, are genetic, and have selective advantage, then the evolutionary development and maintenance of that behavior might be explicable by the theories of Alexander, Hamilton, Trivers, and Wilson.

6. Since none of the properties listed above are demonstrated for humans, chimpanzees, or orangutans, and since there are special biological properties of these three species (cf. 1-4 above) that make the demonstrations listed in 5 extremely unlikely, assertion that the theories of Alexander, Hamilton, Trivers, and Wilson are applicable to humans are at best premature.

In addition, the anthropological generalization made by Wilson has been shown to be invalid for many persistent and viable societies (Sahlins, 1976). It is not the case that humans universally act to benefit their biological kin in the way that is suggested by Wilson.

What is most relevant is Wilson's (1977) description of sociobiology as the "anti-science" of sociology. That is, he asserts the independent status of social science to probably be an illusion based on the failure to realize that biological laws underlie all sociological events.

I can demonstrate the basic weakness of the biological assertions, but if sociology is to avoid being swept away by half-truths, it must develop the theoretical force to withstand *Time* magazine (August 1, 1977) and the popular press, which are (at the moment) espousing Wilsonian sociobiology in a curiously avid way. If sociology does not do this, then, in addition to the class of real problems indicated at the beginning of this paper, we will be inundated with a class of problems raised by quasi solutions, i.e., standards for quality of life will be set by second-rate biology.

This puts the social sciences and, more particularly, sociology, which claims as its province contemporary societies, on the intellectual front line. In the face of Wilson's challenge, it is necessary for sociology to examine what its own theoretical content is and should be. It will be necessary to substitute sociology for methodology.

Conclusions

The title of this part of the book lends itself either to the titillation of the reader by cheerful descriptions of future catastrophes or to considerations of a more serious sort. I have chosen the serious path. Yes, there is a connection among quality of life, resources, and population. The general pattern of the connection is that the greater the material demands made by quality-of-life standards and the greater the number of persons making those demands, the more complicated the problems of resource management. There are technological ways of dealing with these problems, but they do not constitute full solutions in the absence of a theory of quality of life, nor is there any prospect whatever of massive ecological or engineering breakthroughs that can make that problem go away.

On a second level, however, careless discussion of the problems becomes itself a political, intellectual, and ultimately social danger. The social scientists dare not abrogate their intellectual responsibility to consider the very real problem of how standards of quality in life are to be established as management goals and how the political and social systems may intermesh with the ecological and management systems. More particularly, to the degree that the social scientists permit themselves to be panicked by slanted headlines and hysterical generalizations made in the name of, but not out of the substance of, ecology and biology, the political, social, and ecological problems of the present are grossly exacerbated.

My motivation here is to alert social scientists to the fact that time for substantive intellectual advance on their part is very short; without such advance they will be shoved aside by the rush of real and imaginary problems. The inadequacy of resources is no longer a workable excuse. In fact, the resources today probably exceed what will be available tomorrow. The departments of sociology throughout this country have a deep responsibility to the substantive development of their own discipline and can neither rest in the assurance that biologists of the sociobiological or ecological sort are going to solve their problems for them, nor work on the outmoded assumption that masses of chewed data will cause the emergence of theoretical insight.

I am strongly asserting that sociologists must know enough biology to tell the real from the spurious and to understand the problems that biology poses for sociology.[1] In the same sense, it has been customary for many years for biology majors to be required to take a certain amount of chemistry, physics, and mathematics as a routine matter.

Wilson is correct in his concept of biology as the antiscience of sociology. The biologists have accepted the role of antiscience played by chemistry, mathematics, and physics for biology. We are confident as biologists that chemists cannot solve our problems. We also are aware

[1]The work of van den Berghe (1975) demonstrates a freewheeling application of the biological to the sociological by a sociologist.

that they are willing to try, due to their general ignorance of biology, and the only way we can protect ourselves from their well-meaning interference is to make sure that we know enough chemistry to ask the appropriate questions at the appropriate times. Undergraduate biology majors must take chemistry through organic. I suggest that undergraduate sociologists be required to take biology through evolutionary theory, ecology, and genetics. Notice that there have been fruitful contacts between sociology and biology in the past, as in the early days of the Chicago school (Kuklich, 1973).

I am not offering free and unrequested advice to sociologists. This is presumptuous since I am not myself a sociologist, but if I may say so I have always admired sociology and "some of my best friends are sociologists," so I feel entitled to make some comments. Presuming further, I would like to emphasize that what I think is required is that sociology undergraduates actually study in biology departments. That is, I think it would be a grave error if sociology departments attempted to hire biological ecologists and evolutionists to do the training on an in-house basis. I believe that twenty years ago, when it became clear that computers would be needed in sociology, a grave error was made in hiring faculty whose expertise lay primarily in the use of the computer rather than in a concern with sociology itself. With the passage of time and the advance of computer technology, many of these persons have been bypassed by the current movements in computer science, since they were not subject to the constant criticism and interactions of first-class computer scientists, and at the same time they have not been strong producers of basically sociological concepts. It would have been more useful to both sociology and computer science if the problems of sociology had been used to challenge the computers and the process of computation had been a prerequisite for sociologists, in the same way as organic chemistry is for biologists. As it happened, the opportunity for this may have almost been bypassed.

I suggest that there is a new challenge, and that biology, through ecology and evolution, is as vital as elementary psychology to training in sociology. I emphasize that the training of sociologists in biology is valuable not because biology can solve the problems of sociology, but because some knowledge of biology may be of help to the sociologists in solving their own problems. Further, the ecologists are not capable of dealing firmly with problems of resources, population, and quality of life until a major input is provided by sociological theory.

As a biologist and ecologist I am certain that the problems are real. I am also certain that biology cannot provide the full programmatic set of solutions. Solutions will require the activity of sociologists and other social scientists on the highest intellectual level; the search may well stretch the resources of existing sociology departments. I suggest that these departments examine closely how their resources are being used while there is yet time and resources are still available.

The present critical problems of resources, population, and quality of life will be exacerbated in the future. If sociologists permit themselves to be panicked by slanted, overstated, or second-rate biology, or if they fail immediately to consider this general class of problems in a serious way, then the problems of the world will be that much more difficult. Further, sociology itself may be damaged by the spread of erroneous concepts of human society.

Perhaps the fundamental danger is to the integrity of scientific thought. The technical problems of the present and the future can be placed in the hands of engineers and biologists to some degree. We know how to speak to engineers. Do we know how to speak to intellectual heresies and glib fallacies uttered in the name of science?

22

Biology, Meaning, and the Quality of Life

Roy A. Rappaport

THE TERMS "population," "resources," and "quality of life" in the title of this part of the book are problematic. A classical Malthusian formulation seems to lie close to their surface: As population increases resources are depleted and quality of life—whatever that may be—is degraded. Malthusian logic is indubitable. What is always dubious is whether it is sufficient to account for the deterioration of life's quality in particular instances. Events leading up to the so-called "soccer war" between El Salvador and Honduras in 1969 have recently been reviewed by William Durham (1977) and may provide a case in point, for if ever a war seemed to have a Malthusian basis that one did. The average annual growth rate of the Salvadorian population during the preceding decade stood at 3.49 percent, producing one of the highest densities in the hemisphere. Land per person economically engaged in horticulture had been dropping continuously from 9.5 hectares in 1892; by 1971 it had fallen to 2.5 hectares. Local-level data reveal a close inverse correlation between child mortality and family landholding, the rate of death of minors in agricultural families holding less than 1 hectare being almost twice as high as in families holding 3.5 hectares or more, close to one-third dying before reaching their majority. Many peasants were forced off the land and out of the countryside, of course, and by the time hostilities erupted 300,000 of them had migrated to Honduras, where population densities were considerably lower. Most of its surface is, however, too mountainous to cultivate and its soils are generally very poor. During and subsequent to the war these immigrants were rounded up and deported. I have not yet faced the problems of defining quality of life, but it does seem safe to say, other things being equal, that high child-mortality rates are inimical to it and that deportation in itself does little to enhance it.

A fourfold increase in population between 1892 and the time of the war would seem on the face of it to be sufficient to account for land shortages in El Salvador. It is important to note, however, that acreage devoted to food crops had actually been declining steadily since 1955 as land devoted to export crops rose. Moreover, during the same period the land available to the poorest 50 percent of the agricultural population was reduced almost twice as much by the increased concentration of land into the ever-larger holdings of the wealthy as by the effects of population growth. It is also of interest that the Hondurans who pressed for the deportation of the Salvadorians were not peasants. Indeed, interviews with Honduran peasants suggest that they did not perceive the Salvadorians as competitors or even interlopers. The Salvadorians were deported at the instigation of cattlemen who were at the time attempting to expand and enclose their holdings at the expense of peasants, both Honduran and Salvadorian. In Honduras as well as in El Salvador the shortage of land was more an effect of the concentration than of the expansion of population.

It would be easy, in the case of the soccer war, to ascribe demographic and ecological causes to what appeared to be a welter of political and economic problems. It would be closer to the mark to propose that certain demographic and ecological symptoms were effects of economic and political causes. I am led to a related class of misconstructions that may themselves have adverse effects upon the quality of life—those in which ecological processes are conceived in economic terms. I would note in this regard that I take the term "resources," appearing in the title, to be problematic because it may lead us into such fallacy. The Random House *Collegiate* dictionary provides the following definition of "resource" and "resources":

1. A source of supply, source of aid. . . .
2. Resources—the collective wealth of a country or its means of producing wealth.
3. Money or any other property that can be converted into money.

When we use the terms "resource" and "resources" to refer to components of the environment, we tacitly divest them of their properties as elements in the functioning of ecological systems and take to be significant only their direct instrumental value. Such instrumental values are likely to be assigned in economic terms that have nothing to do with either life or its quality. We shall return to these matters latter. For now, I wish to register not simply my distaste for the metaphysic within which components of the world system are regarded primarily as "resources," but would also like to suggest that such a metaphysic, of which formal economics is a manifestation, encourages the use and abuse of biological

systems of all classes and the neglect of moral and aesthetic considerations in general. Whatever may be meant by the phrase "quality of life,"
exploitation does not enhance it.

Having approached the matter of ecological systems, we are led to
the place of the concept of population in ecological rather than demographic formulations. Populations in an ecological sense are constituents of ecosystems, ecosystems being the totals of living organisms
and nonliving substances bound together in matter and energy exchanges within demarcated portions of the biosphere. A population in
the ecological sense is an aggregate of organisms having in common a set
of distinctive means by which they maintain a common set of material
relations with the other constituents of the ecosystems in which they all
participate. Populations have demographic characteristics, of course,
but, from the perspective of the larger system of material exchanges of
which they are components, the demographic characteristics of populations are simply contributory to certain more significant and inclusive
characteristics, namely their matter and energy requirements and their
means for fulfilling them. From the perspective of the ecosystem as a
whole no distinction need be made among the requirements of a human
population as to whether they are the requirements of organisms,
machines, or institutions. What matters is how much matter and energy
is extracted from the ecosystem by a population, in what forms it is
extracted, what sorts of transformation it works upon these materials,
and what effects all of these operations have upon the ecosystem as a
whole.

Obviously quantitative differences of an important sort distinguish one
human population from another. A recent estimate (Cook, 1971) places
per capita energy consumption in contemporary U.S. at around 230,000
K calories per day. Energy consumption among the Kalahari bushmen of
South Africa and the Tsembaga Maring, a horticultural people among
whom I worked in New Guinea (Rappaport, 1968) stands at 2,000 to
3,000 K calories per day (plus whatever is burned as fuel, a matter of
little importance because it is supplied entirely from local and contemporary ecosystemic processes in quantities too small to cause pollution of
any sort).

Differences in energy flux have been associated with notions closely
related to that of life quality, notions such as "standard of living," and a
quarter of a century ago Leslie White took such differences to constitute
cultural evolutionary status, proposing what he called "the basic law of
cultural evolution" as follows:

> Other factors remaining constant culture evolves as the amount of
> energy harnessed per capita per year is increased, or as the efficiency of
> the instrumental means of putting energy to work is increased (L. White,
> 1949:368–69).

This does accord in a general way with mankind's experience. Large, technologically elaborate states do appear later in history and do harness more energy per capita than do small societies of hunters and gardeners. The question is, however, whether cultural evolution can be said to improve life's quality or constitute progress in any other ordinary sense of the word. White and other modern cultural evolutionists have explicitly denied that the notion of progress is intrinsic to the concept of cultural evolution, of course, but progressive implications often do lie close to the surface of their prose—or indeed, on top of it. Speaking of the relationship of anthropology to culture, White wrote:

> The science of Culture is young but full of promise. It is destined to do great things—if only the subject of its study will continue its age old course: onward and upward (L. White, 1949:393).

Twenty years later, Harris (1968) took Sahlins and Service (1960) to task for using White's energetic measure as a criterion of progress, and not only of "successively better adapted sociocultural systems," these being "thermodynamically larger and more efficient" that those they replace. Harris seems hoist on his own petard by his use of comparatives, and it is easy to take a contradictory position. It can be observed, for instance, that Americans are, per capita, entropizing the world seventy-five to one-hundred times as rapidly as the bushmen, not even to mention the polluting concomitants of this higher-energy flux. To put this conversely, as far as the maintenance of human life is concerned, cultural evolution is characterized by declining thermodynamic efficiency. There is no reason to believe that quality of life is to be correlated with thermodynamic efficiency, of course, but neither is there any reason to believe that it is enhanced by inefficiency or, for that matter, by accelerating entropy or increasing pollution.

I have said that seventy-five to one-hundred times as much energy is *required* to support an American as a Bushman or a Maring. Without profound changes in social, political, economic, and technical structure, any significant decrease in the flux of energy through American society would lead to starvation, pestilence, fire, flood, and perhaps war. I would suggest as a kind of Catch-22 corollary of White's law that the further from stable equilibrium the dynamic equilibrium of a system is held, the more vulnerable is that system to disruption and the more serious are the effects of disruption likely to be. I would add here that systemic stability—the ability of systems to maintain and transform themselves adaptively in the face of continuing perturbation—may be reduced not only by increased dependence upon exotic material and energy sources, far-flung delivery systems, and elaborate conversion technologies, but also by reductions in systemic redundancy accompanying the specialization of subsystems, itself a trend facilitated by increased energy capture and also by the increasing role of human management of ecological systems—for humans are more prone to error than the plants that are dominant in most nonanthropocentric systems. Be this as it may, systemic instability is hardly an aspect of the good life by anyone's reckoning. Among other things, the maintenance of intrinsically unstable systems requires disproportionately large commitments of time, energy, and materials that might otherwise be used—or left unused—and their condition also requires more or less continuous monitoring. This monitoring may include some considerable amount of political surveillance, something that some people, at least, would take to be inimical to the quality of their liberties and to their pursuits of happiness, if not of their very lives.

Food energy constitutes less than 2 percent of the energy captured by contemporary American society. Most of the rest powers machinery. While it is undeniable that the expenditure of some of this energy and matter in excess of direct biological need does enhance the quality of life, it would be hard to argue that all of the energy spent and material consumed above and beyond direct biological requirements has such an effect, given, among other things, the noxious side effects of their extraction and use. This is a commonplace. Less obvious is a maladaptive trend that may be a concomitant of certain aspects of cultural evolution, especially the increasing differentiation of specialized subsystems and the increasing elaboration of technology. The basic form has elsewhere been called "escalation," "usurpation," and "overspecification" (Flannery, 1972; Rappaport, 1969). The distribution of power among the increasingly differentiated subsystems of evolving societies is, of course, unequal, tending to concentrate in particular subsystems, especially those most highly industrialized. As they become increasingly powerful these subsystems become increasingly able to elevate their own special goals and interests to positions of predominance in the larger systems of which they are parts. The logical end is for a subsystem or cluster of related subsystems (for instance, that denoted by the label "military-industrial complex") to come to dominate the larger societies of which they are mere parts. This eventuality is nicely summed up in the phrase "What's good for General Motors is good for America." But no matter how benign General Motors might be, what is good for it cannot in the long run be good for America. A society like the United States is, or should be, an adaptive system, that is, one having as its only proper long-term goal one that is so general as to constitute a virtual nongoal, simply its own persistence. To persist in the face of continuous perturbation requires sufficient flexibility to allow continuous self-transformation. For any society to *commit* itself to the maintenance of conditions that may be favorable to the persistence of one of its special-purpose subsystems is not merely to permit special interests to usurp the place of general interest. It is to sacrifice thereby adaptive flexibility, and thus to reduce the range of conditions under which it, as constituted, can persist. The failure of a social system to persist as constituted does not usually result in the extinction of its population, of course, but there is likely to be a period of disorder, privation, and, quite commonly, bloodshed before it reconstitutes itself. Reconstitution may enhance the quality of life, but civil strife and its hardships in themselves surely don't. Orderly evolution, if it is possible, is generally to be preferred to revolution, which in its nature is disruptive and brutal.

Some related concomitants of the process of usurpation should be mentioned. As industrial subsystems become increasingly powerful the quality and utility of their products are likely to deteriorate, for their contribution to society becomes less their product and more their mere operation, providing wages to some, profits to others, and a market for yet others. The product tends to become a by- or even a waste-product of the industrial metabolism, which is ultimately, simply the operation of machines that men serve. To elaborate the metaphor, products come to be related to the firms producing them as feces are to the organisms producing them, and the consumer becomes a coprophage. Neither competition nor an independently established demand serves to regulate or limit industrial metabolism effectively because large industries are not very competitive and they exercise considerable control over the demand to which they are supposedly subject (Galbraith, 1967).

Products characterized by poor quality, rapid obsolescence, and limited usefulness contribute little to the quality of the lives of those who acquire them, but the ultimate consequence of the process of usurpation by industrialized subsystems is more serious. It is not simply that the narrowly defined and short-run interests of those powerful men whom we take to own industry come to prevail. It is that the requirements of the industrial metabolism—the interests of machines, so to speak, that even powerful men serve—become dominant. Machines are no longer extensions of ourselves, as Professor Catton would have it. In the advanced industrial society we become extensions of the machines. It is *their* needs, and not ours, that come to define social goals and to specify social action. Needless to say, the interests of machines and organisms do not coincide. They don't have the same needs for pure air and water, and whereas organisms need uncounted numbers of subtle compounds to remain healthy, the needs of machines are few, simple, and voracious. It is in accordance with the logic and value structure of a world dominated by the gargantuan and simple appetites of machines to rip the top off a complex system like West Virginia to extract a single simple substance like coal.

I have been arguing that a number of social and technical processes are more significantly implicated in the depletion and pollution of what we anthropocentrically call "resources" and in the deterioration of our own life quality than is population growth, but I have not yet indicated what I mean by "quality of life." I have so far been proceeding on the basis of the simple observation that the referent of the term "quality" in the phrase "quality of life" is life, upon the assumption that life is nothing if not biological, and upon the further assumption that anything that is inimical to healthy biological processes is, *prima facie,* inimical to life's quality. This naive approach can be justified on grounds of simple contingency. In the absence of life there can be no differences in quality of life. But any assessment of the quality of life that limits itself to material, or even biological, considerations is surely inadequate. When we speak of the quality of life we generally mean more than biological health. It is here, of course, that problems begin to set in. As Campbell, Converse, and Rodgers (1976), among others, note, the notion is vague, not intrinsically metrical, and highly subjective. Nevertheless there are surely things common to the innumerable variations played by individuals upon this theme.

The Random House *Collegiate* dictionary provides the following definitions, among others, of quality:

1. Character or nature as belonging to or distinguishing a thing.
2. High grade, excellence.

The notion of quality thus seems to subsume the notions of distinction and value, and when we think of comparative quality we think of value-laden distinctions between things and states. Values are, of course, as affective as they are "rational," and it is probably the case that for most people the phrase "quality of life" signifies states of affairs having subjective and emotional components as well as rational and objective ones. Another way to put this is to say that for its quality to be high, life must not only be free of pain and possessed of health sufficient to enjoy the gifts of the senses. It must also be rich in meaning.

I have neither the space nor the qualifications to discuss the meaning of "meaning" in detail. I must note, however, that the terms "meaning," "meaningful," and "quality" do seem closely related. First, the notion of meaning in its simple everyday sense subsumes that of distinction. The meaning of the word "dog" is *dog, dog* being distinct from *cat,* which is signified by the distinct term "cat." Meaning in this low-order sense is closely related to what, in the technical sense, is denoted by the term "information." When, however, we begin to consider not only simple meaning but *meaningfulness,* we become concerned not only with rationally drawn distinctions, but also with emotionally charged values.

Low-order meaning is founded upon distinction, but higher-order meaning is of another sort. The sense of meaning to which the question "What does it all mean?" points when asked by one confronted by a complex mass of information is surely distinct from that of simple distinction. In answering such a question we attempt to discover similarities between apparently disparate phenomena, namely, that which we seek to understand, on the one hand, and that which we already know or at least think we know, on the other. In higher-order meaning these similarities among obviously distinctive phenomena become more significant than the distinctions themselves. The distinctive vehicle of higher-order meaning is metaphor. Metaphor, we may note, enriches the world's meaning, for every term that participates in a metaphor transforms its signification into more than itself, that is, into an icon of other things as well. It is significant that art and poetry rely heavily upon metaphor, a mode of representation that, because of its connotative resonance, is affectively more powerful than straightforward didactic forms.

Whereas low-order meaning is based upon distinction and higher-order meaning is based on similarity, highest-order meaning is grounded in identity or unity, the radical identification of self with other. It is not so much intellectual as experiential and is perhaps most often grasped in religious devotion. Those who have known it may refer to it by such obscure phrases as the "Experience of Being," or "Being Itself," or "Pure Being." They report that although it is nonreferential it is enormously or even ultimately meaningful. It signifies only itself, but it itself is comprehensive. All distinctions seem to disappear into an immediate and undeniable sense of union with others or even with the cosmos as a whole. The ultimately meaningful, it is of interest to note, is devoid of information.

To say that those who know the mystical at first hand take it to have enhanced the quality of their lives may be to trivialize their experience. They understand it to have *founded* their life's meaning and thus to have *defined* its quality. Whatever scientists take mystical experiences to be, it is a simple fact that some people do have them, and that more cultures than don't encourage them, honor them, and grant validity to the insights they provide. They are an important or even crucial component of meaning in those societies and as such are valid. Elsewhere (Rappaport, 1978) I have also argued that mystical experiences may provide deeper and more compelling understandings of perfectly natural aspects of the physical and social world than can be provided by discursive reason alone. Such experiences make palpable to those experiencing them the larger systems of which they are parts and upon which they depend, but are ordinarily hidden from them by the evidence of their senses and the interpretations of their common sense, which tell them of autonomy and separation. Mystical consciousness does not always hide the world from conscious reason behind a veil of illusions. Indeed, it may pierce the veil of illusions behind which unaided rationality hides the world from comprehensive human understanding. Highest-order mystical meaning has an important place, it seems to me, in the adaptive structure of humanity. Its loss not only in itself constitutes deterioration in the quality of subjective experience, but also leaves those deprived of it with less adequate understandings of their relations with the world, increasing the likelihood of their damaging it, and thus themselves. This raises the question of falsity of meaning, a matter to which I shall return shortly.

Quality of life has, in short, biological, cognitive, and affective components. Whether or not it is always appropriate to do so, it is easy to argue that direct systemic relationships pertain between the biological health of individuals and groups on the one hand and the condition of resources and population size, density, and dynamics on the other. It is even plausible to propose that these relationships are causal—that for instance, increases in population size or density exceeding some critical value will result in the depletion of resources and affect health adversely. It would be much more difficult, however, to argue that similar relationships pertain between population dynamics and the meaningfulness of existence and, in my view, it would be mistaken to try. It seems to me to be much more likely that factors affecting the meaningfulness of life are to be found in the internal organization, metaphysics, and epistemology of groups, and in their relations with their environments, than in their population dynamics. Moreover, it is at least as likely that the meanings with which the world is invested affect material conditions as the other way around.

A long line of theologians, philosophers, and social scientists precede me in suggesting that modern society is rather worse off with respect to meaningfulness than tribal society. It is nevertheless worth considering this matter briefly, noting particularly that destruction of meaning may be intrinsic not only to technological elaboration, as has already been implied, but to developments we have taken to be advances in epistemology, computation, and social structure.

We may note here briefly some effects of the most obvious aspects of cultural evolution on people's understandings of their places in nature. In the small-scale technologically undeveloped societies beloved by anthropologists, profound understandings of dependence upon ecosystemic processes often, or even generally, seem to prevail. The pygmies, who live in small groups as hunters and gatherers in the Ituri forest, mystify this understanding in religious terms (C. Turnbull, 1962). The forest as a whole is personified as the God *Ndura*. Its animals, trees, birds, rocks, and streams partake of *Ndura's* divinity and the people consider themselves to be the children of *Ndura*, who, they say, is "mother and father of us all." *Ndura* will provide for them so long as they entertain him/her with song and dance and as long as they act respectfully toward the person of the God by not acting destructively.

The Maring, a horticultural people living in New Guinea (Rappaport, 1968), are also deeply aware of their dependence upon the local ecological system. Moreover, their knowledge of the circulatiries of ecosystemic processes is codified in supernatural terms. These terms inform and give meaning to a ritual cycle that in turn regulates the relations of people with ecosystem in a manner which tends to maintain that ecosystem in a more or less undegraded state. We may note here that the codification of environmental understandings in terms that we would call religious not only enhances the world's meaning through metaphoric and unifying processes but also protects the world from wanton exploitation.

As societies expand and become internally differentiated, the experience of nature changes. No longer is every adult directly engaged in subsistence activity, and thus no longer does everyone experience nature's circularities directly. Each person is personally acquainted with only a small and specialized arc, so to speak, of such a circle, and awareness of the whole disappears. Contemporary societies, moreover, are seldom encompassed by particular ecological associations as tribal societies frequently are. On the contrary, they come to encompass broad ranges of distinct ecological zones. In such a setting a forest is no longer likely to be conceived as a generalized and all-encompassing ecological system but simply as one special element of a more inclusive socioeconomic system. It is no longer "mother and father of us all" as it is to the pygmies, or an indispensable link in the circle of life and death as it is to the Maring, who bush-fallow their gardens. It is likely to be degraded to the status of a resource, an "it" to be exploited.

Consideration of changes in man's view of the world as his social organization changes leads us to consider changes in the way knowledge itself is organized. It seems possible to propose that the relationship between society and ecosystem is not all that has been inverted in the course of cultural evolution. There also seems to have been an inversion in what may be called "the order of knowledge."

Generalizations are dangerous, but it may be suggested that among tribal peoples and in archaic civilizations, sacred knowledge was ultimate. I mean by sacred knowledge knowledge of propositions neither verifiable nor falsifiable in their nature but nevertheless taken to be unquestionable because mystically known or because they are ritually accepted as such (Rappaport, 1971). Concerned with gods and the like, they are typically devoid of terms having material signification, and are thus without sociological specificity. Such propositions do, however, *sanctify* (i.e., certify) other directives expressing social values and also systems of classification that are applied to broad ranges of phenomena that seem to the outsider to be disparate. The Maring classify plants, animals, diseases, persons, activities, states of society, spirits, and spiritual states as "hot" or "cold." The result is that the world is not only laden with agreed-upon values, but also with high-order meaning, if meaning is to be derived from the perception of deep similarity underlying apparently distinctive things and events. Finally, there is knowledge of ordinary material facts, the facts of farming, hunting, cooking. The Maring are as aware as any other cultivators of the special characteristics of particular plants (in which soils they will grow, how long they take to mature, the special treatment they require), but they consider such knowledge to be obvious, transient, and hardly fundamental. Of greater interest is the subsumption of material facts by such classificatory devices as hot/cold classifications and totemic systems through which they are ordered into what Levi-Strauss (1966) calls "logics of the concrete." In such systems material facts become tokens in elaborate and embracing systems of meanings supported by the mysterious but unquestionable sacred.

In modern society, in contrast, ultimate knowledge is knowledge of fact. To be sure, the facts known are subsumed or ordered by scientific generalizations or laws, but these generalizations are always subject to overthrow by the discovery of further facts. Moreover, even perduring generalizations are of limited scope. Those that apply to physical or biological phenomena, for instance, are said not to apply to social phenomena. Attempts to apply generalizations across domains are dismissed as merely analogic or even reductionistic. Thus we come to know more and more about ever more limited domains, but between these domains darkness remains or even extends its sway. As knowledge becomes fragmented meaning is diminished because nothing is any longer an icon of anything else.[1] Moreover, the status of that which in primitive and archaic socieites was taken to be ultimate knowledge becomes anomalous. In a world in which fact constitutes ultimate knowledge, sacred propositions are no longer counted as knowledge at all. They are mere beliefs, and values no more than matters of taste or preference. If high-order meanings are not destroyed they are demeaned, and their influence upon human affairs minimized by "serious" men who give to rationality itself an ever-narrower construction. Knowledge no longer includes the insights of art or religion but is reduced to those of the syllogism, the experiment, or those self-serving mental processes denoted by economists' use of the term "rationality."

It is interesting to consider the semantics of money—money as meaning or substitute for meaning—in light of the fragmentation of knowledge and the degradation of higher-order meaning. Higher-order meaning arises, I have argued, from the discovery of similarities under-

---

[1]This discussion of the fragmentation of knowledge emerged from discussions with Professor Frithjof Bergmann of the Departments of Anthropology and Philosophy of the University of Michigan.

lying distinctions between apparently disparate phenomena. Now money, in terms of which radically disparate things can be assessed, may seem to represent such similarities. This is an illusion. Rather than finding similarities among things that remain distinct, it dissolves whatever is distinctive of anything to which it is applied, thus reducing *qualitative distinctions* to the status of simple *quantitative differences*. The most appropriate answer to questions of the type "What is the difference between a forest and a parking lot?" becomes so many dollars per acre.

In societies dominated by market economies money is a source of meaning or pseudomeaning. In dissolving distinction it reduces meaning to mere difference. Evaluation remains but it becomes nothing more than "the bottom line," the result of the operations of addition and subtraction. Right and wrong, even true and false, are displaced by more and less.

Meaning guides action. To return to a matter raised earlier: In contradiction of the doctrine of cultural relativism, it may be asserted that some of the meanings societies construct are false because they lead those for whom they are meaningful to act in ways that are at variance with the way the world is organized. For instance, it is obvious that the world upon which the simple metric of money is imposed is not as simple as that metric. It is perhaps less obvious that it must not be. Living systems require a great variety of distinct and incommensurable substances to remain viable. Monetization forces the great range of things and processes to which it is applied into a specious commensurability. As such, at the same time that it impoverishes life's meaning it threatens life itself, for the deployment of large amounts of mindless energy under the direction of simpleminded monetary considerations is in its nature unmindful of the uniqueness and incommensurability of elements in the real world upon which life depends, and it is likely to damage them. There is thus a systematic relationship between the meaningful and biological components of life quality.

Let me make clear at the end that I do not deny that increases in population size may have adversely affected life quality in the past and surely threaten to do so in the future. Without doubt it is proper for scholars to concern themselves with population trends and their effects. It nevertheless seems to me that the most significant causes of ecosystemic destruction and of the deterioration of life quality vexing the world today are to be found in the thought and social organization of societies, and not in their population trends.

23

Design and the Quality of Life in a New Community

Suzanne Keller

THE QUALITY OF LIFE is of concern to all Americans. Many believe that this quality has not kept pace with the technical progress that has occurred since World War II. There is a growing sense that certain crucial ingredients of well-being are being neglected in the drive toward material affluence and growth. Beauty, repose, the respect for the natural environment, security in one's home and community, trust among strangers, all seem to be in jeopardy as the century draws to a close.

New communities were in part created to counteract these unwelcome trends by demonstrating the benefits of comprehensive planning and design of the built environment (Burby and Weiss, 1976). The extent to which they have succeeded may be debatable, but it is to their credit that they have drawn collective attention to those aspects of the quality of life in which design plays a crucial role. They thereby forced us to consider how design may accommodate the varied needs of individuals and aggregates. To do full justice to such an endeavor requires information about user needs and design impact as yet in short supply. Save for the famed ecological school of the University of Chicago in the 1920s and 1930s, the social sciences tend to ignore the physical and spatial environment for all except routine descriptive purposes. Architects and planners, on the other hand, assign it a predominant place as a determinant of behavior, but without checking their prejudices against reliable information they often defeat their own best intentions.

In this paper I will try to address the question of the importance of design in the residential assessment of one planned community. It is the first Planned United Development (PUD) in the state of New Jersey, whose development I have tried to follow since its inception in 1970.[1] One of the principal aims of the study was to assess the fit between design in the residential assessment of one planned community. It is the first Planned United Development (PUD) in the state of New Jersey, After some preliminary comments I will discuss selected findings from that study.

However one interprets the quality of life and, admittedly, there is room for disagreement, standards as to what constitutes the good life and resources for attaining it would seem to be at the heart of one's conception. In a major recent study (Campbell, Converse, and Rodgers, 1976:474ff.), Campbell and his associates have noted that satisfactions with key domains of one's life depend on both the objective conditions of the environment in regard to comfort, adequacy, and convenience, and subjective assessments based on personal experience. They found that housing, neighborhood, and the wider community all played an important, even a decisive, part in life satisfactions. Especially salient were the structural conditions of one's dwelling, neighborhood upkeep, public safety, and convenience of access to needed goods and services—all of these obviously dependent on design considerations.

In addition to these specific tangible attributes of the environment, there are more subtle factors at work, involving rules of spatial behavior and definitions of what constitutes attractive and reassuring surroundings. Research has shown that the violation of spatial norms may be a source of considerable physical and mental discomfort (Ittelson, Proshansky, and Winkel, 1974:128ff.). Spatial and territorial integrity contribute to one's sense of physical, psychological, and social self-preservation by giving one a sense of identity and security. Social interaction as well as the effective performance of social roles depend on the physical setting no less than on skill and motivation, and to respect another and to be respected by others involves a favorable physical environment no less than favorable personal dispositions. Physical arrangements, location, centrality, and territoriality contribute to the creation of a sense of community, and ideals of livability and habitability generally involve physical criteria such as environmental complexity, recreational amenities, accessibility of people and places, and the minimization of stress caused by noise, crowding, and pollution (Ittelson, Proshansky, and Winkel, 1974:294–98). In fact, virtually all of the familiar current problems of cities—inner-city ghettoes, the suburban exodus, crime, pollution, and loneliness—have a design aspect and require a concern for design in attempts to solve them.

[1]The study was carried out over a fourteen-month period (1974–1976) under the direction of the author with the aid of an interdisciplinary team of social scientists, photographers, and architects. Its findings are available in a report submitted to the National Science Foundation, whose generous support is hereby acknowledged.

The good life includes good space, a space that is serviceable, accessible, and beautiful. As Hans Blumenfeld has noted:

> The physical environment reacts on the social . . . by facilitating or limiting human relations. In addition, it has a direct influence on health and may have, through its aesthetic aspects, an influence on happiness (Blumenfeld, 1977:461).

And since we depend on the built environment more than on any other as "our lives are spent in houses, offices . . . factories . . . communities" (Ittelson, Proshansky, and Winkel, 1974:341), its texture, appearance, and symbolic meaning are of substantial consequence.

Ittelson and associates suggest that the built environment affects behavior in five principal ways (Ittelson, Proshansky, and Winkel, 1974:343), including: (1) physical and physiological properties to meet basic bodily needs for air, shelter, movement; (2) affective connotations of beauty, orderliness, and comfort; (3) functional suitability for the tasks to be accomplished in a given setting; (4) cognitive meanings and messages of how the environment is to be used and interpreted; and (5) socially—in helping to organize and regulate the activities of individuals and groups. The behavior affected touches on basic aspects of life, including the physical and mental health of individuals, family and household life, and social organization (Ittelson, Proshansky, and Winkel, 1974:364, 366).

Given its qualitative aspects, there is considerable debate over the magnitude and extent of the influence of design, with some according it a determining, others a more modest, role. Still there is little disagreement about the *fact* of the impact of buildings, roads, spaces, and facilities on the attainment of human goals. Design does not guarantee the attainment of these goals, but it contributes to their attainment by facilitating or hindering desired activities and undertakings. Ideally, good design fits the needs and requirements of people; more realistically, it permits them to modify and mold it to suit themselves. Poor design is either unsuitable or inflexible. The fit between design and behavior can hardly be expected to be exact, though its "criticality" varies with different needs (Ittelson, Proshansky, and Winkel, 1974:354), being high for some and low for others. Low criticality gives individual choice freer rein, whereas high criticality makes the role of design more crucial. William Michelson has suggested that the more choices urbanites have as to where they live, work, and play, the more significant becomes the role of design for their quality of life (Michelson, 1975:20–26). Where people have few resources they must make do with what is, though this does not mean that they are immune to the impact of a deteriorated, unattractive, or unsafe environment. It is also possible to take a familiar environment for granted, noticing neither its virtues nor its defects, and so become less sensitive to design as time passes. Clearly more research is needed here.

The significance of design for behavior and the quality of life appears far more obvious when dealing with populations having special problems, such as the blind, the infirm, newcomers, or the aged (R. Scott, 1969:124). For these groups, the design of the environment, its legibility, safety, and ease of locomotion, are unmistakably linked to their survival. Without specially designed aids and a carefully thought through arrangement of spaces and facilities they can readily become immobilized, trapped, distressed, lost. Since all of us are handicapped in some respects, we are all dependent on special design consideration at some point in life.

Design effects also vary over time as individuals may be more sensitive to environmental adequacy in bad weather, let us say, than in good; people at leisure are more tolerant of defective design than people in a hurry; and familiarity makes individuals more tolerant of design imperfections as they either get used to them or modify them.

Good design—like a dress that fits well—enhances the self-satisfaction of those dependent on it. Even poverty may be mitigated by physical upkeep and distinctive landscaping. Design enabled one low-income population to experience greater territorial identification, greater satisfaction with their neighbors, and more positive feelings about safety, layout, and security (Buttimer, 1972:279–318). Becker has shown how the appearance of one's dwelling contributes to the resident's sense of self-respect and status (F. Becker, 1977:chap. 2). By helping to personalize one's environment, design symbolizes the ability to exercise some control over one's world. The absence of such personalization may lead to vandalism and wanton disregard of an environment that seems oblivious to one's presence or needs. In affecting one's ability to be and to be noticed, to control a part of one's life space, and to express important personal and social values, design is clearly related to the quality of life (F. Becker, 1977:23).

Bettelheim has described an appropriate physical setting as the "safe center" from which life can go forward. And his own researches have shown how the built environment may influence the process of getting well, of gaining confidence, of trusting others (Bettelheim, 1974). Indeed, the questions asked of an institutional therapeutic setting are not too different from the questions asked of environments generally:

> Will this place provide ... safety ... ? Will it help create order out of my confusion? ... Will it force me into a mold? Is the building attractive and reassuring enough to become the shell which will protect me ... ? (Bettelheim, 1974:103)

The issues of safety, protection, reassurance, coherence are of concern to everyone at some time. Newman has explored the significance of design for a feeling of safety in low-income residential environments (Newman, 1972), and the desire for safety underlies the establishment of retirement communities as well as the move to new communities.

Indeed, one of the main goals of the New Towns movement has been its endeavor to achieve a better overall quality of life through design. It stressed the creation of visual order, physical integrity, social balance, community participation, and ready accessibility to needed educational, health, and social services. That New Towns did not attain these to the extent hoped for should not detract from their considerable achievements, including the fact that they pioneered in the effort to include design as a way of improving the quality of life.

Thus design defines an environment, symbolizes the availability of resources, and expresses a plan for living. By shaping the spatial contexts in which life takes place it also helps to maintain values to live by. Personal space, privacy, community, concern for others, opportunity for contact and movement—all are dependent on design. In this sense, the creation of desirable and workable physical settings is part of the pursuit—and the attainment—of human happiness.

Tapping the Impact of Design

Before highlighting resident response in one new community, a word about the difficulties involved in obtaining information about the impact of design. Problems of definition, the operationalization of concepts, and the indexes used to ascertain the attitudes of users are just a sample of problematic issues. Experience gained to date suggests that just as there is no uniform or agreed-upon set of concepts and definitions of design, so no single method suffices to yield the desired information. Accordingly, in this study a variety of approaches, including observation, interviews, structured questionnaires, and photography, were utilized. Still it is evident that we have barely begun systematically to explore these key issues.

For one thing, a great deal of what happens in a settlement is not part of the conscious awareness of those who live there, which is why direct questions have serious limitations. Few residents, moreover, in this or any other community know more than a tiny portion of the total environment and cannot therefore give a precise description of how people use that environment. How, then, can one find out about that more general scale, of how children arrive at school, for example, how they enter and leave the building, whether they abide by design directives, and how they modify them? Clearly, observation must supplement more formal techniques.

Observation is also needed for getting at the covert interaction between design and its users, much of which involves an exchange of unspoken messages, signals, and expectations. Designers arrange buildings, facilities, and locales to meet human needs. Their plans are idealized statements of such needs within the constraints of money and knowledge. The population, in actively using—and misusing—the built environment, is revealing its own needs and preferences, which may not match the designers' expectations. It is therefore necessary to devise methods to tap both planning intentions and user reactions, and to assess the one in light of the other.

Design intentions are also often implicit and hard to discern. The time lag between the formulation and the execution of a plan, for example, may unwittingly alter the original objectives, and later attempts to reconstruct design intentions may confront a Rashomon problem of recall. In this study intentions and design objectives were inferred from maps, models, official statements, and advertisements to attract prospective residents, as well as direct interviews with those responsible for bringing the community into being.

Residents' uses were deduced from observation of their activities, the analysis of community records on voting, safety, and expenditures, as well as from extensive in-depth interviews.

At this state of our ignorance, then, there is need for a variety of approaches to this complex problem. It is also advisable to evaluate reactions at more than one point in time and to probe for sensitivity to design with care and subtlety. And even then one is struck by the poverty of the spatial imagination of residents and their inarticulateness in trying to express their feelings about landscape, layout, colors, textures, and shapes. The language of space is as yet poorly developed in the general population despite their desire to speak it. Future studies will need to address this issue head-on.

RESPONSE TO THE DESIGN AMONG ADULTS

The community whose residents were interviewed for this study was the first PUD in the state of New Jersey. Designed to house some 12,000 people on its 700 acres, the predominant housing type was the attached townhouse (1,625 units), followed by apartments (929 units) and single-family houses (137 units) (Keller, 1976).

The postconstruction evaluation that forms the basis for the present paper was conducted over a five-year span, ranging from informal participant observation in 1970, when the first residents moved in, to a formal pilot study in 1971–1972 and a more elaborate full-fledged study between 1974–1976. All told, 250 adults and 80 youths were interviewed in depth, and nearly 1,000 households responded to structured questionnaires based on the lengthy interviews.

The residents, fairly representative of the population usually drawn to such communities, were young (80 percent under thirty-five years of age), college-educated couples with small children who had moved to the community in search of a home of their own, a convenient commute for the male breadwinner, and open space and safety for themselves and their children.

Their appreciation of open space, greenery, and safety is a clue to certain general design preferences. Indeed, their very move to a new, and unfinished, community attests to their sympathies for a design that promised a new way of life. But their sensitivity to design factors was evident in many particulars as well.

First of all, design was what drew most of the newcomers to this community. Among the top five reasons for moving there were the attractions of scale (27 percent), a good commute (26 percent), space for the children to move about and play (16 percent), and safety (16 percent). Burby and Weiss similarly found design factors to be key reasons for moving to new communities (Burby and Weiss, 1976:120). The majority of the residents (70 percent), moreover, felt that the move had been a positive addition to their lives and even more to the lives of their children.

Design also played a role in their appreciation of their individual dwellings and of the community as a whole. The majority liked their houses, being particularly pleased with the interior design (70 percent), and they mentioned the community's location (46 percent), scale (30 percent), recreation (26 percent), and quietness, safety, and privacy (23 percent) as key pluses.

However, just as design features contributed to their satisfaction with the community, so they figured prominently in their complaints. The lack of a community center, for example, was and continues to be a source of frustration. Problems of upkeep of the common grounds and roads and inadequate sanitation services arouse bitterness and resentment beyond the fact that the residents must pay a special fee for these services. The absence of landscaping is deplored by many, as is the bleakness of the play areas and the neglect of the community's appearance. In fact, the substandard enforcement of standards for roads and curbs was part of a list of grievances in a law suit residents brought against the developer and the Trust.

Asked what changes they would make, over half of the residents mentioned modifications at the level of physical design, and design factors were important for their conceptions of an ideal community.

Personal efforts to make the built environment more to their liking showed that the residents were better at criticizing than at creating, a not unfamiliar pattern. Few townhouse dwellers, for example, had finished the basements purposely left unfinished so that they could arrange them as they wished. Even fewer made any notable additions to the outside of their houses, as the photographic monitoring made starkly evident. Nonetheless, it is of interest to note that embellishments, few as they were, were typically added to the private spaces and dwellings, whereas destructions involved public areas and public facilities. This twofold reaction may reflect a tension between the wish for an attractive environment and disappointment with the existing design, the first expressed toward personal possessions, the second toward the community.

Design also contributes to the imagability of a community. This is of special significance in new communities, where part of the initial task of community building involves creating a shared image of community with which residents can identify and around which common experiences and aspirations can coalesce. This objective is faciltated by distinctive design that helps residents relate to the physical terrain, the landscape, and the dwellings as parts of a totality. How and how early this develops in new communities is not well known, but it is of interest to note that something of a perceptual consensus had been established in this community by the fourth year of its life. Asked to select the best, the worst, and the most typical view of the community from among nineteen photographs of it, 31 percent agreed on the worst, 41 percent on the best, and nearly half (47 percent) on the most typical view. The groundwork for a shared physical image has thus been laid.

RESPONSE TO THE DESIGN AMONG YOUTH

Many studies have shown teenagers to be especially critical residents of new communities (Burby and Weiss, 1976:233). Their disaffection, often experienced as boredom, isolation, and anger, takes its toll in the hostility displaced onto the physical environment. Broken windows, defaced lawns, mutilated streetlamps and telephone booths, litter, and deliberate disarray attest to their feelings of discomfort and deprivation.

Looking at the response of the young in this new community, one may discern the crucial role of design for their well-being and attachment to it. The sample consisted of eighty boys and girls, aged thirteen–fifteen, with some as young as eleven and some as old as eighteen. They lived in townhouses with their parents and one or two other children and attended the local public schools in a nearby community.

In exploring the meaning of the move for this middle-class group, design elements were of considerable significance both in their recall of what they most missed in the environment left behind and of what they found in their new one. The young missed facilities and services more than they missed people. In particular, they kept mentioning the transportation facilities, the varied shops, and opportunities for recreation. Problems of adjustment to the new physical setting were felt as a special hardship by as many as one-fourth of the young.

By and large, however, the move was seen as a positive step in their lives and most teenagers readily felt at home in the community where they quickly made "best friends," so their criticism is not due to sour grapes or general discontent. Unlike their parents, moreover, they draw on the entire community for these friendships, citing recreation, shopping, and parking areas as especially conducive to making new social contacts. In fact, they deplore the absence of needed facilities in part because of the restricted social life this implies for them. Thus design and sociability are here clearly and directly interrelated.

As regards their new houses, the majority give them high marks for comfort, privacy, and spaciousness. A chief complaint concerns the size and arrangement of their own rooms, which the majority are fortunate enough to have but which they would like to make bigger, more private, or more attractive. They were also quite critical of such aspects of dwelling design as layout and construction quality and mentioned the areas around the outside of the dwelling as particularly in need of improvement. All told, more than half of the teenagers made specific suggestions about improvements in dwelling design as ways to enhance their lives.

Design considerations are also featured in their overall assessments of the community. Their proposals for changes nearly all involved some design improvements, such as a more diversified and larger scale (21 percent), more recreation and transportation facilities (20 percent), the addition of a teen center (14 percent), better shopping (14 percent), and more attractive grounds and facades. They complained repeatedly of a lack of recreational facilities (26 percent), a sense of being cut off and isolated from other communities (16 percent), too small a scale (15 percent), and inadequate shopping (13 percent).

Some interesting sex differences could be discerned, even though boys and girls were in fairly close agreement in their assessments of the community. Had they the power to make changes in the community, for example, girls would change the scale (25 vs. 16 percent), the shopping (11 vs. 6 percent), and the interiors of their dwellings (15 vs. 0 percent), whereas the boys would add play and sports facilities and alter the exteriors of their dwellings. The girls were also more eager to have a teen center (18 vs. 11 percent) and a movie theater (32 vs. 20 percent) and were far more critical of their rooms (two-thirds vs. one-third) than was true of the boys. Older teens, by the way, were more critical of the community than younger teens.

Comparing the teenagers with their parents' generation, we find adults to be more residentially concentrated in their friendships and to confine their best friends to their own courts (47 vs. 10 percent) or their own quad (37 vs. 28 percent). Youths grumble about isolation (16 vs. 4 percent) and lack of recreational facilities (26 vs. 10 percent), whereas adults are concerned about privacy, construction quality of the dwelling, and the long-range development of the community. And whereas the young stress safety, better facilities, beauty, and comfort as attributes their ideal community should have, their elders are also concerned about a balanced social mix and a sense of community.

There are big discrepancies on boredom—62 percent of the young as against only 23 percent of their elders admitting to frequent boredom—and on loneliness, with more of the young having experienced it (71 vs. 52 percent). When pressed to account for their boredom, they cite a lack of things to do within the community and a lack of transportation facilities to help them get away from it.

Thus the complaints of both generations focus heavily and perhaps surprisingly on various elements of the community's physical design. This was especially true for the young, for whom virtually all expressed shortcomings and desired additions included a design component. Adults were seen to monopolize space and to refuse to share existing facilities fairly. The police and the shopkeepers appeared in an extremely unfavorable light, bent on banishing the young from shops and street corners, which are their favorite gathering places. Their endless refrains about boredom, nothing to do, and no exit all contain explicit criticism of the design of the community and its layout. As a result, the young feel out of place in a community that they consider to have been largely designed for adults and little children but not for them.

Upon reflection, it is striking how prominent a role physical design plays in the lives of the young in suburbia generally. Vandalism, loitering, conflicts over territory, and public misconduct are really inseparable from the attributes of spaces and places. Their inadequacies are a signal to abuse of the built environment, which then further depresses the quality of life that suburbs are bent on providing. And this is of course accentuated in new communities, where expectations are likely to be high.

In sum, teenagers, while appreciative of their new houses and the opportunities for friendships and activities that a new community has to offer, find the community inadequate in regard to needed environmental supports, athletic facilities, movies, and a social center where they can meet friends and make new contacts out of reach of adults. As a result they complain, often bitterly, about the limited opportunities there by comparison with the established urban settings they had come from. At least there they did not need to rely so heavily on their parents to help get them where they wanted to go. They look in vain for more diversified athletic, cultural, and social opportunities in this small, unfinished community, and are impatient to leave it.

Ironically, all that open space for which their parents had moved to the community comes to be experienced as pent-up and confining by its lack of diversity, and the crowded cities come in retrospect to loom as havens of freedom and mobility. Clearly, planning for the needs of teenage residents seems to be significantly related not only to the trials of that awkward age but to the design of the built environment that serves them.

Design Concepts and Realities

Every site plan is also a prescription for a way of living. Its spatial and architectural features rest on assumptions about human behavior and human needs. In the plan of the community under discussion these assumptions were embodied in a number of design concepts to guide its development, including the idea of a self-sufficient territorial community, the neighborhood unit concept, the walking distance idea, and recreational nucleii as foci for a nascent sense of community.

Each of these concepts was to promote the good life and create a sense of community, pride of place, public order, and domestic tranquillity for the inhabitants of this physically compact environment.

An examination of how well these design concepts achieved their aims showed that while such concepts significantly affect the quality of life, they cannot by themselves create it. Of the four concepts reviewed here, only the focus on recreation was unreservedly successful. Each of the others had some basic flaw in either conception or execution that undermined its basic intention.

Consider the idea of a self-sufficient community, for example. Despite its appeal, it became evident from the start that the sparseness of the available facilities meant that residents could not satisfy many of their most basic needs within the community. They were forced to go outside the community for necessities as well as amenities, including shopping, religious worship, health care, and amusements such as movies and concerts.

The problem of providing needed facilities and services is a perennial one in new communities and has varied implications for the kind of community that will develop. The priority extended to completing the dwellings and thus attracting residents means that services and all but elementary shopping will be postponed until a given level of demand has been reached. Yet the consequent resort to facilities outside the community inhibits the development of community feeling that planners try to encourage. The low ratings assigned to the shopping facilities by both adults and teenagers attest to hardships created not only at the practical level of comfort and convenience but also at the symbolic level by diffusing the loyalties needed to create a sense of community.

The neighborhood unit idea, with its hope for microcommunities, proved equally elusive. Indeed, the overriding design feature was not the community's division into four subareas but its bisection by a highway that effectively separated the first two neighborhoods on one side from the two on the opposite side. The residents in each part developed characteristic stances toward what the community had to offer. The significant line of identification was thus not around the individual neighborhood, as intended, but around the larger divisions introduced by the highway. As for the loyalty, local pride, and sociability that neighborhoods are to engender, here, too, the design missed its mark, as these feelings centered not on the entire neighborhood but on much smaller areas near one's home. These were the socially significant areas for the residents, the arenas for their close friendships as well as for the grating frictions of community life.

Finally, there is the circulation pattern designed to accommodate the idea of the self-contained community and the neighborhood units. By making houses, shops, and schools accessible to residents on foot, it was hoped that walking would become a major mode of locomotion in the community. This hope did not materialize as the large majority of the residents, young and old alike, used cars to get about. A focus on walking, so appealing at first glance, confronts a number of difficulties in a modern community. First of all there are the links people forge to people and places outside their residential communities. But there are also certain realities of time and distance within these communities, such as bad weather, illness, lack of time, and multiple destinations, that make the car indispensable. Then there are aesthetic considerations, as residents complained about having nothing beautiful or interesting to see while walking to the shops or the school. Obviously, better design and landscaping could here be used to good effect.

Thus while some residents do like to walk to see friends, get some exercise, or get to a club meeting, the majority do not. The car culture persists and it cannot be banished simply by ignoring it in the design and not providing sufficient parking spaces. The entire notion of a walking-distance community must be reformulated for these cosmopolitan villagers.

Finally, we come to the impact of recreational nodes as focal points of sociability and community. Swimming pools and tennis courts were not only appreciated for their obvious utility but proved to be key points for meeting new people and constituted prime reasons for moving to the community and remaining there. Recreation (26 percent) was second only to the presumed advantages for the children (30 percent) as a top reason for liking the community. Burby and Weiss also stressed the appeal of recreational opportunities in new communities (Burby and Weiss, 1976:238). Men, in particular, took advantage of recreational facilities, and teenagers wished there were a lot more of them. Although pools and tennis courts were well liked, playgrounds received very low ratings from the residents and appear to be little used for their intended purposes. Ill-equipped and inconveniently located, they are ignored by the children in favor of the parking lots and the streets. In all these examples, design obviously affected behavior both negatively and positively.

In sum, physical design affects, though it does not determine, personal well-being and community satisfaction. Design operates in conjunction with economic security, family life, social relationships, and material possessions, though it also has an influence all its own. Traffic congestions, ill-equipped play areas, trampled lawns, and bleak landscapes not only deprive us of pleasure and conveniences in the pursuit of our daily lives, but also depress our spiritual morale.

In no part of the study did design prove to be irrelevant. Size, layout, access, and appearance, all contributed to the residents' satisfactions with the community, just as inadequacies of construction and access, neglect, and visual monotony made for disappointments with it.

Design seems to operate at two main levels, overt and covert. Overtly, it exerts its impact by how well it fits the needs, desires, and fantasies of a given population. Here social research is needed to provide the necessary information base. But design also operates at a more covert level by what it conveys about one's self and one's surroundings. In a culture in which appearance, the package, the glamorous presentation of self is as significant as it is in the United States, community appearance and texture are also statements about self-worth and social significance. This is why the good address is sought quite apart from the shelter it provides and why public housing is so often offensive to those who live in it, despite its structural adequacy. The poverty of design announces their poverty and powerlessness to the world. Thus the appearance of a neighborhood, the richness of a landscape, the texture of the space one inhabits symbolize one's ability to live up to prevalent standards of success and social worth. Ironically, then, a concern with surface appearance may conceal deep-seated needs and anxieties. This is why the image of a community, so heavily dependent on physical features, may be as significant as its substance in its impact on the perceived quality of one's life. Design is not a superfluous frill but a necessary element in feeling pride, pleasure, and comfort in one's community.

VI

On the Multidisciplinary Analysis of Fertility

24

Introduction

The Editors

•

PAPERS IN THE PREVIOUS SECTION have, among other topics, addressed the impact of population growth on resources and on quality of life. In considering the specific demographic components of population growth, however, fertility clearly emerges as the most problematic and critical variable. With declining mortality in non-Western nations, the magnitude of their future population growth will be influenced largely by the rapidity with which fertility declines. Low and constant mortality in Western nations similarly makes fertility the problematic variable in the rates at which their populations grow. While these observations serve simply to underscore the importance of understanding fertility behavior, it is equally apparent that advances in our understanding will depend on the integrated contributions from several disciplines: biology, psychology, sociology, economics, political science, anthropology, and history. From among these several fields, the two papers in this section illustrate the desirability of interdisciplinary efforts by indicating ways in which the perspectives of sociology and economics on fertility would profit from incorporating other disciplinary viewpoints.

Professor N. Krishnan Namboodiri, a sociologist, suggests the potential gains to sociology by viewing reproduction from the investment-consumption perspective of economics; the gains to economics by incorporating sociological perspectives on sequential social pressures influencing fertility behavior; and the gains to both disciplines by including biological perspectives on transitional probabilities of movement from one state to another in the family-building process. Professor Richard A. Easterlin, an economist, not only notes a number of contributions of economics to the understanding of fertility, but also how the

293

characteristic disciplinary perspectives of economics, especially its assumptions of conscious choice and fixed preferences, differ from those of sociology and biology. Allowing deliberate choice and constant tastes to be considered as variables rather than as givens, he argues, would broaden the economist's perspectives so as to enable greater interdisciplinary contributions. Thus both papers reach similar conclusions and argue that the integration of unique disciplinary perspectives on fertility behavior will likely result in a more comprehensive and powerful analytical framework than any one standing alone.

25

On Fertility Analysis: Where Sociologists, Economists, and Biologists Meet

N. Krishnan Namboodiri

How would sociologists go about developing a theoretical framework for fertility analysis? The first part of this essay outlines one sociologist's answer to this question. The second part is devoted to a brief examination of the linkage between the outline presented in the first part and an economic framework for fertility analysis that has attracted considerable attention in recent years. Finally, the third part deals with the question: How does biology fit into the picture? Special attention is given to biometric models of reproduction.

A Sociological Approach to the Study of Fertility

A FEW CONCEPTS: NATURAL AND JURISTIC PERSONS, CORPORATE UNITS

Typically when discussing activities like reproduction, sociologists use terms such as "roles," "rules," and "relationships" (see, e.g., E. K. Wilson, 1971). But I shall adopt a slightly different approach, one that uses terms such as "persons and actions," "events and interests," "rights and resources" (see, in this connection, Coleman, 1974a).

□ I wish to express my appreciation to Bruce K. Eckland, Amos H. Hawley, Gerhard E. Lenski, Duncan MacRae, Richard L. Simpson, and Everett K. Wilson for commenting on an earlier verion of this paper.

A few remarks about some of these terms are in order, first about the term "persons." The legal profession recognizes two types of person, natural persons and juristic persons. Natural persons are creatures like you and me—each legally a bundle of rights and responsibilities. Juristic persons are entities like corporations and councils, trade unions and towns. They are not born from women's wombs, but are creatures of legislative bodies; they have no corpus, and so no one can put them in prison, but they can be put to death by the single stroke of a judge's pen.

For the present purpose I shall use the terms "individuals" and "natural persons" interchangeably, and I shall use the term "corporate units" (see Hawley, 1950:210) in place of "juristic persons." Note that the term "corporate units" stands for juristic persons and more. Thus entities like a friendship pack, a family, and a neighborhood association are all corporate units, irrespective of whether in the eyes of the law they are juristic persons. All compact masses of individuals engaged in any kind of collective activity are corporate units.[1]

There is one thing in common between a natural person and a corporate unit. They both have access to certain resources and are entitled to certain rights. (Some corporate units get their rights and resources from other corporate units, but ultimately all rights and resources belong to natural persons.)

What do we mean by rights and resources? The term "resources" brings to mind money, time, and energy. The membership dues we pay to professional associations, the tax we pay to the local, state, and federal governments, the time we spend in doing chores for charitable organizations, all are illustrative of the flow of resources from natural persons to corporate units. Resources include physical and mental capabilities of individuals and the physical environment's bounty. As for the term "rights," in a real sense it represents freedom to spend one's resources the way one likes.

CONSTRAINTS IMPOSED BY CORPORATE UNITS ON NATURAL PERSONS

When natural persons come together to form a corporate unit, each of them surrenders (invests) certain rights and resources for collective use, in return for whatever the corporate unit has to offer (for consump-

[1]Ethnic, racial, and other such aggregates are not corporate units unless they engage in some kind of collective activity. A similar comment applies to aggregates based on sex, age, color of hair, and other traits.

tion). Thus when a man and a woman enter matrimony, they establish implicitly or explicitly a social contract by which each party agrees to invest certain rights and resources in the corporate unit thus formed. The contract specifies (implicitly or explicitly) the control each person has over the actions of the corporate unit. It also tells what each partner may expect as benefits from the coactions implicated by the formation of the unit. The implicit nature of such contracts deserves to be emphasized. Seldom does one find a marriage contract that specifies, for example, that the husband shall fix breakfast on Mondays, Wednesdays, and Fridays, and the wife shall take care of children born on Tuesdays, Thursdays, and Saturdays.[2] Such explicit specifications go counter to the mutual trust and the romantic relationship that form the bases of most marriages. But it is easily seen that the mutual trust and the love relationship do impose certain constraints on the resources and degrees of freedom of the parties involved and that these constraints are implicit in the marriage contract. Conformity to these constraints is enforced not always by courts of law, but often by informal institutional and interpersonal mechanisms.

It should be remembered that each natural person is a party to as many social contracts as there are corporate units in which he or she holds membership. As noted earlier, these corporate units range from married couple and friendship pack to communes and labor unions, and the granddaddy of them all, the nation-state. Membership in some corporate units involves surrendering only a part of one's alienable resources (e.g., financial investment in a company). There are some units (e.g., communes) that demand practically a total surrender.

To summarize, each of us natural persons is a party to not one but a number of social contracts.[3] Some contracts may be more permanent than others. (Thus one can easily call off a "blind date" with the friend of a friend, but marriage bonds are not as easily broken). Each contract, be it permanent or transitory, takes away a certain amount of resources and degrees of freedom from each natural person who is a party to the contract, leaving that much fewer resources and degrees of freedom available to be used for entering into other contracts.

---

[2]Some young couples reportedly nowadays do sign contracts that specify explicitly in all detail the division of labor between the husband and wife. But this is the exception rather than the rule.

[3]Admittedly the term "contract" is used here in a broad sense. It covers contracts entered into voluntarily (e.g., formal contracts) as well as those entered into involuntarily (e.g., those implicated by one's birth). Some readers might object to lumping different kinds of implicit and explicit contract into a single category. I fail to see, however, any strong reason why explicit and implicit contracts should be separately treated for the present purpose.

SOCIOECONOMIC DEVELOPMENT AND PROLIFERATION OF CORPORATE UNITS

As social and economic development occurs, the number of social contracts to which each natural person is a party increases. This can be seen by: (1) comparing the structural differences between the medieval society and its modern counterpart; and (2) examining the structural changes that accompany industrialization and modernization. In the olden days each natural person was a party to only one contract, the one that bound him or her to the members of his or her family. Only the lowest-level contract was made by natural persons. The rest were made by progressively higher-level units—families forming the city and cities making up the kingdom. The difference between this and the modern social structure is the difference between a nested set of corporate units, with the natural person making only the lowest-order investment decision, and an interlocking set of corporate units, with the natural person (theoretically speaking) as the investor in all cases (Coleman, 1974a).

Now to examine the structural changes that accompany industrialization and modernization. Cumulative change that we call social and economic development involves a progressive division of the total life process into specialized activities. As specialization increases, the number of corporate units also increases to take charge of the specialized activities. A few examples illustrate the idea. What was once a simple matter of consulting a village physician now involves getting help from numerous specialists including a radiologist, a blood analyst, a stool analyst, and a dozen more. Giving birth to a baby used to be a simple matter of finishing the business when the time came, perhaps with the help of an older woman. Nowadays having a baby is a complex set of activities in which the family, the hospital, the insurance company, and a dozen other corporate units are all involved.

To repeat, with economic and social development comes an enormous increase in the number of corporate units (some more permanent than others) in which natural persons typically make investments[4] (in return for actual or expected benefits).

HIERARCHY AMONG CORPORATE UNITS

Among the myriads of corporate units that make up a society, there prevails a hierarchical structure, an ordered arrangement based on

---

[4]The reference is to the fact that the development process, which involves differentiation and specialization, results in the proliferation of corporate units and the multiplicity of membership in them by natural persons.

dominant-subdominant relationships. This is a fundamental notion emphasized in the literature on social structure (see Hawley, 1977, for a discussion of the matter). We shall interpret the presence of a hierarchical structure among the corporate units to mean that natural persons tend to give priority to investment of resources and degrees of freedom in higher-ranked corporate units over investment in lower-ranked ones (in certain nonfamilial units over the familial unit, for example). In practice this simply is a reflection of the greater capability of the higher-ranked units to manipulate the individual effectively. To illustrate how the individual is manipulated, consider how manufacturers of consumer goods try to manage consumer behavior. Many persons have written on the subject. The point emphasized by these writers is that the individual is conditioned to be a consumer, i.e., wants are created in the individual, through relentless propaganda on behalf of goods and services. Every feature of every product is studied for its sale value, and it is then presented with convincing authority and crystallike clarity as the source of social standing, physical health, and overall happiness. Most people fall for the propaganda (Bennett and Kassarjian, 1972:38); some probably won't; but by and large the mass behavior is successfully manipulated, with little danger of enough subjects going astray to impair the management of aggregate consumer behavior[5] (Galbraith, 1967:209ff.).

INVESTMENT IN REPRODUCTION

One can think of having children as a sort of consumer behavior (geared to the satisfaction of the want "to be a parent").[6] The "propaganda" that creates this want is more subtle than the one just described. Through religious teachings, early socialization and training, and actual behavior of relevant others, the individual is cajoled and coerced to want "to be a parent." The effect of all this on reproduction depends upon two factors: (1) how effective and powerful the propaganda for partici-

---

[5]As some readers may see it, propaganda, advertisements, and the like, simply provide the individual with pertinent pieces of information; the individual is free to accept or reject what is presented to him or her. From this standpoint there is no manipulation involved: "People are not passive and plastic to be manipulated at will by Madison Avenue maneuvers," so goes the position statement. In theory, the individual may be thought of as free to accept or reject what he or she is told by the advertisers, but in practice, quite a large proportion of persons exposed to the "propaganda" fall for it, knowingly or unknowingly.

[6]Reproduction can be also thought of as an "occupation." Any job (be it carried out in a town hall, tavern, or at home, be it of the paid kind or of the unpaid variety) can be regarded as an investment-consumption activity. The jobdoer invests certain resources (time, talent, and so on) in return for certain benefits. The benefits may be simply the psychological satisfaction that the job is well done, or resources (e.g., money) that could be used to buy the stuffs (e.g., food) that satisfy certain wants.

pation in competing activities is; and (2) how costly (in terms of investment of resources and degrees of freedom) it is to be a parent. When the levels of these factors are high, reproduction is depressed; if they are both low, reproduction is high. Differential fertility also is to be explained in the same way. Those aggregates in which the levels of the factors just mentioned are low tend to have higher fertility than those aggregates in which the levels of these factors are high. Underlying these propositions is the implicit assumption that the individual gives somewhat lower priority to investment in reproduction than to investment in other activities. This is a dangerous assumption when considered by itself, for in its logical extreme it leads to an anomalous situation wherein there is no provision for reproduction. For this reason we need to temper the assumption with the notion espoused by many a sociologist that there exist in each society norms prescribing what a minimum family size should be. Let us relate this notion to a more basic notion that is commonly discussed in sociology textbooks, namely, that reproduction is a must in order to insure sociocultural continuity. To elaborate: When a baby is born it becomes a party to a social contract. The contract says that the baby shall be provided with a certain amount of human capital, i.e., knowledge, skills, and so on. The family, the community, and the society all are involved in building up the human capital in each individual through socialization and training. Another part of the same contract says that each person shall contribute toward extending the life of the human capital created in that person beyond the lifetime of that person. This is to be done by producing children and contributing to their socialization and training. The contract just mentioned is enforced not in any direct fashion, but indirectly through cultural mechanisms that create and maintain a strong desire on the part of individuals to "have a family," "become a parent," and so on.

When does a person "become a parent"? Not necessarily at the birth of the first child. For example, when emphasis is placed on having at least one son survive the father so as to continue the family line, successful parenthood tends to be defined in terms of a minimum number of children, i.e., a minimum family size that insures a reasonably high probability of leaving at least one male heir. Depending upon the mortality level, it is possible that an average of four or five children may be regarded as a minimum in such situations. This number becomes the family-size threshold below which no one wants to remain, or, to use the term introduced above, the minimum family-size norm.

Until the family-size threshold just mentioned is reached, reproduction wins over if there is a competition between it and other activities for the resources and rights of the persons involved. After the threshold is passed, however, the competitive situation becomes relatively less favorable to reproduction.

A few remarks about the social norms concerning family size are in order.

1. Those who have written on the subject have emphasized the vagueness characteristic of these norms. Thus, for example, according to Freedman (1963:221): "While specifying clearly that childlessness is an unspeakable tragedy and an only child very undesirable, the norm for a particular culture or group may be as vague as 'at least three or four children' or 'as many as possible.'" Because norms are not clear-cut as to how many children a couple ought to have, sanctions are strong only in the case of extreme deviance (childlessness, for example).

2. It is common for sociologists to take the position that norms have a capacity to exert coercion upon behavior of individuals. There are sociologists who feel uncomfortable with attaching coercive capacity to social norms. To these sociologists, a norm is nothing more than a modal pattern of behavior or a statistical fact. Thus the two-child family is a norm to the extent that it is modal. Modal fertility gets altered as behavior changes in response to institutional or other environmental shifts. Put another way, given a social and economic context, there emerges consistent with it a certain family-size distribution of couples, presumably a distribution with a single mode. To account for this distribution one needs to look only at the social and economic context. As the context changes so does the distribution in question. One may ask at this point: How are couples motivated to conform in the aggregate to a certain family-size distribution? It is when confronted with this question that notions such as very high costs (punishments) associated with extreme deviance and rewards for staying close to the mode become appealing.

3. To me, the notion of a family-size threshold below which few couples would wish to remain is a useful one. Irrespective of whether one calls it the minimum family-size norm, it is useful to entertain the idea that remaining below this threshold is likely to be so costly to individual couples that such deviance would be kept to a minimum in the aggregate.

4. The idea of a family-size threshold below which few, if any, would wish to remain is analogous to the notion that consumers will not ordinarily permit their consumption level to drop below a certain floor. This latter notion is emphasized in writings of economists who consider human preferences to be lexicographic in nature. (See Hakansson, 1972; Truelove, 1964. Maslow's [1954] thesis that the basic needs of humans are hierarchical in structure is also of interest in this connection.)

To summarize this part of the paper, reproduction and other human activities can be viewed as investment-consumption behavior, in which the individual invests resources and degrees of freedom in various corporate units (compact masses of individuals engaged in collective activities) in return for what the corporate units have to offer. The individual is constantly faced with the task of deciding which corporate unit to make investments in and which consumption items to (produce and) enjoy. Common sense tells us that such decisions are made sequentially (in the lifetime of the individual), with the actual or expected consequences of decisions already made influencing subsequent decisions. Furthermore, it appears that at all points in the lifetime of the individual investment in certain activities claims priority over investment in others. *This priority ordering is primarily determined by structural features of the society and is reflected in the lexicographic nature of the individual's preference structure.*

Reproduction from Economists' Point of View

A number of years ago Gary Becker (1960) published a paper in which he claimed that he could explain differences in completed family size in terms of differences in prices and incomes, just as he would explain differences in the demand for durables like cars and carpets, refrigerators and record players, washing machines and whatnots. Since then fertility analysis has increasingly become a pastime for many an economist. During the last few years the Becker brand of economic model of fertility has undergone some changes, prompted by the premises of what is often called the new home economics or the new theory of consumer behavior (see, e.g., Michael and Becker, 1973; see also Stigler and Becker, 1977).

THE NEW THEORY OF CONSUMER BEHAVIOR

In the traditional theory, ego maximizes a utility function of the goods and services bought in the marketplace. In the new theory, ego's utility is defined not as a function of "raw" goods and services but as a function of what are called basic commodities (e.g., good health, marital bliss, parental paradise). Ego manufactures all basic commodities using market goods and services, ego's own time, skills, and various other inputs. Formally the utility function can be represented as

$$U = U(Z_1, Z_2, \ldots, Z_n) \tag{1}$$

where Z_i's are basic commodities. Since each Z is manufactured by ego, it is only logical to attach to it a production function, which gives the output in terms of the inputs involved. The production function in its general form can be written as

$$Z = f(X_1, X_2, \ldots, X_k; t_1, \ldots, t_m; R_1, \ldots, R_s) \tag{2}$$

where X's stand for market goods and services, t's for time inputs from ego and others, and R's for pertinent characteristics of ego and others. Production functions of this type are supposed to reflect the state of the production technology. In order to complete the specification of the production of Z's, one should introduce resource constraints, i.e., the limitations imposed by available income, available time, and so on. Given these constraints one can apply the familiar theory of the firm to determine the production behavior. The production and consumption can then be brought together by applying the partial equilibrium theory, assuming that whatever is produced is also consumed.

Note that by substituting the production functions into the utility function, one can get a derived utility function, and every statement about the production function can be translated into an equivalent statement about the derived utility function. In particular, the dependence of production functions on characteristics of persons other than ego is equivalent to stating that ego's utility is dependent on pertinent characteristics of others. This last idea will now be expanded.

PRODUCTION OF "PARENTHOOD"

Let us consider a simple situation involving a single basic commodity, say, Z = "parenthood."[7] The utility function is then a function of a single basic commodity, Z. Hence maximizing the utility function is the same as maximizing Z's production function. Ignoring for the moment time inputs and ego's own characteristics let us write the production function as

$$Z = f(X,R) \tag{3}$$

where X stands for goods and services and R represents pertinent characteristics of the "relevant other."

We shall regard R as the relevant other's expectations about how ego should behave in various situations; in this sense we shall regard R as social norms. For the present purpose, we shall view norms as pieces of information about matters like how many children to have, when to have them, how to raise them, and so on.[8] Now the search for and analysis of

---

[7]As far as I am aware, no one has compiled a list of "basic commodities" that human individuals produce and enjoy. Also, no one seems to have developed any clear guidelines to help decide what is a basic commodity and what is not. Is "parenthood" a basic commodity or is it an ingredient to be used in the concoction of a basic commodity (e.g., old-age security)? Economists do not seem to mind using one thing as a basic commodity in one context and as an input in the production of a basic commodity in another.

[8]The term "norms" has been used in a variety of ways in sociology. One analyst (Gibbs, 1965) identified three different generic definitions of norm in the sociological literature: "A norm in the generic sense involves: (1) a collective evaluation of behavior in terms of what it *ought* to be; (2) a collective expectation as to what behavior *will be;* and/or (3)

information is a costly affair, just as is experimentation with new cures for given ailments. Furthermore, putting into practice behavioral formulas contained in social norms involves resource expenditure. In these senses one can put a value (resource cost) on R. Let P_R be the price (resource cost) per unit R. Then $P_R R$ is the resource equivalent of R.

Let us now write

$$R = h + D \tag{4}$$

where h stands for that part of R in which ego has already made investments, and D the remainder. For a person in childbearing ages, one may think of h as nurture experience (see Easterlin, 1968) and D as peer-group pressures (see Leibenstein, 1977) that have not yet taken hold on ego. Ego's budget constraint can be written as

$$P_X X + P_R h = I \tag{5}$$

where I is ego's income, P_X the price per unit X, and P_R and h have already been defined.

If we note that $h = R - D$, equation (5) can be written as

$$P_X X + P_R R = I + P_R D = S \tag{6}$$

where S represents ego's "social income" (the sum of own income and the imputed value of D).

Sociologists would find it difficult to imagine imputing vague things like nurture experience and peer-group pressures a numerical score so as to obtain a neat quantitative relationship like the ones shown in (5) and (6). To many economists, this is not a problem; they would maintain that influences of nurture experience, peer-group pressures, and so on, can be, for theoretical purposes, thought of in terms of resource costs.

From (6) we can get the following relationship (see G. S. Becker, 1974b:1070):

$$w\eta_X + (1 - w)\,\eta_R = 1 - \alpha \tag{7}$$

where

η_X = own-income elasticity of X (i.e., percent change in X per 1 percent change in I),

---

particular *reactions* to behavior, including attempts to apply sanctions or otherwise induce a particular kind of conduct." (With respect to the obligatory or "ought" aspect of normative behavior, Pope and Namboodiri [1968:8] remarked thus: "If we strip 'ought' and 'should' of their motivational connotations, they refer to 'ends in themselves,' i.e., to consideration of the contemplated act or prospect outside of any preference set or to giving it top priority within a given set." The connection between this interpretation of the "ought" aspect of norm and the postulate that the individual's preference structure is lexicographic in nature should be apparent.

η_R = own-income elasticity of R,

$w = P_X X / S$, the fraction of S that ego uses up in purchasing goods and services, and

$\alpha = P_R D / S$, the share of D in ego's social income.

From (7) it follows that as α, the share of D in S, increases, η_X and η_R become negligible. Thus the greater the share of D in S, the smaller the influence of I on the production of Z (see G. S. Becker, 1974b:1070).

When will D dominate S? Imagine h as nurture experience or norms internalized during the early socialization process. If situational change remains negligible, R will have changed little, all of it having been internalized during adolescence and early adulthood. Under such conditions, D will be trivial. The opposite is likely to be the case if: (1) social change occurs putting ego in a new situation; or (2) memberships in corporate units change as a result of actual (or aspired to) spatial or social mobility, which puts ego in a new (actual or imagined) social setting.

As long as there is little social change, D does not have a marked share in ego's social income. In such situations, the influence of own income on family size is not negligible. In industrially advanced societies, however, D's share in ego's social income is almost always likely to be high. Under such circumstances, it is D, not I, that controls the production of Z. At this point one may exclaim in disbelief: Income effect remains negligible, while social pressures steal the show! To most economists this is unthinkable. Most of them would concede, I hope, that equation (7) and the interpretation given to it are in order. Be that as it may, no economist would fail to point out that the picture remains incomplete until the price (cost) variable is allowed to play its part. In particular, they would point out, a rise in P_R would induce the usual substitution effects away from R. To this many sociologists would take exception, arguing that investment in R, i.e., adherence to norms, is not negotiable, thereby making the usual price (cost) considerations inapplicable. Herein lies the major difference between the two approaches. To most economists, social norms are probably out there, and ego is free to adhere to them or to ignore them; it is simply a matter of price (cost). To many sociologists, ego does not have this freedom; ego is conditioned to adhere to social norms, regardless of price (cost) considerations.

To summarize this (second) part of the essay, the economic perspective outlined above permits the analyst to take into account the influence of social pressures on decisions concerning family growth. But economics has little to say about the nature of social pressures themselves. This falls within the purview of sociologists, who would advance propositions like the following: Social pressures will be for having additional children until the minimum family size prescribed by norms has been reached, after which the pressure will be to avoid additional children and to expend resources in nonchild-related activities, such as status goods consumption (see Leibenstein, 1974). One way of taking into account the notions underlying such propositions is to recognize the lexicographic nature of an individual's preferences and the sequential feature of decision making. Once these are incorporated into models of investment-consumption decisions, there would be more room for sociologists and economists to collaborate. Sociologists could work on the nature of the preference structure, changes, if any, in it over the lifetime of the individual, and the heterogeneity in these respects in the population. The responsibility to elaborate the existing economic models of fertility so as to reflect the results of sociologists' investigations would then fall on economists.

Contributions of Biometricians

How do biological perspectives fit in here, if at all? Let us consider the contributions of biometricians in the area of modeling family-building patterns (see, in this connection, a recent review of the literature by Potter, 1977).

The more comprehensive biological models of family building deal with: (a) the length of interval between consecutive pregnancy terminations, its components, and their determinants; and (b) probabilities of transition from one state to another (e.g., from being a Pill user to the user of no contraception).

Interbirth intervals have several components (see figure 1), including the time added by pregnancy wastage (e.g., abortion). Of particular interest among these components is the length of menstruating interval (the interval between first menses postpartum or postabortum and the date of the next conception). This is influenced by fecundability (monthly probability of conception), which in turn is influenced by age, contraceptive use, viability of sperm and ovum, and so on. (Fecundability is a characteristic of the couple, although commonly it is treated as an attribute of the woman).

Family-planning behavior (i.e., behavior aimed at preventing or postponing births) is incorporated in biometric models by:

1. Suitably lowering fecundability to take into account contraceptive use.
2. Regarding induced abortion as one of the possible pregnancy outcomes.
3. Treating sterilization as a state similar to menopause, end of reproduction, a state from which no escape is possible once one enters it.

Figure 1. Segments of Interbirth Interval, Including Time Added by Pregnancy Wastage

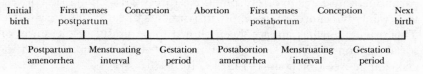

SOURCE: Potter (1975).

4. Making birth-control behavior (contraception, abortion, and sterilization) dependent on parity as well as duration of marriage or interval since last birth, a procedure by which family-size preferences and spacing goals of couples can be taken into account.
5. Treating use of a particular contraceptive (e.g., Pill, IUD, conventional methods, or no contraceptive) as equivalent to being in a particular state.
6. Recognizing that couples learn from experience, i.e., their earlier contacts with contraception and abortion influence their subsequent behavior with respect to these methods of birth control.

The building block of such models is $A_{ij}(x,t)$, the probability of transition from one state (i) to another (j) in a given time period (t), conditional on the fact that the woman is of specific characteristics and history (x) when entering state i.

To do a good job, biometric model builders can use some inputs from economists and sociologists—considerable help in distinguishing appropriate x types, valid information concerning changes over time in family-size preferences (which, incidentally, is linked to changes in the total preference structure), insight as to how experience with contraception and abortion influences the couple's subsequent behavior with respect to these methods of birth control, and so on. Sociologists and economists, on their part, could profitably use biometricians' building blocks, $A_{ij}(x,t)$, or combinations of them (e.g., probability of transition from parity n to parity $n + 1$), for testing the goodness of their theories. For it is the set of transition probabilities of the kind $A_{ij}(x,t)$, or combinations of them, that most elaborate social and economic models of fertility try or should try to explain (see Namboodiri, 1972).

Concluding Remarks

In this paper I have taken the position that reproduction and other human activities can be viewed as investment-consumption behavior in which the individual invests resources and rights in corporate units, like the family, the supermarket, and the state, in return for whatever the corporate units have to offer, sometimes direct satisfaction of the investor's wants but more often simply instruments (means) to satisfy them. This orientation has already been shown to be useful in the study of social phenomena like power, inequality, distribution of justice, and social change (see Coleman, 1974a, 1974b, 1976).

I have suggested that in developing the orientation just mentioned, it be recognized that: (1) investment-consumption decisions are made sequentially over the lifetime of the individual; and (2) at any given point in the lifetime of the investor, investments in certain corporate units are given priority over those in others, this priority order being primarily determined by the hierarchical (i.e., dominant-subdominant) pattern characteristic of the social structure, which presumably is reflected in the lexicographic nature of the individual's preference structure.

There is evidence in the literature that increasing numbers of sociologists have begun to pay attention to this mode of thinking. The same may be said about economists. If appropriate data were available, those who subscribe to the orientation described above would adopt as the explanandum in their analysis the probability of transition of a couple from one state to another, in a fixed time interval, in the family-building process. The explanatory analysis would then involve identifying factors that differentiate couples with respect to these transition probabilities. (A logical member of the set of differentiating [explanatory] factors that one looks for in this connection is the string of events in the couple's life course up to the beginning of the interval in question.) If for convenience we denote the whole set of explanatory factors by the symbol x, we may say that it is $A_{ij}(x,t)$, the probability of transition from state i to j during the time interval t for couples of type x, that forms the appropriate building block of socioeconomic fertility models. Interestingly, the building block of the relatively more comprehensive biometric models of family growth is also $A_{ij}(x,t)$ of the kind just defined. One thus discerns, at least in this respect, a trend toward convergence of the sociological, economic, and biometric approaches to fertility model building.

Severe data problems, however, prevent this trend toward convergence from being anything but slow. Retrospective (survey) data are no doubt available for many populations; they do provide pregnancy and contraceptive-use histories, but they seldom provide the corresponding information on changes in socioeconomic status and other factors. There are also certain technical problems that limit the use of retrospective data for model-building purposes (Potter, 1977). As for prospective data, they are more expensive and more time consuming to collect, and for that reason few such data sets are available.

If there were no data problems, analysts would be able to identify not only the factors that differentiate the probability of transition from one state to another in the family-building process of *a population at a given period in its history,* but also ascertain whether *different sets of differentiating factors come into prominence with institutional and environmental shifts in the society.* When armed with this kind of information, one should be able to answer satisfactorily the question: Why do couples build their families the way they do? Admittedly, as of now we are at some distance away from that stage.

New Directions for the Economics of Fertility

Richard A. Easterlin

DIFFERENT DISCIPLINARY PERSPECTIVES may sometimes promote progress on a subject, but they may also run at cross-purposes. In the last decade the preoccupation of the "economics of fertility" with its own identity has probably served a useful purpose among economists in establishing human fertility as a reputable area of research. But this preoccupation has also resulted, it seems to me, in an undue narrowing of the "economics of fertility," and a consequent alienation from allied work by sociologists and biologists. In this paper I propose some new directions for the economics of fertility that may make the approach more compatible with those of sociologists and biologists than has heretofore been the case.

Let me start with a couple of illustrations that highlight the current difference in disciplinary perspectives. Time series fluctuations in marital fertility and real per capita income are observed to be positively correlated in a premodern society. In other words, when income increases, fertility increases; when income declines, so does fertility. What is the explanation? A biologist, I suppose, would look to physiological factors, such as variations in nutrition and health that might affect female fecundity or frequency of intercourse. A sociologist would acknowledge the possible relevance of the biologist's hypothesis, but would propose additionally the influence of social norms, perhaps the custom, prevalent in some societies, of a wife returning to her parents' home

☐ The research on which this paper reports was funded by NICHHD grant HD-05427, held jointly with Robert A. Pollak and Michael L. Wachter, and Rockefeller Foundation grant 526719. I am grateful for comments to Karen Oppenheim Mason and for assistance to Deborah C. K. Wenger.

when times are bad. The resulting reduction in frequency of intercourse would lower fertility even in the absence of physiological changes stressed by a biologist. What of the economist? He would reason that lower income compels families to cut back on their consumption of a number of goods, and among the goods whose consumption they choose to reduce are children.

Like any illustration, this one doubtless oversimplifies and runs the risk of misrepresentation. Yet it brings out, I believe, an important contrast between the economist's approach and those of the other disciplines. Economics typically views fertility as the exclusive result of conscious choice of family size by parents; the other two disciplines often, though not always, view fertility as not involving conscious choice, as in the illustration above. An economist, James Duesenberry, dramatized this contrast in an oft-quoted statement: "Economics is all about how people make choices. Sociology is all about why they don't have any choices to make" (Duesenberry, 1960:233). While this exaggerates—since sociology does allow for the possibility of conscious choice—it does underscore a fundamental difference in viewpoint.

Let me take one other illustration. Why are American women today having fewer children and working more? A biologist would probably emphasize the mechanisms of fertility control—the pill, IUD, and greater ease of securing an induced abortion. A sociologist, additionally, would look to changes in values and attitudes regarding women's roles. An economist would resist the sociologist's concern with changing attitudes. He would turn instead to changes in the external environment that would alter behavior even in the absence of attitudinal changes, such as a shifting balance between returns from women's home and labor-market activities. And while he would not rule out the possibility that fertility-control innovations are relevant, he would remind one that even in the absence of such innovations there might have been, as in the 1930s, a substantial increase in fertility control because the motivation for limiting family size was strengthened by a change in the environmental circumstances confronting women.

This illustration highlights a second important difference in the approach of economists to the explanation of fertility, namely, the stress on changes in environmental factors, especially market (or "shadow market") conditions, as opposed to subjective attitudes (what economists would label "tastes" or "preferences"), which are typically taken as fixed.[1]

These preconceptions of economics regarding conscious choice and constant tastes, best exemplified in the fertility area by what has been

---

[1] This same contrast is brought out clearly in a discussion by Myron Weiner of approaches to economic growth (Weiner, 1966:9ff.).

called the "Chicago-Columbia approach" (Schultz, 1974), have been of great value in economics in constructing a general and rigorous body of theory, with considerable empirical relevance. As regards fertility behavior, however, I think they are unfortunate. I feel there is persuasive evidence that they lead to a misconception of the mechanisms of fertility determination for a wide segment of the world's population in time and space. And, rather than building bridges, they create a gulf between economics and the other disciplines in the study of fertility. This is especially unfortunate, because with relatively little effort the economist's approach to fertility analysis can be expanded to include the concerns of sociologists and biologists, and when this is done the resulting analytical framework is more powerful than one based on any of the individual disciplines alone.

Let me take up first my reasons for asserting that the usual "deliberate choice" version of the economics of fertility is of limited empirical relevance. Some economists would quarrel with this view, pointing out, for example, that in work on agricultural production behavior in peasant societies, the trend of research has been toward establishing the relevance of conscious decision-making models. And if this is true of farm production in peasant societies, why not also of reproduction?

Reproductive behavior, however, differs from production behavior in an important respect. Babies, since they are a product of sexual intercourse, tend to be produced whether or not they are wanted, whereas rice and wheat do not. Hence a decision to control output would typically require conscious action to limit fertility, such as abstinence, contraception, or induced abortion. If reproductive behavior is a matter of deliberate choice, then one would expect to find evidence of deliberate practice of fertility control. In fact, the evidence points to the general absence, rather than presence, of deliberate fertility control in many times and places.

The evidence available is of two types—survey data in which households report on their knowledge and use of fertility control, and census or other data on actual age-specific fertility rates. The former come mostly from what are known as "KAP surveys"—surveys of the knowledge of, attitudes toward, and practice of fertility control—which have been conducted in a number of countries since World War II. The other body of data relating to the presence or absence of consciously controlled fertility involves inferences from the actual age-specific marital fertility schedule of a population, instead of relying on subjective responses. The technique, which for lack of time will not be described here, was developed by Ansley Coale, based on Louis Henry's work, and, among other things, yields a summary index, m, of the prevalence of deliberate fertility control in a population (Coale and Trussell, 1974).

One may have doubts about either body of evidence. However, results from the two sources turn out to be highly consistent, thus enhancing the credibility of each (Easterlin, Pollak, and Wachter, forthcoming). Both sets of data show very little practice of deliberate fertility control in countries at a premodern or early modern stage of development, whereas for contemporary developed countries both show widespread practice of deliberate control. Also, both sets of data uniformly indicate a greater practice of fertility control in urban than in rural areas. And for the one country where trends can be compared, Taiwan, these two sets of data show similar trends.

The implication of these data is that in many parts of the world, present and past, there has been little or no deliberate family control of fertility. To the extent this is so, the usual economic model, and the mechanisms it emphasizes regarding parents' demands for children, is inapplicable However, this is not to suggest that fertility in these societies is uncontrolled, in the sense that it is at its biological maximum. On the contrary, it is likely that various types of social control reduce fertility below its maximum level. Examples of such controls are an intercourse taboo or prolonged lactation. These practices have the effect of limiting fertility in the society, but they are not usually practiced by couples with that effect in mind. In the terminology of sociologists, the "latent" function of such practices is to limit fertility. However, it is only if the "manifest" function is to limit family size that one can speak of deliberate fertility control.

At this point, one may begin to think I am a traitor to my cause—an economist disputing the empirical relevance of the economics of fertility. This, however, is not my purpose. Rather, as I have mentioned, my aim is to suggest that, with surprisingly little trouble, the economist's approach can be expanded to include the views of sociologists and biologists, and when this is done the result is an overarching framework more useful than that based on any single discipline alone. To the usual economic models, which focus on demand considerations, one merely adds a production constraint (perhaps one should call it a "reproduction" constraint) that reflects the biological relationship between a couple's ability to produce live births and such factors as frequency of intercourse, reproductive span of the household, fertility regulation practices, and the commodities, goods, and practices that govern the probability of conception and the nonsusceptible period of the wife.[2] Coupling the parents' production possibilities with their family-size desires leads one to recognize the possibility of an "excess demand" situation, one in which parents feel they are unlikely to produce as many surviving children as they want. In such a situation it would be rational

[2]Cf. David and Sanderson (1976); Easterlin (1975, 1978); Easterlin, Pollak, and Wachter (forthcoming); Michael and Willis (1976); Tabbarah (1971); Wachter (1972).

for parents to have as many children as they can. Their actual fertility would then depend on the biological conditions and sociological practices stressed by scholars in those two disciplines. A similar outcome would occur even in situations where parents anticipated the likelihood of producing unwanted children, if the subjective drawbacks or monetary costs of fertility restriction outweighed the disadvantages of unwanted children.

These circumstances, leading rationally to an absence of deliberate fertility control at the household level, seem, in fact, to be fostered by conditions in early modern and premodern societies. Infant and child mortality has typically been very high, thus creating doubts that parents will be able to have as many surviving children as they want. And even if parents are motivated to restrict fertility, available methods tend to be limited and are often perceived to have high subjective drawbacks, as, for example, in the case of abstinence. Thus with only a modest modification in the usual economic framework, one admits the possibility of cases of fertility determination in which demand factors are not the cause of fertility variation. These cases are likely to be of substantial empirical importance, especially in premodern and early modern societies, and understanding of them can be significantly enhanced by incorporating in economic models the wealth of sociological and biological research on fertility in such societies.

So far I have dealt with expansion of the economists' model to encompass situations where fertility is unregulated by the individual household. (As mentioned, this does not preclude "social controls" that limit fertility, although they are not usually practiced by individuals with that end in view.) What about the economists' assumption of constant tastes? This assumption is not essential to the economists' framework, although it is sometimes vigorously defended (Keeley, 1975; Stigler and Becker, 1977). The economist's concern here is to avoid the trap so perceptively described by sociologist Kingsley Davis:

> Understanding... has been hindered... by an interpretation of demographic behavior as a response... to some cultural idiosyncrasy such as a particular "value system" or "custom."... Curiously, we do not adopt such an easy way out with respect to mortality. We do not "explain" India's high death rate and Sweden's low death rate by saying that one "values" high mortality and the other low mortality. Yet we sometimes come perilously close to this in regard to other aspects of human demography, especially fertility (Davis, 1963).

Davis' concern is with the use for explanation of "values" (or attitudes or preferences) as an empirically unobservable, and thus untestable, residual—in effect, as a semantic escape from one's ignorance. But values or attitudes are readily handled in an economic framework through varying the form of preference maps or indifference curves. Examples of economists who have worked along these lines are Ronald Lee (1977), Harvey Leibenstein (1974), Peter Lindert (1977), Michael Wachter (1975), and myself (Easterlin, 1973). A central feature of such work is that "tastes" are treated not as a residual, but as an element in fertility determination that is itself systematically formed through observable processes. For example, the studies by Wachter and myself see the post–World War II American fertility swing as the product of the tension between a typical couple's material aspirations (their tastes) and their resources—what might be termed the "relative affluence" of the couple. If a couple's resources are abundant relative to their aspirations, they will feel freer to have children. If their resources are scarce relative to aspirations, they will be hesitant about having children. In assessing resources I use a measure that seeks to capture the earnings outlook for young adult males. For material aspirations I use the income situation in the young adults' families of orientation, specifically, their parents' families when they were growing up, on the theory that the period of adolescent development is critical in the formation of the material aspirations of young adults. This model, combining a resource constraint with a taste or "aspirations" variable, both of which are observable, tracks quite well both the upsurge and subsequent decline in American fertility. Note that in this model there is adopted a view that is highly compatible with sociology, namely, that tastes are formed by one's economic socialization experience, and differences among cohorts in that experience will alter tastes and thereby behavior. This example illustrates the manner in which sociological research on attitude formation can be readily incorporated in an economic model. In fact, the problem in this area, as I see it, is not one of reconciling sociologists' concerns with economists', but the need for more *empirical* research by both sociologists and economists on the factors that shape attitudes and values.

To this point I have tried to identify what I feel are the two critical features of most economic models of fertility that cause sociologists and biologists to pull back from adopting the economists' approach, and justifiably so, in my view. These features are a view of fertility as entirely a matter of deliberate choice by parents and an assumption that attitudes or "tastes" are unvarying. I have also indicated that these shortcomings are not inevitable, and that an economic framework can be expanded to encompass the concerns of sociologists and biologists.

But why should sociologists and biologists bother with an economic framework, expanded or otherwise? I have dwelt so much on the shortcomings of the present economic model of fertility that there may seem to be little advantage at all to adopting the approach. A few words are perhaps in order, therefore, on some of the contributions that have resulted from application to fertility problems of the economic theory of household choice. I shall focus here on conceptual matters relating to the demand for children, and briefly, since these points have been elaborated elsewhere (Easterlin, 1969).

First, economic analysis has reduced the conceptual confusion between cost of children and expenditures per child. As with many economic goods, rising income may promote the acquisition of both greater quantity (more children) and higher quality (greater expenditures per child). A rise in expenditures per child due to higher incomes does not imply cost pressures for reducing the number of children, any more than a rise in expenditures per car, due, say, to a shift as income goes up from a Ford to a Lincoln, justifies inferring that fewer cars will be purchased. Second—a contribution that is attributable especially to research stemming from Gary S. Becker's work—economic theory has led to more explicit recognition both of the competition between children and economic goods for the time of the father and mother and of the value of that time to each parent. In so doing, it has provided a more informed view of the cost of children (cf. Becker, 1965; Mincer, 1963; Lindert, 1977). Third, economic analysis has clarified the nature of the resource constraint relevant to fertility decisions. Due in part to the work just mentioned, there has been increasing recognition that the appropriate income concept is one of "full" or "potential" income that takes account of the time resources of the household. A practical consequence of this has been recognition that observations on total family income may be less pertinent to explaining fertility decisions than measures that better approximate the household's earning potential. For wives (some of whom are not even in the labor force), differences in their observed contributions to family income are a much poorer indicator of differences in their earnings potential than for husbands. Hence measures relating to husband's income alone or to education of the spouses may better approximate variations in the earnings potential of households than does family income, a measure that includes the wife's observed, but not potential, earnings. Finally, partly as a result of refining concepts such as income and cost, economics has clarified causal interrelations. But better understanding of causality has not depended entirely on better concepts. For example, few economists would speak of lower fertility "causing" higher female labor-force participation, or vice versa; rather, economic theory leads to a view of both magnitudes as simultaneously determined by other factors.

These, then, are some of the contributions that have so far resulted from applications of the economic theory of household choice to fertility behavior—greater conceptual clarity and thereby more meaningful measurement of presumptive determinants of behavior such as "costs" and "income" or "resources," and better perception of the causal nexus surrounding fertility behavior. What tends to be left out of the theory as it now stands is the production side of fertility behavior and, on the demand side, systematic attention to preferences. These omissions have substantially limited the empirical relevance of the theory so far. As I have indicated, however, these shortcomings are not inherent in an economic framework, and with relatively modest effort that framework can be expanded to take account of such factors, traditionally the concerns of biologists and sociologists. The result, I feel, would be an approach that is analytically more powerful than that based on any one discipline alone. Moreover, it offers the possibility of cooperative rather than competitive research on fertility.

VII

The Social Sciences and Public Policy

27

Introduction

The Editors

IN THE FACE OF INCREASINGLY complex and intractable societal problems, the social sciences have been called upon to lend their theories, methods, and findings to governmental efforts to improve social and economic conditions. While issues bearing on public policy have appeared repeatedly throughout the book, the four papers in this part address directly the actual and potential policy contributions of the social sciences. Among the important questions raised are: To what extent and in what ways have social science perspectives and findings been used in public policy? Are there neglected yet promising ways in which they can be used? How successful have the social sciences been when they have influenced the direction of public policy?

A common theme in the first two papers is that an aging population, growing age segregation, and structural changes in the family have strained the viability of existing support systems. In view of this situation, Professor Maddox suggests that a potential sociological contribution to public policy lies in its distinctive concern with social change. Arguing that there is a mismatch between the organization of helping resources and services and the needs of an aging population, he notes that sociologists are in a unique position to indicate directions for "guided social change" so as to redress this imbalance. His description of a longitudinal project designed to evaluate the impact of service utilization on functional status serves as a useful illustration. Professor Hareven's focus is on the family and on policy implications that follow from a historical perspective. Her careful review of structural and transitional changes in the family leads her to conclude that policy must recognize the varying needs of successive cohorts of older persons with differing life course experiences. She also points out how the examination of historical changes in intergenerational relations can provide guidelines as to which types of supportive programs are best offered by the public sector and which can remain within the province of the family.

Professor Pelz addresses the basic issue of the actual use of social science findings and perspectives in formulating public policy. He proposes that our common notion of utilization may be too narrow, and he provides several illustrations of how both "hard" and "soft" knowledge have been used instrumentally, conceptually, and symbolically. Based on this expanded perspective, it seems reasonable to conclude that social scientists may be greatly underestimating their impact.

In contrast, Professor Adams acknowledges some of the contributions of economics to public policy (see also Wilensky's paper in this volume, chap. 8, and Heller, 1975), but he argues that theoretical deficiencies and methodological limitations have severely hampered economists in their efforts to provide useful input. His discussion focuses on the neglect of power relationships and the growing preoccupation with methodology as the two major obstacles to the more effective application of economics to public policy.

As a set, then, these papers provide excellent illustrations of both the limits and the potential contributions of the social sciences to public policy and challenge us to consider some long-standing assumptions about their actual role in policy formulation.

28

Sociology, Aging, and Guided Social Change: Relating Alternative Organization of Helping Resources to Well-Being

George L. Maddox

THIS PAPER IS ABOUT two topics that sociologists have neglected—aging and social policy—and about the probability that neglect will be replaced by sustained interest. The forecast appears to be favorable. This is so because the observed neglect does not stem primarily from indifference or from failure to perceive the significance of the issues involved but from some modifiable and changing characteristics of the discipline. Sociologists have experienced prolonged identity crises in recent decades. They have wondered publicly about whether they are scholars or professionals, whether all sociology is really social psychology, about whether they can or should be value free, and about the utility of their theory, the adequacy of their methodology, and the relevance of their conclusions. Sociologists may have been well advised to avoid issues like aging and social policy. The multidisciplinary perspectives characteristically associated with the study of aging, social policy, and worse, the combination of aging as an issue in social policy, challenged a discipline concerned about its identity. Sociologists, when compared with other behavioral and social scientists, have done remarkably little reality testing in trying their hand at systematic research on aging or at evaluation research related to policy. Identity diffusion in sociology, this paper argues, is a state and not a trait. Some reality testing in research on aging, in policy research, and, specifically, in policy research related to guiding societal change triggered by transformations of age distributions will be very beneficial. A particular incentive for stimulating sociological

323

interest in both aging and social policy will surely be the discovery that these topics provide excellent opportunities for the study of social change, a societally important and distinctly sociological concern. This presentation will review briefly why aging, which is a relatively high-priority social issue, and social-policy research on alternatives in guiding change in an aging society are increasingly likely to attract sociologists. The optimistic conclusion drawn from this review will be followed by a description of ongoing multidisciplinary policy research that illustrates the problems and potential of quasi experiments in guided social change as a promising point of departure for a sociology of aging.

The Challenge of an Aging Society

Longevity as a common experience in larger populations is a distinctly modern achievement. The social implications of this achievement and the societal implications of a changing age structure have not escaped the attention of sociologists. The current 10 percent of the U.S. population who are categorized as older is double the proportion at the beginning of this century. The older population continues to grow at a higher rate than any other age category; if zero population growth is achieved or approximated, an estimated 16 percent of the U.S. population will be sixty-five or older in the first quarter of the next century. One-third of this population category will be seventy-five years of age and over (Siegel and O'Leary, 1973). These changes have important social implications. A rapidly aging population challenges existing institutional arrangements in palpable and occasionally dramatic ways. For example, the basic mechanism for income maintenance in late life, social security, initially did not envision so many individuals living so long after retirement. Since the system is designed for instant transfer of funds from persons in the workforce to those who have retired, the changing ratio of workers to nonworkers inevitably escalates the cost of the system to current workers (Kreps et al., 1976). Health-care arrangements that have emphasized specialized acute care in institutions are poorly adapted to caring for the characteristic chronic disability of late life; older persons utilize health-care resources at a rate approximately two and one-half times that of other adults, and current concern about the high cost of care logically focuses particularly on the very high cost of caring for older persons (Shanas and Maddox, 1976; D. W. Anderson, 1976). Over a million long-term-care beds are occupied by debilitating older persons at an annual cost of approximately ten billion dollars; additional thousands of older persons occupy acute- and chronic-care hospital beds. These facts have generated considerable discussion of "alternatives to institutionalization" not only because there is uncertainty about the appropriateness and outcomes of the care but also because of the certainty of the very high cost. The hope that more older persons can be cared for in the community is predicated on the debatable assumption that communities will develop adequate programs for delivering home care and that families and friends can and will continue to be willing to commit private resources for the necessary care. Our social preference for the private automobile as the principal mode of transportation, coupled with a preference for centralized health and welfare services, disadvantages older persons substantially, particularly if they live in suburbs or rural areas (Comptroller General, 1977). Our educational institutions are designed primarily for the young. With minimal sense of incongruity we give "terminal degrees" to very young people, consider continuing education an afterthought, and permit professional schools to devote little or no attention to the implications of an aging society (Butler, 1976).

An aging population and the mismatch of the characteristics of aging persons with existing institutional arrangements could not have escaped the attention of the scientific community. Demographers, in fact, were forecasting socially consequential changes in population composition in the 1920s. Scientific articles on aging began to appear in a wide variety of journals, including sociological ones, in the 1930s. In 1946 the Gerontological Society was founded, in the 1950s a number of academic institutions began systematic research on aging and the aged, and in the last quarter of a century three major sets of handbooks on aging have summarized a substantial amount of research on the biological, psychological, and social scientific aspects of development in the later years (see Maddox and Wiley, 1976). Three White House Conferences on Aging and ten international congresses have been convened. The National Institute on Aging was chartered within the National Institutes of Health in 1974. Yet the systematic study of aging has to a surprising degree remained marginal to the principal interests of established scientific disciplines, particularly sociology. Why so?

Modifiable and Changing Sources of Neglect

A convenient explanation of the observed neglect is that sociologists go where the money is and aging has not, until recently, received much financial support. There is surely a kernel of truth in this cynical wisdom. One can detect some stirring among academics as resources for the study of aging have increased. But funding is, in my estimation, relatively less important in explaining the neglect than two other factors—

the common perception that aging is properly a multidisciplinary enterprise with a strong emphasis on intervention, hence issues of social policy, and that the theoretical and methodological capabilities of sociology as a discipline are not well suited for such intellectual enterprises.

For more than three decades academics from a variety of disciplines have discussed inconclusively the merits of a new discipline, gerontology. A gerontological movement that tended to be aggressively interdisciplinary and to focus on applications of knowledge to the social problems of an aging society generated its own professional societies, journals, and university centers. While not antithetical to disciplinary studies of adult development and aging, the gerontological movement clearly intended to proceed on its own terms.

This emphasis on multidisciplinary problem solving ran counter to the interests of most established academic disciplines in maintaining neat boundaries, in limiting the range of their theoretical paradigms, and in avoiding, if possible, ideological confrontation. Sociology was no exception, as illustrated in a recent volume on sociology and social policy (Demerath, Larsen, and Schuessler, 1975). Sociologists have been quite willing to let other behavioral and social scientists test the potential and limits of applying research to policy formation (see Struening and Guttentag, 1975; Guttentag and Struening, 1975).

Aging, social policy issues in general, and social policy issues specifically related to an aging population do not reduce easily to the intellectual domain of any single academic discipline; there are not many significant problems in any of these areas for sociology to claim exclusively. Moreover, sociology has been handicapped in investigating issues related to aging by both its theory and methodology. Sociologists have used the variable *age* in a relatively mechanical, atheoretical fashion, have given little attention to the process of human development over the life course, and have only recently begun to explore the ways and means to untangle the complex interaction among the variables *age, time of measurement,* and *cohort* (Maddox and Wiley, 1976; Riley, Johnson, and Foner, 1972).

In sum, the multidisciplinary perspective that has characterized the development of gerontology has been uncongenial to a sociology uncertain of its theory, methodology, instrument development, and capacity for generating data appropriate to addressing the issues posed by an aging society. These circumstances have insured minimal interest in both aging and in social policy research on aging. An increasing interest in a sociology of age may, however, be confidently predicted as sociological theory and methodology mature and as a more relaxed discipline does some reality testing of its capacity to advance its legitimate theoretical and methodological interests through research on aging. A key to such developments will be the perception that the aging of society provides an excellent opportunity to study social change, a distinctly sociological concern with which the discipline's theory, methodology, and data bases are increasingly able to cope.

Aging, Social Change, and Social Policy

The significance of aging as a basic issue in the study of social change, and by implication guided social change, has been discussed by Riley, Johnson, and Foner (1972). These authors have laid out the elements in a model of age stratification that stresses the dynamic relationship between the age composition of a society and the allocation of societal resources. In this model, changes in age composition clearly have potential for challenging existing institutional arrangements and the related allocation of societal rewards. Hernes (1976) has elaborated a similar argument, which is summarized in figure 1. In Hernes' dynamic model, macrolevel variables (the structure, opportunity, resources, population characteristics) interact in complex ways with microlevel variables (the properties of actors and their behavior) to produce structural stability and change. Several observations will indicate the relevance of the insights of Riley and her colleagues and of Hernes' paradigm for the illustration of research on aging, and the relationship of alternative organization of helping resources to the well-being of older people with which this presentation will conclude. The problem addressed in this

Figure 1. The Relationship Between Microlevel and Macrolevel

MICROLEVEL		MACROLEVEL
Properties of Actors		*Collective level*
1. Preferences	Incentives, constraints	1. Institutions
2. Capacities	alternatives	2. Reward structure
3. Expectations		
		Material Conditions Aggregations
Behavioral Assumptions		1. Frequencies
1. Optimizing	Action	2. Averages
2. Results—controlled action	choices	3. Variance
		4. Distributions

SOURCE: Hernes (1976).

illustration is timely because the tension currently being generated by the mismatch between the health and welfare needs of older people and existing structure of helping resources is acute. First, observed distributions of well-being in a population are to some degree a function of both age composition and the organization of helping resources (Hernes' aggregations). Second, mismatch between the organization of resources (institutions/rewards structure) perceived to be relevant to well-being (the properties and preferences of actors) might be expected, at least in the United States, to lead to a consideration of alternative arrangements of resources intended to insure or enhance well-being (optimizing, results—controlled action) in the interest of moving the indicators of the well-being of the population in a preferred direction. While we might be interested in the political behavior of the population in correcting a perceived mismatch, we have chosen to concentrate on the behavior of those responsible for managing societal resources.

Sociologists, therefore, might be expected to be particularly interested in opportunities to study the relationships among aging, population change, social change, and the social policy implications suggested by Hernes' paradigm, whether or not they had a disciplinary interest in aging and the aged per se. Such an opportunity is provided, in my estimation, by sociological research intended to inform managers of social programs about alternatives for guiding social change. The scientific maxim, "If one wishes to understand a phenomenon, try to change it," is particularly apt here for those interested in research on guided social change. This is not intended as a recommendation for random social experimentation in the interest of studying social change; this is neither a realistic nor a probable option for sociologists. Rather, as Donald Campbell has argued in his well-known 1969 paper on reforms as experiments (1975b, reprinted), we live in a society in which social experimentation takes place routinely, occasionally on a very large scale (e.g., Haveman and Watts, 1976; Rivlin, 1971). Campbell makes clear his understanding of the acute problems of internal and external validity that plague policy research. But he argues persuasively that most of the basic problems that beset policy research beset social scientific research generally. Under certain conditions quasi-experimental research that is useful for evaluating policy options is possible. As Campbell notes, this is most likely to happen when it is commissioned by "experimentally oriented" managers who are interested in alternative policy options in a broad area of social concern rather than in the evaluation of specific programs to which a political commitment has already been made. An instance of such a favorable circumstance follows. This illustration of a quasi experiment that is relevant to an understanding of guided social change in an area of social significance can be reported only in part because it is in process. But its objectives, essential components, and potential can be described.

Aging, Well-Being, and Alternative Organization of Helping Resources

A federal agency concerned with the high cost of institutionalizing older people asked the Duke Center for the Study of Aging and Human Development to conceptualize the issue and propose research that would generate relevant data on whether and how alternative structuring of helping resources affects the well-being of older persons. In time, the U.S. General Accounting Office received a similar inquiry from the Congress and joined the Duke Center in attempting to respond in a useful way. The occasion for the question were indications at the macrolevel that existing organizations of helping (i.e., health and welfare) resources intended to stabilize or improve the distribution of well-being of the elderly population did not appear to be producing the desired result. Moreover, the existing structure of helping resources appeared to be inconsistent with the microlevel preferences, capabilities, and expectations of that population as expressed in political behavior and by key governmental program managers in their inquiry to us. The questions seemed to be socially important and amenable, to some degree, to sociological analysis, although obviously not totally reducible to a problem that could be addressed by sociologists alone.

Conceptualization of a quasi-experimental research design that would permit the assessment of the impact of alternative organization of helping resources is detailed elsewhere (Maddox, 1972; Pfeiffer, 1975). In brief, the essential elements of the design included both microlevel and macrolevel components recognizably related to Hernes' paradigm for the study of social change (figure 1): (1) a multidimensional classification of the functional status of individuals, a microlevel construct conceptualized equally well as an index of impairment or, conversely, of well-being; and (2) the specification of alternative configurations of service interventions, a macrolevel construct conceptualized as combinations of activities intended to decrease functional impairment and increase well-being. The third essential element of the design was a transition matrix in which individuals of equivalent status exposed to specified interventions could be observed to remain stable or change over time (figure 2). The ultimate objective of the research was to identify the impact of existing options for delivering helping resources on the well-being of older persons. Could suboptimal strategies, either existing or potential, be identified?

The quasi-experimental design we proposed required longitudinal observation of defined populations demonstrably exposed to specified service interventions. The practical problems of implementing such a design cannot possibly be overestimated. The rarity in sociology of data sets that simultaneously provide both microlevel and macrolevel data on defined populations reflects the magnitude of these problems.

Figure 2.   Illustrative Transition Matrix for a Defined Population with a Known
Distribution of Functional States Exposed to Specified Configurations
of Helping Services

Effect of Service Configuration K

Functional Status Class T_2

	1	2	3	.	.	.	.	.	.	n
1										
2										
3										
Functional Status Class T_1 .										
.										
.										
n										

Functional status, conceptualized following Fanshel and Bush (1970), focused on the essential capacity of individuals to perform social roles within an expectable range. This conceptualization is recognizable to the sociologist; so are the technical aspects of developing instruments to measure such a construct. But appropriate measurement of functional status necessarily involves recognition of important substantive components usually considered outside the sociological domain, components such as physical and mental health or the capacity for self-care. The specific components contributing to functional status that were to be measured included social network resources, economic resources, mental health, physical health, and the capacity for the activities of daily living. The emphasis on the multidimensionality of functional status (or well-being) parallels the conceptualization of well-being by Campbell, Converse, and Rodgers (1976), but with an important difference. These authors focused on self-reported, perceived satisfaction, in contrast to our emphasis on the reliably and validly assessed information about the availability of a supportive social network; mobilizable economic resources; cognitive and emotional deficit; physical debility; and limitations in the capacity for self-responsibility. We agree with Campbell and his colleagues that, in order for summary information about well-being to be useful for planning, identification of the specific components that affect the summary indicator is crucial.

Extensive pretesting produced a thirty-five-minute segment of a longer interview schedule that could be administered in both clinical and community settings and could produce reliable and valid classification of individuals. Functional status was recorded on a six-point scale for each of the five dimensions (Fillenbaum, 1975). Functional status could be indexed by either the summation of impairment estimated on each dimension (a Cumulative Impairment Score) or by the derivation of individuals with the same patterns of impairments on each of the five dimensions (equivalency classes), ranging from no impairment on any combination of dimensions.

Both types of summary measure are now available for two probability samples of older persons and will be described below. Before this is done, two caveats are in order. The first involves a practical issue in data reduction. From the perspective of policy analysis it is useful to identify the configurations that underlie a summary index of well-being; this point has been effectively argued by Campbell, Converse, and Rodgers (1976). How much detail is possible and how much is useful? In the case described here, development of the six-point scale for each dimension in order to identify equivalency classes would generate 7,776 (6^5) classes, a trichotomy (unimpaired/mildly impaired/severely impaired) would generate 243 (3^5), and a dichotomy (impaired/unimpaired) would generate a more manageable 32 (2^5). In the two populations studied ($n = 998$ and 1,609), individuals are found empirically in each of 32 equivalency classes but less than half of the 243 classes. The latter option is rather clearly the outside limit of useful differentiation.

The second caveat is especially relevant to concerns of sociologists about valuation and ideological bias in policy research. If one arrays a population either in terms of a Cumulative Impairment Score or in terms of equivalency classes, the array invites the consideration of social preferences about the distribution of functional states. If a manager's choice were simply between a state of well-being or its absence, his preference would be obvious and not significant. The problem is always more complex than this and preferences for various degrees of well-being or the factors that produce well-being are required. The initial issue for the sociological research investigator as well as a manager, however, would not be a determination of personal preference. The initial task would be an identification of options, a recognition that preferences are ultimately involved in resource allocation, and acceptance of the fact that specifying social preferences about resource allocation is inevitably and appropriately a political process. Confusion between personal preference and social preference is neither necessary nor inevitable for the research investigator and is in no way formally implied by an array of variously impaired individuals.

With the first element of the design in place, attention was directed next to the macrolevel variable—the specification of alternative interventions intended to ameliorate functional impairment or well-being status. Again with reference to figure 1, interest concentrated on characterizing observed patterns of resource allocation related to health and welfare, not on the full range of institutional arrangements that might affect individuals exposed to them within a defined period. If such information were available, the basic research question can be addressed straightforwardly: What is the impact on well-being measured at Time 2 of known types, configurations, and quantities of services on an exposed population whose well-being (functional status) is known at Time 1? Classifying and measuring services was, as expected, a difficult task. A standard classification of health and welfare services does not exist in the sociological literature; no acceptable classification was found in the literature of any discipline. The absence of a classificatory scheme reflects the fact that health and welfare services tend to be described most frequently in broad terms of where the service is offered (a hospital, nursing home, or clinic) or by whom (a physician, a nurse, a social worker); moreover, quantification of amount of service given is not standardized. The strategy of measurement adopted was to disaggregate services into generic components that depended to a minimal degree on where the service is offered and by whom. Identification of configurations of services (service packages) and quantification of intensity of exposure were treated as an empirical matter involving the judgments of a wide range of experienced clinicians. The outcome was the twenty-five generic services summarized in Table 1.

This list of generic service components has been validated as, for all practical purposes, exhaustive in the experience of more than one hundred health and welfare agencies serving older persons in Durham, North Carolina, and in Cleveland, Ohio. Additionally, practical consensus has been reached on the basic quantitative units in which these services are offered, permitting both counting and costing (Pfeiffer, 1975; Comptroller General of the United States, 1977). Since reports of services received or perceived to be needed, as distinct from agency records, were desirable, this information was gathered in a social survey interview that requires thirty-five minutes to complete. With the first two elements in the design specified and measurable, consideration of the third element—the transition matrix—is possible and is now in process in Cleveland, Ohio. The initial intention was to develop comparable studies in Durham, North Carolina, and Cleveland, Ohio, but this proved to be impossible for reasons noted below.

Probability samples of persons sixty-five years of age and older were surveyed in Durham in 1973 ($n = 998$) and in Cleveland in 1976 ($n = 1,609$) to determine functional status. Demographic characteristics of these samples appear in table 2. The match between the two populations is reasonably good, although Cleveland has a relatively larger population

T A B L E 1. Generic Components of Helping Services

A. Basic Maintenance Components
1. Living quarters
2. Unprepared foodstuffs
3. Transportation
4. Financial assistance

B. Supportive Care Components
5. Personal care
6. Periodic checking
7. Continuous supervision
8. Meal preparation
9. Homemaker services
10. Legal and protective services
11. Social and recreation activity
12. Employment assistance
13. Education: employment related/ other
14. Coordination of care

C. Remedial Care Components
15. Comprehensive assessment of function
16. Sheltered employment
17. Retraining: job related/other
18. Physical therapy
19. Prostheses
20. Residential relocation
21. Medical care
22. Drug therapy
23. Nursing care
24. General counseling: individual/ family
25. Psychiatric care

SOURCE: Comptroller General of the United States (1977).

NOTE: Each component is specified in terms of objective, range of usual providers, and standard unit of amount of care delivered.

T A B L E 2. Demographic Characteristics of Two Probability Samples of Persons 65 and Over

	CLEVELAND SAMPLE (1976)	DURHAM SAMPLE (1973)
	Percent	
Sex		
Male	38	37
Female	62	63
Age		
65–74	59	68
75 and older	41	32
Race		
White	74	66
Black	26	34
Marital Status		
Single	7	5
Married	40	44
Widowed	46	46
Divorced or separated	7	5
	$n = 1,609$	$n = 998$

TABLE 3. Distribution of Functional Status in Two Populations on Five Dimensions

RATING	SOCIAL		ECONOMIC		MENTAL HEALTH		PHYSICAL HEALTH		ACTIVITIES OF DAILY LIVING	
	Cleveland	Durham	Cleveland	Durham	Cleveland	Durham	Cleveland	Durham	Cleveland	Durham
Excellent or good	70	73	52	44	68	64	41	43	64	64
Mildly or moderately impaired	25	24	46	54	28	32	53	47	30	27
Severely or completely impaired	5	3	2	2	2	4	4	5	9	10

SOURCE: Durham, see Pfeiffer (1975); Cleveland, see Comptroller General of the United States (1977).
NOTE: Excellent/good is equivalent to 1 or 2 on the uniform 6 point scale; mild or moderate impairment, 3 or 4; severe impairment, 5 or 6.

of very old persons and Durham a relatively larger proportion of blacks. With the exception of economic status, the two samples are quite similar in the proportion who are not impaired, moderately impaired, and severely impaired. The distributions are summarized in terms of equivalency classes (table 3) and in terms of the Cumulative Impairment Score (table 4). Tables 3 and 4 make several important substantive points about the distribution of well-being among older persons that are frequently overlooked: (1) a substantial majority are free from severe, debilitating

TABLE 4. Distribution of Cumulative Impairments Scores in Two Populations (Percentages)

CIS*	DURHAM		CLEVELAND	
5	2.4%		1%	
6	5.1		3	
7	6.2		4	
8	7.8		4	
9	8.8		7	
10	8.8		11	
11	8.6		13	
12	7.5		12	
13	8.8		11	
14	8.4		8	
15	6.9		7	
16	4.6		6	
17	4.3	88%	4	91%
18	3.6		3	
19	2.6		3	
20	2.3		1	
21	1.0		1	
22	1.1		1	
23	.05		0	
24	.02		0	
25	.01		0	
26	0		0	
27	.01		0	
28	0		0	
29	0		0	
30	0	12%	0	9%
	n = 998		*n* = 1,609	

SOURCE: Comptroller General of the United States (1977).
*The sum of scores on six-point scales for five dimensions of functional status; 1 = no impairment, 6 = severe impairment.

impairments of functional capability; and (2) there is substantial variability in functional capacity among older persons. In analysis not shown, for instance, well-being is, as expected, negatively correlated with chronological age, but the correlation is a modest .26.

While a pretest of the instrument to document generic services was possible in Durham and established the feasibility of the procedure, implementation of a full-scale survey of services provided in all health and welfare agencies serving the defined samples foundered on a combination of the practical issue of incentives for the helping agencies and the legal issue of confidentiality of records. Both these issues have proved to be surmountable in Cleveland. The U.S. General Accounting Office in Cleveland, with a mandate from the Congress to apply the design outlined above, has just completed a systematic analysis of the services, defined in standard generic components, offered to each individual in the defined population by 118 social agencies during a twelve-month period following an initial determination of functional status. Additionally, Cleveland GAO has merged in the same data file detailed Medicare, Medicaid, and Veterans Administration records of health-care utilization for each person in the defined population. This data file includes a rare combination of microlevel and macrolevel information. With reinterviewing to determine Time 2 functional status of the Cleveland sample completed in the summer of 1977, systematic analysis of the transition matrix is now feasible and is currently underway.

While the full potential of this merging of microlevel and macrolevel data lies in the immediate future, even the preliminary descriptive data from Cleveland provide some tantalizing information about the distribution and use of services. For example, the use of generic definition of services facilitates documentation of extensive duplication of services in agencies serving the same geographic areas, the mismatch between the concentrations of agencies in space, and the spatial concentration of persons whose relatively high functional impairment is demonstrable. In Cleveland social service capability is located in the central city, for instance, in spite of the fact that large numbers of impaired, low-income older persons are demonstrably located in suburban areas. Moreover, large numbers of impaired elderly persons who are eligible for various health and welfare services and whose impairment is documented demonstrably do not use them. For instance, less than half the eligible elderly persons in the sample were using food stamps and supplemental Security Income programs, and there was no record that 29 percent of the eligibles who are medically impaired had used Medicaid. Moreover, the interview schedule secured information from individuals and reliable informants about services being received from family and friends as well as information from agency records. When the total amount of welfare services utilized by the elderly sample in Cleveland during one year was calculated, 80 percent of those services were found to be generated by family and friends, 20 percent by public and private welfare agencies.

The juxtapositioning of measured well-being (impairment ratings) and documented exposure to various combinations of services quantified in standard terms meets the essential conditions of a quasi experiment that permits controlled comparison. The comparisons can be simple (the impact of any service intervention on functional status or well-being) or complex (the impact of quantities of service or various configurations of services). The analysis of the relationship between the existing structure for delivering helping services and the well-being of a defined population is recognizable as an example of program evaluation research, but with an important difference. The research in Cleveland identifies the full range of health and welfare service interventions to which a defined population is exposed, a circumstance rarely achieved in program-evaluation research. This program-evaluation information, in turn, will make possible a more consequential exercise in social policy formulation. What options in the organization of helping resources have the greatest possibility of affecting positively the well-being of older people? The question is a legitimate one for sociologists interested in contributing to the guidelines as well as the understanding of social change. A sociologist's specification of the options and their related probable consequences need not ignore the political process that underlies the determination of social preferences. Investigation of the limits of rationality in decision making is also a legitimate enterprise that can be pursued along with, and not instead of, the policy research described above.

Conclusions

The neglect by sociologists of research on aging and on social policy of relevance for an aging society stems from some modifiable and changing characteristics of the discipline. Theoretical and methodological developments in sociology increase the probability that a sociology of age will become an increasingly attractive area for research. The study of social change, a distinctly sociological problem, provides a particularly important point of departure for future research. The study of social change naturally leads to a consideration of the limits and potential of guided social change and, hence, to policy research. Improving our understanding of how the system of helping services for older persons works, and how it might work more effectively to increase the well-being of these persons, is a consequential societal issue that warrants the best sociology has to offer, and will probably get it.

29

Historical Changes in the Life Course and the Family: Policy Implications

Tamara K. Hareven

THE GROWING CONCERN with old age in our time has tended to focus attention on this stage of life in isolation from the entire life course.[1] Without denying the unique problems of this period of life, it is important to interpret it in a life-course and historical context (Elder, 1978). The recognition of old age as a unique stage of life in the twentieth century is part of a larger historical process involving the emergence of new stages of life and their societal recognition. It is also part of a continuing trend toward age segregation in the family and in the larger society (Hareven, 1976). A historical perspective is useful, therefore, because it sheds some light on long-term developments affecting middle and old age. One of the most important contributions of historical knowledge is its capacity to broaden our understanding of the relationship between individual development and collective behavior of the family unit under changing societal conditions. In this essay I will discuss, first, some of the historical changes in the life course over the past century; second, their relationship to historical changes in the family; and third, the policy implications of such developments.

The timing of life-course transitions has changed significantly in

□ I am indebted to Maltilda Riley for inviting me to participate on the "Life Course" panel and for valuable comments, and to the Center for Population Studies, Harvard University.

[1]The life-course approach, which has been given conceptual coherence by Elder (1975, 1978), has been applied recently to historical data (Hareven, 1978). The collaborative efforts of a number of historians, sociologists, and one demographer have examined the timing of different life-course transitions on a common data set based on late nineteenth-century communities in Massachusetts.

American society over the past two centuries, as have the age configurations of the family unit over the life course of its members (Hareven, 1977; Uhlenberg, 1978). Important changes have also occurred in the synchronization of individual time schedules with the collective timetables of the family unit. Demographic, economic, and cultural factors have combined to account for differences in the timing of such lifecourse transitions as leaving home, entry into and exit from the labor force, marriage, parenthood and postparental stages, and widowhood. An understanding of the nature of these changes is particularly significant in relation to the family's behavior as a collective unit. Because of the familistic character of society in the past, many of the activities that would in our time be considered individual choices were actually tightly meshed with collective family strategies. Under conditions of insecurity, unemployment, migration, and critical life situations, family needs often overpowered individual preferences (Hareven 1975). This change from a familial orientation in the past to a more individualistic orientation in the present is in itself significant for the understanding of discontinuities along the life course and the growing isolation of the elderly in modern society.

As Uhlenberg (1974, 1978) suggests, over the past century several important demographic developments have tended to effect greater uniformity in the life course of American families, and have considerably increased the chances for intact survival of the family unit over the lifetime of its members. As a result of the decline of mortality since the late nineteenth century, there has been a greater chance for children to survive into adulthood, and to grow up with their siblings and with both parents alive. Similarly, women have had a greater chance to survive till adulthood and to fulfill the normatively established script of their family lives, namely, marriage, raising of children jointly with a husband, and survival with husband through the launching stage (Uhlenberg, 1974). For women, these changes, combined with earlier marriage and earlier completion of maternal roles, have meant a more extended period of life without children. At the same time, women's tendency to survive men has resulted in a protracted period of widowhood in later years of life. Men, on the other hand, because of lower life expectancy and a greater tendency to remarry in old age, normally remain married until death (Glick, 1977; Glick and Norton, 1977). Historical investigation of cohorts from 1870 to 1930 has thus shown that an increasing proportion of the population has entered prescribed family roles and, except for divorce, has lived out its life in family units (Uhlenberg, 1974). Contrary to conventional assumptions, there has thus been a growing uniformity in life-course transitions into family roles and survival through the entire family cycle. (The trend in solitary residence since the 1950s suggests a change in this pattern [Kobrin, 1976].)

Given these continuities, why have the middle and later periods of life emerged as problematic? Interestingly, the same demographic factors that are responsible for these continuities have also generated important discontinuities, which have tended to enforce age segregation in American society. These increasing life-course discontinuities over the past century were expressed in the timing of life-course transitions into and out of family roles, and are closely related to the gradual segmentation of the life course into societally acknowledged stages (childhood, youth, adolescence, adulthood, middle age, and old age) (Kett, 1977; Hareven, 1976; Fischer, 1977; Keniston, 1971; Neugarten, 1968). These discontinuities are expressed in the timing of transitions to adulthood, in such areas as family formation and parenthood, entry into the postparental or "empty nest" period, and into old age. Transitions have become more abrupt, rapid, age related, and complex. As Modell, Furstenberg, and Hershberg have shown (1976), over the past century age uniformity in the timing of life-course transitions has been increasingly more marked. By contrast, in the nineteenth century transitions out of the parental home to marriage, to household headship, and to parenthood occurred more gradually and were timed less rigidly. This was expressed in several areas: the time range necessary for a cohort to accomplish such transitions was wider; different transitions (leaving home, marriage, and so on) were not always timed in the same sequence; and there was no consistent congruity among different transitions. Over the past century, transitions to adulthood have become more uniform for the entire population, more rapidly timed, more orderly in sequence, and more definite.

By comparison to the earlier transitions, later transitions such as out of parental roles (the launching of children from the home) have been less uniformly timed. Even in this area there has been an important historical change: The combination of fewer children overall with segregation of childbearing to the early stages of the family cycle and children's leaving home more uniformly earlier in their parents' lives has resulted in a more widespread emergence of the empty nest as a characteristic of middle and old age (Glick, 1977).

In the nineteenth century, later age at marriage, higher fertility, and shorter life expectancy rendered different family configurations from those characterizing contemporary society. These differences were reflected in the following areas: For large families, the parental stage, with children remaining in the household, extended over a longer period of time, sometimes over the parent's entire life. Since children in families were spread along a broad age spectrum, younger children could observe their older siblings and near relatives moving through adolescence and into adulthood. Older siblings in turn trained for adult roles by acting as surrogate parents for younger siblings. Proportionally fewer adults lived alone, in contrast to the emergence of an increasing tendency toward solitary living, especially for women in later years of life (Kobrin, 1976).

In modern society, by contrast, the postparental period comprises one-third or more of the married adult life span (Glick, 1977). Glick concludes that the period of the empty nest has increased over the past eighty years by eleven years (from 1.6 years to 12.3 years): "The couple now entering marriage has the prospect of living together 13 years, or more than one-third of the 44 years of married life that lay ahead of them at the time of marriage" (Glick, 1977:9). Growing sex differentials in mortality above age fifty have made age-structure imbalance and widowhood more important features in women's lives. In this respect, Uhlenberg (1978) has noted that the major change since the late nineteenth century has not been in the emergence of an empty nest as such, but rather in the proportion of a woman's lifetime that this period encompasses. Earlier marriage and earlier completion of childbearing and childrearing on the one hand, and greater survival into older age on the other, have resulted in a higher proportion of a woman's life spent, first, with a husband but without children, and then alone, without either husband or children.

The impact of discontinuities in life-course transitions is further reinforced by increasing discontinuities in labor-force participation. In the nineteenth century entry into and exit from the labor force were only mildly age specific. Children started to work as early as they could, and old men stopped working when they were too old or too feeble to continue. The imposition of compulsory schooling and child labor laws on the one hand, and the introduction of institutionalized retirement on the other, have set clear age boundaries to the work life. These changes not only pushed older people out of the labor force at a specific age, but did so precisely at the point at which their children had already left home, thus depriving them of a familial source of support as well.

The implication of these changes for the middle-aged and the aged are significant: The nineteenth-century patterns of transitions allowed for a wider age spread within the family, and for greater opportunity for interaction among parents and adult children, as well as among other kin. The tendency of children to postpone setting up independent households, or to return to the parental household after marriage, was part of a flexible pattern of family adaptability to insecurity. Family needs and the imperative for exchanges along the life course served as important mechanisms for mutual assistance and for support in old age (M. S. Anderson, 1971). The demographic changes discussed above, combined with the increasing rapidity in the timing of life-course transitions, the increasing separation between an individual's family of orientation and family of procreation, and the introduction of institutionally imposed transitions, have converged to isolate and segregate age groups, with an especially important impact on older people.

Historical Changes in the Family

Recent historical literature has already effectively demolished one of the prevailing explanations for the isolation of the aged in American society, namely, the decline and breakup of traditional extended (especially three-generational) families under the impact of industrialization and urbanization (Laslett and Wall, 1972; Hareven, 1974). The reason for the growing segregation of old people in modern society does not lie, as has been argued, in the breakdown of the "traditional" family. Rather it results from changes in family membership, roles, and expectations, and from changes in the family's interaction with other institutions in the larger society. Along these lines, one of the most important historical developments that has been frequently overlooked is in household membership: namely, the gradual withdrawal of strangers from the family, a process which was almost completed by the late 1930s.

One of the family's most important sources of flexibility and adaptability in the past was the presence of surrogate kin in the household. Boarders and lodgers, mostly in the transitional stage between leaving their family of orientation and setting up their own household, entered exchange relationships with older heads of households, whose own children had left home. The fact that approximately one-fourth to one-third of urban populations in the nineteenth century either boarded with families or took in boarders testifies to the pervasiveness of this practice of economic exchange as a life course and migration phenomenon. Boarding and lodging thus fulfilled the important role of the "social equalization of the family" (Modell and Hareven, 1973). The taking in of strangers into the household met important needs at both stages of the life course: It facilitated transition to independent adulthood (especially where it involved migration) and it provided sources of support and sociability for older heads of households. On the other hand, the withdrawal of strangers from the family in the twentieth century has robbed the family of one of its important sources of fluidity and adaptability to changing economic circumstances.

The second major change in family behavior has been in the nature of kin interaction. The increasing separation between the family of orientation and the family of procreation combined with a growing privatization of the family, and the discontinuities along the life course discussed above all occurred in the context of changes in the quality of kin relations. Prior to the emergence of the welfare state in the twentieth century, family relationships were characterized by a higher degree of kin integration. Kin served as the most essential resource for economic assistance and security and carried the major burden of welfare functions, many of which fall now within the purview of the public sector. Exchange relationships among parents and children and other kin thus provided the major, and sometimes the only, base for security (M. S. Anderson, 1971).

The gradual erosion of instrumental kin relationships has tended to increase insecurity and isolation in old age, especially in areas of need that are not met by public programs. In examining this particular aspect of historical change, it is important to distinguish between kin availability and the nature of kin interaction and support systems. The historical evidence has already shown that the major change did not occur in the decline of coresidence, but rather in the functions that kin fulfilled. Recent historical studies have documented the multiplicity of functions of kin in the nineteenth century, especially their critical role in migration, job placement, and housing (Hareven, 1975, 1978), and in assistance in critical life situations (M. S. Anderson, 1971). Several studies have documented, for nineteenth-century American communities, the tendency of adult children who have left home to locate in the vicinity of their parents during periods of economic crises (Chudacoff, 1978; Chudacoff and Hareven, 1978). These studies suggest that, contrary to prevailing theories, urbanization and industrialization did not break down traditional kinship patterns. There are thus many parallels between the roles of kin in the nineteenth and early twentieth centuries and patterns of kin assistance found by contemporary sociologists in modern American society (Shanas et al., 1968; Sussman, 1976; Litwak, 1960). The difference lies, however, in the degree of integration with kin and the dependence on mutual assistance. While more intensive patterns of kin interaction have survived among first-generation immigrants and working-class families, there has been an overall erosion of instrumental kin relationships and an increasing focus on the nuclear family.

A related development has been the gradual transfer of functions of family welfare, including care for the elderly, to the public sector, a process that culminated in the passage of social security legislation and in subsequent governmental welfare programs. The public institutionalization of care and support of different age groups has drawn firmer boundaries between the family and the community (Bremner, 1956). In American society this shift has generated considerable ambiguity in the expectations for support and assistance for the elderly from their own kin. On the one hand, it is assumed that the welfare state has relieved children from the responsibility of supporting their parents in old age; at the same time, these public measures are not sufficient in the economic area, nor do they provide the kind of support and sociability in areas traditionally provided by the family. It is precisely this ambiguity, and the failure of American society to consummate the historical process of the transfer of functions from the family to the public sector, that is one of the major sources of problems currently confronting old age.

So far this discussion of changes in the timing of life-course transitions and the family has generalized on the entire population. In reality, these historical trends were not experienced uniformly. Different cohorts were affected differently by the changes discussed above (Riley, Johnson, and Foner, 1972). The historical experience of a cohort, particularly its earlier life-course transitions, would seriously affect its adaptability to the conditions it encounters in old age. In addition to variation in socioeconomic factors impinging upon earlier life-course transitions of different cohorts, the following factors affecting the location of cohorts in historical time are of special significance: definitions of age and aging; the availability of institutions outside the family directed toward specific age groups; the nature and pace of transitions into different adult roles; and the emergence of societal regulation governing such transitions (schooling, child labor, and retirement, for example).

Cohorts that experienced erratic and less rigidly age related or institutionalized transitions in earlier life-course stages would respond differently to rigid transitions in old age (such as enforced retirement) from cohorts that entered adulthood through rigidly defined transitions (such as child-labor legislation). Similarly, cohorts that had had no experience with public welfare agencies in early life-course stages would be less adept at interacting with bureaucratic institutions than cohorts that had come of age in the welfare state regime. For example, the first cohort to experience mandatory retirement in the twentieth century would have experienced this discontinuity with greater intensity, since for this cohort sharp discontinuities were absent from earlier stages of the life course (Hareven, 1976).

Policy Implications

One of the most important lessons from history is an understanding of cohort location in historical time. A historical life-course perspective views a cohort not merely as an aggregate of individuals but as an age group moving through history. An understanding of the historical experience of different cohorts could thus help explain their current condition and predict their future needs.

The historical background of life-course transitions of each cohort at earlier stages is relevant to their transition into "old" age. Rather than formulating overall programs for the "aged" and the "elderly," it is important in planning public policy to differentiate among the needs of different cohorts as they are affected by their cumulative life experiences, the pace of their past life-course transitions, and their cultural values. Accordingly, policy planning should be directed not merely toward the specific needs of an age group at one point in time, but also toward subsequent life-course developments and individually initiated changes, such as education, retraining, and housing.

An understanding of the historical model of differentiation between individual choices and the collective needs of the family unit, exemplified most clearly in the growing separation over the past century between one's family of orientation and one's family of procreation, is significant for the development of carefully differentiated programs. One of the important lessons from the historical experience would be that programs directed toward individuals as members of specific *age groups* (the aged, dependent children, unemployed youth) should be differentiated from programs directed toward the entire family unit. The distinction would help public policy discriminate between programs directed specifically to meet the needs of the elderly, for example, and those directed to the family. Thus one would be less likely to run the risk of continuing to reinforce the historical and cultural tendency toward age segregation in American society. While each age group or each stage of the life course requires programs specially oriented toward its characteristic needs, it is also necessary to develop family-oriented programs that strengthen the family as the arena of interaction and socialization of different age groups. A historical perspective could contribute to a more effective balancing of life course–specific individual and family-specific priorities.

Related to the above issue of family policy are changes in the role of kin assistance during critical life situations over the life course (especially during the early stages of the family cycle for child care, and during the later stages for old age). The historical evidence offers a precedent and a comparative model for the understanding of the experience of blacks and newcomers such as Mexicans and Puerto Ricans, whose current family traditions continue or, at times, repeat earlier historical experiences. An understanding of such family traditions and orientations, especially their creative incorporation into policy programs, could render such programs more meaningful and effective.

At the same time, the historical evidence about instrumentality of kin must not be misused in support of proposals to return welfare responsibilities from the public sector to the family without additional support. A careful examination of historical patterns reveals the high price that kin had to pay in order to assist each other in the absence of other forms of societal support. The historical precedent thus offers a warning against romanticizing kin relations, particularly against the attempt to transfer responsibility for children and the elderly back to the family without adequate governmental assistance. Rather than providing justification for such measures, history can provide a model for systematic differentiation between those types of family policy that should remain in the domain of public agencies and those responsibilities that would be best implemented within the province of the family.

30

Some Expanded Perspectives on Use of Social Science in Public Policy

Donald C. Pelz

AMONG WRITERS ABOUT public policy, it has come to be axiomatic that social research in the United States has rarely been applied by public officials at any level. In the introduction to a collection of papers entitled *Using Social Research in Public Policy Making,* Carol Weiss (1977: 5) documents this theme of neglect. For example, a four-volume report by the U.S. House of Representatives Committee on Government Operations (1967) observed that "Existing economic, social and psychological data is rarely utilized in shaping national and local health programs." In the same collection Michael Patton et al. (1977:141) cite a similar consensus among a half-dozen writers regarding the nonutilization or underutilization of evaluation research in social programming.

Some recent investigations, however, suggest that this dismal picture may have arisen from an overly narrow definition of what is meant by social science knowledge and by "utilization" of that knowledge. The thrust of this paper will be to expand the meaning of how social knowledge is defined and used, and to illustrate some of these diverse meanings. In the light of these expanded perspectives, the use of social science knowledge may be more widespread than is generally supposed.

It will be helpful if this discussion is presented in the framework of the matrix of types of knowledge and modes of use shown in figure 1.[1] Definitions of these terms will be taken up as the presentation proceeds. It will be understood that the categories are hardly discrete. In particu-

[1]The first four cells were sketched by Rich and Caplan (1976).

Figure 1. Modes of Knowledge Use

	Type of Knowledge Hard .... Soft	
Mode of utilization		
Instrumental/ engineering	A	B
Conceptual/ enlightenment	C	D
Symbolic/ legitimative	E	F

lar, many distinctions between the extremes of "hard" and "soft" knowledge could be elaborated, as suggested by the dashed lines separating them.

Types of Knowledge: Hard vs. Soft

In a study carried out in 1973–1974 by members of our center, Nathan Caplan and associates (1975) interviewed 204 upper-level officials in nearly all divisions of the U.S. executive branch, to determine ways in which they used social science information in planning policies or programs. Several items obtained self-reported use of social science knowledge, and from these responses a total of 575 instances of use were identified.

In classifying these instances, Caplan and his associates recognized a distinction between two broad types of social science information:[2] *hard* knowledge—"research-based, usually quantitative, and couched in scientific language," and *soft* knowledge—"non-research based, qualitative, and couched in lay language" (Caplan, Morrison, and Stambaugh, 1975: 18). Hard information is illustrated by the content of a technical report or scientific paper—empirical evidence, statistical data, results of scientific experiment or mathematical analysis. Soft information will include general principles and concepts, often expressed in nontechnical language, short phrases, or images.

There is, of course, no sharp demarcation between hard and soft knowledge, but rather a series of gradations. Rigorous research using

[2]For convenience the terms "information" and "knowledge" will be used as roughly interchangeable, although the latter is broader and includes functional relationships and theory in addition to descriptive facts.

meticulously defined measures can generate quantified relationships stated as mathematical functions—all hard types of knowledge. Then as the variables become expressed under popular labels, and as the relationships are translated into loose principles that can be understood by nontechnical audiences, they become softer.

In a preliminary report prepared for an OECD conference on social research and public policies, Caplan (1974: 47) noted that among the 575 examples of knowledge use, 60 percent represented soft information—"basic concepts, general principles, or theory-related ideas (e.g., dissonance reduction, relative deprivation, cultural assimilation)," and 40 percent hard—"more narrowly defined or purpose-specific, usually data-based, information (e.g., program evaluations, the use of psychological tests, statistical rates)."[3]

In addition to the examples coded as utilization for purposes of the study, Caplan found many other illustrations of an even softer character that "really involved the application of secondary-source information, common sense, and social sensitivity, which, as a mixture, might be called a 'social science perspective'" (Caplan, 1974: 53). He observed that how much social science is used in federal decisionmaking depends on how broad a definition of knowledge one employs. "What we have found is that the upper-level decisionmakers who apply the mixture of knowledge that we have called the social science perspective [soft knowledge] far outnumber those who apply the more objective, formalized types of science information as measured in terms of scientific output" [hard knowledge] (p. 53). Furthermore, he found that "this social science perspective . . . appears to play a critical role far more often in upper-level policy decisions than hard 'scientifically' produced information" (p. 54).

On a question regarding major new programs or social policies, over 80 percent of respondents named examples that they felt could be traced to the social sciences—policies such as the all-voluntary army, establishment of the Environmental Protection Agency, revenue sharing, and Head Start. But the decision on whether to undertake these policies was "more likely to depend upon an appraisal of social considerations from the standpoint of the social science perspective" than upon primary source information (p. 55).

An instructive paper by Martin Rein and Donald Schon (1977) gives many illustrations of soft types of knowledge that are useful in policy development. For example, problems will be described within a framework that highlights salient features and ignores others, and binds

---

[3]In this early report Caplan called the two types of information "conceptual" and "instrumental" respectively. In later papers these terms were applied to modes of use (see below) rather than types of knowledge.

them into a "pattern that is coherent and graspable." This process of *framing* is linked to that of *naming;* for example, "the succession of terms, such as *backward, underdeveloped,* and *developing* countries, signifies an underlying frame associated with modernization" (Rein and Schon, 1977: 239). Frames set the stage for allocating blame and proposing remedies. Other illustrations of soft knowledge are the use of *generative metaphors, storytelling, mapping, models,* and *theories.*

Modes of Use: Instrumental vs. Conceptual

Paralleling the distinction between relatively hard and soft types of social science knowledge there emerges a distinction between two contrasting ways in which knowledge is likely to be applied. In a study conducted at the same time as Caplan's, Robert Rich (1975) held repeated interviews with executives in seven federal agencies over an eighteen-month period, to ascertain uses of data generated by the Continuous National Survey (CNS). In this operation, conducted by the National Opinion Research Center (NORC) and funded by the National Science Foundation, national samples were surveyed monthly on critical public issues, with questions tailored by each agency.

In his analysis of the data Rich found it important to differentiate between *instrumental* and *conceptual* utilization—between what he termed "knowledge for action" and "knowledge for understanding." "'Instrumental' use refers to those cases where respondents cited and could document ... the specific way in which the CNS information was being used for decision-making or problem-solving purposes. 'Conceptual' use refers to influencing a policymaker's thinking about an issue without putting information to any specific, documentable use" (Rich, 1977: 200).

Although at first glance it might seem that hard information will be used for an instrumental purpose and soft information for conceptual,[4] it becomes clear that either type of information can be used for either purpose. The instrumental mode deals with a specific decision or action that can be clearly designated, whereas the conceptual mode refers to some change in awareness, thinking, or understanding. In the latter, as stated by Caplan, Morrison, and Stambaugh (1975: 19): "Hard information, past experiences, intuition, values and other considerations all merge to form a frame of reference or perspective within which the social implications of alternative policies of a decision situation are evaluated."

[4]See n. 3, *supra.*

Although Rich and Caplan worked independently, the results of their studies were consistent and supported an interpretation they have elaborated in joint working papers (Caplan and Rich, 1976; Rich and Caplan, 1976). As both authors observed, policy makers found it difficult to identify particular actions or decisions as outputs (instrumental uses) with particular pieces of knowledge as inputs, in a one-to-one matching between input and output. They characterized the shortcomings of such an input/output model (Rich and Caplan, 1976): "First, because knowledge accumulates and builds within organizational memories, some decisions (outputs) are made which seem to be independent of any identifiable, discrete inputs.... Secondly, because knowledge produces [multiple] effects, it is often impossible to trace outputs back to their specific inputs, even when it is possible to identify the universe of informational inputs." They argued that "conceptual uses ... of social science knowledge should not be viewed as failures of policy makers to translate research findings into action," and that other significant functions of knowledge include organizational learning and planning, and the way in which problems are defined.

Superimposing the two types of knowledge on the two modes of use, these authors generated the first four cells of the matrix displayed in figure 1. A traditional perspective on knowledge utilization would focus on cell A in the matrix—that is, hard knowledge is applied in a one-to-one match with a specific action. The investigators observed, however, that this perspective was far from typical in reports of social science use by federal executives. More important was a nontraditional perspective represented in cell D—in which general principles were accumulated through time in a broad framework of understanding about a policy area.

A similar distinction between instrumental and conceptual has been observed by several other researchers. The instrumental use of knowledge is equivalent to what has been called an "engineering" or "technical" or "social-technological" function; the conceptual use of knowledge is equivalent to an "enlightenment" function (see Crawford and Biderman, 1969; Janowitz, 1970; Weiss, 1977; Weiss and Bucuvalas, 1977). The latter investigators observe:

> Thus, the definition of research "use" is broadened. Research that challenges accepted ideas, arrangements, and programs obviously cannot be put to work in a direct and immediate way. It cannot be used instrumentally.... Yet, decisionmakers say it can contribute to their work and the work of other appropriate decisionmakers. It can *enlighten* them (Weiss and Bucuvalas, 1977: 226).

A revealing study on the use of social science by decision makers is reported by Patton *et al.* (1977). For a stratified random sample of twenty program-evaluation studies sponsored by the U.S. Department of Health, Education, and Welfare, detailed interviews were held with decision makers and with evaluators for each study, to find out what impact the studies had had. Questions on impact were broad: effects on program operations, on funding, on policy, and on thinking about the program, as well as on "general thinking on issues that arise from a study, or position papers, or legislation."

The literature on evaluation research gives a pessimistic picture on the extent of its use. In contrast, Patton *et al.* found that fourteen out of eighteen responding decision makers and thirteen out of fourteen responding evaluators felt that the evaluation had indeed had an impact. However, the nature of the impact was different from the conventional meaning of instrumental use:

> Thus, none of the impacts described was of the type where new findings from an evaluation led directly and immediately to the making of major, concrete program decisions [instrumental use]. *The more typical impact was one where the evaluation findings provided additional pieces of information in the difficult puzzle of program action, thereby permitting some reduction in the uncertainty within which any federal decisionmaker inevitably operates* [a form of conceptual use; italics in source] (Patton et al., 1977: 145).

In other words:

> The image that emerges in our interviews is that there are few major, direction-changing decisions in most programming and that evaluation research is used as one piece of information that feeds into a slow, evolutionary process of program development. (Patton et al., 1977: 148)

Third Mode: Symbolic Use

A third broad mode of use may be distinguished from both instrumental and conceptual; Knorr (1977) suggests the term *"symbolic"* use. One aspect may be the use of knowledge as a substitute for decision:

> By initiating, distributing, and publishing a research report, the government official in this case tries to signal to those concerned that something is being done about the problem, while proper decisions and measures that should be taken are postponed or neglected altogether (Knorr, 1977: 171).

A related function is the use of research to legitimate a policy:

> Here the social scientists' data and arguments are used selectively and often distortingly to publicly support a decision that has been taken on different grounds or that simply represents an opinion the decisionmaker already holds (Knorr, 1977: 171).

Weiss (1977) cites additional uses of research that illustrate symbolic or legitimative functions: to provide political ammunition, gain recognition for a successful program, or discredit a disliked policy. She argues that using research to support a predetermined position is neither unimportant nor improper, provided there is no distortion:

> If the issue is still in doubt, what research can do is add strength to the side that the evidence supports. It gives them confidence, removes lingering doubts, and provides an edge in the continuing debate (Weiss, 1977:15).

In the domain of policy making, one suspects that this third mode—symbolic or legitimative use—may in fact be even more prevalent than conceptual use, with instrumental use appearing rarely.

Distinctions among these three uses are, of course, not sharp. There is a shading between instrumental and conceptual uses. If the evidence *persuades* a decision maker to adopt option A rather than B, the use is clearly instrumental. If he has already adopted option B, however, and the evidence *reinforces* his belief in this option, the use is more properly called conceptual.

The demarcation between conceptual and symbolic is also blurred. If information serves to confirm the decision maker's *own judgment* of the situation, we have a conceptual use. If the evidence helps him to justify his position to *someone else*, such as a legislative committee or a public group, the use is symbolic. In symbolic use, also, what may matter is not so much the content of the study as the fact that it was done. By sponsoring the study, regardless of the findings, the agency demonstrates that it is progressive or at least fulfilling its mandate.

Illustrations of Knowledge Use

LOCAL PUBLIC POLICY

The rest of the paper will be given to illustrating these meanings of knowledge and its use, in terms of some current studies at our Center for Research on Utilization of Scientific Knowledge (CRUSK).

My next examples will be drawn from an examination of decisions in local government. Under the sponsorship of the National Science Foundation—RANN program (Research Applied to National Needs), the University of Michigan Biological Station and the Survey Research Center joined forces to collect data on characteristics of inland lakes at the northern tip of Michigan's lower peninsula, the surrounding land, and the local residents, with the objective of using this information to assist decisions affecting the natural environment. CRUSK was involved in developing methods for transmitting this information and in documenting its effects (Pelz, 1977).

The first illustration involves an area of soft knowledge in the natural rather than social sciences—the idea of "wetlands," including marshy areas or solid land with a high water table. Wetlands were once considered the enemy of progress. The pioneers drained the swamps, eradicated malaria, recaptured farmland. Today ecologists recognize that wetlands are a rich habitat for wildlife and a protection against degradation of lakes and streams. The concept of wetlands was frequently included in technical and popular reports of the Biological Station (Pelz, 1977: Appendixes I and II). But wetlands are also eyed by developers; when a marsh is drained or filled and sewered, it becomes valuable residential property.

One tool to control exploitation of wetlands is a zoning ordinance. One township in the study area had a long-standing concern for controlling its population growth. Over several years its leaders had patiently devised a land-use plan with numerous public hearings and incorporation of residents' views; the planning commission then drafted a zoning ordinance (Pelz, 1977: 24–27). The text included a soft piece of knowledge—a definition of wetlands and the need to protect them, which read:

> Natural wetland areas are grown over with grass, and other vegetation which:
>
> —remove nutrients from the waters entering ——— Lake
> —retard the flow of sediment into ——— Lake
> —maintain the established shoreline of ——— Lake
> —encourage the growth of wild plants and animals.
>
> These areas are not suited for general use or habitation by people because preparation for such use requires that the land be dredged, filled, cleared, excavated and drained. These operations destroy the character of natural wetlands and their functions of removing nutrients, retarding sediments, maintaining shoreline, and fostering wildlife, and consequently they lower the quality of the waters.

This passage, then, formed a kind of preamble to the actual regulations. This may be an important way in which soft types of natural or social science find their way into legislation—justifying the purpose or rationale of the action.

In what cell of the knowledge/use matrix does this use fall? I prefer to call it mainly an example of cell D, soft knowledge with a conceptual use; the idea had permeated the thinking of the planning commission so that they incorporated it in their draft. It also provided a symbolic use in cell E, to justify the proposal to the public.

Subsequently the ordinance was approved by the township board in May 1976, and again by public referendum in August. Both of these overt actions illustrate cell B—soft information resulting in an instrumental use.

Another example illustrates the use of hard information, this time in the social survey of residents. In the winter of 1975–1976 the planning commission of one county was examining a proposal by the Department of State Highways to replace existing highways with a limited-access freeway. At public hearings, opposition was expressed. A skeptical chamber of commerce did its own survey of business firms and—perhaps to their surprise—found a slight majority opposing the freeway. At that point data were presented from the Biological Station survey of residents the previous summer: 25 percent favored a freeway, 35 percent wanted to widen existing roads, 40 percent wanted no changes. Given these combined inputs, the planning commission adopted a resolution opposing the freeway. This was a clear example in cell A of the matrix—hard information supporting an instrumental use. Note, however, that the social survey information was only *one of several inputs.* As Rich and Caplan emphasized, it is seldom possible to trace a single decision to a single piece of knowledge in a one-to-one matching between input and output.

AN EXAMPLE OF SYMBOLIC USE

In the late 1960s a series of studies was conducted by the Survey Research Center on national samples of young men of high school age. One set of questions concerned attitudes toward military service, including what enlistment incentives would be effective after ending of the draft (Bachman and Johnston, 1972). Among eleven incentives, the most popular was "four years of college for four years of service." This option was endorsed four-to-one over the next choice of "military pay comparable to civilian pay."

When this finding appeared in 1970, it was apparently ignored by decision makers in the Department of Defense because of its high cost. But in 1977 a congressman cited the finding in support of a similar proposal of his own. The latter example is a symbolic use in cell E of the matrix—hard data used to justify a position already in place, following nonuse by the primary decision makers in cell A. (There may of course have been some conceptual impact on their thinking in cell C, but if so it remains undocumented.)

YOUTH PROGRAM

For several years staff of the Institute for Social Research conducted annual evaluations on the summer camps operated nationwide by the

Youth Conservation Corps (YCC) for young men and women aged fifteen–eighteen, to provide useful service and promote environmental learning (one report is Johnston *et al.,* 1974). Some findings had visible influence on policy. In the first summer, for example, the ratio of males to females was two-to-one, although the data showed that women accomplished and learned as much as men. Citing these data, YCC executives adopted an explicit policy of recruiting equal numbers of women and men—an instrumental use of hard data in cell A.

Another finding was that members who participated more in decisions about camp operations showed more environmental learning. Again an explicit policy was adopted directing camp managers to increase members' participation in decisions about project selection and conduct—another example, apparently, in cell A. How this policy was to be implemented, however, remained a matter of debate—particularly how to reconcile the need for advance planning with the short duration (eight weeks) of the camp. Perhaps there needed to be more conceptual redesign of the program in cells C and D—devising new techniques for operating camps and training managers before a real instrumental use could occur.

A third example illustrates nonuse or at least delayed use. Results from the first year with a before-and-after test of knowledge cast doubt on the amount of environmental learning that occurred. The investigators felt that the test items—directed at a standard national curriculum—often did not reflect the extensive but idiosyncratic learning in local programs, and recommended in 1974 that a single standard test be dropped in favor of local adaptations. This recommendation was ignored, apparently because of administrative needs for scores that could be compared across all camps. Only in 1976 was a process started of recognizing differences in what each camp needed and provided for environmental learning; however, the uniform test continues to be used.

STUDY OF TECHNOLOGY ASSESSMENTS

In another ongoing study, Donald Michael and colleagues are investigating factors that affect the usefulness of the analytical tool called a technology assessment, or TA. A technology assessment seeks to marshal evidence and thinking on the long-range impacts of a given area of technology such as solar energy, offshore energy resources, or electronic transfer of funds. The report tries to document effects in many areas—economic and social as well as technical; it identifies policy options and the potential consequences of each option. The TA draws from hard evidence where available, but much of its content is of a soft character.

In the current project interviews are being held with decision makers and other potential users of TAs to find out what uses have or have not

occurred and why. The following excerpts are culled from early responses and are offered solely to illustrate different kinds of use, with no
conclusion on the prevalence of each.

Mainly Instrumental

Here are two clear examples of instrumental use, in cell B of the
knowledge/use matrix:

> The interview was held just after the respondent had quoted the report
> in testimony he gave for an amendment which entailed one option cited
> in the TA.

> A bill was passed on which the TA was responsible for initiating action. It
> was a thoughtful and in-depth study in which there was a lot of confi-
> dence, and formulated questions for the hearings.

The following comment illustrates a mixture of instrumental and conceptual use—cells B and D of the matrix:

> The TA tended to confirm his perception of what the situation is and
> what needed to be done. It gave confirmation rather than new informa-
> tion. It confirmed [the agency's] perception of the problem and what
> their program activity or role should be.

Mainly Conceptual

The following comment illustrates conceptual use in cell D of the
matrix:

> The TA heavily influenced his cost/benefit analysis in relation to [this
> technology]. It helped him to organize his priorities on policy options . . .
> convinced him that in the area of [energy] storage, a lot had to be done.
> It was useful in solidifying or reinforcing a position already held.

In the following comment, the respondent denied an instrumental effect
but emphasized a conceptual one—cell D of the matrix:

> The TA was not pertinent to what they were *doing* (their work)—i.e., it
> didn't affect their planning. But it was pertinent to their *interests*. It
> solidified their thinking about directions of research in the field.

Mainly Symbolic

The following example illustrates how the existence of the TA had
an effect that must be called symbolic:

> At one time there was a proposal to clamp a moratorium on [this
> technology]. The fact the report existed had the effect of bolstering the
> argument that there would not be a moratorium. The report didn't

change [respondent's] position, which was based on common sense and testimony. The TA as background had some chilling effect on his opponents on the committee, and helped to turn around the decision on the moratorium. The study itself didn't [have an influence], but what did was the fact that some members were aware of the supportive nature of the material contained therein.

Since a specific decision was influenced, one might consider this an instrumental use. But since it was the existence of the TA that mattered more than its content, I prefer to call this use symbolic.

In Summary

A typical conclusion in the literature is that public policy makers have made very little use of social science in their decisions. This view may be due in part to an overly narrow definition of what constitutes "utilization." That concept can be expanded in two ways. First, the type of information may include not only "hard" knowledge in the form of empirical data, but also "soft" knowledge or "social science perspective" in the form of general principles and nontechnical concepts. Second, the modes of utilization may include not only the usual instrumental use in a specific action, but also conceptual use (change in understanding or thinking), and symbolic use (legitimating an existing policy). In terms of these expanded perspectives, utilization of social science knowledge in public policy may be much more widespread than previously supposed.

31

The Contribution of Economics to Public Policy Formulation

Walter Adams

I

IN THEIR IMPACT ON government policy making, economists are often regarded as the most influential among social scientists. If that be so, it is regrettable, because economists of late—particularly academic economists—have had a baneful influence. Indeed, as an economist, I am reluctant to appear in public these days, especially in mixed company.

Without too much exaggeration, I would argue that the economics profession is moribund, if not bankrupt. Substantively, it seems incapable of dealing with the most fundamental economic problems of our time. Methodologically, it is marching down a dead-end primrose path.

A symptom of the malaise: In early 1974, three leading magazines—*Fortune, Business Week,* and *U.S. News & World Report*—assembled a small army of conventional economists to predict what the year would bring. With very few exceptions, they said the stock market would rise; it fell 300 points. They said the inflation rate would decrease; it rose about 12 percent. They said unemployment would peak at 6 percent; it was above 7 percent at year's end and rising. Above all, they said there would be no recession!

A hapless President Ford, you may remember, made the mistake of listening to these economic soothsayers. He launched his ill-fated WIN campaign—Whip Inflation Now—urging people to buy less, to retrench on their consumption of consumer durables, to save more, and so on. That was in the fall of 1974. And by year's end he had to confess error and reverse his position 180 degrees. Suddenly he found himself swamped by the specter of double-digit inflation *and* double-digit unemployment—the sophisticated macro models, built with the latest computer-assisted, econometric models, to the contrary notwithstanding.

II

The failure of the economics profession to understand, let alone cope with, the major economic problem of our time in the United States and the whole Western world, i.e., inflation-in-the-midst-of-recession, is patently obvious. The academic gurus are disoriented and helpless.

Their confusion is the result of the great (and irrelevant) debate of the 1960s between the conservatives in our profession, the so-called Monetarists, following Professor Milton Friedman of the University of Chicago, and the liberals, the so-called Keynesians, following Professor James Tobin of Yale and Professor Walter Heller of the University of Minnesota. (Incidentally, all three men are past presidents of the American Economic Association.) The conservatives and liberals alike had ready prescriptions for dealing with *either* recession *or* inflation. In times of recession, said the conservatives, increase the supply of money in circulation; the liberals wanted to cut taxes and/or increase government expenditures to produce a budget deficit. In times of inflation the conservatives wanted to tighten up on the money supply and raise interest rates; the liberals preferred raising taxes, reducing government spending, and creating a budget surplus. One group advocated reliance on monetary policy, the other reliance on fiscal policy, to produce the desired macro effects on the economy.

Neither group, however, had a policy for dealing with the *simultaneous* occurrence of recession and inflation. Indeed, following their trusted computer models, built on the time-honored GIGO principle (garbage-in-garbage-out), they said that such a phenomenon was theoretically inconceivable. Therefore, it cannot happen; therefore, it is not a problem; therefore, let us continue to behave as if we did not have to worry about it—the real world to the contrary notwithstanding.

And so we proceeded to do what we have done ever since World War II—fight inflation with recession, and recession with inflation. (I remind you that we have suffered through recessions in 1949, 1954, 1958, 1961, 1970, and 1975.) And today, as a daily reading of the *Wall Street Journal* attests, we are still paying a steep price in unemployment and in wasted capacity, which is buying us very little or no progress in unwinding the wage-price spiral. In short, we have not licked the problem of inflation by buying the problem of recession.

Economists, it seems, are immobilized into inaction by a myth, one of those fashionable fads that periodically enthrall every scientific fraternity. It is called the Phillips Curve, according to which society is the victim of an inevitable trade-off between the social goal of full employment and the social goal of price stability. We can get more of one, according to the conventional wisdom, only at the expense of less of the other. Again the battle lines are drawn on the basis of ideological preference. Both goals, say the conservatives, are desirable, but if forced to choose, *at the margin,* let us strive for price stability. Both goals, the liberals agree, are worthy, but if forced to choose, *at the margin,* let us strive for full employment. And so the desultory debate and the cacaphony of irrelevant policy advice continue.

The difficulty is that the conservatives and liberals alike assume that the economy is a mechanistic organism, responding passively and automatically to monetary and fiscal stimuli—that it will behave *as if* it had the structural attributes of "perfect" competition. And, given their belief that the Phillips Curve trade-off is real, that it is an unshakably independent variable, they conclude that policy makers have only one option: to emphasize an antiinflation or an antirecession policy, not both. They perceive the problem as one of economics rather than political economy. They abstract from the existence of concentrated power blocs and structural imperfections in the economy; hence they fail to recognize how these micro phenomena can distort or undermine even the most finely tuned macro policies. Inevitably, therefore, by embracing assumptions inappropriate to institutional reality, they reach defective policy conclusions.

Unlike its founding fathers, modern economics largely ignores the "power" element as a crucial variable in economic statecraft (Galbraith, 1973: 1–11). "Economics lacks a theory of power," says Leonard Silk. "It either ignores the significance of power or seeks ways to minimize the use of power in matters affecting the production and distribution of wealth" (Silk, 1975). Kurt W. Rothschild makes the same point:

> If we look at the main run of economic theory... we find that it is characterized by a strange lack of power considerations. More or less homogeneous units—firms and households—move in more or less given technological and market conditions and try to improve their economic lot *within the constraints of these conditions.* This model has been explored in great detail by modern economic science and very important insights into the working of the market mechanism have been gained. But that people use power to alter the mechanism itself; that uneven power may greatly influence the outcome of market operations; that people may strive for economic power as much as for economic wealth; these facts have been largely neglected (Rothschild, 1971: 7).

And "power" is, of course, at the core of the current inflation. Industrial prices are going up while unemployment is still substantially unreduced, because giant firms in the "administered price" industries have exercised their discretion (i.e., power) to rewrite the "iron laws" of the marketplace. To wit: When demand is weak, when less than 70 percent of capacity is utilized, when the nation is in the midst of a serious recession, these industrial giants, more often than not, refuse to cut prices to stimulate sales. On the contrary, they raise prices, aim at their accustomed target-rate-of-return profit, and cut production and employment. And if their stratagem proves counterproductive, they petition the government for a protectionist bailout. It is a scenario that can be replayed repeatedly and whenever necessary—as long as policy makers can be made to believe that only government spending and budget deficits are the cause of inflation.

It is well recognized, of course, that under certain conditions, i.e., when the resources of the economy are fully employed, increased government spending and budget deficits *do* cause inflation—inflation of a special variety, called "demand-pull" inflation. But this is not the type of inflation we are currently experiencing, simply because the economy is operating far short of full employment. Today's inflation is of the "cost-push" variety, fueled by a seemingly uncontrollable price-wage-price spiral. It is the result of a power grab by highly organized vested interests for a larger share of a fixed pie or a pie growing more slowly than the combined appetites of the interests that desire to devour it. Hence an antiinflation policy based on Phillips Curve assumptions does not come to grips with the basic issue—except, perhaps, at the price of intolerable unemployment levels.

I offer two examples to illustrate the power relationships at the root of the current inflation, which also explain the ineffectiveness of orthodox macro policies of dealing with such inflation. My examples are taken from the "free" sector of the economy (steel) and from the "regulated" sector (airlines).

1. For decades, the steel industry in the United States has been afflicted by the typical maladies of a tight oligopoly. Entry has been at a minimum, or nonexistent. Innovation has been slow, hampered by the bureaucratic dry rot that tends to accompany monopoloid giantism. Price policy has been directed at uniformity and inflexibility, except in an upward direction; while the leadership role has rotated among the oligopolists, the level of product prices has been anything but market determined. Moreover, until 1959 the industry had little to fear from foreign competition, so that the members of its cofraternal, close-knit group felt it safe to follow concerted, tacitly collusive, and consciously parallel price and product policies. Occasional mavericks might from time to time disturb the industry's quiet life but, like others before them, they eventually became members of the club.

Into this well-ordered preserve, where the rules of the game were understood and observed by all parties, surged a rising tide of imports, initiated by the long strike of 1959. Once the industry grasped the fact that these imports were not a temporary phenomenon, and that they were not only securing a U.S. franchise but, more important, disturbing accustomed price relationships and procedures, and indeed undermining the very foundations of the oligopoly, U.S. steelmakers organized themselves for a massive counteroffensive.

First they resurrected a virtually forgotten 1921 statute, and filed antidumping charges against European and Japanese steelmakers. This effort failed. Next they asked Congress to change the rules of the game under the Antidumping Act so as to enhance the probability of obtaining import relief. This effort also failed. Then, using the infant industry argument, they petitioned Congress for "temporary" tariff protection. This effort also failed. Finally, with the support of the United Steel Workers of America, they were able to convince Congress to legislate mandatory import quotas, unless foreign producers agreed to practice "voluntary" restraint in their exports to the U.S. market. This effort succeeded. The European and Japanese steel producers—with the help of friendly persuasion by the U.S. State Department—entered into a Voluntary Restraint Agreement, effective January 1, 1969.

The consequences were predictable. Secure from "excessive" import competition, the domestic steel giants raised prices—dramatically. Thus between January 1960 and December 1968, a period of nine years during which there were no artificial import restraints, the composite steel price index rose 4.1 points—or 0.45 points per year, indicating the moderating effects of imports on domestic prices. In the four years between January 1969 and December 1972, while the VRA was in effect, the steel price index rose 26.7 points—or 6.67 points per year. Put differently, steel prices increased at an annual rate fourteen times greater since the import quotas went into effect than in the nine years prior thereto. According to one study, the VRA caused steel prices to increase by $26 to $39 per ton, meaning that the price of steel would have been 13 to 15 percent lower in the absence of VRA (Adams and Dirlam, 1977).

While the Voluntary Restraint Agreement lapsed in 1974, the U.S. steel industry has continued its drive for protection. It obtained import quotas for its stainless and specialty steel segment in 1976, and is now in the midst of a gigantic public relations campaign to obtain not only import quotas but worldwide "orderly marketing agreements"; in the words of the *Wall Street Journal* (June 20, 1977), it is really "angling for worldwide market rigging and price fixing," i.e., stripped of euphemism, a revival of the old international steel cartel. This effort may yet be crowned with success, especially in the current atmosphere of recession and unemployment.

Two brief observations are relevant: *First,* once the government is perverted into an instrument of privilege creation and privilege dispensing—once it agrees to play a protectionist role, as it recently did in authorizing stainless steel quotas—the industry will feel free to resume its traditional role of óligopolistic price escalation. Note the current spectacle of daily articles in the *Wall Street Journal* reporting sharp declines in steel industry profits: "U.S. Steel's Net Plunges 72% in the First Quarter," "Bethlehem Steel Sees Disappointing Net in Quarter/Cites Need for 5% Price Rise," "National Steel's Profit Drops 63% in First Quarter." What is the industry's response? To raise prices, of course. Demand may be weak, plants may be used only at about 70 percent of capacity, foreign competition may be intense, but the industry's proposed solution is price increases and more price increases—obviously secure in its conviction that the government can be counted on to promulgate the protectionist measures that are necessary to validate the pricing excesses the industry chooses to commit in the market place.

Second, it is noteworthy that the perversion of the government into an instrument of privilege creation is facilitated by the political alliance between management and labor along syndicalist lines. The lobbying for import quotas is now a joint venture, and its effectiveness is largely attributable to this form of tacit vertical collusion. A politician, bent on attaining or retaining public office, knows that, by embracing protectionism, he can count on opulent industrialists for the financing of his campaigns and on labor unions to deliver sizable blocks of votes on election day. It is an impressive formula for political success that only the most stalwart and dedicated servants of the public interest dare to take lightly.

2. The regulated industries are another prototype of government protectionism and built-in cost-push inflation. Here, more often than not, the government protects regulated firms from competition rather than consumers from exploitation.

Take the Civil Aeronautics Board, for example. Like other regulatory commissions, it has the power to limit entry, to control rates, to approve mergers, and to supervise financial practices—powers it has traditionally exercised in a restrictionist, promonopolistic fashion.

But the long arm of the CAB extends only to scheduled airlines, operating in *inter*state commerce. *Intra*state carriers, in large states like Texas and California, are fortunately immune from CAB regulation. They afford an excellent performance yardstick of the excessive rates charged by the CAB carriers—just as the old "nonskeds" and the charters have done for some time. In a recent study, for example, the U.S. Senate Antitrust and Monopoly Subcommittee found

> that the airlines in California and Texas that are not regulated by the CAB offer fares that are 30–50 percent less than those charged by CAB carriers over comparable routes. The 445-mile flight from San Diego to

San Francisco, for example, costs about $30 on intrastate airlines not regulated by the CAB. But, the 400-mile flight from Boston to Washington on a regulated carrier costs about $50. The Subcommittee carefully examined whether these differences were due to regulation, as the critics had been charging, or to other factors. The airlines and the CAB told us that differences in weather, traffic density, and a host of other factors accounted for the difference. But we discovered that those factors accounted for less than one-half the difference in fares....

The secret in California and Texas is deceptively simple: they put more passengers on their planes than the CAB carriers do. This fuller plane, lower fare service seems to be the direct result of greater competition and innovation that comes with freedom from the stranglehold of CAB regulation. In Texas and California these lower fares have stimulated so much extra traffic that there are actually more flights instead of less, and even those flights are somewhat more full....

Studies by both Boeing and Lockheed demonstrated that it is economically and technically possible to provide the lower fare service throughout the United States. With an all-coach seating configuration, for example, profitable cross-country service could be provided in a B-747 flying an average from 50–70 percent full at fares that range from $75 to $95. In fact, World Airways has recently proposed scheduled service coast-to-coast for $89. Unfortunately, the CAB dismissed this application. Meanwhile, the current cross-country CAB-regulated fare is $179. The simple fact is that the CAB has failed to encourage low prices (Congressional Record, 1976: S 6314).

The Interstate Commerce Commission, in its regulation of surface transportation, and especially of the trucking industry, has at least as deplorable a record as the CAB of compromising the public interest. Other "independent" commissions—the FCC, the FPC, the USMC—do not lag far behind (Adams, 1958: 527–43; Green, 1973). Their record lends force to the statement by Lewis Engman, former chairman of the Federal Trade Commission, that "most regulated industries have become federal protectorates, living in the cozy world of cost-plus, safely protected from the ugly spectre of competition, efficiency, and innovation" (Engman, 1974). The organization of these industries and the proclivities of their regulators are anything but an effective mechanism for controlling or moderating the forces of cost-push inflation.

3. In summary, and without belaboring the point with a multiplication of the foregoing examples, it is clear that recessions must be fought by expansionary macro policies—whether they be monetary or fiscal policies, or some combination of the two. It is equally clear that such policies tend to generate inflationary forces that must be brought under control, either by a genuinely competitive market mechanism or by some sort of government regulation. In any event, this means facing up to the power of organized vested interests to manipulate the market and to use

the government, whenever necessary, as an instrument of privilege creation and a mask for monopoly.[1]

III

Turning now to the methodology of contemporary economics, it is clear that the *nouvelle vague* has had much to do with the recent policy triumphs and failures of our discipline. Whatever its other effects may have been, the emphasis on mathematical model building and econometrics has diverted attention from the study and practice of political economy to the pursuit of "economic science."

Undoubtedly the new brand of economics, with the aid of computer technology, has made substantial contributions, especially to the development of operations research and management science. Operations research scholars have done commendable work in refining input-output analysis; developing linear, integer, and quadratic programming; and applying the Markov chains (random walk with absorbing barriers). Welfare economists have explored the inconsistency of group choice (the voting paradox), and experimented with cost-benefit analyses of public investment. Mathematical theorists have developed the existence theorem (the existence and uniqueness of equilibrium), the turnpike theorem (optimal growth patterns), and decomposability theorems. Mathematical forecasters have built more than a dozen econometric models of the American economy—complete with projections of GNP and its individual components.

On the other hand, it must also be recognized that we have paid a price for the benefits obtained. *First,* the mathematical-econometric approach, with its emphasis on abstract model building, has either transcribed into a different (more esoteric) language the tautologies that economists have dealt with for a long time, or developed formulations

---

[1] All this, of course, is not intended to gainsay the formidable contributions of *microeconomic* theory to government policy making by articulating, *inter alia,* the costs of protectionism, the costs and benefits of specific programatic expenditures, the shifting and incidence of particular taxes, and some of the performance consequences of oligopolistic behavior. Nor should it be interpreted to minimize the heroic role of *macroeconomic* theory in forging the bloodless revolution which caused even Milton Friedman and Richard Nixon to confess that "we are all Keynesians now." But the fact remains that economists have not yet developed a new paradigm, integrating micro and macro theory into an operationally useful model that policy makers can mobilize to combat the twin scourges of inflation and recession. It is no reflection on past achievements, therefore, to suggest that the time is nigh for a new and revolutionary breakthrough in policy-oriented economic theory—conscious of the institutional realities of the political economy of power.

based on such unrealistic and confining assumptions that they are of little practical usefulness. Thus the statement that to maximize profits one should operate a firm where marginal revenue equals marginal cost can be expressed as a mathematical theorem. It is a tautology—a theory with zero predictive value that does not represent new economic insights.

The empirical validity or policy relevance of this mathematical model building is a more serious matter. Even Keynes, hardly an incompetent in his command of mathematical tools, decried what he contemptuously referred to as the "pseudo-mathematical" method. "Too large a proportion of recent 'mathematical economics,'" Keynes wrote, "are mere concoctions, as imprecise as the initial assumptions they rest on, which allow the author to lose sight of the complexities and interdependencies of the real world in a maze of pretentious and unhelpful symbols" (Keynes, 1936: 298).

If this was true forty years ago, when the fascination with the "pseudo-mathematical method" was a harmless fad, it is even truer today when that erstwhile fad has become an almost preclusive obsession. "Seldom, in modern positive science, has so elaborate a theoretical structure been erected on so narrow and shallow a factual foundation," writes Wassily Leontief, a Nobel laureate and father of modern input-output analysis.

> Mathematics has without doubt been recognized as the *lingua franca* of economic theory and most of the current work in the field of economic theory is deviated to proofs of formal theorems derivable from more or less arbitrarily chosen sets of axiomatic assumptions and, what is essentially the same, a large-scale production of new mathematical models.... Past experience does not seem to indicate that the most sophisticated of such exercises and the most complicated of mathematical models have made exceptionally noteworthy contributions to the operational understanding of the tangible—as contrasted with the hypothetical—reality (Leontief, 1966: vii).

To this assessment Paul Samuelson, possibly the leading contemporary mathematical economist and also a Nobel laureate, adds this sobering observation: "The first duty of an economist is to describe what is out there: a valid description without a deeper explanation is worth a thousand times more than a clever explanation of nonexistent facts" (Samuelson, 1964: 340).

Second, the overemphasis on the mathematical-econometric approach has resulted in a formidable misallocation of intellectual resources. Economists have tended to ask themselves questions that can be analyzed with their new techniques, rather than finding techniques to deal with the questions they *ought* to ask. They play games they find amusing, rather than contemplate issues that are crucial and pressing. They quantify what appears to be quantifiable, even though it may not be important, and pass up what should be analyzed even though it may be decisive.

As Boulding points out:

> The plain fact is that economists have neglected the study of technical change at the structural and micro level to the point where we are quite incapable of answering many of the most important questions of our day. We have been obsessed with macroeconomics, with piddling refinements in mathematical models, and with the monumentally unsuccessful exercise in welfare economics which has preoccupied a whole generation with a dead end, to the almost total neglect of some of the major problems of our day.... The whole economics profession, indeed, is an example of that monumental misallocation of intellectual resources which is one of the most striking phenomena of our times (Boulding, 1966: 12).

Technique has taken precedence over substance. Economists scurry about, as if they are trying to understand the operation of the internal combustion engine by reading the dials and gauges on the dashboard, instead of lifting the hood and looking at what is underneath. In short, they have not yet learned that algebra and geometry are a complement to, not a substitute for, thought.

Third, the mathematical-econometric approach, aside from its limited usefulness to date, contains within itself the danger of self-delusion and self-deception. Because of its apparent precision and its aura of scientific certainty, it may mislead its "consumers" into thinking that they have obtained an understanding of events and a control over their flow that, in fact, is not true.

Scholars are only now, and belatedly, beginning to discover the pitfalls in their purely mechanical techniques. When they explore the applications of systems analysis to social change—the "living" problems of riot control, waste disposal, urban renewal, and mass transportation, for example—they find that the cool logic of mathematics is less useful than in dealing with the "inertness" of complex military machines. A modern socioeconomic system, such as a city or the transportation complex in the Boston-to-Washington corridor, has little of the "harmonious arrangement or pattern" that the dictionary definition of "system" would imply. Indeed, as the president of the Operations Research Society of America concedes, "As we move closer and closer to human beings, human life, and to its goals, we find that we are dealing with progressively more and more difficult problems." That is why he insists that systems analysis, if it is to be effective, requires "people-oriented people" to work on these problems (*New York Times,* 1968: 28).

In short, mechanical systems analysis and mathematical model building, when applied without sensitivity to the dynamics of an organic social process, may exacerbate rather than remedy the economic ills of our time.

Fourth, the mathematical-econometric approach militates toward a degree of professional superspecialization that, *in extremis,* may result in serious suboptimization. Economic problems are analyzed in a fashion to meet the procrustean exigencies of the method used. They are cast in a narrow frame of reference that abstracts, to whatever extent necessary, from economic reality—i.e., *organic totality*—primarily to maximize the value of the economist's investment in his specialized bag of tools. Because the "scientific" economist has a certain "mind-set" in favor of his own skills, "it is easy for him to leave out essential variables with which he is not familiar." Not recognizing that a little learning may be a dangerous thing, he falls prey to suboptimization—"that is, finding and choosing the best position of part of the system which is not the best for the whole." And so it happens that, trapped by self-imposed overspecialization, "too many experts devote their lives to finding the best way of doing something that should not be done at all" (Boulding, 1966: 10-11).

One consequence of this methodological specialization has been a major redefinition of the scope and function of economic science. Such questions as "What is economics?" and "Who deserves to be called an economist?" elicit some curious answers in the "modern" context. The charmed circle around our profession is ever more tightly drawn; the club is becoming progressively more exclusive; and specialization by method, rather than subject matter, has become the crucial criterion for deciding on inclusion or exclusion.

The cost of overspecialization, which incidentally also infects social sciences other than economics, including, of course, sociology, has been cogently set forth by Alfred North Whitehead—more than fifty years ago. "Each profession makes progress," he said in *Science and the Modern World,* "but it is progress in its own groove. Now to be mentally in a groove is to live in contemplating a given set of abstractions. The groove prevents straying across country, and the abstractions abstract from something to which no further attention is paid. But there is no groove of abstractions which is adequate for the comprehension of human life." The result is a "celibacy of the intellect which is divorced from the concrete contemplation of the complete facts" (Whitehead, 1925: 282-83). Moreover, there is great danger in this overspecialized professionalism, particularly in democratic societies. "The directive force of reason is weakened. The leading intellects lack balance. . . . The task of coordination is left to those who lack either the force or the character to succeed in some definite career. . . . The progressiveness in detail only adds to the danger produced by the feebleness of coordination" (Whitehead, 1925: 283). In short, a narrow professionalism, built on methodological elitism, is not what economists would call a "free good."

Finally, and this is related to all the foregoing defects, the mathematical-econometric approach has changed the "entry conditions" in our profession, and given birth to a new breed of economist. This latter-day "scientist" tends to ignore the simple truism that technique is a means of solving problems as well as a status symbol to impress one's friends—that language is a vehicle for communication as well as an esoteric art. Being "hooked" on a method, he seldom assesses his work in terms of usefulness, relevance, validity, and truth. A methodological addict, he shows singular unconcern with the world as it exists. His standard of success—his payoff matrix—is to impress the tastemakers of an ever-narrowing professional specialty. He is more and more cut off from specialists in other fields, and finds it increasingly difficult to communicate with the lay world. The result is a sort of arpatheid: Economists are no longer able to see the real world, and the world no longer can understand what economists are saying.

What, then, is the upshot of these criticisms? What more can be said than to join Whitehead in his appeal for balance?

> Wisdom is the fruit of balanced development. It is the balanced growth of individuals which it should be the aim of education to secure.... In the Garden of Eden Adam saw the animals before he named them; in the traditional system, children name the animals before they see them.... There is something between the gross specialized values of the mere practical man, and the thin specialized values of the mere scholar. Both types have missed something (Whitehead, 1925: 284–86).

A viable profession must have persons of different talents, using different tools, toiling in its vineyard. Only then can it hope to produce a rich harvest for the society that maintains it, and of which it must be an integral part.

IV

My overall conclusion takes the form of an intuitive prediction: Given present trends in economics, society may decide that economics is too important to be left to the economists; or, it may decide that economics is not important at all.

VIII

The Attitude-Behavior Complex

The Attitude Toward Competition

32

Introduction: Ambiguities in the Attitude-Behavior Relation

Howard Schuman

THIS IS AN EXCELLENT TIME to have a reconsideration of the connection between attitudes and behavior, for there have recently been important changes in our understanding of that relation. Ten years ago it was taken for granted that research showed the relation to be nil—or nearly so—as summarized in a widely cited review by Allan Wicker (1969). That view is still frequently repeated. But both research and theorizing have been extremely active in this area over the past few years, and we now have evidence that the A-B connection can be moderately strong, once theoretical understanding, good measurement on both the attitude and the behavioral sides, and common sense are taken into account (see Schuman and Johnson, 1976). To note one important example, a recent study by Weigel and Newman (1976), which carefully created behavioral as well as attitude scales, produced an A-B correlation of over .60. From the way that study was developed on the basis of theory, there is reason to think that the results represent the general rule, not the exception.

But I would like in my own remarks to stand back a little from current research in order to point up a fundamental ambiguity in the term "attitude" and therefore in the meaning of the attitude-behavior relation, especially when it comes to understanding recent social trends.

From a practical standpoint, "attitudes" are important to social scientists for two seemingly contradictory reasons. First, we often lack good behavioral measures and use attitudes as proxies or substitutes. For example, racial attitude measures from national sample surveys are available going back to the early 1940s, and these provide a valuable record of social change in America over nearly four decades. Lacking equivalent sample surveys of racial behavior, the attitude data furnish primary historical information for the period, though the question then becomes one of how accurately the attitudinal shifts reflect changes in other forms of expression.

The second reason attitudes are important to sociologists is, paradoxically, just the opposite of the first: We sometimes have one or more behaviors available, when in fact what we want is an understanding of underlying attitudes. This second reason may sound less familiar than the first, but a little thought will indicate that it is commonplace. And the paradox tends to disappear—though not quite completely—when one realizes that my first use of "attitude" was primarily in terms of measurement, my second in terms of concept. Let me say a little more about each of these.

My reference to the racial area as an example of the proxy value of attitudes is not a casual one. For sociologists, this has been the main sphere in which research on attitudes and behavior has been pursued. From LaPiere to the present, racial and ethnic attitudes have seemed important to study and accessible to measurement. Most of this research has concerned the relationship at a particular point in time and usually in a laboratory or local setting. But I would like to ask instead about the connection of national time series data on racial attitudes to other forms of racial expression. The attitude record shows remarkable change: Using National Opinion Research Center, Survey Research Center, or other similar data, we find substantial liberalization of white racial attitudes over the past thirty-five years. The relation can be specified further by education, region, and other variables, but for my purpose the national trends are sufficient. (See Greeley and Sheatsley, 1971, and A. Campbell, 1971, for useful reports and analyses.)

But is the attitudinal change more than lip-service liberalization? Is it simply that white respondents in surveys have learned the socially desirable thing to say, and increasingly say it? I do not see how a dispassionate look at racial events, behaviors, and institutional changes over the past thirty-five years can leave any doubt that equally momentous changes have occurred in action as well as in attitude. This is most striking in the South, where legal segregation, disenfranchisement, and open discrimination have disappeared or been radically reduced, and where race relations have undergone what Anthony Lewis (1976) describes as "revolutionary change." The shift is less dramatic in other regions, but I am confident that a careful tracing of events will show that in government, in the armed forces, on television, on college campuses, and in most public spheres of life, racial change in white individual and institutional behavior has occurred at a rapid and visible pace in ways quite consonant with the attitude survey data.

Why is this congruence not recognized? I think there are two quite different reasons.

First, there is a failure to look closely at what white racial attitude data really show. Important attitudinal change in many areas of race relations does not mean complete attitudinal transformation of all aspects of race relations. For example, the fact that residential segregation has changed little over the last several decades does *not* cast doubt on the importance of other types of white racial attitude change. The fact is that measurement of attitudes bearing directly on choice of housing has seldom been adequate to the task. In a recent article, Reynolds Farley and colleagues (1978) have shown that if white attitudes toward residential integration are adequately measured, there is, unfortunately, no conflict between the resulting data and the facts of residential segregation. To put this into the theoretical terms most meaningful to attitude-behavior investigators, one needs to take account of precise attitude-behavior congruence or correspondence—and not simply predict wildly from an attitude trend of one sort to a behavioral trend of an only remotely similar sort.

The other reason that the attitude-behavioral link in recent history is not fully appreciated takes us back to the ambiguity of the term "attitude" and the fact that attitudes are often wanted because *only* behaviors are available—and behaviors are not trusted! The same people who question the validity of attitude measures showing racial liberalization *also* question the meaning of behavioral changes showing racial liberalization. Thus appointments of blacks to high court and cabinet positions are often seen as window dressing; affirmative action programs in colleges are criticized as not pursued with vigor and sincerity; court orders to end segregation are viewed as having limited practical import. In fact, when one examines the criticisms made of liberal white racial behaviors and behavioral change, they are almost identical to the criticisms made of measured attitudes. It is evident that what the critics have in mind is a concept of "true attitudes" that cannot be satisfied by *either* measured attitudes *or* public behaviors.

Moreover, this criticism is in keeping with the way the term "attitude" is generally used outside the social sciences. I have been collecting instances of such usage, and it is clear that the term is rarely employed for surface indicators, whether they are opinions *or* behaviors, but rather for something assumed to be quite basic and close to the heart of truth. For example, my son's report card has a major category called: "poor attitude toward class." A *New York Times* profile of Jody Powell described him as unusually "able to reflect the President's attitudes"—meaning true attitudes. A biography of Henry VIII speaks of "England's attitude" toward the succession to the Habsburg throne in the sixteenth century (Scarisbrick, 1968: 98). Of course, we may not always want to go along with the claim that there is a deeper attitude not revealed by external indicators. Some were rightly skeptical when Earl Butz, on the occasion of his resignation as Secretary of Agriculture, stated: "The use of a bad racial commentary in no way reflects my real attitudes."

In any case, the attitudinal concept may be indispensable to us in referring to an underlying state that represents internal truth, and in this sense of course we must be prepared for discrepancies between "real attitudes" and what people allow themselves to say *or* do. But this is true whether the external indicators are ordinary behaviors or measured attitudes. Indeed, observable behavior in its ineluctable meaning of "public conduct" (R. Williams, 1976) and attitude in the sense of a proxy for behavior could be perfectly correlated, yet both be quite dissociated from attitude as an underlying true state.

What we seem to require then is not the elimination of the attitude concept, but rather the recognition that there are two such concepts—and both are essential to social research and thinking. We hope through good measurement to bring the two meanings of attitude together, but tension between them (and therefore between underlying attitude and observable behavior) is perhaps inevitable, especially in areas where inner feelings and outer demands conflict.

33

Attitudes and Behavioral Prediction: An Overview

Martin Fishbein

REPORTS OF RATHER LOW or nonsignificant relations between attitudinal predictors and behavioral criteria have been accumulating for a period of more than forty years (cf. Wicker, 1969). These negative findings led many investigators to reconsider the nature of the attitude-behavior relation (e.g., Calder and Ross, 1973; D. T. Campbell, 1963; DeFleur and Westie, 1958, 1963; Deutscher, 1966, 1969, 1973; H. J. Ehrlich, 1969; Kelman, 1974a; Rokeach, 1967). In a parallel development, it was possible to discern a growing disenchantment with the attitude concept, and the general consensus was that measures of attitude have little value for the prediction of overt behavior.

Recently, however, social psychology has been witnessing a revival of interest in the relationship between attitude and action (e.g., Brannon, 1976; Liska, 1975; D. J. Schneider, 1976; Schuman and Johnson, 1976). The emerging position seems to be that attitude is only one of many factors determining behavior. While this position reaffirms the importance of attitudes, it leads to the expectation that attitudes will often be unrelated to behavior.

In a number of publications my colleagues and I have presented ideas and data clearly at variance with this assessment of the attitude concept and its utility (Ajzen and Fishbein, 1973; Fishbein, 1967, 1973; Fishbein and Ajzen, 1972, 1974, 1975). The purpose of this paper is to provide an overview of these ideas and then show how they can be incorporated in a more general framework that focuses on the question of correspondence between attitudinal measures and behavioral criteria. More specifically, I will try to show that attitudes and actions are highly correlated when the attitudinal measure corresponds directly to the behavioral criterion under consideration.

Let me begin by briefly reviewing what I believe is currently known about the relations among beliefs, attitudes, intentions, and behavior. To do this it is first necessary to define these terms as they will be used in the present paper.

Definitions

A *belief* is a probability judgment that links some object or concept to some attribute. The terms "object" and "attribute" are used in a generic sense and both terms may refer to any discriminable aspect of an individual's world. For example, I may believe that *cigarettes* (an object) are *harmful to health* (an attribute) or that *my quitting smoking* (an object) will *reduce my capacity to work* (an attribute). The content of the belief is defined by the object and attribute in question, and the strength of the belief is defined by the person's subjective probability that the object-attribute relationship exists (or is true).

An *attitude* is a bipolar evaluative judgment of the object. It is essentially a subjective judgment that I like or dislike the object, that it is good or bad, that I'm favorable or unfavorable toward it. Once again, the term "object" is used in a generic sense. Thus I may have attitudes toward people (e.g., smokers), institutions (e.g., the Federal Trade Commission), events (e.g., the release of the Surgeon General's report on smoking), behaviors (e.g., my quitting smoking), outcomes (e.g., gaining status in the eyes of my friends), and so on.

An *intention* is a probability judgment that links the individual to some action. An intention can be viewed as a person's belief about his or her own performance of a given behavior. Intentions can be general (e.g., I will quit smoking) or specific (e.g., I will not smoke any cigarettes at John's party tonight), and they vary in intensity. Like other beliefs, intentions are usually measured by obtaining some index of the individual's subjective probability that he will perform the behavior in question.

The Relations Among Beliefs, Attitudes, Intentions, and Behavior[1]

Figure 1 presents a brief summary of the relations among beliefs, attitudes, intentions, and behavior with respect to a given object, where

[1]For a more detailed description of the theory and its empirical support, see Fishbein and Ajzen (1975: chap. 6–8); or Ajzen and Fishbein (1973).

Figure 1.   Schematic Presentation of Conceptual Framework Relating Beliefs, Attitudes, Intentions, and Behaviors with Respect to a Given Object

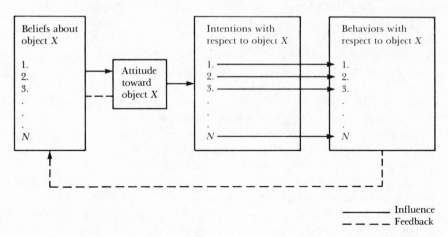

——————— Influence
— — — — Feedback

"object" is used in a more restrictive sense to refer to some type of entity (e.g., a person, thing, policy, or institution). In the figure it can be seen that a person holds many beliefs about any given object (e.g., the church), that is, he associates that object with a variety of attributes. There is now considerable evidence that knowledge of a person's beliefs about an object *and* his attitudes toward the associated attributes allow us to predict accurately his attitude toward the object per se. Notice, however, that it is the *entire set* of salient beliefs that determines the attitude, and *not* any single belief (see Fishbein and Ajzen, 1975: 216–28, for a review of relevant literature). This is an important point because it implies that changing any one belief about an object may not change the person's attitude toward the object.

Once the person has formed an attitude, he is predisposed (i.e., he intends) to perform a variety of behaviors with respect to, or in the presence of, the object. Once again, it must be noted that although his attitude does predispose him to perform a set of behaviors, it does not predispose him to perform any *specific* behavior. I believe this is one of the most important findings to come out of social psychology in the last ten years. In contrast to the previous assumption that changing a person's attitude toward some object would influence some particular behavior with respect to that object, it is now clear that attitudes toward an object may have little or no influence on specific behaviors with respect to that object. Just as attitude is determined by the entire *set* of beliefs a person holds, the attitude only serves to predispose the person to engage in a *set* of behaviors that, when *taken together,* are consistent with the attitude (Fishbein and Ajzen, 1974).

It is important to recognize, however, that figure 1 does *not* imply that there is no relationship between attitude toward an object and intentions to engage in various behaviors with respect to the object. Indeed, it suggests that if one were interested in the totality of intentions a person held with respect to some object, knowledge of a person's attitude would be a useful predictor. That is, the more favorable the person's attitude, the more positive and the fewer negative behaviors he would intend to engage in. To put this somewhat differently, increasing a person's attitude toward some object should increase the *number* of positive behaviors he intends to engage in with respect to, or in the presence of, that object. There is no guarantee, however, that it will increase the person's intention to engage in any particular behavior. Thus, for example, reducing a person's attitude toward cigarettes might increase her intention to prohibit her children from smoking, but not her intention to reduce the number of cigarettes she smokes.

Finally, figure 1 also points out that a person's intention to engage in a specific behavior with respect to an object is the primary determinant of that behavior. That is, the single best predictor of whether or not a person will engage in a particular behavior is his intention with respect to that behavior (see Fishbein and Ajzen, 1975: 368-83, for a review of relevant literature). This does *not* mean that knowledge of a person's intention to perform some behavior will always predict whether or not the person will, in fact, perform that behavior. The performance of a behavior reflects a *decision* on the part of the individual. Unfortunately, the term "decision" has sometimes been used to refer to what a person "intends to do" and, at other times, it has been used to refer to what a person actually does. In this paper the term "decision" will refer only to a person's behavior. We assume that what a person does reflects the decision he made. Thus we know what a person "decided" by observing his behavior.

The term "decision" implies a choice between two or more alternatives. For example, one who has never smoked may have to decide between trying or not trying a cigarette; a current smoker may have to decide between continuing to smoke or quitting. The person's *decision* is reflected in the choice he makes.

Consistent with the notion of a direct relation between intentions and behavior, the decision can be predicted from a knowledge of the person's intentions to perform each of the alternatives (e.g., Ajzen and Fishbein, 1969; Fishbein, Thomas, and Jaccard, 1976). Generally speaking, a person will perform that alternative toward which he or she has the strongest intention.

When a person is confronted with two mutually exclusive and exhaustive alternatives (e.g., to try or not to try a cigarette), knowledge of one of the two intentions will usually be sufficient for predicting the person's decision. This, however, is not the case when more than two alternatives are available or when the individual does not view the alternatives presented as being mutually exclusive and exhaustive. For example, even though a current smoker may have a relatively weak intention to continue smoking at her present level, she may (decide to) do this if her intentions with respect to other alternatives (e.g., quitting) are even weaker. Further, although a person might have a strong intention to continue not smoking, he may still try a cigarette since he may not view these two behaviors as mutually exclusive and his intention to try a cigarette might also be quite strong. In order to understand fully a person's decision, then, it will usually be necessary to investigate his intentions to perform each of the alternative behaviors available to him.

Although figure 1 does not illustrate these relations between intentions toward performing each alternative and the behavioral decision, it does point out that a person's performance of a given behavior is primarily determined by his intention to perform that behavior. Thus everything that was said about the attitude-intention relationship also applies to the attitude-behavior relationship. That is, we can no longer assume that a person's attitude toward an object will be related to any specific behavior the person engages in with respect to the object, but it should be related to the pattern of behavior he performs.

In most cases, however, we are not interested in patterns of behavior but in some specific behavior. Figure 2 presents a brief summary of the factors underlying the performance of a given behavior. In figure 2 we have again oversimplified the situation by indicating that the immediate determinant of any given behavior is the person's intention to engage in that behavior.

Figure 2. Schematic Presentation of Conceptual Framework for the Prediction of Specific Intentions and Behaviors

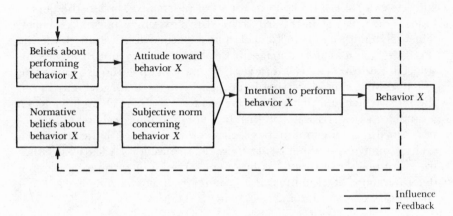

Two major variables have been found to serve as the determinants of an intention: (1) the person's attitude toward her own performance of the behavior in question; and (2) her subjective norm with respect to performing the behavior, that is, her subjective judgment that most people who are important to her think she should or should not engage in the behavior. The relative weights of these determinants vary as a function of the behavior in question and individual difference variables. For some behaviors, the person's intention is based almost entirely on his attitude toward his own performance of the behavior and little or no attention is paid to the prescriptions of important others. For other behaviors, the intention may be based primarily on the prescriptions of important others, and the person's attitude toward her performance of the behavior has little or no influence. Similarly, some people (such as authoritarians) may place more weight on normative influences, while others (such as introverts) may place more weight on attitudinal considerations (see Ajzen and Fishbein, 1973, or Fishbein and Ajzen, 1975: 301–18, for a review of relevant literature.)

Even at this relatively global level, several important points can be made. First, a relatively simple shift in focus from the object the behavior is directed toward to the behavior per se again places importance upon attitude as a predictor of behavior. Note that just as a person's attitude toward an object was viewed as a function of his salient beliefs about the object, a person's attitude toward performing a given behavior is viewed as a function of his salient beliefs about performing the behavior.

Figure 2 also indicates that the subjective norm (like attitudes) is a function of other beliefs. More specifically, a person's judgment that "most people who are important to me think I should/should not perform this behavior" is viewed as a function of his *normative beliefs,* that is, his beliefs that specific referents (be they individuals or groups) think he should or should not engage in the behavior, weighted by his motivation to comply with these referents. It should be noted that, like attitude, the subjective norm is a function of the *set* of (normative) beliefs the person holds, and it is not necessarily related to any single normative belief. Thus changing a person's belief that a particular referent thinks he should (or should not) engage in the behavior may not influence his subjective norm (i.e., his judgment that "most people who are important to me" think I should [or should not] perform the behavior). Further, it should also be noted that even if one were successful in changing a given attitude or a subjective norm, this does not guarantee a change in intention. Once again the intention is seen as a function of both the attitudinal and normative components *and* their relative weights. Clearly, if either the attitudinal or normative component carries little or no weight in the determination of the intention, changing that component will not change the person's intention (Ajzen, 1971).

Finally, it should be noted that figures 1 and 2 imply a causal chain linking beliefs to attitudes, attitudes (and beliefs) to intentions, and intentions to behaviors. It should be clear that one does not change attitudes, intentions, or behaviors directly, but only by changing beliefs that are functionally related to these variables.[2]

To summarize briefly, then, I have argued that a person's attitude toward an object influences the overall pattern of his responses to the object, but it need not predict any given action. According to this analysis, a single behavior is determined primarily by the intention to perform the behavior in question. A person's intention is in turn a function of his attitude toward performing the behavior and of his subjective norm. It follows that a single act is predictable from the attitude toward that act, provided that there is a high correlation between intention and behavior.[3]

As indicated earlier, these arguments can be incorporated into a more general framework that focuses on the question of correspondence between attitudinal predictors and behavioral criteria. It will be shown that a person's actions are found to be systematically related to his attitudes when the nature of the attitudinal predictors and behavioral criteria are taken into consideration.

Attitude-Behavior Correspondence

Attitudes are held with respect to some aspect of the individual's world, such as another person, a physical object, a behavior, or a policy. Although many definitions of attitude have been proposed, most investigators would agree that a person's attitude represents his evaluation of the entity in question. For purposes of the present analysis, only measures that place the individual on a bipolar evaluative or affective dimension will be considered measures of attitude.

Behavioral criteria consist of one or more observable actions per-

---

[2]It should be noted that attitudes can also be changed by changing the evaluation of associated attributes and that subjective norms can also be changed by changing the subject's motivation to comply with the specific referent. However, in both these cases one must again ultimately change beliefs. That is, the evaluation of an associated attribute is nothing more than the person's attitude toward that attribute, and thus a change in this attitude will require changing beliefs about the attribute. Similarly, although the determinants of motivation to comply are still not well understood, it does seem clear that a person's motivation to comply with a given referent is some function of his beliefs about that referent and, in particular, beliefs about the referent's power, prestige, expertise, trustworthiness, and so on.

[3]Even when the intention is primarily under the control of normative consideration, its correlation with attitude toward the action is usually found to be quite high.

formed by the individual and recorded in some way by the investigator. Behavioral acts include attending a meeting, using birth control pills, buying a product, donating blood, and so on.

Attempts to predict behavior from attitudes are largely based on a general notion of consistency. It is usually considered to be logical or consistent for a person who holds a favorable attitude toward some object to perform favorable behaviors, and not to perform unfavorable behaviors, with respect to the object.[4] Similarly, a person with an unfavorable attitude is expected to perform unfavorable behaviors, but not to perform favorable behaviors. The apparent simplicity of this notion is deceptive since there is usually no theoretical basis for the assumption that a behavior has favorable or unfavorable implications for the object under consideration. Obviously, many behaviors have no evaluative implications for a given object.

In most cases a given behavior is assumed to be consistent or inconsistent with a person's attitude on the basis of largely intuitive considerations. In the absence of an explicit and unambiguous definition of attitude-behavior consistency, therefore, many tests of the attitude-behavior relation reduce to little more than tests of the investigator's intuition. From a theoretical point of view, such tests of the relation between arbitrarily selected measures of attitude or behavior are of rather limited value.

The following analysis attempts to specify the conditions under which attitudes can or cannot be expected to predict overt behavior. Our point of departure is the notion that attitudes are held, and behaviors are performed, with respect to certain entities. Two important questions in research on the attitude-behavior relation can then be identified: (1) What are the entities of the attitudinal predictors and of the behavioral criteria? (2) What is the degree of correspondence between the attitudinal and the behavioral entities?

Attitudinal and Behavioral Entities

Attitudinal and behavioral entities may be viewed as consisting of four different elements: the *action,* the *target* at which the action is directed, the *context* in which the action is performed, and the *time* at which it is performed. The generality or specificity of each element depends on the measurement procedure employed.

---

[4]Peabody's (1967) work suggests that the basis for consistency may often be logical or denotative rather than evaluative. However, logical and evaluative consistency are usually confounded and the distinction appears to be of greater theoretical than practical significance.

Behavioral criteria based on single observations always involve four specific elements. That is, a given action is always performed with respect to a given target, in a given context, and at a given point in time. Criteria based on multiple observations of behavior generalize across one or more of the four elements. For example, when the behavioral observations constituting the criterion measure involve a very heterogeneous sample of targets, the target element is essentially left unspecified. However, when the different targets constitute a more homogeneous set, their common attributes determine the target element. When all targets are other human beings, for example, the target element is people in general; when the individuals serving as targets are of the same sex, religion, or race, then males, Jews, or Orientals might constitute the target element.

Similar considerations apply to the definition of the action, context, and time elements. To illustrate, when a very heterogeneous sample of behaviors is observed, the action element is left unspecified. Sometimes, however, the specific acts may represent a more general class of behaviors, such as cooperation, aggression, or altruism. Here, the action element is defined by the class of behaviors.[5]

In conclusion, the measurement procedure determines the behavioral entity. When the same action is observed with respect to heterogeneous targets, in different contexts, and at different points in time, we obtain a behavioral index whose entity is defined only by the action element. The target serves as the entity when heterogeneous behaviors toward the same target are observed in different situations and at different points in time. In a similar manner, indices can be obtained such that the contextual element, the time element, or any combination of elements define the entity for the behavioral criterion.

As in the case of behavioral criteria, attitudes are also directed at entities that may be defined by a single element or by combinations of two or more elements. Attitudinal predictors frequently specify only the target. Attitudes have been measured toward the church, toward various ethnic groups, toward specific persons, and so on, without reference to any particular action, context, or time. However, an investigator can specify an entity in terms of any combination of elements and obtain a measure of attitude toward that entity. For example, an evaluative

---

[5]It is interesting to note that, as in the case of attitudes, personality traits have been found to have little validity for the prediction of specific behaviors (Mischel, 1968; Wiggins, 1973). Personality traits such as dominance or authoritarianism represent general behavioral tendencies without reference to a specific target, context, or time. Given the nature of personality measures, it seems reasonable to suggest that an appropriate behavioral criterion is not a single action but rather an index based on a set of behaviors reflecting the trait in question; target, context, and time should be left unspecified. Data supporting this notion have been reported by Jaccard (1974).

semantic differential could be used to measure attitudes toward targets (Martin Luther King, Jews), toward actions (cooking dinner, cooperating), toward contexts (in St. Mary's Cathedral, at home), toward times (3:00 P.M. tomorrow, August), or toward any combination of elements (cooperating with Jews, cooking dinner at home at 3:00 P.M. tomorrow).

CORRESPONDENCE BETWEEN ATTITUDINAL AND BEHAVIORAL ENTITIES

After defining entities in terms of their elements, we can approach the question of attitude-behavior correspondence. An attitudinal predictor is said to correspond to the behavioral criterion to the extent that the attitudinal entity is identical in all four elements to the behavioral entity. For example, a measure of attitude toward a target such as "my church" (without specification of action, context, or time) corresponds directly only to a behavioral criterion based on the observation of different behaviors with respect to the person's church (e.g., donating money, attending Sunday worship services, participating in church-sponsored activities), in different contexts, and at different points in time. Similarly, when the attitude measure is an evaluation of a specific action toward a given target, such as the attitude toward "donating money to my church," the corresponding behavioral criterion is an index of monetary donations to the person's church based on multiple behavioral observations in different contexts (e.g., at home, in the church) and on different occasions. Alternatively, when the behavioral criterion is a single act, such as the person's attendance or nonattendance of next Sunday's worship service in his church at 10:00 A.M., the corresponding attitudinal predictor would be a measure of the person's evaluation of "attending my church's worship service next Sunday at 10:00 A.M."

CORRESPONDENCE AND THE ATTITUDE-BEHAVIOR RELATION

The main point I wish to make is that the strength of an attitude-behavior relationship depends in a large part on the degree of correspondence between attitudinal and behavioral entities. Although, in theory, correspondence is defined in terms of all four elements of the entities involved, for purposes of the present paper, examination of the target and action elements will be sufficient.

Considering target and action elements alone, two attitudinal predictors can be identified that deserve special attention. The most common measure specifies a given target (be it an object, a person, or an institution) without reference to a particular action. This predictor may be termed *attitude toward a target*. Of less frequent use is the *attitude toward an action*, a predictor that specifies both action and target elements (e.g., attitude toward smoking marijuana).

A similar distinction can be made with reference to behavioral criteria. When the criterion is an index based on observations of heterogeneous behaviors with respect to a given target, only the target element is specified and the resulting measure may be called a *multiple-act criterion*. When only one behavior toward a given target is observed, both target and action elements are specified and we obtain a *single-act criterion*.

The above discussion suggests that attitudes toward targets will predict multiple-act criteria, provided that the attitudinal and behavioral entities involve the same target elements. Similarly, attitudes toward actions are expected to predict single-act criteria if the target and action elements of the attitudinal entity are identical to those of the behavioral entity (cf. Fishbein and Ajzen, 1974, 1975).

Generally speaking, high attitude-behavior correlations cannot be expected in the absence of correspondence between attitudinal and behavioral entities. There is, however, one exception to this rule. Whenever the single-act criterion involves an action that is little more than an evaluation of the target, it should be predictable from a measure of attitude toward the target in question.

The relatively frequent use of petition signing or voting as measures of behavior deserve attention in this context. Under most circumstances both of these behaviors involve little more than expressing an evaluation of the target in question. For example, when a person signs or refuses to sign a petition supporting the legalization of marijuana, the act itself involves little more than the expression of a favorable or unfavorable attitude with respect to the issue. Viewed in this light, a measure of attitude toward the target (legalization of marijuana) should permit satisfactory prediction of the petition-signing behavior.

Similarly, in the United States, the act of voting for a given candidate or issue reflects in large part the voter's evaluation of the candidate or issue under consideration. A measure of attitude toward the candidate or issue would therefore be expected to correlate highly with voting behavior.

Consideration of this kind may also apply to other single-act criteria. That is, a specific act may sometimes have relatively direct evaluative implications for a given target. A procedure for determining such evaluative implications of single-act criteria was discussed by Fishbein and Ajzen (1974). However, even when it can be shown that an action has evaluative implications for the target, the most appropriate predictor of the single-act criterion is the attitude toward the action rather than the attitude toward the target.

In order to test these notions my colleague, Icek Ajzen, and I (Ajzen and Fishbein, 1977) conducted a review of the empirical research that provided data concerning the relation between an evaluative measure of attitude and some behavioral criterion—whether or not these studies were designed to examine the attitude-behavior relation. Studies with inappropriate measures of either the attitudinal predictor or the behavioral criterion were also considered if they were designed to be explicit tests of the relations between attitudes and behavior.

Our review was structured in terms of correspondence in target and action elements. Although it is possible to consider degrees of correspondence in each element, for the sake of simplicity we chose to classify attitudes and behaviors as either corresponding or not corresponding in their targets and actions. For each study reviewed, we identified the target and action elements of the attitudinal and behavioral entities; when the two targets were identical, the attitudinal predictor and the behavioral criterion were classified as corresponding in their target elements. A similar judgment was made with respect to action elements. In keeping with my previous comments, if a single-act criterion involved signing a petition or voting, the action element of the behavioral entity was viewed as unspecified.

Altogether we reviewed 110 studies involving 143 attitude-behavior relations. Of the 143 analyses there were only 45 in which the target and action elements of the attitudinal predictor corresponded directly to the target and action elements of the behavioral criterion; in 19 of these either the attitudinal or the behavioral measure was questionable.

There were twenty-seven comparisons, including some that were made in studies that have received more than their share of attention in reviews of the attitude-behavior relationship (e.g., Katz and Benjamin, 1960; Kutner, Wilkins, and Yarrow, 1952; Rokeach and Mezei, 1966), where there was absolutely no correspondence in either the target or action elements of the attitudinal predictor or the behavioral criterion. Common examples are studies that have measured attitudes toward a racial or religious group (without specifying any action element) and then have used this attitude measure to predict some specific action with respect to, or in the presence of, one or more particular members of that group. Not surprisingly, only one of these twenty-seven comparisons reached a level of statistical significance, and even here the correlation was low.

The greatest number of studies, including many that have been widely cited as examples of the failure of attitudes to predict behavior, had only partial correspondence (e.g., Corey, 1937; DeFleur and Westie, 1958; LaPiere, 1934). Perhaps most typical are those where the target elements of the attitude and behavioral criterion correspond but where there is no correspondence in the action elements. For example, the

T A B L E 1. Effect of Correspondence on the Attitude-Behavior Relation

CORRESPONDENCE		ATTITUDE-BEHAVIOR RELATION		
		Not significant	*Low (r < .40) or inconsistent*	*High (r ⩾ .40)*
None		26	1	0
Partial		20	47	4
High	Questionable measures	0	10	9
	Appropriate measures	0	0	26

NOTE: The cell entries represent number of attitude-behavior relations.

attitude is measured with respect to a particular person or institution—no action element is specified—and the behavioral criterion is a single act directed at or occurring in the presence of that target or institution. That is, the behavioral criterion identifies both a target and an action element while the attitudinal predictor only considers the target.

Table 1 summarizes the results of our review. There it can be seen that when there is no correspondence, there is no relationship. When there is partial correspondence one can, at best, expect only low or inconsistent results. But when the attitudinal and behavioral entities correspond in terms of both target and action elements, high and consistent correlations are obtained. Let me emphasize one point because I think it is of crucial importance. Our analysis is in terms of correspondence, not specificity. It makes little difference to our analysis if the investigator is interested in specific actions or general patterns of behavior. What is crucial, however, is the identification of the target and action elements of the behavioral criterion that you wish to deal with. It makes no difference if these elements are specific, general, or left unspecified—what is important is that the attitude be measured toward the same target and action as that defined by the behavioral criterion. Once this relatively simple task has been accomplished, attitudes consistently and systematically account for a large proportion of the variance in behavior. It is a sad commentary on the state of the art to realize that it has not been the attitude concept that has been at fault for fifty years, but rather the intuitive and speculative hunches of those of us who have tried to utilize the concept. As Herbert Kelman (1974a) has argued, the attitude concept is alive and well; it is attitude research that requires attention.

34

Attitudes, Behavior, and Economics

E. Scott Maynes

THIS PAPER DEALS WITH four topics: (1) attitudes as second-best variables in economics; (2) examples of the use of attitudes in economics; (3) a critical review of a "success" story—the Index of Consumer Sentiment; and (4) an experiment that suggests "calibration" as a possible solution to the measurement problem endemic to attitudes.

Why Attitudes Are Second-Best for Economists[1]

Like Gaul, economics may be divided into three provinces: theory, econometrics, and applied economics. Each subject matter or applied field—e.g., monetary economics, industrial organization, consumer economics—by practice accords different weights to theory, econometrics, and applied knowledge. From these different weights is derived the relative importance of attitudes for that subject-matter field.

In status, theory is clearly "king," its masters being accorded maximum deference often in proportion to the inaccessibility or arcaneness of their product. For graduate students mastery of the received theory is a first-priority goal.

By virtue of long tradition and considerable success, economic theory is characteristically deductive in logic, explicitly or implicitly mathemati-

□ This paper has been improved by the comments and suggestions (some adopted!) of W. Keith Bryant, Clyde H. Coombs, Loren V. Geistfeld, Michael Haines, George Katona, and James Morgan.

I am indebted to Sharyn Beth Adelstein for the data processing and calculations reported in the fourth section, "Calibrating Subjective Scales."

[1]Full disclosure is in order: The author identifies himself as a "behavioral economist."

cal in method, and hence deterministic in outcomes. The use of mathematics enforces parsimony in the number of variables considered and a preference for variables that can be exactly specified, both factors being adverse to the consideration and inclusion of "attitudes."

As a salient example, consider the economist's usual approach to consumer choice. Assume a utility function in which utility, or "satisfaction," depends upon the amount of goods consumed or possessed:

$$U_i = f(X_1, X_2, X_3, \ldots X_n) \tag{1}$$

where

U_i = the utility derived by the ith individual from goods, $X_1 \ldots X_n$
X_n = the amount consumed of good X_n

Ordinarily, the individual is assumed to know the existence of each good as well as the amount of satisfaction it will yield for him. The economist ordinarily avoids efforts to "explain" what it is that determines utility, leaving that task to the sociologist or psychologist.

The consumer is assumed to receive an income, Y_i, whose amount is determined exogenously. This income constitutes his budget constraint. To simplify the problem, it is often assumed that he cannot spend more by going into debt. The consumer is also assumed to know the price of each good available, $P_1, P_2 \ldots \ldots P_n$. Now we can summarize his choice problem: maximize (1) subject to the budget constraint:

$$Y_i = P_1 X_1 + P_2 X_2 \ldots \ldots + P_n X_n \tag{2}$$

By endowing the utility function with plausible properties, $\partial U/\partial P > 0$, $\partial^2 U/\partial^2 P < 0$, we can solve to obtain conditions for utility maximization.

Attitudes and this model? The simple answer is that there is no place for attitudes in this model. Preferences are goods-specific.[2] Of course it is possible that preferences for specific goods could be affected by such higher-order preferences as:

Attitudes, defined (following Katona [Katona Festschrift, 1972: 337]) as "generalized viewpoints with affective connotation, indicating what is good and favorable or bad and unfavorable."
Values, which are preferences of even higher order and longer run, defined by R. M. Williams (1968) as "criteria of discrimination."

But the economic theorist will generally reject this as unnecessary. It is the economist's responsibility to *start* with preferences and to lay bare the

---

[2]In a breakthrough that has proved highly seminal, Kelvin Lancaster (1966) introduced models of consumer choice postulating utility to be a function of the "characteristics" or attributes of goods. As a theorist in good standing, however, he carefully eschewed any attempt to explain the amount of utility derived from a characteristic.

implications of scarcity (as implied by prices and the budget constraint) for consumer choice.

In other domains economic theorists find attitudes equally redundant. In models explaining labor-force participation, utility is a function of the particular activity, e.g., sailing or "loafing." Though attitudes and values might alter preferences for income or for specific activities, economic theorists have felt that it is easier to deal with direct preferences for goods than to grapple with some overriding hierarchy of higher-order preferences. The view that attitudes and values are intrinsically amorphous reinforces this stand. But mostly it is the deductive bent of economic theory that makes theorists view as alien such a thoroughly empirical animal as attitudes.[3]

We turn now to econometrics. *Econometrics* represents the application of mathematics and statistics to the estimation of economic relationships and to the prediction and explanation of economic behavior, both at micro and macro levels. To a certain extent the desire to develop models that "work well" has made pragmatists of some econometricians, leading them to accept alien concepts, such as attitudes, *as long as they help*. For example, the Wharton Quarterly Econometric Model of the U.S., in one of several alternative formulations, incorporates "consumer attitudes" into its automobile and housing demand equations (F. G. Adams and Klein, 1972). This tendency is particularly strong in the case of econometric research and forecasting that must be sold in the market, as opposed to professional journals. In the case of some of the leading journals the theoretical acceptability of econometric models is given more than a little weight and this tends to offset the competitive-pragmatic drive to higher R^2's or likelihood ratios. Add to this the fact that much econometric research—and I will sound like a cynic here—never has to face the test of genuine forward prediction, as contrasted with backward "prediction" or fitting. Hence the discipline of reality is avoided. So we conclude that, while econometrics makes for the acceptance of outside concepts such as attitudes on the part of some practitioners, this tendency fails to affect a very large fraction of econometricians.

Finally, we turn to our third domain—the applied fields. As noted earlier, each of these fields varies in the extent to which theory, econometrics, and applied knowledge are accorded emphasis in teaching and research. In some fields—economic development, for example—it is widely accepted that practitioners, to be effective, must be conversant with many facets of economic reality, and that abstract theory is not sufficient for either the effective functioning of practitioners in the field

---

[3]Very recently some theorists have succeeded in introducing attitudes deductively. This "rational expectations" approach has achieved wide acceptance. It is discussed in the third section, "The Great Success."

or for the development of realistic models by scholars. Such fields are more receptive to attitudes. For others—international trade, for example—theory carries both the practitioner and the scholar a long way.

Finally, we should note that departments of economics are social institutions that competitively differentiate themselves, developing and perpetuating different emphases. Among those that have been more empirical and more interdisciplinary in bent are Michigan and Wisconsin. Within these departments and among the Ph.D.'s they have produced, there tends to exist a more favorable attitude regarding attitudes.

Summing up, the strong deductive tradition coupled with a strong predisposition to regard the determination of utility as a noneconomic matter has led most economists to view attitudes as either wholly alien or second-best. Despite this general view, some economists have encountered and used attitudes in some domains. We now turn to examples of such encounters and such uses.

The Use of Attitudes in Economics: Some Examples

Five examples *explained* in the original paper are *mentioned* here. The first comes from stabilization policy where the "rational expectations" approach endogenizes expectations by specifying in advance how expectations are formed and how "actors" will react to them (Business Week, 1976; Muth, 1961; Sargent and Wallace, 1976). The second is incorporated in the knowledge-attitudes-practice paradigm in economic development. Here attitude changes are viewed as necessary conditions for the adoption of innovations (E. M. Rogers, 1971). The third, the "Easterlin hypothesis," asserts that the marriage and fertility behavior of young persons is greatly influenced by attitudes based on their childhood experiences (Easterlin, 1972; A. C. Kelley, 1972). A fourth citation involves labor-force participation of wives and identifies the husband's attitude toward such participation as an important determinant (Morgan et al., 1962: 112). A final example provides statistical support for the notion that three attitudinal variables—personal efficacy, future orientation, and risk avoidance—contribute importantly as determinants of the mean wage level (G. J. Duncan, 1977).

The Great Success: The Index of Consumer Sentiments

The most conspicuous use and greatest success achieved by attitudes in economics has been the successful forecasting of *all* the postwar economic recessions in the United States by the Survey Research Center's Index of Consumer Sentiments. This represents a record unrivaled by any other forecasting group or method. This consumer anticipations or consumer attitudes approach to forecasting, developed by George Katona in the 1940s and refined in the 1950s, has passed its market "test" with flying colors. At present, four major organizations collect and distribute consumer anticipations data on a regular and large-scale basis—the Survey Research Center of the University of Michigan (since 1947), the National Industrial Conference Board (since 1967), Sindlinger and Company (since 1959), and the Gallup Organization (since 1976). This effort in the U.S. is more than matched by numerous organizations that carry out consumer attitudes surveys in other countries. With this as a prelude, we are ready to examine these consumer attitudes surveys in some detail.

THE PROBLEM

In the late 1940s the overriding macroeconomic challenge for economists was the forecasting and prevention of recessions. The then-vivid memories of the Great Depression of the 1930s together with John Maynard Keynes' (1936) explanation of it conspired to make it so.

While Keynes' genius contributed a generally satisfactory explanation of economic fluctuations, he erred in one major detail: He assigned a passive role to aggregate consumption and hence to consumers. George Katona was among the first to argue the error of Keynes' view and to assert the short-run instability of aggregate consumption expenditures. Working from a background of Gestalt psychology, Katona argued—as early as 1946 (Katona and Likert, 1946) but more completely in 1951 (Katona, 1951)—that "large" expenditures are discretionary, subject to "genuine decisions," as contrasted with habitual behavior. Hence large expenditures should *not* be viewed as automatic responses to changes in the values of such standard economic variables as disposable income.

Instead, Katona would interpose "consumer attitudes" as intervening variables between the standard economic variables and subsequent behavior. The rationale: People's reactions to their environment depend upon their perceptions, their understanding, the context, their expectation—in short, what Katona called their "attitudes." This line of reasoning led Katona to devise a series of surveys that would systematically record shifts in the relevant attitudes of a cross section of American consumers. Suitably quantified, an index of consumer attitudes would provide forecasts of fluctuations in aggregate consumption or provide inputs for such forecasts. These consumer surveys were initiated in

1946; the eighty-eighth such survey was carried out in August 1977.[4] We turn now to the workings of these surveys.

THE CONSUMER ATTITUDES APPROACH

George Katona's expectation that aggregate consumer expenditures—most specifically those items that are "discretionary"—are highly variable has now been confirmed by hard data: Aggregate expenditures on automobiles constitute one of the most volatile components of gross national product (Juster, 1964b); what is more, declines in automobile demand have either triggered or featured all postwar recessions.

For this reason the consumer anticipations approach seeks to forecast changes in aggregate expenditures for either: (1) new automobiles (and parts); or (2) all durable goods.[5] The inputs for the forecast consist of responses to the following attitudinal questions:

Personal Finances #1: We are interested in how people are getting along financially these days. Would you say that you and your family are *better off* or *worse off* financially now than you were a year ago?

Personal Finances #2: Now looking ahead, do you think that *a year from now* you people will be *better off* financially or *worse off,* or just about the same as now?

Business Conditions #1: Now, turning to business conditions in the country as a whole, do you think that during the next twelve months we'll have *good times* financially, or *bad times,* or what?

Business Conditions #2: Looking ahead, which do you say is more likely, that in the country as a whole we will have continuous *good times during the next five years or so,* or that we will have periods of widespread unemployment or depression, or what?

Good Time to Buy Durables: About the things that people buy for their homes—such as furniture, house furnishings, refrigerator, stove, TV, and things like that. Generally speaking, do you think now is a *good* or *bad time to buy* major household items?

Note that, following Gestalt theory, these questions probe much of the cognitive domain, looking both backward and forward in time and taking account of both personal and general business developments.[6]

[4] Since 1957 these surveys have been conducted on a quarterly basis. Not so in the early years.

[5] Some purchases of consumer durables are not discretionary, e.g., auto buyers who "trade in" their old cars regularly, people replacing durables that broke down.

[6] Prior to 1962 the Index included a question on expected price changes. Ambiguities with

Processed into an "Index of Consumer Sentiment," these data become inputs for forecasts, either by themselves or in conjunction with standard economic variables. The expected direction of their influence is straightforward: The more favorable the attitudes registered, the greater will be subsequent discretionary expenditures, *ceteris paribus*.

The differences between attitudinal variables and "ordinary" economic variables such as income or liquid assets are worth noting. First, the information the attitudinal variables contain is much less precise than that for most economic variables, there being no natural metric for an attitude and a three-point Likert scale being a rather crude device.[7] This is clearly a limitation. Second, in a time series, attitudinal variables are most useful at cyclical turning points when "major" developments result in similar changes in attitudes on the part of large groups of consumers, and hence affect the discretionary purchase behavior of many. Third, attitude data are open-ended, allowing the decision maker himself to take account of all possible factors, even those not anticipated when the forecasting model was formulated. This open-endedness should contribute to their robustness in forecasting.[8] Fourth, by their very nature they allow for nonuniform responses to identical stimuli. This property should endow them with a versatility that standard eco-

---

respect to its interpretation led to its elimination from the Index. A principal components analysis by F. G. Adams (1964) revealed that the business conditions questions accounted for most of the variance in the Index during the 1953–1961 period.

The comprehensiveness of the attitudes domain tapped by the Survey Research Center's ongoing program is indicated by the questions asked that are *not* included in the Index. They include:

1. Opinions about extent of price increases expected during next twelve months;
2. Satisfaction with amount of savings;
3. Opinions about the government's economic policy;
4. Heard favorable or unfavorable news of recent changes in business conditions;
5. Current business conditions now as compared with a year ago;
6. Expected change in unemployment;
7. Appraisal of buying conditions for cars;
8. Buying conditions for houses;
9. Expected changes in interest rates.

In addition, the questionnaires probe to ascertain the reasons consumers give for their perceptions, evaluation, and expectations.

[7]Values of 0, 1, 2 are assigned respectively to unfavorable, neutral, and favorable attitudes. Thus for a particular respondent the scale may take values of 0 to 10. The scale is nonresponsive to persistent improvement or persistent deterioration in attitudes: Values less than 0 or more than 10 are impossible.

[8]Some researchers have sought to substitute such "objective" cyclical variables as "stock prices," or "unemployment rate." The advantage of consumer attitudes is that they take account of *any* factor that the decision maker perceives as important and not just those factors that affect stock prices or unemployment rates. Hence, consumer attitudes may *in principle* be expected to be more inclusive and more robust than substitutes of this type. Friend and Adams (1964) found that stock prices and unemployment rate were effective substitutes for consumer attitudes for the 1953–1962 period. As noted below, this result did not prevail over a longer period.

nomic variables lack.[9] We are now ready to examine the forecasting record of consumer attitudes.[10]

THE FORECASTING RECORD OF CONSUMER ATTITUDES

Katona and his associates have argued that consumer attitudes are most helpful in forecasting cyclical turning points. Charts 1, 2, and 3 (pp. 398–400) are responsive to this claim. They depict the simple relationship between the Index of Consumer Sentiment and measures of aggregate discretionary expenditures during the three most severe postwar recessions. Clearly a correlation exists.

For mainstream economists a much more stringent test has been applied: What—if anything—does the Index of Consumer Sentiment add to the predictive ability of a well-specified economic model? The investigation of this problem by Hymans (1970) may be taken as definitive.

Hymans sought to explain aggregate expenditures on new automobiles for 1954–1968 on the basis of the widely accepted stock adjustment model. Briefly, the stock adjustment model asserts that current expenditures on new automobiles represent consumers' efforts to adjust their *current* stock of automobiles to their *desired* stock, the level of their desired stock being a function of income (positive relationship) and automobile prices (negative relationship). Hymans' most relevant result was the following:

$$(1) \quad A = 0.17\, DPI_{-1} - 27.87\, P_{Auto} - 0.12\, Stock_{-1} - 0.77\, Unem_{-1}$$
$$ (7.69) (-4.98) (-4.78) (-4.02)$$

$$+ 1.73\, Strike + 0.30\, Att + 23.07$$
$$ (4.44) (3.85) (3.71)$$

$\bar{R}^2 = 0.965$ Standard error of the estimate = \$1.06B
Durbin-Watson statistic = 1.88

where:

A = consumer expenditures on autos and parts in billions of 1958 dollars, seasonally adjusted at annual rates

DPI_{-1} = real disposable personal income, net of transfers, during the previous quarter

[9]As an example, it seems plausible that a consumer may react more favorably and spend more freely for discretionary products when he expects a given income increase to be permanent. A "temporary" increase might be viewed less favorably and hence produces a smaller or zero increase in spending.

[10]In assessing the record we will rely on data collected by the Survey Research Center, it being the longest and most accessible set.

Chart 1. Consumer Attitudes and Automobile Purchases in the 1957-1958 Recession*

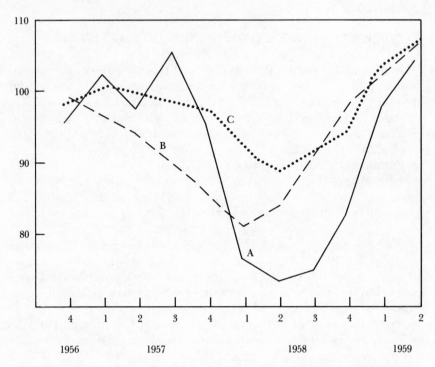

SOURCE: From George Katona, *Psychological Economics* (New York: Elsevier, 1975). Reprinted with permission of the Publisher.

*Interpretation: For the "Index of Consumer Sentiment times Income" variable, the 4th quarter of 1956 = 100; for "New Car Registrations" and "Consumer Durables Expenditures," the first half of 1957 = 100. Data source: Index of Consumer Sentiment from the Survey Research Center; other data: *Survey of Current Business.*

Labels: A New Car Registration
       B Index of Consumer Sentiment times Income
       C Consumer Durables Expenditures

P_{Auto} = ratio of automobile price to other prices, previous quarter

Stock_{-1} = actual auto stock, end of previous quarter

Unem_{-1} = unemployment rate for males twenty years or over, in percent, previous quarter

Strike = assumes values of +1 and +2 in quarters disrupted by auto strikes; otherwise, 0

Att_{-1} = Filtered Index of Consumer Sentiment, assuming actual Index values only in quarters when the change exceeded a threshold value; otherwise, 0

Numbers in parentheses are t statistics

Chart 2. The 1970 Recession: Consumer Attitudes, Disposable Income, and Personal Automobile Expenditures*

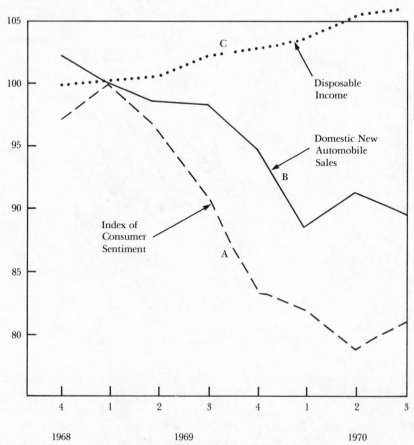

SOURCE: From George Katona, *Psychological Economics* (New York: Elsevier, 1975). Reprinted with permission of the Publisher.

*Interpretation: First quarter of 1970 = 100. Data source: same as Chart 1.

Our focus is on the attitudes variable (Att_{-1}). Note its "filtered" formulation: It takes a positive value only when a "large" change in consumer sentiment is registered. This occurred in seventeen out of sixty-eight quarters. This formulation is consistent with Katona's view that attitudes are important in determining consumer behavior when "major" changes in the personal or business environment are perceived to have taken place. On the other hand, one should not conclude too hastily that this filtered formulation is best. Estimates for other models and other time periods (F. G. Adams and Klein, 1972; Shapiro, 1972) do not support the view that the filtered index performs better than the entire series.

Chart 3.   Index of Consumer Sentiment

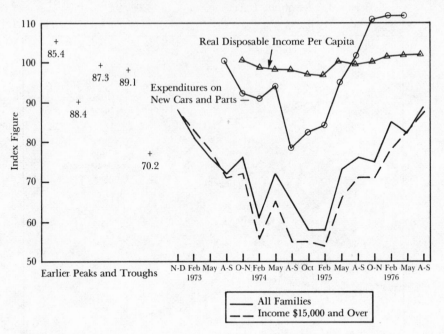

SOURCE: From *Monitoring Economic Change Program* (Ann Arbor: Survey Research Center, University of Michigan, 1976). Reprinted with permission of the Publisher.

Katona observes plausibly: "I do not like the implication that all but 17 of the 68 index measures can be discarded. Sure, predicting turning points is of primary importance, but we always need the reassurance that nothing exceptional has happened and that extrapolations are permissible."[11]

This is a more stringent test than a casual examination might suggest. In the first place, attitudes are *trendless,* while their competitors (income, price, beginning stock, unemployment rate) exhibit strong positive trends over time just as the dependent variable does. Thus it is possible that some of the variation in the dependent variable may be spuriously assigned to an independent variable exhibiting a similar positive trend over time. Second, following the economist's predilection for "objective" variables (especially those that require no special data-collection effort), the unemployment rate has been included though it is not part and parcel of the stock adjustment model. It might be argued that the unemployment rate is a proxy for consumers' perceptions of business conditions, exactly the type of perception that an index of "consumer sentiment" should reflect.

[11]Letter dated September 7, 1977.

On the basis of this and several other lines of investigation, Hymans concluded:

> Changes in consumer sentiment—if properly filtered—do improve the forecasting accuracy of a stock-adjustment model of automobile expenditures. It is apparently possible to forecast ahead at least one quarter (and perhaps further investigation will suggest still longer) on the basis of the current quarter's sentiment index. It is also possible to forecast the *systematic* component of the sentiment index one quarter ahead with the aid of current stock market prices, thus permitting an auto forecast at least two quarters ahead without a forecast of stock market prices (Hymans, 1970: 195).[12]

THE TIME SERIES–CROSS SECTION PARADOX

The consumer attitudes approach was conceived as a solution to the paramount *time series* problem of forecasting and explaining fluctuations over time in aggregate consumption expenditures. But from the very beginning investigators sought to establish a cross-section relationship between the expressed attitudes of individual consumers (representing their households) and their subsequent purchase behavior. Efforts by Klein and Lansing (1955, using 1952–1953 reinterview data), Tobin (1959, also 1952–1953 data), Mueller (1960, using 1954–1956 data), and F. G. Adams (1965, using 1957–1958 data) all failed! It was Adams who, in calling attention to the time series success and the cross-section failure of consumer attitudes, dubbed this phenomenon a "paradox."

So for the first twenty years the consumer attitudes approach was plagued by its inability to explain the concurrent time series success and cross-section failure. The reasons to establish a cross-section relationship? Maynes (1967) argued in 1967 that

> the failure of attitudes at the cross-section level is the consequence of measurement difficulties.... Specifically, I believe that existing techniques fail to eliminate or sufficiently reduce interpersonal differences in scaling of responses to subjective questions. Measurement advances here would be likely to have favorable payoffs not only for the attitudes approach but for any situation where questions are used to elicit subjective data.

---

[12]Recent theoretical work by Westin (1975) asserts that the application of the stock adjustment model to *aggregate* data is inappropriate. As a substitute Westin proposes a "discretionary replacement" model. He then turns to empirical estimation and compares the performance of stock adjustment and discretionary replacement models, including "discretionary" variables with the Index of Consumer Sentiment among them. Unfortunately, his estimates rely on *annual* data, taking them well beyond the predictive period claimed by Katona and his associates. Hence his estimates, though theoretically convincing, have not provided us with a valid test of the predictive value of consumer attitudes.

We shall return to this problem in the fourth section, "Calibrating Subjective Scales."

The "paradox" was partially laid to rest in a 1969 doctoral dissertation by Dunkelberg (1972). Dunkelberg used 1967–1968 data and improved on earlier cross-section studies by using an attitudes index that corresponded more closely to the time series index and a broader definition of discretionary expenditures, eliminating older households from the sample, and taking explicit account of the effects of moving. The result was the detection of a strong attitudes effect:

$$(2) \quad DE = 0.08\, Y_{66} + 0.047\, (Y_{67} - Y_{66}) + 3.34\, \text{Age} + 344.78\, \text{Moved}$$
$$ (0.00) \qquad (0.01) \qquad\qquad\qquad (3.30) \qquad\quad (101.25)$$
$$ + 74.89\, A_{66} + 48.74\, (A_{67} - A_{66}) - 216.01$$
$$ (18.53) \qquad (20.66)$$

$$R^2 = 0.168$$
$$SE = \$1513$$

Numbers in parentheses are estimated standard errors.

where:

DE = total net outlay on cars, durables, additions and repairs to homes, vacations, and sports and hobby equipment during 1967 (discretionary expenditures)

Y_{66} = family disposable personal income for 1966

A_{66} = Index of Consumer Sentiment for January 1967 for sample family

Age = actual age of head of family

Move = 1, if family moved during 1967; otherwise 0

For this sample the attitudes effect is unequivocal. However, Dunkelberg claims that the "decks are stacked" against earlier tests and even this test due to: (1) too long a prediction period (one year); and (2) the random measurement errors cited by Maynes.

THE APPARENT FAILURE: BUYING INTENTIONS

George Katona's other "child" in the attitudes area was the buying intentions approach to forecasting. The idea is simple: If you wish to know whether an individual will purchase an automobile in a given period, ask the decision maker to express his intention to buy. To forecast the aggregate number of purchases, collect such information from a cross section of consumers. A time series index expressing shifts in intention rates should be correlated with aggregate purchases of that commodity.

During the period 1950–1970, the buying intentions approach was much more widely accepted than the consumer attitudes approach. The same cross-section investigations that showed no relation between attitudes and purchase behavior disclosed strong relationships between expressed intentions to buy and subsequent purchases of automobiles as well as houses and "other durables." In 1957–1959 the Tobin article (1959) and the report of a Federal Reserve committee chaired by Arthur Smithies (1955) of Harvard University resulted in the inauguration of the Quarterly Survey of Buying Intentions (1959), conducted by the Bureau of the Census under the sponsorship of the Federal Reserve Board and collecting data on buying intentions from 17,000 households. Bold and imaginative cross-section testing undertaken by F. Thomas Juster (1966) led to the substitution of "subjective probability" questions for the earlier questions and scales ("Do you expect to buy a car within the next twelve months?"; scales: "definitely will buy," "probably," "maybe, depends," "will not buy"). In the 1960s buying intentions were successful in both cross-section and time series tests. (For a detailed review of the attitudes–buying intentions "contest" as of 1967, see Maynes [1967].) Indeed Juster (1964a), the major protagonist of the subjective probability interpretation of buying intentions, asserted and then demonstrated that it was possible to construct a forecasting model consisting wholly of anticipatory data (attitudes plus purchase expectations) that could perform as well as a fully specified objective model (Juster and Wachtel, 1974, 1972).

For the buying intentions approach, there was only one rub. In summer 1969, instead of signaling the forthcoming major downturn in automobile purchases as did the Index of Consumer Sentiment, the U.S. Bureau of the Census' (1969) Current Buying Expectations Survey foretold continued high spending for automobiles. This major failure led to a swift termination of this survey and hence to the demise of this "attitudinal" approach to macroeconomic forecasting. McNeil, Adams, and Juster (McNeil, 1974) provide interesting postmortems on this untimely death.

THE REASONS WHY

This account of consumer attitudes approaches has focused on their predictive record. Katona has argued persuasively that the collection and analysis of data on consumer attitudes make possible the *understanding* of consumer behavior as well as its prediction. A single example shows how this might be useful.

How *should* and how *will* consumers react to expectations of price increases? "Buy now, preemptively," is the unanimous answer given by "rational" expectations, economic theory, students of economics, and professional economists. But consumers have time and time again in the postwar period reacted in exactly the opposite way: Instead of buying in advance they "sat on their hands." Why? Surveys tell us that rising prices make them feel pessimistic and this pessimism causes them to postpone discretionary spending (Katona, 1975: chap. 9).

A SUMMING-UP

That consumer attitudes possess time series (and probably cross-section) predictive value, especially at cyclical turning points, there cannot be the slightest doubt. Nonetheless, they have been accepted more by the business than by the economics community.[13] The reason: Their logic is alien to economic theory and to the deductive tradition of economists.[14] Instead, economists have embraced "rational expectations," assigning it a front and center position.

Calibrating Subjective Scales: Report on a (Possibly) Critical Experiment

Almost by definition, attitudes as "predispositions to actions" are amorphous and no obvious metric seems at hand. (However, cf. Maynes [1972]; Stevens [1966].) As noted above, it was my view that interpersonal differences in the scaling of responses to subjective questions explained (at least in part) the difficulties that behavioral economists encountered, over an entire generation, in seeking to demonstrate a cross-section effect of consumer attitudes on subsequent purchase behavior.

In the interest of interdisciplinary communication this section reports on an experiment in which efforts to "calibrate" subjective data appeared to yield considerable success. It may turn out that this phenomenon and these techniques are already familiar to sociologists (and to psychologists and marketers as well). In that case I will be instructed. But it may turn out that the technique is not known and may prove helpful to sociologists.

[13]Of the major econometric models forecasting GNP, only Wharton includes a consumer attitudes variable. It does this in both its automobile and housing equations (F. G. Adams and Klein, 1972).

[14]The dominant graduate text in macroeconomic theory (Branson, 1972) makes no mention of consumer attitudes and follows Keynes in assigning to aggregate consumption expenditures a passive role. The same observation applies to almost all undergraduate texts in macroeconomics. The older graduate text by Ackley (1960) is a commendable exception in dealing with both problems.

The experiment sought to ascertain whether "fully informed consumers" will make identical quality assessments of a given set of product models. Here we recapitulate only as much of the background of the experiment as is necessary for understanding.

The product set consisted of seventeen varieties of men's ten-speed racing bicycles (e.g., Fuji Road Racer, Peugeot U08). The subjects were twenty-five students in the author's undergraduate class, CEPP 332, "Consumer Decision Making," in fall 1975. The subjects were made "fully informed" by: (1) reading an article on ten-speed bicycles in the January 1974 issue of *Consumer Reports;* and (2) being given test data from the article, coded in a standard form. As a first approximation, quality, G_{ik} (= G for "goodness") was defined as follows:

$$G_{ik} = \sum_{l=0}^{n} (W_{il}) \cdot Ch_{ikl}) \tag{3}$$

where:

W = the relative weight (or importance) assigned to a service characteristic of the bicycle, e.g., the bicycle's wet-braking ability; weights sum to 100

Ch = characteristic score representing the satisfaction derived from the amount of that characteristic embodied in a particular variety of bicycle; characteristic scores may take values from 0 to 10, 10 being the amount of satisfaction derived from the "ideal" bicycle

The subscripts: i denotes the individual making the quality assessment

k denotes the variety (or model) of bicycle

l denotes the characteristic

The model is additive, though sufficiently flexible to accommodate nonadditive relations. Mathematically it is identical with the multiattribute model widely known and used in marketing. For a detailed, though simplified, discussion of the concept of quality defined here, see Maynes (1976b); for a more formal discussion, cf. Maynes (1976a).

As part of being "fully informed," each student had read and been examined extensively regarding the quality model he/she was asked to use. For the experiment his task was to make a numerical quality assessment for each of the seventeen varieties of bicycle that Consumers Union had tested, using the formula above and the materials from *Consumer Reports.* Ten-speed bicycles were thought to be a subject of intrinsic interest to most students, thus leading to more careful performance by the assessors. In all, twelve performance characteristics (bicycle weight, chainguard/kickstand included, extent of pedal reflectors, fenders included, ease of shifting, handling, pedal response, saddle comfort, manufacturing "quality," gearshift range, ease of rolling, wet-brake effectiveness) were weighted and assigned characteristic scores. The multiplicative formula (as scaled) made possible quality scores from 0 to 1,000. Student calculations were checked for accuracy and consistency. Assessments by twenty-five out of twenty-eight students were of acceptable quality and constitute the data on which the analysis is based.

THE RESULTS: THEIR INTERPRETATION AND SIGNIFICANCE

Our analysis will focus only on the final numerical quality scores and not on either the underlying weights or characteristics scores.

TABLE 1. Standard Deviations of Quality Scores for 10-Speed Bicycles; Uncalibrated vs. Calibrated Quality Scores*

PART A: UNCALIBRATED QUALITY SCORES

Percentile	Standard Deviation
10th	86
25th	91
50th	97
75th	111
90th	114
Range	80 to 117
Mean	99

PART B: CALIBRATED QUALITY SCORES

Percentile	Standard Deviation
10th	17
25th	19
50th	22
75th	31
90th	36
Range	15 to 38
Mean	25

*The table reads: "Of 17 varieties of bicycles the standard deviation of the uncalibrated quality scores was 86 for the lowest 10 percent of assessors; 91 for the lowest 25 percent; etc.; the range of standard deviations was from 80 to 117 and the mean was 99, etc."

Chart 4. Mean Scores and Distribution of Scores of 17 Varieties of Men's 10-Speed Bicycles

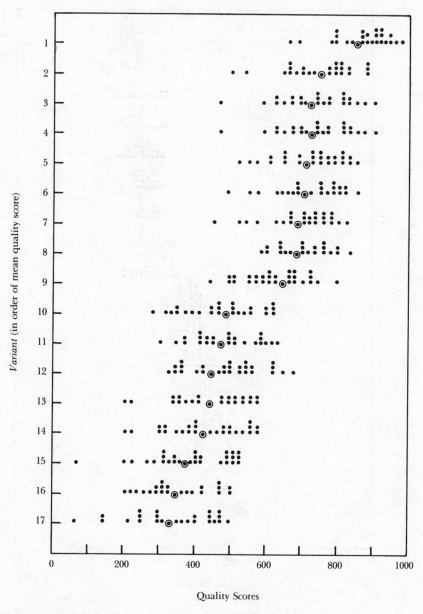

⊚ = mean quality scores.
• = individual observations.

Chart 5.   Final Normalized Mean Scores and Distribution of Scores of 17 Varieties
of Men's 10-Speed Bicycles

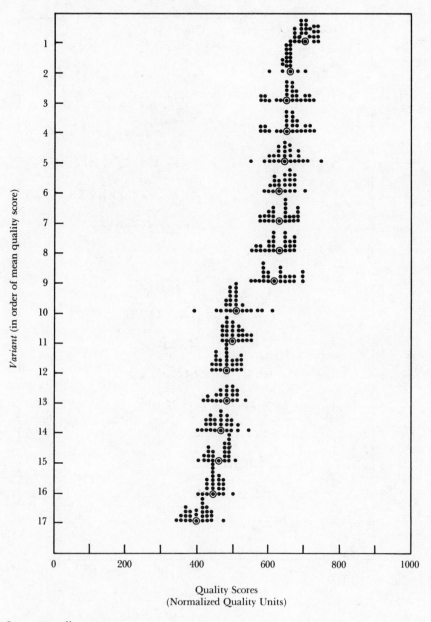

⊙ = mean quality scores.
• = individual observations.

Depicted on chart 4 are the *uncalibrated* quality scores assigned by twenty-five students to each of the seventeen models of ten-speed bicycles. As depicted, they convey most emphatically the impression that this sample of "fully informed consumers" made highly variable assessments of quality. Turn now to chart 5, where the *calibrated* quality scores are depicted. Note that variability of assessments has been drastically reduced to about one-quarter of its chart 4 range. Parts A and B of table 1 show the same result somewhat more precisely. The critical statistic is the before- and after-calibration standard deviation per model averaged over twenty-five assessors. The mean *before-calibration* standard deviation is 99; the mean *after-calibration* standard deviation is 25!

What is going on here? Obviously, assessors have substituted their own "elastic" scale for the apparently precise scale of equation 3. Two kinds of behavior account for the differences between charts 4 and 5:

1. *The "English/Latin" Effect.* Some subjects, endowed with what might be characterized as English or British understatement, made assessments that, on a 0 to 1,000 scale, fell within a narrow range, say 200, while others—the Latins—made assessments that *usually* fell outside the same range. This effect is documented in the standard deviation over all 17 models of the quality scores originally assigned by the 25 assessors. Table 2 shows just how much these standard deviations vary: Note the range of 92 to 278; even the middle 50 percent range from 132 to 231, an almost 1-to-2 ratio.

T A B L E 2 . "English-Latin" Effects: How Standard Deviations of Quality Scores Varied Over Quality Assessors*

PERCENTILE	STANDARD DEVIATION OF THIS ASSESSOR'S SCORES
10th	110
25th	132
50th	165
75th	231
90th	263
Range	92 to 278

*The table reads: "For the lowest 10 percent of assessors (out of 25), the standard deviation for the quality scores they assigned to 17 varieties of bicycles was 110; for the lowest 25 percent, 132; etc. The range in standard deviations was from 92 to 278."

**T A B L E 3 .   Pessimist-Optimist Effects:
How Mean Quality Scores Varied Over
Quality Assessors***

PERCENTILE	MEAN QUALITY SCORE FOR THIS ASSESSOR
10th	463
25th	540
50th	588
75th	620
90th	652
Range	385 to 656

*The table reads: "For the lowest 10 percent of assessors,
the mean quality score assigned was 463 or less; for the
lowest 25 percent, 540 or less; etc. The range in mean
scores was from 385 to 656."

2. *The Pessimist/Optimist Bias.* Apparently some individuals tended
habitually to prefer the lower or "pessimistic" portion of a numerical scale while others preferred the higher or "optimistic"
portion of a numerical scale. The appropriate statistic for documenting this tendency is the mean quality score over the 17 varieties. The distribution of these means over the 25 assessors is
shown in table 3. Again, the tendency is emphatic: Means range
from 385 to 656 while for the middle 50 percent the range runs
from 540 to 620.

To purge the data of these undesirable effects—a process that we
have dubbed "calibration"—we have utilized a commonplace procedure.
We have expressed the quality score assigned to a particular variety in
terms of that individual's standard deviation units. Then, on chart 5 and
part B of table 1, we have reconverted these quality scores expressed in
standard units back into quality scores on the 0 to 1,000 scale by utilizing
the grand mean quality score and the overall standard deviation, based
on *all* the quality scores assigned by *all* the assessors. A numerical example should make this procedure clear:

Assessor #2's quality score for Variety #1	801
Assessor #2's standard deviation (17 bicycles)	125.1
Assessor #2's mean quality score (17 bicycles)	736.1

The score for Variety #1 in Assessor
#2's standard units $0.52 = \dfrac{(801 - 736.1)}{98.7}$

Overall mean quality score (per model)	569.6
Overall mean standard deviation	98.9
Calibrated quality score for Variety #1 for this assessor	$621.0 = (0.52 \times 98.9) + 569.6$

For *this* sample of assessors dealing with *this* problem, calibration designed to eliminate English-Latin and pessimist-optimist effects succeeded in removing about three-quarters of the variation in initial quality scores. It entitles me to claim—I believe—that these assessors demonstrate considerable (though by no means perfect) uniformity in assigning quality scores to these seventeen bicycles.

It seems plausible that many of the numerical and verbal rating scales employed to "measure" attitudes may be subject to similar biases. This experiment raises the possibility that such biases could be eliminated.

Such an achievement would have substantial payoffs: (1) attitudinal effects that have escaped detection might now be identified: (2) the sample size to attain a given level of precision—either in terms of test item questions or number of respondents—might be reduced and still yield a given level of precision; (3) it might become possible to attain that great goal of psychologists and economists—the making of interpersonal comparisons of utility.

35

Attitude and Behavior: A Social-Psychological Problem

Herbert C. Kelman

MY PRIMARY INTEREST in the attitude-behavior controversy focuses on the theoretical status of the concept of attitude and its relationship to action. I bring to this discussion the bias that attitude, or some such concept, is a useful—even essential—tool for social scientists; that it must be conceptualized as an integral part of action; and that such conceptualization presupposes a social-psychological level of analysis.

Current Status of the Attitude-Behavior Controversy

The attitude-behavior controversy has been with us now for over forty years, if we take LaPiere's (1934) classical study as its starting point. In recent years various studies and reviews (e.g., Wicker, 1969) have raised serious questions about the empirical relationship of attitudes to actions. These critiques have led some observers to conclude that measured attitudes (i.e., what people say) are poor predictors of behavior (i.e., what people do); others have gone even further and questioned the utility of the attitude concept as such.

My own assumptions about the status of this controversy, as of 1977, can be summarized as follows:

1. More recent reviews of the empirical evidence suggest solid support for the existence of a reliable, if moderate, association between attitudes and behavior. The excellent chapter by Schuman and Johnson

(1976) has helped to place some of the negative findings in perspective, clarified the criteria to be used in evaluating the association (e.g., by distinguishing between literal consistency and correlational consistency), and shown that the most common finding is one of positive association. A very recent systematic review of the empirical research by Ajzen and Fishbein (1977) shows that the strength of the relationship between attitude and behavior depends on the degree of correspondence between the attitudinal and behavioral entities: When the target and action elements of the two entities correspond to one another, attitude-behavior correlations are consistently high.

2. These reassessments of the empirical evidence allow me to affirm even more strongly than I did before that the validity of the attitude concept is not really at issue. A few years ago the concept was beleaguered with criticisms stemming not only from the attitude-behavior literature but also from studies in the dissonance and self-perception traditions, which suggested that attitudes—being generated by action—were epiphenomenal. This state of affairs led me to devote my presidential address for the American Psychological Association's Division of Personality and Social Psychology to a defense of attitude (Kelman, 1974a). I now feel that there is no longer any need to be defensive. To be sure, there is room for debate about the usefulness and epistemological status of the concept. But whether or not attitudes exist need not occupy us; rather, we should ask whether attitudes "can be conceptualized in ways that yield useful analyses and insightful conclusions about social behavior" (Kelman, 1974a: 316).

3. The relationship between attitudes and behavior is not synonymous with the relationship between words and deeds. Failure to make this distinction has caused unnecessary ambiguities in the attitude-behavior controversy. The two issues are closely related because the best indicators we have for a person's attitudes are his verbal responses to questionnaires or interviews. But we must keep in mind that, theoretically, responses to questionnaires and interviews are behaviors: The questioning situation is a behavioral situation with its own structure, demands, and role requirements. Responses in these situations constitute valid indicators of the "true" underlying attitude (which is, of course, a dispositional concept) only insofar as the investigator takes special precautions to reduce the situational demands of the measurement situation—e.g., by the context he provides, the instructions he gives, the atmosphere he creates, the assurances of anonymity he offers, the types of questions he asks. Many verbal response situations clearly do not meet these criteria and are therefore unsuited to the assessment of underlying attitudes. A good example of a situation unsuited for the assessment of attitudes is the verbal response situation in the LaPiere (1934) study, to which I shall return below.

4. The ability to predict a person's specific action from a measure of his general attitude toward the object of that action (or, as is often the case, toward a larger category to which that object belongs) does not constitute a reasonable test of the attitude-behavior relationship. Certainly, on theoretical grounds, attitudes ought to be associated with behavior, since they are presumed to predispose a person to act toward an object in a particular way. But this merely means that attitude is a determinant of behavior, not that it can serve as a stand-in for behavior (i.e., that assessing general attitudes can substitute for observing specific behaviors). Behavior in a specific situation is determined by a variety of other factors, in addition to attitude toward the object. Moreover, there must be a theoretically meaningful degree of correspondence between the attitude and the behavior if they are to show an association (cf. Ajzen and Fishbein, 1977). It is possible to improve the power of attitude measures to predict a specific action, for example, by directing one's questions to the person's attitude toward performing that particular act instead of his attitude toward the object (cf. Fishbein, 1967; Ajzen and Fishbein, 1970). However, finding the best verbal predictor of a specific overt action is only one part of the agenda in exploring the attitude-behavior relationship. The relationship between general attitudes toward certain social objects and various actions vis-à-vis the object is a legitimate theoretical and empirical issue in its own right. And the question here is not merely *whether* such attitudes are strongly associated with behavior; *when* they are and when they are not is precisely one of the most interesting questions to explore.

The LaPiere Study

With these assumptions about the status of the attitude-behavior controversy in mind, let me now turn—as so many others have done over the past three decades—to the LaPiere study. That study set the tone for the debate on the attitude-behavior issue, and has contributed to some of the ambiguities of that debate to which I have alluded.

Much of the attitude-behavior controversy, it seems to me, is based on a misreading of LaPiere, to which he himself contributed by entitling his article "Attitudes vs. Actions." The contrast in the LaPiere study is between what respondents say on the questionnaire and what they do when the Chinese couple appears at their establishments. He does not—as most of his readers seem to have done—equate the questionnaire responses with attitudes. In fact, he implies that, if anything, the behavioral responses are better indicators of attitude than the questionnaire responses. He basically concludes that what people say they will do (i.e., their verbal response to a symbolic stimulus) does not tell you what they will do—except in situations like voting behavior, where the behavioral situation also involves verbal responses to symbolic stimuli. He does not conclude that attitude is an invalid or useless concept. He merely concludes that questionnaire responses do not necessarily tell us what people's true attitudes are.

In effect, then, the LaPiere study does not really deal with the attitude vs. action contrast, but with the words vs. deeds contrast. The failure to make this distinction has characterized much of the ensuing debate. I am arguing that LaPiere's study, which has been used as the prototype for attitude-behavior research, does not in fact address itself to that issue.

LaPiere's verbal measure cannot be viewed as a measure of attitude. It is clearly a behavioral measure; how a person responds to it has obvious real-life consequences. The questionnaire did not try to elicit private, anonymous responses, but rather public statements about organizational policy. Thus the study deals with the relationship between policy and practice, not with that between attitude and action. Dillehay (1973) and others have pointed out that the respondents to LaPiere's questionnaire were not necessarily the same individuals as those whose behavior was observed. Thus, strictly speaking, the study demonstrates inconsistency between *organizational* policy and practice rather than *individual* saying and doing. On the other hand, most of the establishments studied by LaPiere were small, family-owned businesses. Thus it can reasonably be assumed that, in a large proportion of the cases, the two sets of data were provided by the same individual. The findings are so strong, in the sense that there was virtually no variance in either questionnaire responses or behavior, that they would certainly be significant even if one included only the data for that subset of establishments in which the same individual provided both responses.

Granting, then, that we are dealing with the words and deeds of the same individual, LaPiere's study can be described as a study of the relationship between two behavioral responses in two very differently structured situations, placing the person into two very different roles. In responding to the questionnaire the individual was acting as representative of his organization facing the larger social system; he was expressing organizational policy in what was essentially a public, official context. In the behavioral situation he was also acting in part as representative of the organization; how he acted toward the Chinese couple would certainly affect the reputation of the organization, especially if there were bystanders observing the interaction. Most important, however, he was enacting a role in the microsystem defined by his immediate interaction with the Chinese couple. It would appear that the situational demands—particularly the desire to avoid the embarrassment of turning away a respectable, pleasant, well-behaved couple, presenting themselves as clients expecting to be served—were so strong as to outweigh any other considerations.

LaPiere's striking finding suggests that both of his measurement situations were almost entirely controlled by structural or situational constraints. The questionnaire responses were constrained by organizational policy, which in turn was governed by national norms; the behavioral responses were constrained by the structure of the immediate situation, which in turn was governed by powerful norms of social interaction. Attitudes toward the Chinese, as an individual difference variable, clearly played no role in determining responses in either situation, as evidenced by the lack of variance in both sets of data. That is, virtually all respondents said they would not serve Chinese, and virtually all in fact did serve the Chinese couple. This finding has some interesting implications for the nature of these attitudes at the time, but they are quite different from the implications drawn in much of the work that took off from LaPiere.

Unlike the LaPiere study, much of the subsequent work is indeed relevant to the attitude-behavior issue, but the misreading of LaPiere has set the tone for a good deal of the conceptualization of the attitude-behavior issue that followed. I have dwelt on the LaPiere study because it points so clearly to the effects of social-structural and role requirements on the attitude-behavior relationship. But these have been largely ignored, even by sociologists working in this area—a tendency that began with the error of casting the LaPiere findings in "attitude vs. action" terms. In much of the work, attitudes in their relationship to behavior have been viewed primarily in psychological terms, and occasionally in aggregate terms. These perspectives are certainly relevant, depending on one's purposes. But I would maintain that, overall, a truly relevant conceptualization of the issues requires a social-psychological analysis of attitude, action, and the relationship between the two. By this I mean an analysis that focuses on the intersection between individual processes and social system processes, keeping in mind that social interaction represents the point of intersection between these two types of process.

Propositions for a Social-Psychological Analysis of the Attitude-Behavior Relationship

To clarify what I mean by a social-psychological analysis of the attitude-behavior relationship, let me briefly discuss four "propositions" that underlie such an analysis. My use of the term "propositions" here should not be taken too literally; what I am offering are not formal, testable statements, but general expressions of a point of view. Each of the propositions, as I shall try to indicate, has implications for the nature and strength of the relationship between attitude and action.

1. *Each behavioral situation in which an attitude is put to the test can be viewed as an episode in a continuing socialization process.* It is helpful to view behavioral situations in which attitudes are put to the test as episodes in a continuing socialization process, because this allows us to apply to this problem a general social-psychological framework for conceiving socialization. Within such a framework, socialization is viewed as a process of negotiation between the socializee and "society" (or an organization or institution) as represented by the socializing agent. Each party to the negotiation makes its own demands, which jointly determine the socialization outcome.

Similarly, a specific behavioral situation can be viewed as one in which both the individual actor and the situation make certain demands. One of the demands of the individual is to act out—or to act in accordance with—his attitudes. To oversimplify, as a first approximation, the individual's attitude represents his contribution to the negotiated outcome. It is his preferred basis for action if the choice were entirely his. The attitude has to compete with situational demands, which are essentially of two kinds—corresponding to the two factors that I postulated for LaPiere's questionnaire responses and behavioral responses, respectively: social-structural demands, that is, the requirements of the larger social system (the organization, the society) in whose context this behavioral episode occurs; and interaction demands, that is, the requirements of the immediate microsystem in which the individual participates.

If the person's attitude is in some way incongruent with one or both of these sets of role requirements, it must negotiate with them in producing the behavioral outcome. Clearly, under the circumstances, we cannot expect literal correspondence between attitude and behavior. The degree of correspondence always depends on the relative strength of the competing demands from the individual and from the situation. In conceptualizing attitudes it is important to avoid thinking of the structural and interactional demands as extraneous variables that somehow obscure the functioning of attitudes. Rather, they must be seen as integral parts of the daily life of an attitude, with which it must always be ready to enter into negotiation in the course of producing behavioral outcomes.

2. *Attitude is simultaneously a personal disposition and a societal product.* As a first approximation, I treated attitude as the contribution of the individual to the negotiation process that occurs in an action situation. In actual fact, however, attitude itself is a *social*-psychological concept in the sense that it always has a societal referent. Each individual's attitude is a

product of social interaction, which he shares to a greater or lesser extent
with other members of his diverse groups, organizations, and communities. An individual's attitude is not necessarily a carbon copy of the
attitudes held by fellow group members; there is often considerable
variation in the manifestation of a particular attitude among the members of a group. Nevertheless, when we talk about a social attitude, we
refer to a disposition that acquires a large part of its meaning from its
shared character within a collectivity. In that sense, aggregate attitudes
represent a system property; the attitudes of particular individuals (or
subgroups) represent variants of that system property.

To understand the relationship of attitudes to action we must examine the structure of the particular attitude within the relevant collectivity
and within the individual. Within a collectivity, different attitudes differ
in the degree to which there is room for variability. Certain attitudes are
so closely linked to group goals, or group identity, or concerns for group
survival, that there are strong pressures toward uniformity and little
tolerance for deviation. In those cases action is likely to be controlled to a
high degree by situational demands, and individual attitudes, insofar as
they deviate from the group norm, are often overpowered by these
demands. On the other hand, certain attitudes are seen as matters of
individual taste and preference, or as issues for debate within the collectivity, or as legitimate expressions of differing subgroup interests. In
those cases an individual's attitudes are more likely to compete on an
equal footing with situational demands.

Within the individual, attitudes differ in how individualized they
are—that is, to what degree they have been transformed, in the process
of acquisition and development, from being primarily components of a
social (or role) system to being components of a personal (or value)
system. In this connection, the theoretical distinction among three
processes of social influence—compliance, identification, and
internalization—that I have proposed in earlier writings (cf. Kelman,
1961, 1974b) may be of some relevance. A disposition acquired through
compliance is essentially a tendency to give a particular verbal response,
rather than an attitude per se; a disposition acquired through identification is an attitude that functions primarily as part of the requirements
associated with a particular role; while a disposition acquired through
internalization is an attitude that makes an independent contribution to
the negotiated outcome of action situations. Thus the nature of the
attitude held by a given individual determines the probability that it will
be expressed—or translated into action—in a particular social situation.
Compliance-based dispositions are by definition controlled by situational
demands, whereas internalized attitudes offer the strongest competition
to such demands. Attitudes based on identification are intermediate, in
that they are likely to be expressed to the extent that situational demands

and role requirements bring them into salience. In short, the relationship between attitude and action varies with the degree of independence that a particular attitude has from the situational demands of the action situation.

3. *The effect of structural requirements on behavior is mediated by the definition of the situation in which the attitude is put to the test.* In proposition (1) I treated the pressures and constraints that operate in the behavioral situation as entirely structural. Again, however, I would propose that these constraints are most usefully conceptualized in social-psychological terms. Structural factors—both those derived from the macrosystem (i.e., organizational and societal requirements) and those derived from the microsystem (i.e., requirements of the interaction situation)—are reflected, at the individual level, in the definition of the situation and the perception of the norms and role expectations that govern behavior in that situation.

Definitions of the situation are often subject to considerable individual differences. Hence our ability to predict how an individual will behave in a given situation—or, more precisely, what impact situational requirements will have on his behavior relative to the impact of his own attitude toward the object of the behavior—is greatly enhanced by our knowledge of an individual's definition of the situation (or the distribution of such definitions within the population). Individual differences in definition of the situation are assessed, directly or indirectly, by some of the attitude measures that have been proposed as good predictors of behavior, such as attitude toward the situation (Rokeach, 1969) or attitude toward the act and beliefs about the normative expectations of significant others (Fishbein, 1967).

Even where individual differences in the definition of the situation are minimal, as in the LaPiere (1934) study, it does not mean that attitudinal factors play no part. It simply means that the norms and role requirements of the situation are so strong that there is a high degree of uniformity in defining the situation within the population. Presumably, one might find variations in the definition of even such a powerfully structured situation—and hence variations in behavior—if one went beyond a particular culture or historical period. From a theoretical point of view, it is important to keep in mind that attitudes toward the object are not necessarily inoperative in such situations, but the relationship between attitude and action is attenuated by the uniformity in definition of the situation. However, from a practical point of view, knowing a person's attitude toward the object will add very little to our ability to predict his behavior where the structure of the situation is so powerful that it leaves little room for individual differences in defining it.

4. *Attitude and action are linked in a continuing reciprocal process, each generating the other in an endless chain.* Attitude is not a static psychological

entity that can be separated—functionally or temporally—from the flow of action, but is an integral part of action. It is in the course of action—and more specifically social interaction—that attitudes are formed, tested, and modified or abandoned. Often an action situation provides the occasion for reexamining one's attitudes: The person is exposed to new information about the attitude object, about the position of reference groups, or about the implications of his attitudes for some of his values, and this new information may lead to attitude change. Thus what appears to be an inconsistency between attitude and action may in fact be an indication of attitude change, coming about in the way in which attitude change typically comes about.

Moreover, the action itself may be an integral part of an ongoing attitude change process. Though the person may be acting in a way that is inconsistent with his earlier attitude, the action may reflect an incipient attitude change—a movement toward a new attitude that has not yet been crystallized and to which he has not yet fully committed himself. He may indeed be responding to situational demands, interpersonal pressures, social facilitation, or other extraneous influences, but these may in effect be precipitating an action for which he was already partly prepared. Thus the action situation may represent an opportunity for the individual to adopt a new role that he had been anticipating for some time; or a challenge to make a commitment that he had been toying with but that remained unexpressed because of competing pressures; or a deliberate effort to mobilize internal and external supports for a new level of commitment by creating irreversible consequences and social expectations that would prevent him from backsliding. In short, the person may be ready for change and the action may serve as part of the process of bringing that change into being. Once the action is taken, it helps to sharpen and stabilize the new attitude and to strengthen commitment to it.

Attitude-action inconsistency may thus be, at least in part, an indication of an attitude in flux. The action represents an integral part of the development, testing, and crystallization of new attitudes, which can be understood most fully if we place that action within its social context. This view of the reciprocal relationship between attitude and action is a further illustration of my central point that a social-psychological analysis can provide a fuller and more differentiated picture of the attitude-behavior relationship.

IX

The Social Consequences of Powerlessness

36

Introduction

The Editors

IT IS GENERALLY BELIEVED today that alienation is widespread, especially in the industrial world. Techniques of measurement of alienation range from intensive case studies to public-opinion polls. Though little consensus has built up regarding the reliability and validity of the various measures, or even regarding the definition of what is to be measured, this has not seriously weakened the belief that alienation is a decisive fact of human experience. Indeed, it has been so regarded by many thinkers for two centuries or more.

Among the many dimensions of alienation, powerlessness is perhaps the most discussed and the most studied. It is not defined or measured any more precisely, however, than meaninglessness, normlessness, isolation, or self-estrangement, to use the other dimensions examined in Seeman's important paper (1959).

We agree with the judgment that alienation, even if it can be regarded now more as a sensitizing concept than as a precise variable, deserves careful examination by students of human behavior (see Yinger, 1973). Whether thought of in its general form or in one of its varieties, such as powerlessness, it is a multidisciplinary concept *par excellence*. Philosophy, literature, psychiatry, psychology, theology, political science, and sociology all have substantial literatures dealing with the theme.

The two chapters that follow complement each other nicely. From the perspective of a philosopher, Professor Schacht emphasizes the need for greater clarity in the concepts of power and powerlessness. Until this is achieved, both scholarship and social action are seriously hampered. Professor Geschwender is also concerned with these basic problems of conceptualization, relating them to theoretical issues in political sociology and collective behavior. He then employs his formulation of the concepts of power and powerlessness in a detailed community case study. Perhaps it is appropriate with reference to a topic to which Hegel and Marx have contributed so much to suggest that it is in the dialectic between theoretical clarity and empirical study that our understanding of powerlessness will develop.

37

On Power and Powerlessness

Richard Schacht

"THIS WORLD IS THE WILL to power—and nothing besides! And you yourselves are also this will to power—and nothing besides!" So wrote Nietzsche, a century ago (Nietzsche, 1967: 550). His meaning should not be taken to be obvious, and is misunderstood when his words are construed too simplistically. But if his contention means anything like what it seems to say, and if there is any truth to it, then there is nothing surprising in the preoccupation with power, powerlessness, and related matters on the part of so many people today.

This circumstance may of course be otherwise interpreted; I shall have more to say along these lines shortly. In any event, however, we now find ourselves confronted with a large body of literature, consisting of both theoretical and empirical studies, dealing with social phenomena having to do in various ways with power and powerlessness. In some of this literature the main focus is upon actually obtaining states of affairs, or what might be called the societal facts of the matter, while in other contributions to it the emphasis is upon the perceptions, attitudes, and reactions of different groups with respect to their situations. These may be supposed to be but two sides of the same coin, one "objective" and one "subjective"—and so they undoubtedly are, at least to some extent; but they by no means invariably or even generally exhibit a close (much less exact) fit.

I do not propose on this occasion to discuss any of the empirical data gathered by those who have carried out studies of various specific varieties of power and powerlessness, and their correlates and consequences. What I shall have to say, however, does have some bearing on the interpretation of such data, and on the evaluation of the treatments of these phenomena to be found in the literature as well. For what I propose to do is to examine some of the fundamental issues that arise in connection with the notions of power and powerlessness that social analysts and theorists are wont to employ. And I consider this to be a task of no little importance, both theoretically and practically.

I

First, a preliminary remark. I would urge that care must be taken not to read evaluative meaning into the very notions of power and powerlessness, and to distinguish clearly between the nature of the states of affairs specified by them, on the one hand, and judgments passed with respect to these states of affairs, on the other. Powerlessness per se is no more intrinsically evil or undesirable than power per se is intrinsically good or desirable. An intrinsic negative value cannot be assigned to the former without a counterpart intrinsic positive value being assigned to the latter. And while various sorts of power unquestionably may be assigned instrumental value, or desirability as means to certain further ends, it cannot plausibly be maintained that any of them—not to mention power as such—is of value in its own right, independently of any end or purpose for the attainment of which it might be used. It thus should not be supposed that the discovery of an instance or type of powerlessness is as such the discovery of a situation in need of transformation.

In this connection, it should also be noted that powerlessness bears a very different aspect, even in the eyes of those affected, if the forces in relation to which they are or feel powerless are viewed, e.g., as hostile to them and detrimental to their interests (as in the cases of concentrated economic power or despotic political and military power in the eyes of the exploited, the oppressed, or the subjugated); or, on the contrary, as benevolently disposed toward them or working in their favor (as in the cases of the God of Judeo-Christianity or the ineluctable march of history in the eyes of those who believe and trust in them); or, differently still, as indifferent to them but as rational and as admitting of a degree of manipulation in accordance with their concerns (as in the cases of laws of nature and properties of substances in the eyes of scientists and engineers). I shall not elaborate upon this point, but it ought to be recognized and kept in mind, as a corrective to the common tendency to make sweeping assertions about powerlessness and its effects that apply at most only to certain of its forms and to certain ways of viewing them. And it should alert one to the possibility that any substantive generalizations about powerlessness may turn out to be either untenable or too superficial to be of any value. Indeed, reflection upon examples such as these inclines me to suspect that, as in the case of "alienation" (cf. Schacht, 1970), the variables involved are too numerous to permit the formulation of very many sound and meaningful comprehensive propositions with respect to it.

II

Another general point pertaining to the status of this notion concerns its interpretive character, and the relation between its employment and the social phenomena it is intended to capture. Social relations are phenomena the existence and nature of which are far from being independent of the manner in which the populations with which they are associated understand their lives and circumstances. Rather, they are patterns in a social fabric that is woven upon a warp of strands of meaning, in which are to be found both the accumulated residues of past schematizations of such relations and the results of an ongoing process of their modification and supplementation. They are our collective products, as Hegel long ago observed, and they are transformed as various interpersonal situations and possibilities are endowed with altered or different meanings through changes in the manner in which these are interpretively schematized.

In our society the forms of social inquiry that have emerged in the course of the past several centuries have come to play a significant and expanding role in this process. Social inquiry neither simply mirrors social phenomena in language and thought, nor generally leaves them as it finds them. Broadly regarded, it is society reflecting on itself, affecting itself as it does so. It is an enterprise of societal self-interpretation, in terms of models and metaphors that even in the best of cases contribute to the coloring and structuring of the manifold of self-understanding that informs and partially directs the course of social life.

Thus in the present case it is important to understand that terms such as "power" and "powerlessness," like "alienation," "freedom," and most others in the lexicon of social thought, are not simply the names of various forms of social phenomena whose existence we have detected. Rather, they are interpretive categories that have come to be employed in the schematic comprehension of social events. And the schematization of social phenomena by means of such categories may be of no little consequence, to the extent that participants in social life come to incorporate them into their view of themselves and their world—as has happened in these instances.

This is by no means to say that "powerlessness" is merely a product of the creative imagination of social inquiry, and that there really is no such thing. Social realities are realities of social life, notwithstanding their status as products no less of the interpretive schematization of human affairs than of circumstances obtaining independently of it. But an element of contingency attaches to the fact that certain complex states of affairs are taken to have the significance of forms of "powerlessness," as well as to the import they are understood to have; and this has come about, at least in part, in consequence of a specific instance of the impact of social inquiry upon social consciousness, and thus upon the identity of the social phenomena it seeks to fix in thought.

The implications of these remarks for the matter at hand are large and important. In particular, they should lead to second thoughts about how much of what is asserted about "powerlessness" of one sort or another in the literature is *discovery*, and how much is *recovery*, or the gathering of results the way for which has been prepared by the manner in which social inquiry itself has set the stage. I leave this question open, but I would suggest that it must be faced much more squarely than it generally has been, and the underlying issue taken much more seriously, as discussion of this matter continues.

III

Next I wish to comment briefly upon a much more mundane obstacle to meaningful discussion of power and powerlessness in social-scientific quarters, which ought to have been cleared away long ago. I refer to the continuing adoption and utilization of criteria and tests of powerlessness that are so minimal that virtually everyone who is not either mad or naive is bound to qualify. Consider, for example, questions such as the following, which still are commonly used to measure (and, in effect, to explicate, by operational definition) the notion of "alienation-as-powerlessness" (Kohn, 1976: 116): "Do you feel that most of the things that happen to you are the result of your own decisions or of things over which you have no control?" What a question! For anyone, at any time, in any society, most of the things that happen to one are at least greatly affected by factors over which one has no control, even in cases in which one's decisions do make a difference.

Passing over such other choice items as, "There are things I can do that might influence national policy" (agree or disagree!), I shall comment only on one further example: "How often do you feel powerless to get what you want out of life?" This obviously will depend upon what it is that one wants. But there is so little that anyone *could* "want out of life" that is obtainable regardless of circumstances beyond one's own control, that even those who feel they happen to be getting much of what they want would be naive to credit this result principally to their own capacity to secure it.

Or suppose that powerlessness is conceived, in the words of Melvin Seeman in his now-classical article on alienation, "as the expectancy or probability held by the individual that his own behavior cannot determine the occurrence of the outcomes . . .he seeks" (Seeman, 1959: 784). The consequence, I would suggest, is that (trivial cases of "the occurrence of outcomes sought" aside) *everyone* turns out to be powerless, whether or not all people "hold this expectancy"—as any rational person cognizant of the way things are certainly would and should. For the unqualified capacity to "determine the occurrence" of states of affairs selected from an unrestricted range of contingent possibilities would constitute a form of virtual omnipotence, which we as finite creatures most certainly lack. And powerlessness is here so characterized that it subsumes everything short of such omnipotence.

Now it assuredly is not the aim of Seeman and others to present powerlessness as a corollary of human finitude, and thus as a universally and ineluctably obtaining aspect of the human condition. It is intended to apply selectively, and to admit of quantitative variability as well. This means, however, that care must be taken not to explicate or define the notion of "powerlessness" in a way that results in the interpretive and evaluative assimilation of all cases involving limitations and restrictions upon people's ability to affect what happens in their lives to the extreme or limiting case of utter impotence.

IV

I now turn to another, more fundamental, problem associated with a long-established and deeply entrenched way of thinking of "power" and "powerlessness" that underlies most contemporary discussion of them. In his article on "power" in the recently published *Encyclopedia of Philosophy*, Stanley Benn sums up his treatment of this concept as follows: "To possess power or to be powerful is, then, to have a generalized potentiality for getting one's own way or for bringing about changes (at least some of which are intended) in other people's actions or conditions" (Benn, 1967: 426). Benn does not spell out the implication, but we may do it for him: One may correspondingly be said to be "powerless," in this view of the matter, to the extent that one *lacks* this "generalized potentiality."

The disjunction in this characterization of power and powerlessness is not intended to mark out two different sorts of each, one relating to "getting one's own way" and another quite distinct one relating to "bringing about changes in other people's actions or conditions." The two descriptions may not be referentially coextensive, but they must be admitted to overlap to a very considerable extent—much more considerably, in fact, than it is comfortable to admit. When interests conflict (as they frequently do), one person cannot get his own way without others with whose interests his conflict being unable to get theirs. And if one person is in a position to bring about intended changes in the actions or conditions of other people, it is obvious that these others are to that extent *not* in a position to control *their* actions or conditions.

This complication may be observed to attend the ordinary view of the matter, which Benn's analysis reflects. For "the powerful" are commonly understood to be those people who are in a position to impose their wills on others, or to make decisions on their own that may significantly affect the lives of others, or to do what they want to do at the expense of others without having to concern themselves with that expense. And "the powerless," on the other hand, are correspondingly understood to be those people who are not in such a position, but rather are the unfortunate "others" who must endure such treatment. This way of framing the issue has certain broad implications that ought to be noticed.

In particular, consider the upshot of supposing that everyone numbers either among the powerless or among the powerful (at least in the context of any given domain of human activity), and that one can avoid the condition of powerlessness (in any such domain) only by possessing some significant degree of power in relation to others. To wish or aspire to escape one's condition of powerlessness is then to envision either turning the tables upon those who presently enjoy power over one, or else joining their ranks and thus acquiring a share of the power they enjoy over others in one's present situation. Needless to say, this way of conceiving of power and of what not being powerless involves also would preclude the real possibility of anything approaching a general elimination of powerlessness.

On the other hand, it is worth remarking that the powerlessness of others to affect a person does not necessarily entail that *that* person enjoys any degree of power in relation to *them*. And if powerlessness were conceived simply to be a function of the extent to which one is *subject to the power of others*, rather than as a matter of one's inability to impose one's will upon them, then powerlessness would be diminished precisely to the extent that the power anyone is able to achieve in relation to others is restricted. The consequence of taking *this* view of the matter is that, paradoxical though it might seem, the only way to minimize powerlessness would be to minimize power. For it is only if none are power*ful* in relation to others that none will be power*less* relative to others.

This suggestion warrants brief elaboration. Rather than making so much of a person's ability to get his own way regardless of what that might entail, one might think of powerlessness along the lines of a *loss of autonomy and liberty,* to be contrasted with a notion of power linked to the idea of the greatest degree of autonomy and liberty that would be possible for all. The remedy for powerlessness so construed would not be to "give more power" to the powerless in order that they might thereby replace, join, or achieve a "balance of power" with the erstwhile powerful. Rather, it would be to impose strict limits on autonomy and liberty, and so on the power anyone might have—and in particular to eliminate the possibility of some people getting their own way at the expense of others. This idea is hardly a new one; it is as old as social contract theory. But it bears recalling in this context, and should at least be taken into consideration in thinking about the values in the name of which "powerlessness" might be protested.

V

In any event, it must be admitted that "powerlessness" can meaningfully be considered to *be an issue* only in relation to a contrasting condition of some humanly attainable sort. There are many things about life and the world (and ourselves) that we cannot change, either alone or in concert with others. And it seems to me to be essential to distinguish between forms of powerlessness that might realistically be diminished and those that cannot, for practical social reasons as well as for purposes of conceptual and theoretical clarity. For the failure to do so can lead to the growth of expectations and demands that cannot possibly be fulfilled, giving rise in turn to dangerous frustrations, suspicions, and dispositions to which demagogues may appeal and turn to their advantage.

A century and a half ago, Hegel wrote—with similar concerns in mind—that "it is not what *exists* that makes us vehement and causes us suffering; rather, it is what is *not* as it *should* be," in the judgment of those reflecting upon their situation. It was his conviction that the philosophical "comprehension of what exists" reveals that in many cases it "must be" as it is, and so *cannot* be otherwise, at least under the historical conditions obtaining at a given time. Contrary to what is often said of him, Hegel did not hold that one who achieves this comprehension will cease to regard *any* existing state of affairs as objectionable, and will instead affirm everything that is the case just as it is. But he did think that there are a great many instances in which acceptance of what exists is the only reasonable stance, and thus where such comprehension should serve to "promote a more tranquil attitude toward it, together with a moderate toleration of it in word and deed" (Hegel, 1923: 5; my translation).

It may be that Hegel erred in the treatment he accorded to many specific states of affairs; even so, however, the general point still stands (as Marx himself clearly saw.) If we acknowledge, as he and most other philosophers have urged we must, that "ought" implies "can," then we must also recognize that whatever "cannot" be otherwise than it is may not reasonably be held to be something that *ought* to be otherwise. In such cases protest is out of place, demands for betterment are pointless, and remedies attempted will be ineffectual if not actually harmful. And I would suggest that a number of forms of powerlessness constitute instances of this sort.

VI

In short, a state of affairs can properly be considered objectionable only if it is one about which something can be done. It does not suffice, however, merely to draw this distinction. For among those cases of forms of powerlessness about which something *can* be done, it is further crucial to distinguish those with respect to which it is at least arguable that something *should* be done from those that do not admit of such criticism. It would be no less unfortunate for people to refuse to reconcile themselves to *any* potentially eliminable form of powerlessness to which they might be subject, than it would be for them to resign themselves passively to *all* of those that might happen to obtain. Many people do lack certain sorts of power that they conceivably could have under altered— and alterable—circumstances, and that certain other people may in point of fact possess. But in at least some such cases they have no legitimate grounds on which either to claim entitlement to the forms of power at issue, or to condemn their possession by others.

The common association of the ideas of power and powerlessness with the ability or inability to impose one's will upon other people, noted earlier in my discussion, provides a case in point. There are many respects in which some people may be said to have power over others, and conversely to be subject to the power of others, and alternatively to lack power over them. But powerlessness in the last-mentioned sense cannot reasonably be complained of, since its alleviation in one's own case would of necessity involve one's attainment of a position of dominance in relation to others. And the ability to impose one's will upon others is not as such something to which anyone can reasonably claim to be entitled. It is no inalienable human right, but rather at most a contingently acquired capacity, the legitimacy of which requires always to be established by reference to ends and values transcending individual self-interest and desires. In the absence of any such special justification, this ability is not to be regarded as legitimate, and so cannot legitimately be demanded or aspired to. In short, in considering what sort of attitude is warranted with respect to powerlessness, one must consider what sorts of power people can and cannot justifiably seek. And it would seem reasonable to suppose that, *ceteris paribus,* they must admit of potential *universalizability* in order to satisfy this condition.

On the other hand, it is by no means the case that forms of power that are not and do not admit of being enjoyed in equal measure by all concerned are in principle objectionable. The *ceteris paribus* qualification above is an important one. Special justifications of various arrangements in which some people can and do exercise various types of control of influence that other people lack, and that affect these others, are not only possible but rather common. And I consider it important to recognize that this is so, and to guard against the tendency to blur the distinction between these and other cases in which a lack of power on the part of some in relation to others is discernible. The evaluative criterion of potential universalizability may be thought of as having a general *prima facie* applicability in all cases, but it *can* be overridden by other evaluative considerations, which may in various circumstances warrant the assignation of certain powers to some and their denial to others.

More specifically, many institutions, which serve to promote the attainment of a wide range of human values, essentially involve an inequitable distribution of powers, reserving forms of influence and control to some while denying them to others. And by seizing upon the existence of avoidable forms of powerlessness in such cases, while neglecting to consider the contexts in which they occur, the significance of the institutions of which they are features is only too easily misunderstood. Indeed, it might even be argued that the condemnation of *all* practices in which such inequities exist is in effect a recipe for a new barbarism, since their general elimination would entail the elimination of the institutional conditions of the possibility of large portions of social and cultural life.

I shall not pursue this issue here. It is clearly of the greatest importance to do so, but in order to address it adequately, it would be necessary to deal with a variety of problems much too large and complex to be confronted on this occasion. My remarks in this connection have been intended simply to call attention to it, and so to suggest the necessity of viewing the existence of forms of power and powerlessness in a larger perspective. Factors beyond the circumstance that some people happen to lack forms of power that certain others have (and that conceivably could be possessed by all in equal measure) may be of no little relevance to the question of how such situations are properly to be viewed. And I might add that the significance of the way in which instances of "power-lessness" in such cases are broadly perceived can hardly be overestimated in considering the viability and future course in our society.

VII

The notion of "powerlessness" is also problematical in a different and more fundamental respect, in view of considerations relating to what "can in principle" be done by anyone, and thus to the reality of "power" insofar as it is humanly attainable. The kind of power at issue here may be abstractly characterized in terms of one's ability to control or influence courses of events that impinge upon or constitute what happens in one's life. Much hinges, therefore, upon the nature of the events focused upon, and also upon the type and extent of control or influence with respect to them that is envisioned. In general, the degree of control or influence a person can have upon some course of events will inevitably be limited by that person's particular constitution, and by the extent to which it is also conditioned by natural and sociohistorical circumstances and dependent upon what other people do. And it must be recognized that these limits are very extensive where all but the more modest of intentions one may have are concerned, for virtually everyone and under almost any realistically imaginable conditions. This point should be taken seriously; it has important implications.

For some people, things may sometimes or often turn out the way they want them to. As was earlier remarked, however, it is only in those rare cases in which people succeed in disciplining themselves to want next to nothing in particular to come about that it is anything more than an illusion to attribute this result exclusively or even primarily to their own agency. It may often be that things would not have turned out the way these people wanted them to if they had not applied themselves energetically to that end; but it does not follow from this that the results are attributable to that application rather than to the obtaining of any other conditions. A necessary condition is frequently far less than a suffic-ient one; in the realm of human action, this is almost invariably the case where the relation of individual exertions to the realization of individual objectives is concerned.

Either as a reality or as an attainable possibility, therefore, the idea of power in the sense of *decisive personal control* over courses of events per-taining to what happens in the course of one's life is largely a myth when applied to matters of any real moment. And if the powerlessness that may be defined as the lack of such power is not itself likewise a myth, the idea of its eliminability or significant alleviation is. Personal *influence* of varying degrees can be and sometimes is a reality; it may be diminished or extended through a variety of sorts of possible modification of the relevant circumstances. But it can never be extensive enough, in any except rather trivial cases, to admit of anything more than a relative contrast with complete impotence.

All human beings are thus powerless, in the sense of being unable to exert decisive personal control over what happens in their lives. On the other hand, power may reasonably be attributed to anyone who is able to have any degree and form of such influence, in the same measure as the scope of this possible influence. In *this* sense, *no one* is utterly powerless, although the extent of that power enjoyed by most is not very great, and undoubtedly in the case of many could be considerably enlarged without either unfairness to others or detrimental effects upon social and cultural life. Its general enlargement, moreover, while possible, can only be brought about, I submit, in the context of the development of an appropriate network of *institutions*.

This is a point of sufficient importance to warrant brief elaboration. Institutions are commonly thought of as impediments to the attainment of personal influence, serving only to exacerbate the powerlessness of nearly everyone. It is not institutions as such that are the villains of the piece, however, for they are no less essential to the solution—insofar as a solution is to be found—than they are part of the problem. They may invariably limit what people can do, in one way or another. Yet they alone can establish the conditions in which large numbers of people, whose lives will inevitably impinge upon each other, can collectively attain and secure for themselves a substantial domain within which each can enjoy personal influence. The circumstance has long been recog-. nized in certain philosophical quarters, and was made much of by Hegel; unfortunately, it has all too frequently been inadequately appreciated.

The sort of power presently under consideration, and in relation to which the notion of powerlessness can perhaps best be understood, may once more be usefully related to several other concepts that have long occupied a central place in social thought: those of *liberty* (or freedom) and *autonomy* (or self-determination). The former is generally regarded as involving the ability to do as one chooses and the absence of constraint, while the latter is usually taken to have to do with independence of externally imposed regulation and the selection of one's own manner of life. Power conceived in terms of personal influence does not simply reduce to these two concepts, but it can be thought of as building upon them. Thus it may be construed as a matter of being able to affect a course of events through actions of one's choosing and in a manner pursuant to some objective one has determined upon.

It is not my intention further to explore these interrelations here, although such an exploration would surely prove to be of considerable interest. My chief reason for touching upon these matters again at this point is that they serve to underscore the importance of exercising the caution I have been urging in the handling of the ideas of power and powerlessness. For, like liberty and autonomy, power is not and cannot be unconditioned and unrestricted in human life. If conceived absolutely, none of these notions is validly predicable of human existence, and none of them can meaningfully be employed to characterize the way human life should or even could be. The sooner the limited and conditioned nature of all actual and attainable human liberty, autonomy, and power is recognized, the better their understanding will be, and the more useful and significant these notions will become. And the same is true of the institutional presuppositions of their general attainment, preservation, and greatest possible enhancement.

This is not a matter of purely theoretical importance, for misunderstandings along these lines can have profound practical consequences as well. Thus the widespread acceptance of a "myth of power" that takes flight from reality, and promotes dissatisfaction with anything short of some degree or form of personal influence upon events that is in point of fact an impossible dream, can lead to the disintegration of the very social arrangements that hold the greatest promise of sustaining and extending people's actual ability to affect courses of events relating to what happens in their own lives. And in this connection, the careers of the ideas of liberty and autonomy—or more properly, of certain "myths" of liberty and of autonomy that emerged in the past few centuries—may prove instructive. For it is arguable that each in some measure contributed, in a perversely dialectical way, to the emergence and temporary triumph of certain political developments (in France under Napoleon and in Germany under Hitler) of an opposite character, which were profoundly antithetical to attained and attainable forms of them. And it could be suggested that the same sort of thing also has already occurred at least once in this century in connection with a certain myth of "power" (in the Soviet Union under Stalin). Nor should it be supposed that these dangers are safely behind us, for in various forms, the same myths are with us still.

In short, these specific historical cases aside, I would urge that the ideal can prove, in the real world of human affairs, to be the enemy of both the possible and the actual. Extreme and absolutistic conceptions of such principles, which take leave of the practicable and assume mythical proportions, can only too easily contribute to the emergence of contrary social developments through their power to distort people's perceptions, alter their commitments, and dispose them to courses of action or inaction that in reality serve to further such developments. A strong dose of realism would thus appear to be in order for anyone who would make an issue of liberty and constraint, or of autonomy and heteronomy, or of power and powerlessness.

VIII

The social-theoretical heart of the matter under consideration, as I see it, is to determine the kind and degree of personal influence upon what occurs in their lives to which members of a society such as our own might reasonably aspire, where "reasonably" is understood to mean both realistically, fairly, and with due regard to the importance of other social and cultural values. In this paper, however, I have not attempted to develop such an account. My chief concerns have been to try to reformulate the issue at hand in a manner rendering it more amenable to fruitful exploration and sound treatment, and to offer a kind of prolegomenon to the undertaking of this formidable and important task. Much else could also be said in this connection, however, and I shall conclude with a few additional observations along these lines.

It is crucial to recognize further that the topic of power and powerlessness is by no means simply a social-theoretical one. I began with a reference to Nietzsche, who held that a "will to power" constitutes the most fundamental of all human psychological dispositions (and indeed is an intrinsic feature of life itself). I return to him now, at the conclusion of my discussion, to suggest that he raises a number of issues in this connection with which any such account must come to terms, and to draw attention to certain implications of this fact. These issues are, first, whether human beings are so constituted that the attainment and exercise of some significant degree of power is a basic requirement of our human nature, which if unmet must be expected to have pathological consequences; and second, whether (if this is so) the requisite degree of power can only be achieved by some at the expense of others, or instead can at least conceivably be achieved by all simultaneously and harmoniously.

Nietzsche's position with respect to the first issue obviously was affirmative. With respect to the second, he appears to have been inclined toward the former alternative—with the consequence that human life in his view not only is but always will be characterized by a struggle for power, with both creative and destructive manifestations, and involving disparities and shifting relations of power and powerlessness. And the pathological consequences he considered to be the inevitable issue of the latter, in cases in which no devious alternative routes to the attainment of power are discovered, begin with resentment of the powerful, and take either outwardly or inwardly directed destructive forms. On the other hand, Nietzsche saw the temporary frustration of the "will to power," which prompts a search for alternative forms of its satisfaction, as the motor of social, cultural, and intellectual development, and as the impetus to the emergence of all higher forms of human spiritual life.

There is much that is of interest in what he has to say along these lines. My main reason for making reference to him here, however, is not primarily to draw attention to this fact. Rather, it is to indicate by way of an example how much depends upon the resolution of a number of larger and more fundamental issues relating to human nature and social life, in the understanding of power and powerlessness. It will not suffice to consider simply what forms of power are and are not individually and generally attainable, what forms of powerlessness are and are not eliminable, and what normative considerations are appropriate to the evaluation of various possible alternative social arrangements involving them. One must also take into consideration the status and modifiability of dispositions to seek to acquire and exercise power in different forms—and further of second-order reactive dispositions associated with the blockage of the former, as well as the possibility and consequences of the repression and/or sublimation of both, and so on. On one level at least, these may be conceived as psychological questions; but they ultimately lead to philosophical ones, ranging from the fundamental structures of human reality to the character of genuinely human existence.

In short, it seems to me that Nietzsche was quite right to regard power and powerlessness in their various forms not only as social phenomena, admitting of social-theoretical analysis, but also and at the same time as phenomena with a variety of other dimensions, requiring to be understood further in the perspectives of both biological and psychological investigation, and finally within the context of a comprehensive philosophical anthropology. His specific conclusions, with respect to power and powerlessness specifically and to human nature generally, are of course quite another matter. But the issues he calls upon us to face do not stand or fall with them. It should by no means be supposed, moreover, that these issues have been clearly and satisfactorily resolved by others, leaving to us merely the task of interpreting specific phenomena accordingly. And especially when dealing with matters of such moment as power and powerlessness, we pass over such larger issues at our peril.

38

On Power and Powerlessness: Or with a Little Help from Our Friends

James A. Geschwender

MY ASSIGNED TOPIC IS the social consequences of powerlessness but, while very important, such a discussion is premature. We must first rethink the concepts of power and powerlessness. Most sociologists would include power on their list of key concepts for sociological analysis. My own list would include power, exploitation, class, nation, consciousness, conflict, and social change, among others. Each concept has meaning only as related to the others within a theoretical framework that recognizes the dynamic nature of society. Each concept—and their interrelations—must be seen as fluid and changeable as all are constantly reshaped by the interplay of social forces. Power must be recognized as an objective property of collectivities rather than individuals and as a phenomenon that may be created, destroyed, or altered in magnitude. Social analysis within this theoretical tradition should always be located within particular sociohistorical settings.

It is not my intention to develop such a theory in this paper. I shall first attempt to demonstrate the inadequacy of the two dominant formulations of power and powerlessness (that of the social psychologists and the political sociologists), briefly comment on a more promising but still less than satisfactory formulation (that related to collective behavior and social movements), and then briefly describe the fight of Waiahole and Waikane (Hawaii) residents to retain their life style. The latter material

□ The data portion of this paper is based upon research done while on sabbatical leave from the State University of New York and was partially supported by a fellowship from the National Endowment for the Humanities and a research grant from the National Institute for Mental Health.

will be used to illustrate the weaknesses in existing treatments and to point the way toward a better formulation of power and powerlessness. In concluding, I will suggest that existing formulations by social psychologists and political sociologists may have some utility in the revised approach to the study of power.

The Social Psychological Approach

Recent decades have seen two major lines of emphasis in sociological research on power and powerlessness. The dominant line of inquiry has followed from Melvin Seeman's (1959, 1972) classic discussion of alienation in which powerlessness was defined as one of the five (later six) types of alienation. I will limit myself to some general comments, as Seeman (1972, 1975) has already summarized the work in this area. Powerlessness is defined as a subjective state of individuals—an expectancy that one cannot determine one's future social outcomes (Seeman, 1972:472). While there is general recognition that a strong correlation between sensed and actual powerlessness cannot be assumed, there is still a tendency to assume that they are associated (Seeman, 1972: 507). Consequently, much scholarly effort has been expended developing objective indices or scales of powerlessness as a subjective state. These indices have been correlated with factors believed to lead to a sense of powerlessness, with behavioral consequences, or with other subjectively defined types of alienation. Other studies have suggested reanalyzing the concept into the dimensions of sensed personal efficacy and sensed political efficacy.

Few scholars attempt to measure the association between objective power and subjectively defined powerlessness, although Lippitt, Polansky, and Rosen (1954) demonstrated an association between self-defined, other-attributed, and observer-defined patterns of influence in a group setting. It is generally recognized that perceptions of powerlessness are changeable, but Hunt and Hardt (1969) are among the very few who have tested the impact of experience upon perceptions. None of the existing work has indicated any awareness of the fact that meaningful social power is not possessed by individuals but rather by social collectivities ranging from small community groupings to social classes.

Political Sociology and Power

Political sociologists have always been more concerned than social psychologists with power as an objective phenomenon. It is true that their measures are indirect and often employ perceptions as indices, but their primary objective has always been to assess real power. Terry N. Clark (1975) describes the current state of community power studies— the arena in which political sociologists have best displayed their conceptions of power:

> Probably the best known debate of earlier years involved Hunter, Dahl, and their respective followers. Reputational and decisional methods were viewed as conflicting means to the same end: answering the question of who governs? ... With time, however, the fact that they were studying distinct phenomena has become clearer. Hunter's basic concern was *power,* conceived of as the potential for influence. Dahl's concern was *influence,* conceived of as making explicit decisions among alternatives Hunter's reputational method, inquiring of the potential import of various actors, operationalized power. Dahl's decisional method, focussing on particular actors in reaching specific decisions, operationalized influence. Similarly, a *power structure,* as the patterned distribution of power, may be distinguished from a *decision-making* structure, or the patterned distribution of influence in a social system.
>
> Third, and distinct from power and influence, is *base resources....* Base resources are the actor's properties or facilities that may be converted into power or influence. Some obvious examples are money, high social status, and verbal skills. Appropriate measures vary for different base resources. However, an important class of base resources consists of those deriving from occupancy of a particular social status—mayor, city councilman, bank president, etc. One simple procedure for gauging such base resources has been termed the positional method: it generates a list of statuses occupied by leading individuals in a community (T. N. Clark, 1975: 274).

These are the three dominant approaches to the study of community power. Each is oriented toward determining some aspect of an actual distribution of power in a given community. The best work in each tradition recognizes that power may be possessed by collectivities as well as by individuals. However, all three approaches suffer in that they are unable to assess power in relation to social change. They tend to view power distributions as static. The decision-making approach is a bit more dynamic in that it follows an issue over time and can chart the activation of actors and social processes as it moves toward resolution. Nevertheless, it tends to be restricted to issues and decisions that arise within the social system rather than those that arise as challenges to the system. It could be used to chart the manner in which new coalitions create or seize power not previously possessed, but there is little evidence of actual use for this purpose.

Political sociologists have also exhibited a concern with power in numerous political participation studies, but the relationship between participation and power remains problematic. Alford and Friedland (1975)

provide an excellent discussion of the relationship and suggest a potentially useful definition of power:

> Power is held by those who benefit over time from the operation of
> social, economic, and political structures. Power is not held by those who
> win in a given electoral battle or attempt to influence a decision. . . . Our
> definition has the advantage of referring to concrete behavior—not the
> behavior of those seeking benefits, but of those who, consciously or
> unconsciously, intentionally or unintentionally, act in such a way as to
> confer benefits upon one group rather than another. Therefore, we
> argue that power should not be assumed to follow from participation.
> Power and participation are independent although causally related
> phenomena. . . . Participation may be associated with power, but power
> can exist without participation. . . . Participation may occur without
> power . . . and powerlessness can exist without participation. . . . While
> the creation of . . . structural power requires participation, its effects are
> often to reduce the need for participation by dominant groups (Alford
> and Friedland, 1975: 431–32).

Political Sociological and Social Psychological Approaches Compared

The approach toward the study of power used by political
sociologists resembles that of the social psychologists in having both virtues and shortcomings, but differs in primary emphasis. The social psychologists are primarily concerned with powerlessness as a subjectively
defined individual attribute, while the political sociologists are primarily
concerned with power as an objective attribute that may be possessed
either by individuals or social collectivities. These two approaches supplement one another and enable us to make some determination regarding both the nature of power as actually existing within a given social
system and as subjectively perceived by the system participants. However, even in combination, they are inadequate in that they do not fully
analyze the relation of power to social change and tend to treat power as
a static or relatively fixed phenomenon that is neither created nor destroyed.

Collective Behavior and Social Movements

The field of collective behavior and social movements can best be
described as having a unifying perspective rather than an integrated
theory (see Marx and Wood, 1975). Neil Smelser (1963) provided the

most ambitious attempt at a general theory of collective behavior, but the results proved less than satisfactory. There is an emerging consensus on a perspective that views collective behavior and social movements as collective problem-solving efforts on the part of those sharing a community of interests, confronted by a common problem, and excluded from legitimate channels of redress. There is an unfortunate tendency for researchers to specialize in narrowly defined topics that are analyzed in isolation.

We have many excellent studies on the nature of grievances, strains, social structures, and so on, that may spark the search for a collective solution to a shared problem. We also have many studies of the mobilization process, the leadership and the following, the role of ideology, the development of strategy and tactics, and relations between the movement and the public. Others have concentrated on the study of career patterns of social movements and what happens to them after they either achieve their objectives or fail to do so over an extended period of time.

There are numerous case studies of individual movements that attempt to analyze the interrelations among the concepts cited above. These only partially overcome the problem caused by treating a unity as if it were made up of discrete parts. They must be supplemented by more good comparative analyses of social movements along the lines of the excellent analysis of agrarian revolutions by Jeffery Paige (1975). Let us now turn to a case history that may prove valuable in helping us to understand the conceptualization of power and powerlessness required for good social analysis. This is a very sketchy account of events based upon my own research. Data were collected through participant observation, interviews with participants, newspaper accounts, propaganda literature, and official government documents.

Waiahole and Waikane Valleys

Waiahole and Waikane are two rural Hawaiian valleys located on the windward side of Oahu (urban Honolulu is on the leeward side). There is a scattering of small individually owned plots of land in the valleys, but most land is owned by the heirs of Lincoln McCandless, who began acquiring land in 1890. The McCandless land is leased in small plots on a month-to-month basis (evictions may legally take place with a twenty-eight-day notice) to persons who normally live on it and either farm it as a full-time occupation or to supplement income from outside jobs.

Robert N. Anderson (1974) found that most persons in the valleys have lived in their present residences for an extended period of time (41 percent for over twenty years, 17 percent between ten and nineteen years, 42 percent less than ten years). This actually understates the extent of permanency as it does not consider the children of valley residents who, upon maturity, set up their own housekeeping, or those who have changed residences within the two valleys. Anderson (1974) also found the valley residents to be ethnically mixed (46 percent pure or part Hawaiian, 20 percent of Japanese ancestry, 17 percent Filipino, 12 percent Haole or Caucasian, and 5 percent other); to have a skewed age distribution, with only 37.1 percent of all residents (16.8 percent males and 20.3 percent females) in their most productive years between twenty and fifty-five; and to have significantly lower family incomes than Oahu as a whole despite a high proportion of multiple-income families.

THE POWER DISTRIBUTION, JANUARY 1974

Let us now consider the situation as of early 1974. On December 1, 1973, the McCandless heirs submitted to the state a letter of intent to rezone 1,337 acres of agricultural land in Waiahole and Waikane (752 acres to urban and 585 acres to rural or large-lot residential-use classifications). Despite allegations that Lincoln McCandless used immoral, unethical, and quasi-legal methods in acquiring the land, the landlord had clear title and the legally unchallengeable right to sell the land and evict the tenants. The potential developer would have the right to develop the small amount of land along the highway and near the Waiahole school currently zoned urban without any rezoning. He would also have the legal right to develop land zoned agricultural into two-acre lots for luxury homes or apply to have it rezoned urban for a small-lot residential development. Historical precedent in recent years found more and more rural valleys such as Waiahole and Waikane being rezoned urban and developed to accommodate a growing population. There is a continued need for new housing but also great, and growing, reluctance to take land out of sugar or pineapple production because of their importance as cash commodities.

The entire weight of law, economic rationality, and past precedent lay on the side of those seeking development. This was supplemented by the great wealth of the potential developer. The residents did not appear to possess any resources that would enable them to resist successfully. They also possessed the social characteristics (e.g., low education, low income, and minority status) that are believed to be associated with a high degree of sensed powerlessness. Thus any reasonable social scientist would anticipate that the land would be sold to developers, the tenants evicted, and the region developed for residential purposes. Let us now contrast these perfectly reasonable expectations with the actual course of events.

THE COMMUNITY RESPONSE

Subsequent events may be broken into three phases. During the first phase the community sought information and organized itself; it next sought support from the larger Hawaiian public; and finally the very nature of the struggle became transformed as the residents came to see their fight as one segment of a larger struggle. This series of changes took place against a backdrop of landlord and developer maneuvering, governmental deliberations, and the actions of outsiders. This is not the place for a full account of such events, but they will be selectively reported as they bear upon our present concern.

Phase One

In January and February of 1974 residents of the valleys, although unaware of the landlord's letter of intent, were made uneasy by an increasing frequency of large, expensive cars driving down their rural roads with passengers who appeared to be businessmen from Japan. These feelings were exacerbated when Robert Anderson (hired by the potential developer) conducted a survey of the area that he represented as an "objective academic study." The residents became afraid that the land might be sold to Japanese investors and developed for tourist or commercial purposes. They were uncertain how to find out just what was happening but Sei Serikaku, a farmer who leased land in the valley, had a nephew who was an experienced community organizer and who was currently running a religiously oriented youth project in Kahaluu (the valley immediately adjacent to Waiahole). Bob Nakata, the nephew, was approached and agreed to do what he could to discover what was going on. He went to the state Land Use Commission and discovered the letter of intent.

Word about the prospective development was spread to the various tenants and small landowners in the valleys and discussions began as to how best to resist. A general meeting of Waiahole and Waikane residents was held on April 8, 1974, and the Waiahole-Waikane Community Association (WWCA) was formed, a steering committee organized, and monthly meetings scheduled. Bobby Fernandez was elected president at the meeting on May 6. The WWCA incorporated the full range of ethnic and economic diversity found in the valleys, but the first steering committee was composed primarily of small landowners and large farmers. They developed a strategy of opposition and sought public support. Some early support was received from Bob Nakata, residents of Kahaluu valley, and persons associated with the Ethnic Studies Program at the University of Hawaii. With these exceptions, the valley residents were alone in their struggle at this stage.

Phase Two

The full implications of the development plans became more apparent with the submission of a revised rezoning request on June 30, 1974. It and subsequent elaborations described the development program as involving three five-year stages culminating in 6,700 housing units and a total residential population of 20,000 persons. The first stage would be limited to construction in only a small section of Waikane. The WWCA worked to make the general public acquainted with the details of the plans and to force them to consider the implications. It became easier and easier to attract supporters to the cause of the residents of the valleys as more and more of the public pondered the implications for urban sprawl, environmental damage, increased congestion on the highways, destruction of agriculture, and the accelerated demise of what has been loosely described as the "Hawaiian life style."

The tremendous growth of Oahu's population has combined with increased tourist pressure to cause drastic changes in the environment in a relatively short space of time. The urban concentration has rapidly spread outward from the center of Honolulu. Rural valley after rural valley has been taken over for either residential or tourist use. Water quality has rapidly deteriorated. Highway congestion has long since gone beyond the tolerable stage and there is no place to build additional highways without massive destruction of environmentally and/or historically important sites. The best of the remaining agricultural land is concentrated in the cash crops of sugar and pineapple. Consequently, Hawaii has to import most of its food and is vulnerable to shipping interruptions.

Much lip service has been paid in recent years to the effort to make Hawaii agriculturally self-sufficient. The environmental movement was very strong in Hawaii during the 1960s and continues to have an important influence. The development of Waiahole and Waikane would produce increased erosion, flood threats, increased pollution for a deteriorating Kaneohe Bay, and would remove two of the few remaining natural areas of Oahu. It would also remove from agriculture two productive valleys (producing over half of Hawaii's sweet potatoes and the majority of Oahu's bananas along with a variety of other crops). Thus it is not surprising that the WWCA was able to attract many supporters to their struggle to remain in Waiahole and Waikane and to keep the valleys in agriculture.

Supporters were drawn from a variety of middle-class and student groups. They were, for the most part, sincerely concerned individuals with a respect for law, order, and government. They wished to influence public policy but wished to do so in an orderly manner. They were willing to express their beliefs, contact politicians, sign petitions, make donations, and do what they could to retain the present character of Waiahole and Waikane so far as possible within the limits determined by legality and good taste. The State Land Use Commission held hearings on the proposal to rezone Waiahole and Waikane on October 10 and 21. Many valley residents and their supporters attended the meetings. Public pressure had been influential in getting Honolulu's Mayor Frank Fasi, Hawaii's Governor George Ariyoshi, and other public figures to indicate varying degrees of support for their cause. On December 20, 1974, the State Land Use Commission voted without dissent to deny the rezoning request. However, this did not end the matter.

On December 31 the McCandless heirs assigned all of their interests in Waiahole and Waikane to one of their members, Mrs. Loy McCandless Marks, in exchange for land she held on leeward Oahu. In May she subsequently sold a portion of Waikane to developer Joe Pao, who also purchased options on the rest of the 2,868 acres that she owned in Waiahole and Waikane. Waikane tenants received a letter from Mrs. Marks on June 2, 1975, informing them of the land transfer and notifying them that existing leases were canceled and new ones would have to be negotiated with Pao Investment Corporation. The next day Waiahole tenants received letters informing them of rent increases ranging from 50 to 750 percent. The WWCA membership agreed not to pay the new rents but instead to deposit rent at the old rate into a trust account pending resolution of their situation. A move was made to destroy the unity of the WWCA when Mrs. Marks offered Waiahole tenants (Waiahole was not part of the first five-year plan) new one-year leases at lower rents than previously set. This offer was accepted by a few tenants but most rejected it.

Phase Three

In August the Waiahole tenants who had not signed new leases received eviction notices. On the same day Joe Pao filed a request with the City Department of Land Utilization to develop 130 large house lots in Waikane. Both this and a later revised version of the request were rejected. The residents of the valleys became increasingly sophisticated in their understanding of the nature of power and the workings of law and the government. They came to believe that particular decisions on rezoning or land utilization were final only if they lost. Every time they won the developers would simply back off for a while and then submit a revised request that might stand a better chance of approval. The developers had sufficient money and other resources that they could put Waiahole and Waikane on the back burner to be periodically reheated. In the meantime they would use their influence backstage upon commission members, politicians, and other key influentials. Commission members could ultimately be replaced if not influenced.

However, a single decision against Waiahole-Waikane would mean the end of the struggle if the residents chose to be law-abiding, respectable citizens. Consequently, a struggle emerged within the WWCA as to the best line of activities. Disagreements emerged over with which outsiders to form linkages, over ultimate objectives, over strategy and tactics, and even over ideology. A group, largely made up of workers, developed within the association, calling itself "Up in Arms" and advocating a more militant, class-oriented line. They sought to unite with other worker and community groups in common struggle for shared interests and they forged closer ties with radical groups in Hawaii.

A committed group of political activists had been developing in Hawaii ever since the 1960s. These were people with a sophisticated political orientation, a commitment to building a just society, a dedication that would be reflected in almost total involvement in any struggle once undertaken, and a willingness to risk their personal well-being for a cause in which they believed. This band of radicals was a most important catalyst in helping to pull together the entire Waiahole-Waikane movement. One such person was Pete Thompson, who was associated with the Ethnic Studies Program at the University of Hawaii and had a history of activism in support of community groups fighting in their own behalf. Thompson was among the first to offer his services to Waiahole-Waikane in 1974. He then left for an extended trip to the Peoples Republic of China but resumed his association with the WWCA upon his return.

There were several organizations of radicals in Hawaii, but the most significant in terms of the Waiahole-Waikane struggle was the Revolutionary Communist Party (RCP). A number of radicals who had previously been associated with the Revolutionary Union joined together with other activists to form the RCP in the fall of 1975. Very early in its existence the RCP defined the Waiahole-Waikane struggle as a key element in the emerging class struggle in Hawaii. These political activists offered their services to the WWCA but at no time did they attempt to take over leadership. Advice was given when requested. Decisions were made by the WWCA steering committee and membership. However, the activists carried the decisions out to the larger community and helped to put them into practice. They helped to develop a broad base of class allies throughout Oahu and in some of the outer islands. Those who were workers carried the message of Waiahole-Waikane back to the workplace with them. The unemployed talked to other unemployed workers. Students started an educational campaign on the campus. GIs communicated with other GIs. Gradually an entire set of support organizations was built all across the state, representing persons from a variety of walks of life but mostly workers, students, the unemployed, and welfare rights advocates.

In each case the members of the political cadre helped to develop the political analysis and interpretation of events so that people could see the relationship of their own cause to that of Waiahole-Waikane. The residents of Waiahole and Waikane, in turn, lent their support to other struggles in exchange for the opportunity to talk about their own situation. A broad-based movement of workers with feelings of class solidarity emerged. One might also note that the level of political consciousness and sophistication of the WWCA membership grew as the struggle continued. It is impossible to state whether it was the presence of the political cadre or the nature of the struggle that caused this development, but it can probably be traced to the two factors in interaction.

There was a gradual alteration in lines of activity within the WWCA. Initially there was a division of labor, with some elements participating in increasingly militant demonstrations while others sought to continue the more respectable attempts to influence key politicians. The former group increasingly formed alliances with the newly emerging support groups and increasingly defined themselves as participating in a common class struggle. This transition became complete with a change in composition of the steering committee early in 1976. Many, but not all, of the small landowners and larger farmers left the steering committee, to be replaced by workers who had been part of Up in Arms. With this shift in leadership the WWCA became fully committed to carrying on the fight for Waiahole-Waikane as part of a larger class struggle, and the working relationship with the RCP was strengthened. Many of the middle-class supporters remained as supporters, but the new working-class allies became of greater overall significance.

Meanwhile, the battle continued. A series of dates were set and reset for the eviction of the Waiahole tenants. An application was made to rezone a portion of Waikane for urban use. The tenants affected by the proposed Waikane changes were granted delays in their eviction date until all legal appeals were exhausted. Proposals and counterproposals were made, but January 3, 1977, was eventually set as the date to evict some eighty-six Waiahole tenants. On January 2 a tent city was set up in Waiahole valley. Tents were erected by student groups (the Revolutionary Student Brigade and Students United for Land and Housing), worker groups (representing pineapple workers, sugar workers, the unemployed, and civil service workers), youth groups, GIs, and supporters without affiliation. On January 3 the sheriff served writs of possession effective immediately. The writs were accepted but the road leading into the valley was blocked by an arm-linked mass of several hundred people. No attempt was made to enforce the order that day.

By Tuesday, January 4, people began drifting away and the force in tent city became token. Teams were sent out to leaflet and picket throughout Oahu during rush hours. The public was informed of events and asked to phone public officials demanding intervention to prevent the evictions. Around 11:00 P.M. on January 4 word came to the camp that the police were on their way to carry out the eviction order. The tenants, the camp residents, and an "on-call reserve force" mobilized and blocked a half-mile stretch of the Kamehameha Highway, preventing all access to the valley. This blockade also stopped traffic on windward Oahu, as the highway is the only auto route connecting it with the rest of the island. The blockade lasted for over an hour until trusted police sources gave assurance that no police eviction team would come. Public pressure forced the governor to intervene. He set up a meeting of all concerned parties for Friday, January 7, during which Mrs. Marks agreed to delay evictions until March 1 to allow time to work out a nonviolent solution.

The ensuing fifty days were event-filled. The State Land Use Commission held hearings on February 9 and 10 on the application to rezone a portion of Waikane for urban use. A large number of Waiahole-Waikane residents, their allies, and supporters attended the hearings. Both the state of Hawaii and the city and county of Honolulu testified in opposition to the rezoning request. Rallies and demonstrations were held and new compromises were proposed. Finally, on February 26, 1977, Governor Ariyoshi announced that the state would buy 600 acres of Waiahole valley for six million dollars. The state would develop the mountainous terrain at the head of the valley for recreational use and would develop the remainder under a village agricultural scheme. A new residential village would be constructed, land would be developed for agriculture outside the village, long-term leases would be granted, and first priority would be granted to present tenants.

This plan was not a complete victory for the WWCA. The state could not purchase the valley unless Pao and his development corporation (Windward Partners) failed to exercise their purchase option, scheduled to expire in mid-November. It was generally assumed that Pao would not buy Waiahole unless Waikane were rezoned urban. Late in July the State Land Use Commission rejected the request to rezone Waikane. To date no subsequent action has been taken with regard to the purchase option. The state plan did not include the land on the ocean side of Kamehameha Highway in Waiahole (affecting about twelve families) and did not provide for the nine families threatened with eviction in Waikane. At the time of this writing (October 1977) it is expected that Windward Partners will allow their option to lapse and that the state will proceed with its purchase plans. The Hawaii Housing Authority announced on August 13 the establishment of a planning team to design the Waiahole project, but no further details are as yet available.

Discussion

Thus while they did not get everything they wanted, the WWCA won a major victory. In January 1974 it seemed evident that the valley residents were powerless to prevent the loss of their land and forced relocation—probably to the city, as rural land was rapidly becoming nonexistent. Yet by 1977 they were able to coerce the state into buying Waiahole for six million dollars and committing another large, but unspecified, sum to its development. They also were able to prevent Waikane from being rezoned urban. This is a tremendous change in objective levels of power possessed over three years.

It is important that we as sociologists have a theoretical and conceptual scheme that enables us to analyze what happened. This power came from somewhere. It was not created out of thin air. The residents of Waiahole and Waikane valleys did not suddenly gain control of large amounts of base resources not previously possessed. The source of the new power has to be located in the social organization that was created and the allegiances that were formed in the course of the struggle. It is precisely these types of phenomenon that existing social psychological work on powerlessness and political sociological work on power are incapable of handling. Arthur Field (1970) proposed the concept of "people power" for precisely this purpose, but neither he nor anyone else ever developed it. In fact, his original formulation only referred to the power of numbers of people and ignored the dimension of social organization.

It is only in the oft-maligned area of collective behavior and social movements that even the rudiments of a viable, complete approach to power can be found. The collective behavior–social movement area provides a useful starting point. There is a general recognition that power is a collective attribute. Social movement analysts examine the mobilization of segments of a class, nation, or community that normally lack the ability (are powerless) to force the existing social order to respond to their collective needs. Scholars analyze the techniques through which movements attempt to create power and exert sufficient leverage so as to coerce a desired response from representatives of the established order. At its best, this type of analysis takes place within a framework of concern for the larger process of social change. It is precisely this type of approach, when combined into a larger theoretical framework, that could enable us to make sense out of the Waiahole-Waikane experience.

HISTORICAL BACKGROUND

A complete understanding of Waiahole-Waikane would require an analysis of Hawaiian history from the time of earliest European settlement (see Daws, 1968; Fuchs, 1961). The Europeans came as missionaries and traders but remained to alienate the land, proletarianize the Hawaiians, establish plantation agriculture, and import labor from China, Japan, and the Philippines under contracts favorable to planter interests. Work was hard, working conditions bad, and rewards to labor minimal. There was a tendency for each of the racial groups (i.e., Hawaiians, Japanese, Chinese, and Filipinos) initially to interpret their experience as national exploitation at the hands of Haoles (Caucasians) rather than class exploitation at the hands of capitalists. The earliest forms of resistance were national in form and were not without evidence of tensions among racial minorities as well as between them and the Haole elite.

Hawaii remained under the political and economic control of a tightly knit little oligarchy until World War II. The end of the war brought an economic challenge by the ILWU that unionized a large portion of the territory's labor force with a class-oriented ideology. A political challenge was launched by Japanese Americans under the leadership of a group of young men who had served in the military during the war. These two groups joined together to revitalize the Democratic party and build it to the point where it usurped political control from the Republicans. The dominance of the old elite was further undermined when outside capitalists, first from mainland United States and later from Japan, were able to break through barriers and begin a program of investment in Hawaii. The one thing that remained secure in the hands of the old ruling elite was their monopoly over the land. Even here, their orientations changed and they began to see the possibility of selling land and/or developing it for profit rather than retaining it as a combination capital investment and status symbol. This is what made possible both the contemplated development of Waiahole-Waikane and the possibility for viable resistance to such plans.

NATIONALISM AND THE ORGANIZATION OF WAIAHOLE-WAIKANE

The first step in building a successful movement to resist planned development was for Waiahole-Waikane to organize itself. This was not without its problems. The community was multinational in a state with a high degree of national consciousness. This worked two ways. The majority of the residents were non-Haole and could see their present experiences as a continuation of Haole exploitation. Thus nationalism could help to stimulate the will to resist. However, at the same time there existed a certain amount of tension among the different national groups that could impede the development of a unified community resistance movement. Waiahole-Waikane was fortunate in that the first outsiders to offer aid were personally acceptable because of local ties (e.g., kinship, race, previous contact), demonstrated their commitment through a previous history of community activism, and espoused a social analysis stressing the primacy of class over nation. This was reinforced by observation of, and experience with, various situations such as the destruction of an earlier eviction-resistance movement (Kalama Valley) through internal dissent caused by narrow nationalism. These factors combined to enable Waiahole-Waikane to overcome national differences and form a united community movement.

WAIAHOLE-WAIKANE CREATES POWER

The first step toward the development of power came with the self-organization of the community and the formation of the WWCA. This by itself would not have been enough. Even with the community solidly organized and willing to fight, it is unlikely that Waiahole-Waikane could have stood off the political clout of developers or prevented legal evictions. As is often the case, the group that was initially activated into positions of leadership consisted of the higher-status and economically better-off segments of the community. They pursued strategies designed to attract supporters from the cooptable public and to influence actions of state and city agents. Turner's (1970) classic analysis of movement strategies does an excellent job of laying out the relation of a movement to the public. However, he fails to distinguish between supporters and allies. The WWCA at this stage attracted supporters from that segment of the public that empathized with their problem and was willing to lend aid. This aid was useful but was restricted to that which was legitimate and respectable. In contrast, after the leadership of the WWCA changed to include more workers, the entire orientation shifted. The WWCA sought allies who would unite with the WWCA because they recognized that the struggle of the WWCA and their own struggles were part of a more general one. They united as class allies in a larger struggle against capital. The degree of commitment of allies is much greater than that of supporters, in part because they expect a similar commitment in return.

The WWCA did not develop any significant amount of real power during the period of moderate leadership and middle-class support. They were able, with the aid of their supporters, to generate sufficient influence to entice government agencies to make desired decisions. However, it was generally believed by the larger public that the landlord and the developer had the law on their side and that they would ultimately win. A degree of real power was created once the movement took on a clear class character and the WWCA developed class allies. The WWCA and its allies were able to coerce the state into purchasing the land, and the developers were permanently halted. It was no longer a case of persuasion but one of coercion through confrontation. It was clearly demonstrated that the people united can create power where none existed previously, and that this power can be used to bring about some social change, no matter how limited.

Conclusions

This has been just a brief sketch of the type of theoretical approach that could be used to analyze developments such as Waiahole-Waikane. It requires the use of a concept of power that is defined in objective terms and that is located in social collectivities or classes rather than in individuals. The definition of power used by Alford and Friedland (1975) is appropriate for use here providing that it is modified to recognize the dynamic fluid nature of power. It must allow for power to grow, shrink, be created, and be destroyed. The approaches to the study of power utilized by political sociologists in community power studies can provide useful information regarding power structures as they exist at any given moment in time, but it must be recognized that these are merely stop-action views of a dynamic process. This type of research can also provide useful information regarding those vested interests that will attempt to marshal their power to resist social change and loss of privilege.

The social psychological approach to powerlessness can be useful in analyzing the mobilization of participants and the attraction of allies in the course of movement development. One can gain an understanding of the process of recruitment providing one is careful not to confuse individual perceptions of power and powerlessness with actual power that is always possessed by collectivities. Research in this area should also attempt to ascertain the relationship among ideological systems, perceptions of power, and recruitment into change-oriented movements. A closely related problem area is the relation among class consciousness, national consciousness, and either potential for developing actual power or subjective perceptions of power.

This paper has not gone very far in developing the requisite theory or in analyzing the single case of Waiahole-Waikane. Neither of these was my primary objective. Nor would either task be possible in a paper of this limited scope. My objective was to clarify a bit more the nature of the concept of power, how it must be defined, and the type of theory into which it must be integrated, before we can meaningfully attempt to determine the social consequences of powerlessness. I believe that I have accomplished this limited objective.

X

On Social Change: Modernity and Countermodernity

Introduction

The Editors

MOST OF THE PAPERS in this volume deal, directly or indirectly, with social change. Many social issues become major—matters of great concern and the focus of attention—precisely because social changes have broken up accustomed interactions and institutional arrangements.

In the following two papers, social change is the focus of attention. Building on his well-known studies of modernization, Professor Inkeles examines the interactions between institutional change and the tendencies of individuals. He outlines various models of possible futures that might emerge from those interactions. What he sees is a much more complex set of possibilities than many earlier studies, using a fixed and limited conception of modernization, envisaged. Inkeles also observes that rapid change continues in societies that have already industrialized. Some are entering a period during which movements that can be called postmodern—opposed to many of the values associated with the centuries-long process of modernization—have appeared.

These movements are part of what Professor Yinger has called countercultures. In the final chapter he explores the structural and personal sources of these efforts drastically to redefine the true, the good, and the beautiful, to use terms by which various forms of countercultural protests can be characterized. Tendencies toward such protest are endemic in human societies, Yinger argues, including even small and relatively isolated tribal societies. They become major expressions of societal upheaval, however, under conditions of rapid occupational and demographic change and as a result of the weakening of shared meanings and values. Once set in motion, countercultures often become agents of change, both directly by taking the lead in adopting values and patterns of behavior that later diffuse through a society, and indirectly by setting unintended processes in motion. On the whole, the major social issues that countercultures express are not defined so much by the manifest content of their new value systems as by the spotlight they throw on the values and practices of the societies against which they rebel.

40

The Future of Individual Modernity

Alex Inkeles

THE INSTITUTIONAL, STRUCTURAL, AND CULTURAL arrangements that define the modern include a set of attitudes, values, opinions, and modes of feeling and acting in interpersonal relations that may be thought of as an ethos, a frame of mind, or a personality type. This element has been neglected relative to the study of structural change. We have just begun to get some grasp of what the modern individual is like, and what makes a person modern.[1] Yet we are already being asked to indicate what is the future of individual modernity. But before turning to that future we need to be clear as to what we mean by individual modernity.

Individual modernity is defined by a set of psychosocial characteristics that cohere as a syndrome. It is customary to specify both a set of external social indicators and, separately, a set of psychological characteristics that mark the modern individual. The "objective" attributes include being relatively better educated through exposure to formal schooling, participating more in communal and public life in the active citizen's role, being exposed to the message of the mass media, working in the technologically more advanced and organizationally complex productive enterprises, being physically and socially mobile. Some would add to this list having urban as against rural residence.

Very much less studied are the subjective aspects of this syndrome. In our initial research on individual modernity we found an empirical syndrome of personal qualities having basically the same content and structure in all the six countries we studied.[2] Subsequently the same

[1]See Lerner (1966); Kahl (1968); Inkeles and Smith (1974).

[2]The Harvard-Stanford research on individual modernity was conducted in Chile and Argentina, India and East Pakistan, and Nigeria and Israel. In each country a sample was taken of industrial workers, urban nonindustrial workers, and village agriculturalists, up to 1,000 in number. For details see Inkeles and Smith (1974).

syndrome has been identified in more than a dozen additional countries, including the United States and Canada. It is, moreover, found at all occupational and educational levels, and from the oldest segments of the population down to children tested at third-grade level in Brazil.[3] By considerable compression one can reduce the elements to a few main components.[4]

1. *A strong sense of personal and social efficacy.* The more modern individual stands at the other pole from the passive and fatalistic. He or she believes that alone, or in concert with others, one can act to influence the course of one's own life, the fate of one's community, or even the actions of nature. Such individuals take initiatives and act to improve their condition, that of their family, and of their community.

2. *Independence from traditional authorities,* and autonomous decision making, particularly when deciding about the conduct of one's personal life. When selecting a spouse, job, or career, such individuals will decide for themselves rather than allowing parents, elders, or similar authorities to determine their choice.

3. *Openness to new ideas and experiences.* This is expressed in interest in technical innovation; in support of scientific exploration of hitherto sacred or taboo subjects such as the forces that determine whether a baby will be a boy or girl; in readiness to meet strangers; and in acknowledging the right of women to take advantage of opportunities outside the household.

4. *Being an informed, active, participant citizen.* In the newly emerging countries this expresses itself in adopting new identities as a member of newer, larger, political entities beyond family, village, and clan. Everywhere it involves taking an interest in public affairs, especially those beyond the purely parochial; joining organizations; keeping informed about the news; noting and otherwise taking an active part in the political process.

Additional elements of attitude and value change that define modernity involve the orientation to time, to personal and social planning, to the rights of dependents and subordinates, and to the relevance of formal rules as a basis for running things.

Later clinically oriented research has indicated that at deeper-lying levels of personality the more modern individual is cognitively more flexible, is more field independent, is equipped with greater ego strength, and is somewhat above average in compulsiveness.

[3]See Holsinger (1973); Suzman (1973).

[4]The themes that make up the modernity syndrome are described in some detail in chapter 7 of Inkeles and Smith (1974). For a description of a short form of the scale of individual modernity that is based on fifteen or fewer questions, and can be administered in less than ten minutes, see Smith and Inkeles (1966); also see Appendix B of Inkeles and Smith (1974).

Psychological modernity is then a complex, multifaceted, and multidimensional syndrome. Although it is found in all societies, and at all levels of those societies, it tends to be much more concentrated in those countries that are economically more developed. This is, in part, a contextual effect, but it results mainly from the fact that in such societies there is a greater concentration of the institutional forces that make individuals more modern, such as schools, factories and cooperatives, mass media, cities, and mass markets. Exposure to those institutions produces individuals who are more modern than their compatriots, whether they are located in more or less developed countries. Thus in our six-nation study our index of exposure to modernizing institutions generally produced 2 to 3 percent of modern men at the lowest decile, rising steadily until at the tenth decile of exposure 80 to 90 percent of the men scored as modern, regardless of which country was under study.

Interaction of Institutional Change and Individual Modernity

If individual modernity depends mainly on the nature of the sociocultural systems in which people live, and the distribution of experience within those systems, then to read the future of individual modernity we need to predict the future of society. Alas, no one can do that with precision, and certainly not for the long term. But we can specify a range of scenarios with reasonable estimates of the probability of their occurring in the short term. And for each of those scenarios, in turn, we can, with much more confidence, suggest the fate of individual modernity.

IMAGES OF TOTAL CASTASTROPHE

In this age we cannot exclude from the set of scenarios having claim to probability several that can only properly be described as cataclysms. Such potential total disasters could come in two forms:

Cataclysm I offers death by suffocation. This is the Club of Rome model—it anticipates a breakdown of the world system as population overtakes food and other resources, which leads to the end of industrial civilization. The result is presumably a Hobbesian war or an Armageddon.

Cataclysm II takes the form of a nuclear holocaust, which produces a quicker, but no less certain, end of civilization as we know it.

Both scenarios promise the end of individual modernity as now constituted. Except for some deviant individuals or subcultures, the extinction of individual modernity would probably be almost complete within one or two generations, because the structural forms generating and supporting the type would be destroyed. It is unlikely that mankind would return to the Stone Age, or even to a condition equivalent to that of contemporary primitives, but impoverished settled agriculture under sociopolitical conditions similar to those of feudalism seems a not improbable prospect. Attitudes and values would then develop in tune with the system, colored by fear and anxiety persisting from the memory and mythology of the precipitating cataclysm. Passivity, fear of the stranger and the new experience, severe subordination of the individual to group norms linked to survival, the exercise of tyrannical personal power, all would come to prevail.

THE STEADY-STATE OR NO-GROWTH MODEL

This supposes that forces calling for, and seeking to install, no growth succeed. The result would be not destruction of the present system, but rather its petrification. Institutions, relational patterns, the relative gap between less and more developed countries would be preserved.

Just as the no-growth steady-state model would freeze the absolute and relative inequalities of the present world system, just so would it act to fix the existing differentials in the distribution of modern qualities in the world population. On the world scale, high levels of individual modernity would be overwhelmingly concentrated in the most developed countries. The elite strata within the less developed countries would manifest modernity levels similar to those in the advanced countries, so long as these elites had access to modernizing experiences at levels comparable to those enjoyed by their opposite numbers in advanced countries, discounting some for the contextual effects produced by the poverty of their countries. But the great masses of the populations in the poor countries, cut off from increased exposure to modernizing influences, would remain at levels of traditionalism similar to those that now prevail.

However, conversion to no growth might also produce some major unanticipated deviations from present patterns. Since the currently advanced sector has not lived in a steady state for some 500 years, there is very little precedent to guide us. Frustration over inhibited achievement drives, a gradual constriction of cognitive openness, depression and lassitude replacing instrumental activism, diversion of energy to pleasure seeking or escape into hallucinatory searches for the absolute, all seem plausible outcomes, at least for significant segments of the population.

But we need not pursue this line too assiduously, because it seems to me highly implausible to assume that the world will accept a no-growth steady-state approach within the framework of anything like the present, or any immediately foreseeable, world order.

LONG-TERM DEVELOPMENT MODELS

These also come in several versions. Two of the scenarios express a great dream—one revolutionary, the other evolutionary.

The Radical's Dream

In this scenario a series of revolutions, or one global breakthrough, establishes socialist countries everywhere. China and Russia settle their differences, and a reborn U.S. and Europe join them in instituting social justice everywhere, redistributing resources, maximizing participation and communalism, rationing produce, eliminating waste, and so on.

The Liberal's Dream

This calls for balanced growth that gets the poorer countries out of their desperate plight without seriously impoverishing the most advanced countries or significantly eroding their present political and cultural patterns. The gap between rich and poor is not quite eliminated but is greatly narrowed. More important, the absolute levels of living in the less developed countries are raised so that by today's standards they live reasonably well—with 3,000 calories of food daily, eight to twelve years of education per child, reasonable housing, clean water, adequate health care, and so on. All this is accomplished with due speed, say in twenty years, without violence, based on spontaneous economic forces and political goodwill supplemented by moderate global regulation to control pollution and constrain exploitation. Democratic party systems prevail, free movement of people and especially ideas is relatively unimpeded, and so on.

OUTCOMES OF THE DREAM MODELS

The radical and the liberal dreams make many common assumptions about the institutional structure of future societies. On this basis our theory predicts common outcomes at the level of individual psychology regardless of differences in the politicoeconomic context. Among the institutional developments expected by both models are:

1. Greatly diffused and much longer exposure to formal education for the average person.
2. Substantial expansion of mass media and great growth in popular exposure.
3. Increased industrialization, especially technicalization, miniaturization, materials substitution in the mode of the plastic revolution.
4. Mechanization and industrialization of agriculture and food production.
5. Vast population shifts to urban and suburban centers.
6. Maintenance of high levels in, and probably expansion of, basic and especially applied scientific research.
7. Great growth of public services as implementation of the revolution of rising entitlements progresses.[5]

If these structural shifts occur, they should be reflected in substantial changes in the levels, but not the content, of individual modernity among all the peoples affected, but especially in the populations of the now less developed countries. Increased levels of modernity would presumably be manifested over the entire range of dimensions covered by the concept of individual modernity, from active public participation, through openness to new experience, to women's rights. Moreover, these increases in individual modernity would take similar form and would occur at comparable rates whether either the radical or the liberal dream came to pass.

To many it will seem a curious, and surely a profoundly mistaken, belief to assume that the future of individual modernity would be basically the same in a socialist as in a capitalist world. Without extensive testing of our modernity scales in socialist countries we cannot assert this proposition without risk of plausible challenge. The evidence available so far, however, indicates that the clearly more important determinants of psychological modernity are individual exposure to a set of relatively standard institutional inputs, such as schools; factories, offices, and laboratories; cooperative farms; the mass media; and modern cities. This is not to say there are no demonstrated contextual effects at the societal level. We already have available evidence about one such effect based on differentiating the six countries in our original study on a scale of relative economic development. In that test 21 percent of the explained variance was accounted for by the country factor, a modest but not inconsequential figure next to the 79 percent accounted for by the set of individual experiences such as education and occupation.[6]

---

[5]For an evaluation of the extent and force of the popular expectation of ever-greater entitlement to an ever-increasing range of services and goods from education through health to legal aid, see Inkeles (1977a).

[6]See Inkeles (1977b).

Evidence aside, we can, of course, speculate about the differences in the individual modernity syndrome that might result from the conditions specified by the radical and the liberal dreams.

Let us assume, for this purpose, the Chinese rather than the Russian version of the radical dream were to prevail. In that case, differences might emerge on the dimensions that follow.

Individualism

This difference, of a particular kind, has been part of the modernity syndrome in virtually all the countries tested so far. However, individualism as it enters into the modernity syndrome does not mean rugged individualism in the classic American sense. Rather the scale measures independence from control by parents, village elders, or other traditional authority figures, especially as concerns intimate associations as in the choice of spouse or job. Nevertheless, it is reasonable to assert that, in the nonsocialist countries studied so far, increased individualism emerges as a concomitant of increasing modernity.

It seems likely that in socialist countries of the Chinese type this element of the syndrome would be either muted or would be quite displaced by a greater emphasis on collectivism. We have in mind the stories from journalists and visitors who consistently report that when they ask young people in China, "What do you want to be when you grow up?" the children reply with astounding regularity, "I want to become whatever the party (or country) wants me to become."

Antiauthoritarianism

One indicator of liberating oneself from traditionalism consists in challenging the right of received authority to command obedience merely by right. Although antiauthoritarianism, in this sense, was not explicitly defined as part of the modernity syndrome, it is a quality that seems to suffuse the modernity scale. Moreover, when standard tests of antiauthoritarianism are correlated with tests of modern attitudes, they regularly show strong positive correlations. My reading of the Chinese model of authority suggests that, under it, antiauthoritarianism would be much more weakly, and perhaps even negatively, correlated with other elements of the modernity syndrome.

Equalitarianism

The syndrome measured by our scale of individual modernity, which we call the OM scale, tests one's concern for the dignity of those weaker and less prestigeful, readiness to accord women rights equal to those of men, and insistence that in local rule the opinion and vote of all should count equally. We read this set of responses as indicating a strong equalitarian tendency to be part of the modernity syndrome.

Again, how one predicts the fate of this disposition in the radical dream depends on how one reads the social reality of Communist China. For myself, I see the authority of the Communist party and of its local representatives, and the concept of the leadership role of the "proletarian vanguard," as decidedly nonequalitarian. On the other hand, there is the Chinese espousal of communal principles, their extensive organization of cooperatives, their emphasis on consensus, and the strong leveling tendencies in both Communist ideology and practice. Keeping those facts in mind, one might well be led to anticipate that those more modern in attitude on the other elements of the syndrome would, if the radical dream became reality, be more strongly inclined to equalitarianism than would individuals living in the liberal's dream world.

Even if these adjustments to the special conditions of the Chinese model of communism were to take place, I believe it would still be true that of all the questions and themes that together measure individual modernity, some 80 to 90 percent would have more or less the same weight in the typical individual profile were *either* the radical or the liberal dream to come to pass. Both would bring in their train a strong sense of personal efficacy; openness to new experience; valuing of technical competence; heightened interest in public affairs; positive attitudes toward limiting family size and practicing birth control; being an active, participant citizen; greater knowledge of national and worldwide places, persons, and events; and other elements of the modernity syndrome as already manifested elsewhere in our historical experience.

MORE REALISTIC MODELS

I believe that neither the radical nor the liberal dream will come to pass in the next twenty years or so. Instead, we are likely to witness a scene not profoundly different from that which has filled the world's stage during the last twenty or twenty-five years. Some of the less developed countries will continue frozen in poverty and neglect; some will see some minor degree of improvement in the condition of life; the majority will make slow but steady progress; and some few will experience a great surge of development. The major developed countries of the world will, with intermittent crises, probably continue to grow at modest rates, maintaining the main features of their politicoeconomic systems as now constituted, although progressing further in the direction of centralization, regulation, public welfare, and other forms for diffusing public entitlements. Possibly one or two new members will be added to the club of the advanced, as Japan won its way in the era just past, but in general its composition will remain basically the same.

For the set of more developed countries and possibly some of the newcomers to the club of the affluent, we may anticipate three main trends.

First, we expect the progressive incorporation into the modern sector of the presently marginal populations—rural black and white Appalachians in the United States; the Ainu in Japan; the oriental Jews in Israel; some portion of the tribal people and the untouchables in India.

Second, a modest increase in the *average* level of individual modernity as educational levels, exposure to mass media, travel, and other modernizing influences continue to rise, except as they may have reached a saturation point in the most advanced countries.

Third, substantial increases in the frequency and diffusion of the qualities of the postmodern man. This type should not be confused with the individuals involved in the ecological movement, with health foods, organic gardening, bicycle riding, and jogging. All those are essentially congruent with the syndrome of individual modernity. Indeed, in their expression of a heightened sense of efficacy, their affirmation of personal autonomy, their experimental openness to new experience, and their desire to adapt and direct science and technology to new goals, they may be said to manifest the qualities of psychological modernity in the highest degree.

Instead, by postmodern I mean being increasingly oriented to passive rather than active roles; ready to surrender personal autonomy to collective control; suspicious or defeatist about all forms of science; seeking mystical experience or release from sensation through drugs or violence; hostile to any sort of fixed schedule; skeptical about the payoff for personal or social planning. So marked are some of these tendencies, and so much at variance with the main elements of the modernity syndrome, that they might more accurately be described as antimodern.

Such qualities were previously found in a U-shaped distribution, strong mainly among the most advantaged youth and simultaneously in some of the most disadvantaged segments of the population. But these tendecies also had, and continue to have, considerable fascination for many middle-class youths. The high point may have been reached in the 1960s, but this wave's future is problematic in the extreme. Marked resurgence of such tendencies would pose considerable challenge to the modernity syndrome and, indeed, could undermine the psychological base on which modern large-scale society rests.

Analogous developments, albeit specific to their social setting, may be anticipated in the so-called socialist countries. The tendencies I have called antimodern are already sufficiently widespread as to be frequently described and discussed in the Soviet press. The pattern includes avoidance of regular work; pursuit of illegal trading, especially in objects of West European provenance; and exaggerated costume, again with a preference for "exotic" items like blue jeans and printed tee shirts. As in the West, these styles seem to attract, with differentiation in the content and mode of expression, both the young people from the most advantaged and those in the more disadvantaged segments of the society.

However, of much greater importance for the future of the socialist countries will be the extent and the fate of the movement for greater freedom and self-expression. This group, often called the dissidents, bears important resemblance to those who make up the ecology movement in the U.S. and Western Europe, but in other respects is distinctive. The critical point, however, is that it is quite inappropriate to classify them as a variant of the postmodern personality. On the contrary, I see these dissidents as quintessentially modern individuals in conflict with a social system that in many respects has failed to adapt its institutional forms, in particular its political practice, to the level of development that characterizes the society in other respects, such as its technological complexity, its dependence on scientific research, and its pervasive system of popular education. The intellectual opposition in the Soviet Union urges greater freedom of expression, openness to new ideas, innovation and experimentation in institutional forms, more opportunity for individual mobility, fuller actual rather than symbolic participation in the public decision-making process. All this is eminently modern. By contrast, the style of the Soviet regime is traditional, indeed, antimodern. Just as the unevenness of development in the U.S. is reflected in our failure to eliminate poverty and unemployment, so it is part of the uneveness of development of the Soviet Union that it continues relatively unchanged its particular forms of legal and intellectual oppression long after the system has, in other respects, developed modern forms of organization and modes of operation common to other large-scale, advanced, industrial societies.

Conditions Specific to the Less Developed Countries

To deal with the specific conditions manifested in the less developed countries, we again need a differentiated scenario. The fate of individual modernity in a country such as Haiti will obviously be vastly different from that in Cuba. And these are, clearly, not the only models. The problem is further complicated by the prospect that nations will not necessarily remain in the same structural category for a long period, but will shift from one to another, at times with confusing rapidity.

Nevertheless, certain major sets of societies do encompass a considerable number of cases, which permits imposing some order and justifies the expectation of some regularity of outcome. We may distinguish several future conditions for different sets of the less developed countries, along with consequently differentiated propects for the future of individual modernity.

First, there are the countries frozen or locked into backwardness, isolated, forgotten. Their poverty is expressed in GNP per capita of under $100, and electric consumption per capita of under twenty kilowatts per year. Their desperation is expressed in life expectancies at birth under forty, food consumption under 2,100 calories per day, and a ratio of less than one teacher for every two thousand of population. And their isolation is reflected in a total value of exports and imports of no more than $20 to $30 per person per year. In this set we have Haiti in the Caribbean; in Africa, Somalia and Chad; in Asia, the Indonesian part of Borneo, Burma, Laos, and Afghanistan; while in Latin America, Bolivia might qualify. Such societies are, fortunately, ever fewer in number, and we may hope the category will disappear. But to expect that outcome by 2000 is probably too sanguine.

These are the societies profoundly burdened by the most extreme poverty, the most unpromising physical setting, the most severe paucity of resources, those often chillingly designated the "international basket cases." Education, technical change, mobility, a flow of information, free movement of ideas and people are either infeasible or actively prevented by the authorities. Very little change can be expected, and that affecting only a very thin veneer of those at the interface with the outside world. In these countries today's average scores for individual modernity will be much the same twenty years hence.

Closely related to the frozen lands are the countries where structural change is extremely slow, but where certain elements—such as the military, or an exporting sector, along with the trading and service groups that support them—have created enclaves of differentiated activity bearing some resemblance to the rationality of modern organization. In Latin America, Ecuador and Honduras might qualify; in Africa, Nigeria, the Ivory Coast, or Morocco; in Asia, Indonesia or Sri Lanka; and in the Middle East, Jordan or Iraq.

In these countries even the nominally "modern" sector will be found suffused with sentiments typical of traditional societies. Their modernity will be severely limited to certain realms of action, most notably technical and administrative, and will in no significant degree carry over to reduce social injustice or personal privilege.

Fortunately, the bulk of the developing nations do not fall in the category of the isolated or the near isolated. The unevenness of their development makes it extremely difficult, nevertheless, to treat them as a coherent set. They do, of course, have some features in common. Among these are:

>moderate rates of economic growth;
>rapid, almost explosive, expansion of their education programs;
>intense urbanization, product largely of a massive flow of population out of the countryside;
>burgeoning of mass communication;
>economic infrastructures of roads, harbors, railroads, air- and seaports steadily, often rapidly, expanding;
>reasonably stable and moderately effective central civil service apparatus.

Having much in common, this middle range of countries is still markedly differentiated on many dimensions:

>*politically,* they vary from relatively stable and effective democracies, through all combinations of fluctuating and ineffective party and military regimes, to relatively stable and effective autocratic and dictatorial rule;
>*economically,* they range from relatively open, classically capitalist, free-market economies, through all manner of mixture of the state and private sector, to relatively complete socialism or, more accurately, state capitalism;
>*culturally,* they range from ideologically committed, religiously fanatic, totalistic systems, to relatively open, laissez-faire, even libertarian, orientations;
>*in stratification terms,* they include societies ranging from the most rigid hierarchies and steep pyramids, to those of relative equality in the distribution of power and income.

While acknowledging the existence of this structural differentiation and its significance in political and economic terms, I believe that such contextual forces will, in themselves, not have great impact on the process of individual modernization. The critical factor in that process, the prime determinant of the rate of individual change, will be the extent to which individuals are exposed to the "schools for modernity" such as formal education, factories, modern offices, and other rationalized work settings; the mass media; domestic and foreign travel; and urban conglomerations. In direct proportion to their contact with such institutions and experiences, individuals will become more efficacious, more open to new experience, more active participants in the political process, more flexible cognitively, and in other ways will manifest the qualities of the individual who is psychosocially modern.

Some allowance should perhaps be made for special situations of greatly accelerated economic and social development creating environments highly stimulating to the growth of individual modernity above and beyond what would be predicted solely on the basis of individual levels of education or occupation. Such a situation may currently exist in Taiwan, Singapore, Hong Kong, Brazil, and the People's Republic of China, and will likely develop in some new settings in the next two decades.

Persistent Questions and Lingering Doubts

These main scenarios being duly sketched, there remain several questions of a more general nature about the future of individual modernity that deserve at least brief responses.

IS EVERYBODY TO BECOME MODERN?[7]

Since modernity, as I conceive it, is not an absolute but a relative state, this question cannot be answered exactly as it has been put. But insofar as education, industrial or bureaucratic employment, mass media exposure, and other modernizing experiences spread, to that degree more and more people will become more modern than they are now. This process is pervasive and, barring the two cataclysms sketched earlier, I believe it comes as near to being inexorable as any social process can be.

Actually, it *is* possible to express individual modernity in absolute rather than relative terms. One could, for example, arbitrarily classify as modern everyone who gave the modern answer to half or more of the questions on a modernity measure such as the OM scale.[8] Using our experience with the scale so far, we could effectively calculate the proportion who might be expected to score as modern in future years by basing our calculation on estimates of what the social characteristics of the world's population will be like at various later points in time. These projections might be rather discouraging. In virtually all countries the absolute numbers of individuals going to school, or going to school longer, increase regularly. That produces an *absolute* increase in the number of modern individuals. But in some of the less developed coun-

---

[7]For an exchange of views on this theme see Hagen (1976) and Inkeles (1976).

[8]To facilitate making comparisons among different national populations we have scored the OM scale on an absolute "right or wrong" basis, rather than in the relative fashion utilized in creating the scales as reported in Inkeles and Smith (1974). In this form we call the scale not OM, but IM, to stand for "International Modernity." See Inkeles (1977b).

tries huge population growth has meant that the proportion of the total population having attained minimum levels of schooling has failed to rise or has even decreased. The consequence is that there is a *relative* decline in the *proportion* of modern individuals. Unless we can provide education for a larger proportion of the global population, therefore, it will be a very long time indeed before everyone is psychologically modern.

CAN ONE SKIP STAGES TO CLOSE THE GAP?

The gap in physical wealth separating the most from the least advantaged nations is much greater than that separating them on measures of individual modernity. Nevertheless, the gap is substantial and, as in the case of wealth, we hope to reduce it and, if possible, close it entirely.

Those who start with less cannot hope to catch up unless those who are ahead gain more slowly than those who are behind. Interestingly enough, this seems to be happening in the economic sphere, since the average growth rate of GNP for the most advanced countries tends to be below that of the less developed. A similar "ceiling effect" seems to operate in the case of individual modernity. Those who start with the lowest levels of individual modernity gain most rapidly, given equal-unit increments of exposure to modernizing institutions.

Still, the regular processes will be very slow and indeed protracted. Many people have the sense that the world's expectant people cannot wait that long. They wonder if there is not some way in which people can skip stages, going directly and immediately from psychological traditionalism to psychological modernity, as they might skip the long-distance telephone wire and go directly to line-of-sight microwave transmission.

Since individual modernity has no apparant stages, but rather is a continuous and seemingly seamless web, the very notion of skipping stages seems hardly applicable. Acceleration, however, is another matter. Many individuals and groups seem to have moved with exceptional speed from the lowest to quite high points on the scale of individual modernity within a generation, within a life span, or even within a decade. Such changes, however, depend on providing the individuals concerned with more extensive exposure to the modernizing experiences provided by education, modern employment, and mass media exposure. Alas, to increase the availability of such experiences obviously requires that we solve very imposing challenges of a politicoeconomic nature. And even if the general *diffusion* of modernizing experiences can be very much increased, that will only influence how *many* people are modernized and how *far* they are modernized. It seems unlikely that it can affect how *fast* they are individually modernized. To produce a person moderately high on the modernity scale, scored in absolute terms, seems to take at least six to eight years of schooling, or more than double that exposure to work in a modern productive enterprise, or some appropriate combination of the two. It is evidently a slow process, and we know no obvious way greatly to accelerate it.

DOES THE SPREAD OF THE MODERNITY MEAN THE END OF THE TRADITIONAL?

Few issues arouse more apprehension and generate more misconceptions. Much confusion could be avoided if we could forgo our propensity to use the terms "traditional" and "modern" as global, undifferentiated concepts that can have almost any meaning. As I have defined individual modernity in my work, it refers to a broad syndrome of qualities, but one finite and specific. Other realms of value and forms of social interaction cannot safely be assumed automatically to follow the patterns observed with our measures. One should, therefore, be extremely cautious about projecting onto the conception of the "modern" popular and casually arrived at notions that have not been systematically tested empirically.

For example, it is regularly and widely assumed that becoming modern automatically carries with it decreasing respect for the aged, and increasing unwillingness to assume the burden of care for the elderly. But the research evidence available indicates this is a mistaken assumption. This is not to say that modernity brings no changes in one's orientation to parents and elders. On the contrary, our data show that increasing modernity does express itself in resistance to having one's elders decide who is the right person to marry or which is the right job to take. But this specific expression of independence from parents cannot safely be generalized to all other forms of relation with elders and kin.[9]

A very wide range of religions, kinship patterns, sexual relations, styles of dress, forms of recreation, types of housing and living arrangement, modes of intimate interpersonal relations, forms of linguistic expression, scheduling of daily activity, preferences in diet, and other numerous elements of culture are quite compatible with the industrial order and with other aspects of the modern institutional system. Among these many culture patterns compatible with modernity are some that would commonly be considered traditional. Other patterns mistakenly abandoned or officiously driven out in the first waves of modernization

[9]For evidence that respect for, and readiness to care for, parents and elders persists in the presence of the greater autonomy characteristic of modern individuals, see Bengtson et al. (1975).

may well make their way back. For example, industrialization and westernization in Japan drove the Japanese businessman out of his kimono into the Western business suit, but not out of the geisha house. Retaining the latter, perhaps otherwise deplorable, evidently did not impede his business acumen. And in the future he may retain the geisha while restoring the kimono without losing his share of the world market.

In the political games of life and society there are always circumstances making for strange bedfellows. Traditional authorities may use modern individuals to support and even strengthen their traditional controls, and modern individuals may seek to capture the force at the command of traditional authority to advance their modernizing objectives.

ARE THERE NO MASSIVE COUNTERTENDENCIES TO STOP OR AT LEAST OFFSET THE MARCH OF MODERNITY TRIUMPHANT?

Of course there are. Modernity must be recognized as being at least as fragile and vulnerable as any other general historical tendency. Either of the two cataclysms sketched above would very likely bring it to a complete halt, and might well eliminate it. Insofar as it comes to be seen not as a mere social process, but rather as some sort of social movement, it may become the object of ideological warfare designed to halt or even to eradicate it. Rightest movements are the most obvious sources from which antimodern campaigns might emanate, but modernism seems not less attractive as a target for both orthodox Marxism and the New Left. Finally, there is the possibility that individual modernity as we have conceived and measured it may itself become tomorrow's traditionalism, a historical anachronism no longer appropriate to the structural features of some as yet unimagined future society radically different in form and content from any we have yet known.

MODERNITY: GOOD OR EVIL?

Some may consider it morally insensitive to have come so far without saying whether modernity is good or bad. I do not see how one can make that judgment without specifying some personal standard of value. The question is rather like asking whether the Industrial Revolution was good or bad. Most likely those who see the consequences of the Industrial Revolution as, on balance, good will also affirm the goodness of individual modernity.

So far as the specific qualities making up the syndrome of individual modernity are concerned, one would probably find general agreement, at least in liberal circles, that modernity is preferable to traditionalism. This judgment would surely apply to open-mindedness, to cognitive flexibility, and to respect for the feelings of those less powerful than oneself. But when it comes to efficacy, to faith in science, or to interest in technical innovation, many, young and old, will begin to hold back their approbation, seeing in these qualities the seedbed that ultimately came to nourish great engines of destruction, such as hydrogen bombs, breeder reactors, strip mining, and pesticides like DDT.

It can convincingly be argued that the qualities of the modern have in their more exaggerated, Faustian, form a potential for producing demonic impulses. I would deny that Hitler or Stalin, Khadafy or Amin, in any significant degree embodies or symbolizes the qualities of individual modernity. But we all have our own frequent nightmare of the demonic villain who will cement all the river banks, or dam all the wild rivers, or cut down all the virgin forests, or bulldoze all the cherished architectural monuments, or turn all the friendly little family groceries and restaurants into supermarkets or fast-food chains. These tendencies are real. To some they are, moreover, not mixed blessings, but rather genuinely desirable manifestations of modernization and progress. And the impulses just described are surely among the less demonic that we can mention or that others have conceived and pursued in the name of modernity.

Acknowledging all this, one may nevertheless believe that without the modern spirit a much poorer future, indeed, one may say a much worse fate, awaits humanity. Being in the condition we are now in, to opt for a return to the mentality of traditionalism would win us not a hoped-for return to a bucolic idyll, but rather to a Hobbesian state of nature. Indeed, we are beyond the point where such a choice is possible. The real choice is no longer between modernism and traditionalism. It is, rather, between one combination of modernism or another—either a modernism linked to a passion for power and to a bottomless greed, resting on torture and erecting monuments to tyranny, or a modernism restrained by humility and tempered by humanism. Let us hope that the choice will be ours to make.

41

Countercultures and Social Change

J. Milton Yinger

DURING THE LAST FIFTEEN YEARS, few topics have attracted more attention, both of social scientists and of the general public, than the sharp challenges to prevailing values brought by the hippies and the yippies, the religious movements based on Oriental perspectives, the communards, and the many other deviations from established ways of doing things that have come to be referred to as "the counterculture." Although these are often described as rare, if not indeed unique, social movements, I have been struck with the extent to which a great many nearly universal phenomena have a countercultural quality and are better understood if one examines them from the perspective of countercultural theory. These make up a heterogeneous list: religious sectarianism and heresy; alienation; Freudian and other depth psychologies, with their conception of a characterological underworld, filled with impulses and tendencies in sharp contradiction to the conscious life of the ego and the normative order of the superego; youth groups and generation conflicts; communes and utopias; modernization and revolutions; rites of rebellion and rituals of reversal in tribal societies; protests against discrimination; social change. Each of these, and several other topics that I shall not list, are better understood if one examines their countercultural elements. My aim is to examine a few of these topics to see what they may contribute, when studied by use of the concept of counterculture, to our understanding of society.

□ Adapted from the presidential address, American Sociological Association, September 5, 1977. I am deeply grateful to the National Endowment for the Humanities for a Fellowship for Independent Study and Research, to Oberlin College for a sabbatical leave, and to Clare Hall, Cambridge University, for appointment as Visiting Fellow.

Now this is a paradoxical way to study sociology. The central questions have always been: How can we account for social order, granted our egocentricity and the scarcity of many valued things? And how is change from one system of order to another brought about? I am suggesting that as a complement to those questions we look for explanations of disorder, hoping that a new perspective will increase our understanding.

Following the more usual way of looking at things, social theorists have developed three partially competing theories of social order:

1. It is a product of a mutually shared normative system—a blueprint for action that has been internalized by a set of persons in interaction.
2. It is a product of reciprocity and exchange, of perceived mutual advantages.
3. It is a consequence of the power of some to command the behavior of others.

Statements such as these are best seen as analytic. A given interaction, a specific social situation is likely to be a product of all three factors, although one may predominate. Norms may be exploited for power purposes; exchange arrangements may get "frozen" into culture; power long exercised may take on the trappings of authority—a cultural concept.

Quarrels among theorists over the "true" or "basic" source of order seem pointless. The task is to measure the range of empirical mixtures of norms, power, and reciprocity and then to explore the conditions under which these mixtures occur. The mixtures undergo continual change, hence the study of social order must at the same time be a study of social change.

This is where countercultures come in. Some individuals and groups feel particularly strongly that the social order is unable to bring them the accustomed or the hoped-for satisfactions. Depending on their social location and on their personal tendencies, they attack, strongly or weakly, violently or symbolically, the frustrating social order—that is, the normative-power-reciprocity system. The nature of the attack varies widely, with some believing that they have been caught in very bad bargains, others that they are being exploited by unjust and unwise leaders or rulers, and still others emphasizing that they are surrounded by a shoddy system of norms and values. All three elements are found in most protest movements, even though they can be distinguished analytically. Giving the terms sharper and more limited meanings than they ordinarily carry, we can say that reform movements are efforts to change the social bargains—the exchange rates; rebellions are attempts to change the rulers and the bases of power; and countercultural movements are attempts drastically to reorganize the normative bases of order. Revolutions, which are rare and usually require several decades, include all three.

Our concern here is with normative systems in sharp opposition to the prevailing culture, and with the groups and individuals who are proponents and carriers of the oppositional culture. Attention to social organization and social structure must be complemented, we have come to agree, by attention to the fact that conflict is endemic, presenting a need for synthesis. Similarly, the emphasis on normative integration, on culture as a governing blueprint, must be modified by *continuous* attention to countercultures, while working toward synthesis. I am suggesting a cultural dialectic: Every normative system contains the seeds of its own contradiction. This is not propounded as a truth, of course, but as a point of departure, a fruitful way to begin the study of societies.

In the current emphasis on power and exchange, contemporary sociology is largely unaware of the deeply nonrational forces at work in all societies, forces that are built around symbol, ritual, and myth. Most of us are ready to recognize the unconscious and nonrational aspects of individual life, but pay too little attention to the counterpart on the societal level—the shared myths and rituals by which we collectively strive to avert crises or deal with them if they come. We can think of culture on its most abstract and mythical level as a paradigm that selects, interprets, and powerfully affects our impressions and feelings and desires. When culture begins to leave many questions unanswered and many needs unfilled, when individuals suspect their own emotions and experience only a blurred identity, the cultural system may be pushed aside (Tiryakian, 1974: 1–15). Periods of cultural crisis (a potential at any time), of anomie, are not simply periods of loss of faith, but of struggle toward some new way to deal with the threat or reality of crisis and chaos.

The Definition of Counterculture

In the seventeen years since I proposed the term, several explicit and dozens of implicit definitions of "counterculture" have been offered.[1] We can begin to sketch out the parameters of the concept by examining some of these definitions.

[1] I preferred and used the Latin prefix, hence "contraculture." But the voice of the people has spoken, and the usual spelling, by about three to one, is now counterculture. To my ear, contraculture is more mellifluous. I also wanted to avoid suggesting a close parallel with counterrevolution and counterreformation, with their rather specific connotations of returning to an earlier situation. Yet, like Mark Twain, I have no sympathy for those ignorant people who know only one way to spell a word.

There are fundamentally two ways of defining what a counterculture is, the first on an ideological level and the second on a behavioral level. On the ideological level, a counterculture is a set of beliefs and values which radically reject the dominant culture of a society and prescribe a sectarian alternative. On the behavioral level, a counterculture is a group of people who, because they accept such beliefs and values, behave in such radically nonconformist ways that they tend to drop out of the society (Westhues, 1972: 9-10).

The statement that countercultural groups tend to drop out of society is problematic, as Westhues recognizes. Some do; others stay engaged, hoping to change society and its values; others look inward, searching for their souls, but not leaving society.

Some definitions proceed mainly by illustration. Contrast minor variations on a cultural theme, Fred Davis suggests, with sharp variations:

The gang boy configuration . . . fits nicely Yinger's notion of a contraculture; its very meaning and existential quality inhere in its members' patterned deviation from the dominant American cultural pattern. . . . Hippies, too, are an instance *par excellence* of a contraculture whose *raison d'être* . . . lies in its members' almost studied inversion of certain key middle class American values and practices (F. Davis, 1971: 4).

Davis then spells out these contradictions of value and practice in some detail:

. . . *immediacy* contra past preoccupation and future concern; the *natural* . . . contra the artificial . . .; the *colorful* and *baroque* contra the classical, contained, and symmetrical; the *direct* contra the mediated, interposed, or intervening . . .; the *spontaneous* contra the structured; the *primitive* contra the sophisticated; the *mystical* contra the scientific . . . (F. Davis, 1971: 14-15).

There is a tendency to stereotype both the dominant and the hippie standards in Davis' description, as in many discussions of countercultures, in order to draw the sharpest possible contrast; but he does capture the ideological tone of at least one variant of contemporary countercultures.

Some definitions proceed from an opposite perspective:

Today's pop counterculture, especially among the young, is an awesome mix of maximum mindlessness, minimum historical awareness, and a pathetic yearning for (to quote Chico Marx) strawberry shortcut. To hell with established religions, with science, with philosophy, with economics and politics, with the liberal arts—with anything that demands time and effort. Dig the rock beat, kink up your sex life, meditate, tack a photo of Squeaky Fromme on the wall (Gardner, 1975: 46).

Amid the abundance of such descriptions and definitions, pro and con, it is difficult to reestablish the concept of counterculture as a useful part of a scientific vocabulary. Some use it as a word of opprobrium, an indication of incivility, depravity, heresy, or sedition. For others counterculture means hope and salvation, a unique and perhaps final opportunity to get humankind off the road to destruction. Some devotees with whom I have talked are offended when I suggest that countercultures have occurred in many times and places. Their response is a "religious" objection to any doubt cast on the uniqueness of their experience. They are implicitly supported by the host of writers who, in recent years, have discussed "the" counterculture. Others are aware of the frequency with which countercultures have appeared but, not wanting to reduce the enthusiasm of current participants, they play down the historical parallels and emphasize the uniqueness of contemporary oppositional movements.

Certainly every counterculture has unique elements that for some purposes are appropriately the focus of attention. However, I shall be climbing up the abstraction ladder—often, it may appear to you, to dizzying heights—to see the similarities. The term "counterculture" is appropriately used

> whenever the normative system of a group contains, as a primary element, a theme of conflict with the values of the total society, where personality variables are directly involved in the development and maintenance of the group's values, and wherever its norms can be understood only by reference to the relationship of the group to a surrounding dominant culture (Yinger, 1960: 629).

This definition leaves several questions unanswered: Should we speak of countercultures when second-level or subterranean values of a society are raised by some segment of that society to a primary place? The apocalyptic visions, populism, and evangelical fervor of American student radicals, Matza notes (1961), are part of the dominant tradition. When these "counterthemes" are carried to an extreme, however, they are "publicly denounced." Delinquent youth can also draw on a subterranean tradition of the dominant society. The search for a thrill, the use of "pull," and aggression are scarcely limited to delinquents; they are secondary values of the dominant society (Matza and Sykes, 1961). At some point an exaggerated emphasis on a value becomes a countervalue by virtue of the exaggeration. We are dealing with a variable, and only careful study can tell us at what point an exaggerated value becomes countercultural, as indicated by the consequences of its use.

How is deviant behavior distinguished from countercultural behavior? The latter is only one form of deviation, nonconformist and not aberrant, in Merton's terms (Merton and Nisbet, 1966: chap. 15). It is also supported by the norms and values of a group. When counterculture is used to refer to deviation whether or not it is nonconformist and group supported, we are prevented from distinguishing behaviors that, although sometimes similar on the surface, are different in causes and consequences.

Is not the whole concept of counterculture riddled with class and ethnic bias in pluralistic societies? There is a growing tendency to view urban societies as so diverse culturally that each segment is, at the most, countercultural to the other segments. Empirical study tends to support the view, however, that most youths as well as adults hold quite closely to the values of the larger society (Kandel and Lesser, 1972; National Children's Bureau, 1976; Yankelovich, 1974; Wattenberg, 1974). The degree of cultural diversity is not an either-or question and countercultural theory must deal with the range of social situations, from those where value coherence and agreement are high to those where the common core is small (see R. M. Williams, 1970: chap. 10). *To the degree that* the total society has a shared culture, there can be reciprocal countercultures. And each subsociety can also have countercultures.

How counter must a statement or action be (assuming it to be expressive of some norm or value of a group) before we shall consider it countercultural? In the most limiting sense, we might say it has to be specifically a *reversal* of the established value. Note the use of such terms as "polarity," "reversal," and "inversion" in the definitions I have cited. Berger and Berger (1971: 20) speak of "diametric opposition." Indeed these ideas are central to the original concept of counterculture (Yinger, 1960).

We have no way of saying with certainty, however, that sharply oppositional statements and actions are 180 degrees different from prevailing values. We have only the beginnings of a sociometry of dominant values (as in the work of Rokeach, 1973; Yankelovitch, 1974; R. M. Williams, 1970; McCready and Greeley, 1976), and of measurement and scaling of countercultures (Musgrove, 1974; Wuthnow, 1976b; Wieder and Zimmerman, 1974; Spates, 1976; Spates and Levin, 1972; Wattenberg, 1974; Starr, 1974).

Varieties of Countercultures

One might organize material for a study of countercultures in various ways. We could build on an analysis of human behavior that has proved to be useful in several other fields. Years ago Karen Horney (1937) noted that neurotics tend to struggle with their anxieties in three different ways: by attack, by withdrawal, or by a search for shelter and protection. Charles S. Johnson (1943) skillfully described the ways in which minority-group members dealt with discrimination by aggression, avoidance, or acceptance. Turner and Killian (1957) develop a highly analogous interpretation of power-oriented, value-oriented, and participation-oriented social movements. There is a further close parallel in Weber's description (1963) of prophetic, ascetic, and mystical sects.

I shall not develop this valuable theoretical convergence more than to say that countercultural groups quite clearly fall into the same threefold pattern, not the twofold activist-withdrawal categories ordinarily used. The closest comparison is with types of sect. The radical activist counterculturalist is the prophet who "preaches, creates, or demands *new* obligations," to use Weber's words. In typological terms, the communitarian utopian is the ascetic who withdraws into a separated community where the new values can be lived out with minimum hindrance from an evil society. Neither of these descriptions fits the mystics searching for the truth, and for themselves. Realization of their values requires, in their view, that they turn inward. They do not so much attack society as disregard it, insofar as they can, and float above it in search of enlightenment. "The enemy is within each of us," says Charles Reich (1970: 356-57).

Although every countercultural group tends to be a mixture, the strains and the splits they experience often result from sharply contrasting views of the best way to realize their oppositional values. When at the 1969 Woodstock festival, for example, Abbie Hoffman tried to generate political action by saying that the festival was meaningless until a radical "rotting in jail" was freed, a member of The Who rock band, in the words of *Rolling Stone*, "clubbed Hoffman off the stage with his guitar" (Denisoff and Levine, 1970). From the perspective of prophetic counterculturalists, the tendency of many participants in the "New Left" to define political problems in terms of personal issues, often in the language of alienation, seems a terrible deflection from the basic goal of achieving a society based on new values (Lasch, 1969; Clecak, 1973). In theory, if not always in their own ideologically guided behavior, they share Weber's view that "he who seeks the salvation of the soul, of his own and others, should not seek it along the avenue of politics" (Weber, 1946: 126).

A group may seek to mix the mystical-experiential and the ascetic communal countercultural modes, until it is clear that the search for wisdom and the ultimate trip doesn't get the corn planted or the groceries bought, whereupon the group breaks up, or some members leave for a setting more in keeping with their inclinations. In recent years persons who had sought salvation through drugs and unrestrained sex have sometimes turned to ascetic and highly restrained religious groups—the Divine Light Mission, or Hare Krishna, or Meher Baba (K. Kelley, 1973; Judah, 1974; Zaretsky and Leone, 1974; Glock and Bellah, 1976; Robbins and Anthony, 1972).

Other than this brief reference, I will not follow what can be called the sectarian way of organizing the discussion of oppositional cultural movements. We can develop more meaningful comparisons and more useful general principles by examining the following questions:

Are there drastic shifts in the criteria and the methods by which a group claims to *know* what is true, good, and beautiful?

Are there drastic shifts in the standards of what are *held to be* true, good, and beautiful?

In the traditional categories of philosophy, we can define countercultures in terms of their epistemologies, their ethics, and their aesthetics.

1. Truth, today's counterculturalists declare, is not attained by arid research but by mystical insight. It is found in populist, homespun wisdom, in antiuniversities, in direct experience with the cosmos, in meditation, in chants, in drugs, in sensory deprivation, in sensitivity to the messages of the intuitive right hemisphere of the brain—all this set over against science, technology, the knowledge of the expert, and cold rationality.

Attacks on the intellectual establishment are scarcely new, of course. The Taborites denounced the masters of Prague University in the fifteenth century. In England, during the period preceeding the Civil War, itinerant interrupters, professionally skilled hecklers, moved among the churches, which were indissolubly linked with the universities, and despite legal difficulties, denounced the self-righteousness of the pastors and their greed in taking tithes (Hill, 1975: 105–6). Truth, they declared, was not the monopoly of the clergy, but could be given to anyone through an inner light. It would require little shifting of terms to use this set of activities and claims to describe a free university in London or Berkeley in the 1960s.

At the end of World War II H. G. Wells declared that "mind is at the end of its tether." Today we see even more clearly that some of our deepest problems come from application of scientific findings. The countercultural epistemology appears in response to this predicament. Pursue a sense of mystery and fantasy, embrace the occult, meditate, unlock the truth that is in you (N. O. Brown, 1966; Roszak, 1973; Smith, 1976).

Belief in the occult and the pursuit of understanding through mystery are, of course, persistent elements in human history. But their strength alternates, with waves of mysticism occurring when a society has experienced, as Tiryakian has put it, "a loss of confidence in established symbols and cognitive models of reality. . . . Occult practices are appealing, among other reasons, because they are seemingly dramatic opposites of empirical practices of science and of the depersonalization of the industrial order" (Tiryakian, 1972, 510, 494; see also Gellner, 1974; Wuthnow, 1976a).

The way was paved for the countercultural epistemology of our time by the long tradition of unmasking in European and American thought (along with other sources). Do not trust appearances or presumed objective truth, for there are deeper realities, say Hume, Marx, Niezsche, Freud, Pareto, and many others. Truth requires that we bring these deeper realities to light (see Mannheim, 1936; Merton, 1968). If this unmasking laid the groundwork for the sociology and psychology of knowledge in the thought of some persons, it supported the search for truth through mysticism and the occult among others for whom science itself has been unmasked. (My statement itself, of course, is a hypothesis in the sociology of knowledge).

2. Countercultural ethics contradict the values of the dominant society as sharply as countercultural epistemology. Proponents of one, however, are often not proponents of the other. Those who oppose the established ways to truth may be quite conservative in their definitions of the good life; while those who condemn the morality of the establishment may be quite comfortable with its epistemology. The search for a "new head" has much more often been associated with quietism, introversion, and withdrawal from an evil world than with efforts to change it; but ethical counterculturalists challenge the world with new visions of the good life.

To the seventeenth-century English Ranters, the prevailing moral law was not binding on true believers. "I know nothing unclean to me," Clarkson wrote, "and therefore what Act soever I do, is acted by that Majesty in me," (quoted in Cohn, 1970: 312). "Do your own thing" is a somewhat less elegant way of putting it. Many Quakers and Ranters went naked through the streets and into churches—no segregated nudist beach for them (Cohn, 1970; Hill, 1975). Abiezer Coppe and his more effervescent followers were a free speech movement, using obscenity as a weapon; they affirmed the rightness of sex before marriage and attacked the monogamous family; they supported the use of drugs to heighten spiritual vision (though it was alcohol and the new drug tobacco); they dismissed the prevailing doctrines of the church and its structure of authority; they rejected private property in favor of communism.

To the contemporary counterculturalists, what feels good is good. This sometimes collides with another principle: If it is good to the establishment, it is bad for us. Since the establishment takes a somewhat ambiguous middle position with regard, for example, to aggression and sex, countercultural groups have to push away from the center, toward pacifism and celibacy or toward violence and sexual exhuberance, meanwhile claiming that the establishment is not in the center, but actually occupies the opposite pole from the one being held up as good. Counterculturalists do not escape the common human tendency to make their enemies, as well as their leaders, into what they need them to be—need them in an effort to justify their actions and handle their ambivalences.

3. A culture is as fully defined by its aesthetic standards as by its epistemology and its ethics. In many ways the opposition of artists has been negative, in the sense that they have held societies and their cultures up to fundamental criticism more than they have affirmed the values of a counterculture. Yet some oppositional art by its very creation defines an aesthetic counterculture, by using forms and sounds and ideas that formerly were taboo. As culture rather than as criticism, the contemporary counterculture scarcely runs the gamut. Its range is more nearly from yoga to yogurt to zen. The appeal to chaos and dissonance and the overwhelming of the senses correspond with many experiences of our time; but when that point has been made, we may begin to demand of our artists that they help us find—help us experience—some new sense of order and consonance.

I have said "help us experience" because it is not art as argument, but art as experience that more strongly carries the countercultural (or the cultural) impact. "The world doesn't fear a new idea," D. H. Lawrence wrote. "It can pigeonhole any idea. But it can't pigeonhole a new experience" (quoted by Trilling, 1966: xvii). In a society whose major values are intact, the artistic experience, though filled with turmoil and agony, becomes in the last analysis an affirmation of those values. In a society torn by doubt, much of the art—often including some of the best—will take us into a different world. The pilgrim in Dante's *Divine Comedy* moved from low to high, into a kind of rebirth. Samuel Beckett has his heroes, if that is the word, still *Waiting for Godot* as the curtain falls. The protagonist of Kafka's fable is no nearer *The Castle* at the end of his journey than at the beginning.

As experience, many novels and plays in the "theatre of the absurd," using that term in a broad sense, are countercultural comments on the world. (See Esslin, 1973, for a more restricted usage.) Even this absurdity that we dramatize, they say, makes sense by comparison with our sorry state. Let a brief comment on Jean Giraudoux's *The Madwoman of Chaillot* stand for a number of works that despite their differences, affirm that to understand the world, we shall have to turn our usual perceptions upside down. With a wonderfully comic touch, Giraudoux holds the rich, the power hungry, the presumably successful up to ridicule. The industrialist, the general, the broker, the southern fundamentalist minister, and the commissar are seen as truly mad. They are about to destroy Paris and the world as they seek to get the oil they believe is under the city, while the "madwoman" and her eccentric friends recognize the absurdity in the powerful and try to stop them.

I shall only point to some of the other forms of aesthetic

counterculture—those drastic efforts to redefine the beautiful, to break away from old standards that seem not only to inhibit the imagination but to confirm the whole culture within which they are embedded. Most great musicians push back the boundaries of the received tradition and are sometimes regarded as countercultural by defenders of the prevailing classicism. Early in the twentieth century Schönberg, Stravinsky, and many others turned against the romantic tradition, as did many of their literary contemporaries, to explore the farthest possibilities of dissonance—one is tempted to say, in a world filled with crashing sounds and disharmonies.

Seen against the history of music, it comes as no surprise that popular as well as classical forms can drastically challenge prevailing standards. The contemporary counterculture in music, to be sure, seems to bring a much more powerful dissent, both in the sharpness of its reversal of standards and the breadth of its influence. The enormous power of the electronic media to give voice to new sounds, the economic resources to produce them and listen to them, the depth of the disenchantment and its expression in so many other ways, all support the musical protest of our time. For some, of course, rock music is entertainment, fad, and declaration of independence, or it is a source of great profit (Eisen, 1969: xiii). For others, however, it is the chief ritual of a new life; it is community; it is religion. The whole culture complex—the music, lyrics, volume, artifacts, audience, set, and setting—facilitates, as Harmon puts it, "an unprecedented questioning of basic cultural values and institutions" (1972: 81). The "acid rock" groups have given coverage and confirmation to the use of drugs; the lyrics define a new morality—roughly stated as "All the things they said were wrong are what I want to be"; the festivals bring together a community that supports the new values; the music itself declares that the old harmonic and well-modulated sounds of the past are the sounds of a repressive society.

Candidates for Countercultures

Why are some people drawn to the new epistemological, ethical, and aesthetic standards while others are repelled by them? A theory of countercultures must connect oppositional normative movements with individual personalities. Freud saw us all as good candidates for behavior that contravenes the norms because, as he put it, "what we call our civilization is largely responsible for our misery" (1962: 33) by blocking strongly motivated activities. "We are so made," he wrote, "that we can derive intense enjoyment only from a contrast and very little from a state of things. Thus our possibilities of happiness are already restricted by our constitution. Unhappiness is much less difficult to experience" (1962: 23–24). Durkheim had earlier made a similar point. One can only be disillusioned, he remarked, if one moves toward a point that "recedes in the same measure that one advances. . . . This is why historical periods like ours, which have known the malady of infinite aspiration, are necessarily touched with pessimism" (Durkheim, 1973: 40).

We all know, from experience and experiment, how readily we accommodate to new standards of enjoyment, so that what seemed pleasant yesterday is now unacceptably bland. "Where pleasure is concerned, humans are insatiable animals, shifting their criterion level upward when the level of pleasurable input increases, so that once again experience is scored as one-third pleasure, one-third pain, and one-third blah" (D. T. Campbell, 1975a: 1121). We do not make equally quick adaptation to any downward pull of experience. There is nothing more painful, as Veblen noted, than a retreat from a standard of living.

Granted this principle, a society that enormously raises the aspirations but only modestly raises the pleasures of its members, or some of its members, is furnishing an essential ingredient of protest. In this context, Erik Erikson, using perhaps the most useful psychological analogue for counterculture, develops the term "negative identity." In an often desperate choice between being a failure, a nobody, an "invisible man," and being a shockingly visible antihero, a person to reckon with, some choose the latter, expressing their frustration "in a scornful and snobbish hostility toward the roles offered as proper and desirable in one's family or immediate community" (Erikson, 1968: 172–74).

Erikson tends to assume that a negative identity is pathological. It may be wiser to reserve one's judgment on that issue, asking in each instance what a person is being negative against, what balance of creativity and inanity is found in the available positive identities, and what the consequences are for the individual and society in the various choices. Such self-feelings may be part of the character not only of the neurotic, but also of the prophet or the highly creative person who finds the preferred identities too closely bound to an unacceptable society. It is not only that individuals may be alienated—societies may be alienating. One psychiatrist, "when asked what he thought the best therapy was for students who had been severely alienated by the Vietnam war, replied, 'Stop the damn war!' " (Bloy, 1969: 651).

Those driven to define themselves in terms that quite reverse the standards of their time and place are often torn by ambivalence (on ambivalence see Merton and Barber, 1963; Room, 1976). Redl and Wineman note that often the "delinquent ego" has the task of "duping its own superego," so that "delinquent impulsivity can be enjoyed tax-free from feelings of guilt" (Redl and Wineman, 1951: 144).

Perhaps the reciprocal of this is the need of a participant in the dominant society—one who is also ambivalent about dominant values— for duping his own id. The "long-haired, ne'er-do-well, pot smokers" are the hidden and repressed parts of his own life—the dreams and fantasies of freedom from routine, inhibition, and the demands of work. By making advocates of such freedoms seem abhorrent, one can more easily resist temptation.

This interpretation ought not to be pushed too far in either direction, however. Genuine value conflicts exist, and the opponents are those who hold contrary values, not the hidden selves.

Although persons with feelings of negative identity are symptoms of and sources of countercultures, it is necessary to distinguish the individual from the group level (Yinger, 1965). Not all those with negative identities support countercultural values or groups; not all who support countercultures have negative identities. Under some conditions, however, persons struggling with problems of identity and leaning toward a negative formulation are drawn into a social movement that validates their self-definitions and thus aids in the repression of the doubt and guilt that characterize ambivalent feelings (A. K. Cohen, 1955: 59–65; Klapp, 1969).

Rituals of Opposition as Countercultures

If countercultures are a continuing part of human experience, rooted in characterological and social constants, one should find them, in one form or another, in all societies. Their strength can be expected to vary widely, along with their specific or precipitating causes, but they should be found everywhere, in incipient or highly developed form.

This argument is put to its most severe test in its application to small, tribal societies, relatively isolated from contact with other societies. Many authors have described the role reversals and the rituals of rebellion and opposition that are not only permitted but sometimes required of persons occupying certain positions. Related to them are the saturnalia, the feasts of fools, the charivaris that come down to us from, at least, the days of classic Greece and Rome.

From James G. Fraser's *The Golden Bough* to Arnold van Gennep's *Rites of Passage* (1960), to the works of Max Gluckman, Victor Turner, Jack Goody, Edward Norbeck, Peter Rigby, T. O. Beidelman, and many others, we have had a steady flow of ethnographic description and a variety of interpretations of rituals of opposition and of role reversals. Many American Indian tribes had burlesque ceremonies during which clowns "parodied serious rituals, introduced obscenity into sacred places... , and showed open disrespect for the gods themselves" (Wallace, 1966: 136). A striking feature of the organization of the Zulu "is the way in which they openly express social tensions" by licentious behavior and role reversals (Gluckman, 1963: 112).

Such activities can be matched in the medieval and contemporary worlds. By the late fifteenth century All Fools' Days were banned by the cathedrals, but they were picked up by laymen, by families, by craft guilds or "societés joyeuses," who planned ribald festivals, "Abbeys of Misrule." Lyon had a Judge of Misrule and a Bench of Bad Advice; Rouen's Abbot had serving him the Prince of Improvidence, the Cardinal of Bad Measure, Bishop Flatpurse, Duke Kickass, and the Grand Patriarch of Syphilitics (N. Davis, 1971: 41–44).

Needless to say we have Halloween, football weekends, Mardi Gras, New Year's Eve, and twenty-four-hour rock concerts, all tolerated and to some degree protected by the agents of the official culture. Less obviously, but perhaps more powerfully, some teaching, particularly in the humanities and the social sciences, can be seen as a ritual of opposition attacking the established order and describing, or implying, an alternative cultural world.[2] In a brilliant essay, "On the Teaching of Modern Literature," Lionel Trilling (1966: 3–30) observed that most of the best of modern literature is subversive, filled with "strange and terrible . . . ambivalence toward the life of civilization." From Blake and Wordsworth to Nietzsche, Conrad, Lawrence, Gide, Yeats, and Joyce (make out your own list) there runs a "bitter line of hostility" toward the dominant culture. By the time students have read Nietzsche's *The Birth of Tragedy,* Conrad's *Heart of Darkness,* and Dostoevsky's *Notes from Underground,* they seem ready, as Trilling put it, to engage in "socialization of the antisocial, or the acculturation of the anti-cultural, or the legitimation of the subversive" (1966: 25).

Such study—and the exams on the material—are a kind of ritual of rebellion, allowing strongly countercultural feelings and ideas to be expressed, but within a culturally permitted and ritualized frame of reference—the classroom—where participants see themselves and are seen as in a liminal phase, to use Gennep's term, surrounded by cultural ambiguities as they move from one social position to another.

How can we account for these sanctioned, even sponsored, deviations from the established cultures, these culturally circumscribed countercultures? They are most commonly seen as cultural inventions that serve, whatever their origins, as lightning rods. Gluckman (1954) described rituals of rebellion that blatantly subverted the usual moral and sexual norms as cathartic release mechanisms that lowered anger and resent-

[2]Particular circumstances make a given discipline "a fulcrum for the rejection of established social arrangements" (Ladd and Lipset, 1975:73). During earlier periods the physical sciences were also a source of radical challenge.

ment. It seems paradoxical, Wallace notes, that some people should be permitted, even required, to do the "wrong" thing, the culturally forbidden. "The paradox, however, is only a seeming one, for the ultimate goal is still the same: the maintenance of order and stability in society" (Wallace, 1966: 135).

These explanations seem to me to be incomplete. Rites of rebellion do not resolve the contradiction, but give voice to strongly ambivalent feelings. They often contain sharp criticisms of the social order, allowing some persons to express values that stand as potential reversals of the dominant values. This keeps such values alive while not compelling the participants to see themselves wholly in terms of them. Such rituals also allow the orthodox, the "straights," to see and hear and sense the force behind alternative ways, perhaps breaking their cultural isolation and rigidity. As Victor Turner puts it, describing the contemporary "rock" experience: "The structure-dissolving quality of liminality is clearly present" (Turner, 1974: 263). He then goes on to note that the "rock" experience is ancient, arguing against those who suppose that contemporary rock music, with its accompanying group experiences and multiple stimuli, is unique:

> Anthropologists the world over have participated in tribal "scenes" not dissimilar to the rock "scene" . . . "synnaesthesia," the union of visual, auditory, tactile, spatial, visceral, and other modes of perception. . . , is found in tribal ritual and in the services of many modern religious movement. Arthur Rimbaud, one of the folk heroes of the counterculture, would have approved of this as *"un deréglement ordonné de tous les sens,"* "a systematic derangement of the senses" (Turner, 1974: 264).

As a writer for the *Oracle* put it: "Imagine *tasting* G-minor."

Social Change and Countercultures

Countercultures are variously regarded as engines of social change, symbols of change, or mere faddist epiphenomena. There are several ways to examine this disagreement.

COUNTERCULTURES AS MUTATIONS

One way to study the connection between social change and oppositional movements is to glance at genetic mutations, which stand as powerful analogies to countercultures. If we take them as suggestive hints about similar processes that occur on the cultural level, these analogies can help us to describe, if not to explain, countercultures.

Biological systems are self-reproducing, but they are not closed systems. In addition to natural genetic variations they experience drastic discontinuities. Most mutations are maladaptive, and individuals whose genes are thus modified are less likely to survive or reproduce than more standard members of the species so long as the environment remains relatively stable. If there are significant changes in the environment, however, deviant individuals—those carrying the mutant gene—may have a survival advantage.

Some cultural deviations can be seen as the mutations of a society's normative system. Since it is difficult to believe, however, that the individual-societal-environmental system is as well balanced as the organism-environment system, we ought not to assume that most cultural deviation, like most mutation, is maladaptive. Nor should we assume the opposite, after the fashion of those who believe that any kind of change is preferable to stability. Some cultural deviations, like most mutations, are lethal.

Most social scientists today believe that rigidity is a greater threat than are cultural mutations. As Donald Campbell has argued in an important paper (1975a), social scientists and psychologists may be overeager "to discover and believe antitraditional, antirepressive theories"; they may be especially receptive to "the prohedonic message of liberation."

The old ways, of course, may contain social adaptations that have become destructive under new sets of circumstances. Pressure against the traditional cultures, however, comes not only from their failures to adapt to new circumstances, but also from the hedonic individualism and self-centeredness that are the product of biological selection. The continuing task, Campbell argues, is to arrive at a minimax solution or a stable compromise between the needs and requirements of the biological and the social systems. (See also Meddin, 1976).

Social norms the world over seek to limit selfishness, greed, and dishonesty, even though it can be argued that biological evolution favors individuals who practice them. "Look out for your own interests" may be as important as "thou shall not covet," Campbell observes, but spontaneous compliance with the former generally makes normative reinforcement unnecessary.

This is a powerful argument, but I would emphasize somewhat more than Campbell does the rigidity built into social systems. He notes that in Moses' day, as in ours, honoring one's parents could have been carried to dysfunctional lengths, "but such excesses were so little of a social problem that 'Thou shalt show independence from thy parents' was usually omitted from the limited list of reiterated commandments" (1975a: 1118). Usually omitted, perhaps, but not always. Several centuries after Moses, a charismatic prophet with countercultural tendencies declared:

"For I have come to set a man against his father, and daughter against her mother, and a daughter-in-law against her mother-in-law; and a man's foes shall be those of his own household (Matt. 10:35 and 36).

This quotation prompts me to suggest that major countercultural mutations often—I am tempted to say in the majority of cases—appear as religious movements. "The sect," says Werner Stark, "is typically a contraculture" (1967: 129). To say that many cultural mutations are religious is not to say that they are good—or that they are bad. Most persons would probably agree that certain prophetic movements with which they identify have been major forces in transforming an unjust or otherwise inadequate social order. Not many are inspired with awe, however, by hearing from the Church of Satan that greed, pride, envy, anger, gluttony, lust, and sloth are cardinal virtues, not the seven deadly sins (Moody, 1974; Alfred, 1976). In noting that many countercultures are religious, I want simply to emphasize that those involved connect them with the fundamental problems of existence.

COUNTERCULTURES AS THE RESULT OF SOCIAL CHANGE

Major countercultural movements are, in the first instance, indicators of a society experiencing severe stress. The common tendency today to associate countercultures only with the middle and upper classes fails to see that they are often a two-pronged attack on the established culture, expressing different kinds of stress. On one side we get the countercultures of the privileged who say, in effect: Here are values we can respect, that give us a sense of meaning. On the other side are the countercultures of the deprived, who say: Here are values we can attain, that give us a sense of control.

Thinking of countercultures as the dependent variable, we see many kinds of social change that upset the moving equilibrium of a social order, the structural-cultural-characterological balance of a given time, and make the appearance of countercultural movements more likely (none of these is a sufficient cause; some may be necessary; all are interdependent):

1. Drastic reorganization of the way people make their livings. These ways are closely bound up with shared values and norms, with the power distribution, and with accustomed reciprocities.

2. Changes in the size, location, age distribution, and sex ratio of a population. Insofar as a low average age is a factor, the most highly industrialized societies can expect a reduction of countercultural inventiveness, for better or worse. The average age in the United States is now twenty-nine—up from twenty-five a decade ago—and may be nearly thirty-five by the end of the century, if present trends continue. The

graying of American may prove to be a more accurate prediction than the "greening of America."

3. Rapid importation of new ideas, techniques, goods, and values from "alien" societies or from earlier periods.

4. Sharp increase in life's possibilities, hopes, dreams, and actualities, followed by a plateau, actual loss, or serious threat of loss. This has long been recognized as a factor in revolutions. Countercultural movements do not typically occur when desired values are becoming more difficult to attain, despite the ideology of the protesters, but when they have become more accessible over a period of time, although at a rate slower than the increase in demand. The result is a stronger sense of relative deprivation.

5. Lower participation in intimate and supporting social circles—families, neighborhoods, work groups (Hendin, 1975; Berger and Berger, 1971). Many counterculturalists, ranging from the utterly deprived to the "poor little rich kids," share in common a broken bond between parents and children that predisposes the latter to many forms of negativism. Some turn the negative impulses inward, which in our time has meant a sharp increase in rates of anxiety and suicide; or they may find support for turning the hostility outward. Feuer (1969) speaks of the deauthorization of the older generation as the major cause of the coalescing of individual oedipal problems into a shared revolt. He is one-sided in his interpretations and imprecise in his discussion of the sources of such deauthorization, though it seems reasonable to note its interdependence with the other sources of countercultures we have noted. The loss of intimacy between generations does not seem to have been overcome by the "love" generation, whose children are usually neglected in the name of permissiveness, much as they themselves were neglected (Yablonsky, 1968: 302–15; Rothchild and Wolf, 1976).

6. An increase in the number of "antinomian" persons, or those with negative identities, or in the strength of tendencies in those directions.

7. A loss of meaning in the deepest symbols and rituals of society, or, if you will, a religious crisis (Wuthnow, 1976b). In a recent study of over a thousand university students in six countries (Yinger, 1977), I found that 60 percent believed that problems of meaning were the most fundamental issues facing humanity. The present crisis of meaning is now generations old, and many feel, with Matthew Arnold (1907: 321), that they are

> Wandering between two worlds, one dead,
> The other powerless to be born....

Many of those caught in such a situation grasp for faith; they invent what they can (glorious religions are seldom the outcome), and they borrow meaning systems that seem uncorrupted by the society around them.

We need a theme?   then let that be our theme:
that we, poor grovellers between faith and doubt,
the sun and north star lost, and compass out,
the heart's weak engine all but stopped, the time
timeless in this chaos of our wills—
that we must ask a theme, something to think,
something to say, between dawn and dark,
something to hold to, something to love (Aiken, 1970: 666–67).*

We are moved by the poet more than by prosaic facts, but I think we need to guard against pluralistic ignorance—a shared belief in pseudo facts. It may be that a moderate reduction in the sense of shared fundamental values is so threatening that we are drawn to those sensitive voices warning of imminent danger.

8. Such social and personality factors as we have mentioned create the context in which countercultures are likely to occur, but at least one other element is needed: communication among those with predispositions and living in situations that can precipitate countercultural values.

COUNTERCULTURES AS THE SOURCE OF SOCIAL CHANGE

When we turn the question around, to ask how and to what degree countercultures are the cause of social change, we come to some of the most critical problems of sociological theory. With respect to recent American countercultures, a basically functionalist interpretation is now commonly given. Chief Justice Warren Burger of the United States Supreme Court recently declared "that turbulent American youth, whose disorderly acts he once 'resented,' actually had pointed the way to higher spiritual values" (*Cleveland Plain Dealer,* May 29, 1976: 5-A). Philip Slater writes that a basic characteristic of successful social systems is the presence of devices that keep alive alternatives antithetical to the dominant emphases:

> These latent alternatives usually persist in some encapsulated and imprisoned form ("break glass in case of fire"), such as myths, festivals, or specialized roles. . . . Such latent alternatives are priceless treasures and must be carefully guarded against loss (Slater, 1971: 110–11).

Well, some of them are priceless treasures and others are lethal bombs, but we may not be able to have one without the other. Slater's argument is close to Durkheim's interpretation of crime, which, Durkheim declared, is necessary to the evolution of morality and law: "In order that the originality of the idealist whose dreams transcend his

*From Conrad Aiken, *Time in the Rock* (New York: Oxford University Press, 1970). Reprinted by permission of the Publisher.

century may find expression, it is necessary that the originality of the criminal, who is below the level of his time, shall also be possible. One does not occur without the other" (1938: 70–71). And of course Durkheim goes on to say that crime not only implies that new ways are open; it may even be an anticipation of new collective sentiments. Socrates was a criminal, but he helped pave the way for a new morality.

I am uncomfortable with such unqualified functionalist views. Countercultures may stimulate the growth of highly resistant antibodies in society that make wise and necessary changes less likely. Opposition to the bizarre may deflect attention from basic needs; it may furnish those most resistant to change with superficially strong moral arguments, not to mention allies.

Antithetical groups do not escape each other's influence. We take on the face of the adversary, as the French proverb puts it, whether we wish to or not. Or, more technically, culture and counterculture are bound together in linked evolution. Under conditions of lowered legitimacy and loss of faith, efforts on the part of the dominant society to repress new norms and values can lead to deviation-amplification, not to a reaffirmation of the established norms and values. Efforts to coopt the deviants can, by legitimating their more moderate practices, have the same effect. Thus we need to complement Durkheim's view of the way deviation strengthens a group by an evolutionary view of the way it modifies a group. "If you're not part of the solution, you're part of the problem" is one of today's slogans. Gerlach and Hine offer us a similar notion: "If you're not part of a mutation, you are part of the environment which selects for or against it. No one can escape an evolutionary role" (1973: 260). Deviant ideas that become the operative values of a group tell us, at the least, something about the stresses faced by the members of that group. On another level, they can tell us something about the larger system, indicating points of inadequacy. On still another level, they can prove to be new values required to meet a new situation.

The changes in values and norms propounded by countercultures cannot proceed far without concomitant changes in social structure and character. Most revolutions show that structural change is more likely to be carried through than cultural change. In the early stages revolutions usually contain a counterculture, carried along by a utopian conception of a new world. But those whose first concern is the transfer of power may believe this objective is threatened by demands for a new culture (A. Cohen, 1974: chap. 3). After the transfer of power—often carried out in the name of new values—the new rulers don't seem very different from the old. From czar to commissar is not so far. Radicals fight the revolution; conservatives write the constitution.

The indirect effects of countercultures are probably more important than the direct and intended effects. The protest movements of mid-seventeenth-century England created a dissenting *tradition* that has out-lasted some of the content of particular dissenting movements. This tradition has strongly influenced English, and American, history ever since (see Baltzell, 1972: 217–18).

Insofar as some upper-middle-class WASPs and Jews persist in their opposition to and withdrawal from technological society, Berger and Berger observe (1971), they are less likely to modify that society drasti-cally than to create new room at the top for the sons and daughters of manual workers—"The Blueing of America." "If Yale should be hopelessly greened," the Bergers write, "Wall Street will get used to recruits from Fordham or Wichita State. Italians will have no difficulty running the RAND Corporation, Baptists the space program" (1971: 23).

Conclusion

Someone has said that every country gets the Socialist party it de-serves. It is equally true that every society gets the countercultures it deserves, for they do not simply contradict, they also express the situa-tion from which they emerge—pushing away from it, deploring its con-tradictions, caricaturing its weaknesses, and drawing on its neglected and underground traditions. If we shudder at the illegal drug problem, we ought more carefully to study our rates of alcoholism and lung cancer and the results of the use of other legal mind-altering drugs. If we shudder at the Manson family or the Symbionese Liberation Army, we ought to do more than contemplate the violence we do to some of our children in the ghetto or to the Vietnamese. If we shudder at the Church of Satan, we should at the same time note the aberrant violations of basic values by "respectable" people, violations that such nonconformist cults have transposed into virtues.

Lest I seem to be confirming only the negative image of countercul-tures, let me add: If we applaud the emphasis on gentleness and love, on conservation and sharing, on self-reliance and self-discovery that charac-terizes many oppositional movements today, we should recognize that these, too—although expressed in the context of drastic value reversals—borrow from the dominant culture even as they oppose it.

The most important lesson from the study of countercultures is not what it tells us about our times—or any specific time—but what it tells us about the human condition. In some ways such a study underlines the points made by conservatives: The social fabric is delicate, it is based on long experience, it is built on constant factors in human life. Therefore, don't touch. This is often the wrong conclusion, however. Because the social fabric is delicate, we need continually to weave in new threads. A cultural-countercultural confrontation, a consequence of changing conditions and inflexible structures, is a costly way to proceed. We need to learn how to respond to early warning signals rather than waiting for overcompensating attacks powered by ambivalence and anger.

In my judgment we are in the midst of a major civilizational transformation. The critical issue that humankind faces today is: How do we create a rolling adjustment to the incredibly rapid and drastic changes taking place on the planet? We're faced with the problem of rebuilding the station, relaying and changing the gauge of the tracks, and accommodating vastly more passengers, while still keeping the trains running. Some say: Don't change; civilization can be breached too easily; or, in the language of the train analogy, patch up the station a bit, but don't tamper with the basic structure. Others say: Stop the trains; the building isn't worth saving; it's about to collapse; we need a clean field on which to build anew. That is the position taken by countercultures. If we think of them as art forms, we may find that, like other forms of art ranging from the sublime to the ugly, they highlight, dramatize, and anticipate drastic problems. Whether as "voices crying in the wilderness" or as symptoms of major disorders—unintended warnings and illustrations of what may lie ahead—countercultures require the most intensive study by those whose aim and task it is to study societies and to see them whole.

References

AARON, HENRY J.
   1967 "Social security: International comparisons." In Otto Eckstein (ed.), Studies in the Economics of Income Maintenance. Washington: The Brookings Institution.

   1975a "Alternative ways to increase work effort." Pp. 161–88 in Irene Lurie (ed.), Integrating Income Maintenance. New York: Academic Press.

   1975b Who Pays the Property Tax? Washington: The Brookings Institution.

ABOUD, F. E., AND D. M. TAYLOR
   1971 "Ethnic and role stereotypes: Their relative importance in person perception." Journal of Social Psychology 85:15–27.

ACKERMAN, FRANK, et al.
   1972 "The extent of income inequality in the United States." Pp. 207–18 in Richard C. Edwards, M. Reich, and T. E. Weisskopf (eds.), The Capitalist System: A Radical Analysis of American Society. Englewood Cliffs, N.J.: Prentice Hall.

ACKLEY, GARDNER
   1960 Macroeconomic Theory. New York: Macmillan.

ADAMS, F. GERARD
   1964 "Consumer attitudes, buying plans, and purchases of durable goods: A principal components, time-series approach." Review of Economics and Statistics (Nov.): 347–55.

   1965 "Production with consumer attitudes: The time series-cross section paradox." Review of Economics and Statistics (Nov.): 367–78.

ADAMS, F. GERARD, AND LAWRENCE R. KLEIN
   1972 "Anticipations variables in macro-econometric models." In Katona Festschrift: 289–320.

ADAMS, WALTER
   1958 "The role of competition in the regulated industries." American Economic Review 48 (May): 527–43.

ADAMS, WALTER, AND JOEL B. DIRLAM
1977 "Import quotas and industrial performance." In H. W. deJong and A. Jacquemain (eds.), Welfare Aspects of Industrial Markets. The Hague: Martinus Nijhoff: 153–81.

AIKEN, CONRAD
1970 Time in the Rock. New York: Oxford University Press.

AJZEN, ICEK
1971 Attitudinal vs. normative messages: An investigation of the differential effects of persuasive communications on behavior. Sociometry 34:263–80.

AJZEN, ICEK, AND MARTIN FISHBEIN
1969 "The prediction of behavioral intentions in a choice situation." Journal of Experimental Social Psychology 5:400–16.
1970 "The prediction of behavior from attitudinal and normative variables." Journal of Experimental Social Psychology 6:466–87.
1973 "Attitudinal and normative variables as predictors of specific behaviors." Journal of Personality and Social Psychology 27:41–57.
1977 "Attitude-behavior relations: A theoretical analysis and review of empirical research." Psychological Bulletin 84:888–918.

ALBA, R. D.
1976 "Social assimilation among American Catholic national-origin groups." American Sociological Review 41:1030–46.

ALEXANDER, R. D., AND P. W. SHERMAN
1977 "Local mate competition and parental investment in social insects." Science 196:494–500.

ALFORD, ROBERT R., AND ROGER FRIEDLAND
1975 "Political participation and public policy." Pp. 429–79 in Alex Inkeles (ed.), Annual Review of Sociology, vol. I. Palo Alto: Annual Reviews.

ALFRED, RANDALL H.
1976 "The Church of Satan." Pp. 180–202 in C. Y. Glock and R. N. Bellah (eds.), The New Religious Consciousness. Berkeley: University of California Press.

ALLPORT, G. W.
1954 The Nature of Prejudice. Reading, Mass.: Addison-Wesley.

ALLPORT, G. W., AND L. POSTMAN
1947 The Psychology of Rumor. New York: Holt.

AMERICAN CORRECTIONAL ASSOCIATION
1960 "Declaration of principles." American Journal of Correction 22:10.

ANCELIN, JACQUELINE, AND BERNARD DUMAS
1974 "The societal context for social welfare." Pp. 1–73 in Alfred Kahn and Sheila Kamerman (eds.), Cross-National Studies of Social Service Systems 1. New York: Columbia School of Social Work.

ANDERSON, D. W.
1976 "Reflections on the sick aged and the helping systems." In B. L.

Neugarten and R. J. Havighurst (eds.), Social Policy, Social Ethics and the Aging Society. Washington: Government Printing Office.

ANDERSON, MICHAEL S.
1971 Family Structure in Nineteenth Century Lancashire. Cambridge, England: Cambridge University Press.

ANDERSON, ROBERT N.
1974 Waiahole-Waikane: A socioeconomic profile. Report submitted to the Hawaii State Land Use Commission.

ANDREWS, FRANK M., AND STEPHEN B. WITHEY
1977 Social Indicators of Well-Being: Americans' Perceptions of Life Quality. New York: Plenum Publishing Corporation.

ANONYMOUS
1832 "Punishment of Death—Wakefield on Newgate." The Quarterly Review 47 (March and July): 170–216.

ARNOLD, MATTHEW
1907 Poetical Works. London: Macmillan.

BABCOCK, BARBARA ALLEN, ANN FREEDMAN, ELEANOR HOLMES NORTIN, AND SUSAN ROSS
1975 Sex Discrimination and the Law. Boston: Little, Brown.

BACHMAN, J. G., AND J. JOHNSTON
1972 "The all-volunteer armed force, not whether but what kind." Psychology Today 6 (October):113–16, 128.

BAILEY, WILLIAM C.
1975 "Murder and capital punishment: Some further evidence." American Journal of Orthopsychiatry 45 (July):664–88.

BAILYN, L. L.
1970 "Career and family orientations of husbands and wives in relation to marital happiness." Human Relations 23:97–113.

Bakke v. *The Regents of the University of California*
18 C. 3d 34.

BALTZELL, E. DIGBY
1972 "Epilogue: To be a phoenix—reflections on two noisy ages of prose." American Journal of Sociology 78:202–20.

BANE, MARY JO
1976 Here To Stay: American Families in the Twentieth Century. New York: Basic Books.

BANKS, W. C., G. V. McQUARTER AND J. PRYOR
1977 "In consideration of a cognitive-attributional basis for stereotypy." Princeton University: Unpublished manuscript.

BARTH, F. (ed.)
1969 Ethnic Groups and Boundaries, The Social Organization of Cultural Differences. Boston: Little, Brown.

BARTH, MICHAEL, GEORGE CARCAGNO, AND JOHN PALMER
1974 Toward an Effective Income Support System. Madison, Wisc.: Institute for Research on Poverty.

BATESON, P.
   1978   "Where does our behavior come from?" In R. Monro (ed.), The Bio-
          sciences and Society. Liverpool: University of Liverpool.

BAUER, RAYMOND A. (ed.)
   1966   Social Indicators. Cambridge, Mass.: M.I.T. Press.

BAYLISS-SMITH, TIM
   1974   "Constraints on population growth: The case of the Polynesian outlier
          atolls in the precontact period." Human Ecology 2 (September): 259–
          96.

BEATTIE, CHRISTOPHER
   1974   Minority Men in a Majority Setting: Francophones and Anglophones.
          New York: McClellan and Stewart.

BECCARIA, CESARE
   1880   "Crimes and Punishments." In James Anson Farrer (ed.), Crimes and
          Punishments. London: Clatoo and Windus.

BECKER, FRANKLIN D.
   1977   Housing Messages. Stroudsberg, Pennsylvania: Dowden, Hutchinson
          and Ross, Inc.

BECKER, GARY S.
   1960   "An economic analysis of fertility." In National Bureau of Economic
          Research, Demographic and Economic Changes in Developed Coun-
          tries. Princeton, N.J.: Princeton University Press.
   1965   "A Theory of the allocation of time." Economic Journal 75, no. 229
          (Stepember):493–517.
   1974a "Crime and punishment: An economic approach." in G. S. Becker and
          W. M. Landes (eds.), Essays in the Economics of Crime and Punish-
          ment. New York: Columbia University Press.
   1974b "A theory of social interactions." Journal of Political Economy 42
          (December):1063–93.

BECKER, H. S.
   1974   "Labelling theory reconsidered." In S. Messinger et al. (eds.), The
          Aldine Crime and Justice Annual—1973. Chicago: Aldine.

BEDAU, HUGO ADAM (ed.)
   1967   The Death Penalty in America. Garden City, N.Y.: Anchor/Doubleday.

BELL, WENDELL
   1974   Comparative research on ethnicity, a conference report. Social Science
          Research Council Items 28, no. 4 (December):61–4.

BELL, WENDELL, AND WALTER E. FREEMAN (eds.)
   1974   Ethnicity and Nation-Building. Beverly Hills, California: Sage.

BENGTSON, VERN L., JAMES J. DOWD, DAVID H. SMITH, AND ALEX INKELES
   1975   "Modernization, modernity, and perceptions of aging: A cross-cultural
          study." Journal of Gerontology 30, no. 6:688–95.

BENN, STANLEY
   1967   "Power." In Paul Edwards (ed.), The Encyclopedia of Philosophy, vol.
          6. New York: Macmillan and The Free Press.

BENNETT, PETER D., AND HAROLD H. KASSARJIAN
1972   Consumer Behavior. Englewood Cliffs, N.J.: Prentice-Hall.

BERGER, PETER L., AND BRIGITTE BERGER
1971   "The blueing of America." New Republic (April 3):20–23.

BERKOWITZ, L.
1969   "Social motivation." In G. Lindzey and E. Aronson (eds.), The Handbook of Social Psychology, 2d ed., vol. 3. Reading, Mass.: Addison-Wesley.

BERLINER, JOSEPH S.
1957   Factory and Manager in the U.S.S.R. Cambridge: Harvard University Press.

BETTELHEIM, BRUNO
1974   A Home for the Heart. New York: Knopf.

BIBB, ROBERT
1977   "Sexual inequality of earnings in metropolitan blue-collar labor markets." Ph.D. dissertation, University of Illinois.

BILLER, H. B.
1971   Paternal Deprivation. Lexington, Mass.: Heath.

BLACK, R. D. C., et al. (eds.)
1972   "The marginal revolution in economics." History of Political Economy 4 (Fall), no. 2.

BLACKWELL, JAMES E.
1974   "Role behavior in a corporate structure: Black sociologists in the ASA." Pp. 341–67 in James E. Blackwell and Morris Janowitz (eds.), Black Sociologists. Chicago: University of Chicago Press.

BLALOCK, H. M., JR.
1956   "Economic discrimination and Negro increase." American Sociological Review 21:584–88.

BLAU, PETER
1964   Exchange and Power in Social Life. New York: Wiley.
1968   "Interaction: Social exchange." Pp. 452–58 in David L. Sills (ed.), International Encyclopedia of the Social Sciences, vol. 7. New York: Macmillan and The Free Press.

BLAU, PETER, AND OTIS DUDLEY DUNCAN
1967   The American Occupational Structure. New York: Wiley. Reprinted 1978, The Free Press.

BLOY, MYRON B., JR.
1969   "Alienated Youth, the counter culture, and the chaplain." Pp. 649–63 in Donald R. Cutler (ed.), The Religious Situation. Boston: Beacon.

BLUMENFELD, HANS
1977   "Criteria for judging the quality of the urban environment." Pp. 458–81 in Louis K. Lowenstein (ed.), Urban Studies. New York: The Free Press.

BONGER, WILLIAM ADRIAN
1916   Criminality and Economic Conditions. Boston: Little, Brown.

1936   An Introduction to Criminology. London: Methuen and Company.

BONJEAN, C. M., et al.
1967   Sociological Mesurement: An Inventory of Scales and Indices. San Francisco: Chandler.

BOSSARD, J. H. S., AND E. S. BOLL
1956   The Large Family System. Philadelphia: University of Pennsylvania Press.

BOTKIN, D., S. GOLUBIC, B. MAGUIRE, B. MOORE, H. MOROWITZ, AND L. SLOBODKIN
Forth- Report from The National Science Foundation Summer Study on
coming Space Biology and Medicine.

BOUDON, RAYMOND
1973   Education, Opportunity, and Social Inequality. New York: Wiley.

BOUGHEY, ARTHUR S.
1975   Man and the Environment: An Introduction to Human Ecology and Evolution, 2d ed. New York: Macmillan.

BOULDING, KENNETH
1966   "The economics of knowledge and the knowledge of economics." American Economic Review 56 (May):1-13.

BOWERS, WILLIAM J.
1974   Executions in America. Lexington, Massachusetts: D. C. Heath.

BOWRING, JOHN (ed.)
1843   The Works of Jeremy Bentham, vols. 1, 2, and 3. Edinburgh: William Tait.

BRANNON, R.
1976   "Attitudes and the prediction of behavior." Pp. 145-98 in B. Seidenberg and A. Snadowsky (eds.), Social Psychology: An Introduction. New York: The Free Press.

BRANSON, WILLIAM H.
1972   Macroeconomic Theory. New York: Harper & Row.

BRAZELTON, T. B.
1976   Toddlers and Parents. New York: Dell.

BREMNER, ROBERT H.
1956   From the Depths: The Discovery of Poverty in the United States. New York: New York University Press.

BREWER, M. B., AND D. T. CAMPBELL
1976   Ethnocentrism and Intergroup Attitudes: East African Evidence. Beverly Hills, California: Sage.

BRIEF FOR PETITIONER, No. 76-811, U.S. SUPREME COURT, OCTOBER. TEXAS
1977   The Regents of the University of California v. Allan Bakke: Paul J. Mishkin, Jack B. Owens, Donald L. Reidhaar, Counsel; Archibald Cox, of Counsel, pp. 13-14.

BRIGGS, VERNON
1975   "Mexican workers in the U.S. labor market: A contemporary dilemma." International Labour Review 112 (November):351-68.

BRIGHAM, J. C.
1971 "Ethnic stereotypes." Psychological Bulletin 76:15–38.

BRIMMER, ANDREW
1976 "The economic position of blacks in 1976." Special Report No. 9. Washington: National Commission for Manpower Policy.

BRINTON, CRANE
1965 Anatomy of Revolution. New York: Vintage Books.

BRONSON, M., AND B. WHITING
1972 A Comparison of the Social Behavior of Brookline and Kikuyu Two Year Olds. Unpublished manuscript.

BROWN, LESTER R.
1974 The Global Politics of Resource Scarcity, Development Paper 17. Washington: Overseas Development Council.

BROWN, NORMAN O.
1966 Love's Body. New York: Random House.

BRUNER, EDWARD M.
1976 "Tradition and modernization in Batak Society." In George DeVos (ed.), Responses to Change. Princeton, N.J.: Van Nostrand Reinhold.

BRUSH, STEPHEN B.
1975 "The Concept of carrying capacity for systems of shifting cultivation." American Anthropologist 77 (December):799–811.

BRYCE-LAPORTE, ROY S.
1972 "The black immigrant: experience of invisibility and inequality." Journal of Black Studies 3 (September):29–56.
1973 "The black immigrants." Pp. 44–61 in Peter Rose, Stanley Rothman, and William Wilson (eds.), Through Different Eyes. London: Oxford University Press.

BRYCE-LAPORTE, ROY S., AND DOLORES MORTIMER (eds.)
1976 Caribbean Immigrants to the United States. Washington: Smithsonian Institution (RIIES Occasional Papers no. 1).

BRYCE-LAPORTE, ROY S., AND CLAUDEWELL S. THOMAS (eds.)
1976 Alienation in Contemporary Society. New York: Praeger.

BUCHANAN, JAMES
1970 The Public Finances, 3d ed. Homewood, Illinois: Richard D. Irwin.

BUCK, GARY L., AND ALVIN L. JACOBSON
1968 "Social evolution and structural-functional analysis: An empirical test." American Sociological Review 33:343–55.

BURBY, RAYMOND J., AND SHIRLEY F. WEISS
1976 New Communities USA. Lexingon, Massachusetts: D. C. Heath.

Business Week
1976 "How expectations defeat economic policy." November 8:74–76.

BUTLER, R. N.
1976 "Medical schools should pay more attention to the aged." American Medical News, May 24:5–6.

BUTTIMER, A.

1972 "Social space and the planning of residential areas." Environment and Behavior 4:279–318.

BYE, RAYMOND T.

1919 Capital Punishment in the United States. Philadelphia: The Committee on Philanthropic Labor of Philadelphia.

CALDER, B. J., AND M. ROSS

1973 Attitudes and Behavior. Morristown, N.J.: General Learning Press.

CAMPBELL, ANGUS

1971 White Attitudes toward Black People. Ann Arbor, Michigan: Institute for Social Research.

CAMPBELL, ANGUS, PHILIP E. CONVERSE, AND WILLARD L. RODGERS

1976 The Quality of American Life: Perceptions, Evaluations, and Satisfactions. New York: Russell Sage Foundation.

CAMPBELL, DONALD T.

1963 "Social attitudes and other acquired behavioral dispositions." Pp. 94–172 in S. Koch (ed.), Psychology: A Study of a Science, vol. 6. New York: McGraw-Hill.

1967 "Stereotypes and perception of group differences." American Psychologist 22:812–29.

1975a "On the conflicts between biological and social evolution and between psychology and moral tradition." American Psychologist 30:1103–26.

1975b "Reforms as experiments." In E. L. Struening and M. Guttentag (eds.), Handbook of Evaluation Research, vol. 1. Beverly Hills, California: Sage.

CANADA-PARLIAMENT, JOINT COMMITTEE OF THE SENATE AND HOUSE OF COMMONS ON CAPITAL AND CORPORAL PUNISHMENTS AND LOTTERIES

1956 Final Report on Capital Punishment. Ottawa: Queen's Printer and Controllers of Stationery.

CANTRIL, H.

1941 The Psychology of Social Movements. New York: Wiley.

CAPLAN, N.

1974 "The use of social science information by federal executives." Pp. 46–67 in G. M. Lyons (ed.), Social Research and Public Policies—The Dartmouth/OECD Conference. Hanover, N.H.: Public Affaris Center, Dartmouth College.

CAPLAN, N., A. MORRISON, AND R. J. STAMBAUGH

1975 The Use of Social Science Knowledge in Policy Decisions at the National Level. Ann Arbor, Michigan: Institute for Social Research.

CAPLAN, N., AND R. RICH

1976 "Institutional insularity and bureaucratization: The process and consequence of information policy at the national level." Paper delivered at the OECD Conference on Dissemination of Economic and Social Development Research Results, Bogotá, Colombia, June.

CARNEGIE COMMISSION ON HIGHER EDUCATION

1970 A Chance to Learn. New York: McGraw-Hill.

CAUDILL, WILLIAM, AND GEORGE A. DEVOS
1956 "Achievement, culture and personality: The case of the Japanese Americans." American Anthropologist 58:1102-26.

CENTRAL STATISTICAL OFFICE
1975 Social Trends no. 6, 1975. London: HMSO. Pp. 115ff.

CHLUMSKY, JIRI
1974 "The distribution and redistribution of income during the life cycle." Pp. 1-15 in Expert Group on the Structure of Income Distribution and Implications for Social Development, European Social Development Program, pt. 2. New York: United Nations.

CHUDACOFF, HOWARD P.
1978 "Non-private newlyweds: familial extension in the first stage of the family cycle." In Tamara K. Hareven and Maris Vinoviskis (eds.), Demographic Patterns and Family Processes in Nineteenth Century America. Princeton: Princeton University Press.

CHUDACOFF, HOWARD P., AND TAMARA K. HAREVEN
1978 "The later years of life and the family cycle." In Tamara K. Hareven (ed.), Family Transitions and the Life Course in Historical Perspective. New York: Academic Press.

CICOUREL, AARON L., AND JOHN I. KITSUSE
1963 The Educational Decision-Makers. Indianapolis: Bobbs-Merrill.

CLARK C. W.
1975 "The economics of whaling: A two species model." Simulation Councils Proceedings Series, vol. 5, no. 1. Pp. 111-19 in G. S. Innes (ed.), New Directions in the Analysis of Ecological Systems, pt. 1.

CLARK, KENNETH
1965 Dark Ghetto. New York: Harper & Row.

CLARK, L. R.
1962 "The general biology of Cardiaspina Albitextura (Psyllidae) and its abundance in relation to weather and parasitism." Australian Journal of Zoology 10 (December):537-86.
1964 "The population dynamics of Cardiaspina Albitextura (Psyllidae)." Australian Journal of Zoology 12 (December):362-80.

CLARK, MARGARET
1959 Health in the Mexican-American Culture. Berkeley: University of California Press.

CLARK, TERRY N.
1975 "Community power," Pp. 271-95 in Alex Inkeles (ed.), Annual Review of Sociology, vol. I. Palo Alto: Annual Reviews.

CLARK, TERRY N. (ed.)
1968 Community Structure and Decision-Making, Comparative Analyses. San Francisco, California: Chandler Publishing Co.

CLARK-STEWART, A.
1978 "And daddy makes three: The father's impact on mother and young child." Child Development 49 (June).

CLECAK, PETER
  1973   Radical Paradoxes: Dilemmas of the American Left: 1945–1970. New York: Harper & Row.

COALE, ANSLEY J., AND R. JAMES TRUSSELL
  1974   "Model fertility schedules: Variations in the age structure of childbearing in human populations." Population Index 40, no. 2 (April):185–258.

COCKBURN, CHRISTINE, AND DOLMER HOSKINS
  1976   "Social security and divorced persons." International Social Security Review 29, no. 2:111–51.

COHEN, ABNER
  1974   Two-Dimensional Man. Berkeley: University of California Press.

COHEN, ALBERT K.
  1955   Delinquent Boys. New York: The Free Press.

COHN, NORMAN
  1970   The Pursuit of the Millennium: Revolutionary Millenarians and Mystical Anarchists of the Middle Age. New York: Oxford University Press.

COLEMAN, JAMES S.
  1966   Equality of Educational Opportunity. Washington, D.C.: Department of Health, Education, and Welfare, Office of Education.

  1974a   Power and the Structure of Society. New York: Norton.

  1974b   "Review essay: Inequality, sociology, and moral philosophy." American Journal of Sociology 80 (November):739–64.

  1976   "Individual rights and the state: A review essay." American Journal of Sociology 82 (September):428–42.

COMMISSION OF THE EUROPEAN COMMUNITIES
  1974   Women and Unemployment in the United Kingdom, Ireland, and Denmark. Cranfield: R. B. Cornu.

  1977   "Report from the commission to the council on the European plan of pilot schemes to combat poverty, 1976." COM (76) 718 Final Brussels.

COMMITTEE ON THE STATUS OF RACIAL AND ETHNIC MINORITIES IN SOCIOLOGY
  1977   "The status of racial and ethnic minorities in sociology." Footnotes (August): special supplement.

COMPTROLLER GENERAL OF THE UNITED STATES
  1977   Report to the Congress: The Well-Being of Older People in Cleveland, Ohio. Washington, D.C.: General Accounting Office.

CONFERENCE OF EUROPEAN MINISTERS RESPONSIBLE FOR FAMILY AFFAIRS
  1971   Single Parents with Dependent Children. Stockholm: Council of Europe.

CONGRESSIONAL BUDGET OFFICE
  1977   "Poverty status of families under alternative definitions of income." CBO Background Paper #17. Washington, D.C.: Government Printing Office.

CONGRESSIONAL RECORD
  1976   122 (May 3): S 6295–S 6315.

COOK, EARL
1971 "The flow of energy in an industrial society." Scientific American 225, no. 3:134–44.

COREY, S. M.
1937 "Professed attitudes and actual behavior." Journal of Educational Psychology 28:271–80.

COUGHLIN, RICHARD M.
1977 "Ideology and social policy: A comparative study of the structure of public opinion in eight rich nations." Ph.D. dissertation, University of California, Berkeley.

COWGILL, DONALD OLEN
1949 "The theory of population growth cycles." American Journal of Sociology 55 (September):163–70.

CRAWFORD, E. T., AND A. D. BIDERMAN
1969 "The functions of policy-oriented social science." Pp. 233–43 in E. T. Crawford and A. D. Biderman (eds.), Social Scientists and International Affairs. New York: Wiley.

CROSBY, F.
1976 "A model of egoistical relative deprivation." Psychological Review 83:85–113.

CUTRIGHT, PHILLIPS
1965 "Political structure, economic development, and national social security programs." American Journal of Sociology 70 (March):537–50.

DAGI, T. F.
1976 "Cause and culpability." Journal of Medicine and Philosophy 1:349–71.

DAVID, PAUL A., AND WARREN C. SANDERSON
1976 "Contraceptive technology and family limiting behavior: Toward a quantitative history of the diffusion of contraceptive practices in America, 1850–1920." Unpublished paper.

DAVIES, JAMES C.
1962 "Towards a theory of revolution." American Sociological Review 27:5–19.

DAVIS, ALLISON W., AND ROBERT J. HAVIGHURST
1947 Father of the Man: How Your Child Gets His Personality. Boston: Houghton Mifflin.

DAVIS, FRED
1971 On Youth Subcultures: The Hippie Variant. New York: General Learning Press.

DAVIS, JAMES A.
1959 "A formal interpretation of relative deprivation." Sociometry 22:280–96.
1964 Great Aspirations. Chicago: Aldine.

DAVIS, KINGSLEY
1945 "The world demographic transition." Annals of the American Academy of Political and Social Science 273 (January):1–11.

1963   "The theory of change and response in modern demographic history."
        Population Index 29, no. 4 (October):345-66.

DAVIS, NATALIE Z.
1971   "The reasons of misrule: Youth groups and charivaris in sixteenth-
        century France." Past and Present 50:44-75.

DAWS, GAVIN
1968   Shoal of Time. Honolulu: University Press of Hawaii.

DEAUX, K., AND T. EMSWILLER
1974   "Explanation of successful performance on sex-linked tasks: What is
        skill for the male is luck for the female." Journal of Personality and
        Social Psychology 29:80-85.

DE BEAUVOIR, S.
1962   The Prime of Life. Cleveland: World Book.

DEFLEUR, M. L., AND F. R. WESTIE
1958   "Verbal attitudes and overt acts: An experiment on the salience of
        attitudes." American Sociological Review 23:667-73.
1963   "Attitude as a scientific concept." Social Forces 42:17-31.

DELPÉRÉE, ALBERT
1975   "The influence of the economic recession on social policy," Interna-
        tional Social Security Review 28, no. 3:215-28.

DEMERATH, N. J., O. LARSEN, AND K. SCHUESSLER (eds.)
1975   Social Policy and Sociology. New York: Academic Press.

DENISOFF, R. SERGE, AND MARK H. LEVINE
1970   "Generations and counter-culture: A study in the ideology of music."
        Youth and Society 2:33-58.

DE QUIROS, C. BERNALDO
1911   Modern Theories of Criminality. Boston: Little, Brown.

DEUTSCHER, I.
1966   "Words and deeds." Social Problems 13:235-54.

1969   "Looking backward: Case studies on the progress of methodology in
        sociological research." American Sociologist 4:35-41.

1973   What We Say/What We Do: Sentiments and acts. Glenview, Illinois:
        Scott, Foresman.

DEVOS, GEORGE A.
1975   "Affective dissonance and primary socialization: Implications for a
        theory of incest avoidance," Ethos 3 (Summer):165-82.

1976   "Affective dissonance and primary socialization: Implications for a
        theory of incest avoidance." In Theodore Schwartz, ed., Socialization as
        Cultural Communication. Berkeley: University of California Press.

1977   "Selective permeability and reference group sanctioning: Psychological
        continuities in role degradation." Address delivered at the meetings of
        the American Sociological Association. Chicago, Illinois.

n.d.   Change in Culture, Personality and Society. Unpublished manuscript.

DeVos, George A. (ed.)
1973 Socialization for Achievement: Essays on the Cultural Psychology of the Japanese. Berkeley and Los Angeles: University of California Press.
1976 Responses to Change. Princeton, N.J.: Van Nostrand Reinhold.

DeVos, George A., and Hiroshi Wagatsuma
1966 Japan's Invisible Race: Caste in Culture and Personality. Berkeley: University of California Press.
n.d. Heritage of Endurance. Unpublished manuscript.

Dillehay, Ronald C.
1973 "On the irrelevance of the classical negative evidence concerning the effect of attitudes on behavior." American Psychologist 28:887-91.

Dillman, Don A., and Kenneth R. Tremblay, Jr.
1977 "The quality of life in rural America." Annals of the American Academy of Political and Social Science 429 (January):115-29.

Doering, S. G., and D. R. Entwisle
1975 "Preparation during pregnancy and ability to cope with labor and delivery." American Journal of Orthopsychiatry 45 (October):825-37.
1977 The First Birth. Unpublished manuscript.

Doering, S. G., D. R. Entwisle, and D. C. Quinlan
1977 "Husband participation in labor and delivery and the woman's birth experience: A multivariate analysis." Unpublished manuscript.

Dostoyevsky, F.
1950 The Brothers Karamazov. New York: Random House.

Douglas, Jack D. (ed.)
1971 The Technological Threat. Englewood Cliffs, N.J.: Prentice-Hall.

Duesenberry, James S.
1960 "Comment." Pp. 231-35 in Universities-National Bureau Committee for Economic Research, Demographic and Economic Change in Developed Countries. Princeton, N.J.: Princeton University Press.
1967 Income, Saving, and the Theory of Consumer Behavior. New York: Oxford University Press.

Duncan, B. L.
1976 "Differential social perception and attribution of intergroup violence: Testing and lower limits of stereotyping of blacks. Journal of Personality and Social Psychology 34:590-98.

Duncan, Greg J.
1977 "Paths to economic well-being." In Greg J. Duncan and James N. Morgan (eds.), Five Thousand American Families—Patterns of Economic Progress, vol. 5. Ann Arbor, Michigan: Survey Research Center.

Duncan, Otis Dudley, David Featherman, and Beverly Duncan
1972 Socioeconomic Background and Achievement. New York: Seminar Press.

Dunkelberg, William C.
1972 "The impact of consumer attitudes on behavior: A cross-section study." In Katona Festschrift:347-71.

DURAN, J. J.
1974 "The ecology of ethnic groups from a Kenyan perspective." Ethnicity
       1:43–64.

DURHAM, WILLIAM HAYNES
1977 Scarcity and survival: The ecological origins of conflict between El
       Salvador and Honduras. Ph.D. dissertation, University of Michigan.

DURKHEIM, EMILE
1933 The Division of Labor in Society. New York: Macmillan.
1938 The Rules of Sociological Method. Chicago: University of Chicago
       Press.
1973 Moral Education. New York: The Free Press.

DWORKIN, RONALD
1977 "Why Bakke has no case." New York Review of Books (November
       10):15.

EASTERLIN, RICHARD A.
1968 Population, Labor Force and Long Swings in Economic Growth: The
       American Experience. New York: Columbia University Press.

1969 "Towards a socioeconomic theory of fertility: A survey of recent re-
       search on economic factors in American fertility." Pp. 127–51 in S. J.
       Behrman, Leslie Corsa, Jr., and Ronald Freedman (eds.), Fertility and
       Family Planning: A World View. Ann Arbor, Michigan: University of
       Michigan Press.

1973 "Relative economic status and the American fertility swing." Pp. 120–
       223 in Eleanor B. Sheldon (ed.), Family Economic Behavior: Problems
       and Prospects. Philadelphia: Lippincott.

1975 "An economic framework for fertility analysis." Studies in Family Plan-
       ning 6 (March):54–63.

1978 "The economics and sociology of fertility: A synthesis." In Charles Tilly
       (ed.), Historical Studies of Changing Fertility. Princeton, N.J.: Prince-
       ton University Press.

EASTERLIN, RICHARD A., ROBERT A. POLLAK, AND MICHAEL L. WACHTER
Forth- "Toward a more general economic model of fertility determination:
coming Endogenous preferences and natural fertility." In Universities-National
        Bureau Committee for Economic Research, Population and Economic
        Change in Less Developed Countries.

ECKHARDT, KENNETH
1968 "Deviance, visibility, and legal action: The duty to support." Social
       Problems 15 (Spring):470–77.

EDWARDS, R. Y., AND C. DAVID FOWLE
1955 "The concept of carrying capacity." Transactions of the North Ameri-
       can Wildlife Conference 20 (March):589–602.

EELLS, K., A. DAVIS, et al.
1951 Intelligence and Cultural Differences: A Study of Cultural Learning
       and Problem Solving. Chicago: University of Chicago Press.

EHRLICH, H. J.
1969 "Attitudes, behavior, and the intervening variables." American Sociologist 4:29–34.

EHRLICH, ISAAC
1974 "Participation in illegitimate activities: An ecnomic analysis." In G. S. Becker and W. M. Landes (eds.), Essays in the Economics of Crime and Punishment. New York: Columbia University Press.
1975 "The deterrent effect of capital punishment: A question of life and death." American Economic Review 6 (June):397–417.
1977 "Capital punishment and deterrence: Some further thoughts and additional evidence." Journal of Political Economy 85 (August): no. 4.

EHRLICH, ISSAC, AND JOEL GIBBONS
1977 "On the measurement of the deterrent effect of capital punishment and the theory of deterrence." Journal of Legal Studies 6 (January): No. 1.

EHRLICH, PAUL R.
1968 The Population Bomb. New York: Ballantine Books.

EHRLICH, PAUL R., ANNE H. EHRLICH, AND JOHN P. HOLDREN
1973 Human Ecology: Problems and Solutions. San Francisco: W. H. Freeman and Company.

EIDELBERG, PHILIP GABRIEL
1974 The Great Rumanian Peasant Revolt of 1907, Origins of a Modern Jacquerie. Leiden: E. J. Brill.

EISEN, JONATHAN (ed.)
1969 The Age of Rock: Sounds of the American Cultural Revolution. New York: Random House.

EISENSTADT, S. N.
1971 "Continuities and changes in systems of social stratification." Pp. 61–81 in Bernard Barber and Alex Inkeles (eds.), Stability and Social Change. Boston: Little, Brown.

ELDER, GLEN H., JR.
1974 Children of the Great Depression. Chicago: University of Chicago Press.
1975 "Age differentiation and the life course." In Annual Review of Sociology, vol. 1, chap. 2. Palo Alto, California: Annual Reviews.
Forth- "Family history and the life course." In Tamara K. Hareven (ed.),
coming Family Transitions and the Life Course in Historical Perspective. New York: Academic Press.

EMBER, C.
1973 "Feminine task assignment and the social behavior of boys." Ethos 1:424–39.

ENGMAN, LEWIS
1974 Address before the Detroit Economic Club. October 7. Mimeographed.

ENLOE, CYNTHIA
1973   Ethnic Conflict and Political Development. Boston: Little, Brown.

ERIKSON, ERIK H.
1950   Childhood and Society. New York: Norton.
1966   "The concept of identity in race relations: Notes and queries." In T. Parsons and K. B. Clark (eds.), The Negro American. Boston: Houghton Mifflin.
1968   Identity: Youth and Crisis. New York: Norton.

ESMAN, MILTON J.
1973   The management of communal conflict." Public Policy 21:49–78.

ESSLIN, MARTIN
1973   The Theatre of the Absurd. Woodstock, N.Y.: Overlook Press.

EUROPEAN COAL AND STEEL COMMUNITY, EUROPEAN ECONOMIC COMMUNITY, AND EUROPEAN ATOMIC ENERGY COMMUNITY
1974   Report on the Development of the Social Situation in the Community in 1973. Brussels-Luxembourg.
1975   Report on the Development of the Social Situation in the Community in 1975. Brussels-Luxembourg.

EUROSTAT
1974   Social Accounts 1970–1972. Luxembourg: Eurostat.

EVANS, J. L.
1968   Affect and the Attribution of Causation. Master's thesis, University of Alberta.

FABIUS, L.
1976   "The economy and social security in a period of inflation and recession." International Social Security Review 29, no. 3:215–27.

FAIRCHILD, HENRY PRATT
1939   People: The Quantity and Quality of Population. New York: Holt.

FANSHEL, S., AND J. W. BUSH
1970   "A health-status index and its application to health-services outcomes." Operations Research 18 (June):1021–25.

FARLEY, REYNOLDS, HOWARD SCHUMAN, SUZANNE BIANCHI, DIANE COLESANTO, AND SHIRLEY HATCHETT
Forth-   "Chocolate city, vanilla suburbs: Will the trends toward racially sepa-
coming   rate communities continue?" Social Science Research.

FEIRING, C., AND J. TAYLOR
Forth-   "The influence of the infant and secondary parent on maternal becoming   havior: Toward a social systems view of infant attachment." Merrill Palmer Quarterly.

FERBER, MARIANNE, AND HELEN LOWRY
1977   "Woman's place: National differences in the occupational mosaic." Journal of Marketing 41 (July):23–30.

FERNANDEZ, RONALD (ed.)
1977   The Future as a Social Problem. Santa Monica, California: Goodyear Publishing Company.

FERRI, ENRICO
1917 Criminal Sociology. Boston: Little, Brown.

FEUER, LEWIS
1969 The Conflict of Generations. New York: Basic Books.

FIELD, ARTHUR
1970 Urban Power Structures. Cambridge: Shenckman.

FILLENBAUM, G.
1975 "Reliability and validity of the OARS multidimensional functional assessment questionnaire." In E. Pfeiffer (ed.), Multidimensional Functional Assessment: The OARS Methodology. Durham, North Carolina: Duke University Center for the Study of Aging and Human Development.

FISCHER, DAVID H.
1977 Growing Old in America. New York: Oxford University Press.

FISHBEIN, MARTIN
1967 "Attitude and the prediction of behavior." Pp. 477–92 in M. Fishbein (ed.), Readings in Attitude Theory and Measurement. New York: Wiley.
1973 "The prediction of behavior from attitudinal variables." Pp. 3–31 in C. D. Mortensen and K. K. Sereno (eds.), Advances in Communication Research. New York: Harper & Row.

FISHBEIN, MARTIN, AND ICEK AJZEN
1972 "Attitudes and opinions." Annual Review of Psychology 23:487–544.
1974 "Attitudes toward objects as predictors of single and multiple behavioral criteria." Psychological Review 81:59–74.
1975 Belief, Attitude, Intention, and Behavior: An Introduction to Theory and Research. Reading, Mass.: Addison-Wesley.

FISHBEIN, MARTIN, K. THOMAS, AND J. J. JACCARD
1976 "Voting behavior in Britain: An attitudinal analysis." Occasional Papers in Survey Research 7, SSRC Survey Unit, London, England.

FISHER, IRVING
1909 Report of National Vitality, Its Wastes and Conservation. Washington, D.C.: Government Printing Office.

FISHER, R. A.
1930 The Genetical Theory of Natural Selection. Oxford: Clarendon Press.
1954 Statistical Methods for Research Workers, 12th ed. New York: Hafner.

FISHMAN, JOSHUA A.
1972 Language in Sociocultural Change. Stanford, California: Stanford University Press.

FLAMM, FRANZ
1974 Social Services and Social Work in the Federal Republic of Germany. Frankfurt/Main: Eigenverlag des Deutschen Vereins für Öffentliche und Private Fürsorge.

FLANNERY, KENT
1972   "The cultural evolution of civilizations." Annual Review of Ecology and
        Systematics 3:399–426.

FLYNN, MARILYN
1973   "Assistance to the poor: Our English legislative heritage." Mimeog-
        raphed.
1975   "Perspectives on America's social security system." Public Welfare 33
        (Fall):17–22.
1977   "Public assistance, social insurance, and social policy in industrialized
        nations: Options for the future." Paper presented in Public Policy
        Seminar, University of Illinois at Urbana-Champaign.

FORM, WILLIAM
1976a   Blue Collar Stratification: Autoworkers in Four Countries. Princeton:
        Princeton University Press.
1976b   "Conflict within the working class: The skilled as a special interest
        group." Pp. 51–73 in Lewis Coser and Otto Larson (eds.), The Uses of
        Controversy in Sociology. New York: The Free Press.

FORM, WILLIAM, AND JOAN HUBER
1976   "Occupational power." Pp. 751–806 in Robert Dubin (ed.), Handbook
        of Work, Organization, and Society. Chicago: Rand McNally.

FORST, BRIAN E.
1977   "The Deterrent Effect of Capital Punishment." Minnesota Law Review
        61 (May):743–67.

FOUNDATION FOR CHILD DEVELOPMENT
1977   National Survey of Children: Summary of Preliminary Results. New
        York: Foundation for Child Development.

FOURASTIÉ, JEAN
1960   The Causes of Wealth. New York: The Free Press.

FRANCIS, E. K.
1976   Interethnic Relations: An Essay in Sociological Theory. New York:
        Elsevier.

FREEDMAN, RONALD
1963   "Norms for family size in underdeveloped areas." Proceedings of the
        Royal Society, B159, part 974:220–34.

FREEMAN, RICHARD B.
1971   The Market for College-Trained Manpower: A Study in the Economics
        of Career Choice. Cambridge: Harvard University Press.

FREUD, SIGMUND
1962   Civilization and Its Discontents. New York: Norton.

FRIEDMAN, MILTON
1957   A Theory of the Consumption Function. Princeton, N.J.: Princeton
        University Press.

FRIEDRICH, C. J.
1963   "Justice, the political act." In C. J. Friedrich and J. Chapman (eds.),
        Justice, Nomos VI. New York: Atherton.

FRIEND, IRWIN, AND F. GERARD ADAMS
1964 "The predictive ability of consumer attitudes, stock prices, and non-attitudinal variables." Journal of the American Statistical Association 59 (December):987–1005.

FRISBIE, W. PARKER, AND L. NEIDERT
1977 "Inequality and the relative size of minority populations: A comparative analysis." American Journal of Sociology 82:1007–30.

FUCHS, LAWRENCE H.
1961 Hawaii Pono. New York: Harcourt, Brace.

FUSFELD, DANIEL
1974 "The basic economics of the urban and racial crisis." Pp. 43–70 in Joan Huber and Peter (Paul) Chalfant (eds.), The Sociology of American Poverty. Boston: Schenkman.

GALBRAITH, JOHN K.
1967 The New Industrial State. Boston: Houghton Mifflin.
1973 "Power and the useful economist." American Economic Review 63 (March):1–11.

GALLIHER, J. F., AND J. L. McCARTNEY
1977 Criminology: Power, Crime, and Criminal Law. Homewood, Illinois: Dorsey.

GALLIMORE, R., A. HOWARD, AND C. JORDAN
1969 "Independence training among Hawaiians: A cross-cultural study." In H. C. Lindgren (ed.), Contemporary Research in Social Psychology. New York: Wiley.

GAMSON, WILLIAM A.
1968 Power and Discontent. Homewood, Illinois: Dorsey.
1975 The Strategy of Social Protest. Homewood, Illinois: Dorsey.

GARDNER, MARTIN
1975 Review of Powers of Mind, by Adam Smith. New York Review of Books 22:46.

GAROFALO, RAFAELE
1914 Criminology. Boston: Little, Brown.

GELBER, SYLVA
1975 "Social security and women: A partisan view." International Labour Review 112 (December):431–44.

GELLNER, ERNEST
1974 Contemporary Thought and Politics. London: Routledge and Kegan Paul.

GENNEP, ARNOLD VAN
1960 The Rites of Passage. Chicago: University of Chicago Press.

GENOVESE, EUGENE D.
1974 Roll, Jordan, Roll: The World the Slaves Made. New York: Pantheon Books.

GERLACH, LUTHER P., AND VIRGINIA H. HINE
   1973   Lifeway Leap: The Dynamics of Change in America. Minneapolis:
          University of Minnesota Press.

GIBBS, JACK P.
   1965   "Norms: The problems of definition and classification." American
          Journal of Sociology 70 (March):586–94.

GILLESPIE, W., IRWIN
   1976   "On the redistribution of income in Canada." Canadian Tax Journal 24
          (July–August):419–450.

GIRAUDOUX, JEAN
   1947   The Madwoman of Chaillot. New York: Random House.

GLAZER, NATHAN
   1975a Affirmative Discrimination: Ethnic Inequality and Public Policy. New
          York: Basic Books.

   1975b "The universalization of ethnicity: Peoples in the boiling pot." En-
          counter 44:8–17.

GLAZER, NATHAN, AND DANIEL P. MOYNIHAN
   1970   Beyond the Melting Pot: The Negroes, Puerto Ricans, Jews, Italians,
          and Irish of New York City. Cambridge: Harvard University Press and
          M.I.T. Press, 2d rev. ed. (1st ed. 1963).

GLENN, NORVAL D.
   1966   White gains from Negro subordination. Social Problems 14:159–78.

   1964   The relative size of the Negro population and Negro occupational
          status. Social Forces 43:42–49.

GLICK, PAUL C.
   1947   "The family cycle." American Journal of Sociology 12:164–74.

   1955   "The life cycle of the family." Marriage and Family Living 18:3–9.

   1977   "Updating the life cycle of the family." Journal of Marriage and the
          Family 39 (February):5–13.

GLICK, PAUL C., AND ARTHUR J. NORTON
   1977   "Selected data from 'Marrying, divorcing and living together in the
          U.S. today.'" Prepared for Family Economic Behavior Seminar. Ameri-
          can Council on Life Insurance.

GLICK, PAUL C., AND ROBERT PARKE, JR.
   1965   "New approaches in studying the life cycle of the family." Demography
          2:187–212.

GLOCK, CHARLES Y., AND ROBERT N. BELLAH (eds.)
   1976   The New Religious Consciousness. Berkeley: University of California
          Press.

GLUCKMAN, MAX
   1954   Rituals of Rebellion in South-East Africa. Manchester: Manchester
          University Press.

   1963   Order and Rebellion in Tribal Africa. New York: The Free Press.

GOODE, WILLIAM
1963 World Revolution and Family Patterns. New York: The Free Press.

GORDON, MILTON M.
1964 Assimilation in American Life: The Role of Race, Religion, and National Origins. New York: Oxford University Press.

GOSLIN, DAVID A.
1963 The Search for Ability: Standardized Testing in Social Perspective. New York: Russell Sage Foundation.

GRANT, M.
1916 The Passing of the Great Race or the Racial Basis of European History. New York: Charles Scribner's Sons.

GRANIER, R., AND J. P. MARCIANO
1975 "The earnings of immigrant workers in France," International Labour Review 112 (February):143–66.

GREAT BRITAIN—PARLIAMENT
1907 "Judicial statistics, England and Wales, 1905." In Accounts and Papers (52). London: HMSO.

GREBLER, LEO, JOAN MOORE, AND RALPH GUZMAN
1970 The Mexican-American People. New York: The Free Press.

GREELEY, ANDREW M.
1974 Ethnicity in the United States: A Preliminary Reconnaissance. New York: Wiley.

GREELEY, ANDREW M., AND PAUL B. SHEATSLEY
1971 "Attitudes toward racial integration." Scientific American, December:13–19.

GREEN, MARK J. (ed.)
1973 The Monopoly Makers. New York: Grossman Publishers.

GROGAN, D., AND J. HUNT
1977 "Digestive proteases of two species of wasps of the genus *Vespula*." Insect Biochemistry 7:191–96.

GROSSMAN, ALLYSON SHERMAN
1977 "Almost half of all children have mothers in the labor force." Monthly Labor Review 100 (June):41–44.

GUINDON, HUBERT
1964 Social unrest, social class and Quebec's bureaucratic revolution. Queen's Quarterly 71:150–62.

GULLAND, J. A.
1974 The Management of Marine Fisheries. Seattle: University Washington Press.

GURR, TED R.
1969 Cross-National Studies of Civil Violence. Washington, D.C.: The American University Center for Research in Social Systems.
1970 Why Men Rebel. Princeton, N.J.: Princeton University Press.
1972 "The calculus of civil conflict." Journal of Social Issues 28:27–47.

GURWITZ, S. B., AND K. A. DODGE
1977 "Effects of confirmations and disconfirmations of stereotyped-based attributions." Journal of Personality and Social Psychology 35:495–500.

GUTMANN, DAVID
1972 "The premature gerontocracy: Themes of aging and death in the youth culture." Social Research 39 (Autumn):416–48.

GUTTENTAG, M., AND E. L. STRUENING (eds.)
1975 Handbook of Evaluation Research, I. Beverly Hills, California: Sage.

HAGEN, EVERETT E.
1976 "Becoming modern: The dangers of research governed by preconceptions." History of Childhood Quarter 3 (Winter):411–21, 435–37.

HAKANSSON, NILS H.
1972 "Sequential investment-consumption strategies for individuals and endowment funds with lexicographic preferences." In James L. Bicksler (ed.), Methodology in Finance-Investments. Lexington, Mass.: Lexington Books.

HALEY, A.
1976 Roots. Garden City, N.Y.: Doubleday.

HALSEY, A. H. (ed.)
1977 Heredity and Environment. New York: The Free Press.

HALSEY, A. H., JEAN FLOUD, AND C. A. ANDERSON (eds.)
1961 Education, Economy, and Society: A Reader in the Sociology of Education. New York: The Free Press.

HAMILTON, D. L.
1976 "Cognitive biases in the perception of social groups." In J. S. Carroll and J. W. Payne (eds.), Cognition and Social Beahvior. Hillsdale, N.J.: Erlbaum.

HAMILTON, D. L., AND R. K. GIFFORD
1976 "Illusory correlation in interpersonal perception: A cognitive basis of stereotypic judgments." Journal of Experimental Social Psychology 12:392–407.

HAMILTON, W. D.
1964 "The genetical theory of social behavior." Journal of Theoretical Biology 7:1–52.
1972 On the Ecology and Behaviour of the African Elephant. Ph.D. dissertation, Oxford University.

HANSARDS PARLIAMENTARY DEBATES
1868 Third Series, V. CXCI. London: Cornelius Buck.

HARDESTY, DONALD L.
1977 Ecological Anthropology. New York: Wiley.

HARDIN, G.
1968 "The tragedy of the commons." Science 162:1243–48.

HARDIN, G. (ed.)
1969 Population, Evolution and Birth Control: A Collage of Controversial Ideas. San Francisco: W. H. Freeman and Co.

HAREVEN, TAMARA K.
1974 "The family as process: The historical study of the family cycle." Journal of Social History 7:322–29.

1975 "Family time and industrial time: Family and work in a planned corporation town, 1900–1924." Journal of Urban History 1:365–89.

1976 "The last stage: Historical adulthood and old age." Daedalus (Fall):13–27.

1977 "Family time and historical time." Daedalus (Spring):13–27.

HAREVEN, TAMARA K. (ed.)
1978 Family Transitions and the Life Course in Historical Perspective. New York: Academic Press.

HAREVEN, TAMARA K., AND MARIS VINOVSKIS (eds.)
1978 Demographic Patterns and Household Processes in Nineteenth Century American Communities. Princeton, N.J.: Princeton University Press.

HARMON, JAMES E.
1972 "The new music and counter-cultural values." Youth and Society 4:61–83.

HARPER, FOWLER V., AND JEROME H. SKOLNICK
1962 "Note: Legal and social impediments to intermarriage." Problems of the Family. Indianapolis: Bobbs-Merrill.

HARRIS, MARVIN
1968 The Rise of Anthropological Theory. New York: Crowell.

HAVEMAN, R. H., AND H. W. WATTS
1976 "Social experiments as policy research: A review of negative income tax experiments." In G. V. Glass (ed.), Evaluation Studies, I. Beverly Hills, California: Sage.

HAWLEY, AMOS H.
1950 Human Ecology: A Theory of Community Structure. New York: Ronald Press.

1977 "Hierarchy in human systems." In Perspectives on Adaptation, Environment, and Population. Washington: Department of Health, Education, and Welfare.

HAWLEY, AMOS H. (ed.)
1975 Man and Environment. New York: The New York Times Company.

HEADY, HAROLD F.
1975 Rangeland Management. New York: McGraw-Hill.

HEBERT, ROBERT F.
1977 "Edwin Chadwick and the economics of crime." Economic Inquiry 15 (October):539–50.

HECHTER, MICHAEL
1975 Internal Colonialism: The Celtic Fringe in British National Development. Berkeley and Los Angeles: University of California Press.

HECLO, HUGH
1974   Modern Social Politics in Britain and Sweden. New York: St. Martin's Press.

HEGEL, G. W. F.
1923   "Die Verfassung Deutschlands." In Georg Lasson (ed.), Schriften zur Politik und Rechtsphilosophie. Leipzig: Felix Meiner.

HEIDENHEIMER, ARNOLD J.
1976   "Professional unions, public sector growth, and the Swedish 'equality policy.'" Comparative Politics 7 (October):49–73.

HEIDENHEIMER, ARNOLD, HUGH HECLO, AND CAROLYN TEICH ADAMS
1975   Comparative Public Policy: The Politics of Social Choice in Europe and America. New York: St. Martin's Press.

HEIDER, F.
1958   The Psychology of Interpersonal Relations. New York: Wiley.

HELLER, WALTER
1975   "What's right with economics?" American Economic Review 65 (March):1–26.

HENDIN, HERBERT
1975   The Age of Sensation. New York: Norton.

HERNES, G.
1976   "Structural change in social processes." American Journal of Sociology 82 (November):513–47.

HERZOG, E., AND C. E. SUDIA
1973   "Children in fatherless families." In Betty E. Caldwell and Henry N. Ricciuti (eds.), Review of Child Development Research, vol. 3. Chicago: University of Chicago Press.

HETHERINGTON, E. M.
1972   "Effects of father absence on personality development in adolescent daughters." Developmental Psychology 7:313–26.
1977   "Aftermath of divorce." In J. H. Stevens, Jr., and Marilyn Mathews (eds.), Parent-Child Relations. Washington: NAEYC.

HIBBS, DOUGLAS A.
1973   Mass Political Violence: A Cross-National Analysis. New York: Wiley.

HILL, CHRISTOPHER
1975   The World turned Upside Down: Radical Ideas during the English Revolution. Harmondsworth, Middlesex, England: Penguin.

HOBSBAWN, E. J.
1965   Primitive Rebels. New York: Norton.

HODGE, R. W., P. M. SIEGEL, AND P. H. ROSSI
1966   "Occupational prestige in the United States." Pp. 322–34 in R. Bendix and S. M. Lipset (eds.), Class, Status and Power, 2d ed. New York: The Free Press.

HODGE, R. W., D. J. TREIMAN, AND P. H. ROSSI
1966 "A comparative study of occupational prestige." Pp. 309–21 in R. Bendix and S. M. Lipset (eds.), Class, Status and Power, 2d ed. New York: The Free Press.

HOLLINGSHEAD, A. B.
1949 Elmtown's Youth: The Impact of Social Classes on Adolescents. New York: Wiley.

HOLSINGER, DONALD B.
1973 "The elementary school as modernizer: A Brazilian study." International Journal of Comparative Sociology 14 (September–December):180–202.

HOLZMAN, FRANKLYN
1955 Soviet Taxation. Cambridge: Harvard University Press.

HOMANS, GEORGE C.
1958 "Social behavior as exchange." American Journal of Sociology 63 (May):597–606.
1961 Social Behavior: Its Elementary Forms. New York: Harcourt, Brace.

HORNEY, KAREN
1937 The Neurotic Personality of our Time. New York: Norton.

HOROWITZ, D. L.
1975 "Ethnic identity." In N. Glazer and D. P. Moynihan (eds.), Ethnicity: Theory and Experience. Cambridge, Mass.: Harvard University Press.

HOUGHTON, W. E. (ed.)
1966 The Wellesley Index of Victorian Periodicals, 1824–1900. Toronto: University of Toronto Press.

HOWARD, A.
1974 Ain't No Big Thing. Honolulu: University Press of Hawaii.

HOWELL, JOSEPH T.
1973 Hard Living on Clay Street: Portraits of Blue-Collar Families. Garden City, N.Y.: Anchor/Doubleday.

HOWEY, R. S.
1960 The Rise of the Marginal Utility School, 1870–1889. Lawrence: University of Kansas Press.

HROCH, MIROSLAV
1968 Die Vorkaempfer der nationalen Bewegung bei den kleiner Voelkern Europas, Eine vergleichende Analyse zur gesellschaftlichen Schichtung der patriotischen Gruppen. Prag: Universita Karlova, Acta Universitatis Carolinae philosophica et historica. Monographia 24. 171 S.

HUBER, JOAN, AND WILLIAM H. FORM
1973 Income and Ideology: An Analysis of the American Political Formula. New York: Macmillan and Free Press.

HUNE, SHIRLEY
1977 Pacific Migration to the United States. Washington, D.C.: Research Institute on Immigration and Ethnic Studies, Smithsonian Institution.

HUNT, C. L., AND L. WALKER
   1974   Ethnic Dynamics: Patterns of Ingergroup Relations in Various
          Societies. Homewood, Illinois: Dorsey.

HUNT, DAVID F., AND R. H. HARDT
   1969   "The effect of upward bound programs on the attitudes, motivations,
          and academic achievement of Negro students." Journal of Social Issues
          25 (Summer):117-29.

HUTCHINSON, E. P.
   1956   Immigrants and Their Children, 1850-1950. New York: Wiley.

HYMAN, HERBERT
   1942   "The psychology of status." Archives of Psychology 38, no. 269
          (June):1-94.

HYMAN, HERBERT, CHARLES R. WRIGHT, AND JOHN SHELTON REED
   1975   The Enduring Effects of Education: Chicago: University of Chicago
          Press.

HYMANS, SAUL H.
   1970   "Consumer durable spending: Explanation and prediction." Brookings
          Papers on Economic Activity 2:173-206.

INKELES, ALEX
   1976   "Remaining orthodox: A rejoinder to Everett Hagen's review-essay of
          Becoming Modern." History of Childhood Quarter 3 (Winter):422-35.

   1977a "Rising expectations: Revolution, evolution or devolution?" Pp. 25-37
          in Howard R. Bowen (ed.), Freedom and Control in a Democratic
          Society. New York: American Council of Life Insurance.

   1977b "National differences in individual modernity." Comparative Studies
          in Sociology 1, no. 1.

INKELES, ALEX, AND DAVID H. SMITH
   1974   Becoming Modern: Individual Change in Six Developing Countries.
          Cambridge: Harvard University Press.

International Brotherhood of Teamsters v. United States
   1977   45 L. W. 4506.

INTERNATIONAL LABOUR OFFICE
   1964   The Cost of Social Security, 1958, 1960. Geneva.

   1972   The Cost of Social Security. Seventh International Inquiry, 1964-1966.
          Geneva.

   1976   The Cost of Social Security, 1966-1971. Geneva.

INTERNATIONAL SOCIAL SECURITY ASSOCIATION (ISSA)
   1975   "Income maintenance for one-parent families," International Social
          Security Review 28, no. 1:3-60.

INTERNATIONAL SOCIAL SECURITY REVIEW
   1976   "International news." International Social Security Review 29, no.
          2:196-97.

ISAJIW, W. W.
   1974   "Definitions of ethnicity." Ethnicity 1:111-24.

ITTELSON, WILLIAM H., HAROLD M. PROSHANSKY, AND GARY H. WINKEL
1974   An Introduction to Environmental Psychology. New York: Holt, Rinehart.

JACCARD, J. J.
1974   "Predicting social behavior from personality traits." Journal of Research in Personality 7:358-67.

JACOBSON, ALVIN L.
1973   "Intrasocial conflict: A preliminary test of a structural-level theory." Comparative Political Studies 6:62-83.

JAMES, EDWARD, AND ANDRÉ LAURENT
1974   "Social security: The European experiment." Social Trends, no. 5.

JANOWITZ, MORRIS
1970   Political Conflict: Essays in Political Sociology. Chicago: Quadrangle Books.

JASSO, GUILLERMINA, AND PETER H. ROSSI
1977   "Distributive justice and earned income." American Sociological Review 42 (August):639-51.

JENCKS, CHRISTOPHER, et al.
1972   Inequality: A Reassessment of the Effects of Family and Schooling in America. New York: Basic Books.

JOHNSON, BEVERLY, AND HOWARD HAYGE
1977   "Labor force participation of married women, March 1976." Monthly Labor Review 100 (June):32-36.

JOHNSON, CHARLES S.
1943   Patterns of Negro Segregation. New York: Harper & Row.

JOHNSTON, J., D. LINGWOOD, W. MORRIS, AND R. MARANS
1974   An Evaluation of the 1973 Youth Conservation Corps. Ann Arbor: Institute for Social Research, University of Michigan.

JONES, E. E.
1976   "How do people perceive the causes of behavior?" American Scientist 64:300-5.

JONES, E. E., AND V. A. HARRIS
1967   "The attribution of attitudes." Journal of Experimental Social Psychology 3:1-24.

JONES, E. E., D. E. KANOUSE, H. H. KELLEY, R. E. NISBETT, S. VALINS, AND B. WEINER (eds.)
1971   Attribution: Perceiving the Causes of Behavior. Morristown, N.J.: General Learning Press.

JOYCE, JAMES
1928   Portrait of the Artist as a Young Man. New York: Modern Library.

JUDAH, J. STILLSON
1974   Hare Kirshna and the Counterculture. New York: Wiley.

JUSTER, F. THOMAS
   1964a Anticipations and Purchases: An Analysis of Consumer Behavior.
         Princeton, N.J.: Princeton University Press.
   1964b Household Capital Formation and Financing, 1897–1962. New York:
         National Bureau of Economic Research.
   1966 "Consumer buying intentions and purchase probability: An experi-
         ment in survey design." Journal of the American Statistical Association
         61 (September):658–96.

JUSTER, F. THOMAS, AND PAUL WACHTEL
   1972 "Uncertainty, expectations and durable goods demand models." In
         Katona Festschrift:321–45.
   1974 "Anticipatory and objective models of durable goods demand." Ex-
         plorations in Economic Research 1, no. 2 (Fall):340–92.

KAHL, JOSEPH A.
   1968 The Measurement of Modernism: A Study of Values in Brazil and
         Mexico. Austin: University of Texas Press.

KAHN, HERMAN, WILLIAM BROWN, AND LEON MARTEL
   1976 The Next 200 Years: A Scenario for America and the World. New
         York: Morrow.

KAHNE, HILDA
   1975 "Economic perspectives on the roles of women in the American econ-
         omy." Journal of Economic Literature 13 (December):1249–92.

KANDEL, DENISE B., AND GERALD S. LESSER
   1972 Youth in Two Worlds. San Francisco: Jossey-Bass.

KANOUSE, D. E., AND L. R. HANSON, JR.
   1971 "Negativity in evaluations." In E. E. Jones, D. E. Kanouse, H. H. Kelley,
         R. E. Nisbett, S. Valins, and B. Weiner (eds.), Attribution: Perceiving
         the Causes of Behavior. Morristown, N.J.: General Learning Press.

KANTER, R. M.
   1977 "Some effects of proportions on group life: Skewed sex ratios and
         responses to token women." American Journal of Sociology 82:965–90.

KARDINER, ABRAM, AND LIONEL OVESEY
   1962 The Mark of Oppression. Cleveland and New York: World Publishing
         Company.

KATONA FESTSCHRIFT: BURKHARD STRUMPEL, JAMES N. MORGAN, AND ERNEST
ZAHN (eds.)
   1972 Human Behavior in Economic Affairs: Essays in Honor of George
         Katona. Amsterdam: Elsevier.

KATONA, GEORGE
   1951 Psychological Analysis of Economic Behavior. New York: McGraw-
         Hill.
   1975 Psychological Economics. New York: Elsevier.

KATONA, GEORGE, AND RENSIS LIKERT
   1946 "Relationship between consumer incomes and saving." Review of Eco-
         nomic Statistics 28 (November):197–99.

KATZ, I., AND L. BENJAMIN
1960 "Effects of white authoritarianism in biracial work groups." Journal of Abnormal and Social Psychology 61:448–56.

KAUFMAN, JACOB, J., AND TERRY G. FORAN
1971 "The minimum wage and poverty." Pp. 508–23 in John F. Burton et al. (eds.), Readings in Labor Market Analysis. New York: Holt, Rinehart.

KEELEY, MICHAEL
1975 "A comment on 'An interpretation of the economic theory of fertility.'" Journal of Economic Literature 13, no. 2 (June);461–67.

KELLER, SUZANNE
1976 Twin Rivers: Study of a Planned Community. Washington: National Science Foundation (NSF Grant G1 41 311).

KELLEY, ALLEN C.
1972 "A response to Easterlin." Pp. 224–31 in Eleanor B. Sheldon (ed.), Family Economic Behavior: Problems and Prospects. Philadelphia: Lippincott.

KELLEY, H. H.
1967 "Attribution theory in social psychology." In D. Levine (ed.), Nebraska Symposium on Motivation 15. Lincoln: University of Nebraska Press.

1973 "The process of causal attribution." American Psychologist 28:107–28.

KELLEY, KEN
1973 "Blissed out with the perfect master." Ramparts 12:32–35, 50–57.

KELMAN, HERBERT C.
1961 "Processes of opinion change." Public Opinion Quarterly 25:57–78.

1974a "Attitudes are alive and well and gainfully employed in the sphere of action." American Psychologist 29:310–24.

1974b "Social influence and linkages between the individual and the social system: Further thoughts on the processes of compliance, identification, and internalization." Pp. 125–71 in James T. Tedeschi (ed.), Perspectives on Social Power. Chicago: Aldine.

1977 "The Conditions, criteria, and dialectics of human dignity." International Studies Quarter 31 (September):529–52.

KENISTON, KENNETH
1971 "Psychological development and historical change." Journal of Interdisciplinary History 2 (Autumn):329–45.

KETT, JOSEPH
1977 Rites of Passage: Adolescence in America, 1790 to the Present. New York: Basic Books.

KEYNES, JOHN M.
1936 The General Theory of Employment, Interest and Money. New York: Harcourt, Brace.

KING, ROBERT R.
1973 Minorities under Communism: Nationalities as a Source of Tension among Balkan Communist States. Cambridge, Mass.: Harvard University Press.

KIRK, DUDLEY
1971 "A new demographic transition?" In National Academy of Sciences (eds.), Rapid Population Growth. Baltimore: Johns Hopkins Press.

KLAPP, ORRIN E.
1969 Collective Search for Identity. New York: Holt, Rinehart.

KLASSEN, D. F.
1975 "Cesarean section rates: Time, trends, and comparisons among hospital sizes, census regions, and teaching and nonteaching hospitals." PAS Reporter 14 (December 15).

KLEIN, LAWRENCE R., AND JOHN B. LANSING
1955 "Decisions to purchase consumer durable goods." Journal of Marketing 20 (October):109-32.

KNORR, K. D.
1977 "Policymakers' use of social science knowledge: Symbolic or instrumental?" Pp. 165-82 in C. H. Weiss (ed.), Using Social Research in Public Policy Making. Lexington, Mass.: Heath.

KOBRIN, FRANCES E.
1976 "The fall in household size and the rise of the primary individual in the United States." Demography 13 (February):127-38.

KOESTLER, A.
1945 The Yogi and the Commissar. New York: Macmillan.

KOHN, MELVIN L.
1976 "Occupational structure and alienation." American Journal of Sociology 82 (July):111-30.

KREBS, EDITH
1975 "Women workers and the trade unions in Austria: An interim report." International Labour Review 112 (October):265-78.

KREPS, J. M., J. J. SPENGLER, R. L. CLARK, AND S. HERREN
1976 Economics of a Stationary Population: Implications for Older Americans. Durham, N.C.: Duke University Center for the Study of Aging and Human Development.

KUKLICK, H.
1973 "A 'scientific revolution': Sociological theory in the United States, 1930-1945." Sociological Inquiry 43:3-22.

KUTNER, B., C. WILKINS, AND P. R. YARROW
1952 "Verbal attitudes and overt behavior involving racial prejudice." Journal of Abnormal and Social Psychology 47:649-52.

KUZNETS, SIMON
1966 Modern Economic Growth: Rate, Structure and Spread. New Haven: Yale University Press.

LACHENMEYER, C. W.
1971 The Language of Sociology. New York: Columbia University Press.

LADD, E. C., JR., AND S. M. LIPSET
1975 The Divided Academy: Professors and Politics. New York: McGraw-Hill.

LAMPMAN, ROBERT J.
1968 "National wealth: II. Distribution." Pp. 59–63 in David L. Sills (ed.), International Encyclopedia of the Social Sciences, vol. 11. New York: Macmillan and Free Press.

LANCASTER, KELVIN
1966 "A new approach to consumer theory." Journal of Political Economy 74 (April):132–57.

LAND, KENNETH
1975 "Social indicator models: An overview." Pp. 5–36 in Kenneth Land and Seymour Spilerman (eds.), Social Indicator Models. New York: Russell Sage Foundation.

LANE, DAVID
1976 The Socialist Industrial State: Toward a Political Sociology of State Socialism. Boulder, Colorado: Westview Press.

LAPIERE, RICHARD T.
1934 "Attitudes vs. actions." Social Forces 13:230–37.

LAROQUE, PIERRE
1969 "Social security in France." Pp. 171–89 in Shirley Jenkins (ed.), Social Security in International Perspective. New York: Columbia University Press.

1972 "Women's rights and widows' pensions." International Labour Review 106 (July):1–10.

LASCH, CHRISTOPHER
1969 The Agony of the American Left. New York: Knopf.

LASLETT, PETER, AND RICHARD WALL (eds.)
1972 Household and Family in Past Time. Cambridge, England: Cambridge University Press.

LAWRENCE, D. H.
1951 Sons and Lovers. New York: Harper.

LAWS, R. M., I. S. C. PARKS, AND R. C. B. JOHNSTONE
1975 Elephants and Their Habitat. Oxford: Clarendon Press.

LEE, CHANGSOO, AND GEORGE A. DEVOS
n.d. Koreans in Japan. Unpublished manuscript.

LEE, RONALD
1977 "Fluctuations in U.S. fertility, age structure, and income." Population Studies Center, University of Michigan (July).

LEIBENSTEIN, HARVEY
1974 "An interpretation of the economic theory of fertility: Promising path or blind alley?" Journal of Economic Literature 12 (June):457–79.

1975 "The economic theory of fertility decline." Quarterly Journal of Economics 89 (February):1–31.

1977 "The economic theory of fertility—survey, issues and considerations." International Union for the Scientific Study of Population, International Population Conference, Mexico, 2:49–64.

LEKACHMAN, ROBERT
1975   "Managing inflation in a full employment society." Annals of the American Academy of Political and Social Science 418 (March):85–93.

LE MAGAZINE MACLEAN
1963   "Pour ou contre l'independence du Quebec," November:23–26, 80–82.

LENSKI, GERHARD, AND JEAN LENSKI
1974   Human Societies: An Introduction to Macrosociology, 2d ed. New York: McGraw-Hill.

LEONTIEF, WASSILY
1966   Essays in Economics. New York: Oxford University Press.

LEOPOLD, ALDO
1943   "Deer irruptions." Transactions of the Wisconsin Academy of Sciences, Arts and Letters 35:351–66.

LEPPER, M. R., AND D. GREENE
1975   "Turning play into work: Effects of adult surveillance and extrinsic rewards on children's intrinsic motivation." Journal of Personality and Social Psychology 31:479–86.

LERNER, DANIEL
1966   The Passing of Traditional Society: Modernizing the Middle East. New York: The Free Press.

LEVINE, DONALD M., AND MARY JO BANE (eds.)
1975   The "Inequality" Controversy: Schooling and Distributive Justice. New York: Basic Books.

LEVINE, ROBERT A., AND DONALD T. CAMPBELL
1972   Ethnocentrism: Theories of Conflict, Ethnic Attitudes, and Group Behavior. New York: Wiley.

LEVINE, ROBERT A., N. H. KLEIN, AND C. R. OWEN
1967   "Father-child relationships and changing life styles in Ibadan, Nigeria." In H. Miner (ed.), The City in Modern Africa. New York: Praeger.

LÉVI-STRAUSS, CLAUDE
1966   The Savage Mind. Chicago: University of Chicago Press.

LEVITAN, SAR
1969   The Great Society's Poor Law. Baltimore: Johns Hopkins University Press.

LEVITAN, SAR, WILLIAM B. JOHNSTON, AND ROBERT TAGGART
1975   Still a Dream: The Changing Status of Blacks Since 1960. Cambridge, Mass.: Harvard University Press.

LEVITAN, SAR, AND ROBERT TAGGART
1976   The Promise of Greatness. Cambridge, Mass.: Harvard University Press.

LEWIS, ANTHONY
1976   "It works." New York Times Magazine, July 4:26.

LEWONTIN, R.
1974   The Genetic Basis of Evolutionary Change. New York: Columbia University Press.

LIEBERSON, STANLEY, AND LYNN K. HANSEN
1974 "National development, mother tongue diversity, and the comparative study of nations." American Sociological Review 39:523–41.

LIEBOW, ELLIOT
1967 Tally's Corner. Boston: Little, Brown.

LIGHT, IVAN
1972 Ethnic Enterprise in America: Business and Welfare Among Chinese, Japanese and Blacks. Los Angeles: University of California Press.

LIJPHART, AREND
1975 The Politics of Accommodation: Pluralism and Democracy in the Netherlands. Berkeley: University of California Press.

LILJESTRÖM, RITA, CUNILLA FÜRST MELLSTRÖM, AND GILLAN LILJESTRÖM SVENSSON
1975 Sex Roles in Transition: A Report on a Pilot Program in Sweden. Trans. Carol Walden. Stockholm: Swedish Institute.

LINDERT, PETER
1977–78 Fertility and Scarcity in America. Princeton, N.J.: Princeton University Press.

LIPPITT, RONALD N., N. POLANSKY, AND S. ROSEN
1954 "The dynamics of power," Human Relations 5, no. 1:37–64.

LISEIN-NORMAN, M.
1974 "Wages and family benefits in the European community: Recent trends in purchasing power." International Social Security Review 27:517–56.

LISKA, A. E. (ed.)
1975 The Consistency Controversy: Readings on the Impact of Attitude on Behavior. New York: Wiley.

LITWAK, EUGENE
1960 "Occupational mobility and extended family cohesion." American Sociological Review 25:385–94.

LLOYD, B. B.
1966 "Education and family life in the development of class identification among the Yoruba." In P. C. Lloyd (ed.), New Elites of Tropical Africa. London: Oxford University Press.
1970 "Yoruba mothers' reports of child-rearing." In Philip Mayer (ed.), Socialization: The Approach from Social Anthropology. London: Tavistock.

LOCKWOOD, WILLIAM G.
1975 European Moslems, Economy and Ethnicity in Western Bosnia. New York: Academic Press.

LODISH, RICHARD
1976 Cross-Age Relationships in an After-School Center: An Observational Study of Children's Interactions with and Perceptions of Different Age Groups. Ph.D. dissertation, Harvard University.

LORBER, J.
1977 "Beyond equality of the sexes: The question of the children." In B. J. Stein, J. Richman, and N. Hannon (eds.), The Family. Reading, Mass.: Addison-Wesley.

Loving v. *Virginia*
1967 388 U.S. 1.

LUNDSGAARDE, H. P.
1977 Murder in Space City: A Cultural Analysis of Houston Homicide Patterns. New York: Oxford University Press.

LURIE, IRENE
1975 "Integrating income maintenance programs: Problems and solutions." Pp. 1–38 in Irene Lurie (ed.), Integrating Income Maintenance Programs. New York: Academic Press.

LYDALL, HAROLD
1968 The Structure of Earnings. London: Oxford at the Clarendon Press.

LYNN, D. B.
1974 The Father: His Role in Child Development. Belmont, California: Wadsworth.

McADOO, HARRIET
1977 "The ecology of internal and external support systems in black families." Paper presented at the Conference of Research Perspectives in the Ecology of Human Development. Ithaca, N.Y.: Cornell University.

McCLELLAND, D. C.
1961 The Achieving Society. Princeton, N.J.: Van Nostrand Reinhold.

MACCOBY, ELEANOR E., AND C. N. JACKLIN
1974 The Psychology of Sex Differences. Stanford, California: Stanford University Press.

McCREADY, WILLIAM C., WITH ANDREW H. GREELEY
1976 The Ultimate Values of the American Population. Beverly Hills, California: Sage.

MacDONALD, ARTHUR
1910 "Death penalty and homicide." American Journal of Sociology 16 (July):1088–1160.

McNEIL, JOHN
1974 "Federal programs to measure consumer purchase expectations, 1946–73: A post-mortem." Journal of Consumer Research (December:1–10. (F. Gerard Adams and F. Thomas Juster, "Commentaries on McNeil's Post-Mortem." Ibid.:11–15.)

MADDOX, G. L.
1972 "Interventions and outcomes: Notes on designing and implementing an experiment in health care." International Journal of Epidemiology 1 (Winter):339–45.

MADDOX, G. L., AND J. WILEY
1976 "Scope, concepts, and methods in the study of aging." In R. Binstock and E. Shanas (eds.), Handbook of Aging and the Social Sciences. Princeton, N.J.: Van Nostrand Reinhold.

MALCOLM X (WITH ALEX HALEY)
1966 The Autobiograph of Malcolm X. New York: Grove Press

MALTHUS, ROBERT
1798 An Essay on the Principle of Population as it Affects the Improvement of Society. London: J. Johnson.

MANN, D., L. F. WOODWARD, AND N. JOSEPH
1961 Educating Expectant Parents. New York: Visiting Nurse Service of New York.

MANNHEIM, KARL
1936 Ideology and Utopia. New York: Harcourt, Brace.

MARMOR, T. R., MARTIN REIN, WITH SALLY (BOULD) VAN TIL
n.d. "Post-war European experience with cash transfers, pensions, child allowances, and public assistance." Pp. 259–92 in The President's Commission on Income Maintenance Programs: Technical Studies. Washington: Government Printing Office.

MARSHALL, RAY
1974 "The economics of racial discrimination: A survey." Journal of Economic Literature 12 (September):849–71.

MARX, GARY T., AND JAMES L. WOOD
1975 "Strands of theory and research in collective behavior." Pp. 363–428 in Alex Inkeles (ed.), Annual Review of Sociology, vol. I. Palo Alto, California: Annual Reviews.

MARX, KARL
1956 "Capital punishment." In T. B. Bottomore and M. Rubel (eds.), Karl Marx, Selected Writings in Sociology and Social Philosophy. London: C. A. Watts and Company, Ltd.

MASLOW, ABRAHAM H.
1954 Motivation and Personality. New York: Harper.

MASTERS, STANLEY H.
1975 Black-White Income Differentials: Empirical Studies and Policy Implications. New York: Academic Press.

MATZA, DAVID
1961 "Subterranean traditions of youth." Annals of the American Academy of Political and Social Science 338:102–18.

MATZA, DAVID, AND GRESHAM SYKES
1961 "Juvenile delinquency and subterranean values." American Sociological Review 26:712–19.

MAYNES, E. SCOTT
1967 "An appraisal of consumer anticipations approaches to forecasting." American Statistical Association, 1967 Proceedings of the Business and

Economic Statistics Section. Washington, American Statistical Association:114-23.

1972   "The power of the consumer." In Katona Festschrift: 399-419.

1976a   "The concept and measurement of product quality." Pp. 529-60 in Nestor E. Terleckyj (ed.), Household Production and Consumption: Studies in Income and Wealth vol. 40. New York: National Bureau of Economic Research.

1976b   Decision-Making for Consumers: An Introduction to Consumer Economics, chap. 3. New York: Macmillan.

MEADE, J. E.
1973   "The Inheritance of inequalities, some biological, demographic, social, and economic factors." Third Keynes Lecture in Economics. Proceedings of the British Academy 19:3-29. London: Oxford University Press.

MEDDIN, JAY
1976   "Human nature and the dialectics of immanent sociocultural change." Social Forces 55:382-93.

MENNINGER, K.
1968   The Crime of Punishment. New York: Viking.

MERTON, ROBERT K.
1938   "Social structure and anomie." American Sociological Review 3:672-82.

1968   Social Theory and Social Structure, 3rd ed. New York: The Free Press.

1972   "Insiders and outsiders; A chapter in the sociology of knowledge." American Journal of Sociology 78 (July):9-47.

MERTON, ROBERT K., AND ELINOR BARBER
1963   "Sociological ambivalence." Pp. 91-120 in Edward A. Tiryakian (ed.), Sociological Theory, Values and Sociocultural Change: Essays in Honor of Pitirim A. Sorokin. New York: The Free Press.

MERTON, ROBERT K., AND ROBERT A. NISBET (eds.)
1966   Contemporary Social Problems. New York: Harcourt, Brace.

MICHAEL, ROBERT T., AND GARY S. BECKER
1973   "On the new theory of consumer behavior." Swedish Journal of Economics 75 (December):378-96.

MICHAEL, ROBERT T., AND ROBERT J. WILLIS
1976   "Contraception and fertility: Household production under uncertainty." Pp. 27-94 in Conference on Research in Income and Wealth, Household Production and Consumption, Studies in Income and Wealth, vol. 40. New York: National Bureau of Economic Research.

MICHELSON, WILLIAM
1975   "Urbanism as ways of living: The changing views of planning research." Ekistics 40:20-26.

MILL, JAMES
n.d.   "Jurisprudence." In Essays on Government, Jurisprudence, Liberty of the Press, and the Law of Nations. London: J. Innes.

MILL, JOHN STUART
1907 Utilitarianism, 15th ed. London: Longmans, Green.

MILLER, HERMAN P.
1964 Rich Man, Poor Man. New York: Crowell.
1975 "Inequality, poverty, and taxes." Dissent 22 (Winter):40–49.

MILLS, C. WRIGHT
1951 White Collar: The American Middle Class. New York: Oxford University Press.

MINCER, JACOB
1963 "Market prices, opportunity costs, and income effects." In Measurement in Economics: Studies in Mathematical Economics and Econometrics in Memory of Yehuda Grunfeld. Stanford, California: Stanford University Press.

MISCHEL, W.
1968 Personality and Assessment. New York: Wiley.

MODELL, JOHN, FRANK FURSTENBERG, AND THEODORE HERSHBERG
1976 "Social change and transitions to adulthood in historical perspective." Journal of Family History 1:7–32.

MODELL, JOHN, AND TAMARA K. HAREVEN
1973 "Urbanization and the malleable household: Boarding and lodging in American families." Journal of Marriage and the Family 35:467–79.

MONSON, T. C., AND M. SNYDER
1977 "Actors, observers, and the attribution process." Journal of Experimental Social Psychology 13:89–111.

MOODY, EDWARD, J.
1974 "Magical therapy: An anthropological investigation of contemporary satanism." Pp. 355–82 in Irving I. Zaretsky and Mark P. Leone (eds.), Religious Movements in Contemporary America. Princeton, N.J.: Princeton University Press.

MOORE, WILBERT E.
1951 Industrialization and Labor: Social Aspects of Economic Development. Ithaca, New York: Cornell University Press.

MORGAN, JAMES N., DAVID H. MARTIN, WILBUR J. COHEN, AND HARVEY E. BRAZER
1962 Income and Welfare in the United States. New York: McGraw-Hill.

MOSTELLER, FREDERICK, AND DANIEL P. MOYNIHAN (eds.)
1972 On Equality of Educational Opportunity: Papers Deriving from the Harvard University Faculty Seminar on the Coleman Report. New York: Random House.

MOY, JOYANNA, AND CONSTANCE SORRENTINO
1975 "Unemployment in nine industrial nations, 1973–1975." Monthly Labor Review 98 (June):9–18.

MUELLER, EVA
1960 "Consumer attitudes: Their influence and forecasting value." Pp. 149–80 in National Bureau of Economic Research, The Quality and

Economic Significance of Anticipations Data. Princeton, N.J.: Princeton University Press.

MULLOY, WILLIAM
1974   "Contemplate the navel of the world." Americas 26 (April):25-33.

MUNSINGER, H. L.
1964   "Meaningful symbols as reinforcing stimuli." Journal of Abnormal and Social Psychology 68:665-68.

MURDOCH, W., AND A. OATEN
1975   "Population and food: Metaphor and reality." Bio Science 25:561-67.

MUSGRAVE, RICHARD
1959   The Theory of Public Finance. New York: McGraw-Hill.

MUSGROVE, FRANK
1974   Ecstasy and Holiness: Counter Culture and the Open Society. Bloomington, Indiana: Indiana University Press.

MUTH, JOHN F.
1961   "Rational expectations and the theory of price movements." Econometrica 29 (July):315-35.

NAMBOODIRI, N. KRISHNAN
1972   "Some observations on the economic framework for fertility analysis." Population Studies 26 (July):185-206.

NASH, J.
1976   "Historical and social change in the perception of the role of the father." Pp. 65-87 in M. E. Lamb (ed.), The Role of the Father in Child Development. New York: Wiley.

NATIONAL ACADEMY OF SCIENCES
1976   Toward a National Policy for Children and Families. Washington: National Academy of Sciences.

NATIONAL CHILDREN'S BUREAU
1976   Britain's Sixteen-Year-Olds. London: National Children's Bureau.

NESVOLD, BETTY A.
1969   "Scalogram analysis of political violence." Comparative Political Studies 2:172-94.

NETTLER, G.
1972   "Quinney on 'The Violence Commission.'" Contemporary Sociology 1:204.

1978   Explaining Crime, 2d ed. New York: McGraw-Hill.

NEUGARTEN, BERNICE L. (ed.)
1968   Middle Age and Aging: A Reader in Social Psychology. Chicago: University of Chicago Press.

NEWMAN, OSCAR
1972   Defensible Space. New York: MacMillan.

New York Times
1968   "Systems Analysts Baffled by Problems of Social Change," March 24.

NICHOLSON, A. J.
  1954   "An Outline of the Dynamics of Animal Populations." Australian Journal of Zoology 2 (May):9-65.

NIETZSCHE, FRIEDRICH
  1967   The Will to Power, trans. Walter Kaufmann (ed.) and R. J. Hollingdale. New York: Random House.

NIKOLSKY, G. V.
  1963   The Ecology of Fishes. London: Academic Press.

NISBETT, R. E., C. CAPUTO, P. LEGANT, AND J. MARECEK
  1973   "Behavior as seen by the actor and as seen by the observer." Journal of Personality and Social Psychology 27:154-65.

NOWELL-SMITH, P. H.
  1967   Ethics. Oxford: Basil Blackwell.

OBERHEU, HOWARD   1976   "The typical family compared with the afdc family." Social and Rehabilitation Record 3 (July/August):6-8.

ODUM, EUGENE P.
  1971   Fundamentals of Ecology, 3d ed. Philadelphia: W. B. Saunders.

OECD
  1975   "Effect of tax and welfare schemes on worker's incomes." In The OECD Observer #74. Paris: OECD.
  1976   "Income distribution in OECD countries," by Michael Sawyer. OECD Economic Outlook—Occasional Studies (July).
  1977   The Treatment of Family Units in OECD Member Countries Under Tax and Transfer Systems. Paris: OECD.

OGBURN, WILLIAM F.
  1956   "Technology as Environment." Sociology and Social Research 41 (September-October):3-9.

ORNATI, OSCAR
  1974   "Migrant Labor." Pp. 175-77 in Encyclopedia Britannica 12, 15th ed. Chicago: Encyclopedia Brittanica, Inc.

ORTEGA Y GASSET, J.
  1946   Concord and Liberty. New York: Norton.

OSGOOD, C. E., et al.
  1957   The Measurement of Meaning. Urbana: University of Illinois Press.

OSMOND, MARIE WITHERS, AND CHARLES GRIGG
  1975   "Correlates of poverty: The interaction of individual and family characteristics." Paper presented at the annual meeting of the American Sociological Association, San Francisco.

PADFIELD, HARLAND, AND ROY WILLIAMS
  1973   Stay Where you Were: A Study of Unemployables in Industry. Philadelphia: Lippincott.

PAIGE, JEFFERY M.
  1975   Agrarian Revolution: Social Movements and Export Agriculture in the Underdeveloped World. New York: The Free Press.

PALEY, WILLIAM
   1822   The Principles of Moral and Political Philosophy. London: T. David-
          son, Whitefriars.

PARDUCCI, A.
   1968   "The relativism of absolute judgments." Scientific American 219:84–
          90.

PARETO, VILFREDO
   1935   The Mind and Society, vol. 3. New York: Harcourt, Brace.

PARKE, ROSS
   Forth- Perspectives on Father-Infant Interaction.
   coming

PARKE, ROSS, AND O'LEARY, S. E.
   1976   "Father-mother-infant interaction in the newborn period: Some find-
          ings, some observations, and some unresolved issues." In K. Riegel and
          J. Meacham (eds.), The Developing Individual in a Changing World,
          vol. 2: Social and Environmental Issues. The Hague: Mouton.

PARKIN, FRANK
   1971   Class Inequality and Political Order. New York: Praeger.

PARRISH, B. B. (ed.)
   1973   Fish Stocks and Recruitment, Rapp. et Proces-Verbaux des Reunions.
          Cons. Int. Pour L'Exploration de la Mer, vol. 164. Charlottenlund
          Slut-Danemark.

PARSONS, TALCOTT
   1977   The Evolution of Societies. Englewood Cliffs, N.J.: Prentice-Hall.

PASSEL, PETER
   1975   "The deterrent effect of the death penalty." Stanford Law Review 61
          (November):61–80.

PATTON, M. Q., P. S. GRIMES, K. M. GUTHRIE, N. J. BRENNAN, B. D. FRENCH, AND
D. A. BLYTH
   1977   "In search of impact: An analysis of the utilization of federal health
          evaluation research." Pp. 141–63 in C. H. Weiss (ed.), Using Social
          Research in Public Policy Making. Lexington, Mass.: Heath.

PEABODY, D.
   1967   "Trait inferences: Evaluative and descriptive aspects." Journal of Per-
          sonality and Social Psychology Monograph 7, whole no. 644.

PEASE, JOHN, WILLIAM FORM, AND JOAN HUBER RYTINA
   1970   "Ideological currents in American stratification literature," American
          Sociologist 5 (May):127–37.

PECHMAN, JOSEPH A.
   1971   Federal Tax Policy, rev. ed. Washington, D.C.: The Brookings Institu-
          tion.

PECHMAN, JOSEPH A., AND BENJAMIN A. OKNER
   1974   Who Bears the Tax Burden? Washington, D.C.: The Brookings In-
          stitution.

PEDERSEN, F. A., B. J. ANDERSON, AND R. L. CAIN
1977 "An approach to understanding linkages between the parent-infant and spouse relationships." Paper presented at the meetings of the Society for Research in Child Development, New Orleans (March).

PEDERSEN, F. A., AND K. S. ROBSON
1969 "Father participation in infancy." American Journal of Orthopsychiatry 39:466-72.

PELZ, D. C.
1977 Utilization of Environmental Knowledge on Northern Michigan. Ann Arbor: Institute for Social Research, University of Michigan.

PEN, JAN
1971 Income Distribution: Facts, Theories, Policies. New York: Praeger.

PERELMAN, CHAIM
1967 Justice. New York: Random House.

Perez v. *Sharp*
1948 Supreme Court of California, 32 Cal (2nd series) 711, 198, P. 2d 17.

PERRY, CHARLES
1975 Impact of Manpower Training Programs in General and on Minorities and Women. ETA-ORD-NTIS. Philadelphia: University of Pennsylvania Press.

PETTIGREW, T. F.
1964 A Profile of the Negro American. Princeton, N.J.: Van Nostrand Reinhold.
1967 "Social evaluation theory: Convergences and applications." In D. Levine (ed.), Nebraska Symposium on Motivation: 1967. Lincoln: University of Nebraska Press.
1971 Racially Separate or Together? New York: McGraw-Hill.
1973 "Racism and the mental health of white Americans." Pp. 91-126 in C. Willie, B. M. Kramer, and B. S. Brown (eds.), Racism and Mental Health. Pittsburgh: University of Pittsburgh Press.

PETTIGREW, T. F. (ed.)
1975 Racial Discrimination in the United States. New York: Harper & Row.

PFEIFFER, E. (ed.)
1975 Multidimensional Functional Assessment: The OARS Methodology. Durham, N.C.: Duke University Center for the Study of Aging and Human Development.

PHELPS-BROWN, HENRY
1977 The Inequality of Pay. Oxford: Oxford University Press.

PHETERSON, G. I., S. B. KIESLER, AND P. A. GOLDBERG
1971 "Evaluation of the performance of women as a function of their sex, achievement and personal history." Journal of Personality and Social Psychology 19:114-18.

PINKNEY, ALPHONSO
1976 Red, Black, and Green: Black Nationalism in the United States. Cambridge: Cambridge University Press.

POPE, HALLOWELL, AND N. KRISHNAN NAMBOODIRI
   1968   "Decisions regarding family size: Moral norms and the utility model of social choice." Research Previews 15 (April):6-17.

POPPER, K. R.
   1967   The Open Society and Its Enemies, vol. 2. New York: Harper.

POTTER, ROBERT G.
   1975   "Changes of natural fertility and contraceptive equivalents." Social Forces 54 (September):36-51.

   1977   "Uses of models in evaluating changing effects of conception behavior." In International Union for the Scientific Study of Population, International Population Conference, Mexico, 1:273-85.

PRYOR, FREDERICK L.
   1968   Public Expenditure in Capitalist and Communist Nations. Homewood, Illinois: Irwin.

   1973   Property and Industrial Organization in Communist and Capitalist Nations. Bloomington: Indiana University Press.

RABUSHKA, A., K. A. SHEPSLE
   1972   Politics in Plural Societies: A Theory of Democratic Instability. Columbus, Ohio: Charles E. Merrill.

RADZINOWICZ, LEON
   1957   A History of the English Criminal Law, vol. 3. New York: Macmillan.

   1966   Ideology and Crime. New York: Columbia University Press.

RAGIN, CHARLES
   1977   "Class, status, and 'reactive ethnic cleavages,' the social bases of political regionalism." American Sociological Review 42:438-50.

RAINWATER, LEE
   1966   "Crucible of identity: The Negro lower-class family." Daedalus 95 (Winter):172-216.

   1974   What Money Buys: Inequality and the Social Meaning of Income. New York: Basic Books.

RAPPAPORT, ROY A.
   1967   "Ritual regulation of environmental relations among a New Guinea people." Ethnology 6 (January):17-30.

   1968   Pigs for the Ancestors. New Haven: Yale University Press.

   1969   "Sanctity and adaptation." Paper prepared for Wenner-Gren Conference on the Moral and Aesthetic Structure of Human Adaptation, Burg Wartenstein, Austria. Reprinted in Io no. 9 (1970) and Coevolution Quarterly 1 and 2 (1974).

   1971   "The sacred in human evolution." Annual Review of Ecology and Systematics 2:23-44.

   1976   "Liturgies and lies." Yearbook for the Sociology of Religion and Knowledge 10:75-104.

1978 "Adaptation and the structure of ritual." In V. Reynolds and N. G. Blurton Jones (eds.), Human Behavior and Adaptation. Society for the Study of Human Biology Symposia, vol. 18. London: Taylor and Francis.

REDL, FRITZ, AND DAVID WINEMAN
1951 Children Who Hate. New York: The Free Press.

REGAN, D. T., et al.
1974 "Liking and the attribution process." Journal of Experimental Social Psychology 10:385-97.

REICH, CHARLES A.
1970 The Greening of America. New York: Random House.

REIN, M., AND D. A. SCHON
1977 "Problem setting in policy research." Pp. 235-51 in C. H. Weiss (ed.), Using Social Research in Public Policy Making. Lexington, Mass.: Heath.

REPORT OF FEDERAL RESERVE CONSULTANT COMMITTEE ON CONSUMER SURVEY STATISTICS
1955 (Smithies Committee). Washington, D.C.: Government Printing Office.

REUBENS, BEATRICE
1970 The Hard-To-Employ: European Programs. New York: Columbia University Press.

REYNAUD, JEAN-DANIEL
1975 "Trade unions and political parties in France: Some recent trends." Industrial and Labor Relations Review 28 (January):208-25.

RICH, R. F.
1977 "Selective utilization of social science related information by Federal policy-makers." Inquiry 13 (September):239-45.

RICH, R. F., AND N. CAPLAN
1976 "Instrumental and conceptual uses of social science knowledge and perspectives: Means/ends matching versus understanding." Paper delivered at the OECD Conference on Dissemination of Economic and Social Development Research Results, Bogotá, Columbia, June.

RICHMOND, A. H.
1974 "Language, ethnicity and the problem of identity in a Canadian metropolis." Ethnicity 1:175-206.

RIESMAN, DAVID (WITH NATHAN GLAZER AND REUEL DENNEY)
1958 The Lonely Crowd: A Study of the Changing American Character. New Haven: Yale University Press.

RILEY, M. W., M. E. JOHNSON, AND A. FONER
1972 Aging and Society, III: A Sociology of Age Stratification. New York: Russell Sage Foundation.

RIMLINGER, GASTON
1971 Welfare Policy and Industrialization in Europe, America, and Russia. New York: Wiley.

RIVLIN, ALICE
1971   Systematic Thinking for Social Action. Washington, D.C.: The Brookings Institution.

ROBBINS, THOMAS, AND DICK ANTHONY
1972   "Getting straight with Meher Baba: A study of mysticism, drug rehabilitation and postadolescent role conflict." Journal for the Scientific Study of Religion 11:122-40.

ROGERS, EVERETT M., WITH F. FLOYD SHOEMAKER
1971   Communication of Innovations: A Cross-Cultural Appraisal, 2d ed. New York: The Free Press.

ROGERS, PAUL (ed.)
1976   Future Resources and World Development. New York and London: Plenum Press.

ROKEACH, MILTON
1967   "Attitude change and behavior change." Public Opinion Quarterly 30:529-50.

1969   Beliefs, Attitudes, and Values. San Francisco: Jossey-Bass.

1973   Nature of Human Values. New York: The Free Press.

ROKEACH, MILTON, AND L. MEZEI
1966   "Race and shared belief as factors in social choice." Science 151:167-72.

ROOM, ROBIN
1976   "Ambivalence as a sociological explanation: The case of cultural explanations of alcohol problems." American Sociological Review 41:1047-65.

ROSALDO, M. Z., AND L. LAMPHERE (eds.)
1974   Women, Culture, and Society: A Theoretical Overview. Stanford, California: Stanford University Press.

ROSEN, B. C., AND R. C. D'ANDRADE
1959   "The psychosocial origins of achievement motivation." Sociometry 22:185-218.

ROSS, HEATHER, AND ISABEL SAWHILL
1975   Time of Transition: The Growth of Families Headed by Women. Washington, D.C.: Urban Institute.

ROSS, L. D.
1977   "The intuitive psychologist and his shortcomings: Distortions in the attribution process." In L. Berkowitz (ed.), Advances in Experimental Social Psychology 10. New York: Academic Press.

ROSS, L. D., T. M. AMABILE, AND J. L. STEINMETZ
1977   "Social roles, social control, and biases in social-perception processes." Journal of Personality and Social Psychology 35:485-94.

ROSSI, PETER, AND KATHERINE LYALL
1977   Reforming Public Welfare: A Critique of the Negative Income Tax Experiment. New York: Russell Sage Foundation.

ROSZAK, THEODORE
1969   The Making of a Counter Culture. Garden City, N.Y.: Doubleday.

1973   Where the Wasteland Ends: Politics and Transcendence in Postindustrial Society. Garden City, N.Y.: Doubleday.

ROTHBART, M., S. FULERO, C. JENSEN, J. HOWARD, AND P. BIRRELL
Fortn-   "From individual to group impressions: Availability heuristics in stercoming |eotype formation." Journal of Experimental Social Psychology.

ROTHCHILD, JOHN, AND SUSAN BERNS WOLF
1976   The Children of the Counter-Culture. Garden City, N.Y.: Doubleday.

ROTHSCHILD, KURT W.
1971   Power in Economics. London: Penguin.

ROYAL COMMISSION
1975   Distribution of Income and Wealth, Report #1. London: HMSO.

ROYAL COMMISSION ON CAPITAL PUNISHMENT
1953   Report. London: HMSO.

RUNCIMAN, WALTER G.
1966   Relative Deprivation and Social Justice. London: Routledge and Kegan Paul.

RUSSELL, D. E. H.
1974   Rebellion, Revolution, and Armed Force. New York: Academic Press.

RYAN, SELWYN D.
1972   Race and Nationalism in Trinidad and Tobago: A Study of Decolonialization in a Multiracial Society. Toronto: University of Toronto Press.

RYS, VLADIMIR
1966   "Comparative studies of social security: Problems and perspectives." Bulletin of the International Social Security Association (July/August):242-68.

SAHLINS, MARSHALL
1976   The Use and Abuse of Biology: An Anthropological Critique of Sociobiology. Ann Arbor: University of Michigan Press.

SAHLINS, MARSHALL, AND ELMAN SERVICE (eds.)
1960   Evolution and Culture. Ann Arbor: University of Michigan Press.

SAMUELSON, PAUL
1964   "A brief survey of post-Keynesian development." In R. Lekachman (ed.), Keynes' General Theory: Reports of Three Decades. New York: St. Martin's Press.

SARGENT, THOMAS, AND NEIL WALLACE
1976   "Rational expectations and theory of economic policy." Journal of Monetary Economics (April):169-84.

SCARISBRICK, J. J.
1968   Henry VIII. Berkeley: University of California Press.

SCHACHT, RICHARD
1970   Alienation. Garden City, N.Y.: Doubleday.

SCHACHTER, S.
1959   The Psychology of Affiliation. Stanford, California: Stanford University Press.

SCHERMERHORN, R. A.
   1970   Comparative Ethnic Relations: A Framework for Theory and Re-
          search. New York: Random House.

SCHEWE, DIETER, KARLHUGO NORDHORN, AND KLAUS SCHENKE
   1972   Survey of Social Security in the Federal Republic of Germany. Trans.
          Frank Kenny. Bonn: Federal Minister for Labour and Social Affairs.

SCHIFFMAN, H., AND R. WYNNE
   1963   Cause and Affect. Princeton: Educational Testing Service, RM-63-7.

SCHILLER, BRADLEY R.
   1973   The Economics of Poverty and Discrimination. Englewood Cliffs, N.J.:
          Prentice Hall.

SCHNEIDER, D. J.
   1976   Social Psychology. Reading, Mass.: Addison-Wesley.

SCHNEIDER, HAROLD K.
   1974   Economic Man: The Anthropology of Economics. New York: The Free
          Press.

SCHNEIDER, W., AND R. M. SHIFFRIN
   1977   "Controlled and automatic human information processing: I. Detec-
          tion, search, and attention." Psychological Review 84:1-66.

SCHOEN, ROBERT, AND WILLIAM URTON
   1977   "Marriage, divorce, and mortality: The Swedish experience." Proceed-
          ings of the International Union for the Scientific Study of Population.

SCHOOLER, D.
   1972   "Birth order effects: Not here, not now!" Psychology Bulletin 78:161-
          75.

SCHUESSLER, KARL
   1952   "The deterrent influence of the death penalty." Annals of the Ameri-
          can Academy of Political and Social Science 284 (November):54-62.

SCHULTZ, THEODORE W.
   1961   "Investment in human capital." American Economic Review 51:1-17.

SCHULTZ, THEODORE W. (ed.)
   1974   Economics of the Family: Marriage, Children and Human Capital.
          Chicago and London: University of Chicago Press for National Bureau
          of Economic Research.

SCHULZ, JAMES, GUY CARRIN, HANS KRUPP, MANFRED PESCHKE, ELLIOTT SCLAR,
AND J. VAN STEENBERGE
   1974   Providing Adequate Retirement Income: Pension Reform in the
          United States and Abroad. Hanover, Mass.: University Press of New
          England.

SCHULZ, WILLIAM, AND LOWELL HARRISS
   1959   American Public Finance, 7th ed. Englewood Cliffs: Prentice-Hall.

SCHUMAN, HOWARD, AND MICHAEL P. JOHNSON
   1976   "Attitudes and behavior." Pp. 161-207 in Alex Inkeles (ed.), Annual
          Review of Sociology. Palo Alto, California: Annual Reviews.

SCHWENDINGER, H., AND J. SCHWENDINGER
1975 "Defenders of order or guardians of human rights?" In I. Taylor et al. (eds.), Critical Criminology. London: Routledge and Kegan Paul.

SCOTT, HILDA
1974 Does Socialism Liberate Women? Experiences from Eastern Europe. Boston: Beacon.

SCOTT, ROBERT A.
1969 The Making of Blind Men. New York: Russell Sage Foundation.

Scott v. *State*
1869 39Ga.

SEARS, PAUL B.
1975 "Environmental equilibrium and the quality of life." Pp. 212–28 in William R. Burch, Jr., and Herbert Bormann (eds.), Beyond Growth: Essays on Alternative Futures. New Haven: Yale University School of Forestry and Environmental Studies Bulletin No. 88.

SEEMAN, MELVIN
1959 "On the meaning of alienation." American Sociological Review 24 (December):783–91.
1972 "Alienation and engagement." Pp. 467–527 in A. Campbell and P. E. Converse (eds.), The Human Meaning of Social Change. New York: Russell Sage Foundation.
1975 "Alienation studies." Pp. 91–123 in Alex Inkeles (ed.), Annual Review of Sociology, vol. I. Palo Alto, California: Annual Reviews.

SELLIN, THORSTEN
1959 The Death Penalty. Philadelphia: The American Law Institute.
1961 "Capital punishment." Federal Probation 25 (September):3–11.

SELLIN, THORSTEN (ed.)
1967 Capital Punishment. New York: Harper & Row.

SELZNICK, PHILIP S.
1969 Law, Society, and Industrial Justice. New York: Russell Sage Foundation.

SERVICE, ELMAN
1962 Primitive Social Organization: An Evolutionary Perspective. New York: Random House.

SEWELL, WILLIAM H., AND ROBERT M. HAUSER
1974 Education, Occupation, and Earnings: Achievement in the Early Career. New York: Academic Press.

SEXTON, PATRICIA CAYO
1977 Women and Work. R & D Monograph 46. Washington, D.C.: Department of Labor.

SHANAS, ETHEL G., ET AL.
1968 Old People in Three Industrial Societies. New York: Atherton.

SHANAS, E., AND G. L. MADDOX
1976 "Aging, health and the organization of health resources." In R.

Binstock and E. Shanas (eds.), Handbook of Aging and the Social Sciences. Princeton, N.J.: Van Nostrand Reinhold.

SHAPIRO, HAROLD T.
1972 "The index of consumer sentiment and economic forecasting: A reappraisal." In Katona Festshcirft: 373–96.

SHEPPARD, HAROLD L., AND A. HARVEY BELITSKY
1966 The Job-Hunt: Jobseeking Behavior of Unemployed Workers in a Local Economy. Upjohn Institute for Employment Research. Baltimore: Johns Hopkins Press.

SHERIF, MUZAFER, AND CAROLYN W. SHERIF
1964 Reference Groups: Exploration into Conformity and Deviation of Adolescents. New York: Haprer & Row.
1967 Social Interaction: Process and Products. Chicago: Aldine.

SHIFFRIN, R. M., AND W. SCHNEIDER
1977 "Controlled and automatic human information processing: II. Perceptual learning, automatic attending, and a general theory." Psychological Review 84:127–90.

SIEGEL, J. S., AND W. E. O'LEARY
1973 "Some demographic aspects of aging in the United States." Current Population Reports, Series P. 23:43.

SIEGENTHALER, JÜRG
1975 "Current problems of trade-union party relations in Switzerland: Reorientation versus inertia." Industrial and Labour Relations Review 28 (January):264–81.

SILK, LEONARD
1975 "Market versus state." New York Times, February 19, 1975.

SINGER, S. FRED (ed.)
1971 Is There an Optimum Level of Population? New York: McGraw-Hill.

SKOLNICK, JEROME H.
1969 The Politics of Protest: A Task Force Report Submitted to the National Commission on the Causes and Prevention of Violence. New York: Simon and Schuster.

SLATER, PHILIP
1971 The Pursuit of Loneliness: American Culture at the Breaking Point. Boston: Beacon.

SLOBODKIN, LAWRENCE
1972 "On the inconstancy of ecological efficiency and the form of ecological theories. Pp. 291–306 in E. S. Deevey (ed.), Growth by Intussusception: Ecological Essays in Honor of G. Evelyn Hutchinson. Trans. Conn. Acad. Arts and Sciences, vol. 44.
1977 "Problems on the border between biological and social sciences." Michigan Discussions in Anthropology 2:124–37.

SLOBODKIN, LAWRENCE B., AND ANATOL RAPOPORT
1974 "An optimal strategy of evolution." Quarterly Review of Biology 49 (September):181–200.

SMELSER, NEIL J.
1963   Theory of Collective Behavior. New York: The Free Press.

SMITH, ADAM
1976   Powers of Mind. New York: Random House.

SMITH, ADAM
1777   The Theory of Moral Sentiments, 6th ed. Dublin: Printed for J. Beatty and C. Jackson.

1896   Lectures on Justice, Police, Revenue, and Arms. Edited by Edwin Cannan. Oxford: Clarendon Press.

1939   An Inquiry into the Nature and Causes of the Wealth of Nations. New York: Modern Library.

SMITH, DAVID H., AND ALEX INKELES
1966   "The OM scale: A comparative socio-psychological measure of individual modernity." Sociometry 29 (December):353–77.

SNYDER, M., AND W. B. SWANN
Forth-   "Behavioral confirmation in social interaction: From social perception
coming   to social reality." Journal of Experimental Social Psychology.

SOLTOW, LEE
1975   Men and Wealth in the U.S., 1850–1870. New Haven: Yale University Press.

SOLZHENITSYN, A. I.
1975   "Words of warning to America." U.S. News & World Report 79 (July 14):44–50.

SPATES, JAMES L.
1976   "Counterculture and dominant culture values: A cross-national analysis of the underground press and dominant culture magazines." American Sociological Review 41:868–83.

SPATES, JAMES L., AND JACK LEVIN
1972   "Beats, hippies, the hip generation and the American middle class: an analysis of values." International Social Science Journal 24:326–53.

SPECTOR, A. J.
1956   "Expectations, fulfillment, and morale." Journal of Abnormal and Social Psychology 52:51–56.

SPIRO, MELFORD E.
1970   Kibbutz: Venture in Utopia, 2d ed. New York: Schocken Books.

STANFORD EVALUATION CONSORTIUM
1976   "Review essays: Evaluation of the Handbook of Evaluation Research." In G. V. Glass (ed.), Evaluation Studies, I. Beverly Hills, California: Sage.

STARK, WERNER
1967   The Sociology of Religion: A Study of Christendom, vol. 2. New York: Fordham University Press.

STARR, JEROLD M.
1974   "The peace and love generation: Changing attitudes toward sex and violence among college youth." Journal of Social Issues 30:73–106.

State v. *Hariston*
1869   63 N. C. 451.

STEIN, BRUNO
1976   Work and Welfare in Britain and the U.S.A. New York: Wiley, Halstead Press.

STEIN, HOWARD F., AND ROBERT F. HILL
1973   "The new ethnicity and the white ethnic in the United States: An exploration in the psycho-cultural genesis of ethnic irredentism." Canadian Review of Studies in Nationalism 1:81–105.

STEPHAN, G. EDWARD
1970   "The concept of community in human ecology." Pacific Sociological Review 13 (Fall):218–28.

STEPHEN, JAMES FITZJAMES
1883   A History of the Criminal Law of England, 3 vols. London: Macmillan.

STERN, E., AND S. KELLER
1953   "Spontaneous group reference in France." Public Opinion Quarterly 17:208–17.

STEVENS, S. S.
1966   "A metric for the social consensus." Science 151 (February)530–41.

STIGLER, GEORGE J.
1965   Essays in the History of Economics. Chicago: University of Chicago Press.

STIGLER, GEORGE J., AND GARY S. BECKER
1977   "De gustibus non est disputandum." American Economic Review 67, no. 2 (March):76–90.

STORMS, M. D.
1973   "Videotape and the attribution process: Reversing actors' and observers' points of view." Journal of Personality and Social Psychology 27:165–75.

STRODBECK, FRED
1958   "Family interaction, values, and achievement." Pp. 135–94 in David C. McClelland (ed.), Talent and Society: New Perspectives on the Identification of Talent. Princeton, N.J.: Van Nostrand Reinhold.

STRYKER, S.
1977   "Development in 'two social psychologies': Toward an appreciation of mutual relevance." Sociometry 40:145–60.

STRUENING, E. L., AND M. GUTTENTAG (eds.)
1975   Handbook of Evaluation Research, I. Beverly Hills, California: Sage.

SUMNER, W. G.
1906   Folkways. New York: Ginn.

SUSSMAN, MARVIN B.
1959   "The isolated nuclear family: Fact or fiction?" Social Problems 6:333–40.
1963   "Parental aid to married children: Implications for family functioning." Marriage and Family Living 24:320–32.

1976 "The family life of old people." Pp. 218–43 in Robert H. Binstock and Ethel Shanas (eds.), Handbook of Aging and the Social Sciences. Princeton, N.J.: Van Nostrand Reinhold.

SUTHERLAND, EDWIN H.
1973 "Murder and the death penalty." In Karl Schuessler (ed.), Edwin H. Sutherland on Analyzing Crime. Chicago: University of Chicago Press. Reprinted from Journal of Criminal Law and Criminology 15 (1925).

SUZMAN, RICHARD M.
1973 "Psychological modernity." International Journal of Comparative Sociology 14 (September–December):273–87.

TABBARAH, RIAD B.
1971 "Toward a theory of demographic development." Economic Development and Cultural Change 19, no. 2 (January):257–77.

TAEUBER, IRENE B.
1960 "Japan's demographic transition re-examined." Population Studies 14 (July):28–39.

TAIRA, KOJI, AND PETER KILBY
1969 "Differences in social security development in selected countries." International Social Security Review 2:139–53.

TAJFEL, H.
1969 "Cognitive aspects of prejudice." Journal of Social Issues 25:79–97.

TANNENBAUM, ARNOLD S., et al.
1974 Hierarchy in Organizations. San Francisco: Jossey-Bass.

TARDE, GABRIEL
1912 Penal Philosophy. Boston: Little, Brown.

TAYLOR, I., et al.
1973 The New Criminology. London: Routledge and Kegan Paul.

TAYLOR, S. E.
Forth- "The token in the small group: Research findings and theoretical
coming implications." In J. Sweeney (ed.), Psychology and Politics. New Haven, Conn.: Yale University Press.

TAYLOR, S. E., AND S. T. FISKE
1975 "Point of view and perceptions of causality." Journal of Personality and Social Psychology 32:439–45.
1977 "Salience, attention, and attribution: Top of the head phenomena." Unpublished manuscript. Harvard University.

TAYLOR, S. E., S. T. FISKE, M. M. CLOSE, C. E. ANDERSON, AND A. J. RUDERMAN
1976 "Solo status as a psychological variable: The power of being distinctive." Unpublished manuscript. Harvard University.

TAYLOR, S. E., AND J. H. KOIVUMAKI
1976 "The perception of self and others: Acquaintanceship, affect, and actor-observer differences." Journal of Personality and Social Psychology 33:408–8.

TAYNOR, J., AND K. DEAUX
1973 "When women are more deserving than men: Equity, attribution and

perceived sex differences." Journal of Personality and Social Psychology 28:360–67.

TEICH, ALBERT H. (ed.)
1977   Technology and Man's Future, 2d ed. New York: St. Martin's Press.

TEMIN, PETER
1966   "Labor scarcity and the problem of American industrial efficiency in the 1850's." Journal of Economic History 26:277–98.

TENENBAUM, SUSAN
1977   "Work and welfare: None of this is anti-feminist?" Women's Washington Representative 2 (12 June):1–2.

THIBAUT, J. W., AND H. RIECKEN
1955   "Some determinants and consequences of the perception of social causality." Journal of Personality 25:115–29.

THOMPSON, WARREN S.
1935   Population Problems, 2d ed. New York: McGraw-Hill.
1942   3d ed.
1953   4th ed.
1965   5th ed., with David T. Lewis.

THORELLI, HANS B.
1955   The Federal Antitrust Policy. Baltimore: Johns Hopkins Press.

THUROW, LESTER C.
1975   Generating Inequality: Mechanisms of Distribution in the U.S. Economy. New York: Basic Books.

TILLY, C., L. TILLY, AND R. TILLY
1975   The Rebellious Century, 1830–1930. Cambridge, Mass.: Harvard University Press.

TINBERGEN, JAN
1975   Income Distribution: Analysis and Policies. Amsterdam: North-Holland.

TIRYAKIAN, EDWARD A.
1972   "Toward the sociology of esoteric culture." American Journal of Sociology 78:491–512.
1974   On the Margin of the Visible: Sociology, the Esoteric, and the Occult. New York: Wiley.

TITMUSS, RICHARD
1969   "New guardians of the poor in Britain." Pp. 151–70 in Shirley Jenkins (ed.), Social Security in International Perspective. New York: Columbia University Press.
1962   Income Distribution and Social Change. Toronto: University of Toronto Press.

TITTLE, CHARLES R., AND CHARLES H. LOGAN
1973   "Sanctions and deviance." Law and Society Review 7 (Spring):371–92.

TOBIN, JAMES
1959 "On the predictive value of consumer intentions and attitudes." Review of Economics and Statistics 41 (August):1-11.

TOSH, PETER
1977 Equal Rights. New York: Columbia Records, Columbia Broadcasting System.

TRAIN, RUSSELL E.
1972 "The quest for environmental indices." Science 178 (13 October):121.

TRILLING, LIONEL
1966 Beyond Culture: Essays on Literature and Learning. London: Secker and Warburg.

TRIVERS, R. L., AND H. HARE
1976 "Haplodiploidy and the evolution of the social insects." Science 191:249-63.

TRUELOVE, ALAN
1964 A Multi-stage Investment Process. RM-4025. Santa Monica, California: The Rand Corporation.

TURNBULL, COLIN
1962 The Forest People. New York: Natural History Press.

1972 The Mountain People. New York: Simon and Schuster.

TURNBULL, JOHN, ARTHUR WILLIAMS, AND EARL CHEIT
1973 Economic and Social Security, 4th ed. New York: Ronald Press.

TURNER, RALPH H.
1951 "The relative position of Negro males in the labor force of large American cities." American Sociological Review 16:524-29.

1970 "Determinants of social movement strategies." Pp. 145-64 in Tamotsu Shibutani (ed.), Human Nature and Collective Behavior: Papers in Honor of Herbert Blumer. Englewood Cliffs, N.J.: Prentice-Hall.

TURNER, RALPH H., AND LEWIS M. KILLIAN
1957 Collective Behavior. Englewood Cliffs, N.J.: Prentice-Hall.

TURNER, VICTOR W.
1974 Dramas, Fields, and Metaphors. Ithaca, N.Y.: Cornell University Press.

TVERSKY, A., AND D. KAHNEMAN
1974 "Judgment under uncertainty: Heuristics and biases." Science 185:1124-31.

UHLENBERG, PETER
1974 "Cohort variations in family life cycle experiences of U.S. females." Journal of Marriage and the Family 34:284-92.

1978 "Changing configurations of the life course." In Tamara K. Hareven (ed.), Family Transitions and the Life Course in Historical Perspective. New York: Academic Press.

ULMAN, LLOYD, AND ROBERT J. FLANAGAN
1971 Wage Restraint: A Study of Income Policies in Western Europe. Berkeley: University of California Press.

UNITED STATES BUREAU OF THE CENSUS

1959 Quarterly Survey of Consumer Buying Intentions. Washington: Government Printing Office.

1966 "Income Distribution in the U.S." by H. P. Miller (a 1960 census monograph). Washington, D.C.: Government Printing Office.

1969 Current Population Reports, Consumer Buying Indicators, Series P-65, No. 27 (August 22).

1976 "Persons of Spanish origin in the United States, March 1975." Current Population Reports. Series P. 20, No. 290. Washington, D.C.: Government Printing Office.

UNITED STATES BUREAU OF LABOR STATISTICS

1970 Bulletin 1657: Youth Unemployment and Minimum Wages.

UNITED STATES COMMISSION ON CIVIL RIGHTS

1974 Women and Poverty. Washington, D.C.: Government Printing Office.

UNITED STATES DEPARTMENT OF JUSTICE, BUREAU OF PRISONS

1954 Federal Prisons, 1953. Leavenworth: U.S. Penitentiary.

1966 "Executions 1930–1965." National Prisoner Statistics, no. 39 (June).

UNITED STATES DEPARTMENT OF LABOR

Forth- "Labor force participation rates adjusted to United States concepts,
coming nine countries, 1960–1976."

UNITED STATES HOUSE OF REPRESENTATIVES, COMMITTEE ON GOVERNMENT OPERATIONS, RESEARCH AND TECHNICAL PROGRAMS SUBCOMMITTEE.

1967 The Use of Social Research in Federal Domestic Programs, 4 vols. Washington, D.C.: Government Printing Office.

UNITED STATES HOUSE OF REPRESENTATIVES, COMMITTEE ON THE JUDICIARY

1972 Capital Punishment Hearings (serial no. 29). Washington, D.C.: Government Printing Office.

VAN DEN BERGHE, PIERRE L.

1967 Race and Racism: A Comparative Perspective. New York: Wiley.

1975 Man in Society: A Biosocial View. New York: Elsevier.

VANNEMAN, R. D., AND T. F. PETTIGREW

1972 "Race and relative deprivation in the urban United States." Race 13:461–86.

VELDKAMP, GÉRARD

1973 "The coherence of social security policy." International Labour Review 108 (November):357–70.

WACHTER, MICHAEL L.

1972 "Government policy towards the fertility of the poor." Fels Center of Government Discussion Paper no. 19, July.

1975 "A time series fertility equation: The potential for a baby boom in the 1980's." International Economic Review 16 (October):609–24.

WAGAR, J. ALAN

1970 "Growth versus the quality of life." Science 168 (5 June):1179–84.

WALLACE, ANTHONY F. C.
1966　Religion: An Anthropological View. New York: Random House.

WALLERSTEIN, IMMANUEL
1974　The Modern World-System: Capitalist Agriculture and the Origins of the European World-Economy in the Sixteenth Century. New York: Academic Press.

Wall Street Journal
1977　Editorial, June 20.

WALSTER, E., E. BERSCHEID, AND G. W. Walster
1973　"New directions in equity research." Journal of Personality and Social Psychology 25:151–76.

WARNER, WILLIAM LLOYD
1941–59　The Yankee City Series, vol. 1. New Haven: Yale University Press.

WARNER, WILLIAM LLOYD, ROBERT HAVIGHURST, AND MARTIN B. LOEB
1944　Who Shall Be Educated? The Challenge of Unique Opportunity. New York and London: Harper and Brothers.

WARNER, WILLIAM LLOYD, AND LEO SROLE
1945　The Social Systems of American Ethnic Groups. New Haven: Yale University Press.

WATSON, J.
1977　"Who attends prepared childbirth classes? A demographic study of CEA classes in Rhode Island." Journal of Obstetrical, Gynecologic and Neonatal Nursing 6:36–39.

WATTENBERG, BEN J.
1974　The Real America: A Surprising Examination of the State of the Union, rev. ed. New York: Putnam.

WEBER, MAX
1946　From Max Weber, Hans Gerth and C. Wright Mills, eds. New York: Oxford University Press.
1963　The Sociology of Religion. Boston: Beacon.

WEIGEL, RUSSELL H., AND LEE S. NEWMAN
1976　"Attitude-behavior correspondence by broadening the scope of the behavioral measure." Journal of Personality and Social Psychology 33:793–802.

WEINER, MYRON (ed.)
1966　Modernization: The Dynamics of Growth. New York: Basic Books.

WEINFELD, M.
1977　"Determinants of ethnic identification of Jews, Slavs, and Italians in Toronto: The assimilationist model. Unpublished manuscript. Harvard University.

WEISS, C. H. (ed.)
1977　Using Social Research in Public Policy Making. Lexington, Mass.: Heath.

WEISS, C. H., AND M. J. BUCUVALAS
1977 "The challenge of social research to decision making." Pp. 213-33 in C. H. Weiss (ed.), Using Social Research in Public Policy Making. Lexington, Mass.: Heath.

WEISSKOPF, THOMAS E.
1972 "Capitalism and inequality." Pp. 125-33 in Richard C. Edwards, M. Reich, and T. E. Weisskopf (eds.), The Capitalist System: A Radical Analysis of American Society. Englewood Cliffs, N.J.: Prentice-Hall.

WELLER, LEONARD
1974 Sociology in Israel. Westport, Conn.: Greenwood Press.

WELLISCH, KAREN
1977 "Washington report: Welfare: The non-decision." Spokeswoman 7 (June 15):6-7.

WESTHUES, KENNETH
1972 Society's Shadow: Studies in the Sociology of Countercultures. Toronto: McGraw-Hill Ryerson.

WESTIN, RICHARD B.
1975 "Empirical implications of infrequent purchase behavior in a stock adjustment model." American Economic Review (June):384-96.

WHITE, BURTON, AND JEAN CAREW
1973 Experience and Environment. Englewood Cliffs, N.J.: Prentice-Hall.

WHITE, LESLIE
1949 The Science of Culture. New York: Farrar, Strauss.

WHITEHEAD, ALFRED N.
1925 Science and the Modern World. New York: Macmillan.

WHITING, B., AND C. P. EDWARDS (ed.)
n.d. Sex Differences and Modernization: A Comparative Study of Children's Behavior.

WHITING, B., AND J. W. M. WHITING
1975 Children of Six Cultures: A Psychocultural Analysis. Boston: Harvard University Press.

WHITING, B., J. W. M. WHITING, AND J. HERZOG (eds.)
n.d. Social Change in the Village of Ngecha, Kenya.

WHITING, J. W. M.
1964 "Effects of climate on certain cultural practices." In W. Goodenough (ed.), Explorations in Cultural Anthropology. New York: McGraw-Hill.
1971 "Causes and consequences of body contact." Paper presented at annual meeting of the American Anthropological Association.

WHITTAKER, ROBERT H.
1975 Communities and Ecosystems, 2d ed. New York: Macmillan.

WICKER, ALLAN W.
1969 "Attitudes vs. actions: The relationship of verbal and overt responses to attitude objects." Journal of Social Issues 25, no. 4:41-78.

WIEDER, D. LAWRENCE, AND DON H. ZIMMERMAN
1974 "Generational experience and the development of freak culture." Journal of Social Issues 30:137–61.

WIGGINS, J. W.
1973 Personality and Prediction: Principles of Personality Assessment. Reading, Mass.: Addison-Wesley.

WILENSKY, HAROLD L.
1962 "Labor and leisure: Intellectual traditions." Industrial Relations 1 (February):1–12.

1964a "Mass society and mass culture: Interdependence or independence." American Sociological Review 29 (April):173–97.

1964b "Varieties of work experience." Pp. 125–54 in Henry Borow (ed.), Man in a World at Work. Boston: Houghton Mifflin.

1967 "Careers, counseling, and the curriculum." Journal of Human Resources 2 (Winter):19–40.

1975a The Welfare State and Equality: Structural and Ideological Roots of Public Expenditures. Berkeley: University of California Press.

1975b "The 'welfare mess.'" Unpublished manuscript.

1976 "The 'new corporatism,' centralization, and the welfare state." In Professional Papers in Contemporary Political Sociology. Beverly Hills, California: Sage.

WILENSKY, HAROLD L., AND CHARLES N. LEBEAUX
1965 Industrial Society and Social Welfare. New York: Russell Sage Foundation, 1958; enl. paperbound ed., New York: The Free Press–Macmillan.

WILES, P. J. D.
1962 The Political Economy of Communism. Cambridge: Harvard University Press.

1974 Distribution of Income: East and West. New York: Elsevier.

WILLIAMS, COLIN H.
1976 "Cultural nationalism in Wales." Canadian Review of Studies in Nationalism 4:15–37.

WILLIAMS, RAYMOND
1976 Keywords: A Vocabulary of Culture and Society. New York: Oxford University Press.

WILLIAMS, ROBIN M., JR.
1968 "The concept of values." In David M. Sills (ed.), International Encyclopedia of the Social Sciences. New York: The Free Press.

1969 "Sociology and social change in the United States." Pp. 151–61 in Irving L. Horowitz (ed.), Studies in Comparative International Development. Beverly Hills, California: Sage.

1970 American Society. New York: Knopf.

1972 "Conflict and social order: A research strategy for complex propositions." Journal of Social Issues 28:11–26.

1975a "Race and ethnic relations." Pp. 125–64 in A. Inkeles, N. Smelser, and J. S. Coleman (eds.), Annual Review of Sociology, vol. 1. Palo Alto, California: Annual Reviews.

1975b "Relative deprivation." Pp. 355–78 in Lewis Coser (ed.), The Idea of Social Structure: Papers in Honor of Robert K. Merton. New York: Harcourt, Brace.

1976 "Relative deprivation versus power struggle? 'Tension and structural' explanations of collective conflict." Cornell Journal of Social Relations 11:31–38.

WILSON, E. O.
1971 The Insect Societies. Cambridge, Mass.: Belknap Press.

1975 Sociobiology: The New Synthesis. Cambridge, Mass.: Belknap Press.

1977 "Biology and the social sciences." Daedalus 106:127–40.

WILSON, EVERETT K.
1971 Sociology: Rules, Roles and Relationships, rev. ed. Homewood, Illinois: Dorsey Press.

WINTERBOTTOM, M.
1958 "The relations of need for achievement to learning experiences in independence and mastery." In J. W. Atkinson (ed.), Motives in Fantasy, Action and Society. Princeton, N.J.: Van Nostrand Reinhold.

WRIGHT, ERIK O., AND LUCA PERRONE
1977 "Marxist class categories and income inequality." American Sociological Review 42 (February):32–55.

WUTHNOW, ROBERT
1976a "Astrology and marginality." Journal for the Scientific Study of Religion 15:157–68.

1976b The Consciousness Reformation. Berkeley: University of California Press.

YABLONSKY, LEWIS
1968 The Hippie Trip. New York: Pegasus.

YANKAUER, A.
1958 Pregnancy, Childbirth, the Neonatal Period and Expectant Parent Classes. Albany, N.Y.: Bureau of Maternal and Child Health, New York State Department of Health.

YANKELOVICH, DANIEL
1974 The New Morality: A Profile of American Youth in the 70's. New York: McGraw-Hill.

YINGER, J. MILTON
1960 "Contraculture and subculture." American Sociological Review 25:625–35.

1965 Toward a Field Theory of Behavior. New York: McGraw-Hill.

1973 "Anomie, alienation, and political behavior." Pp. 171–202 in Jeanne Knutson (ed.), Handbook of Political Psychology. San Francisco: Jossey-Bass.

1976   "Ethnicity in complex societies: Structural, cultural and characterological factors." Pp. 197–216 in L. A. Coser and O. N. Larsen (eds.), The Uses of Controversy in Sociology. New York: The Free Press.

1977   "A comparative study of the substructures of religion." Journal for the Scientific Study of Religion 16 (March):67–86.

YOUNG, MICHAEL (ed.)
1975   Poverty Report 1975. London: Temple Smith.

ZAJONC, ROBERT, AND G. B. MARKUS
1975   "Birth order and intellectual development." Psychology Review 82:74–88.

ZARETSKY, IRVING I., AND MARK P. LEONE
1974   Religious Movements in Contemporary America. Princeton, N.J.: Princeton University Press.

ZUBROW, EZRA B. W.
1971   "Carrying capacity and dynamic equilibrium in the prehistoric Southwest." American Antiquity 36 (April):127–38.

1975   Prehistoric Carrying Capacity: A Model. Menlo Park, California: Cummings Publishing Company.

Name Index

Newman, Lee S., 373
Newman, Oscar, 281
Nicholson, A. J., 243
Nietzsche, Friedrich, 425, 437, 438, 484, 489
Nikolsky, G. V., 259
Nisbet, Robert A., 480
Nisbett, R. E., 43
Nixon, Richard, 163, 365
Norbeck, Edward, 488
Nordhorn, Karlhugo, 118
Norton, Arthur J., 339
Nowell-Smith, P. H., 170
Nydegger, Corinne, 217
Nydegger, William, 217

Oaten, A., 255
Odum, Eugene P., 234
Ogburn, William F., 236
Okner, Benjamin A., 106, 128
O'Leary, S. E., 202
O'Leary, W. E., 324
Ornati, Oscar, 118
Ortega y Gasset, José, 162
Osgood, C. E., 161
Osmond, Marie Withers, 121
Ovesey, Lionel, 15
Owen, C. R., 223

Packer, Arnold, 125
Padfield, Harland, 90
Paige, Jeffery M., 59, 443
Paley, William, 173, 174
Palmer, John, 116
Pao, Joe, 447, 450
Parducci, A., 47
Pareto, Vilfredo, 175, 177, 484
Parke, Ross, 201, 202
Parkin, Frank, 52
Parks, I. S. C., 251
Parrish, B. B., 254
Parsons, Talcott, 247
Passel, Peter, 188
Pasteur, L., 176
Patton, Michel Q., 346, 350, 351
Peabody, D., 384
Pease, John, 110
Pechman, Joseph A., 106, 124, 128

Pederson, F. A., 202, 212
Pelz, Donald C., 322, 346, 353
Pen, Jan, 90, 94, 111
Perelman, C., 170
Perk, Ralph, 34
Perrone, Luca, 98
Perry, Charles, 122
Pettigrew, Thomas Fraser, 4, 5, 25, 29, 32–36, 46, 56, 71–76, 78, 80, 81
Pfeiffer, E., 329, 332, 334
Phelps-Brown, Henry, 90, 93, 94, 98, 99, 101, 103, 104
Pheterson, G. I., 47
Pinkney, Alphonso, 58
Polansky, N., 440
Pollak, R. A., 310, 313
Pope, Hallowell, 304
Popper, Karl, 160
Postman, L., 39
Potter, R. G., 306–308
Powell, Jody, 375
Proshansky, Harold M., 278, 279
Pryor, J., 40, 42–46, 95, 114

Quinlan, D. C., 214

Rabushka, A., 59
Radzinowicz, Leon, 174, 175
Ragin, Charles, 58
Rainwater, Lee, 90, 96, 102, 103
Rapoport, Anatol, 236
Rappaport, Roy A., 230, 231, 265, 267. 269, 272, 274
Redl, Fritz, 487
Reed, John Shelton, 90
Regan, D. T., 163
Reich, Charles, 482
Rein, Martin, 116, 348, 349
Reubens, Beatrice, 116
Reynaud, Jean-Daniel, 118
Ricardo, David, 175
Rich, R. F., 346, 349, 350, 354
Richmond, A. H., 30
Riecken, H., 40, 42
Riesman, David, 16
Rigby, Peter, 488
Riley, Matilda W., 326, 327, 338, 344
Rimlinger, Gaston, 110

Subject Index